This book may be kept

FOURTEEN D

# THE ENVIRONMENT OF MARKETING BEHAVIOR

# The Wiley Marketing Series

WILLIAM LAZER, Advisory Editor *Michigan State University*

# THE ENVIRONMENT OF MARKETING BEHAVIOR

*Selections from the Literature*

**SECOND EDITION**

**Robert J. Holloway**
*Professor of Marketing*
*University of Minnesota*

Southern Baptist College
FELIX GOODSON
LIBRARY
Walnut Ridge, Ark.

**Robert S. Hancock**
*Dean, School of Business*
*Southern Illinois University*

John Wiley & Sons, Inc., New York · London · Sydney · Toronto

Copyright © 1964, 1969 by John Wiley & Sons, Inc.

All rights reserved. No part of this book may
be reproduced by any means, nor transmitted,
nor translated into a machine language without
the written permission of the publisher.

10 9 8 7 6 5 4 3 2 1

Library of Congress Catalog Card Number: 73-77835
Cloth: SBN 471 407135 Paper: SBN 471 407143

Printed in the United States of America

35,738

658.8008
H728e

# *Preface*

S ince the original publication of this book in 1964, the changing social and economic factors affecting marketing indicate a need for this edition. While many of the original articles are retained, new and equally provocative points of view are included among the selections.

Students and academicians at several colleges and universities have been most constructive in the comments concerning the strengths and weaknesses of our original work. In analyzing these suggestions, some sections of this volume are strengthened and one new area of marketing concern added. Particularly noteworthy are the new selections dealing with the Economic Aspects of Consumer Behavior; the inclusion of a selection on the culture market (reading number 19); the new selections and expansion of some sections that are designed to be more stimulating; and, finally the addition of a number of challenging issues in Part V. In that section the student is introduced to a few socially sensitive questions, namely, the researching of the race/poverty problem, cigarette smoking, and a criticism of the chemical industry. These and other issues will be with our students for some years to come, and some perspective, or at least a point of discussion, may be helpful to them.

The editors again found their original criteria of selection sound and of prime guidance in compiling this edition. It was and still is our contention that basic concepts are the foundation of the learning process. Hence, our criteria for selections remains as follows: (1) that the article contribute to the basic framework and knowledge of marketing, (2) that the article be more or less timeless insofar as the concepts expressed, and/or (3) that the article be one around which discussion or controversy could evolve in the classroom setting.

The wisdom of these criteria seems verified by the use of the original selections by beginning marketing students and by the many comments from our academic colleagues. With the selections cast within the framework of marketing as explained in our "A Comment on the Study of Marketing" (pp. 00), beginning marketing can be a stimulating and intellectually challenging subject.

In reproducing the selections, it was necessary to take some liberties with them. All of the articles are not reprinted in their entirety, some footnotes and other reference materials were deleted, and minor editorial adjustments were necessary to fit them more appropriately to the size and style limitations of this book. For

v

these liberties and the permission to reprint the articles, we are indebted to the authors and publishers. And, for the many helpful suggestions from students and the suggested improvements from our numerous colleagues, we are most appreciative.

*R. J. Holloway*
*R. S. Hancock*

# Contents

# III.  DIRECTING THE MARKETING EFFORT, 253

# IV.  INTERNATIONAL MARKETING AND ECONOMIC DEVELOPMENT, 369

## V. MARKETING IN PERSPECTIVE AND CHALLENGING ISSUES, 399

# THE ENVIRONMENT OF MARKETING BEHAVIOR

# A Comment on the Study of Marketing

Marketing as an academic discipline and as a major function of business enterprises has taken on increased dimensions during the last two decades. Both the academic community and the business community have come to recognize the study of marketing as fundamental to one's understanding of the business process and his conceptual framework of our social and economic system. Whereas someone might be successfully involved with some segment of marketing without formal training, it is doubtful that he would understand all its complexities, its subtleties, and its relationships to other economic functions. And, without exposure and study of marketing as an orderly body of knowledge, one would probably not have an aggregative concept of the abundant research possibilities posed by the marketing system.

As one studies marketing, he will be struck by the difficulty of developing a precise definition of marketing and perhaps even more difficulty in comprehending its dimensions. An explanation for this is needed. Perhaps an explanation of what marketing is in its broadest sense may reconcile this potential dilemma.

Marketing is a social and economic phenomenon that exists by virtue of the nature of man. As any society evolves beyond the subsistence level of existence, marketing (or trade) comes into being. As a society moves through progressively more advanced stages of development, man responds by building institutions; devising social, economic, and political systems and engaging in those activities essential to economic progress. The precise character and dimensions of marketing differ from one society to another, and this is explained, at least in part, by the degree of specialization practiced. If the possessions and abilities of all people were the same, there would be no exchange, and hence, no need for a marketing structure and its attendant activities. Fortunately, this is not the case, and most societies are characterized by people possessing different abilities and different goods—thus, exchange ensues and a marketing structure of some dimension develops. Similarly, marketing activities anchored in the marketing structure are carried on. Marketing, then, involves markets, marketing institutions, marketing systems, and marketing activities—all of which have been devised to carry

1

on the task of meeting society's material and service needs through its marketing structure.

Marketing as an integral part of our social and economic processes is not a narrow, precisely defined discipline. Rather, marketing is an eclectic discipline. That is, it is a discipline that recognizes and synthesizes those doctrines, methods, and principles contributory to an understanding of marketing phenomena. Scholars from many fields have made significant contributions to marketing thought. For example, economics, sociology, psychology, anthropology, law, philosophy, and history all represent disciplines from which important segments of marketing knowledge have been drawn. Marketing scholars have been adaptive in their application of selected doctrines to improve and formulate marketing thought.

By the very nature of marketing in a society, it will be influenced by the environment in which it is carried on. The environment of marketing also represents a number of forces that generate change in a marketing structure, and furthermore, these forces influence the character of marketing activities. If these forces and the environment of marketing explain its existence, character, and dimensions, it is probably most desirable to begin a study of marketing within such a framework.

As the title of this book suggests, major emphasis is given to the environment of marketing and the way in which the environment influences the behavior of marketing. Just what is the environment of marketing? What are the forces that generate change in marketing? In answer to these questions a rough schema, or model, of an introductory course in marketing might be like that shown below.

The model depicts the environment of marketing as being social, economic, legal, ethical, technological, and physical. The social aspects of marketing take on importance, because markets involve people who are conditioned and influenced by several forces and their interrelationships. Their behavior in the marketplace is most properly analyzed in terms of demographic factors, psychological influences, and the impact of their traditions and culture.

The economic aspects of marketing are of twofold importance. First, the economic condition of consumers contributes to their behavior and makes it possible for other influences acting on them to be realized. When the economic status of consumers is combined with the social aspects of society, the impact of their behavior in the marketplace becomes a reality of major significance to marketers. Second, firms operating in the market and firms moving goods into the market do so in an atmosphere of competition with price functioning as the core to exchange transactions. In this way the economic dimension is broadened, and the economic environment of the firm becomes a market force worthy of consideration.

All social and economic activities are carried on in a legal and an ethical framework. These segments of our model are concerned with the probabilities and permissive aspects of market behavior. The legal environment influences the character of pricing, competitive activities, market control, and promotional strategies. The ethical behavior (or lack of it) in the marketplace is a more nebulous subject. From one society to another, this aspect may be expected to vary by virtue of traditions, the mores of society, and the values of a society.

Technology is another force influencing marketplace behavior. Technology puts pressures on a marketing system to which it must adjust, and similarly, technology has much to do with the products distributed and their eventual acceptance.

The physical environment of marketing includes the institutional structure. Intermediaries of all types are included in this concept, and it is recognized that the structure of the intermediaries influences the physical movement of goods to their possession by a consumer.

When marketing is cast in this framework, the marketing activities of the firm should ideally correspond to its environment. As a result, Part III, "Directing the Marketing Effort," is developed within a research context followed by the major marketing activities that can be designed to adjust to and meet an ever-changing environment.

Part IV deals with a number of international facets of marketing and especially, economic development. Underdeveloped countries face particularly difficult problems because their market activities and market structures are too deficient to absorb much more than a painfully slow rate of change. Marketing and its essential activities are paramount to economic development, but are often not recognized as a priority in the social and economic climate even though a nation gives much emphasis to uplifting the economic status of its domestic economy.

Finally, Part V of this volume raises a number of challenging issues which students in our colleges and universities today should find relevant to their lives tomorrow. Each issue raised presents a problem of wide interest, without simple solutions. These are some of the challenges that students reading this material will face as they embark on their careers. May they find the acceptable solutions.

# The Focus of Marketing

The first section of this volume introduces the student to the character and nature of marketing. The selections, all by eminent contributors to marketing knowledge, focus on the nature and origin of trade, on marketing problems, and on basic marketing concepts. In this section, the reader can gain an overview of marketing and consider diverse points of view.

Most of the emphasis in marketing is cast within the free enterprise framework. Some contrasts between marketing in a free enterprise system and a planned economic system are presented in the last two readings.

# A. The Role of Marketing in Society

## 1. Notions About the Origins of Trading

GEORGE W. ROBBINS

The origins of trade have been the concern of economists and anthropologists in the past in order to trace or to relate the present functions of trade to their primeval beginnings and to discover the basic character of this economic usage. While this preoccupation with origins is disappearing from the scientific literature, it is not uncommon to find its implications and assumptions in the more popular literature of business, and particularly on the subject of salesmanship.

References are often made to premises concerning the origin of trading as a means of explaining or analyzing the ethical position of modern selling, imputing to present practices in the market place the circumstances and virtues of an assumed primeval genesis. It is, for example, not uncommon to hear trading spoken of as universal and natural. On the other hand, anthropological evidence reveals primitive cultures with a complete lack of competitive trading and with insignificant exchange practices.

In the face of these opposing positions, it is desirable to examine the various notions concerning the origins of trading and to appraise them in the light of their usefulness in the analysis of trading in our own society. It is possible to do this without a true chronological history of trading, or without attempting to formulate an organic-evolutionary concept of trading which takes the form of extracting from succeeding cultures certain common characteristics, with the conclusion that these have been

passed down the lingering trail of institutional patterns.

Indeed, it should be evident that the accurate establishment of the origins of any human activity must await sufficient evidence from archaeological diggings.[1] The dearth of this evidence precludes a chronology that starts at the beginning. It is more profitable to avoid an historical recital in favor of an attempt to penetrate the internal logic of trading.

Our concern here is with the efficacy of employing, as either inarticulate or expressed premises, notions about the origins of trading in the evaluation of present-day trading practices from a functional or an ethical viewpoint. Is an understanding of the origins of trade an essential matter in the study of the ethics of selling and buying? Will it help to answer the problems of honesty and efficiency in selling? Does it throw light on the problems of the contests and conflicts of trading today in the economic institution?

It should be clearly understood that this inquiry differs from, and is not in conflict with, the study of trade history as it can be established through adequate records.[2] It relates to those

‡‡ SOURCE: Reprinted by permission from the *Journal of Marketing* (National Quarterly Publication of the American Marketing Association), Vol. 11, No. 3, January 1947, pp. 228–236.

[1] See Melville J. Herskovits, *The Economic Life of Primitive Peoples* (New York: Alfred A. Knopf, 1940), Pt. I, for detailed comment on methodology in economics and anthropology.

[2] As for example: Clive Day, *A History of Commerce* (New York: Longmans, Green, 1938); George Burton Hotchkiss, *Milestones of Marketing* (New York: Macmillan, 1938); N. S. B. Gras, *An Introduction to Economic History* (New York: Harper, 1922).

histories only insofar as their authors employ reference to origins; and it is, of course, possible to treat a matter historically without assuming an organic evolution based on obscure beginnings.

It is well to keep in mind that we are concerned with trading—buying and selling—as a matter of social behavior rather than as a technical process in marketing. It is essential to assume that trading is not a fortuitous or whimsical phenomenon, but rather an observable datum governed by laws of behavior that are subject to discovery. Moreover, it is no part of assumption here that trading is good or bad, strong or weak, or favorable to any given environment. These matters must emerge only as conclusions based on adequate observation of group activity in a definable situation.

### THE MEANING OF TRADING

The term "trading" may mean many things to say that a trade is an act of effecting an exchange, barter, transfer of title, persuasion, or even deception. It is not an oversimplification to say that a trade is an act of effecting an exchange of goods or services between a seller and a buyer; indeed, such a statement involves complexities of subtle premises. What lies both before and after the trade is of interest to this inquiry. The mere fact of communication between two individuals is a relatively superficial datum

It may be helpful to clarify the thing we are discussing by examining definitions. Confusion will be avoided if it is remembered that a trade is a two-sided shield—it is both a purchase and a sale. While it is a popular misconception that the initiative in trading is largely with the seller, it is irrelevant to our purposes which side we take for reference. For the sake of brevity, only the selling side will be defined; and even the uninitiated may fill in a parallel definition of buying.

There are at least three types of definitions of *sale* which serve to illustrate the usual approaches to selling:

(1) The legal: "Sale is an agreement by which one of the two contracting parties, called the 'seller,' gives a thing and passes title to it, in exchange for a certain price in current money, to the other party, who is called the 'buyer' or 'purchaser,' who on his part, agrees to pay such a price." [3]

(2) The vocational: A sale is the exchange of goods or services resulting from the exercise of the art of salesmanship.

(3) The professional: A sale is an exchange of goods or services resulting from rivalry in the productive effort of creating demand and of rendering service in the satisfaction thereof.

The legal definition leads to a concept of trading that is narrow and restricted mainly to the technical fact of title transfer in a society characterized by a highly refined property concept. It fails to provide for the student of the economic or sociological aspects of trading adequate attention to the circumstances precedent or subsequent to that transfer. [4]

The vocational approach to selling, on the other hand, emphasizes the importance of the arts of persuasion rather than their functional position. By contrast, what may be called the professional approach calls attention to the fundamental circumstance of human wants and of the existence of rivalry in the performance of the services that create and satisfy those wants. [5] It is not concerned with the contractual character of the sale; for contract is a usage of convenience, and the vast majority of sales are completed without the parties being aware that a legal contract is involved. Likewise, it does not deny that there is an important body of arts practiced by both sellers and buyers, which are effective in lubricating the process; but these arts are chiefly vocational techniques (however difficult to master). The professional approach places emphasis on the fundamental creative functions of selling in a highly competitive society.

---

[3] Walter A. Shumaker and George Foster Longsdorf, *The Cyclopedic Law Dictionary* (3rd ed.; Chicago: Callahan, 1940), p. 992.

[4] This is not to say that the law has little influence on selling, but rather to emphasize that a legal definition is necessarily a cautious one and is more likely to represent a careful attempt to classify a concept rather than to penetrate it. It should be recognized, of course, that the law does place the intention of the parties to a contract in an important position as distinct from the transfer to title. See Nathan Isaacs, "Sales," *Encyclopaedia of the Social Sciences* (New York: Macmillan, 1931), VIII, pp. 511–516.

[5] By calling this approach "professional," it is not necessarily implied that selling is a profession. However the social responsibility of the seller today certainly suggests a professional attitude, and it is clear that the acceptance of business as a profession will only follow, not precede, the adoption of such an attitude on the part of sellers. Cf. Louis Dembritz Brandeis, *Business—a Profession* (Boston: Small, Maynard, 1914), pp. 1–12.

While varying in approach, these three familiar concepts of selling have in common the functional position of selling in a society whose economic institution is characterized by a high degree of competitive effort—in short, a society like our own. In juxtaposition to these definitions, another, more fundamental, approach may be more suggestive of the real character of trading. A trade must always be a human relationship involving the behavior patterns of at least two persons.[6]

Hence, it is basically a *communication* and should be viewed as a part of the sociological field of communication.[7] It is subject to all the status barriers which define and separate individuals and groups. Again, any trade must be *cooperative* in the sense that two or more persons are acting together to achieve a new relationship which manifestly could not be achieved by each acting alone. Furthermore, every trade is an *organization* because it is a system, formal or otherwise, of consciously coordinated activities of at least two persons.[8] And lastly, the term is confined to situations where the ends are economic in order to exclude the multitude of other human relations which, without this modification, would fall unwanted into the area of our present concern.

Thus, we may define trading as a cooperative organization in communication to achieve economic ends. This definition carries no connotations with respect to the characteristics which may surround trading as the result of differing practices, usages, instruments, and mores to be found in the economic institution either at different times or in different locations. Like all other organizations in communication, trading belongs to a social institutional pattern, and becomes a part of the usages of that pattern. Specifically, it is part and parcel of the system of regulating economic contest and conflict, and

is itself subject to contests and conflicts with usages of the other social institutions, marital, familial, educational, recreational, religious, scientific, and governmental.[9]

From the historical viewpoint, any inquiry into the nature of trading, to be significant, must be one that takes cognizance of the particular institutional fabric of which it is a part. To say that trading in our society today has its roots in the behavior of our primeval ancestors, or to say that this notion is confirmed by the habits of our "contemporary ancestors,"[10] the non-literate primitives now living, is to stretch the latitudes of scientific inquiry to the point of incredulity.

Yet it is true that many practitioners of selling base an important part of their philosophy on premises concerning the origins of trading that comprise the substance of these ideas. It is precisely this basic mistake of many writers on salesmanship that led them to attitudes which provoked the well-known, pointed, and inescapable criticism of salesmanship by Clarence Darrow.[11]

## THE MAJOR HYPOTHESES

No one disputes the antiquity of trading; but the exact point and conditions of its origins provide the subject of consideration by many writers whose attempts may be classified in seven main hypotheses. Not a few students of anthropology and economics alike have supported one or more of these assumptions without even the benefit of tacit recognition of the implications.

### (1) *Trading Is Instinctive*

It is perhaps most widely held that "to trade, or 'swap' is an inborn trait in the human being."[12] A variation of this view was expressed by Sombart, who believed that some have an inherent capacity to become traders (undertakers) while others do not. "Either you are born a bourgeois or you are not. It must be in the blood, it is a natural inclination."[13]

---

[6] This is the case even where impersonal or even mechanical implements are employed, (e.g., corporations, agents, or vending machines).

[7] Communication is "the process of exchanging commonly understood ideas, facts, or usages by means of language, visual presentation, imitation, suggestion." Constantine Panunzio, *Major Social Institutions* (New York: Macmillan, 1939), p. 529.

[8] This concept has been used effectively by Chester I. Barnard in his interesting analysis of business organization. See, "Comments on the Job of the Executive," *Harvard Business Review*, XVIII, Spring 1940, pp. 295–308. See also his *The Functions of the Executive* (Cambridge: Harvard University Press, 1938).

[9] Constantine Panunzio, *op. cit.*, p. 7.

[10] Melville J. Herskovits, *op. cit.*, p. 35.

[11] "Salesmanship," *The American Mercury*, V, August 1925, pp. 385–392.

[12] Charles H. Fernald, *Salesmanship* (New York: Prentice-Hall, 1937), pp. 44 ff.

[13] Werner Sombart, *The Quintessence of Capitalism* (London: T. Fisher Unwin, 1915), p. 205.

This palpable view is undoubtedly a sufficient explanation to many salesmen; it is certainly a comfortable refuge from the penetrating criticism of some of the ancient and modern practices of the market place. If it is "natural" to sell, then the criticism of traders is comment out of hand. But the evidence of scientific anthropology gives little support to this notion.

Not a few evidences exist to show that primitive peoples have existed for long periods without competitive trading.[14] The industrial civilization of the Incas is a striking case in point.[15] Polish peasants for centuries did not know the meaning of buying and selling between members of the same community. Their knowledge of trading came entirely from contacts with outsiders; and their resistance to selling has survived, since "even today, peasants dislike to trade with neighbors."[16]

While it is a rare culture that does not produce some exchanges of commodities on occasion, it is rather common to find that among primitives trading, insofar as it possessed any formal existence, arises mainly to facilitate exchange between members of different groups rather than between individual members of the same group.[17] In a culture where the institutions support a strict control of production and allocation of wealth, trading between individuals in the society becomes unnecessary, as in the case of the Incas, or vastly restricted, as in the case of Soviet Russia in the early years at least, where other stimuli than private profit were dominant.[18]

One would expect few psychologists to rank so complex a phenomenon as trading with fundamental instincts of self-preservation and sex as a basic drive. Unlike these fundamental urges, trading is not universal, intensive, or repetitive. And while it is true that trading appeared early in many different places and independently under different circumstances, these facts serve no more to demonstrate instinctiveness of trading than does the simultaneous scattered growth of the family institution prove that marriage is instinctive. Not only is this hypothesis too simple and superficial, but adherence to it may even retard the ability of present-day sales management to cope with its functional responsibilities.

## (2) *Trading Grew Out of Warfare*

This "hostility" hypothesis has trading growing out of war between clans or tribes. It pictures primitive man as essentially warlike because of the pressure of population on the means of subsistence. It assumes that warfare has economic roots, and that it is inevitable when man searches for the satisfaction of elemental wants. The reasoning follows that whereas man could satisfy his wants by warring on his neighbor, he soon learned that trading was an alternative possibility that had merit from the standpoint of group survival.[19]

This hypothesis has many faults, not the least of which is that it leads us into the difficult path of analyzing the origins of war, a path that is as rugged and unmarked as any other that goes in the direction of primeval origins. It is sufficient here to record that the hostility notion runs afoul of evidence of trading where war is unknown, as well as testimony pointing to the conclusion that both war and trading appear to develop from the same circumstances, and independently of each other. War was unknown among some primitives who carried on a rudimentary form of trade, notably the Eskimo and the Semang of the Malay Peninsula.[20]

The Arapesh tribe of New Guinea, naturally easy-going and yet pitted against physical barrenness that might be expected to produce

---

[14] Melville J. Herskovits, *op. cit.*, pp. 17–19.

[15] Elizabeth Ellis Hoyt, *Primitive Trade, its Psychology and Economics* (London: Kegan Paul, Trench, Trubner, 1926), p. 141.

[16] W. I. Thomas and F. Znaniecki, *The Polish Peasant in Europe and America*, 1927, as quoted by E. L. Thorndike, *Human Nature and the Social Order* (New York: Macmillan, 1940), p. 633.

[17] Melville J. Herskovits, *op. cit.*, pp. 133 ff.

[18] William Henry Chamberlin, "The Planned Economy," *Red Economics* (Boston: Houghton Mifflin, 1932), pp. 9 ff. See also M. Ilin, *New Russia's Primer* (Boston: Houghton Mifflin, 1931), II, and XIII.

[19] It is interesting that the opposite view is widely held also; namely, that trading inevitably leads to warfare. Elizabeth Ellis Hoyt cites evidence to support both views, *op. cit.*, VII.

The fact that war and trade often appeared together as effect and cause may have been attributable to the fact that the traders (foreigners) were usually more advanced culturally than those on whom they called and thus had a higher capacity to injure [cf. Max Radin, *Manners and Morals in Business* (New York: Bobbs-Merrill, 1939), pp. 89 ff]. But they also should have had a higher capacity to serve, which may well have prevented conflicts!

[20] Margaret Mead, "Primitive Society," *Planned Society* (New York: Prentice-Hall, 1937), p. 16.

strong rivalry for survival, finds great adventure in producing for others and actually regards it a sin to eat one's own kill. Motivation is achieved without competitive rivalry or war by a custom of having an official "insulter" for each man to taunt him publicly for his failure to produce feasts. So dreadful is this torture in the face of his peaceful nature, that a man looks forward to his reward—release from his "insulter" and retirement when his son reaches puberty. Thus, at least one primitive culture has institutionalized its lack of aggressiveness and self-interest, both of which would seem to be of some importance in the origin of either competitive trading or war.[21]

Nor is it easy to relate war and trading in the face of the fact that in many primitive peoples the rewards for war are personal and psychological rather than economic, and take the form of prestige supported by the evidence of another feather in the cap or another enemy's scalp on the belt. And the persistence of war, not only among primitives but in our own society, is difficult to explain if it is to be argued that trading supplanted war because of its demonstrated superior contributions to group survival; for wars have almost always provided a serious interference with economic life. Indeed, it seems well to avoid any attempt to relate trade to war as a fruitless inquiry in which observable data are altogether too lacking to support reasonable conclusions.[22]

### (3)  *Trading Originated in Predation*

The "predatory" hypothesis is closely allied with the hostility notion. Because there are a few primitive tribes, such as the Bushman and the Apache, whose economies were regularly dependent upon the capture of wealth from other tribes,[23] and because there are a few evidences that modern business "is a complex and well-integrated series of frauds,"[24] some observers may conclude that trading began with the extraction of tribute and has never suc-

ceeded in getting away from the original predatory pattern.

The difficulty here lies in the abundance of evidence, historical and anthropological, that trading flourished between peoples who were entirely friendly and to whom the idea of tribute never seemed to occur. Moreover, predatory activities are not confined to the economic institution, but pervade the other social institutions as well. Indeed, political leaders, whether they be the heads of primitive tribes or of literate nations, have been among the most notorious tribute-extracting racketeers of history, and their predacity on merchants has all too often throttled trade.[25]

### (4)  *Trade Grew Out of Friendly Gift-Giving*

This "friendship" hypothesis is an explanation in diametrically the opposite vein. Professor Hoyt cites many examples of friendly gift-giving in primitive society and suggest that this practice may have led to learning the utility of exchange.[26] In primitive societies where the ownership of things was strongly identified with personal or group spiritual entity, the giving of gifts to neighboring tribal chiefs must indeed have stemmed from a genuine gregarious feeling and friendly goodwill.[27] The cynical view that a wise chieftain would buy off the predatory nature and power of his neighbor with gifts is not sufficient to explain the facts of anthropological research.

It is perhaps sufficient here to note that both war-making and gift-giving were means of communication, either or both of which may have been helpful in the discovery of trading. Professor Hoyt's emphasis on gift-giving as an origin of trading is supported by logic; for the atmosphere of gift-giving is a congenial one in which man may learn to perceive the utility of exchange.

---

[21] *Ibid.,* p. 23.

[22] A more fruitful approach to the question of war and trade will be found in Lionel Robbins, *The Economic Causes of War* (London: J. Cape, 1940).

[23] Margaret Mead, *op. cit.,* pp. 17 ff.

[24] J. B. Matthews and R. E. Shallcross, *Partners in Plunder* (Washington, New Jersey: Consumers' Research, 1935), p. 400. See also Clarence Darrow, *op. cit.*

[25] N. S. B. Gras, *Business and Capitalism* (New York: F. S. Crofts, 1939), pp. 307 ff. See also Miriam Beard, *A History of the Business Man* (New York: Macmillan, 1938), *passim.*

[26] *Op. cit.,* p. 104 and Part IV.

[27] To say that gift-giving is entirely a matter of goodwill or altruism, however, is to overstate the matter; for no matter how freely a gift is given, its presentation in primitive societies appears nearly always to create an obligation which, if neglected by the recipient, leads to loss of prestige or social disapprobation, which is a strong factor in shaping action. Cf. Herskovits, *op. cit.,* p. 134.

## (5) Trading Originated with the "Silent Trade"

Silent trade is well-known to anthropologists as an early means of economic communication, and it appears in many isolated places among primitives. In this crude form, trade is initiated when one group leaves its wares on a promontory and retires from sight to permit another group to come out of hiding to inspect the goods and deposit its offering in return.[28]

Silent trade seems to have prevailed (1) where contact was between peoples of widely different cultures, (2) where languages were different, and (3) where fear or distrust was even more highly felt than were the economic motives of the intercourse. While the silent trade is an important fact in early communication, it throws little light on the real origins of trading. Its existence proves, however, that trading did occur between peoples who were motivated by neither the desire to make friends nor the will to annihilate.

It should also be recognized that neither party to the silent trade would have acted had he failed to develop an evaluation of the exchanged wares entirely apart from his own spirit or soul. Some degree of objectivity was implicit. Moreover, it is not plausible that this form of trading was an expression of instinct; it was discovered, developed, and learned as a crude but effective usage in the framework of the existing social institutions.

## (6) Trading Arose from Surpluses

Some students have suggested that trading originated because of the pressure of surplus goods resulting from the early division of labor in the primitive family or tribe.[29] Presumably the relative scarcity of goods was apparent in the periodic surpluses made available either through the efforts of nature or man. The plethora of cattle against the dearth of fodder may have suggested a gain from the exchange of cattle for fodder that was plentiful in a neighboring area.

This explanation fails on a number of grounds. There is practically no evidence that surpluses were accumulated by primitive families or clans excepting for anticipated emergencies.[30] Indeed, it is probable that excesses of things to eat or wear or use were regarded as "free goods" with respect to which transferable control did not even suggest itself until after trading as an instrument of communication developed. Moreover, much of the early trade in all parts of the world was in rare and exotic items "for which the demand was largely an expression of arbitrary value."[31] The primitive trading in ornaments and trinkets which gave their owners social prestige can hardly be said to stem from surpluses.

Too, a rational and administrative division of labor in primitive tribes, assumed in this hypothesis, cannot conceivably have preceded the need for it; and this need certainly compels outside markets as a *sine qua non*. The superficial explanation posed by the surplus hypothesis is to be found in the contemporary and popular notion that foreign trade exists because of surpluses resulting from the division of labor when in fact it is quite the other way around.

## (7) Trading Grew Out of the Development of the Property Concept

Tracing the origin of trading to the growth of the concept of property is a preoccupation of those who see in the exaggerated manifestations of trading in our society an overemphasis on private ownership. It is not appropriate to our purposes here to enter the controversy over the inequalities of property ownership or over the ways by which the function of property may be molded in the interests of social progress and public welfare.

It is merely essential to point out that in the manner in which the function of property is conceived as an end in terms of private advantage, special privilege, and exploitation will have a profound bearing on the practices in the market place. That many of these practices are subject to question today is not gainsaid; but to attack trading as a major evil growing out of the property concept is to engage in ardent speculation.

If by property we refer to the claim which gives transferable control over things,[32] then the property concept is best explained by the relative scarcity of these things in terms of the con-

---

[28] N. S. B. Gras, "Barter," *The Encyclopaedia of the Social Sciences* (New York: Macmillan 1933), II, pp. 468 ff. Elizabeth Ellis Hoyt, *op. cit.*, pp. 133 ff. Max Radin, *op. cit.*, pp. 81 ff.

[29] Edward D. Page, *Trade-Morals*, 2nd. rev. ed. (New Haven: Yale University Press, 1918), p. 58. See also Charles H. Fernald, *op. cit.*, pp. 44 ff.

[30] Max Radin, *op cit.*, pp. 85 ff.

[31] *Ibid.*

[32] Frederic B. Garver and Alvin H. Hansen, *Principles of Economics*, rev. ed. (Boston: Ginn, 1937), pp. 29 ff.

351738

SOUTHERN BAPTIST COLLEGE LIBRARY

test for individual and group survival.[33] While it is true that the extensive and complex exchange in our society presupposes a well-developed concept of property, it is far from true that crude trading could never have existed without even a simple property concept. Indeed, the very definition of property as anything with exchange value implies clearly that it is the need and practice of trading which called the property concept into use and aided materially in shaping its character. To say that property value existed before the fact of exchange is to indulge in a hopeless confusion of ideas and terms.

Trading and property concepts are both man-made and have developed in close relationship. They have certain characteristics in common: (1) both are dependent on the recognition of scarcity values; (2) both presuppose a divorcement of possessions from the individual's spiritual identity—an objective valuation of things; (3) both emerge from the same set of factors and must be explained in terms of a larger institutional concept.

Hence, to say that trading originated in the property concept and is a usage of property is to misinterpret the origins of both while leaving the essential character of each shrouded in confusion. In short, it is another example of the futility of tracing origins without the supporting evidences of observable data.

## A RATIONAL EXPLANATION OF TRADING

The one thing in common which all of these hypotheses of the origins of trading have is a high degree of speculation unsupported by the accumulation of empirical data. It should be clear that any logic based upon premises like these is not acceptable to the social scientist. Indeed, social science has long since abandoned the methodology suggested by such speculations as those we have been examining.

If an explanation of trading is needed, it is to be found in the nature of man and of his adaptation to his environment through the institutions he builds. The universal, abiding, and repetitive characteristics of man to learn, to explore, to satisfy his curiosity, and to live with groups of other men have led him into an ever-expanding circle of experiences from which he has developed his learning and his patterns of

associated living.[34] These attributes undoubtedly stem from the character of man's genes as distinguished from those of other animals. The explanation of trading lies neither in man's instincts nor his intelligence alone, but must be seen in terms of the patterns of the accumulated deposits of his activities in associated living.[35]

The essential prerequisite to trading, original or otherwise, is the development of the ability to valuate things in terms of other things rather than in terms of spiritual or mystical beliefs—to objectify and emancipate one's belongings from his spiritual self and soul.[36] But this ability is by no means a guarantee that trading will be carried on in a society unless the folkways and mores are receptive to the changes which it imposes in the patterns of living.

Trading may be said to have been a slow discovery, made at a relatively early stage by peoples the world over, that followed the intellectual advance of valuation and which, in turn, vastly stimulated that advance, that grew out of the practices of associated living and, in turn, greatly affected these practices.

As contrasted with the other means of acquiring things, trading is by all odds the most complex. It is unique in that it alone is a two-way transaction.[37] The fact that trading has grown to such prominence and complexity as one of the dominant means of acquiring things is attributable, in part at least, to its relative survival value and to the character of the prevailing institutional patterns of which it is a part.

## CONCLUSION

The answers to our original questions may now be seen in better perspective. Although it would be the height of pedantic scepticism to

---

[33] Constantine Panunzio, *op. cit.*, p. 216.

[34] A highly imaginative, yet penetrating essay on this fundamental character of man as opposed to other animals is to be found in Clarence Day, *This Simian World* (New York: A. A. Knopf, 1936).
[35] Constantine Panunzio, *op. cit.*, pp. 143 ff.
[36] Elizabeth Ellis Hoyt, *op. cit.*, Pt. IV. That this emancipation is universally or wholly accomplished today (or, indeed, should be) is not suggested. Contemporaries have "priceless" trinkets and sometimes order them interred with their remains. Businessmen have been known to defy the logic of the case by insisting on the use of their own photographs as trademarks.
[37] The other means are strictly one-way: appropriation from nature, seizure from others, cultivation and making with the hands, gifts and inheritance, and gambling. H. K. Nixon, *Principles of Selling* (New York: McGraw-Hill, 1942), pp. 41 ff.

deny validity to a hypothesis because of the absence of all conceivable verification, nevertheless, the main assumptions examined all fall in the same category of speculation without adequate empirical verification, and they involve an outmoded methodology in the social sciences.

Even by the most tolerant sense of proportion and broad feeling for the evidence, any conceivable proof of the kinship of modern competitive trading to the earliest forms of barter and exchange would fail to offer a basis for a discussion of either ethics or efficiency of trading unless it be considered in a particular institutional framework. Consequently, it is not to be argued that the ethics of selling in our own society can be related to that of the societies in which origin may have occurred.

As a basis for the evaluation of the ethics of selling and buying in our own society, the concept that trading is a cooperative organization in communication for the purpose of achieving economic ends is one that properly expresses the internal logic of trading. For it implies in trading a concept in the economic institution whose usages entail a continuing contest and conflict with other concepts and usages prevailing in all of the social institutions. This view of trading permits one to proceed with an examination of the ethics of trading in our own society without the hindrance of a cloak of prejudgment drawn about it by speculation with respect to the ultimate origins of trading usages.

# 2. Some Problems in Market Distribution
ARCH W. SHAW

## THE ACTIVITIES OF BUSINESS

When a workman in a factory directs the cut of a planer in a malleable steel casting, he applies motion to matter with the purpose and result of changing its form.

When a retail clerk passes a package of factory-cooked food over the counter to a customer, he applies motion to matter with the purpose and result of changing its place.

When a typist at her desk makes out an invoice covering a shipment, she influences the motion of that material or merchandise, not directly to change its form or place, but indirectly to facilitate changes of one or both kinds.

Isolate any phase of business, strike into it anywhere, and invariably the essential element will be found to be the application of motion to matter. This may be stated, if you will, as the simplest ultimate concept to which all the activities of manufacturing, selling, finance and management can be reduced.

Starting with this simple concept, it is at once evident that we have an obvious and easy basis for the classification of business activities —a simplifying, unifying principle from which to proceed rather than some mere arrangement by kind or characteristic of the materials, men, operations and processes in the various departments of a business enterprise.

The nature of the motion does not of itself supply the key to this basic classification. For

◆ SOURCE: Reprinted by permission from *Harvard Business Review*, Vol. 40, No. 4, July-August 1962, pp. 113–122. © 1962 by the President and Fellows of Harvard College; all rights reserved.

while the action may be characteristic of one part of a business and not duplicated elsewhere, like the pouring of molten metal in a foundry or the making up of a payroll, it may, in contrast, be common to all the departments into which the organization is divided, such as the requisition of a dozen pencils or a box of paper clips. It is not until we single out the common fundamental element and inquire, "What is the purpose of this motion?" that we find the key.

I do not wish to exaggerate the importance of this simple and apparently obvious concept; but for me it has opened a way to locate the activities of business and disclose their relations to one another and to their common object, and so has proved a device of daily use. For the final function of the classification, as it is the practical problem of all business, is to identify those motions which are purposeless, so that they may be eliminated, and to discover those motions, old or new, which are of sound purpose, so that they may be expedited.

When, upon studying an individual motion or operation in itself and in relation to the other associated activities, no satisfactory answer can be found to the question, "What is its purpose?", you have strong grounds for assuming that it is a non-essential and useless motion. It may have the sanction of house tradition or trade custom, but its superfluous character persists and the wisdom of eliminating it becomes plain. Conversely, a new motion proposed for adoption, though never before tried in the trade, may still have value. Purpose again is the decisive test. From the social standpoint, any motion which has no valid purpose or result is economically useless and wrong. The effect of employing such a motion in business, like the effect of omitting a useful motion, is to limit profits that otherwise might rise.

So the purpose of the analysis, from the manager's point of view, is not alone to position the activities of business and develop their relationship, but also to order his thinking so that he can more readily see what activities he should discontinue and what others he should encourage, perfect, or add.

This does not always mean a reduction in the total number of motions. In our roundabout system of production, with its minute subdivision of labor, it is possible to make a greater number and variety of motions and distribute them over a longer period of time, yet increase the eventual output or decrease the cost through the group effectiveness of all the motions.

In the three operations already mentioned—those of the factory workman, the retail clerk, and the office typist—each application of motion was for an economically valid purpose and each instance was typical of one of the three great groups of business activities:

1. The activities of production, which change the form of materials.

2. The activities of distribution, which change the place and ownership of the commodities thus produced.

3. The facilitating activities, which aid and supplement the operations of production and distribution.

Whatever the nature or kind of any business activity, its final effect is one of these three.

## METHODS OF DISTRIBUTION

In the early stages of our industrial history, sales were made in bulk. At all stages in distribution, the purchasers saw the actual goods before the sale was made.

Later sale by sample appeared. The purchaser bought goods represented to be identical with the sample he was shown. The introduction of this method of sale was necessitated by the widening of the market and was made possible by improvement in commercial ethics and increasing standardization of product. The purchaser had to have confidence not only in the producer's honest intention to furnish goods identical with the sample, but also in his ability to produce identical goods. Hence, increasing uniformity in product through machine meth-ods of applying standard materials in its manufacture was a factor in the increase of sale by sample.

Sale by description is the most modern development in distribution. Here an even higher ethical standard is required than for sale by sample. Moreover, sale by description requires a higher level of general intelligence than sale in bulk or sale by sample. Sale by description in its modern development is, in a sense, a by-product of the printing press.

All three methods of sale are in use in modern commercial life. The consumer still makes a large part of his purchases under a system of sale in bulk. He sees the goods before he buys them. The middleman, buying in larger quantities, generally purchases from sample. But sale by description becomes each year more important in every stage of the distribution system.

The root idea in sale by description is the communication of ideas about the goods to the prospective purchaser by spoken, written or printed symbols and facsimiles. This method takes the place of the sight of the goods themselves or a sample of them. It is obvious that this requires that the purchaser shall have sufficient intelligence to grasp ideas either through spoken, written or printed symbols.

The ideas to be conveyed to the prospective purchaser in sale by description are such as will awaken an effective demand for the commodity in question. The awakening of demand is the essential element in selling. It must be remembered, however, that the distributor has the further task of making it possible to gratify that demand by making the goods physically available to the buyer.

With sale in bulk, this problem merges with the selling, since the goods are physically present when the sale is made; while in sale by description the physical distribution of the goods is a problem distinct from the awakening of demand. And it is a problem that requires equal attention, for it is obviously useless to awaken the demand unless the goods to satisfy it are available.

As demand creation is the initial step in distribution, it is necessary to consider the agencies for this purpose available to the merchant-producer. There are three general agencies to be considered: (1) middleman, (2) the producer's own salesman, and (3) advertising, direct and general. The business man faces the problem of what agency or combination of agencies is the most efficient for the creation of demand and the physical supply of his particular commodity.

The number of possible combinations of methods and agencies renders the problem of the producer-merchant an intricate one. It will be seen that he has a difficult task in analyzing the market with reference to his goods, and in working out that combination of methods and agencies which will give him the most efficient system of applying motion to achieve distribution.

The middleman is a by-product of a complex industrial organization. The chart of Fig. 1 shows in rough outline the evolution of the middleman from the early period when producer dealt directly with consumer, to the appearance of the orthodox type of distribution (late in the Eighteenth Century and in the first quarter of the Nineteenth Century) when a complicated series of middlemen existed.

In the more primitive barter economy, the producer deals directly with the consumer, and middlemen take no part in the transaction. In the medieval period, as the handicrafts become specialized occupations under a town-market regime, the producer is a retailer and sells directly to the consumers. As the market widens, a division of labor becomes necessary, and the merchant appears as an organizer of the market.

Steadily the market widens until business confronts both national and world-wide markets. The merchant is no longer a single intermediary between the producer and the consumer. The merchant who takes the goods from the producer disposes of them to retail merchants who in turn distribute them to consumers. After a long period, we find the producers gradually strengthening their financial position, and freeing themselves from the control of a single merchant. They become merchant-producers. They assume the burden of production, and dispose of the product to various wholesalers, who in turn sell to retailers and they to the consumers. As a world market appears, the producer disposes of a part of his product to the export merchant.

In the early days of the factory system, shown in the chart of Fig. 2, we find that the producers have lost their character as merchants and are devoting themselves to the problems of production. The selling agent appears as a link in the chain of distribution to relieve the producer from the task of selling his product. He distributes it among wholesalers, who in turn distribute it to retailers, and the retailers to the consuming public. This may be termed the orthodox pattern in distribution, a pattern almost universal thus far in the Nineteenth Century.

Conversely, as the long period of development from a system of barter economy to the early decades of the factory system showed a continuous tendency toward increase in the number of middlemen intervening between the producer and the consumer, so recent years have shown a growing tendency to decrease the number of successive steps in distribution. Fig. 2 is an attempt to show diagrammatically the

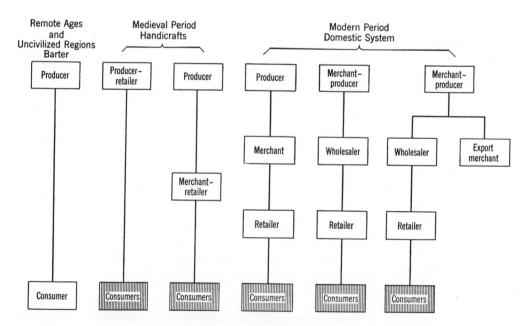

FIG. 1.   Evolution of the middleman.

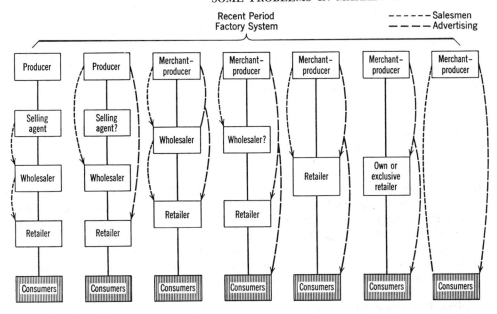

FIG. 2.    An apparent tendency to reduce the number of successive middlemen.

development of this apparent tendency to decrease the number of middlemen.

The most extreme step in the process is the complete elimination of middlemen, and the sale direct from the merchant-producer to the consumer, either by advertising alone or by salesmen supplemented by advertising.

It should be emphasized that the analogy between direct salesmen and advertising is very close. Each agency is largely used to enable the producer to take over one function of the middleman, that is, the selling function. And in each case the root idea is the same. The producer seeks to communicate most directly to the prospective purchaser, through one or the other agency, or a combination of the two, such ideas about his goods as will create a conscious demand for them. The direct salesman and advertising are different modes of accomplishing the same end.

Advertising, then, may properly be regarded either as a substitute for middlemen and salesmen, or as auxiliary to them in the exercise of the selling function. Owing to the rise of sale by description and the increasing differentiation of commodities, it tends to displace in whole or in part these other agencies in many lines of distribution.

Advertising may be said to build up three general classes of demand: (1) expressed conscious demand, (2) unexpressed conscious demand, and (3) subconscious demand. Expressed conscious demand means present sales; unexpressed conscious demand means future sales; subconscious demand means a fertilizing of the field so that future selling efforts will be more fruitful. Unexpressed conscious demand and subconscious demand are difficult to measure but must always be taken into account in any consideration of the efficiency of advertising as a selling agency.

What has gone before has been by way of analysis. The general problem of distribution, the present-day differentiation of products, the price policies open to the producer, the methods of sale, and the three chief selling agencies have all been subjected to brief review. This has been essential because neither economists nor business men have previously made such an analysis.

The social significance of the problem calls for emphasis also. While a more systematic handling of distribution means to the business man greater business success, a better organization of distribution with maximum economy of motion means to society the prevention of an enormous annual waste.

## CONSIDERATIONS OF THE MARKET

The business man faces a body of possible ·purchasers, widely distributed geographically, and showing extremes of purchasing power and felt needs. The effective demand of the indi vidual consumer depends not alone upon his purchasing power but also upon his needs, conscious or latent, resulting from his education, character, habits, and economic and social environment. The market, therefore, splits up into economic and social strata, as well as into geographic sections.

The producer cannot disregard the geographic distribution of the consuming public. He may be able to sell profitably by salesmen where the population is dense, while that method of sale would be unprofitable where population is sparse. If a sound system of distribution is to be established, the business man must treat each distinct geographic section as a separate problem. The whole market breaks up into differing regions.

Equally important is a realization of what may be termed the market contour. The market, for the purposes of the distributor, is not a level plain. It is composed of differing economic and social strata. Too seldom does the business man appreciate the market contour in reference to his product.

Nor does the merchant-producer always realize how intricate is his problem as to the agency or combination of agencies that will be most efficient in reaching his market.

The business man often adopts one method of reaching his market and becomes an advocate of it, entirely disregarding other methods.

While the method adopted may be more efficient than any other single method, it is apparent that a method which is relatively efficient in reaching one area may be inefficient in reaching another. So a system of distribution which has proved effective in reaching one economic stratum may be relatively inefficient when employed to reach a different economic stratum in society. Each distinct area and economic stratum may have to be treated as a separate problem.

A sound selling policy will require as its basis a careful analysis of the market by areas and strata, and a detailed study of the proper agency or combination of agencies to reach each area and stratum, taking into account always the economic generalizations expressed in the law of diminishing returns. It must also take into account not only the direct results obtained from the use of one or another agency over a short period, but also the less measurable results represented by the unexpressed conscious demand and subconscious demand which may facilitate future selling campaigns.

The crux of the distribution problem is the proper exercise of the selling function. The business man must convey to possible purchasers through one agency or another such ideas about the product as will create a maximum demand for it. This is the fundamental aim whatever the agency employed.

*Editor's Note*: The reader may be interested to know that Shaw's original material was published in the *Quarterly Journal of Economics* (1912) and in a book by Arch W. Shaw. *Some Problems in Market Distribution* (Harvard University Press, 1915).

# 3. Some Concepts of Markets and Marketing Strategy

ROLAND S. VAILE

## THE BASIC DEFINITION OF MARKETING

"Marketing covers all business activities necessary to effect transfers in the ownership of goods and to provide for their physical distribution." [1] "Marketing includes all the activities involved in the creation of place, time, and possession utilities." [2] "Marketing, in the full sense of the word, must involve change in ownership; physical movements merely facilitate this change or make possible the use of the commodity by the new owner. All the rights, privileges, and responsibilities, either of use or of further sale, attach to ownership and are passed on with change in ownership." [3]

These three definitions, taken from many, pretty well represent the concept of marketing although perhaps sale of services merits more specific inclusion. Change in ownership is all important. Physical movement is facilitating. Place, time, and possession utilities are involved, but their development requires marketing only when change of ownership is also involved.

There are many other instances in which the creation of place utility does not involve marketing. For example, place utility and only place utility is created in bringing crude oil from the bottom of a deep well to a surface tank, and yet that process is not usually included in marketing. Actually the sinking of an oil well and pumping oil from it have much in common with the laying of a pipeline and pumping oil through it. Both result in place utility, but one pair is classed with marketing and the other with production. The same point might be made with coal mining, potato digging, and many other activities which result only in place utility, but which are commonly thought of as part of production rather than marketing.

## CONCEPT OF A MARKET

The term "market" may be used to designate:

(1) The place where a sale is made.

(2) The area in which a particular supply usually is sold, or the area from which a particular supply generally is procured.

(3) The particular institutions or channels that carry on the marketing processes.

(4) The complex set of forces that result in a certain price being paid for a particular bill of goods or service.

Legal controversy exists concerning the locus of a market in the geographic sense. Is the market for cement, for example, at the point where it is made, or where it is used? The primary focus of the forces of demand is at the latter point, surely, although some of the basing-point discussions seem to contend otherwise. One basic question involved is whether different proportions of common costs may properly be covered by identical sales in markets with differing demands. Retail pricing certainly results in differing contributions to common costs from

[1] T. N. Beckman and others, *Principles of Marketing* (New York: Ronald Press, 1957), p. 4.

[2] P. D. Converse and others, *Elements of Marketing* (New York: Prentice-Hall, 1952), p. 1.

[3] Roland S. Vaile and others, *Market Organization* (New York: Ronald Press, 1930), p. 43.

‡‡ SOURCE: Reprinted by permission from *Changing Structure and Strategy in Marketing* edited by Robert V. Mitchell (Bureau of Economic and Business Research, University of Illinois, 1958), pp. 17–29.

the sale of different items. To what extent and under what conditions would similar leeway be appropriate between different geographic markets? In other words, is there anything necessarily nefarious in "freight absorption" per se? No completely satisfying answer has been given to this question.

A conspicuous change during the past generation is seen in the growth of individual firms through integration, both horizontal and vertical. Firms that have expanded horizontally have tended also to integrate vertically. According to data summarized in *Fortune*, six merchandising firms each had sales of over $1 billion in 1956. Each of these is engaged predominantly in retailing, but each also has undertaken many activities usually considered as wholesaling, as well as some manufacturing. Our concepts and definitions in this field are made archaic by these developments, and our statistics do not permit precise chronological comparison. Moreover, the question still is moot as to the conditions under which a firm should be permitted to own or control its principal customers so that a large portion of its "sales" are merely paper transactions.

The growth of our great suburban shopping centers and of supermarket self-service retailing is made possible, of course, by the high-income, automobile age. Rather than a move toward economy in the use of total social resources, it appears to be grossly inefficient, as is, in fact, practically every do-it-yourself program. These movements are reversions away from the principle of specialization. They can be tolerated only because specialized technology already has resulted in high productivity and considerable unused personal time and energy, together with widely dispersed ownership of idle capacity in quasi-industrial goods like washing machines and automobiles. (The importance of the automobile in our abundant economy is highlighted by the fact that six of the ten national firms with largest 1956 sales are engaged in automobile manufacture and petroleum production while three others have the automobile business as a principal customer.)

Of course there are some sociological considerations connected with do-it-yourself programs, and perhaps the sociological gains outweigh any economic inefficiency. Measurement of the net effect on our culture involves value judgment that is beyond the scope of this paper. Suffice it to say that the opportunity cost of many do-it-yourself programs is pretty low while some economic use is made of otherwise unemployed labor and equipment. The alterna-

tive use of that potential capacity may be a rather low-grade consumption activity. In any case the public seems to have accepted the trend philosophically and with considerable enthusiasm.

Melvin Copeland suggested a generation ago that consumer goods are purchased as convenience, shopping, or specialty goods, and that stores tend to concentrate on one of these lines.[4] This tendency has led to a mixing of the conventional lines of groceries, drugs, and household gadgets into a fairly complete stock of convenience goods in modern supermarkets. That this development has been going on for some time is shown by the following quotation from Chester Haring:

Of course, lines are being added to the stocks of nearly all retail merchants, but the greatest change is taking place in the drug, grocery, cigar, and five-and-ten-cent stores. While each of these groups is doing its largest business in its natural field, each is encroaching upon the fields of others, and also into entirely new fields. In short, these four classes of stores seem to be making up a new class which we may call "convenience stores."[5]

In the nearly thirty years since that statement was written, change in the concept of the most appropriate market institutions has continued. The supermarkets and the suburban shopping centers are dominant in the fashion of the moment. Completely automatic service in supermarkets is in the pilot stage and may become the fashion for tomorrow. Evidently the ultimate physical and institutional pattern for market distribution still is to be conceived and evolved. As one result our retail statistics are badly muddled, and for most useful analysis they should be reported in much greater detail.

Changes in the commodity mix are not confined to retailing. In many cases manufacturers are taking on new lines. This may be done to give more price lines as in the case of the Edsel. It may be done to improve the seasonal distribution of demand or because the firm has funds to invest and decides to spread its risks. Whatever the reasons, it appears that the concept of the market for an individual firm is broadening and specialization by manufacturers on a limited line of commodities is being reduced.

Of course many manufacturers have long undertaken to reach different segments of their

---

[4] *Principles of Merchandising* (New York: A. W. Shaw, 1924).
[5] *The Manufacturer and His Outlets* (New York: Harper, 1929), p. 176.

market with differentiated products. For example, canners, flour millers, some tire manufacturers, and others have sold their products both under their own brands and under wholesaler or retailer brands. Sometimes the product offered under several brands has been essentially identical, but through this multiple-brand strategy additional segments of the total market have been reached. This practice constitutes a form of semisecret, intra-firm competition, often with only minor physical differences among the products.

As individual firms have grown in size and have added to their lines of products, many of them have undertaken more direct and obvious intra-firm competition. This strategy is conspicuous, of course, in the automobile field. General Motors, for example, not only offers different named cars in different price lines, but there is considerable overlap of prices among the different makes. Strenuous rivalry exists among the retail agents that sell the several makes—as strenuous, perhaps, among the separate units of GM as between them and the members of the Ford or Chrysler families. Competition among the products of a single company is well illustrated, also, in Procter and Gamble where the sales division is organized on a competitive product basis. Recently, intra-firm product competition has become keen with cigarette manufacturers, especially following the wide introduction of the filter and mentholated brands. This practice of differentiating the products of a single seller makes it possible to satisfy the tastes and whims of segregated markets. One result is an increase in total company sales, as illustrated by the huge volume of such organizations as General Motors or Procter and Gamble. Sometimes, but not always, it permits some price discrimination.

Money makes markets. This aspect of markets deserves and receives close attention. The flow of income is of great importance to market potentials. Changes in the flow of income are reflected closely by changes in retail purchases. Forecasts of future changes in income directly affect the volume of industrial expenditures. Increases in income generally are accompanied by changes in the percentage of savings and investment. Conversely, neither increases nor decreases in income flow result immediately in equal changes in consumption expenditure. Increases and decreases in credit have much the same immediate effects as do changes in income flow. Thus when income falls, an increase in consumer credit may temporarily offset the

effect of the fall. These points are elementary, of course, and call for no amplification here.

It may be pointed out, however, that both government and private agencies have made available an increasing amount of data on income, past, present, and future. These data include the well-known estimates of GNP, national income, disposable personal income, average individual and family income, and so on. Of considerable use to some branches of marketing is the MacFadden estimate of discretionary purchasing power. All these data are available in both current and constant-value dollars. Studies in consumer economics are available to indicate many of the relations between changes in income and the accompanying changes in its use. These correlations are of great value in the planning of business decisions affecting marketing.

Perhaps it almost goes without saying, however, that relationships between income and expenditures change over the years. This is illustrated, for example, by the well-known fact that until recently the percentage of consumer income spent on food has decreased as income increased, while the reverse sems to have occurred in the past decade. Perhaps this is merely a statistical illusion due to changes in the form in which food is bought, but at least it points a finger of caution against stubborn adherence to past or present relations.

## CONCEPT OF COMPETITION

Discussions among economists have been fruitful in developing, modifying, and clarifying concepts that are useful in the description and understanding of marketing as well as in the making of marketing decisions. (I am impressed by the extent to which recent management research has been devoted to how management decisions are made rather than to the decisions themselves.) A sharp dichotomy between competition and monopoly was neither realistic nor very useful in practical affairs. The newer concepts of monopolistic competition, oligopoly, workable competition, and administered prices are much more pertinent to actual business situations. The idea of cross-elasticity of demand has gained in acceptance and application to the analysis of specific market situations. So also has the idea of the kinked demand curve.

Understanding of these concepts seems to have an increasing influence on pricing policies of individual firms. However, the relation of costs to pricing policy and the influence of full costs, marginal costs, allocation of common costs, break-even analysis, and similar matters on specific prices still is somewhat moot.

In 1927 Wesley Mitchell wrote as follows: "The prices ruling at any moment for the infinite variety of commodities, services, and rights which are being bought and sold constitute a system in the full meaning of that term. That is, the prices paid for goods of all sorts are so related to each other as to make a regular and connected whole. Our knowledge of these relations is curiously inexact. . ."[6] Our knowledge of these relations is still inexact, but the economists' clarification and market research have at least helped toward an understanding of how some of them come about.

The concept or strategy suggested by Edwin G. Nourse in *Price Making in a Democracy*[7] is still hotly argued. Who should get how much of the advantage from technological improvements in production—stockholders of large firms, owners of small businesses, wage earners through wage increases, or consumers through lowered prices? Nourse argues for a large share to the consumer directly, Walter Reuther favors higher wages, some neo-Keynesians want high dividends to attract capital for an ever expanding economy. The consensus has not jelled yet. Relative prices unquestionably are of major importance in marketing strategy, but no one knows just how or to what extent they should be used.

One of the changes in the applied use of a concept as a marketing strategy is seen in the case of the single price. The basic policy of one price to all was introduced by many merchants in the nineteenth century. It gained considerable acceptance, enough so that it was considered the general policy. Trade-in allowances, package deals, trading stamps, and other devices have eroded some of the rigidity so that a recent article carried the title "One Price— Fact or Fiction?" and the implication that fiction was more nearly the case. Marshall Field is using trade-in allowances even with pots and pans!

The distinction between price competition, product-quality competition, and non-price competition still is somewhat foggy. Marketing strategies include attempts to increase sales (and profits) through lowering price, through change in product, or through mere sales effort

with no change in either price or product. Perhaps the latter is the true non-price competition. Probably in most real-life situations two or more of the three strategies are in use at the same time, but it is useful for the marketing analyst to consider their effects separately.

## SALES PROMOTION

For the purposes of this paper I have divided marketing strategies into three classes, namely:

(1) Direct price competition (just discussed briefly).

(2) Product development and change (merely mentioned).

(3) Sales promotion (now to be discussed).

Attempts to sell an existing product at an established price involve many sophisticated strategies. Included are such obvious things as personal selling, advertising, and merchandise fairs. Specific tactics may change with time. In 1923, for example, Daniel Starch defined advertising as "selling in print."[8] Since the advent of radio and TV, new methods of advertising have been adopted and the definition has been broadened.

As I wrote in 1927, however, "It must be clearly recognized that 'advertising' is but a convenient name for certain forms of persuasion applied to buying and selling. At many points the economic arguments would apply with equal force to the arousing of desire . . . whether the technique used was 'advertising' or 'personal selling.' In such cases the choice between the two would be merely one of relative costs. With this in mind it seems unnecessary to define advertising; each reader may include in this category whatever technical activities suit his fancy."[9]

Probably it is likewise unnecessary to define sales promotion. It may be pointed out, however, that in addition to various forms of publicity, the extension of credit, as in installment selling, may be used as a sales-promoting stratagem. When consumer credit is expanded, consumer purchasing is stimulated as with any other form of sales promotion. Moreover, it follows that there is an increase in inflationary pressure.

In 1928 Paul Nystrom wrote that "there seems to be little to indicate that any important

---

[6] *Business Cycles* (New York: National Bureau of Economic Research, 1927).

[7] Washington: The Brookings Institution, 1944.

[8] *Principles of Advertising* (New York: A. W. Shaw, 1923), p. 5.

[9] Vaile, *Economics of Advertising* (New York: Ronald Press, 1927), p. 3.

trend of fashion has ever been changed by any form of sales promotion." [10] Probably this statement still holds so far as the *direction* of any trend is concerned. On the other hand, the *rate* of acceptance or decline of a fashion may be affected by sales promotion. Because of these phenomena, sales-promoting effort usually is correlated directly with industrial fluctuations, with increased effort when sales are easy to make, and with decreased effort when selling is difficult. This holds true, certainly, both for advertising and for extension of installment credit. Thus instability of economic activity is furthered by sales promotion. The over-all data suggest little change in this situation over the years. The burden placed on the monetary system and other possible devices for the control of industrial fluctuations is increased by sales promotion. The question may well be raised whether, as a general concept or stratagem, sales promotion should or could be used as an aid toward industrial stability. Some individual firms appear to have successfully used it in this manner.

"In December 1923 there were no less than ten manufacturers of milk chocolate who unqualifiedly advertised their products as 'the best.' Such a condition is possible because there is no definite standard of 'best.'" [11] Today an equal number of cigarette brands are advertised as having "the best taste." Apparently the use of claims that can neither be proven nor disproven is a continuing stratagem. This is one way that advertisers continue to play up what Borden has called the "hidden qualities" of goods.

Another stratagem that seems, if anything, to have grown in use is reference to scientific evidence. This is an age in which science is popular —as Anthony Standen tells us, Science is a Sacred Cow! Unfortunately, not all of the evidence used by advertisers is actually pertinent to the consumer's problem, but if it helps persuade him to buy, it has accomplished its purpose. Thus sales promotion continues to be opportunistic and to prey upon the gullible.

So long as these practices are continued it is doubtful that consumers are helped by advertising to make wiser or more rational choices in their general purchasing. In fact, I see little in today's advertising strategy, at least at the consumer level, to modify my 1927 statement that "if education were the principal claim of

advertising as it is now practiced, it would be an enormously wasteful enterprise." [12] Of course, as George French said years ago, "The major function of advertising is to persuade," [13] and this it seems to do pretty effectively with categorical and emotionally slanted claims.

In 1926 Clare Griffen wrote, "The third phase of the [automobile] industry will be one in which . . . annual sales will go largely to replace cars that have been eliminated from use. A majority of the industries of the United States have been in this . . . stage for a long time. . . ." [14] In 1927 I made a companion point in connection with the sales promotion of the California Fruit Growers Exchange. [15] In this case a wide expansion of supply was possible. In fact, while sales promotion had successfully expanded demand, supply had increased at about the same rate, leading to the conclusion that individuals who had owned orange orchards in 1905 had just about maintained a status quo so far as the purchasing power of the net income from these orchards was concerned. More recent data indicate that this result has been continued for another thirty years. In other words, in the long run, at least in this case, the rate of return on invested capital has not been increased by sales promotion.

Perhaps in each of these cases the professor was overly conservative or even pessimistic. Certainly the automobile industry has not yet, thirty-one years later, reached a mere replacement basis; and when control of supply is more practical, some brand advertising continues to be accompanied by high rates of return on invested capital even after more than thirty years of continuous promotion. While the two illustrations suggest the inevitable long-range result of specific sales promotion, aggressive businessmen refuse to accept the inevitable, thank goodness!

This discussion is both too broad and too episodic for successful summary or statement of specific conclusions. In closing, therefore, let me merely say that marketing is a living, growing organism. As it grows, its behavior sometimes is erratic and whimsical. Our understanding of its problems has increased materially, as has our ability to direct its further development. As with much of evolution, however, constructive and lasting change often is slow in coming.

---

[10] *Economics of Fashion* (New York: Ronald Press, 1928), p. 36.

[11] Vaile, *op. cit.*, p. 49.

[12] *Ibid.*, p. 59.

[13] *Advertising* (New York: Ronald Press, 1924).

[14] "The Evolution of the Automobile Market," *Harvard Business Review*, July, 1926, pp. 407–408.

[15] Vaile, *op. cit.*, Chap. 7.

# B. Marketing in Free and Planned Economies

## 4. *Soviet Economic Growth*

FRANCIS M. BODDY

CAPITALISM AND SOVIET COMMUNISM

If we take the view that in the economic race between the Soviet Union and the United States the basic resource factors (except for the deficiency in Soviet agriculture) are about equal, the outcome may be determined largely by the relative efficiency with which the two economies can be managed. Here, of course, direct comparisons are difficult because of the striking organizational differences between the two systems: one is a mixed-market economy, the other is, basically, a centrally planned state socialism. Nevertheless, both the US and the USSR come up with answers to essentially the same questions. Each of them has to make decisions concerning:

1. Who shall use the available natural resources? For what purposes? How intensively? At what locations?

2. How much of current resources shall be directed to the production of investment goods —and of what kinds?

3. How shall the remaining available capital goods and labor supply be used? What goods and services shall be produced for current consumption?

4. How shall the output for current consumption be distributed to the consumers?

5. How shall resources and output be allocated between private or personal consumption and public or group consumption?

‡‡ SOURCE: Reprinted by permission from *Soviet Union: Paradox and Change* edited by Robert T. Holt and John E. Turner (New York: Holt, Rinehart and Winston, Inc., 1962), pp. 62–89.

The distinctive characteristics of capitalism and Soviet Communism can be illustrated by the location of the decision-making power in the economy and by the forces that determine how these decisions are made.

### Features of Capitalism

1. Ownership and control of natural resources, capital goods, and personal labor lies with individuals or firms owned by individuals. These are the private property rights of a capitalistic society. Such rights may be temporarily (or permanently, except for labor) assigned to other persons by mutual agreement. This is the *right of contract*.

2. The organization and fundamental direction of the economic processes of production, exchange, and consumption are accomplished by the market system. This is, first of all, a system for the collection and dissemination of *information* as to current supplies and demands and market prices; and it is, secondly, a system of processes and institutions by which the exchanges of the goods and services are arranged for and accomplished. Under capitalism the market system is not directly planned nor are the prices fixed by the government or by any organized groups, but arise spontaneously and react freely to the economic actions of all the individual persons or firms in the economy.

3. The income of each individual and firm is determined basically by the market valuation of the contribution of that individual's (or firm's) labor, or of his other owned resources, to the economic output of the system.

4. Hence the economic incentives that lie behind economic decisions are (a) income for the owners of resources, (b) profits for the business firms, and (c) individual desires and satisfactions for the consumers.

In modern western capitalism generally, and in the United States, government has become an important economic sector. For defense, and for a variety of other governmental activities, the governments purchase large quantities of materials and products and hire large numbers of employees through the markets. In addition, governments of capitalist countries plan their policies of taxation and expenditure, as well as their monetary policies, in such a way as to promote full employment of resources and stability in overall economic conditions. In carrying out these activities, however, the governments have generally acted through the markets and have not used direct controls or "fixed" the market results.

In spite of the governmental effects, and in some cases controls, on the free market, however, a basic characteristic of western capitalism is the dominant role played by the free market in directing the whole economic process.

### Features of Soviet Communism

1. All natural resources and all capital goods are owned collectively, that is, by the state; and the direction of their use, as well as the use of the labor of all individuals, lies with the state.

2. The organization and direction of the economic processes of resource use, production, and distribution is directly controlled by the state, although each consumer is permitted to choose, to a large degree, how he shall spend his income for the goods or services available to the consumer.

3. The incomes of individuals come solely from payments for personal contributions to the production of goods and services, and the rates of payment are determined by the state. No individuals are permitted to own or to receive the income from natural resources or capital goods (except for the "private plots" permitted to the farmers), or to hire other individuals for productive or income-earning activities.

4. The market processes and institutions are firmly and centrally controlled by the state, and the forces of supply and demand do not control market prices or economic decisions. Rather, prices and economic decisions conform to the central directive—the economic plan of the

state. In the actual operation of Soviet Communism, this complete economic control and direction by the state is somewhat tempered by the economic and political necessities of permitting some degree of individualism, particularly in the agricultural sector, and permitting some freedom of choice to consumers. Some small areas of private property exist (for example, the small "private plots" allotted to the collective farmers and private ownership of some livestock). Moreover, in recent years the collective farms have been freed from the system of compulsory delivery of their produce to state agencies at state-set prices, and they may sell their output directly in consumer markets if they wish. But these are minor exceptions. The basic pattern is centralized state control over all significant economic decisions.

From this brief sketch of the two economic systems, the primary differences are apparent. First, the contrast of individual versus state ownership and control over resources; second, the contrast of a free-market system versus central planning as a means of organizing the economic life of the society.

In a mixed-market economy there is no overall economic plan that directs each individual or firm in its economic activities. Decisions on who shall make how much of what for whose consumption are decentralized. The quality and quantity of production in a given firm or industry are determined over time by the interaction of the forces of supply and demand. The future plans for a firm are made by the management as it estimates future demand for its products in relationship to anticipated costs. The resources needed for production are bought at a price determined by the market; the products produced are sold at a price determined by the market.

In the Soviet Union, on the other hand, the plans for each operating unit (the *enterprise*) are handed down from above. The resources needed for production are sent to the enterprise at a fixed-price according to the plan—management does not (in theory, at least) have to procure them. Finished products are distributed through the marketing outlets according to the plan at a price set by the plan. The plan for a firm is a segment of the plan for an industry (before 1957) or for an area (after 1957) that, in turn, is a part of the master plan for the entire economy.

To the uninitiated observer of these two different economic systems, the planned economy, in which all important decisions are centrally made by relatively few men, may seem to be the model of rational and efficient order; and a free economy may appear as a disordered array in which hundreds of thousands of entrepreneurs are making independent decisions, with only disorder and inefficiency as the inevitable results. But reality may be quite the reverse. The market mechanism in a free economy is an integrating force of great power, providing the entrepreneur with the information necessary to make rational decisions concerning the most efficient use of resources in his firm.

When in a free-market system the economy is running along at something like full employment; when general economic conditions are relatively stable, so that decision-makers have reason to be confident of their future plans; and when free competition is the dominant characteristic of the market relationships; then the economy has, in its market system, an operating process that leads to an efficient allocation of resources that, in turn, produces a maximum of desired products and services.

In fact, of course, and in spite of the effort of governments to maintain the desirable conditions, the system works far from perfectly. Unemployment obviously signals failure to achieve as much output as can and should be produced. Monopoly is neither fully prevented nor perfectly regulated when it does arise. And the rapid changes in technology and in consumer and governmental demands keep the system continually off balance. Nevertheless, free-market system achieves a very high degree of economic efficiency and preserves the highest levels of individual human freedoms.

Part of the job of the designers of a planned and centrally controlled economy is to develop incentives and mechanisms that will achieve the efficient allocation of economic resources to achieve *their* economic objectives. What they need, therefore, is a plan or set of plans that will do for their economy what the market largely does for western economies. The complexity of the problem of detailed allocation of all economic resources by a central plan may be illustrated by a vastly oversimplified example, using a very simple "economy," and posing the problem arising out of a single planned change for the coming plan period.

## AN ILLUSTRATION OF THE PLANNERS' PROBLEM

One way to illustrate the difficulty of allocating resources in a planned system is to set up an input-output table for a simple economy (Table 1). This simple hypothetical economy consists in its entirety of five sectors (metal, machinery, fuel, agricultural products, and labor). The table shows the number of units of the products (outputs) of each sector required by each of the other sectors.

Across the top of the resulting table are listed sectors that consume the products of each producing sector. For example, the figures in the machinery column (reading down) show the units of output of each of the producing sectors that are consumed during the year by the machinery sector in the creation of its output. In order to make 200 units of machinery, it takes 65 units of metal, 25 units of machinery, 5 units of fuel, 10 units of agricultural produce, and 200 units of labor. The same sectors as producing sectors are listed down the side (except that the output, labor, is used as a title instead of the title of the consuming units, households). One can read across a row and find in each column the disposition of the output of that sector. The disposition of the total output of 50 units of fuel is shown by the figures in each column in the row labeled "Fuel."

An input-output table can be constructed on the basis of past records of actual operations of the economy or from knowledge of the tech-

TABLE 1. A Simple Model of an Economy

| Producing Sectors | Consuming or Using Sectors | | | | | Total Output |
|---|---|---|---|---|---|---|
| | Metal | Machinery | Fuel | Agric. | Households | |
| Metal | 10 | 65 | 10 | 5 | 10 | 100 |
| Machinery | 40 | 25 | 35 | 75 | 25 | 200 |
| Fuel | 15 | 5 | 5 | 5 | 20 | 50 |
| Agriculture | 15 | 10 | 50 | 50 | 525 | 650 |
| Labor | 100 | 200 | 100 | 550 | 50 | 1000 |

nical and engineering requiremnts of the available techniques for producing each product.

We can show the basic problem of a planner who is concerned with setting future production targets in each sector by looking at this table. (The establishment of such goals is, of course, one of the things the Soviet economic plan does.) Suppose that the planners decide to increase next year the amount of machinery to be made available to the household sector by 20 units. Since the total machinery output is 200 units, this is an increase of 10 percent in the total output of machines. This increase in production will require a 10-percent increase of all of the products needed to make machines: 6.5 units of metal, 0.5 unit of fuel, 1 unit of agricultural produce, and 20 units of labor, *plus* 2.5 additional units of machinery (it takes machines to make machines). Thus the other units of inputs into the machine sector will have to be increased by an additional 1.25 percent. But this is only the beginning of the computations. The additional units of metal that are required to make the additional units of machines will require increased inputs into the metal sector of the economy. Thus we can see that a change in just one column in the table requires a change in many other columns. If our planners were trying to set new goals for each of the products used by each of the other sectors, there would be hundreds of computations to make in this simple five-sector economy.

While even this simple illustration seems complex enough, the problem of Soviet planners is unimaginably more complex. Our five-sector input-output table must be replaced by one containing thousands of sectors. (A thousand-sector table would have one million entries, although many would consist of zeros.) The computational problem would be impossible if it were not for the development of high-speed electronic computers. Even these, however, could not effectively handle an input-output model that would recognize the need to break down the calculations to particular enterprises within the product classes and economic sectors. In many respects, however, the computational problem is the easy one. It is even more difficult to get the information needed to construct such a table, particularly in a rapidly changing economy where technological developments and increased labor productivity are constantly modifying the input-output relationships. Estimates have to be used, and errors in estimating even a few of the required inputt-output relationships will generate errors through the system. Inaccuracies of this sort will result in nonfulfillment of an output plan, or in a waste of resources or both.

As the planner runs through the computations of the input-output requirements necessary to fulfill a specified final output list, he may well find bottlenecks in the form of shortages of plant capacity, of raw materials or fuels, or of labor. This would call for a recasting of the plan to allocate more resources to break these bottlenecks by increasing investment in the critical areas, which will mean that lower output goals must be planned in the final-goods sectors. Sometimes, indeed, it may not be feasible to provide the inputs called for by a plan, and the goals may have to be adjusted to bring them within the limits imposed by resources and technology.

After the major outlines of the problem of economic decision-making in a planned economy have been laid out, there still remains the question of what administrative structure is to be established to carry out the plan that has been decided upon.

## IS THERE A SUBSTITUTE FOR THE MARKET?

The Soviet Union is certainly not going to adopt, in the foreseeable future, all the features of a market system. Economic priorities will still be set by the political leaders in Moscow. But if the maturing economy is to achieve the level of efficiency necessary to maintain growth rates in the seven to nine percent range, the regime may have to borrow some of the techniques of the market system to provide rapid, accurate information on the relative scarcity of the factors of production. In other words, some type of pricing system will have to be developed in which prices reflect relative scarcity and real costs of production.

The Communist rulers have already taken a few timid steps in this direction. The freeing of the collective farms from the compulsory delivery of produce is one example. The farm manager has the option of selling produce in a market, and thus prices in the market to some degree affect his planting and investment decisions—to the extent that he is permitted to exercise any discretion. The manipulation of market prices by the planners may thus to some degree replace "the plan" as the main directive over the farmers.

In many ways, a more interesting adaptation has been in the consumer-goods sector of the economy. In the past, the typical manner in which the USSR planned the distribution of consumer goods was to estimate net disposable income in each republic and to provide the amount of consumer goods and/or to set the prices in such a way as to absorb this income. There was only the crudest concern for product mix and none at all for individual differences in tastes and styles. This method proved effective in an austere economy, in which consumer goods were so short in supply that the consumers had little alternative to accepting what was available. As incomes rose and as larger quantities of goods became available, however, consumers could afford to be more discriminating. A woman with enough clothes to meet her basic needs might save her money and wait until the dress style she wanted became available. A man could afford to be more particular about the quality and style of a suit. The result was that although most types of consumer goods remained scarce, some embarrassing surpluses began to appear. Indeed, certain products scarcely moved off the shelves.

In order to correct this situation, the system was modified. Now retail trade officials in the several republics are beginning to *order* the consumer goods they want from the producers or wholesalers, rather than merely distributing the goods sent to them on the basis of the economic plan. At this point, however, the retail-trade officials begin to encounter some of the fundamentals of a freshman course in the economics of the market. Since demand depends on price, the suit that will barely sell for 100 rubles may sell very well at 50. The retail-trade officials, to make the new approach an improvement, must have some device for measuring consumer demand and determining its elasticity for a wide range of products. The best and most efficient way (perhaps the only adequate way) of obtaining measures of these factors is through a market in which the consumer can use his "ruble ballot," and in which the prices are permitted to respond to supply and demand.

By 1961 surpluses in certain capital goods were also beginning to appear. The obvious solution to this problem would also be to allow factory management and *sovnarkhoz* officials to bid for their own capital goods. Here again certain elements of a market would have to be introduced to facilitate the making of a rational choice. But a decision on which capital goods should be purchased involves a consideration that is rarely present in a consumer-goods transaction; there is a range of alternative choices that would involve a different mix of capital and manpower, according to the production process in which the capital goods are to be used. The manager will want to choose the most efficient mix, but what criteria does he have to guide him?

A simple case will illustrate the problem. Suppose the *sovnarkhoz* in a region having an iron and steel complex decides to open a new iron mine and must provide for transporting the ore to the furnaces. The alternatives might be an electrified railway, a steam railway, or a road to accommodate heavy-duty trucks. Let us assume that the initial cost for the electric railway is 12,500,000 rubles; for the steam railway, 5,000,000 rubles; and for the truck highway (including the trucks), 2,000,000 rubles. The annual operating costs (including depreciation) of the electric railway are 250,-000 rubles; of the steam railway, 750,000 rubles; and of the truck highway, 1,000,000 rubles. Which alternative is the most rational and efficient? One can answer this question if he knows the marginal costs of capital in the economy. In a market economy, interest rates provide a good measure of such costs.

Not only is there nothing really comparable in the Soviet economy, but Soviet rulers have steadfastly refused to accept the idea of interest rates, regarding them as a feature of the exploitative capitalistic system. One of the fundamental themes of classical Marxist doctrine, to which lip service is still being paid, is the labor theory of value. The official ideology, in other words, denies that there can be anything like a cost of capital. If capital "costs nothing" in investment decisions, capital costs tend in fact to become enormous. This is one of the reasons for the "gigantomania" that is so characteristic of many Soviet productive enterprises. If the economy is to reach optimal efficiency, capital costs will have to be calculated as a part of investment decisions. If they are to be calculated, they must be measured. If they are to be measured, there is no really good substitute for introducing the concept of interest rates, which, in turn, must be sensitive to supplies of and demands for capital if they are to be reliable guides in decision-making.

In short, we are arguing that if the Soviet economy, rapidly increasing in complexity, is to achieve the efficiency necessary for continuing rapid economic growth, certain characteristics of the market will have to be introduced to provide reliable guides for rational economic decisions. The market, however, is not an "automatic" decision-making system. Knowing how to use the information derived from market operations requires the professional skills of the economist or of the western type businessman more than it does the talents of the successful bureaucrat or politician. For the intricate economic machine to operate efficiently, economic decision-making will probably have to become the job of economic managers rather than of politicians. The price the political elite may have to pay for economic efficiency is the diminution of some of their control over the economy.

Khrushchev has shown a strong pragmatic bent. To him the critical question is, "Will it work?" This has led him to steer the whole Soviet system, and particularly its economic system, in directions far from those indicated by Marx and Lenin.

The strength of the income incentive in persuading men to work effectively seems to have so impressed him that he told the Twenty-second Party Congress in 1961 that the present "socialist" rule (Article 12 of the Soviet Constitution)—"Work in the USSR is a duty and a matter of honor for every able-bodied citizen in accordance with the principle: 'He who does not work, neither shall he eat' "—would continue as a supreme principle under Communism as well.

Given this strong practical approach, the current Soviet regime may well permit or even encourage moves in the direction of a decentralized and partly market-controlled economy that will be heretical to the ideological Communists.

## THE OUTCOME OF THE ECONOMIC RACE

The programs that the Soviet regime may have to adopt in order to win such a race, however, may in time have great impact upon the structure of Communist control over the society. We have suggested that the problems of maintaining and measuring economic efficiency in a mature economy may ultimately call for the adoption of a decentralized and, to a significant degree, market-controlled economic organization. The discussion of "synthetic" or "shadow" prices in the context of mathematical-economic analysis of economic problems by Soviet economists themselves; the use of prices rather than the plan to control and direct agricultural production; the struggle to find some "true measure" of economic costs of production; and the continued emphasis on the further decentralization of economic decision-making in the Party Program for the Twenty-second Party Congress—all these give some indication that modifications in the economic machinery may be in process. The state will undoubtedly retain ownership of the basic resources and monopoly over all economic enterprises; what is suggested here is that the *means* of control may move toward a modified market system.

If this development occurs to any significant extent, it will lead to a further strengthening of the use of economic incentives for the workers and a consequent further rise in the influence of the consumer in the system. It will also tend to attach greater importance to successful decentralized "managers" rather than to the central "planners" as key personnel in the economic system. Shifts in the locus of decision-making away from the center in the economic sphere may even be accompanied by changes in the pattern of control in other areas of Soviet life. Whether in fact such developments take place depends upon the way in which the Party moves to maintain its power. Khrushchev may discover, however, that the type of people upon whom he must depend in the economic race have a different political and psychological outlook from those of the ordinary Communist functionary. If this is true, and if such personnel begin to gain a bigger voice in decision-making, the structure of the dictatorship itself may undergo some modification over time.

# 5. The Role of the Market

ZDENĚK KODET

If anyone wanted to briefly express the essential purpose of our efforts to introduce the new system of economic management, he would have to list as one of the main aims the creation of conditions for the operation of the market mechanism. In this connection, there now arise a number of theoretical and practical questions. While it is impossible to give an exhausting answer to all of these problems, I shall at least try to answer some of them.

First of all, there is the question of the role of the market as one of the driving forces of the mechanism of socialist economy, as the stimulus and source of economic initiative. We know that under the administrative centralized model of management the economic pressure of the market is replaced by the administrative imposition of a technocratically viewed plan. By excluding or formalizing the market, the plan deprives itself of the possibility of rationally influencing the economy. In solving clashes of interests resulting from economic reality, administrative pressure cannot replace economic coercion resulting from market relations.

The replacement of economic pressure by administrative coercion has gradually led and still leads to the elimination of stimuli of socialist economic development. Mutual competition between socialist commodity producers, i.e. enterprises, and even between individual persons has been weakened and deformed. This is proved by the present formal character of socialist emulation. The elimina-

♦ SOURCE: Reprinted by permission from *New Trends in Czechoslovakia Economics*, Pragopress, Prague 6, Slavickova 5, edited by Ladislav Jenik, pp. 67–88.

tion of economic stimuli and the lack of innovations is particularly adversely reflected in the introduction of the achievements of science and technology into production.

However, the overestimation of the effects of administrative pressure in the economic sphere has not only economic but also socio-political consequences. This, I think, is the basic cause of the decline of such values as labour discipline, labour morale, social responsibility etc. This is also the source of the present underestimation of the role played by the human factor not only in its capacity of being the ultimate goal of production but also as a factor in the process of production. The lack of economic pressure creates unsocialist phenomena in the sphere of production and eventually in the entire society. Their elimination and the solution of serious social problems must be sought basically in the economic sphere although, naturally, it cannot be reduced to this sphere only.

Socialist economy cannot normally function for a prolonged period without the operation of the law of values of the market mechanism. This is proved by the present situation of economic theory as well as by our past economic development. Under socialism, the market must be the main source of the driving forces of economic development; the market provides the main stimuli of economic growth, economic initiative and the spirit of enterprise. Nothing can replace the market in this respect.

Value relation and the market must form the basis for emulation (competition) between individual persons and between socialist commodity producers, i.e. enterprises. The mechanism of the market will enable the solution of economic contradictions in a flexible and operative way and will thus create conditions for a far greater flexibility in the entire mechanism of the operation of socialist economy. Our experience shows that without the influence of the market this mechanism is rigid, inflexible, and unable to adapt itself to changing conditions as quickly as necessary.

I think it is no exaggeration to say that the market mechanism is also one of the main conditions for the planned regulation of the process of reproduction in the scale of the entire society. Theoretical study and our present practical experience supply convincing evidence that it is very difficult, if not impossible, to achieve a planned management of socialist economy without the mechanism of the market. The economic categories of the market create objective correctives of subjectivism in planning; they create the "economic basis" for these correctives and stable starting points providing a reliable basis for the plan.

I do not intend to give a detailed characteristic of the relationship between the plan and the market under socialism, nor do I want to overestimate the role of the market. I believe that—in theory and particularly in practice—this danger is not by far imminent in this country; in fact, it is rather the reverse.

We do not perhaps as yet fully realize—in economic theory and in the practical implementation of the new system—the impact of the introduction and the operation of the mechanism of the market in our economy. Frequently, we still consider the market as merely an unequal complement of the present mechanism of planning. It is, of course, theoretically correct to assert—as is frequently done —that the plan must rectify the defects or the shortsightedness of the market, that the market is unable to give a long-range orientation to enterprises, particularly in the field of investments etc. This situation will evidently exist also in this country when the introduction of the new system reaches the state we call the final shape of this system. Essentially, there is no market in our economy, it has to be created. *Will not the newly created mechanism of the market—at least for a certain time —have to rectify the defects of a technocratically viewed and schematically implemented system of planning?* My answer to this question is in the positive and I believe that for some time to come the plan and the market

must be viewed as two equivalent principles on which we want to build the economic mechanism of the new system of management. The market as well as the most perfect existing mechanisms of planning on the scale of the entire society have certain defects. These shortcomings must be known, they must be realized and as far as possible (it will not evidently be possible to do so completely) they must be eliminated by mutually complementing the plan and the market.

The transition from "non-market" to "market" economy is greatly complicated by the fact that we want and must achieve it with the burden of past errors and shortcomings— i.e. under conditions of deep economic disproportions making the economy generally unbalanced. Although the creation of conditions for the operation of market relations is rendered more difficult by the improper economic balance, there can at the same time be no doubt that it cannot be eliminated without the operation of the market. Under the present situation, the market is the basic prerequisite for creating and maintaining a proper balance in our economy.

I believe that this "vicious circle" must be eliminated by efforts both from below and from the top, by solving micro-problems as well as macroproblems. *However, from the factual point of view and from the point of view of timing, priority should be held by solutions from below, which should begin in enterprises and bring about a change in the scope of their interests.* One of the most important prerequisites for this is that enterprises should be sufficiently independent in decision-making and in their economic activities in order that they be really able to act as commodity producers and that they might be exposed to the pressure of the market. However, our enterprises will not this year have the necessary degree of "free" decision-making and we cannot, consequently, expect them to act as producers of commodities and to work along the principle of economic calculation.

✳  ✳  ✳

At the same time, however, the consequences of the decisions made by enterprises as regards the way how they use their means must have an impact on them—a positive or a negative impact—and must influence their future decisions. This principle of the new system of management has been so frequently repeated that it sounds nearly like a banality. In spite of this, however, some of its consequences are frequently ignored; this particularly concerns the interrelation between this principle and the economic independence of enterprises. A restriction of the economic independence of enterprises makes it impossible to delegate to them full responsibility for their economic activities, it slows down the creation of an effectively operating market and does not create conditions for influencing the decision-making in enterprises from the centre.

I believe that *if the market is to exert complex economic pressure on the producer, the independence of enterprises in changing factors of production, in selecting production programmes, in price-setting and in taking decisions on wages must be substantially greater than that attained this year in the course of the first steps of the new system.* These important rights of enterprises are not only the condition for a functioning market but also for the establishment of the proper balance in our economy by means of value instruments. The most important of them is evidently the price.

Prices can influence the restoration and the maintenance of the proper balance only if they are *flexible*. The restoration and the maintenance of flexible prices and of flexibility in the entire price system indispensably require that, to a certain necessary extent, decisions on prices be made by the commodity producers themselves, i.e. by enterprises. As soon as a certain limit in decision-making as regards changes in the prices of individual products or price levels is exceeded in the sense that these decisions are made by central bodies which are unable to ensure that prices quickly respond to the market, the price system becomes inflexible, prices cease to react to the demand and the supply and the market does not function.

\* \* \*

The principle of a flexible response of prices to the market is to a certain extent interrelated with problems concerning the *determination of the type of price* which is one of the decisive criteria of proportionality in market economy. It is probable that this is not only the question of a central decision on the type of the price, even if the optimum alternative is worked out by mathematical methods. *The type of the price is given and influenced by the pattern of the market and at the same time influences it* (under the term "pattern of the market" I understand primarily the degree of concentration and specialization in

production). Therefore, our considerations as regards the correctness and incorrectness of a certain type of price will be eventually verified by the normally functioning market.

\* \* \*

## THE MARKET AND INVESTMENTS

The process of restoring the market from below must be of course accompanied by a number of measures taken in the centre, in the macrostructure. We particularly refer to such decisions as determining the share of accumulation and consumption in the national income and determining the rates of growth and the size of investments involved. In this case, too, the adopted measures will have to be—of course temporarily—subordinated to the aim of creating a balanced economy and of thus narrowing down the gap between resources and needs and creating conditions for a functioning market.

*I believe that, to a certain extent, greater effectiveness of investments also depends on a functioning market. The economic pressure of the market must restore the criteria of economic effectiveness also in the sphere of investments.* It is impossible to imagine a system of management based on a functioning market from which investments or the effect of their economic activities would be artificially excluded.

In the sphere of investments, centralism in taking decisions on investments is not being substantially relaxed this year. Nevertheless, the achievement of an economic solution makes it necessary in this sphere also to *establish a direct economic relationship between the means advanced for investments and their effect.* Economic organizations, especially enterprises, must finance investments, on which they decide, from their own resources or by credit. At the same time, however, they must, by their long-term activities ensure the reproduction of the funds advanced for investments. The economic mechanism must ensure a direct impact—whether positive or negative—of the economic effect on the organization or the enterprise which has decided on the investment. This must eliminate the anonymity in the present way of making the entire society bear the economic consequences of capital construction.

If these principles are to be implemented, the right to decide about investments must be to a much greater extent transferred to economic organization which can be held economically responsible. Decisions on investments, on the way they will be financed, the formation of prices, etc., will then become part of the market relations operating in the entire economy.

\* \* \*

## THE STRUCTURE OF THE MARKET

If we want to appreciate the role of the market in our country, it is particularly important to study its *structure*. An analysis of our industrial structure over the past years shows that organizational concentration of the basis of productions is growing. In 1958, many hundreds of enterprises were reorganized into 250 economic production units and, in 1964, their number declined to 236. Of these, about 90 branch enterprises were created on July 1, 1965 under the new organization of the technical productive basis. However, organizational concentration is merely one of the many conditions for the growing concentration of production, for concentrating more and more elements of the process of work in a single system of cooperation in production. Analyses show that concentration of production has been stagnant over the past years and is still stagnant. *This makes it possible to conclude that there was an increasing contradiction in this country between growing organizational concentration in the basis of production, on one hand, and the process of economic concentration of production proper, which was stagnant, on the other hand.*

\* \* \*

At the same time, small, so-called unprofitable enterprises and workshops frequently used to be closed down in a rash manner and without justification in the past. For instance in the food industry, the number of local production units declined from about 44,000 in 1948 to some 5000 in 1965, i.e. by about nine-tenths. A similar development took place in other branches as well. The effectiveness of small enterprises and workshops was measured only according to the fulfillment of the indices of the plan, especially of productivity of labour; as a consequence of this, they naturally appeared to be "unprofitable." No sufficient account was taken of the role they played on the market in satisfying needs and in balancing the demand and supply.

The process of specialization in production developed in a similar way. Under the model of centralized administrative management, the process of specialization was reduced to shifting production programmes more or less arbitrarily from one producer onto the other. Under these conditions, the division of production programmes was naturally stimulated exclusively from the top.

This has led to a *distinctive state of monopolization* in our production. Its specific features could be briefly characterized as follows:

(a) Its predominant feature is its administratively organizational character resulting from the operation of the model of centralized administrative management and from a certain conception of the economic and organizational function of the State. This is reflected in the criteria applied in creating the present institutional structure of the technical productive basis and of central bodies of management in general, as well as in the factors stimulating its development; these were and continue to be predominantly of an external, non-economic character. *Consequently, this monopolization is not the result of the economic concentration of production itself.*

(b) As to its type, it is a *monopoly of the offer:* the whole party of the offer uses its exclusive monopoly position in relation to the party of the demand, i.e. of consumption. This monopoly has emerged as a result of the operation of the model of centralized administrative management which maintains its long-term existence. The fact that demand is generally greater than supply weakens the competition between producers, their competition for raising the productivity of work and for cutting down production costs or, in brief, for providing the conditions of production. This weakens the internal stimuli of economic progress.

(c) If, on the basis of a legal administrative act (e.g. a directive plan) the State reserves the production of a certain product or branch or even of all branches and main products to certain enterprises only, it provides them with a monopoly in the offer. At the same time, however, in this way it substantially restricts the possibility of extending the production of the given products beyond the scope of the fixed producers and thus provides them with a *permanent monopoly as regards production costs;* this is one of the factors slowing down technical progress.

\* \* \*

I think that certain negative features of our organizational monopolization could be eliminated by the operation of market relations. *Above all, it is necessary to gradually overcome the contradictions between concentration in the field of organization and concentration of production. The market is, among other things, also the source of internal impulses from the sphere of the production for raising the concentration of production. Enterprises would then integrate not only as a result of decisions coming from the top but primarily on the initiative from below.* They would get economically interested in the most various forms of associations—in research, in the sphere of circulation, in production etc. The effectiveness of this process, which evidently will have to be accelerated also by measures taken at the centre, will in this way be subject to economic criteria.

The operation of the market will also provide economic criteria for organizational concentration and for institutional changes in the managerial organism in general. Unfortunately, we did not have these criteria even at the time of last year's changes in the organization of the technical productive basis. *In carrying out organizational changes in the technical productive basis, greater account must be taken of the real concentration of production in the individual branches. Further, it is impossible to raise organizational concentration without raising concentration of production. The sharp differences in the level of concentration of production in the individual branches will evidently have to be taken into account in solving the question where the dividing line should be drawn in these branches between management based on cost accounting and administrative management. This dividing line should evidently not be the same in all branches.* This has also a direct bearing on the question of the optimum size of the unit to be managed on the basis of the cost accounting system.

I think we should also have a different approach to the question of the *usefulness of the existence of independent small and medium-sized enterprises.* In advanced capitalist countries there are, besides big monopolies, also thriving small and medium-sized enterprises which are in no way outsiders. Theoretical analyses show that this feature must be considered in connection with the operation of the mechanism of the market and with its structure. The present state of technical achievements, discontinuity in the growth of supply etc. make it necessary that, besides giant monopolies, there should exist—as a normal feature—independent small and medium-sized enterprises. I naturally do not want to draw simplified analogies with present-day capitalism. But I think that it would be correct —precisely in connection with the introduction of the mechanism of the market—to consider, also in this country, the *justification for the existence of small and medium-sized enterprises satisfying the specific needs of those purchasing for production and for individual purposes. These independent socialist enterprises would not have to be subordinated to any branch management or ministry but their work would be influenced exclusively by the general economic "rules of the game."*

In the light of these solutions, *the problem of using the competition between producers as one of the stimuli of progress,* would naturally assume a different character. The present organizational monopolization is frequently presented as being in contradiction to the possibility of taking advantage of this form of competition. The elimination of the administrative features of monopolization would create conditions for abolishing the "ration system" economy in raw materials and other material; it would make it possible to gradually enable the producer to freely choose his supplier, to eliminate the administrative method of setting up marketing territories and to replace it by a territorial division based on economic considerations, to create an effective organization for supplying the market with means of production etc. The solution of these problems—together with the elimination of the still existing legal ballast in the sphere of circulation—would make it possible to effectively use the competition between producers as one of the important stimuli promoting innovations and economic growth.

# The Environment and Forces of Marketing

A. Sociological and Anthropological Aspects
B. Psychology of Consumer Behavior
C. Economic Aspects of Consumer Behavior
D. Fashion and Culture
E. The Legal Framework
F. Ethical Considerations
G. Competition and Economic Environment
H. Technological Developments and Marketing
I. The Institutional Framework of Marketing

Marketing functions within a complex, dynamic, and demanding environment. Deeply ingrained cultural patterns of behavior mesh with contemporary forces such as technological change. Consumption patterns are influenced by economic capabilities and by social and psychological motivations to satisfy wants and to achieve ever-changing aspirations.

It is the task of marketing to link producer and consumer within our environment. To this end, marketing institutions continually adjust to the environmental needs as they carry on their functions.

The readings in Part II have been selected because they develop the perspective of the marketing environment. An appreciation and understanding of this environment helps one immeasurably to perceive marketing in its proper focus.

# A. Sociological and Anthropological Aspects

## 6. Social Classes and Spending Behavior
### PIERRE MARTINEAU

All societies place emphasis on some one structure which gives form to the total society and integrates all the other structures such as the family, the clique, voluntary association, caste, age, and sex groupings into a social unity.

Social stratification means any system of ranked statuses by which all the members of a society are placed in some kind of a super-ordinate and subordinate hierarchy. While money and occupation are important in the ranking process, there are many more factors, and these two alone do not establish social position. The concept of social class was designed to include this process of ranking people in superior and inferior social position by any and all factors.

### CLASS SYSTEM

It has been argued that there cannot be a class system existent in America when most individuals do not have the slightest idea of its formal structure. Yet in actuality every individual senses that he is more at home with and more acceptable to certain groups than to others. In a study of department stores and shopping behavior, it was found that the Lower-Status woman is completely aware that, if she goes into High-Status department stores, the clerks and the other customers in the store will punish her in various subtle ways.

"The clerks treat you like a crumb," one woman expressed it. After trying vainly to be waited on, another woman bitterly complained

‡‡ SOURCE: Reprinted by permission from the *Journal of Marketing* (National Quarterly Publication of the American Marketing Association), Vol. 23, No. 2, October 1958, pp. 121–130.

that she was loftily told, "We thought you were a clerk."

The woman who is socially mobile gives considerable thought to the external symbols of status, and she frequently tests her status by shopping in department stores which she thinks are commensurate with her changing position. She knows that, if she does not dress correctly, if she does not behave in a certain manner to the clerks, if she is awkward about the proper cues, then the other customers and the clerks will make it very clear that she does not belong.

In another study, very different attitudes in the purchase of furniture and appliances involving this matter of status were found. Middle-Class people had no hesitancy in buying refrigerators and other appliances in discount houses and bargain stores because they felt that they could not "go wrong" with the nationally advertised names. But taste in furniture is much more elusive and subtle because the brand names are not known; and, therefore, one's taste is on trial. Rather than commit a glaring error in taste which would exhibit an ignorance of the correct status symbols, the same individual who buys appliances in a discount house generally retreats to a status store for buying furniture. She needs the support of the store's taste.

In a very real sense, everyone of us in his consumption patterns and style of life shows an awareness that there is some kind of a superiority-inferiority system operating, and that we must observe the symbolic patterns of our own class.

Lloyd Warner and Paul Lunt have described a six-class system: the Upper-Upper, or old families; Lower-Upper, or the newly arrived; Upper-Middle, mostly the professionals and successful businessmen; Lower-Middle, or the white collar salaried class; Upper-Lower, or the wage earner, skilled worker group; and Lower-Lower, or the unskilled labor group.[1] For practical purposes, in order to determine the individual's class position, Warner and his associates worked out a rating index, not based on amount of income but rather on type of income, type of occupation, house type, and place of residence.

Athough the Warner thesis has been widely used in sociology, it has not generally been employed in marketing. As a matter of fact, some critics in the social sciences have held that, since Warner's thesis rested essentially on studies of smaller cities in the 10,000-25,000 class, this same system might not exist in the more complex metropolitan centers, or might not be unravelled by the same techniques. Furthermore, many marketers did not see the application of this dimension to the individual's economic behavior, since the studies of Warner and his associates had mostly been concerned with the differences in the broad patterns of living, the moral codes, etc.

## SOCIAL CLASS IN CHICAGO

Under Warner's guidance, the *Chicago Tribune* has undertaken several extensive studies exploring social class in a metropolitan city, and its manifestations specifically in family buying patterns. The problem was to determine if such a social-class system did exist in metropolitan Chicago, if the dimensions and the relationships were at all similar to the smaller cities which were studied before the far-reaching social changes of the past fifteen years. The studies were undertaken to see if there were any class significances in the individual family's spending-saving patterns, retail store loyalties, and his expressions of taste in typical areas such as automobiles, apparel, furniture, and house types.

It seems that many an economist overlooks the possibility of any psychological differences

between individuals resulting from different class membership. It is assumed that a rich man is simply a poor man with more money and that, given the same income, the poor man would behave exactly like the rich man. The *Chicago Tribune* studies crystallize a wealth of evidence from other sources that this is just not so, and that the Lower-Status person is profoundly different in his mode of thinking and his way of handling the world from the Middle-Class individual. Where he buys and what he buys will differ not only by economics but in symbolic value.

It should be understood, of course, that there are no hard and fast lines between the classes. Implicit in the notion of social class in America is the possibility of movement from one class to another. The "office boy-to-president" saga is a cherished part of the American dream. Bobo Rockefeller illustrates the female counterpart: from coal miner's daughter to socialite. As a corollary of the explorations in class, the study also tried to be definitive about the phenomenon of social mobility—the movement from one class to another.

There are numerous studies of vertical mobility from the level of sociological analysis, mostly by comparing the individual's occupational status to that of his father. There are also studies at the level of psychological analysis. This study attempted to combine the two levels, to observe the individual's progress and also to understand something of the dynamics of the mobile person as compared to the stable individual. The attempt was to look both backward and forward: tracing such factors as occupation, place of residence, and religion back to parents and grandparents, and then where the family expected to be in the next five or ten years, what were the educational plans for each son, each daughter, a discussion of future goals.

Because this article is confined primarily to social class, this section may be concluded by saying that the studies show a very clear relationship between spend-saving aspirations and the factors of mobility-stability.

## FRAMEWORK OF STUDY

Following are Warner's hypotheses and assumptions for the study:

I. *Assumptions about symbols and values and about saving of money and accumulation of objects.*

---

[1] W. Lloyd Warner and Paul Lunt, *The Social Life of a Modern Community* (New Haven: Yale University Press, 1950). Also, W. Lloyd Warner, Marchia Meeker, and Kenneth Eells, *Social Class in America* (Chicago: Science Research Associates, 1949).

Our society is acquisitive and pecuniary. On the one hand, the values and beliefs of Americans are pulled toward the pole of the accumulation of money by increasing the amount of money income and reducing its outgo. On the other hand, American values emphasize the accumulation of objects and products of technology for display and consumption. The self-regard and self-esteem of a person and his family, as well as the public esteem and respect of a valued social world around the accumulator, are increased or not by such symbols of accumulation and consumption.

The two sets of values, the accumulation of product symbols and the accumulation (saving) of money, may be, and usually are, in opposition.

*General working hypotheses* stemming from these assumptions were: (1) People are distributed along a range according to the two-value components, running from proportionately high savings, through mixed categories, to proportionately high accumulation of objects. (2) These value variations conform to social and personality factors present in all Americans.

**II.** *Assumptions about product symbols, savers, and accumulations.*

American society is also characterized by social change, particularly technological change that moves in the direction of greater and greater production of more kinds and more numerous objects for consumption and accumulation.

*Hypothesis.* New varieties of objects will be most readily accepted by the accumulators, and most often opposed by the savers.

**III.** *Assumptions about the social values of accumulators and savers.*

American society is characterized by basic cultural differences, one of them being social status. Social class levels are occupied by people, some of whom are upward mobile by intent and fact. Others are non-mobile, by intent and fact. The values which dictate judgments about actions, such as the kinds of objects which are consumed and accumulated, will vary by class level and the presence or absence of vertical mobility.

**IV.** *Assumptions about the personal values of accumulators and savers.*

The personality components are distributed through the class levels and through the mobility types. By relating the social and personality components, it is possible to state a series of hypotheses about accumulators and savers as they are related to the object world around them, particularly to objects which are new and old to the culture, those which are imposing or not and those which are predominantly for display or for consumption.

At the direct, practical level, all of these theoretical questions can be summarized by one basic question: *What kinds of things are people likely to buy and not buy if they are in given class positions and if they are or are not socially mobile?* In other words, what is the effect on purchasing behavior of being in a particular social class, and being mobile or non-mobile?

If this is the crucial question, theoretically grounded, then a whole series of hypotheses can be laid out concerning values about money and values about buying various kinds of objects for consumption and for display. Some of these are:

1. *There will be a relationship between values held by a particular subject and the extent to which particular products exemplify those values.*
2. *There is a differential hierarchy of things for which it is worth spending money.*
3. *Veblen's theory that conspicuous expenditure is largely applied to the Upper Class is erroneous. It runs all the way through our social system.*

From these statements certain other hypotheses follow:

4. *At different class levels, symbols of mobility will differ.*

There is a differential hierarchy of things on which it is worth spending money. Class and mobility will be two of the dimensions that will differentiate—also personality and cultural background.

5. *The place in the home where these symbols will be displayed will shift at different class levels.*

The underlying assumption here is that there is a hierarchy of importance in the rooms of the house. This hierarchy varies with social class, mobility, age, ethnicity. The studies also revealed clear-cut patterns of taste for lamps, furnishings, house types, etc.

6. *The non-mobile people tend to rationalize purchases in terms of cost or economy.*

In other words, non-mobile people tend to be oriented more toward the pole of the accumulation of money. Purchases, then, are rationalized in terms of the savings involved.

The basic thesis of all the hypotheses on mobility is this: Whereas the stable individual would emphasize saving and security, the behavior of the mobile individual is characterized by spending for various symbols of upward movement. All of the evidence turned up indicates that this difference in values does exist, and furthermore that notable differences in personality dynamics are involved. For instance, the analysis of how families would make investments shows that stable people overwhelmingly prefer insurance, the symbol of security. By contrast, the mobile people at all levels prefer stocks, which are risk-taking. In Warner's words, the mobile individual acts as if he were free, white, and twenty-one, completely able to handle the world, and perfectly willing to gamble on himself as a sure bet to succeed.

## CLASS PLACEMENT

Returning to the factor of social class, in this study class placement was based on a multistate probability area sample of metropolitan Chicago, involving 3,880 households. It was found that the matter of placement could not be done by the relatively simple scoring sufficient for the smaller cities. To secure house typings, it was necessary to provide the field investigators with photographs covering a wide range of dwelling types, all the way from exclusive apartments to rooms over stores. Because of the very complexity of metropolitan life, occupations provided the biggest problem. To solve this operational problem, it was necessary to construct an exhaustive list of occupational types involving degree of responsibility and training required by each. The data finally used to calculate the Index of Status Characteristics (ISC) were:

(weighted by 5)
  Occupation (from 1 to 7 broad categories)
(weighted by 4)
    Sources of Income (from 1 to 7 types)
(weighted by 3)
      Housing Type (from 1 to 7 types)

The sum of the individual's weighted scores was used to predict his social class level as follows:[2]

| ISC Scores | Predicted Social Class Placement |
|---|---|
| 12-21 | Upper Class |
| 22-37 | Upper-Middle Class |
| 38-51 | Lower-Middle Class |
| 52-66 | Upper-Lower Class |
| 67-84 | Lower-Lower Class |

The study very clearly shows that there is a social-class system operative in a metropolitan area which can be delineated. Furthermore, class membership is an important determinant of the individual's economic behavior, even more so than in the smaller city. The one department store in the smaller city may satisfy almost everyone, whereas in the metropolitan city the stores become sharply differentiated.

This is the social-class structure of Metropolitan Chicago, typifying the transformation of the formerly agrarian Midwestern cities from Pittsburgh to Kansas City into a series of big milltowns:

| | |
|---|---|
| Upper and Upper-Middle | 8.1% |
| Lower-Middle | 28.4% |
| Upper-Lower | 44.0% |
| Lower-Lower | 19.5% |

While the Old Families and the Newly Arrived are still recognizable as types, they constitute less than 1 per cent of the population. A similar study in Kansas City turned up so few that they could not be counted at all. On the other hand, we see the emergence of a seventh class, the Upper-Lower "Stars" or Light-Blue Collar Workers. They are the spokesmen of the Upper-Lower Class groups—high income individuals, who have the income for more ostentatious living than the average factory worker but who lack the personal skills or desire for high status by social mobility.

There is certainly a rough correlation between income and social class. But social class is a much richer dimension of meaning. There are so many facets of behavior which are explicable only on a basis of social class dynamics. For instance, this analysis of the purchase of household appliances in Chicago over a four-

---

[2] Dr. Bevode McCall helped to solve the ISC scoring problem for Metropolitan Chicago.

year period shows a very different picture by income and by class:

Nine Appliance Types—Four-Year Period

By Income

| | |
|---|---|
| Over $7,000 | 36.2% |
| 4,000-6,999 | 46.0% |
| Under 4,000 | 17.8% |

By Social Class

| | |
|---|---|
| Upper and Upper-Middle | 16.6% |
| Lower-Middle | 29.2% |
| Upper-Lower | 45.7% |
| Lower-Lower | 8.5% |

Income analysis shows that the lowest income group represents an understandably smaller market, but nevertheless a market. Social-class analysis highlights a fundamental difference in attitudes toward the home between the two lower classes. The Upper-Lower Class man sees his home as his castle, his anchor to the world, and he loads it down with hardware—solid heavy appliances—as his symbols of security. The Lower-Lower Class individual is far less interested in his castle, and is more likely to spend his income for flashy clothes or an automobile. He is less property-minded, and he has less feeling about buying and maintaining a home.

Several *Tribune* studies have explored the way of life and the buying behavior in many new suburbs and communities. All of them quickly become stratified along social-class and mobility dimensions, and, therefore, differ tremendously among themselves. *Fortune* has reported on Park Forest, Illinois, a Middle-Class suburb of 30,000 and only ten years old. It is characterized by high degrees of both upward and geographical mobility. The people are overwhelmingly those who had moved from other parts of the United States, who had few local roots, and who consequently wanted to integrate themselves in friendship groups. But this was not typical of the new Lower-Status suburbs where the women did relatively little fraternizing. It was not typical of the new Upper-Middle Class mobile suburbs where the people were preoccupied with status symbols, not in submerging themselves in the group.

One new community had crystallized as being for Higher-Status Negroes. This was a resettlement project with relatively high rents for Negroes. Eighty-five per cent of them had come from the South where social class was compressed. But, as soon as they came to Chicago, the class system opened up and they were anxious to establish a social distance between themselves and other Negroes. Almost all of them said they enjoyed the "peace and quiet" of their neighborhood, which was their way of insisting that they were not like the "noisy" Lower-Class Negroes. They deliberately avoided the stores patronized by other Negroes.

## CHOICE OF STORE

All of these studies reveal the close relation between choice of store, patterns of spending, and class membership. In the probability sample delineating social class, such questions were asked in the total metropolitan area as:

"If you were shopping for a good dress, at which store would you be most likely to find what you wanted?"
"For an everyday dress?"
"For living room furniture?"
"At which store do you buy most of your groceries?"

To assume that all persons would wish to shop at the glamorous High-Status stores is utterly wrong. People are very realistic in the way they match their values and expectations with the status of the store. The woman shopper has a considerable range of ideas about department stores; but these generally become organized on a scale ranking from very High-Social Status to the Lowest-Status and prestige. The social status of the department store becomes the primary basis for its definition by the shopper. This is also true of men's and women's apparel stores, and furniture stores, on the basis of customer profiles. The shopper is not going to take a chance feeling out of place by going to a store where she might not fit.

No matter what economics are involved, she asks herself who are the other customers in the store, what sort of treatment can she expect at the hands of the clerks, will the merchandise be the best of everything, or lower priced and hence lower quality? Stores are described as being for the rich, for the average ordinary people, or for those who have to stretch their pennies.

The most important function of retail advertising today, when prices and quality have become so standard, is to permit the shopper to make social-class identification. This she can do from the tone and physical character of the advertising. Of course, there is also the factor of psychological identification. Two people in the same social class may want different stores. One may prefer a conservative store, one may want the most advanced styling. But neither will go to stores where they do not "fit," in a social-class sense.

In contrast to the independent food retailer, who obviously adapts to the status of the neighborhood, the chain grocers generally invade many income areas with their stores. Nevertheless, customer profiles show that each chain acquires a status definition. The two largest grocery chains in the Chicago area are A. & P. and Jewel; yet they draw very different customer bodies. A. & P. is strong with the mass market, whereas Jewel has its strength among the Middle Class.

While the national brand can and often does cut across classes, one can think of many product types and services which do have social class labels. The Upper-Middle Class person rarely travels by motor coach because none of his associates do so, even though there is certainly nothing wrong with this mode of transportation. On the other hand, even with low air-coach fares, one does not see many factory workers or day laborers on vacation around airports. Such sales successes as vodka and tonic water, and men's deodorants and foreign sports cars, were accomplished without benefit of much buying from this part of the market.

## COMMUNICATION SKILLS

There is also a relation between class and communication abilities which has significance for marketing. The kind of super-sophisticated and clever advertising which appears in the *New Yorker* and *Esquire* is almost meaningless to Lower-Status people. They cannot comprehend the subtle humor; they are baffled by the bizarre art. They have a different symbol system, a very different approach to humor. In no sense does this imply that they lack intelligence or wit. Rather their communication skills have just been pressed into a different mold.

Here again, style of advertising helps the individual to make class identification. Most of the really big local television success stories in Chicago have been achieved by personalities who radiate to the mass that this is where they belong. These self-made businessmen who do the announcing for their own shows communicate wonderfully well with the mass audience. While many listeners switch off their lengthy and personal commercials, these same mannerisms tell the Lower-Status individual that here is someone just like himself, who understands him.

Social Research, Inc., has frequently discussed the class problem in marketing by dividing the population into Upper-Middle or quality market; the middle majority which combines both the Lower-Middle and Upper-Lower; and then the Lower-Lower. The distinction should be drawn between the Middle Classes and the Lower-Status groups. In several dozen of these store profiles, there is scarcely an instance where a store has appeal to the Lower-Middle and Upper-Lower classes with anything like the same strength.

It would be better to make the break between the Middle Class, representing one-third of the population and the Lower-Status or Working-Class or Wage-Earner group, representing two-thirds of metropolitan Chicago. This permits some psychological distinctions to be drawn between the Middle-Class individual and the individual who is not a part of the Middle-Class system of values. Even though this is the dominant American value system, even though Middle-Class Americans have been taught by their parents that it is the only value system, this Lower-Status individual does not necessarily subscribe to it.

## WHO SAVES, WHO SPENDS?

Another important set of behavioral distinctions related to social class position was revealed in the "save-spend aspiration" study. The question was asked: "Suppose your income was doubled for the next ten years, what would you do with the increased income?" This is a fantasy question taken out of the realm of any pressing economic situation to reflect aspirations about money. The coding broke down the answers to this question into five general categories: (1) the mode of saving, (2) the purpose of saving, (3) spending which would consolidate past gains, meet present defensive needs, prepare for future self-advancement, (4) spending which is "self-indulgent-centered," (5) spending which is "house-centered."

Here are some of our findings:[3] The higher the individual's class position, the more likely is he to express some saving aspirations. Conversely, the lower his class position, the more likely is he to mention spending only. Moreover the higher the status, the more likely is the individual to specify *how* he will save his money, which is indicative of the more elaborate financial learning required of higher status.

Proceeding from the more general categories (such as saving versus spending only) to more specific categories (such as non-investment versus investment saving and the even more specific stock versus real estate investment, etc.) an increasingly sharper class differentiation is found. It is primarily *non-investment* saving which appeals to the Lower-Status person. Investment saving, on the other hand, appeals above all to the Upper-Status person.

Investors almost always specify how they will invest. And here in mode of investment are examples of the most sharply class-differentiated preferences. Intangible forms of investment like stock and insurance are very clearly distinguished as Upper-Status investments. Nearly four times as many Upper-Middles select insurance as would be expected by chance, whereas only one-fifth of the Lower-Lowers select it as would be expected by chance. By contrast, Lower-Status people have far greater preference for tangible investments, specifically ownership of real estate, a farm, or a business.

To sum up, Middle-Class people usually have a place in their aspirations for some form of saving. This saving is most often in the form of investment, where there is a risk, long-term involvement, and the possibility of higher return. Saving, investment saving, and intangible investment saving—successively each of these become for them increasingly symbols of their higher status.

The aspirations of the Lower-Status person are just as often for spending as they are for saving. This saving is usually a non-investment saving where there is almost no risk, funds can be quickly converted to spendable cash, and returns are small. When the Lower-Status person does invest his savings, he will be specific about the mode of investment, and is very likely to prefer something tangible and concrete— something he can point at and readily display.

Turning from mode of saving to purpose of

saving, very significant class relationships are likewise evident. Consider the verbalization of saving purpose. Lower-Status people typically explain why one should save—why the very act of saving is important. On the other hand, Middle-Class people do not, as if saving is an end-in-itself, the merits of which are obvious and need not be justified.

Spending is the other side of the coin. Analysis of what people say they will spend for shows similar class-related desires. All classes mention concrete, material artifacts such as a new car, some new appliance. But the Lower-Status people stop here. Their accumulations are artifact-centered, whereas Middle-Class spending-mentions are experience-centered. This is spending where one is left typically with only a memory. It would include hobbies, recreation, self-education and travel. The wish to travel, and particularly foreign travel, is almost totally a Middle-Class aspiration.

Even in their fantasies, people are governed by class membership. In his day-dreaming and wishful thinking, the Lower-Status individual will aspire in different patterns from the Middle-Class individual.

## PSYCHOLOGICAL DIFFERENCES

This spending-saving analysis has very obvious psychological implications to differentiate between the classes. Saving itself generally suggests foresightedness, the ability to perceive long-term needs and goals. Non-investment saving has the characteristics of little risk-taking and of ready conversion, at no loss, into immediate expenditures—the money can be drawn out of the account whenever the bank is open. Investment spending, on the other hand, has the characteristics of risk-taking (a gamble for greater returns) and of delayed conversion, with possible loss, to expenditures on immediate needs.

Here are some psychological contrasts between two different social groups:

### Middle-Class
1. Pointed to the future
2. His viewpoint embraces a long expanse of time
3. More urban identification
4. Stresses rationality
5. Has a well-structured sense of the universe
6. Horizons vastly extended or not limited
7. Greater sense of choice-making
8. Self-confident, willing to take risks
9. Immaterial and abstract in his thinking
10. Sees himself tied to national happenings

[3] The saving-spending aspiration analysis was carried out by Roger Coup, graduate student at the University of Chicago.

Lower-Status

1. Pointed to the present and past
2. Lives and thinks in a short expanse of time
3. More rural in identification
4. Non-rational essentially
5. Vague and unclear structuring of the world
6. Horizons sharply defined and limited
7. Limited sense of choice-making
8. Very much concerned with security and insecurity
9. Concrete and perceptive in his thinking
10. World revolves around his family and body

## CONCLUSIONS

The essential purpose of this article was to develop three basic premises which are highly significant for marketing:

I. *There is a social-class system operative in metropolitan markets, which can be isolated and described.*

II. *It is important to realize that there are far-reaching psychological differences between the various classes.*

They do not handle the world in the same fashion. They tend not to think in the same way. As one tries to communicate with the Lower-Status group, it is imperative to sense that their goals and mental processes differ from the Middle-Class group.

III. *Consumption patterns operate as prestige symbols to define class membership, which is a more significant determinant of economic behavior than mere income.*

Each major department store, furniture store, and chain-grocery store has a different "pulling power" on different status groups. The usual customers of a store gradually direct the store's merchandising policies into a pattern which works. The interaction between store policy and consumer acceptance results in the elimination of certain customer groups and the attraction of others, with a resulting equilibration around a reasonably stable core of specific customer groups who think of the store as appropriate for them.

Income has always been the marketer's handiest index to family consumption standards. But it is a far from accurate index. For instance, the bulk of the population in a metropolitan market today will fall in the middle-income ranges. This will comprise not only the traditional white collar worker, but the unionized craftsman and the semi-skilled worker with their tremendous income gains of the past decade. Income-wise, they may be in the same category. But their buying behavior, their tastes, their spending-saving aspirations can be poles apart. Social-class position and mobility-stability dimensions will reflect in much greater depth each individual's style of life.

# 7. The Concept of Reference Group Influence

## FRANCIS S. BOURNE

On the common sense level the concept says in effect that man's behavior is influenced in different ways and in varying degrees by other people. Comparing one's own success with that of others is a frequent source of satisfaction or disappointment. Similarly, before making a decision one often considers what such and such a person or such and such a group (whose opinion one has *some* reason to follow) would do in these circumstances, or what they would think of one for making a certain decision rather than another. Put in these ways, of course, reference group influence represents an unanalyzed truism which has long been recognized. The problem to which social scientists have been addressing themselves intensively only for the last two decades, however, concerns the refinement of this common sense notion to the end that it might be applied meaningfully to concrete situations.

The real problems are to determine which kinds of groups are likely to be referred to by which kinds of individuals under which kinds of circumstances in the process of making which decisions, and to measure the extent of this reference group influence. Towards this end empirical researches have been conducted in recent years which have at least made a start in the process of refining the reference group concept.

Reference group theory as it has developed has become broad enough to cover a wide

‡ SOURCE: Reprinted by permission from *Group Influence in Marketing and Public Relations* edited by Francis S. Bourne (Ann Arbor, Michigan: Foundation for Research on Human Behavior), 1956, pp. 1, 2, 7–11.

range of social phenomena, both with respect to the relation of the individual to the group and with respect to the type of influence exerted upon the individual by the group in question.

### Kinds of Reference Groups

Reference groups against which an individual evaluates his own status and behavior may be of several kinds.

They may be *membership* groups to which a person actually belongs. There can be small face-to-face groups in which actual association is the rule, such as families or organizations, whether business, social, religious, or political. On the other hand, there can be groups in which actual membership is held but in which personal association is absent. (For example, membership in a political party, none of whose meetings are personally attended.)

Reference groups may be *categories* to which a person automatically belongs by virtue of age, sex, education, marital status and so on. This sort of reference group relationship involves the concept of role. For example, before taking a certain action an individual might consider whether this action would be regarded as appropriate in his role as a man or husband or educated person or older person or a combination of all of these roles. What is involved here is an individual's perception of what society, in general or that part of it with which he has any contact, expects people of his age, or sex, or education or marital status to do under given circumstances.

They may be *anticipatory* rather than actual membership groups. Thus a person who aspires to membership in a group to which he does *not* belong may be more likely to refer to it or compare himself with its standards when making a decision than he is to refer to the standards of the group in which he actually belongs but would like to leave. This involves the concept of upward mobility. When such upward mobility is sought in the social or business world it is ordinarily accompanied by a sensitivity to the attitudes of those in the groups to which one aspires, whether it involves the attitudes of country club members in the eyes of the aspiring non-member or the attitudes of management in the eyes of the ambitious wage earner or junior executive.

There are also negative, *dissociative* reference groups. These constitute the opposite side of the coin from the anticipatory membership groups. Thus an individual sometimes avoids a certain action because it is associated with a group (to which the individual may or may not in fact belong) from which he would like to dissociate himself.

### Influence on Individual Behavior

Reference groups influence behavior in two major ways. First, they influence *aspiration levels* and thus play a part in producing satisfaction or frustration. If the other members of one's reference group (for example, the neighbors) are wealthier, more famous, better gardeners, etc., one may be dissatisfied with one's own achievements and may strive to do as well as the others.

Second, reference groups influence *kinds* of behavior. They establish approved patterns of using one's wealth, of wearing one's fame, of designing one's garden. They set tabus too, and may have the power to apply actual sanctions (for example, exclusion from the group). They thus produce *conformity* as well as *contentment* (or discontentment).

These two kinds of influence have, however, a good deal in common. Both imply certain perceptions on the part of the individual, who attributes characteristics to the reference group which it may or may not actually have. Both involve psychological rewards and punishment.

## DIFFERENT KINDS OF DECISIONS AND REFERENCE GROUP INFLUENCE

### Marketing and Reference Group Relevance

As has already been suggested, the reference group constitutes just one of the many influences in buying decisions, and this influence varies from product to product. How then does one determine whether reference group influence is likely to be a factor in buying behavior in connection with a given product or brand? Research has been conducted on the various factors that influence buying behavior with reference to several products, and out of this have emerged some general ideas about how reference group influences may enter into purchasing.

Buying may be a completely individualistic kind of activity or it may be very much socially conditioned. Consumers are often influenced by what others buy, especially those persons with whom they compare themselves, or use as reference groups.

The conspicuousness of a product is perhaps the most general attribute bearing on its susceptibility to reference group influence. There are two aspects to conspicuousness in this particular context that help to determine reference group influence. First the article must be conspicuous in the most obvious sense that it can be seen and identified by others. Secondly it must be conspicuous in the sense of standing out and being noticed. In other words, no matter how visible a product is, if virtually everyone owns it, it is not conspicuous in the second sense of the word. This leads to a further distinction: reference groups may influence either (a) the purchase of a product, or (b) the choice of a particular brand or type, or (c) both.

The possible susceptibility of various product and brand buying to reference group influence is suggested in Figure 1. According to this classification a particular item might be susceptible to reference group influence in its purchase in three different ways, corresponding to three of the four cells in the above figure. Reference group influence may operate with respect to product alone (Brand + Product −) as in the upper left cell, or it may operate both with respect to brand and product (Brand + Product +) as in the upper right cell, or it may operate with respect to product but not brand (Brand − Product +) as in the lower right cell.

Only the "minus-minus" items of the kind illustrated (Brand − Product −) in the lower left cell are not likely to involve any significant reference group influence in their purchase *at the present time*.

What are some of the characteristics that place an item in a given category, and what sig-

Reference Group Influence Relatively:

|  | Weak − | Strong + |  |
|---|---|---|---|
| **Strong +**<br><br>Reference<br>Group<br>Influence<br>Relatively:<br><br>**Weak −** | Clothing<br>Furniture<br>Magazines<br>Refrigerator (type)<br>Toilet soap | Cars\*<br>Cigarettes\*<br>Beer (prem. vs. reg.)\*<br>Drugs\* | + <br><br>Brand<br>or<br>Type |
|  | Soap<br>Canned peaches<br>Laundry soap<br>Refrigerator (brand)<br>Radios | Air conditioners\*<br>Instant coffee\*<br>TV (black and white) | − |
|  | − | + |  |

Product

FIG. 1.   Products and brands of consumer goods may be classified by the extent to which reference groups influence their purchase. *Source*: Bureau of Applied Social Research, Columbia University (Glock, unpublished).

\* The classification of all starred products is based on actual experimental evidence. Other products in this table are classified speculatively on the basis of generalizations derived from the sum of research in this area and confirmed by the judgment of seminar participants.

nificance do such placements have for marketing and advertising policy?

*"Product-plus, brand-plus" items.* Autos constitute an article where both the product and the brand are socially conspicuous. Whether or not a person buys a car, and also what particular brand he buys, is likely to be influenced by what others do. This also holds true for cigarettes, for drugs (decisions made by M.D.'s as to what to prescribe) and for beer with respect to type (premium vs. regular) as opposed to brand. Cigarettes and drugs, however, qualify as "plus-plus" items in a manner different from cars.

For example, while the car belongs to a class of products where brand differentiation is based at least substantially on real differences in attributes, the cigarette belongs to a class of product in which it is difficult to differentiate one brand from another by attributes: hence attributes are ascribed largely through reference group appeal built up by advertising. Popular images of the kinds of people who smoke various brands have been created at great cost, and in some cases additional images are being created to broaden a particular brand's market. In the case of drugs, it was found that the reference group influencing *whether* the product was

used was different from that influencing the particular *brand* selected. Reference group influence was found to be prominent in determining whether or not beer was purchased at all, and also in determining whether regular or premium beer was selected. It did not appear to influence strongly choice of a particular brand.

*"Product Plus, Brand Minus" Items.* Instant coffee is one of the best examples of this class of items. Whether it is served in a household depends in considerable part on whether the housewife, in view of her own reference groups and the image she has of their attitudes towards this product, considers it appropriate to serve it. The brand itself in this instance is not conspicuous or socially important and is a matter largely for individual choice. In the case of air conditioners, it was found that little prestige attached to the particular brand used, and reference group influence related largely to the idea of purchasing the product itself. Analysis in one city revealed that the purchase of this often "visible from the outside" product was concentrated in small neighborhood areas. Clusters of conditioners were frequently located in certain rows and blocks. In many cases clusters did not even cross streets. Immediate neighbors

apparently served as a powerfully influential group in the purchase of these appliances. In this general class may also be found the black and white TV set, with its antenna often visible on the outside of the house. As the saturation point in black and white TV set ownership rapidly approaches, however, the influence of reference groups may soon become minor, and the product can then be put in the "brand minus, product minus" quadrant, along with refrigerators. Color TV may remain in the "brand plus, product minus" quadrant, with type (color) rather than brand per se the element which is strongly related to reference groups.

*"Product Minus, Brand Plus" Items.* This group is made up essentially of products that all people or at least a very high proportion of people use, although differing as to type or brand.

Perhaps the leading example in this field is clothing. There could hardly be a more socially visible product than this, but the fact that everyone in our society wears clothing takes the *product* out of the area of reference group influence. The *type* of clothing purchased is, however, very heavily influenced by reference groups, with each subculture in the population (teenagers, zootsuiters, Ivy League collegians, western collegians, workers, bankers, advertising men, etc.) setting its own standards and often prescribing within fairly narrow limits what those who feel related to these groups can wear. Similarly, though not quite as dramatically, articles like furniture, magazines, refrigerators and toilet soap are seen in almost all homes, causing their purchase in general to fall outside of the orbit of reference group influence. The visibility of these items, however, coupled with the wide variety of styles and types among them make the selection of particular kinds highly susceptible to reference group influence.

*"Product Minus, Brand Minus", Items.* Purchasing behavior in this class of items is governed largely by product attributes rather than by the nature of the presumed users. In this group neither the products nor the brands tend to be socially conspicuous. This is not to say that personal influence cannot operate with respect to purchasing the kind of items included in this group. As with all products, some people tend to exert personal influence and others tend to be influenced by individual persons. Reference groups as such, however, exert relatively little influence on buying behavior in this class

of items. Examples of items in this category are salt, canned peaches, laundry soap and radios. It is apparent that placement in this category is not *necessarily* inherent in the product itself and hence is not a static placement. Items can move in and out of this category.

While it is true that items which are essential socially inconspicuous, like salt and laundry soap, are natural candidates for this category, it is not entirely out of the realm of possibility that through considerable large scale advertising and other promotional efforts images of the kind of people who use certain brands of salt or laundry soap could be built up so as to bring reference group influence into play on such items, much as has been the case with cigarettes. The task here would be more difficult, however, since the cigarette is already socially visible. On the other hand, items such as radios and refrigerators which are conspicuously visible and whose purchase was once subject to considerable reference group influence have now slipped into this category through near saturation in ownership.

### Implications of Strong and Weak Reference Group Influence for Advertising and Marketing

It should be stressed again that this scheme of analysis is introduced to show how reference group influence might enter into purchasing behavior in certain cases. It cannot be regarded as generally applicable to marketing problems on all levels. There is still a need to know more precisely where many different products or brands fit into this scheme. Attempts to fit products and brands into the classification above suggest research that needs to be done to obtain more relevant information about each product.

Assuming, however, that a product or brand has been correctly placed with respect to the part played by reference groups in influencing its purchase, how can this help in marketing the product in question?

Where neither product nor brand appear to be associated strongly with reference group influence, advertising should emphasize the product's attributes, intrinsic qualities, price, and advantages over competing products.

Where reference group influence is operative, the advertiser should stress the kinds of people who buy the product, reinforcing and broadening where possible the existing stereotypes of users. This involves learning what the stereotypes are and what specific reference groups enter into the picture, so that appeals can be "tailored" to each major group reached by the different media employed.

Although it is important to see that the "right" kind of people use a product, a crucial problem is to make sure that the popular image of the product's users is as broad as possible without alienating any important part of the product's present or potential market in the process. Creating or reinforcing a stereotype of consumers which is too small and exclusive for a mass-produced item may exclude a significant portion of the potential market. On the other hand, some attempts to appeal to new groups through advertising in mass media have resulted in the loss of existing groups of purchasers whose previous (favorable) image of the prod-uct-user was adversely affected. One possible means for increasing the base of the market for a product by enlarging the image of its users is to use separate advertising media through which a new group can be reached without reducing the product's appeal to the original group of users. Another method might be to appeal to a new group through cooperative advertising by a number of companies producing the product, possibly through a trade association. This would minimize the risk to an individual producer who, trying to reach a new group of users through his own advertising (women as opposed to men or wealthy as opposed to average people, for example), might antagonize people who had a strong need to identify with the *original* image of the product's kind of user.

# 8. America's Tastemakers

## THE TARGET IS THE CONSUMER

At the center of our perplexities as market researchers has been the realization that no matter how sophisticated our methods of analysis, no matter how ingenious our mathematical models, the events we are trying to predict are human events. It is consumer behavior that determines sales trends, industry performance, national indices—and not vice versa.

Management, of course, has always operated on this fact. By improving products, by developing new ones, by advertising and promotion and corporate reputation building, by training an effective sales staff, by virtually all its activities in short, management aims to influence consumer behavior. Past sales trends, etc., are studied only as guides to accomplishing this.

From whatever angle we approach the problem, therefore, we come back to the same base: the consumer and his needs, desires, aspirations, likes and dislikes, tastes, and pocketbook. In brief, to a very complex matter of human behavior.

In recognition of this reality, market research has bent its efforts increasingly on studying King Consumer. Here again, there has been a genuine growth in knowledge, sophistication, technique. But here too our growing skills and insight seem to reveal ever more serious problems that limit our ability to predict.

❖ SOURCE: Reprinted by permission from *Tastemaker Research Report No. 1* (Princeton, New Jersey: Opinion Research Corporation, April 1959).

## WHY TRADITIONAL CONSUMER IDENTIFICATION LIMITS PREDICTIVE POWER

Researchers have noted three major flaws in the standard background analyses used in consumer research. One of them has to do with the built-in assumptions that are entailed. The second flaw has to do with the way we use categories—we work with aggregates of *characteristics* of people, not with aggregates of whole individuals. Third, our categories may appear to stay the same in size, while the people in them change radically. Or the categories may change, without revealing which persons are doing the changing.

## WHERE IS OUR SOCIETY HEADING?

Our concern here is not philosophy or the long sweep of history, but the way people manage their lives.

Where are we as a people moving? Toward what new dimensions of experience, of aspirations, of taste and custom and habit? How can we best ascertain this?

In the free society of America there is no single man at the helm. We are a vast collection of societies: big governments and little governments, religious bodies and educational institutions, corporations and partnerships, clubs and lodges and sewing circles.

## WHO ARE THE LEADERS?

Within every society there is a leadership elite. For our purposes, which are those of prediction, the critical question is one of identification.

The time-honored means—identifying leaders by title—does not serve us well. Titles designate leadership *roles;* they do not tell us how individuals behave in those roles.

Bearing these difficulties in mind, the nature of the task may be set forth in successive steps as follows:

1. If we are to predict changing consumption patterns in our society, we must get wind of upcoming social change—changes arising in the whole society, in its values, its way of life, its activity patterns.

2. If we are to predict social change, we must be able to identify those individuals most responsible for it—the leadership elite for change.

3. If we are to identify the leadership elite, we must search for the golden cord that binds the dynamic individual and his society together.

## THE DIMENSIONS OF KINSHIP MOBILITY

The "break with the past" has long been a feature of the American psychology. We have termed this complex phenomenon "Kinship Mobility." Included within it are these increasing trends in American life:

1. The disappearance of what anthropologists call "the extended family"—a tightly-knit group of people of all generations related by blood, often living under the same roof, usually in the same community.

2. The dominance of what is called "the nuclear family"—man, wife, and dependent children—as the basic social unit.

3. The geographical spreading of blood relatives from the local neighborhood to towns and cities across the map—a process affecting even parents and their grown children to an increasing degree.

4. The continued growth of occupational shifting between generations. Both sons and daughters are increasingly likely to be following an occupation different from that of their parents.

5. The continuing rapid increase in educational difference between Americans and their parents and grandparents.

In all of the standard demographic categories, in short—ranging from place of residence, ethnic background and social ties to income, education and family size—the American is increasingly shaking loose from blood ties and moving out into the world on his own.

## A NEW SET OF SPECTACLES: MOBILITY

In searching for a common denominator, to characterize our society, have we not overlooked *the fact of movement and change itself?*

If we are to gain predictive power over our changing environment, we clearly are in bad need of a new way of viewing it, a new set of spectacles. As a summary way of stating it, we will call this hypothetical common denominator in modern society "Mobility."

Since what we are attempting to develop is a scientific theory of marketing (and ultimately of social change in other spheres), we must set forth as precisely as we can what is meant by the term mobility.

As used in this research, *the term mobility refers to movement of the individual or group in relation to his human and physical environment.*

### THE TASTEMASTER THEORY

The central thread of our modern society is mobility. The leadership elite is that group of people who possess this quality in greater degree than do other people.

Having identified significant aspects of mobility that characterize our mobile society, we can now proceed to identify the people who possess them in greater degree than do others. We will call them The High Mobiles. The means of identifying them may be described, in highly condensed form, as follows:

*Prime Characteristics of The High Mobiles Compared With Other Americans*

1. They travel more and change residence more often.

2. They show more movement through the occupational structure.

3. They are more likely to change their economic status.

4. They associate with a wider variety of people, of different types.

5. They move through more educational levels and institutions.

6. They move through more intellectual influences.

7. They are more selective and variable in their politics.

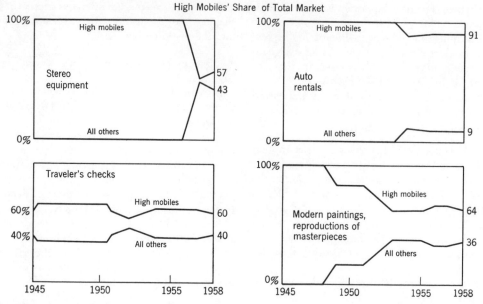

FIG. 1.   Research on the tastemaker theory shows that high mobile households strongly dominate present "fledgling" markets.

8. In these various dimensions, they have moved a greater distance from their family of birth.

The High Mobiles are not to be identified by any one or two main characteristics. It is the *pattern* of their mobility that serves to distinguish them.

Our search for a predictive approach to changing U.S. markets then leads us to these three steps:

1. Identify the High Mobiles.
2. Determine the changing pattern of their values.
3. Relate the High Mobile value patterns to the ways in which they are expressed in styles, tastes, and ultimately product preference.

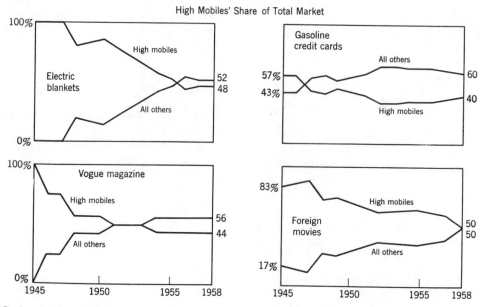

FIG. 2.   As the market broadens, high mobile households naturally account for a dwindling share of the total market.

eas.[2] Many of the same patterns noted have
een found in cross-sectional samples of the
.S. Negro and white population, as well as
some local surveys.

## BASIC DILEMMA OF NEGROES

Negroes as a group have accepted the
alues of the majority white middle-class cul-
are, but are at a disadvantage in acquiring
ie goods which represent some of these
alues.

In other words, *the basic dilemma of Ne-
roes is whether to strive against odds to
ttain these middle-class values (and the goods
hich come with them) or to give in and live
ithout most of them.*

It is easy to listen to the rising, increasingly
ilitant, voices of American Negroes com-
ined with the voices of African nationalism,
id to conclude that the American Negro has
ot accepted white middle-class values, or
iat he may even be alienated from the white
ulture. However, even the publications of the
lack Muslims reveal strong emphasis on the
alues of temperance and achievement, along
ith some racist content.

Certainly it is the consensus of both Negro
id white students of the American Negro that
egroes have accepted white middle-class
alues.[3]

For convenience, we have been discussing
egroes and whites as though they were two
istinct groups, each of which is in turn homo-
eneous. This is, of course, not so; but we are
ying to emphasize some major trends and
ertainly various Negroes respond differently
the "basic dilemma" mentioned above.

### Differences in Consumption Patterns

Any discussion of the Negro market needs
be based on general differences in Negro-
hite consumption patterns. A combination of
cietal restraints and cultural traditions leads
egroes to underspend, as compared with
hites of equal income, in four major areas:
ousing, automobile transportation, food, and
edical care (excluding certain categories of
roprietary medicines). See Table 1.

This pattern of spending less on housing,
itomobile transportation, food, and medical
ire makes available to Negroes *proportion-
ely* more money for the purchase of goods
an is available to whites of comparable in-
me. Thus, Negroes at a given level of in-

**TABLE 1. Negro Versus White
Spending Behavior
Controlled by Income**

|  | Negro Spending Versus White Spending |
| --- | --- |
| Food | Less |
| Housing | Less |
| Clothing | More |
| Recreation and leisure | Mixed |
| Home furnishing | More |
| Medical | Less |
| Auto transportation | Less |
| Non-auto | More |
| Savings | More |
| Insurance | Less |

SOURCE: Marcus Alexis: "Some Negro-White
Differences in Consumption," *American Journal
of Economics and Sociology,* Vol. 21, January
1962, pp. 11–28.

come repeatedly have been found to spend
more on clothing, furniture, and alcoholic beverages than do whites of the same income.

### Symbolic Importance of Goods

The once prevalent stereotype that Negroes
were uninterested in, or incompetent to judge,
the quality of goods has long been displaced—
with the contrary image now of Negroes being
extremely interested in quality, and being
even more concerned with the symbolic value
of goods than are whites. Although this idea
may sometimes be overdrawn, it seems close
to the truth. Table 2 shows the proportion of
white and Negro women in New York and
Cleveland who scored high on a scale of
fashion-consciousness.[4] Negro women were at

**TABLE 2. Proportion of Negro and White
Women Showing "High-Fashion Interest"** [a]

| Family Income | Negro Women % | No. | White Women % | No. |
| --- | --- | --- | --- | --- |
| Under $3,000 | 34% | (113) | 21% | (216) |
| $3,000- 4,999 | 38 | (115) | 36 | (416) |
| $5,000- 7,500 | 56 | ( 99) | 47 | (938) |

[a] Of the Negro women who had $3,000 family in-
come, 34% were "high fashion" in orientation.

[2] Made available through the cooperation of
Browne-Vintners, Inc., distributors of White Horse
Scotch.
[3] For example, Thomas F. Pettigrew, *A Profile of
the Negro American* (Princeton: D. Van No-
strand, 1964), Chapters 1 and 2.
[4] Same reference as footnote 1.

# 9. The Marketing Dilemma of Negroes

RAYMOND A. BAUER,
SCOTT M. CUNNINGHAM,
and
LAWRENCE H. WORTZEL

The distinctive nature of the Negro revolution is that it is not a revolution to overthrow the established order so much as it is a revolution to achieve full membership in that order.

Because material goods have such an important symbolic role in American society, the acquisition of material goods should be symbolic to the Negro of his achievement of full status. This is not to say that all product categories have such a symbolic function for Negroes. In general, though, the symbolic status attributed to products by Negroes parallels that attributed to these products by whites.

Some exceptions, however, give the Negro market some distinctive characteristics. For example, it would appear that toilet soap, particularly as associated with deodorizing properties, has special importance for Negro women as compared with white women. Perhaps this is only a reflection of the middle-class dictum about cleanliness being next to godliness, perhaps also a reaction to the belief that Negroes smell different than whites.

The background of both the Negro revolution and the Negro's behavior in the marketplace is, of course, his relatively low socio-economic status. Despite an absolute income increase in Negro income since World War II, it is a moot point as to whether the Negro's relative position has improved. While two-thirds of Negroes reported a family income

below $4,500 in the 1960 census third of the white families did educational, occupational, and hoi vations are also severe. These are factors which account for the N creasing concentration in Nortl "ghettos."

The socio-economic factors are s that it may be asked whether there market in any meaningful sense. any special characteristics which the Negro from any other lower-inc educated, and geographically group?

The answer is yes. And while education are the most important are not the only ones.

## SOURCES OF DATA

The hypotheses developed here from reanalyses of over a dozen s local and national, which have b during a period beginning in 196!

To preserve continuity for the illustrative data will be drawn fro studies: a survey of women's shop in New York and Cleveland,[1] and male buyers of Scotch in Nort

♦ SOURCE: Reprinted by permission from *Journal of Marketing*, (National Quarterly Publication of the American Marketing Association) Vol. 29, July 1965, pp. 1–6.

[1] Stuart U. Rich, with the assistance Portis, Jr., *Shopping Behavior of Dep Customers*. (Boston: Division of Re vard University Graduate School of ministration, 1963.) The data presen sult of reanalysis of the original data, found in Rich and Portis.

least as fashion-conscious or more so than white women.

For another product category, liquor, a Negro family is likely to spend about 1.25 times as much money on alcoholic beverages as a white family with the same per capita income.[5] But the figures on buying Scotch are even more interesting.

Negroes drink at least 25% of the Scotch consumed in the United States, although they represent only 11% of the population. *Chicago Tribune* panel data (1961) indicate that 16.8% of Negro families report buying Scotch, compared with 9.3% of white families. The distributors of White Horse have found that the average Negro Scotch drinker reports drinking almost twice as many drinks of Scotch per week as the average white Scotch drinker.

These data suggest that Negro *per capita* consumption of Scotch is *three times* as much as that consumed by whites. Other estimates have been of the same order.

Is Scotch related to status among Negroes? On a series of questions generally assumed to be related to the idea of Scotch as a high-status drink, Negroes indicate that drinking of Scotch is associated with high status. But perhaps a more crucial question is whether these attitudes vary according to whether a Negro sees himself moving upward or downward in society. We find that self-perceived mobility—that is, perceiving one's self as higher, the same, or lower in social class than one's father—is closely related to attitudes toward Scotch and toward reporting that one is a regular Scotch drinker.

Within the Negro group, such attitudes are much more highly correlated with self-perceived mobility than with present income. Those Negroes who see themselves as moving upward from their fathers' position in society are most likely to give answers which indicate they regard Scotch as a "status" drink, and

are most likely to report being regular Scotch drinkers.

### Segmentation Within the Negro Market:

To repeat what was stated above, the "basic dilemma" of the Negro is whether to strive against odds for middle-class values as reflected in material goods, or to give in and live more for the moment. It is the response of Negroes to this dilemma that creates two categories of persons whom we have labeled "strivers" and "nonstrivers." In turn, their responses to goods of high symbolic value, leads to an interesting segmentation of the Negro market.

Let us assume, therefore, that Negro women who are high on the scale of fashion-consciousness and Negro men who report they are regular Scotch drinkers are "strivers," and that the others are "nonstrivers," and then see where this leads us.

Table 3 shows relationships between fashion interest and social activities outside the respondent's family. The pattern suggested by these data is: Among white women, social activities outside the family are almost entirely a function of family income, whereas for Negro women, once they have been identified by degree of interest in fashion, income no longer plays a role in the Negro group.

In every income category, those Negro women high on fashion-consciousness are twice as likely to take part in social activities outside the family as are low-fashion-conscious Negro women.

These data indicate that by comparing Negro women on the basis of interest in fashion, we have identified women with two basically different orientations toward the world outside

---

[5] George Fisk, *Leisure Spending Behavior* (Philadelphia: University of Pennsylvania Press, 1963), p. 145.

**TABLE 3. Social Activities Outside the Family**

| | Negroes | | | | Whites | | | |
|---|---|---|---|---|---|---|---|---|
| Income | High Fashion | No. | Low Fashion | No. | High Fashion | No. | Low Fashion | No. |
| Under $3,000 | 54%[a] | (38) | 25% | (46) | 30% | ( 45) | 29% | (120) |
| $3,000-$5,000 | 46 | (44) | 21 | (27) | 44 | (150) | 38 | (161) |
| $5,000-$7,000 | 53 | (56) | 28 | (24) | 54 | (440) | 48 | (281) |

[a] Of 38 high-fashion Negroes who had income under $3,000, 54% were involved in community activities.

TABLE 4.    Combining Shopping with Other Activities
Controlled by Income

| Activity While Shopping[a] | Negroes | | White | |
|---|---|---|---|---|
| | Fashion-Consciousness | | Fashion-Consciousness | |
| | High | Low | High | Low |
| Lunches | 11%[b] | 3% | 7% | 3% |
| Theatre | 15 | 4 | 4 | 4 |
| Seeing friends | 7 | .... | 6 | 3 |
| Errands | 3 | 5 | 2 | 3 |
| Other | 5 | 3 | 7 | 4 |
| Don't combine shopping with other activities | 60 | 84 | 73 | 83 |
| Number = | (136) | (98) | (626) | (581) |

[a] Multiple responses permitted.

[b] Of the 136 high-fashion-conscious Negro women, 11% reported eating lunch when they went shopping.

the family. One group is actively engaged with the outside world; the other is more withdrawn from the world. This proposition would not be so interesting if it were not for the fact that this is *not* true for the white women in this sample.

The same sort of relationship holds for a whole series of questions on shopping habits: High-fashion-conscious Negro women are more than twice as likely as low-fashion-conscious Negro women to report that they shop with others. Also, they are likely to combine shopping with social and recreational activities (see Table 4).

In short, the high-fashion-conscious Negro women (in the Rich-and-Portis shopping study) express their greater involvement with the world outside of the family in their shopping activities. Such differences among white women are in the same direction; but the differences, in general, are less than half the magnitude, either absolutely or relatively, as those among Negro women.

Thus, the Negro strivers are more actively engaged in the world about them than the nonstrivers; and shopping and attitudes toward symbolically important goods (interest in fashion) reflect this "striving" attitude.

### Anxiety About Shopping

Shopping can be an especially serious business for a social group that is moving up in society and very concerned with whether their funds are sufficient for buying the goods to which they aspire. We have found that Negro

women are less likely to mention the secondary aspects of shopping—convenience, politeness of salesgirls, crowds, and so on—than white women. Rather, Negro women concentrate more on the economic transaction of exchanging dollars for goods. Compared with white women, what Negroes *like* best about shopping is getting new things and finding bargains; but they also are more likely to say that what they *dislike* about shopping is spending money!

Our discussion of shopping as an especially serious business for Negroes leads us to the expectation that there is a greater degree of anxiety among Negroes with respect to making shopping decisions generally. Table 5 shows

TABLE 5.    Proportion Having Difficulty
Making Shopping Decisions
Controlled by Income

| | Negroes | | Whites | |
|---|---|---|---|---|
| | Fashion-Consciousness | | Fashion-Consciousness | |
| | High | Low | High | Low |
| | 39%[a] | 29% | 25% | 23% |
| N = | (158) | (110) | (1,472) | (979) |

[a] Of the 158 high-fashion-conscious Negroes, 39% reported having difficulty making shopping decisions.

that Negro women in general report greater difficulty than white women, in making buying decisions. This becomes most acute among those Negroes who are "most involved" in the product category. The Negro women "strivers" are more committed to goods of high symbolic value (we identified them by their interest in fashion), more involved with the world outside the family, and show more concern over making shopping decisions.

A parallel may be found in the market for Scotch. Negroes are more likely than whites to report having an established brand preference, and at least as likely to specify a particular brand of Scotch when ordering a drink (see Table 6). Furthermore, the regular Scotch drinkers, both Negro and white, are more brand-conscious than occasional Scotch drinkers.

In response to the statement: "To obtain a good Scotch you have to order an old reliable brand," the regular drinkers among the whites are somewhat more likely to reject this statement.

This pattern conforms to a trend that has been discussed in marketing circles, namely, that persons more experienced with a product type probably will display their "expertise" by departing from accepted brands. But among Negroes, the reverse is true in the present instance. It is the regular drinkers, those most engaged in the product category, who report being reliant on the brand-name for assurance

of getting a good Scotch (see Table 7).

The inference we draw is that the regular Negro drinker of Scotch, in contrast with his white "opposite number," is more anxious about the possibility of making a mistake. His greater familiarity with the product (compared with the occasional drinker) does not decrease his reliance on brand names to avoid a mistake. This is analogous to the finding above, that fashion-conscious Negro women are more likely to report having difficulties in making buying decisions.

### Discussions

We have indicated that Negroes show a simultaneous high degree of involvement in material goods of high symbolic value, and a degree of anxiety associated with exchanging scarce resources for goods about which one does not want to make a mistake. Among Negroes, this leads to a good deal of talking about shopping. Negro women are more likely to say they find it useful to talk with someone when they have trouble making shopping decisions than are white women (52% v. 36%).

#### TABLE 6.   Brand Preference for Scotch
#### Controlled by Income

| | Negro Drinkers | | White Drinkers | |
| | Regular | Occasional | Regular | Occasional |
|---|---|---|---|---|
| Brand preferences | | | | |
| "firmly established" | 71%[a] | 51% | 67% | 46% |
| (No. =) | (94) | (107) | (243) | (375) |
| Specify brand of Scotch | | | | |
| when ordering in bars, | | | | |
| clubs, restaurants | 79%[b] | 64% | 77% | 55% |
| (No. =) | (93) | (101) | (241) | (389) |

[a] Of the 94 Negro regular Scotch drinkers, 71% claim that their brand preferences are firmly established.

[b] Of the 93 Negro regular Scotch drinkers, 79% claim to specify a particular brand of Scotch when ordering in bars.

#### TABLE 7.   Reliance on Brand Name
#### Controlled by Income

| | Negro Drinkers | | White Drinkers | |
| | Regular | Occasional | Regular | Occasional |
|---|---|---|---|---|
| State that to obtain | | | | |
| a good Scotch you | | | | |
| have to order an | | | | |
| old reliable brand | 61%[a] | 53% | 49% | 60% |
| (No. =) | (98) | (114) | (247) | (416) |

[a] Of the 98 Negro regular drinkers of Scotch, 61% agreed with the statement.

Furthermore, to the extent that they are involved with the world outside their family, they are more likely to turn to it for guidance. As can be seen from Table 8, high-fashion-conscious Negro women are much more likely to talk with and go shopping with friends than with husbands. This trend is not nearly so strong among the white group.

As to the market for Scotch, Negroes are more likely to report that they initiated and took part in discussions about brands of Scotch. Furthermore, regular drinkers (both Negro and white) are generally more likely to take part in such discussions than occasional drinkers.

Since regular Scotch drinkers have more friends who are also regular Scotch drinkers, they have more opportunities to talk about Scotch than do occasional Scotch drinkers (and in fact they do talk more). After performing a statistical manipulation to equalize the number of regular Scotch drinkers each group has among its friends, we can look at their discussion habits as they would be if everyone had about the same opportunity to talk. This is the basis for the data presented in Table 9.

The data in this table indicate that the regular Negro drinkers of Scotch are *not* appreciably more likely to report having heard of a brand recommended than the occasional drinkers of Scotch among the Negroes. However, they are at least four times as likely as occasional drinkers to report having heard a brand criticized.

This suggests that the regular Negro drinkers of Scotch are principally concerned with in-

TABLE 8.    1.    Proportion Finding it Helpful to Discuss Shopping
with Various Types of Persons

|  | Negroes | | Whites | |
|  | Fashion-Consciousness | | Fashion-Consciousness | |
| Person | High | Low | High | Low |
|---|---|---|---|---|
| Friend | 55%[a] | 32% | 30% | 20% |
| Husband | 5 | 8 | 9 | 11 |
| Other or no one | 45 | 60 | 51 | 69 |
| (No. =) | (158) | (110) | (1472) | (979) |

[a] Of the 158 Negroes who were high-fashion-conscious, 55% found it helpful to discuss shopping with their friends.

2.    Choice of Shopping Companions

|  | Negroes | | Whites | |
|  | Fashion-Consciousness | | Fashion-Consciousness | |
| Companion | High | Low | High | Low |
|---|---|---|---|---|
| Friend | 48%[a] | 34% | 37% | 27% |
| Husband | 9 | 32 | 23 | 24 |
| Other or no one | 43 | 34 | 40 | 49 |
| (No. =) | (98) | (56) | (517) | (400) |

[a] Of the 98 high-fashion Negroes who took someone with them when shopping, 48% selected a friend as a companion.

TABLE 9.    Word-of-Mouth Activity Relative to Scotch
Controlled by Friendship Patterns

|  | Negro Drinkers | | White Drinkers | |
|  | Regular | Occasional | Regular | Occasional |
|---|---|---|---|---|
| Heard brand recommended | 42% | 39% | 51% | 39% |
| Heard brand criticized | 25 | 6 | 21 | 11 |
| (No. =) | (98) | (114) | (247) | (416) |

formation that will help them to avoid mistakes. This fits with the picture sketched above of the regular Negro drinkers of Scotch being especially anxious about not making mistakes.

## IMPLICATIONS

The data about drinking of Scotch fit the contemporary stereotype of high brand loyalty among Negroes. However, an all embracing notion of Negroes being brand loyal is, judging from our other studies, often too simple.

There are whole product categories, for example, facial tissues, which appear *not* to have high symbolic value with respect to middle-class cultural values (at least in the eyes of Negroes). In this product category none of the phenomena discussed with respect to Scotch and fashion have been found.

Furthermore, the Negro market is by no means homogeneous as to involvement with products of high symbolic importance. In fact, it is split between the strivers and nonstrivers.

Again, in some product categories, such as women's fashion, the same dynamics that might elsewhere lead the strivers among the Negroes to rely on brand names for reassurance drives them rather to other sources of information such as talking with friends.

Finally, in areas where brand names are important, Negroes tend to be brand-conscious, rather than brand-loyal. In the Scotch market we found evidence of Negroes being under cross-pressures—on the one hand, they had their own favorite brands; but on the other hand, they also reported being involved in many more discussions in which competing brands were recommended.

Compared with whites, Negroes show more concern, more anxiety, and more ambivalence over spending money for material goods. In this connection, it will be remembered that what the women liked most about shopping was getting things, and what they liked least was spending money.

While some Negroes will become increasingly secure in their status, it is probable that a growing proportion will become strivers as their expectations rise to the point where they work for a full place in American life. The proportion of nonstrivers will probably decrease as aspirations rise in general. But until Negroes' opportunities are brought in line with their aspirations, the basic dilemma we have discussed will remain.

# 10. Anthropology's Contributions to Marketing

CHARLES WINICK

The relative slowness of anthropologists and marketers in finding common ground is surprising.[1] Anthropologists have served as colonial administrators, in foreign-aid programs, and in other situations requiring a special sensitivity to foreign cultures. They have also developed sales-training procedures which involve the analysis of the rate of speech of salesmen with potential customers, through devices which measure the rate of interaction between people talking.[2] Another specialized industrial situation in which anthropologists have worked involves the application of their knowledge of the field of anthropometry or measurement of the body, in the design of products like chairs and knobs.[3]

Other anthropologists have worked in applied fields such as: reactions to disaster, the operation of internment and relocation centers, mental health, medical care, labor-management relations,[4] the culture of a factory,[5] community organization, social work,[6] military government, the cultural change associated with economic development,[7] contact between cultures, the nature of small-town life, behavior in extreme situations, the study of culture at a distance,[8] the reconstruction of the themes of a culture, relations among minority groups, the social structure of a hospital,[9] American national character,[10] and television.[11]

Although anthropologists have published their findings on America in very accessible formats,[12] there has been little discussion of how their findings could be applied to marketing problems.[13] One advertising publication has

---

[1] John Gillin, "The Application of Anthropological Knowledge to Modern Mass Society," *Human Organization*, Vol. 15, Winter 1957, pp. 24–30.
[2] Eliot D. Chapple, "The Interaction Chronograph," *Personnel*, Vol. 25, January 1949, pp. 295–307.
[3] Earnest A. Hooton, *A Survey In Seating* (Cambridge: Harvard Department of Anthropology, 1945).
[4] Charles R. Walker, *The Man on the Assembly Line* (Cambridge: Harvard University Press, 1952).
[5] Eliot Jaques, *The Changing Culture of A Factory* (New York: Dryden Press, 1953).

‡‡ SOURCE: Reprinted by permission from the *Journal of Marketing* (National Quarterly Publication of the American Marketing Association), Vol. 25, No. 5, July 1961, pp. 53–60.

[6] Franklin K. Patterson, Irving Lukoff, and Charles Winick, "Is Society the Patient," *Journal of Educational Sociology*, Vol. 30, October 1956, pp. 106–112.
[7] Almost every issue of *Economic Development and Cultural Change* carries relevant articles.
[8] Margaret Mead and Rhoda Metraux, *The Study of Culture At A Distance* (University of Chicago Press, 1952).
[9] Charles Winick, "The Hospital As A Social System," *New York State Nurse*, Vol. 26, January 1954, pp. 9–13.
[10] David M. Potter, *People of Plenty* (University of Chicago Press, 1954).
[11] Charles Winick, *Taste and the Censor In Television* (New York: Fund For the Republic, 1959).
[12] Margaret Lantis, editor, "The U.S.A. As Anthropologists See It," *American Anthropologist*, Vol. 57, December 1955, pp. 1,113–1,380.
[13] Richard C. Sheldon, "How The Anthropologist Can Help The Marketing Practitioner" in W. David Robbins, editor, *Successful Marketing at Home And Abroad* (Chicago: American Marketing Association, 1958), pp. 209–304.

published an article on the possibility of using anthropology in advertising.[14] The journal of applied anthropology, formerly called *Applied Anthropology* and now called *Human Organization,* almost never carries any material on marketing; and the national journal, *American Anthropologist,* also ignores the subject.

## ANTHROPOLOGY, SOCIOLOGY, AND PSYCHOLOGY

Anthropology is usually defined as the study of man. Such a definition is so all-inclusive that the field is generally divided into four subfields: archeology, cultured anthropology, linguistics, and physical anthropology. Archeology is concerned with the historical reconstruction of cultures which no longer exist. Cultural anthropology examines all the behaviors of man which have been learned, including social, linguistic, technical, and familiar behaviors; often it is defined as the study of man and his works. Linguistics is the comparative study of the structure, interrelationships, and development of languages. Physical anthropology is concerned with human biology and the development of the human organism, with special interest in race differences.

When anthropology is employed in marketing, it is usually cultural anthropology which is relevant. Cultural anthropology began with the study of primitive cultures, and its comparative analyses documented the different ways in which cultures have solved their problems of living.

Cultural anthropology has much in common with psychology and sociology. All three are concerned with the examination of man in his cultural setting. They differ in the emphases which they place on different elements of the relationship between a person and his environment. It can be said that all human behavior essentially is a function of the interrelations of personality, the social system, and culture.

Oversimplifying, psychology is concerned with personality, sociology addresses itself to the social system, and anthropology explores the culture. The interdisciplinary field of social psychology may draw on all three of these fields, and there are integrated social psychology texts which do so.[15]

A sharper focus on the differences among these three social sciences may be obtained by speculating on how each of the three might look at a family.

The psychologist would be interested in the personal adjustment and emotional health of each member of the family. He would want to examine their attitudes, mutual perceptions, and motivational systems. Their happiness or lack of it would interest him.

The sociologist would be concerned primarily with the dimensions of role and status within the family and with the number of different kinds of families. He would examine how the social structure created various kinds of internal arrangements which made it possible for the family to exist. He would be interested in the norms of behavior and the stresses and strains shown by the deviations from the norm and resulting from role conflict. He would study class membership as well as the rates of various kinds of behavior, such as the birth rate.

The cultural anthropologist would examine the technological level which the culture had reached and the interrelations of technology with culture. He would scrutinize the procedures for inheritance of property and how kinship was reckoned and described, and how the spouses got to know each other. He would study the family's food and housing. He would be interested in the language level and dialects and in who talked to whom. He would be concerned with how the age of different members of the family affected their behavior, and with trends in illnesses. He would study how the culture "rubbed off" on the family unit. The anthropologist thus does not have information which it would be impossible for the sociologist or psychologist to obtain, but he has a special sensitivity to certain facets of social life.

The sociologist and psychologist bring a powerful and varied arsenal of concepts and approaches to the study of social life. In what ways is the anthropologist able to contribute insights and experience toward the science of "marketology," and to what extent may they not be immediately accessible, for example, to the sociologist?[16] The anthropologist is especially

[14] Alan S. Marcus, "How Agencies Can Use Anthropology in Advertising," *Advertising Agency,* Vol. 49, September 14, 1956, pp. 87–91.

[15] Steuart Henderson Britt, *Social Psychology of Modern Life* revised edition (New York: Rinehart, 1949). S. Stanfeld Sargent and Robert C. Williamson, *Social Psychology* (New York: Ronald Press, 1958).

[16] Robert Bartels, "Sociologist and Marketologists," *Journal of Marketing,* Vol. 24, October 1959, pp. 37–40; Christen T. Jonassen, "Contributions of Sociology to Marketing," *Journal of Marketing,* Vol. 24, October 1959, pp. 29–35.

trained to have empathy with groups other than his own and to "tune in" on their patterns of culture. Inasmuch as his training has exposed him to a wide variety of cultures, he can take a global view of a situation and see it in the context of a larger background. His training makes him sensitive to cross-cultural differences which may be of crucial importance in many different situations, because his entire training is geared toward awareness of such differences.

Anthropology has less of the factionalism which characterizes psychology and sociology. This is not to suggest that all is serene in anthropology or that it has never been troubled by theoretical or methodological issues. However, even though anthropologists may disagree on something like the exact value of the contribution of a particular anthropologist, they would generally agree on what the cultural anthropologist looks for, and there are standardized check lists on how to view a culture.[17] In contrast, a psychologist's allegiance to the Gestalt, behaviorist, psychoanalytic, learning-theory, or perception schools is likely to influence what he does with a given problem. A sociologist's commitment to the structure-function, historical, ecological, "middle range," environmental-determinism, or demographic schools would largely determine the emphases of his approach to a problem. Since such divergent schools are less likely to exist in cultural anthropology, it is probable than anthropological guidance on a given marketing problem would be relatively consistent.

## WHAT THE ANTHROPOLOGIST KNOWS

The anthropologist is specifically trained to study national character, or the differences which distinguish our national group from another. He should be able to provide measures for distinguishing the subtle differences among a Swede, a Dane, and a Norwegian; or between a Frenchman and an Englishman; or a Brazilian and an Argentinian; or between a typical resident of Montreal and one of Toronto. The anthropologist is also a specialist in the study of subcultures. He would be able, in a city like New York, to differentiate the patterns of living of such disparate but rapidly homogenizing groups as Puerto Ricans, Negroes, Italo-Americans, Jews, Polish-Americans, and Irish-Americans.

Because almost any large community consists of a variety of subcultures, this awareness of subcultural trends can be especially useful. A more subtle area of special interest to anthropologists is the silent language of gesture, posture, food and drink preferences, and other nonverbal cues to behavior.[18]

Related to this is the anthropologist's professional interest in languages and symbols. He might, for example, be especially concerned about why a particular shape has special significance as a symbol in a society, or how the structure of a language or a regional speech pattern was related to how people think.[19]

Another area of concern to the anthropologist, because of its symbolic meanings has to do with "rites de passage" or the central points in a person's life at which he may ritually be helped to go from one status to another, for example, birth, puberty, or marriage.[20]

Taboos represent a continuing area of interest to the anthropologist.[21] Every culture has taboos or prohibitions about various things, such as the use of a given color, or of a given phrase or symbol. The anthropologist is aware of the larger values of a culture, which represent the substratum of custom which is taken for granted and the violation of which represents a taboo.

The anthropologist's method is primarily the exposure of his highly developed sensitivity to the area in which he is working, via observation and extended interviews with informants. Projective tests have also been widely used in anthropological studies. The anthropologist can bring a wealth of insight to marketing situations.

## USE OF ANTHROPOLOGY IN MARKETING

There are at least three kinds of situations in which the knowledge of the anthropologist has been employed in marketing: specific knowledge; awareness of themes of a culture; sensitivity to taboos.

---

[17] Royal Anthropological Institute, *Notes and Queries on Anthropology* (London: The Institute, 1956).

[18] Edward T. Hall, *The Silent Language* (New York: Doubleday, 1959).

[19] Benjamin Lee Whorf, *Collected Papers on Metalinguistics* (Washington: Department of State Foreign Service Institute, 1952).

[20] Jan Wit, *Rites De Passage* (Amsterdam: De Windroos, 1959).

[21] Franz Steiner, *Taboo* (London: Cohen and West, 1957).

## Specific Knowledge

Here are a few cases in which the specific knowedge of an anthropologist was applied to marketing situations.

A manufacturer of central heating equipment was planning to introduce central heating to an area which previously had used other heating. Since people generally grow up to accept a certain approach to heating which they take for granted, introduction of the new central heating posed marketing problems in coping with deeply imbedded consumer resistance to what would be a major innovation. An anthropologist was able to draw on his knowledge of the folklore and symbolism of heat and fire in order to suggest methods of presenting the new system, so as to make it as consonant as possible with the connotations of heat, even though the nature of the heating method had changed radically. There was considerable consumer resistance to the central heating, but it decreased substantially after the first year.

In addition to a marketing problem, the introduction of central heating also posed problems of public policy which the manufacturer had to overcome before he could obtain approval for the introduction of the heating equipment. The area was one which suffered from a declining birth rate, and officials were concerned about the extent to which central heating might cause the birth rate to decline further, because of their belief that heated bedrooms would cause a decline in sexual activity and ultimately in births.

The anthropologist was able to point to some cultures in which the birth rate had declined and some in which it had not done so after the introduction of central heating. The anthropologist's data made it possible for the manufacturer of the central-heating equipment to discuss its probable effects realistically with the appropriate officials.

Another field in which the anthropologist has specific knowledge that other social scientists are not likely to have is that of clothing and fashion. The only empirical study of the fashion cycle in woman's clothing which has successfully been used for predictive purposes by clothing manufacturers was conducted by anthropologists.[22] In marketing situations, the anthropologist has often been able to combine his special knowledge of the needs of the body for clothing of various kinds at different ages, his sensitivity to what technology makes possible and his awareness of fashion.

For example, an anthropologist was consulted by a leading manufacturer of overalls for young children, a product which had remained unchanged for decades. He examined the product in the light of the special needs of children who wear overalls, the growing use of washing machines to launder the overalls, their relative frequency of laundering, and contemporary technology. He suggested that the overall straps have a series of sets of metal grippers instead of buttons, thus making it possible to use different sets of grippers as the child grew instead of tying or knotting the straps. Noting that the straps often fall off the shoulders when children played, he suggested that the shirts which children wore under the overalls have either a loop for the straps to pass through or a synthetic fastener which faced matching material on the strap, so that the shoulder of the shirt could be pressed against the strap and remain attached to it until shoulder strap and shirt were pulled apart.

He also recommended that the seams of the overalls, previously single stitched, be double stitched like those of men's shirts, which have to withstand frequent launderings. The double-stitched overalls would be less likely to come apart as a result of frequent launderings in a washing machine. These recommendations were adopted, and within a few years substantially changed and expanded the nature of the overall market for young children. The children's parents were more pleased with the overalls because they lasted longer and looked better on the children, and they were far more functional than before.

The special knowledge of the anthropologist has been called into play where there are special subcultural groups to which the marketer wishes to address himself. One beer manufacturer wished to extend his market share among Negroes in a large eastern city in the United States. He was advised about reaching this group by an anthropologist who was familiar with the special subculture of Negroes, and who pointed to the profound effects of Negroes' caste membership on their purchasing behavior. The ambiguity of their role has led many Negroes to be especially aware of articles that have status connotations and of whether a brand symbolizes racial progress. Examination of the manufacturer's marketing program by

[22] Jane Richardson and Alfred L. Kroeber, *Three Centuries of Women's Dress Fashions* (Berkeley: University of California Press, 1940).

the anthropologist led to several recommendations for change. The manufacturer began to help in the support of several major social events related to the arts in Negro communities, and to stress that the beer was a national brand with quality-control procedures. He changed the content of his advertising in the direction of enhancing its status and quality connotations. These changes were all directed toward improving the status connotations of the beer to Negroes.

Guidance on related problems with respect to the Puerto Rican and Jewish markets has also been used constructively. Since 35 to 40 per cent of the population of the United States consists of minority subcultures, the anthropologist's contributions may be considerable.

Another situation had to do with the selection of specific symbols for various purposes. A major manufacturer of women's products was uncertain about whether to continue using the Fleur de Lis emblem on his package. Anthropological analysis of the symbol suggested that its association with French kings and other cultural connotations of maleness made it more masculine than feminine. The anthropologist's recommendations were confirmed by subsequent field testing.

In a related case, a manufacturer of women's cosmetics conducted an anthropological study of the comparative symbolism in our culture of women's eyes and mouth, which suggested that the eye tends to be experienced as a relatively protecting organ while the mouth tends to be experienced as more nurturing. This knowledge of the differences between the special meanings of eye and mouth could constructively be used in marketing the products, and especially in advertising. The advertising explicitly and implicitly mentioned the role of the eye in protection of the woman. It stressed the role of the mouth as the organ which both symbolically and literally gives love. This replaced the manufacturers' previous advertising, in which both eye and mouth were treated in the same way, as organs which could be made beautiful.

### Awareness of Themes

The anthropologist has functioned in situations in which he can use his special understanding of themes of a culture, oftentimes taken for granted.

A major chain of candy shops was suffering a decline in sales. A marketing-research study had established that the brand was usually bought as a gift, either for others or as a gift for the purchaser. The chain was unable to develop any ways of using this finding that were not hackneyed. Anthropological guidance on the symbolism of gift-giving enabled the chain to develop merchandising, packaging, and advertising formats for the gift theme. Anthropological study of the connotations of the major holidays suggested themes for window displays, and advertising of the candy in conjunction with the holidays. The chain's marketing strategy was revised on the basis of the anthropological interpretation and clarification of the marketing-research study. Anthropologists are the only social scientists who have systematically studied gift-giving and gift-receiving.[23]

Another example of anthropological interpretation of a marketing-research study was provided by a shirt manufacturer. The study had established that women buy more than half of men's shirts in a particular price range. The anthropologist was able to interpret this finding in the light of several anthropological studies of the relations between husbands and wives in America. The manufacturer had been thinking of placing advertising for his men's shirts in selected women's magazines. The anthropologist was able to point to a number of studies of husband-wife relations which suggested growing resentment by men over the extent to which women had been borrowing and buying men's clothing, and which suggested that the proposed advertising campaign might not be propitious.

Another anthropologist's special sensitivity to the "rites de passage" helped a shoe manufacturer whose sales were declining because of aggressive foreign and domestic competition. The anthropologist was able to point to the extent to which shoes represent major symbols of our going from one stage of life to another, and to assist the manufacturer in developing methods for using the relationship between shoes and "rites de passage."[24]

A landmark along the road of an infant becoming a child usually is found between the ages of 4 and 6 when he can tie his own shoe laces. The manufacturer developed some pamphlets and other instructional material for

[23] Marcel Mauss, *The Gift* (London: Cohen and West, 1954).

[24] Charles Winick, "Status, Shoes, and the Life Cycle," *Boot and Shoe Recorder*, Vol. 156, October 15, 1959, pp. 100–202.

parents on how to help children to learn to tie their shoe laces. Distribution by local retailers contributed toward making parents favorably aware of the brand's line for children in this age group.

The teenager signalizes her entrance into a new social world by her first high heels. Window displays and advertising which explicitly stressed the new social activities of the teenager wearing her high heels, and naming specific shoe models after teenage social events ("The Prom") contributed toward associating the manufacturer's name with the excitement of the new world symbolized by the high heels.

Older people see the wearing of special "old people's shoes" as the ultimate reminder that they are becoming old. The manufacturer was able to redesign his line for older people so that it retained its special health features but still looked as stylish as any adult shoe, and had no visible stigma of "old people's shoes."

### Sensitivity to Taboos

Marketers may unwittingly violate a taboo, whether cultural, religious, or political, especially in selling overseas. Blue, for example, is the color for mourning in Iran and is not likely to be favorably received on a commercial product. Green is the nationalist color of Egypt and Syria and is frowned on for use in packages. Showing pairs of anything on the Gold Coast of Africa is disapproved. White is the color of mourning in Japan and, therefore, not likely to be popular on a product. Brown and gray are disapproved colors in Nicaragua. Purple is generally disapproved in most Latin American markets because of its association with death. Feet are regarded as despicable in Thailand, where any object and package showing feet is likely to be unfavorably received.

The anthropologist can cast light on taboos and on their opposite: favored colors and symbols. The reason for the people in a country or an area liking or not liking a particular color or symbol may be a function of political, nationalist, religious, cultural, or other reasons.

### SOME APPLICATIONS IN CANADA

Canada represents a special opportunity for the application of anthropology in marketing situations. Twenty-nine per cent of the country's entire population is in French-speaking Quebec, and over half of this number know no English. Canada thus offers a changing kind of

bilingual and culture contact situation with major cross-cultural differences for anthropological analysis.

Both the farm community and the industrial community of Quebec have been studied by anthropologists.[25] The re-evaluation of the nature of Quebec family and community life sparked by Dean Phillipe Garigue of the University of Montreal and a team at Laval University has led to renewed interest in Quebec on the part of anthropologists. Their studies have produced considerable information on styles of life in Quebec which should be translatable into marketing data on pricing policies, colors, package size, flavor and taste of various food items, tetxure of fabrics, automobile symbolism, product scents, and related subjects.

### Specific Knowledge

Perhaps the most frequent occasion for the anthropologist to demonstrate specific knowledge in Canada has to do with language. One laundry-soap company had point-of-sale material on its soap describing it as extra strong and the best one to use on especially dirty parts of wash ("les parts de sale"). After sales of the soap had declined, an anthropologist who was called in by the company pointed out that the phrase is comparable to the American slang phrase "private parts." This kind of mistake might have been avoided if anthropological guidance had been available before sales declined.

Some products do not sell well in Quebec because the English name may be almost unpronounceable to a French speaker, or the name of the product may be meaningless even when translated idiomatically. Even the English spoken in Montreal differs somewhat from the English spoken in Toronto, creating potential hazards for the marketers who may not know, for example that a "tap" in a "flat" in Toronto is likely to be a "faucet" in a Montreal "apartment."

### Awareness of Themes

A study done by an anthropologist for a food manufacturer demonstrated the relationship between the purchases of certain food items and the gradual decline of the wood-burning stove which used to be a staple of Quebec farm

---

[25] Horace Miner, *St. Denis* (University of Chicago Press, 1939); Everett C. Hughes, *French Canada In Transition* (University of Chicago Press, 1943).

kitchens. The wood stove would almost always have a stew pot ("pot au feu") simmering all day. Various ingredients were put into the pot to provide flavor. With the introduction of gas and electric kitchen ranges, it not only became relatively expensive to keep the stew pot going but the simmering could not be sustained because the pot would tend to boil rather than simmer.

This change was accompanied by some radical adjustments in food consumption which were of great relevance to food marketing. The manufacturer was able to begin distribution of canned soups and stews which soon found a very large market and rapidly replaced the "pot au feu."

### Taboos

Alertness to taboos was illustrated by an anthropologist's suggestion to a manufacturer of canned fish for changing a series of advertisements which were appearing in Quebec magazines and newspapers. The same advertisement was run repeatedly. The advertisements showed a woman in shorts playing golf with her husband. The caption read that the woman would be able to be on the golf links all day and still prepare a delicious dinner that evening if she used the product. Every element in the adver-

tisement represented a violation of some underlying theme of French Canadian life; the wife would not be likely to be playing golf with her husband, she would not wear shorts, and she would not be serving the particular kind of fish as a main course. In this case, the anthropologist was consulted *after* the series had been running for awhile.

### THE MARKETER AS AN ANTHROPOLOGIST

A good case could be made for the thesis that marketing researchers do more anthropological research on modern cultures than do anthropologists. Marketing researchers are studying national character, subcultures, themes, and ways of life. The kind of information which marketing-research studies seek on how peope live and what products they use represent first-rate material for the cultural anthropologist.

The questionnaire, panel, audit, sales analysis, and other methods of modern marketing differ in degree but not in kind from the trained observations of the anthropologist, but there is no reason why the two methods cannot complement each other. Greater communication between these two fields can and should lead to mutual enrichment of both.

# B. Psychology of Consumer Behavior

## 11. Psychological Dimensions of Consumer Decision

WALTER A. WOODS

Motivational research has grown at such a great pace because consumer attitudes and behavior are so important in solving marketing and advertising problems. But motivational research as commonly practiced has often been undisciplined and even capricious. Psychological and sociological theories are often ignored. Old dimensions, often inadequate, are not replaced with new dimensions to provide a systematic way of looking at the consumer.

One reason is a common tendency to miss the differences between motivational and psychological research. Today the two terms are often used incorrectly as interchangeable.

As a result of these errors in definition, other psychological points are often understressed. Theories of consumer behavior have tended to ignore important determinants such as habit, cognition, and learning.[1]

### CONSUMER DIMENSIONS VERSUS PRODUCT DIMENSIONS

Consider two distinct processes which work to determine that a particular product will be bought or consumed: (1) The process of motivation—someone is hungry and needs food. (2) The process of discrimination—the hunger

is satisfied by selecting particular foods, or particular brands of foods.

This is oversimplification, of course. To be sure, the factors underlying eating (food consumption) are motivational. Theoretically, people eat for several reasons: they are hungry, they are bored, it is time to eat, or they require an outlet for some psychological force.

But what a person (or group) eats at a particular time is usually outside the realm of this kind of motivation. Cereal may be eaten at breakfast because (1) cereal is always eaten for breakfast (habit); (2) the cereal box was in view as breakfast was considered (impulse); (3) cereal is "healthy" (motivation); or (4) everyone else was having cereal (social pressure).

As to why cereal was available in the household, there are other possibilities: (1) cereal is always purchased (habit); (2) there was no cereal but mother wanted a change (cognition plus motivation); (3) cereals are inexpensive (cognition); or (4) the young son shopped with her, and he liked the package (impulse).

As to brand selected, there are also several possibilities: (1) the same brand is "automatically" purchased (habit); (2) brand X is considered best (cognition); or (3) brands of "big" manufacturers are preferred (motivation).

Contrast this with the purchase of a car, where there is a basic need for transportation (motivation), and a secondary need for ownership. When we inquire as to make of car, the question, "What car for what purpose?", is raised. New reasons come into play: cost and economy (cognition), appearance (impulsivity), prestige (motivation).

---

[1] An attempt to remedy this is represented in James A. Bayton, "Motivation, Cognition, Learning—Basic Factors in Consumer Behavior." *Journal of Marketing*, Vol. 22, January 1958, pp. 282–289.

‡‡ SOURCE: Reprinted by permission from the *Journal of Marketing* (National Quarterly Publication of the American Marketing Association), Vol. 24, No. 3, January 1960, pp. 15–19.

Cereals and cars are different. Habitual and rational forces are more at work with cereals, irrational forces with cars. Consumers identify with and get more involved emotionally with automobiles than with cereals. All consumer behavior is motivated, but actual choices made to satisfy motives may depend on other psychological variables. Motivation, per se, is most often a secondary factor in consumer choice, although it underlies all consumer behavior. Two sets of factors determine the choices which are made: personality of the purchaser, and character of the product. There are thus two sets of variables:

1. Consumer variables, the differences among consumers in their habits, cognitive structure, and motives which cause them to behave differently in purchase situations.

2. Differences among products in "demand character" which cause consumers to become more ego-involved with some products than with others.

## CONSUMER VARIABLES

Consumers pass through an organizing and integrating process during which patterns of behavior are established with respect to purchasing and product use. The newly married woman brings certain attitudes to her new home, but she has no set ways of running her new home. Because of the major recurring problems of personal, family, and social growth, she solves her minor problems by establishing routines (a motive common to everyone).[2] Frequently these routines are established without awareness or deliberate intent.

Among the behaviors frequently relegated to routine are menu planning and preparation, and shopping. Once housewives have routinized these activities, they become relatively "closed" to new product introductions and to brand promotion.

But no consumer solves all problems at the same time. For example, the problem of cake baking may persist long after the problem of coffee preparation is solved. Also, problems are not solved once and for all. The problem of storing perishables may be solved by a new refrigerator; but the problem may recur if, for

instance, the family grows in size and more space is needed.

Thus, particular buying habits persist because they have solved some household problems, and they continue until changes in circumstances or outlook present new problems. No published studies are known which discuss the extent to which such behavior (habit-determined behavior) exists, but for some product areas about 60 per cent of the market may be habit dominated.

On the other hand, consumer behavior may remain unstable. Brands and products may be freely changed on the basis of rational factors (cognitive behavior) such as price or convenience. One study suggests that cognitive behavior exists in about 20 per cent of the market.[3]

The cognitive-habit dimension does not explain all purchasing behavior. Purchasing decisions may be made on the basis of other forces. Two such types of behavior may be identified: behavior in response to *affective* appeal and behavior in response to *symbolic* appeal.[4] Although these behavior types are often loosely grouped together as "irrational," they do differ.

Response to affective appeals is probably best described as "impulsive" behavior. As used here, it refers to reactions to product qualities which are primarily physical. Included would be such qualities as color, design, flavor, odor. For example, a shopper impulsively purchases candy because of its inherent physical appeal; or a shopper impulsively selects an automobile because of the inherent appeal of its color and design.

Response to symbolic appeals might best be termed "emotional" behavior. As used here, it refers to behavior which is generated by thinking about the meaning of a product purchase rather than the function of the purchase. Thus, the perceived prestige of owning a Cadillac may be more important in bringing about its purchase than is the function which the Cadillac would serve. This is irrational behavior.

This discussion of consumer variables has suggested that particular people tend consist-

[2] As exemplified by the principle, referred to in psychological literature as "The Principle of Least Effort"; see G. K. Zipf, *Human Behavior and the Principle of Least Effort* (Boston: Addison-Wesley, 1949).

[3] Ben Gedalecia, "The Communicators: An All-Media Study"; a report made at the 3rd Annual Advertising Research Foundation Conference, November 14, 1957.

[4] The term "cathectic," as used by T. Parsons, E. A. Shils, and others in *Toward a General Theory of Action* (Cambridge: Harvard University Press, 1951), pp. 8–12, appears to include both "affective" and "symbolic" as used here.

ently to behave in particular ways. Although it is unlikely that a given consumer always reacts in one way rather than another, people do react predominantly in one way rather than in other ways. The market for consumer products probably is composed of:

1. *A habit-determined group* of brand loyal consumers, who tend to be satisfied with the last purchased product or brand.

2. *A cognitive group* of consumers, sensitive to rational claims and only conditionally brand loyal.

3. *A price-cognitive group* of consumers, who principally decide on the basis of price or economy comparisons.

4. *An impulse group* of consumers, who buy on the basis of physical appeal and are relatively insensitive to brand name.

5. *A group of "emotional" reactors,* who tend to be responsive to what products symbolize and who are heavily swayed by "images."

6. *A group of new consumers,* not yet stabilized with respect to the psychological dimensions of consumer behavior.

This discussion of consumer variables has been concerned with behavior and *not* with attitudes. Behavior and attitudes are not the same. A favorable attitude toward a TV message is not the same thing as in-store purchasing of the product advertised.

## PRODUCT VARIABLES

Superimposed across the entire gamut of consumer cognition and motivation is the character of the product itself. Some products have the capacity to get consumers ego-involved to a high degree. That is, consumers identify with the product. Other products have this capacity to a lesser degree. Still other products depend on their sensory appeal, and others on the function they perform.

Thus, the demands of products on the consumer fall into three classes:

A. Demands of ego-involvement in the external symbols which the product conveys. ("All executives ride in big cars like mine.")

B. Hedonic demand. ("It's so beautiful, I can't resist it.")

C. Functional demands. ("Here it is Tuesday again; we may as well have tuna casserole for dinner.")

Although product variables have been studied to a much lesser degree than consumer

variables and less is known about them, it is possible to describe rather unambiguous variables of this sort. Group A above can be broken down into four sub-classes of products where ego-involvement is at issue: (1) prestige products; (2) maturity products; (3) status (or membership) products; (4) anxiety products. These four, along with B and C, provide six psychological product classes.

*1. Prestige Products. Prestige products are those which themselves become symbols.* The product not only *represents* some image or personality attribute, but *becomes* that attribute. For example, ownership of a Cadillac is not only a symbol of success, but is evidence of success. Products which fall into this class include automobiles, homes, clothing, furniture, art objects, newspapers, and magazines.

The function which these products serve is to extend or identify the ego of the consumer in a direction consistent with his self-image, in such a way as to give him individuality.

*2. Maturity Products.* Maturity products are those which because of social customs are typically withheld from younger people. The initial use of such products symbolizes a state of maturity on the part of the consumer. Intrinsic product merit is not a factor, at least in the beginning stages of use. Products in this category include cigarettes, cosmetics, coffee, beer, and liquor.

*3. Status Products.* Status products serve the function of imputing class membership to their users. The intrinsic merit of products in this class is an important factor in continued usage. However, consumers tend to select "big-name" brands because they believe such brands impute "success," "substance," "quality," or similar attributes. "Bigness," in turn, is often imputed from familiarity or frequency of exposure of the consumer to the brand. Packaged food and gasoline are often in this category. While prestige products connote leadership, status products connote membership.

*4. Anxiety Products.* Anxiety products are those products which are used to alleviate some presumed personal or social *threat.* Products in this category include soaps, dentifrices, "health" foods, perfumes, and razors. This group of products involves ego-defense, whereas the three preceding categories are concerned with ego-enhancement.

*5. Hedonic Products (or Product Features).* Hedonic products are those which are highly dependent on their sensory character for their appeal. Moreover, their appeal is immediate and highly situational. This category includes snack items, many types of clothing, pre-sweetened cereals. Visual (style) features of any product fall within this area; automobile design and color are examples.

**6. Functional Products.** Functional products are those products to which little cultural or social meaning has, as yet, been imputed. Included in this category are the staple food items, fruits, vegetables, and also most building products.

The differences between these product classes have important implications for competitive marketing. Where ego-involvement can be developed, a high degree of interest can be won on the basis of product image. This, in turn, means a high susceptibility to "other-brand" image and a less habit-bound audience. For such products, marketing success hinges heavily on motivational selling.

On the other hand, where involvement is low, loyalty to one's brand must be achieved differently. Product image becomes unimportant, while product identity and familiarity become very important. Once loyalty is established, threat from "other-brand" penetration is considerably less than with "ego-involving" products. Moreover, "other-brand" success will be much more costly for the "other" manufacturer to achieve, since the other brand must get through on the basis of cognitive appeals to a habit-bound, closed-out audience. For this reason, "lead time" becomes a highly important requirement for success of a product whose appeal is primarily functional or hedonic.

## INTERRELATIONS OF VARIABLES

It might seem that the above listed person variables and product variables are two views of the same panorama. But this is not the case.

The psychological character which a product has is a true character which has been imputed to it by society as a whole through long periods of time, and is independent of the psychological character (or personality) of particular individuals. For example, no matter whether the consumer be "habit determined," "cognitive," or "impulsive," he will still acknowledge that Cadillacs do convey prestige connotations of some sort, and that cosmetics do represent a means of conveying "maturity."

Yet, while product variables and person variables represent two sets of variables, it is also true that interrelations do exist. The very nature of impulsivity as a personality characteristic leads to greater susceptibility to products with hedonic appeal. Similarly, social needs will lead to association with products with status connotations.

Although interrelations may exist between these two sets of variables, treatment as a duality is necessary in the development of marketing programs. A true differentiation is required in order to distinguish between market (or consumer) segmentation and product description. A study of consumer variables leads to a description of the market in terms of consumer segments and needs. A study of product variables leads to a definition of product concept and product attributes. Both are required in the development of a product philosophy.

# 12. Behavioral Models for Analyzing Buyers

PHILIP KOTLER

In times past, management could arrive at a fair understanding of its buyers through the daily experience of selling to them. But the growth in the size of firms and markets has removed many decision-makers from direct contact with buyers. Increasingly, decision-makers have had to turn to summary statistics and to behavioral theory, and are spending more money today than ever before to try to understand their buyers.

Who buys? How do they buy? And why? The first two questions relate to relatively overt aspects of buyer behavior, and can be learned about through direct observation and interviewing.

But uncovering *why* people buy is an extremely difficult task. The answer will tend to vary with the investigator's behavioral frame of reference.

The buyer is subject to many influences which trace a complex course through his psyche and lead eventually to overt purchasing responses. This conception of the buying process is illustrated in Figure 1. Various influences and their modes of transmission are shown at the left. At the right are the buyer's responses in choice of product, brand, dealer, quantities, and frequency. In the center stands the buyer and his mysterious psychological processes. The buyer's psyche is a "black box" whose workings can be only partially deduced. The marketing strategist's challenge to the behavioral scientist is to construct a more specific model of the mechanism in the black box.

◆ SOURCE: Reprinted by permission from the *Journal of Marketing*, (National Quarterly Publication of the American Marketing Association) Vol. 29, October 1965, pp. 37–45.

Unfortunately no generally accepted model of the mechanism exists. The human mind, the only entity in nature with deep powers of understanding, still remains the least understood. Scientists can explain planetary motion, genetic determination, and molecular behavior. Yet they have only partial, and often partisan, models of *human* behavior.

Nevertheless, the marketing strategist should recognize the potential interpretative contributions of different partial models for explaining buyer behavior. Depending upon the product, different variables and behavioral mechanisms may assume particular importance. A psychoanalytic behavioral model might throw much light on the factors operating in cigarette demand, while an economic behavioral model might be useful in explaining machine-tool purchasing. Sometimes alternative models may shed light on different demand aspects of the same product.

What are the most useful behavioral models for interpreting the transformation of buying influences into purchasing responses? Five different models of the buyer's "black box" are presented in the present article, along with their respective marketing applications: (1) The Marshallian model, stressing economic motivations; (2) The Pavlovian model, learning; (3) the Freudian model, psychoanalytic motivations; (4) the Veblenian model, social-psychological factors; and (5) the Hobbesian model, organizational factors. These models represent radically different conceptions of the mainsprings of human behavior.

## THE MARSHALLIAN ECONOMIC MODEL

Economists were the first professional group to construct a specific theory of buyer be-

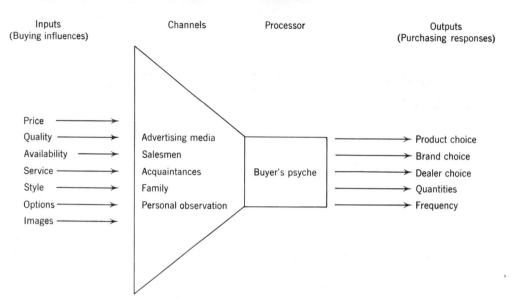

FIG. 1. The buying process conceived as a system of inputs and outputs.

havior. The theory holds that purchasing decisions are the result of largely "rational" and conscious economic calculations. The individual buyer seeks to spend his income on those goods that will deliver the most utility (satisfaction) according to his tastes and relative prices.

The antecedents for this view trace back to the writings of Adam Smith and Jeremy Bentham. Smith set the tone by developing a doctrine of economic growth based on the principle that man is motivated by self-interest in all his actions.[1] Bentham refined this view and saw man as finely calculating and weighing the expected pleasures and pains of every contemplated action.[2]

Bentham's "felicific calculus" was not applied to consumer behavior (as opposed to entrepreneurial behavior) until the late 19th century. Then, the "marginal-utility" theory of value was formulated independently and almost simultaneously by Jevons[3] and Marshall[4] in England, Menger[5] in Austria, and Walras[6] in Switzerland.

Alfred Marshall was the great consolidator of the classical and neoclassical tradition in economics; and his synthesis in the form of demand-supply analysis constitutes the main source of modern micro-economic thought in the English-speaking world. His theoretical work aimed at realism, but his method was to start with simplifying assumptions and to examine the effect of a change in a single variable (say, price) when all other variables were held constant.

He would "reason out" the consequences of the provisional assumptions and in subsequent steps modify his assumptions in the direction of more realism. He employed the "measuring rod of money" as an indicator of the intensity of human psychological desires. Over the years his methods and assumptions have been refined into what is now known as *modern utility theory*: economic man is bent on maximizing his utility, and does this by carefully calculating the "felicific" consequences of any purchase.

¶ As an example, suppose on a particular evening that John is considering whether to prepare his own dinner or dine out. He esti-

[1] Adam Smith, *An Inquiry into the Nature and Causes of the Wealth of Nations*, 1776 (New York: The Modern Library, 1937).

[2] Jeremy Bentham, *An Introduction to the Principles of Morals and Legislation*, 1780 (Oxford, England: Clarendon Press, 1907).

[3] William S. Jevons, *The Theory of Political Economy* (New York: The Macmillan Company, 1871).

[4] Alfred Marshall, *Principles of Economics*, 1890 (London: The Macmillan Company, 1927).

[5] Karl Menger, *Principles of Economics*, 1871 (Glencoe, Illinois: Free Press, 1950).

[6] Leon Walras, *Elements of Pure Economics*, 1874 (Homewood, Illinois: Richard D. Irwin, Inc., 1954).

mates that a restaurant meal would cost $2.00 and a home-cooked meal 50 cents. According to the Marshallian model, if John expects less than four times as much satisfaction from the restaurant meal as the home-cooked meal, he will eat at home. The economist typically is not concerned with how these relative preferences are formed by John, or how they may be psychologically modified by new stimuli.

Yet John will not always cook at home. The principle of diminishing marginal utility operates. Within a given time interval—say, a week —the utility of each additional home-cooked meal diminishes. John gets tired of home meals and other products become relatively more attractive.

John's *efficiency* in maximizing his utility depends on the adequacy of his information and his freedom of choice. If he is not perfectly aware of costs, if he misestimates the relative delectability of the two meals, or if he is barred from entering the restaurant, he will not maximize his potential utility. His choice processes are rational, but the results are inefficient.

### Marketing Applications of Marshallian Model

Marketers usually have dismissed the Marshallian model as an absurd figment of ivory-tower imagination. Certainly the behavioral essence of the situation is omitted, in viewing man as calculating the marginal utility of a restaurant meal over a home-cooked meal.

Eva Mueller has reported a study where only one-fourth of the consumers in her sample bought with any substantial degree of deliberation.[7] Yet there are a number of ways to view the model.

From one point of view the Marshallian model is tautological and therefore neither true nor false. The model holds that the buyer acts in the light of his best "interest." But this is not very informative.

A second view is that this is a *normative* rather than a *descriptive* model of behavior. The model provides logical norms for buyers who want to be "rational." Although the consumer is not likely to employ economic analysis to decide between a box of Kleenex and Scotties, he may apply economic analysis in deciding whether to buy a new car. Industrial buyers even more clearly would want an economic calculus for making good decisions.

A third view is that economic factors operate to a greater or lesser extent in all markets, and, therefore, must be included in any comprehensive description of buyer behavior.

Furthermore, the model suggests useful behavioral hypotheses such as: (a) The lower the price of the product, the higher the sales. (b) The lower the price of substitute products, the lower the sales of this product; and the lower the price of complementary products, the higher the sales of this product. (c) The higher the real income, the higher the sales of this product, provided that it is not an "inferior" good. (d) The higher the promotional expenditures, the higher the sales.

The validity of these hypotheses does not rest on whether *all* individuals act as economic calculating machines in making their purchasing decisions. For example, some individuals may buy *less* of a product when its price is reduced. They may think that the quality has gone down, or that ownership has less status value. If a majority of buyers view price reductions negatively, then sales may fall, contrary to the first hypothesis.

But for most goods a price reduction increases the relative value of the goods in many buyers' minds and leads to increased sales. This and the other hypotheses are intended to describe average effects.

The impact of economic factors in actual buying situations is studied through experimental design or statistical analyses of past data. Demand equations have been fitted to a wide variety of products—including beer, refrigerators, and chemical fertilizers.[8] More recently, the impact of economic variables on the fortunes of different brands has been pursued with significant results, particularly in the case of coffee, frozen orange juice, and margarine.[9]

But economic factors alone cannot explain all the variations in sales. The Marshallian model ignores the fundamental question of how product and brand preferences are formed. It represents a useful frame of reference for analyzing only one small corner of the "black box."

[7] Eva Mueller, "A Study of Purchase Decisions," Part 2, *Consumer Behavior, The Dynamics of Consumer Reaction*, edited by Lincoln H. Clark (New York: New York University Press, 1954), pp. 36–87.

[8] See Erwin E. Nemmers, *Managerial Economics* (New York: Wiley, 1962), Part II.

[9] See Lester G. Telser, "The Demand for Branded Goods as Estimated from Consumer Panel Data," *Review of Economics and Statistics*, Vol. 44 (August, 1962), pp. 300–324; and William F. Massy and Ronald E. Frank, "Short Term Price and Dealing Effects in Selected Market Segments," *Journal of Marketing Research*, Vol. 2 (May, 1965), pp. 171–185.

## THE PAVLOVIAN LEARNING MODEL

The designation of a Pavlovian learning model has its origin in the experiments of the Russian psychologist Pavlov, who rang a bell each time before feeding a dog. Soon he was able to induce the dog to salivate by ringing the bell whether or not food was supplied. Pavlov concluded that learning was largely an associative process and that a large component of behavior was conditioned in this way.

Experimental psychologists have continued this mode of research with rats and other animals, including people. Laboratory experiments have been designed to explore such phenomena as learning, forgetting, and the ability to discriminate. The results have been integrated into a stimulus-response model of human behavior, or as someone has "wisecracked," the substitution of a rat psychology for a rational psychology.

The model has been refined over the years, and today is based on four central concepts—those of *drive, cue, response,* and *reinforcement.*[10]

*Drive.* Also called needs or motives, drive refers to strong stimuli internal to the individual which impels action. Psychologists draw a distinction between primary physiological drives—such as hunger, thirst, cold, pain, and sex—and learned drives which are derived socially—such as cooperation, fear, and acquisitiveness.

*Cue.* A drive is very general and impels a particular response only in relation to a particular configuration of cues. Cues are weaker stimuli in the environment and/or in the individual which determine when, where, and how the subject responds. Thus, a coffee advertisement can serve as a cue which stimulates the thirst drive in a housewife. Her response will depend upon this cue and other cues, such as the time of day, the availability of other thirst-quenchers, and the cue's intensity. Often a relative change in a cue's intensity can be more impelling than its absolute level. The housewife may be more motivated by a 2-cents-off sale on a brand of coffee than the fact that this brand's price was low in the first place.

*Response.* The response is the organism's reaction to the configuration of cues. Yet the same configuration of cues will not necessarily produce the same response in the individual. This depends on the degree to which the experience was rewarding, that is, drive-reducing.

*Reinforcement.* If the experience is rewarding, a particular response is reinforced; that is, it is strengthened and there is a tendency for it to be repeated when the same configuration of cues appears again. The housewife, for example, will tend to purchase the same brand of coffee each time she goes to her supermarket so long as it is rewarding and the cue configuration does not change. But if a learned response or habit is not reinforced, the strength of the habit diminishes and may be extinguished eventually. Thus, a housewife's preference for a certain coffee may become extinct if she finds the brand out of stock for a number of weeks.

Forgetting, in contrast to extinction, is the tendency for learned associations to weaken, not because of the lack of reinforcement but because of nonuse.

Cue configurations are constantly changing. The housewife sees a new brand of coffee next to her habitual brand, or notes a special price deal on a rival brand. Experimental psychologists have found that the same learned response will be elicited by similar patterns of cues; that is, learned responses are *generalized.* The housewife shifts to a similar brand when her favorite brand is out of stock. This tendency toward generalization over less similar cue configurations is increased in proportion to the strength of the drive. A housewife may buy an inferior coffee if it is the only brand left and if her drive is sufficiently strong.

A counter-tendency to generalization is *discrimination.* When a housewife tries two similar brands and finds one more rewarding, her ability to discriminate between similar cue configurations improves. Discrimination increases the specificity of the cue-response connection, while generalization decreases the specificity.

### Marketing Applications of Pavlovian Model

The modern version of the Pavlovian model makes no claim to provide a complete theory of behavior—indeed, such important phenomena as perception, the subconscious, and interpersonal influence are inadequately treated. Yet the model does offer a substantial number of insights about some aspects of behavior of considerable interest to marketers.[11]

---

[10] See John Dollard and Neal E. Miller, *Personality and Psychotherapy* (New York: McGraw-Hill, 1950), Chapter III.

[11] The most consistent application of learning-theory concepts to marketing situations is found in John

An example would be in the problem of introducing a new brand into a highly competitive market. The company's goal is to extinguish existing brand habits and form new habits among consumers for its brand. But the company must first get customers to try its brand; and it has to decide between using weak and strong cues.

Light introductory advertising is a weak cue compared with distributing free samples. Strong cues, although costing more, may be necessary in markets characterized by strong brand loyalties. For example, Folger went into the coffee market by distributing over a million pounds of free coffee.

To build a brand habit, it helps to provide for an extended period of introductory dealing. Furthermore, sufficient quality must be built into the brand so that the experience is reinforcing. Since buyers are more likely to transfer allegiance to similar brands than dissimilar brands (generalization), the company should also investigate what cues in the leading brands have been most effective. Although outright imitation would not necessarily effect the most transference, the question of providing enough similarity should be considered.

The Pavlovian model also provides guide lines in the area of advertising strategy. The American behaviorist, John B. Watson, was a great exponent of repetitive stimuli; in his writings man is viewed as a creature who can be conditioned through repetition and reinforcement to respond in particular ways.[12] The Pavlovian model emphasizes the desirability of repetition in advertising. A single exposure is likely to be a very weak cue, hardly able to penetrate the individual's consciousness sufficiently to excite his drives above the threshold level.

Repetition in advertising has two desirable effects. It "fights" forgetting, the tendency for learned responses to weaken in the absence of practice. It provides reinforcement, because after the purchase the consumer becomes selectively exposed to advertisements of the product.

The model also provides guide lines for copy strategy. To be effective as a cue, an advertisement must arouse strong drives in the person. The strongest product-related drives must be identified. For candy bars, it may be hunger;

for safety belts, fear; for hair tonics, sex; for automobiles, status. The advertising practitioner must dip into his cue box—words, colors, pictures—and select that configuration of cues that provides the strongest stimulus to these drives.

## THE FREUDIAN PSYCHOANALYTIC MODEL

The Freudian model of man is well known, so profound has been its impact on 20th century thought. It is the latest of a series of philosophical "blows" to which man has been exposed in the last 500 years. Copernicus destroyed the idea that man stood at the center of the universe; Darwin tried to refute the idea that man was a special creation; and Freud attacked the idea that man even reigned over his own psyche.

According to Freud, the child enters the world driven by instinctual needs which he cannot gratify by himself. Very quickly and painfully he realizes his separateness from the rest of the world and yet his dependence on it.

He tries to get others to gratify his needs through a variety of blatant means, including intimidation and supplication. Continual frustration leads him to perfect more subtle mechanisms for gratifying his instincts.

As he grows, his psyche becomes increasingly complex. A part of his psyche—the id—remains the reservoir of his strong drives and urges. Another part—the ego—becomes his conscious planning center for finding outlets for his drives. And a third part—his super-ego—channels his instinctive drives into socially approved outlets to avoid the pain of guilt or shame.

The guilt or shame which man feels toward some of his urges—especially his sexual urges—causes him to repress them from his consciousness. Through such defense mechanisms as rationalization and sublimation, these urges are denied or become transmuted into socially approved expressions. Yet these urges are never eliminated or under perfect control; and they emerge, sometimes with a vengeance, in dreams, in slips-of-the-tongue, in neurotic and obsessional behavior, or ultimately in mental breakdown where the ego can no longer maintain the delicate balance between the impulsive

---

A. Howard, *Marketing Management: Analysis and Planning* (Homewood, Illinois: Richard D. Irwin, Inc., revised edition, 1963).

[12] John B. Watson, *Behaviorism* (New York: The People's Institute Publishing Company, 1925).

power of the id and the oppressive power of the super-ego.

The individual's behavior, therefore, is never simple. His motivational wellsprings are not obvious to a casual observer nor deeply understood by the individual himself. If he is asked why he purchased an expensive foreign sports-car, he may reply that he likes its maneuverability and its looks. At a deeper level he may have purchased the car to impress others, or to feel young again. At a still deeper level, he may be purchasing the sports-car to achieve substitute gratification for unsatisfied sexual strivings.

Many refinements and changes in emphasis have occurred in this model since the time of Freud. The instinct concept has been replaced by a more careful delineation of basic drives; the three parts of the psyche are regarded now as theoretical concepts rather than actual entities; and the behavioral perspective has been extended to include cultural as well as biological mechanisms.

Instead of the role of the sexual urge in psychic development—Freud's discussion of oral, anal, and genital stages and possible fixations and traumas—Adler[13] emphasized the urge for power and how its thwarting manifests itself in superiority and inferiority complexes; Horney[14] emphasized cultural mechanisms; and Fromm[15] and Erickson[16] emphasized the role of existential crises in personality development. These philosophical divergencies, rather than debilitating the model, have enriched and extended its interpretative value to a wider range of behavioral phenomena.

### Marketing Applications of Freudian Model

Perhaps the most important marketing implication of this model is that buyers are motivated by *symbolic* as well as *economic-functional* product concerns. The change of a bar of soap from a square to a round shape may be more important in its sexual than its functional connotations. A cake mix that is advertised as involving practically no labor may alienate housewives because the easy life may evoke a sense of guilt.

Motivational research has produced some interesting and occasionally some bizarre hypotheses about what may be in the buyer's mind regarding certain purchases. Thus, it has been suggested at one time or another that:

1. Many a businessman doesn't fly because of a fear of posthumous guilt—if he crashed, his wife would think of him as stupid for not taking a train.

2. Men want their cigars to be odoriferous, in order to prove that they (the men) are masculine.

3. A woman is very serious when she bakes a cake because unconsciously she is going through the symbolic act of giving birth.

4. A man buys a convertible as a substitute "mistress."

5. Consumers prefer vegetable shortening because animal fats stimulate a sense of sin.

6. Men who wear suspenders are reacting to an unresolved castration complex.

There are admitted difficulties of proving these assertions. Two prominent motivational researchers, Ernest Dichter and James Vicary, were employed independently by two separate groups in the prune industry to determine why so many people dislike prunes. Dichter found, among other things, that the prune aroused feelings of old age and insecurity in people, whereas Vicary's main finding was that Americans had an emotional block about prunes' laxative qualities.[17] Which is the more valid interpretation? Or if they are both operative, which motive is found with greater statistical frequency in the population?

Unfortunately the usual survey techniques—direct observation and interviewing—can be used to establish the representativeness of more superficial characteristics—age and family size, for example—but are not feasible for establishing the frequency of mental states which are presumed to be deeply "buried" within each individual.

Motivational researchers have to employ time-consuming projective techniques in the hope of throwing individual "egos" off guard. When carefully administered and interpreted, techniques such as word association, sentence completion, picture interpretation, and role-playing

---

[13] Alfred Adler, *The Science of Living* (New York: Greenberg, 1929).

[14] Karen Horney, *The Neurotic Personality of Our Time* (New York: Norton, 1937).

[15] Erich Fromm, *Man For Himself* (New York: Holt, Rinehart & Winston, 1947).

[16] Erik Erikson, *Childhood and Society* (New York: Norton, 1949).

[17] L. Edward Scriven, "Rationality and Irrationality in Motivation Research," in Robert Ferber and Hugh G. Wales, editors, *Motivation and Marketing Behavior* (Homewood, Illinois: Richard D. Irwin, Inc., 1958), pp. 69–70.

can provide some insights into the minds of the small group of examined individuals; but a "leap of faith" is sometimes necessary to generalize these findings to the population.

Nevertheless, motivation research can lead to useful insights and provide inspiration to creative men in the advertising and packaging world. Appeals aimed at the buyer's private world of hopes, dreams, and fears can often be as effective in stimulating purchase as more rationally-directed appeals.

## THE VEBLENIAN SOCIAL-PSYCHOLOGICAL MODEL

While most economists have been content to interpret buyer behavior in Marshallian terms, Thorstein Veblen struck out in different directions.

Veblen was trained as an orthodox economist, but evolved into a social thinker greatly influenced by the new science of social anthropology. He saw man as primarily a *social animal*—conforming to the general forms and norms of his larger culture and to the more specific standards of the subcultures and face-to-face groupings to which his life is bound. His wants and behavior are largely molded by his present group-memberships and his aspired group-memberships.

Veblen's best-known example of this is in his description of the leisure class.[18] His hypothesis is that much of economic consumption is motivated not by intrinsic needs or satisfaction so much as by prestige-seeking. He emphasized the strong emulative factors operating in the choice of conspicuous goods like clothes, cars, and houses.

Some of his points, however, seem overstated by today's perspective. The leisure class does not serve as everyone's reference group; many persons aspire to the social patterns of the class immediately above it. And important segments of the affluent class practice conspicuous underconsumption rather than overconsumption. There are many people in all classes who are more anxious to "fit in" than to "stand out." As an example, William H. Whyte found that many families avoided buying air conditioners and other appliances before their neighbors did.[19]

Veblen was not the first nor the only investigator to comment on social influences in behavior; but the incisive quality of his observations did much to stimulate further in-

vestigations. Another stimulus came from Karl Marx, who held that each man's world-view was determined largely by his relationship to the "means of production." [20] The early field-work in primitive societies by social anthropologists like Boas [21] and Malinowski [22] and the later field-work in urban societies by men like Park [23] and Thomas [24] contributed much to understanding the influence of society and culture. The research of early Gestalt psychologists —men like Wertheimer, [25] Köhler, [26] and Koffka [27] —into the mechanisms of perception led eventually to investigations of small-group influence on perception.

### Marketing Applications of Veblenian Model

The various streams of thought crystallized into the modern social sciences of sociology, cultural anthropology, and social psychology. Basic to them is the view that man's attitudes and behavior are influenced by several levels of society—culture, subcultures, social classes, reference groups, and face-to-face groups. The challenge to the marketer is to determine which of these social levels are the most important in influencing the demand for his product.

#### Culture

The most enduring influences are from culture. Man tends to assimilate his culture's mores and folkways, and to believe in their absolute rightness until deviants appear within his culture or until he confronts members of another culture.

[18] Thorstein Veblen, *The Theory of the Leisure Class* (New York: Macmillan, 1899):
[19] William H. Whyte, Jr., "The Web of Word of Mouth," *Fortune,* Vol. 50 (November, 1954), pp. 140 ff.
[20] Karl Marx, *The Communist Manifesto,* 1848 (London: Martin Lawrence, Ltd., 1934).
[21] Franz Boas, *The Mind of Primitive Man* (New York: Macmillan, 1922).
[22] Bronislaw Malinowski, *Sex and Repression in Savage Society* (New York: Meridian Books, 1955).
[23] Robert E. Park, *Human Communities* (Glencoe, Illinois: Free Press, 1952).
[24] William I. Thomas, *The Unadjusted Girl* (Boston: Little, Brown, 1928).
[25] Max Wertheimer, *Productive Thinking* (New York: Harper & Brothers, 1945).
[26] Wolfgang Köhler, *Gestalt Psychology* (New York: Liveright Publishing Co., 1947).
[27] Kurt Koffka, *Principles of Gestalt Psychology* (New York: Harcourt, Brace, 1935).

### Subcultures

A culture tends to lose its homogeneity as its population increases. When people no longer are able to maintain face-to-face relationships with more than a small proportion of other members of a culture, smaller units or subcultures develop, which help to satisfy the individual's needs for more specific identity.

The subcultures are often regional entities, because the people of a region, as a result of more frequent interactions, tend to think and act alike. But subcultures also take the form of religions, nationalities, fraternal orders, and other institutional complexes which provide a broad identification for people who may otherwise be strangers. The subcultures of a person play a large role in his attitude formation and become another important predictor of certain values he is likely to hold.

### Social Class

People become differentiated not only horizontally but also vertically through a division of labor. The society becomes stratified socially on the basis of wealth, skill, and power. Sometimes castes develop in which the members are reared for certain roles, or social classes develop in which the members feel empathy with others sharing similar values and economic circumstances.

Because social class involves different attitudinal configurations, it becomes a useful independent variable for segmenting markets and predicting reactions. Significant differences have been found among different social classes with respect to magazine readership, leisure activities, food imagery, fashion interests, and acceptance of innovations. A sampling of attitudinal differences in class is the following:

¶ Members of the *upper-middle* class place an emphasis on professional competence; indulge in expensive status symbols; and more often than not show a taste, real or otherwise, for theater and the arts. They want their children to show high achievement and precocity and develop into physicists, vice-presidents, and judges. This class likes to deal in ideas and symbols.

Members of the *lower-middle* class cherish respectability, savings, a college education, and good housekeeping. They want their children to show self-control and prepare for careers as accountants, lawyers, and engineers.

Members of the *upper-lower* class try to keep up with the times, if not with the Joneses. They stay in older neighborhoods but buy new kitchen appliances. They spend proportionately less than the middle class on major clothing articles, buying a new suit mainly for an important ceremonial occasion. They also spend proportionately less on services, preferring to do their own plumbing and other work around the house. They tend to raise large families and their children generally enter manual occupations. This class also supplies many local businessmen, politicians, sports stars, and labor-union leaders.

### Reference Groups

There are groups in which the individual has no membership but with which he identifies and may aspire to—reference groups. Many young boys identify with big-league baseball players or astronauts, and many young girls identify with Hollywood stars. The activities of these popular heroes are carefully watched and frequently imitated. These reference figures become important transmitters of influence, although more along lines of taste and hobby than basic attitudes.

### Face-to-face Groups

Groups that have the most immediate influence on a person's tastes and opinions are face-to-face groups. This includes all the small "societies" with which he comes into frequent contact: his family, close friends, neighbors, fellow workers, fraternal associates, and so forth. His informal group memberships are influenced largely by his occupation, residence, and stage in the life cycle.

The powerful influence of small groups on individual attitudes has been demonstrated in a number of social psychological experiments.[28] There is also evidence that this influence may be growing. David Riesman and his coauthors have pointed to signs which indicate a growing amount of *other-direction*, that is, a tendency for individuals to be increasingly influenced

---

[28] See, for example, Solomon E. Asch, "Effects of Group Pressure Upon the Modification & Distortion of Judgments," in Dorwin Cartwright and Alvin Zander, *Group Dynamics* (Evanston, Illinois: Row, Peterson, 1953), pp. 151–162; and Kurt Lewin, "Group Decision and Social Change," in Theodore M. Newcomb and Eugene L. Hartley, editors, *Readings in Social Psychology* (New York: Henry Holt Co., 1952).

by their peers in the definition of their values rather than by their parents and elders.[29]

For the marketer, this means that brand choice may increasingly be influenced by one's peers. For such products as cigarettes and automobiles, the influence of peers is unmistakable.

The role of face-to-face groups has been recognized in recent industry campaigns attempting to change basic product attitudes. For years the milk industry has been trying to overcome the image of milk as a "sissified" drink by portraying its use in social and active situations. The men's-wear industry is trying to increase male interest in clothes by advertisements indicating that business associates judge a man by how well he dresses.

Of all face-to-face groups, the person's family undoubtedly plays the largest and most enduring role in basic attitude formation. From them he acquires a mental set not only toward religion and politics, but also toward thrift, chastity, food, human relations, and so forth. Although he often rebels against parental values in his teens, he often accepts these values eventually. Their formative influence on his eventual attitudes is undeniably great.

Family members differ in the types of product messages they carry to other family members. Most of what parents know about cereals, candy, and toys comes from their children. The wife stimulates family consideration of household appliances, furniture, and vacations. The husband tends to stimulate the fewest purchase ideas, with the exception of the automobile and perhaps the home.

The marketer must be alert to what attitudinal configurations dominate in different types of families, and also to how these change over time. For example, the parent's conception of the child's rights and privileges has undergone a radical shift in the last 30 years. The child has become the center of attention and orientation in a great number of households, leading some writers to label the modern family a "filiarchy." This has important implications not only for how to market to today's family, but also on how to market to tomorrow's family when the indulged child of today becomes the parent.

### The Person

Social influences determine much but not all of the behavioral variations in people. Two individuals subject to the same influences are not likely to have identical attitudes, although these attitudes will probably converge at more points than those of two strangers selected at random. Attitudes are really the product of social forces interacting with the individual's unique temperament and abilities.

Furthermore, attitudes do not automatically guarantee certain types of behavior. Attitudes are predispositions felt by buyers before they enter the buying process. The buying process itself is a learning experience and can lead to a change in attitudes.

Alfred Politz noted at one time that women stated a clear preference for G.E. refrigerators over Frigidaire, but that Frigidaire continued to outsell G.E.[30] The answer to this paradox was that preference was only one factor entering into behavior. When the consumer preferring G.E. actually undertook to purchase a new refrigerator, her curiosity led her to examine the other brands. Her perception was sensitized to refrigerator advertisements, sales arguments, and different product features. This led to learning and a change in attitudes.

### THE HOBBESIAN ORGANIZATIONAL FACTORS MODEL

The foregoing models throw light mainly on the behavior of family buyers.

But what of the large number of people who are organizational buyers? They are engaged in the purchase of goods not for the sake of consumption, but for further production or distribution. Their common denominator is the fact that they (1) are paid to make purchases for others and (2) operate within an organizational environment.

How do organizational buyers make their decisions? There seem to be two competing views. Many marketing writers have emphasized the predominance of rational motives in organizational buying.[31] Organizational buyers are represented as being most impressed by cost, quality, dependability, and service factors. They are portrayed as dedicated servants of the organization, seeking to secure the best terms. This view has led to an emphasis on

[29] David Riesman, Reuel Denney, and Nathan Glazer, *The Lonely Crowd* (New Haven, Connecticut: Yale University Press, 1950).

[30] Alfred Politz, "Motivation Research—Opportunity or Dilemma?", in Ferber and Wales, same reference as footnote 17, at pp. 57–58.

[31] See Melvin T. Copeland, *Principles of Merchandising* (New York: McGraw-Hill, 1924).

performance and use characteristics in much industrial advertising.

Other writers have emphasized personal motives in organizational buyer behavior. The purchasing agent's interest to do the best for his company is tempered by his interest to do the best for himself. He may be tempted to choose among salesmen according to the extent they entertain or offer gifts. He may choose a particular vendor because this will ingratiate him with certain company officers. He may shortcut his study of alternative suppliers to make his work day easier.

In truth, the buyer is guided by both personal and group goals; and this is the essential point. The political model of Thomas Hobbes comes closest of any model to suggesting the relationship between the two goals.[32] Hobbes held that man is "instinctively" oriented toward preserving and enhancing his own well-being. But this would produce a "war of every man against every man." This fear leads men to unite with others in a corporate body. The corporate man tries to steer a careful course between satisfying his own needs and those of the organization.

### Marketing Applications of Hobbesian Model

The import of the Hobbesian model is that organizational buyers can be appealed to on both personal and organizational grounds. The buyer has his private aims, and yet he tries to do a satisfactory job for his corporation. He will respond to persuasive salesmen and he will respond to rational product arguments. However, the best "mix" of the two is not a fixed quantity; it varies with the nature of the product, the type of organization, and the relative strength of the two drives in the particular buyer.

Where there is substantial similarity in what suppliers offer in the way of products, price, and service, the purchasing agent has less basis for rational choice. Since he can satisfy his organizational obligations with any one of a number of suppliers, he can be swayed by personal motives. On the other hand, where there are pronounced differences among the competing vendors' products, the purchasing agent is held more accountable for his choice and probably pays more attention to rational factors. Short-run personal gain becomes less motivating than the long-run gain which comes from serving the organization with distinction.

The marketing strategist must appreciate these goal conflicts of the organizational buyer. Behind all the ferment of purchasing agents to develop standards and employ value analysis lies their desire to avoid being thought of as order-clerks, and to develop better skills in reconciling personal and organizational objectives.[33]

### SUMMARY

Think back over the five different behavioral models of how the buyer translates buying influences into purchasing responses.

Marshallian man is concerned chiefly with economic cues—prices and income—and makes a fresh utility calculation before each purchase.

Pavlovian man behaves in a largely habitual rather than thoughtful way; certain configurations of cues will set off the same behavior because of rewarded learning in the past.

Freudian man's choices are influenced strongly by motives and fantasies which take place deep within his private world.

Veblenian man acts in a way which is shaped largely by past and present social groups.

And finally, Hobbesian man seeks to reconcile individual gain with organizational gain.

Thus, it turns out that the "black box" of the buyer is not so black after all. Light is thrown in various corners by these models. Yet no one has succeeded in putting all these pieces of truth together into one coherent instrument for behavioral analysis. This, of course, is the goal of behavioral science.

---

[32] Thomas Hobbes, *Leviathan*, 1651 (London: G. Routledge and Sons, 1887).

[33] For an insightful account, see George Strauss, "Tactics of Lateral Relationship: The Purchasing Agent," *Administrative Science Quarterly*, Vol. 7 (September, 1962), pp. 161–186.

# 13. The Autonomy of the Consumer

NELSON N. FOOTE

Depression and war, fascism and communism, have taught us that freedom and equality must have an economic content if they are to be real to the mass of the people. This content Americans are getting in the growth of the "middle market." Some 1953 issues of *Fortune* provide numerous texts to illumine this assertion. In the August 1953 issue, carrying Mr. Whyte's critique of the loss of individuality among the interchangeable Park Foresters, appears the first of a series on the changing American market. Therein is presented the economic background for this intriguing cultural phenomenon: a nationwide multiplication of middle-income families, a correlative shrinking of upper and lower income groups, a substantial rise in real income every year, and, as a result, a mounting ratio of discretionary income. As the *Fortune* editors note, the American today has more things to be independent *about* than ever before.

Conventionally, consumer sovereignty is conceived as an all-or-none matter. Among economists it refers to the right of the consumer to buy or not to buy. In this sense, it might be said that his sovereignty is what the psychological warriors of business are bent on reducing. Consumer autonomy, however, is not an all-or-none possession. For by autonomy I mean the consumer's self-determined use of his sovereignty, his utilization of the opportunity to create his own style of spending.

In general, the autonomy of the consumer

has probably been increasing. It is less important for consumer research to document the current trend, however, than to ascertain the conditions under which autonomy develops optimally. For I submit that *the researcher and his employer have more to gain from cultivating the autonomy of the consumer than from discouraging or frustrating it.*

Let us suppose a fully autonomous researcher, deeply interested in consumer behavior, supplied with unlimited resources, and ready to choose the problems of most interest to himself.[1] What would they be?

It would make a great deal of difference who the researcher is. I speak here as a family sociologist. Most of the research on consumer behavior has been done by psychologists and economists, but it is not mere professional bias that leads me to urge that the sociologist and the cultural anthropologist have much to offer. It is the sociologists who have given greatest attention to the effects of stratification upon the behavior exhibited as styles of life within our society. And it is the anthropologists who have given most attention to styles of life in comparing whole societies, not merely in the fine arts as done by the art historian but across the whole breadth of culture.

The psychologist and the economist alike tend to start from individuals and proceed to aggregates of individuals, with insufficient attention to the processes by which these aggre-

⌗ SOURCE: Reprinted by permission from *Consumer Behavior: The Dynamics of Consumer Reaction*, edited by Lincoln H. Clark (New York University Press, 1955), pp. 15–24.

[1] This article is based on a paper given at the second annual conference of The Committee for Research on Consumer Attitudes and Behavior, September 17, 1953.

gates become formed into really social phenomena like classes and communities, institutions, and associations. I cannot claim that the sociologists have done much better. For instance, I have not yet seen a satisfactory way of treating families statistically as constellations rather than as mere combinations of individuals, though fortunately I do know of several persons who are working on this. Census definitions take into account about eighteen different types of living units; they include dependency and relationship characteristics but omit the social-psychological aspects, which are of greatest interest from the standpoint of consumption. What seems badly needed is research on group factors in consumer behavior that will deal with phenomena falling between, let us say, brand preferences at one end of the scale and the national consumption function, as theoretical economists call it, at the other. The home economists should have stepped in here long ago, but they have been so dominated by ideas of productive efficiency that they have contributed little in this area. Their current reorientation toward the family may, however, cause them to come up with something before long.

## IDENTIFICATION WITH CONSUMER URGED

Assuming that this hypothetical researcher is a sociologist or group psychologist, I would paradoxically urge that he identify with the object of his study, the consumer himself. This is normally not done; usually the researcher takes his employer's attitude and tries to anticipate and outwit the consumer.

But we now have before us a consumer less predictable than before. Even if we still wanted to outwit him, we would have to enter into his thinking, his doubts, changes, growth, and fickleness. But the job is much more that of helping the consumer, by creating a stability or predictability congenial to him. Why hunt in a dark room for the famous black cat that isn't there? If we are to study regularities in behavior, I think we will be able to find far more by helping create them, rather than simply by searching for them.

To create them will mean that the researcher will *participate with the consumer in the orderly development of consistent patterns of choice*. His role would not be that of a bird dog engaged in sniffing out unsaturated markets; it would be the much more professional—and even artistic—role of experimentation in the creative

development of markets. Instead of simply boosting sales, he could simultaneously help make distribution more efficient and thus continue to justify his services.

With autonomy as our theme and identification with the consumer as our starting point, the variations upon our theme will be specific research hypotheses, arbitrarily set at ten. Because economics seems so basic, we shall start from the income end and work over to psychology. But, throughout, the emphasis will be upon the social conditions for development of style in consumption.

### Increase in the "Middle Market"

*1. As real income continues to rise, the "middle market" will continue to grow, almost regardless of national fiscal policy.*

Whatever may have been true in the past, the Protestant ethic of striving and straining, of scrimping and saving, is no longer necessary to the continuous advance of real income. From here on out that advance will come principally through technical improvement, the conditions for which have already been built into our institutional structure in the endless frontier of engineering colleges and industrial research centers. The effect of these is cumulative. For the mass of people, the significance of this fact has still not been fully grasped. They still do not realize that we can all get ahead without exertion and self-denial. I could go further in undermining puritan mores by pointing out that large amounts of idle reflection are an important aid in creativity, and creativity is the basic capital of industry of the future.

As real income goes up, the motivation to enhance personal income and accumulate property will level off. This curvilinear feature of the motivation to increase one's income can already be observed among individual deviants, but it will be found more frequently among whole groups, as in shortening of hours, the multiplication of vacation and holiday clauses.

Progressive taxation, union wage bargaining, and the relative increase of salaried positions have probably received more than their share of credit, for the equalization of family income in the last decades. Given the increased security, which makes saving against catastrophe pointless, the craving for expansion of income is likely to approach some kind of ceiling for most people. This ceiling will no doubt continue to drift upward due to distribution of the benefits of enhanced productivity, but the pursuit of wealth for its own sake has already lost its former status as the be-all and end-all of human existence for masses of Americans. Leisure seems already preferable to work for all but the fortunate few whose professions are their hobbies.

Almost as important as the number of people drawing middle incomes is the increasing stability of these incomes. For the person on salary or annual wage is the one who can truly budget, who has the best chance of creating an orderly style of spending his income. The relative equality of incomes in this middle range likewise reduces the pressure to compete in primarily quantitative terms with others. Conspicuous consumption is on the decline, while the development of qualitatively distinctive taste is on the upgrade.

All this presents for the researcher a need to analyze styles of spending among people of more or less equal income. Problems of calculating the effect of changes of income upon aggregate patterns of spending will remain for the economist, and there is an inviting opportunity here for some genuinely experimental research in economics—something in which the dismal science has hitherto been peculiarly lacking. But the most novel and exciting research, even in the field of income distribution, will be in the study of that nonutilitarian calculus by which the values of leisure limit and condition the individual pursuit of income until a point of indifference is reached.

### Increase in Leisure Time

2. *As this point, at which leisure becomes preferable to further work, recedes, considerations of time expenditure will further condition money expenditure in consumer behavior.*

The puritanical injunction that "time is money" will no doubt continue in force in factories and offices where people are paid for their time. Off the job, however, it is being reversed to read "money is time," in the sense that the worker, as his income goes up, becomes able to bid against his employer for his own time. The more money he makes per hour—a function of productivity as much as of distribution—the more time he can take off. And what he does after hours may or may not be exhibited in cash expenditures.

For the consumption researchers who must serve a commercial employer, purchasing behavior is what counts. But even this can best be understood against the background of non-purchasing behavior. Once the consumer gets beyond the point at which he is governed mainly by anxiety to survive, the consumption of time may become the basic common denominator of consumer behavior.

Currently there is a booming market in do-it-yourself items. This market could not have been predicted by extrapolations from other expenditures, but a theory of the place of crafts in any complete regime of play would afford a basis for fairly precise and detailed anticipation of where and when it will develop further. In doing it for himself, the consumer does not simply calculate the cost of a paper hanger against his own rate of pay but the interest and value of the play and creativity involved. One of the great, under-recognized values of home ownership is the play it gives to the pursuit of home crafts. Thus the growth of suburbs is not simply to be accounted for in terms of the tax structure of cities not to be halted except by economic catastrophe.

We know that the so-called laws of expenditure on food, clothing, housing, medical care, and the like, keep breaking down in the face of new conditions. Engels' law on the proportion of income spent on food, for example, apparently depended upon a set of cultural conditions. As long as they obtained, the law was "verified" in many repeated studies. But now it appears that many of our "middle-incomers" have increased the proportion they spend on food. This suggests that the social rituals of cooking and eating are being elaborated into an art of boundless proportions; not only is cooking becoming more and more efficient, it is becoming an end in itself. It consumes increasing time, attention, and ingenuity; attracts a more and more critical and appreciative audience; requires improved techniques for achieving aesthetic ends.

There is still need for further study of family budgets; also some of the archaic categories need to be refined, to take account of matters like reciprocal gift giving, philanthropy, and the value of self-produced items. We must take into account large quantities of consumption not directly purchased—free public services, receipt of charity, non-profit institutional services, bequests of goods, being a dependent, unpaid services to others. Then there are tax exemptions and illegal gains and chance winnings. Some qualitative analysis of borrowing and saving is also called for, to distinguish the effort and cost devoted to stabilization of expenditure. Just as there is food and "food," there is saving and "saving."

Here again we may see at work not a traditional motive of thrift or an unwise use of credit, but a steady effort by consumers to work out a self-conscious and orderly pattern of spending—a genuine standard of living, albeit of developing one—over and above their interest in stabilizing income. But, beyond these improvements in analysis of money budgets, the big call, theoretically at least, is for time-budget studies. The time spent with children by a mother, as against the time spent with organizations to which she belongs, may more truly index her values than the amount of money she spends on either.

### Increased Effect of the Stage of the Family Cycle

*3. As this enlarging market of middle-income consumers becomes more stable and homogeneous, it will become progressively more differentiated in terms of stages of the family cycle.*

The high and rising rate of physical and social mobility among the American population is tending to break down traditional communities of custom and taste. To count upon any new and regularizing differentiations to appear in this squirming mass might seem futile. Evidence is accumulating, however, that patterns already visible are going to become more pronounced.

As Mr. Whyte has noted, most families found in suburbs like Park Forest live there only during a certain period in their careers. The very rate of mobility helps to account for the internal homogeneity, the external distinctiveness, of such suburbs. Birds of a feather can more readily flock together than before. What are the feathers that guide their flocking? Within the middle-income group, the most visible appears to be the stage of the family cycle. This correlates with the development of personal careers, but it is family, not occupation, that stands out in determining one's residence and style of consumption. As we look around, we find suburbs, neighborhoods, even single apartment buildings, that consist homogeneously of young-married couples, young parents, middle-aged people, bachelor girls and boys, empty-nesters, and the retired. It is easier to move than to rebuild, and thus people in metropolitan areas (and who is not?) tend to segregate themselves voluntarily among their peers. Among peers the old way of selecting friends on the basis of propinquity can once more operate without one demeaning one's autonomy.

Not the census categories, which classify families as combinations of individuals, but the family-stage categories seem the more appropriate for consumption research. Take, for example, the varieties of dependency. Internal Revenue definitions are almost beside the point if what we are interested in is the development of style of spending. Where is the authority and the leadership in the family? Children, especially adolescents, are often the missionaries of change. The psychological structure of a family in which the wife works or has another source of income than her husband is quite different from the traditional patriarchy in which wife and children are not only dependents but subordinates.

### Increased Need for Criteria of Judgment

*4. As freedom of choice in expenditure increases in the tangible form of discretionary income and time, the need for explicit criteria of judgment will become more consciously felt among consumers.*

Any sudden or even rapid accession of wealth is likely to lead for a time to behavior like that of Molière's famous bourgeois gentleman. This is a nation of nouveaux riches, one might say, and it is to be expected that its buying will appear whimsical, uninformed, suggestible, unbalanced, and full of admitted mistakes. It is not to be expected that this awkward phase will last indefinitely, however, for criticism and the correction of error are incessant. I would not say we are swamped with wealth, but I would say the rate of stimulation to spend has run ahead of our rate of assimilation.

Better judgment is needed, and the more the consumer develops it, the more likely is he to be autonomous. And the more autonomous he is given a chance to become, the better judgment he is likely to develop. He needs to become able to state what he likes and what he does not and why. This implies practice in criticism. If sellers are as tender to criticism as Bernard De Voto alleges, they are not likely to take kindly to the proposition that they have an interest in developing the judgment of the consumer. I hope De Voto is wrong, though I half fear he may be right. Sellers may pine only for ways to control consumer decision making.

### New Wants Develop

*5. As income and leisure increase, not only are old wants more fully satisfied but new wants are created.*

In market research, it is an undeserved compliment to the consumer to assume that he always and infallibly knows what he wants, that he can articulate his wants accurately in answer to questions, and that what he says will match what he later does. At the same time, it is an undeserved disparagement of his judgment and an intrusion of his autonomy to assume the role of trying to mold his wants to suit the seller. Concretely, the middle ground between these alternatives is best illustrated in the collaboration between seller and buyer that has developed markets of adepts for high-fidelity recordings, power woodworking tools, garden seeds, backyard barbecue equipment, and books.

Wants are not given. Once learned or acquired, they may remain quite stable, but many wants are not stable and none are permanent. They are generally in a constant process of elaboration, definition, integration, realization, fluctuation. One's wants are very much influenced by the other persons with whom he identifies himself. Rhetoric directed at producing an identification is often as effective in creating a new want as direct stimulation of existing wants or associations with previous values.

It would be valuable to explore the whole conception of wants in terms of psychological theory. But, at least, we should raise a question about the very title of the Committee for Research on Consumer Attitudes and Behavior, under whose auspices these papers are presented. If by the phrase "attitudes and behavior" it is implied that attitudes are entities resident in the consumer that may be discovered and utilized to explain his behavior, I would say the conception involved is highly debatable. I think the exploration of motivation, using the concept of identification, is going to be far more fruitful than employment of the concept of attitude. In particular, when we talk of the creation of wants as a social process in which one party creates wants in another or both participate in developing their wants, we must get around to the psychology of rhetoric, which is inevitably a psychology of identification, not of pre-existent attitudes or static preferences.

In conceiving of the growth of a market, it makes a great deal of difference whether that market is conceived as a mass of more or less unrelated individuals or as a structured and organized network of interpersonal and intergroup relationships. Even when markets are treated in terms of income levels, social strata, regions and age groupings, it may still be true that people in these categories are nonetheless conceived pretty much as individual agents rather than as members of identifiable group formations. I think all practical strategies are based on some assumption about the nature of society, and certain familiar conceptions of society are quite unrealistic and frequently ambiguous. On the one hand, they posit an isolated, thinking individual, who is to be influenced by rational appeals to his self-interest. On the other hand, his autonomous capacity for critical acceptance or rejection of group values and fashions is discouraged by the notorious tactics of band-wagon appeals, glittering generalities, the "plain-folks" device, and the testimonials originally indicted by the Institute for Propaganda Analysis.

### Need for a Style of Life

6. *As wants develop for a wider array of goods and services, the need for their unification through a satisfying and coherent style of living, based on aesthetic rather than economic criteria, becomes increasingly manifest.*

One of my former students who became a union organizer wrote me recently the following reflections on what is happening among the people she serves.

That is why unionism has its appeal to me. It has the seeds for the developing of the workers' control of those factors that affect his life, give him a voice in determining those decisions. But unionism, in its quest for more and more, doesn't necessarily bring a sense of well-being to many workers caught up in the never-ending acquisition of gadgets, of latest models, of newest fashions, of passive recreation. How to rechannel the values people have so that they don't spend at routine work their valuable hours of life supporting cars and television sets but engage in pursuits that do develop their own potentialities; so that they don't sit back, having their entertainment spooned out to them, but have a hand in creating their own? Boredom is a problem to think about with the trend toward more leisure hours, earlier retirement, longer life.

It is a striking turn of events when a union organizer becomes as concerned about boredom off the job as on it. The two are very much related, but there is no opportunity here to deal with boredom on the job or even to do more than touch upon its relationship to boredom during leisure. The important point is: the mule can be as harassed and driven by a bewildering array of carrots as by the stick. In fact, there are already prophets to deplore the fractured multiplicity of life under constant bombardment of consumers' goods, prophets who recommend a return to rigorous simplicity. But who could without malice urge another depression or another escape from freedom? Save to these reactionaries, the problem is not that of simplification but of organization.

The organization of a style of life is not a simple product of rational deduction. It requires countless decisions contingent one on the other. As a process, it is more like the practice of art than of algebra. The artist is not governed by scarcity of paints but by self-imposed criteria. To be sure, if we think of expenditure, there is a definite vocabulary, grammar, and syntax. Rules are necessary to give some form to the composition, but the rules only set limits, they do not determine content. One can criticize an insufficient diet from the standpoint of the biochemistry of nutrition, but neither biochemistry nor guilt feelings provide a sufficient basis for planning artistic menus. Neither can mere recipes for tasty dishes form the basis for a satisfying style of eating. We are now hearing that obesity is the nation's number one health problem. Obesity, thus, rather well serves to symbolize the importance of developing a discriminating style of consumption.

As with diet, most patterns of consumption are family-wide customs rather than individual habits. The development of style in consumption, however, ought to start as near to the individual as it can without being unrealistic. Food habits are a case in point. Whether habit or custom, some researchers conceive their problem as that of overcoming resistance to change.

But food habits are neither more recalcitrant nor more pliable than most other consumer behavior. Everyone knows the fight that children can put up against being forced to eat something they do not like. They do not become less resistant as adults. It is just that no one pushes them any more (unless it be their own consciences). On the other hand, children and adults will put almost anything in their mouths, especially if encouraged by others whose example they esteem and trust. The development of any style of consumption involves as much the organization of groups of people in concerted patterns of action as it does the more intellectual subordination of purchasing decisions to autonomous styles of living.

## Development of an Individual Style

*7. As the autonomy of consumers develops, it is going to produce a renewed concept of style as belonging to specific persons and groups.*

Style as popularly conceived is a mass phenomenon almost synonymous with fashion—transitory, shallow, anonymous. There is a large element of chance and uncertainty in its manifestations, which gives rise to a speculative fever for windfall profits through "playing the market right" or getting an edge on rivals in quick exploitation of nascent fads. All this gives to contemporary style a synthetic, ephemeral, and irresponsible character, which is continually deplored by critics.

To critics of aristocratic pretensions, there is a ready retort. The growth of the mass market has made it possible to put finer and finer things into the hands of more and more people. Given time and the continued working of the beneficent forces of advertising and mass production, the masses will graduate from low-brow to at least middle-brow levels of taste. The standard example is the sale of records of classical music.

This standard retort is satisfactory as far as it goes, but it fails to answer a more fundamental criticism. The critics and defenders of popular culture tend to focus upon the vocabulary of consumption, to criticize the qualities of the objects and events purchased, and to berate buyer or seller or someone else for their low standards or praise him for high ones. But the far more important issue is whether the standard that the seller or buyer follows is genuinely his own. If it is his own, it should and would be more continuous, more cumulative, more authentic; in other words, it would be a style and not a fashion. It would not necessarily be more individualized, though this too would be more likely. Some persons create styles uniquely expressive of themselves, but these styles tend rather soon to get adopted by others. If style is conceived as pertaining to persons rather than products, its development runs no conflict with mass production and entails no return to custom work. It may mean that the producer who aspires to make and market fine things can increasingly afford to do so.

The consumer is able nowadays to select from a wider range of sources than ever before. That is the glory of the modern market: it gives us the whole world to choose from. But let there be choice, rather than mere collective whim. Let a pattern of choice be created self-consciously among the items we buy. That is what I mean when I say that regularities in buying behavior are more likely to be created than to be discovered through research. Research can provide the basis for evaluating experiments in the development of style, for the development of judgment, autonomy, and creativity. I think we need to develop measures of these three abilities more than we need further refinements in the measurement of preference.

The consumer needs help, however, in the development of his style, and not help of a patronizing sort any more than condemnation. He needs the help of the humanities as much as that of the social sciences.

The humanities in our colleges and universities, however, are unfortunately about the last remaining refuge of the obsolete class-mass division of culture. It may be that the humanities departments are beyond hope of redemption. Home economics colleges offer only slightly more basis for optimism, owing to their rural connections. Perhaps quite new educational institutions will have to be created to aid the contemporary consumer, and perhaps the merchandiser himself—if he can honor the autonomy of the consumer—will be able to help in creating them. I doubt if any of our present commercial institutions, ostensibly devoted to raising the standards of consumership, as yet qualify, though some of the better consumer magazines, and especially certain of the new critics of consumption who appear in their columns, are beginning to show the way.

### Professionalizing Marketing Skills

8. *As the autonomy of consumers develops, the occupations of advertising, marketing, merchandising, and selling will become more professionalized.*

In order to complete a circuit, communication requires a two-way flow of information. The role of market research, like that of these other intermediary occupations, may be seen as that of completing the flow of communication between producer and consumer.

Both the consumer and the producer may be viewed as engaged in creative activity. One is making a specific product. The other is fashioning a whole style of life. If they are to collaborate, they need to communicate. Failure to do so frustrates the aims of both. In the days of village enterprise and custom work, they could communicate face to face. With mass production and mass markets, we have the reign of commodities as rather eloquently and provocatively described by Karl Marx.

However, we cannot go back to handicrafts and county fairs while retaining the benefits of modern technology. And after all, the do-it-yourself phenomenon is primarly a form of recreation, with no prospect of putting General Foods or General Electric or General Mills out of business. Rather, the power of the consumer to express his wants in his own way will increasingly become a means of restoring communication between himself and the producer. This implies that all who play a part in the function of distribution must see themselves not merely as merchants but as channels of communication, of criticism and appreciation, of teaching and demonstration.

Such a prophecy may seem to contradict certain evident trends toward reducing the numbers and cost of sales personnel. I do not think it does. Merchandising can move toward self-service further than it has, but that will only increase the need for communication, not obviate or diminish it.

Something quite positive can be said, as a matter of fact, for the steady divorce of selling (*and of sales research*) from specific products. The strategic intermediary position of the distributive trades has not been sufficiently utilized, because the interests of the producer in simple expansion of sales have tended to dominate both the intermediaries and ultimately the consumer, despite the verbal emphasis on service and consumer sovereignty. As the consumer's autonomy increases, however, there is a benevolent circle or spiral, through which the intermediaries can increase their autonomy also. As this happens, producers can shift their attention from the marketing of specific products to the cultivation of the consumer's style. To use David Riesman's phrase, they tend to become "taste counselors." Their customers, as in the professions, meanwhile begin to take on the characteristics of a clientele. Instead of the commercial vocabulary, which implies gloating over maneuvering consumers into "impulse buys" and "tie-in sales," a professional vocabulary of objectivity and impartiality, a professional ethics of merited trust, are likely to be the newer sources of pride, as they are among architects.

As with persons, so with institutions. When the department store can achieve a sufficient degree of independence from manufacturers, it has the opportunity to take the part of the consumer and to market goods on their merits. I think it is more likely that stores will develop along this line than that the average consumer will sit down and study Consumers Union reports. We have something like taste counseling already in specialty shops, such as certain men's clothing stores, sporting goods departments, and travel agencies. I have found myself willing to pay the price that includes the competent professional advice of salesmen in these establishments, because I trusted them to guide the development of my taste, rather than to pursue the short-run benefits of loading me with things I was not sure I wanted. I doubt if I am unique in responding favorably to this kind of treatment.

Who are the taste counselors who exhibit this professional competence, independence, and integrity? The kind of person who best resembles what I have in mind is the unhampered writer for the less commercial magazines or the free-lance independent. Names like these come to mind: Russell Lynes, Jane Nickerson, Duncan Hines, Edward Tatnall Canby, John Crosby. At the local level, everyone can name his own trusted face-to-face mentors, employed by this store or that newspaper, or simply an amateur. It is worth mentioning that, as the professionalization of salesmanship occurs, it will become evident that the judgment of these taste counselors will be of the greatest value to industrial designers in all fields.

Manufacturers have discovered, one could almost say stumbled into the realization, that in the long run good design is as much in their interest as in that of the consumer. Before long they may find that close liaison between their design departments and the taste counselors is in their interest also and that the professional integrity and independence of these professions is as worthy of being cherished as is academic freedom in the universities. Selling in the old sense of mere expansion of sales may have had its place in a certain phase of the development of the national economy. With the approach of some kind of regularly evolving equilibrium between the values of work and play, the relation of intermediary persons and institutions to the array of producers and the array of style groups must almost inevitably be transformed. Observations of its manifold emergence in other fields make me almost smugly secure in predicting the professionalization of salesmanship.

Commercial institutions and the advertising media will principally employ these taste counselors, but it will still take a university to train

them. As yet, I do not know a single school that is fully capable of doing so. Probably we will have to staff such a school by hiring the best of the self-taught ones. In the university environment, they can compare and systematize, as they cannot now, under conditions of still greater protection of their autonomy. Out of such really interdisciplinary thought and research, we may then get our general science of consumption, our general theories of work and play, our positive criteria for the criticism of popular taste, our experiments in the development of judgment.

### Development of Consumer Leadership in Style

9. *As the development of style in spending becomes more self-conscious and critical, leadership in the creation and propagation of style will develop among consumers themselves, making them less dependent on counselors.*

At present the phenomena of indigenous leadership in style are visible in popular culture only in patches and in connection with particular products. The vogues in dresses, haircuts, and mammary glands seem to be set as much by movie and television queens as by the designers. I do not know whether the vogue in loud, tieless sport shirts for men is traceable to Harry Truman or Dwight Eisenhower, to Bing Crosby or Arthur Godfrey, but in general there is not even yet what could be called the development of style in clothing among men, despite the fact that their taste is less fickle than that of women. Genuine growth of style through identification of large numbers with important personalities is visible in the fine arts, as in the influence of Hemingway in writing or Le Corbusier in architecture. But about the only place where fine art has really permeated mass taste to a substantial degree is in the field of furniture and tableware. American interiors have been vastly improved as a result, and today one can no longer speak of a single modern style in these fields, but recognizes considerable differentiation as he takes in the shows and the literature. These differing modern styles are coming to be identified with particular designers who develop followings. This differentiation of style is likely to become far more common as consumers take an interest in the quality of their own purchasing decisions and become equipped with resources and training for interrelating these decisions according to chosen master-themes.

This image of man constructively engaged in formulating himself is in sharp contrast to the well-known caricature of the consumer as a container of definitely satiable wants, whose only aim in life is to reach the zero point of tension. To involve man in the creation of a major style is to demand of him a commitment of which he is not often thought capable. Yet, the original development of Gothic style called for real sacrifice, and today there are communities whose inhabitants tax themselves equally hard to realize the values they have for the schooling of their children.

Public buildings in the United States used to be little short of monstrous, and they still exhibit a false dependence upon classical and medieval styles. I hope to see in my time the appearance of styles of consumption as authentically expressive of our time as Gothic and Corinthian were of theirs, styles that spread across all the categories of consumption—food, clothing, housing, transportation, association, hygiene, education, recreation, government, and family life.

We do not have to sit and pray for the return of the golden days. Social science is something they did not have in classical times, and no people anywhere ever had the quantity of resources available to us. What we do not have and need desperately to recapture is the creativity at the grass roots, and the identification with creativity at the level of genius and leadership, which some other times have had. I think that research can do something with the problem of engendering creativity in consumption as it has with creativity in production. We cannot all be poets and prophets, but there is vast need for explorers and inventors, for teachers and critics, in every community. If we can ascertain the conditions for reproducing such creativity, we may be able in this generation to gain a community better than that the Lynds pictured in their compelling indictment of the commercial civilization of Middletown.

### Development of Consumers Organizations

10. As the autonomy of consumers increases, a variety of consumer organizations will arise through which consumers may exert their power in markets.

These remarks may appear subversive to the average seller who fears that such a step will bring the American way of life tumbling down around his ears. But what is wrong about organizing the consumer? And is it really against the interests of commerce for the consumer to organize? Management felt it was against its interests for employees to organize, yet it now admits that the wide distribution of purchasing power has much to do with the continuation of prosperity.

I have no idea what forms consumer organization will take. There are numerous rudimentary forms of consumer organization that may furnish some clues, but I am quite skeptical of the hopes and claims of their partisans. Too many of them are already declining because of their adherence to outdated concepts of merely helping the consumer to save his money or of protecting him from the alleged confidence men who operate the nation's business.

Perhaps the policy era of consumer behavior will be ushered in by the unions' extending their function. More likely, however, are analogous organizations that will represent different kinds of consumers. Thus, we might get bodies like the Arts Council of Great Britain to criticize and encourage the standards achieved in the entertainment field. We already have the PTA, such as it is, as a medium for expression and advancement of consumer wants in education. Our rod and gun clubs do a very good job of promoting the interests of their members before state legislatures, as do the automobile clubs.

The unions offer a second analogy. For the autonomous researcher, the organization of consumers offers no cause for alarm. Arbitrators and the rule of reason came into their own in industrial relations when the power of management was equalized by the power of unions. Similarly, the influence of the professional intermediary between producer and consumer will reach its height when the autonomy of organized consumers countervails the power of the now increasingly less competitive, more and more organized producers.

What I do not doubt is that the American genius for organization will operate in the field of consumption as in all other fields of contemporary activity, and that it will construct channels through which the will of consumers will more directly and efficaciously be brought to bear upon the making of distribution policy. As that happens, our hypothetical autonomous researcher who begs to cultivate the autonomy of the consumer will have to beg no longer. At that point, the producer and seller will be begging the researcher for predictions of what turn consumer policy will take next. And consumer behavior will no longer be merely the aggregate of collective decisions by individuals, more or less cajoled in loose herds, but policy in the self-conscious, affirmative sense that demands execution by responsible agents.

# C. Economic Aspects of Consumer Behavior

## 14. Rational Behavior and Economic Behavior

GEORGE KATONA

While attempts to penetrate the boundary lines between psychology and sociology have been rather frequent during the last few decades, psychologists have paid little attention to the problems with which another sister discipline, economics, is concerned. One purpose of this paper is to arouse interest among psychologists in studies of economic behavior. For that purpose it will be shown that psychological principles may be of great value in clarifying basic questions of economics and that the psychology of habit formation, of motivation, and of group belonging may profit from studies of economic behavior.

A variety of significant problems, such as those of the business cycle or inflation, of consumer saving or business investment, could be chosen for the purpose of such demonstration. This paper, however, will be concerned with the most fundamental assumption of economics, the principle of rationality. In order to clarify the problems involved in this principle, which have been neglected by contemporary psychologists, it will be necessary to contrast the most common forms of methodology used

◆ SOURCE: Copyright 1953 by the American Psychological Association. Reprinted by permission from the author and the American Psychological Association, *Psychological Review*, Vol. 60, No. 5, 1953, pp. 307–317.

in economics with those employed in psychology and to discuss the role of empirical research in the social sciences.

### THEORY AND HYPOTHESES

Economic theory represents one of the oldest and most elaborate theoretical structures in the social sciences. However, dissatisfaction with the achievements and uses of economic theory has grown considerably during the past few decades on the part of economists who are interested in what actually goes on in economic life. And yet leading sociologists and psychologists have recently declared "Economics is today, in a theoretical sense, probably the most highly elaborated, sophisticated, and refined of the disciplines dealing with action" (15, p. 28).[1]

To understand the scientific approach of economic theorists, we may divide them into two groups. Some develop on a priori system from which they deduce propositions about how people *should* act under certain assump-

---

[1] The quotation is from an introductory general statement signed by T. Parsons, E. A. Shils, G. W. Allport, C. Kluckhohn, H. A. Murray, R. R. Sears, R. C. Sheldon, S. A. Stouffer, and E. C. Tolman. The term "action" is meant to be synonymous with "behavior."

tions. Assuming that the sole aim of business-men is profit maximization, these theorists deduce propositions about marginal revenues and marginal costs, for example, that are not meant to be suited for testing. In developing formal logics of economic action, one of the main considerations is elegance of the deductive system, based on the law of parsimony. A wide gap separates these theorists from economic research of an empirical-statistical type which registers what they call aberrations or deviations, due to human frailty, from the norm set by theory.

A second group of economic theorists adheres to the proposition that it is the main purpose of theory to provide hypotheses that can be tested. This group acknowledges that prediction of future events represents the most stringent test of theory. They argue, however, that reality is so complex that it is necessary to begin with simplified propositions and models which are known to be unreal and not testable.[2] Basic among these propositions are the following three which traditionally have served to characterize the economic man or the rational man:

1. The principle of complete information and foresight. Economic conditions—demand, supply, prices, etc.—are not only given but also known to the rational man. This applies as well to future conditions about which there exists no uncertainty, so that rational choice can always be made. (In place of the assumption of certainty of future developments, we find nowadays more frequently the assumption that risks prevail but the probability of occurrence of different alternatives is known; this does not constitute a basic difference.)

2. The principle of complete mobility. There are no institutional or psychological factors which make it impossible, or expensive, or slow, to translate the rational choice into action.

3. The principle of pure competition. Individual action has no great influence on prices because each man's choice is independent from any other person's choice and because there are no "large" sellers or buyers. Action is the result of individual choice and is not group-determined.

Economic theory is developed first under these assumptions. The theorists then introduce changes in the assumptions so that the theory may approach reality. One such step consists, for instance, of introducing large-scale producers, monopolists, and oligopolists, another of introducing time lags, and still another of introducing uncertainty about the probability distribution of future events. The question raised in each case is this: Which of the original propositions needs to be changed, and in what way, in view of the new assumptions?

The fact that up to now the procedure of gradual approximation to reality has not been completely successful does not invalidate the method. It must also be acknowledged that propositions were frequently derived from unrealistic economic models which were susceptible to testing and stimulated empirical research. In this paper we shall point to a great drawback of this method of starting out with a simplified a priori system and making it gradually more complex and more real—by proceeding in this way one tends to lose sight of important problems and to disregard them.

The methods most commonly used in psychology may appear at first sight to be quite similar to the methods of economics which have just been described. Psychologists often start with casual observations, derive from them hypotheses, test those through more systematic observations, reformulate and revise their hypotheses accordingly, and test them again. The process of hypotheses-observations-hypotheses-observations often goes on with no end in sight. Differences from the approach of economic theory may be found in the absence in psychological research of detailed systematic elaboration prior to any observation. Also, in psychological research, findings and generalizations in one field of behavior are often considered as hypotheses in another field of behavior. Accordingly, in analyzing economic behavior[3] and trying to understand rationality, psychologists can draw on (a) the theory of learning and thinking, (b) the theory of group belonging, and (c) the theory of motivation. This will be done in this paper.

---

[2] A variety of methods used in economic research differ, of course, from those employed by the two groups of economic theorists. Some research is motivated by dissatisfaction with the traditional economic theory; some is grounded in a systematization greatly different from traditional theory (the

most important example of such systematization is national income accounting); some research is not clearly based on any theory; finally, some research has great affinity with psychological and sociological studies.

[3] The expression "economic behavior" is used in this paper to mean behavior concerning economic

## HABITUAL BEHAVIOR AND GENUINE DECISION MAKING

In trying to give noneconomic examples of "rational calculus," economic theorists have often referred to gambling. From some textbooks one might conclude that the most rational place in the world is the Casino in Monte Carlo where odds and probabilities can be calculated exactly. In contrast, some mathematicians and psychologists have considered scientific discovery and the thought processes of scientists as the best examples of rational or intelligent behavior.[4] An inquiry about the possible contributions of psychology to the analysis of rationality may then begin with a formulation of the differences between (a) associative learning and habit formation and (b) problem solving and thinking.

The basic principle of the first form of behavior is repetition. Here the argument of Guthrie holds: "The most certain and dependable information concerning what a man will do in any situation is information concerning what he did in that situation on its last occurrence" (4, p. 228). This form of behavior depends upon the frequency of repetition as well as on its recency and on the success of past performances. The origins of habit formation have been demonstrated by experiments about learning nonsense syllables, lists of words, mazes, and conditioned responses. Habits thus formed are to some extent automatic and inflexible.

In contrast, problem-solving behavior has been characterized by the arousal of a problem or question, by deliberation that involves reorganization and "direction," by understanding of the requirements of the situation, by weighing of alternatives and taking their consequences into consideration and, finally, by choosing among alternative courses of action.[5] Scientific discovery is not the only example of such procedures; they have been demonstrated in the psychological laboratory as well as in a variety of real-life situations. Problem solving

results in action which is new rather than repetitive; the actor may have never behaved in the same way before and may not have learned of any others having behaved in the same way.

Some of the above terms, defined and analyzed by psychologists, are also being used by economists in their discussion of rational behavior. In discussing, for example, a manufacturer's choice between erecting or not erecting a new factory, or raising or not raising his prices or output, reference is usually made to deliberation and to taking the consequences of alternative choices into consideration. Nevertheless, it is not justified to identify problem-solving behavior with rational behavior. From the point of view of an outside observer, habitual behavior may prove to be fully rational or the most appropriate way of action under certain circumstances. All that is claimed here is that the analysis of two forms of behavior—habitual versus genuine decision making—may serve to clarify problems of rationality. We shall proceed therefore by deriving six propositions from the psychological principles. To some extent, or in certain fields of behavior, these are findings or empirical generalizations; to some extent, or in other fields of behavior, they are hypotheses.

1. Problem-solving behavior is a relatively rare occurrence. It would be incorrect to assume that everyday behavior consistently manifests such features as arousal of a problem, deliberation, or taking consequences of the action into consideration. Behavior which does not manifest these characteristics predominates in everyday life and in economic activities as well.

2. The main alternative to problem-solving behavior is not whimsical or impulsive behavior (which was considered the major example of "irrational" behavior by nineteenth century philosophers). When genuine decision making does not take place, habitual behavior is the most usual occurrence: people act as

---

matters (spending, saving, investing, pricing, etc.). Some economic theorists use the expression to mean the behavior of the "economic man," that is, the behavior postulated in their theory of rationality.

[4] Reference should be made first of all to Max Wertheimer who in his book *Productive Thinking* uses the terms "sensible" and "intelligent" rather than "rational." Since we are mainly interested here in deriving conclusions from the psychology of

thinking, the discussion of psychological principles will be kept extremely brief.

[5] Cf. the following statement by a leading psychoanalyst: "Rational behavior is behavior that is effectively guided by an understanding of the situation to which one is reacting." French adds two steps that follow the choice between alternative goals, namely, commitment to a goal and commitment to a plan to reach a goal.

they have acted before under similar circumstances, without deliberating and choosing.

3. Problem-solving behavior is recognized most commonly as a deviation from habitual behavior. Observance of the established routine is abandoned when in driving home from my office, for example, I learn that there is a parade in town and choose a different route, instead of automatically taking the usual one. Or, to mention an example of economic behavior: Many businessmen have rules of thumb concerning the timing for reorders of merchandise; yet sometimes they decide to place new orders even though their inventories have not reached the usual level of depletion (for instance, because they anticipate price increases), or not to order merchandise even though that level has been reached (because they expect a slump in sales).

4. Strong motivational forces—stronger than those which elicit habitual behavior—must be present to call forth problem-solving behavior. Being in a "crossroad situation," facing "choice points," or perceiving that something new has occurred are typical instances in which we are motivated to deliberate and choose. Pearl Harbor and the Korean aggression are extreme examples of "new" events; economic behavior of the problem-solving type was found to have prevailed widely after these events.

5. Group belonging and group reinforcement play a substantial role in changes of behavior due to problem solving. Many people become aware of the same events at the same time; our mass media provide the same information and often the same interpretation of events to groups of people (to businessmen, trade union members, sometimes to all Americans). Changes in behavior resulting from new events may therefore occur among very many people at the same time. Some economists (for instance, Lord Keynes, see 9, p. 95) argued that consumer optimism and pessimism are unimportant because usually they will cancel out; in the light of sociopsychological principles, however, it is probable, and has been confirmed by recent surveys, that a change from optimistic to pessimistic attitudes, or vice versa, sometimes occurs among millions of people at the same time.

6. Changes in behavior due to genuine decision making will tend to be substantial and abrupt, rather than small and gradual. Typical examples of action that results from genuine decisions are cessation of purchases or buying waves, the shutting down of plants or the building of new plants, rather than an increase or decrease of production by 5 or 10 per cent.[6]

Because of the preponderance of individual psychological assumptions in classical economics and the emphasis placed on group behavior in this discussion, the change in underlying conditions which has occurred during the last century may be illustrated by a further example. It is related—the author does not know whether the story is true or fictitious—that the banking house of the Rothschilds, still in its infancy at that time, was one of the suppliers of the armies of Lord Wellington in 1815. Nathan Mayer Rothschild accompanied the armies and was present at the Battle of Waterloo. When he became convinced that Napoleon was decisively defeated, he released carrier pigeons so as to transmit the news to his associates in London and reverse the commodity position of his bank. The carrier pigeons arrived in London before the news of the victory became public knowledge. The profits thus reaped laid, according to the story, the foundation to the outstanding position of the House of Rothschild in the following decades.

The decision to embark on a new course of action because of new events was then made by one individual for his own profit. At present, news of a battle, or of change of government, or of rearmament programs, is transmitted in short order by press and radio to the public at large. Businessmen—the manufacturers or retailers of steel or clothing, for instance—usually receive the same news about changes in the price of raw materials or in demand, and often consult with each other. Belonging to the same group means being subject to similar stimuli and reinforcing one another in making decisions. Acting in the same way as other members of one's group or of a reference group have acted under similar circumstances may also occur without deliberation and choice. New action by a few manufacturers will, then, frequently or even usually not be compensated by reverse action on the part of others. Rather the direction in which the economy of an entire country moves—and often the world economy as well—will tend to be subject to the same influences.

After having indicated some of the contributions which the application of certain psycho-

---

[6] Some empirical evidence supporting these six propositions in the area of economic behavior has been assembled by the Survey Research Center of the University of Michigan.

logical principles to economic behavior may make, we turn to contrasting that approach with the traditional theory of rationality. Instead of referring to the formulations of nineteenth century economists, we shall quote from a modern version of the classical trend of thought. The title of a section in a recent article by Kenneth J. Arrow is "The Principle of Rationality." He describes one of the criteria of rationality as follows: "We can imagine the individual as listing, once and for all, all conceivable consequences of his actions in order of his preference for them" (1, p. 135). We are first concerned with the expression "all conceivable consequences." This expression seems to contradict the principle of selectivity of human behavior. Yet habitual behavior is highly selective since it is based on (repeated) past experience, and problem-solving behavior likewise is highly selective since reorganization is subject to a certain direction instead of consisting of trial (and error) regarding all possible avenues of action.

Secondly, Arrow appears to identify rationality with consistency in the sense of repetition of the same choice. It is part and parcel of rational behavior, according to Arrow, that an individual "makes the same choice each time he is confronted with the same set of alternatives" (1, p. 135).[7] Proceeding in the same way on successive occasions appears, however, a characteristic of habitual behavior. Problem-solving behavior, on the other hand, is flexible. Rationality may be said to reflect adaptability and ability to act in a new way when circumstances demand it, rather than to consist of rigid or repetitive behavior.

Thirdly, it is important to realize the differences between the concepts action, decision, and choice. It is an essential feature of the approach derived from considering problem-solving behavior that there is action without deliberate decision and choice. It then becomes one of the most important problems of research to determine under what conditions genuine decision and choice occur prior to an action. The three concepts are, however, used without

differentiation in the classical theory of rationality and also, most recently, by Parsons and Shils. According to the theory of these authors, there are "five discrete choices (explicit or implicit) which every actor makes before he can act"; before there is action "a decision must always be made (explicitly or implicitly, consciously or unconsciously)."

There exists, no doubt, a difference in terminology, which may be clarified by mentioning a simple case: Suppose my telephone rings; I lift the receiver with my left hand and say, "Hello." Should we then argue that I made several choices, for instance, that I decided not to lift the receiver with my right hand and not to say "Mr. Katona speaking"? According to our use of the terms decision and choice, my action was habitual and did not involve "taking consequences into consideration."[8] Parsons and Shils use the terms decision and choice in a different sense, and Arrow may use the terms "all conceivable consequences" and "same set of alternatives" in a different sense from the one employed in this paper. But the difference between the two approaches appears to be more far-reaching. By using the terminology of the authors quoted, and by constructing a theory of rational action on the basis of this terminology, fundamental problems are disregarded. If every action by definition presupposes decision making, and if the malleability of human behavior is not taken into consideration, a one-sided theory of rationality is developed and empirical research is confined to testing a theory which covers only some of the aspects of rationality.

This was the case recently in experiments devised by Mosteller and Nogee. These authors attempt to test basic assumptions of economic theory, such as the rational choice among alternatives, by placing their subjects in a gambling situation (a variation of poker dice) and compelling them to make a decision, namely, to play or not to play against the experimenter. Through their experiments the authors prove that "it is feasible to measure utility experimentally" but they do not shed light on the

---

[7] In his recent book Arrow adds after stating that the economic man "will make the same decision each time he is faced with the same range of alternatives": "The ability to make consistent decisions is one of the symptoms of an integrated personality."

[8] If I have reason not to make known that I am at home, I may react to the ringing of the telephone by fright, indecision, and deliberation (should I

lift the receiver or let the telephone ring?) instead of reacting in the habitual way. This is an example of problem-solving behavior characterized as deviating from habitual behavior. The only example of action mentioned by Parsons and Shils, "a man driving his automobile to a lake to go fishing," may be habitual or may be an instance of genuine decision making.

conditions under which rational behavior occurs or on the inherent features of rational behavior. Experiments in which making a choice among known alternatives is prescribed do not test the realism of economic theory.

## MAXIMIZATION

Up to now we have discussed only one central aspect of rationality—means rather than ends. The end of rational behavior, according to economic theory, is maximization of profits in the case of business firms and maximization of utility in the case of people in general.

A few words, first, on maximizing profits. This is usually considered the simpler case because it is widely held (a) that business firms are in business to make profits and (b) that profits, more so than utility, are a quantitative, measurable concept.

When empirical research, most commonly in the form of case studies, showed that businessmen frequently strove for many things in addition to profits or in place of profits, most theorists were content with small changes in their systems. They redefined profits so as to include long-range profits and what has been called nonpecuniary or psychic profits. Striving for security or for power was identified with striving for profits in the more distant future; purchasing goods from a high bidder who was a member of the same fraternity as the purchaser, rather than from the lowest bidder— to cite an example often used in textbooks—was thought to be maximizing of nonpecuniary profits. Dissatisfaction with this type of theory construction is rather widespread. For example, a leading theorist wrote recently:

If *whatever* a business man does is explained by the principle of profit maximization—because he does what he likes to do, and he likes to do what maximizes the sum of his pecuniary and non-pecuniary profits—the analysis acquires the character of a system of definitions and tautologies, and loses much of its value as an explanation of reality.

The same problem is encountered regarding maximization of utility. Arrow defines rational behavior as follows: ". . . among all the combinations of commodities an individual can afford, he chooses that combination which maximizes his utility or satisfaction" (1, p. 135) and speaks of the "traditional identification of rationality with maximization of some sort" (2, p. 3). An economic theorist has recently characterized this type of definition as follows:

The statement that a person seeks to maximize utility is (in many versions) a tautology: it is impossible to conceive of an observational phenomenon that contradicts it. . . . What if the theorem is contradicted by observation: Samuelson says it would not matter much in the case of utility theory; I would say that it would not make the slightest difference. For there is a free variable in his system: the tastes of consumers. . . . Any contradiction of a theorem derived from utility theory can always be attributed to a change of tastes, rather than to an error in the postulates or logic of the theory (16, pp. 603 f.).[9]

What is the way out of this difficulty? Can psychology, and specifically the psychology of motivation, help? We may begin by characterizing the prevailing economic theory as a single-motive theory and contrast it with a theory of multiple motives. Even in case of a single decision of one individual, multiplicity of motives (or of vectors or forces in the field), some reinforcing one another and some conflicting with one another, is the rule rather than the exception. The motivational patterns prevailing among different individuals making the same decision need not be the same; the motives of the same individual who is in the same external situation at different times may likewise differ. This approach opens the way (a) for a study of the relation of different motives to different forms of behavior and (b) for an investigation of changes in motives. Both problems are disregarded by postulating a single-motive theory and by restricting empirical studies to attempts to confirm or contradict that theory.

The fruitfulness of the psychological approach may be illustrated first by a brief reference to business motivation. We may rank the diverse motivational patterns of businessmen by placing the striving for high immediate profits (maximization of short-run profits, to use economic terminology; charging whatever the market can bear, to use a popular expression) at one extreme of the scale. At the other extreme we place the striving for prestige or power. In between we discern striving for security, for larger business volume, or for profits in the more distant future. Under what kinds of business conditions will motivational patterns tend to conform with the one or the other end of the scale? Preliminary studies would seem to indicate that the worse the

---

[9] The quotation refers specifically to Samuelson's definition but also applies to that of Arrow.

business situation is, the more frequent is striving for high immediate profits, and the better the business situation is, the more frequent is striving for nonpecuniary goals (see 8, pp. 193-213).

Next we shall refer to one of the most important problems of consumer economics as well as of business-cycle studies, the deliberate choice between saving and spending. Suppose a college professor receives a raise in his salary or makes a few hundred extra dollars through a publication. Suppose, furthermore, that he suggests thereupon to his wife that they should buy a television set, while the wife argues that the money should be put in the bank as a reserve against a "rainy day." Whatever the final decision may be, traditional economic theory would hold that the action which gives the greater satisfaction was chosen. This way of theorizing is of little value. Under what conditions will one type of behavior (spending) and under what conditions will another type of behavior (saving) be more frequent? Psychological hypotheses according to which the strength of vectors is related to the immediacy of needs have been put to a test through nationwide surveys over the past six years.[10] On the basis of survey findings the following tentative generalization was established: Pessimism, insecurity, expectation of income declines or bad times in the near future promote saving (putting the extra money in the bank), while optimism, feeling of security, expectation of income increases, or good times promote spending (buying the television set, for instance).

Psychological hypotheses, based on a theory of motivational patterns which change with circumstances and influence behavior, thus stimulated empirical studies. These studies, in turn, yielded a better understanding of past developments and also, we may add, better predictions of forthcoming trends than did studies based on the classical theory (see footnote 10). On the other hand, when conclusions about utility or rationality were made on an a

priori basis, researchers lost sight of important problems.[11]

## DIMINISHING UTILITY, SATURATION, AND ASPIRATION

Among the problems to which the identification of maximizing utility with rationality gave rise, the measurability of utility has been prominent. At present the position of most economists appears to be that while interpersonal comparison of several consumers' utilities is not possible, and while cardinal measures cannot be attached to the utilities of one particular consumer, ordinal ranking of the utilities of each individual can be made. It is asserted that I can always say either that I prefer A to B, or that I am indifferent to having A or B, or that I prefer B to A. The theory of indifference curves is based on this assumption.

In elaborating the theory further, it is asserted that rational behavior consists not only of preferring more of the same goods to less ($2 real wages to $1, or two packages of cigarettes to one package, for the same service performed) but also of deriving diminishing increments of satisfaction from successive units of a commodity.[12] In terms of an old textbook example, one drink of water has tremendous value to a thirsty traveler in a desert; a second, third, or fourth drink may still have some value but less and less so; an nth drink (which he is unable to carry along) has no value at all. A generalization derived from this principle is that the more of a commodity or the more money a person has, the smaller are his needs for that commodity or for money, and the smaller his incentives to add to what he has.

In addition to using this principle of saturation to describe the behavior of the rational man, modern economists applied it to one of the most pressing problems of contemporary American economy. Prior to World War II the American people (not counting business firms) owned about 45 billion dollars in liquid assets (currency, bank deposits, government bonds)

---

[10] In the Surveys of Consumer Finances, conducted annually since 1946 by the Survey Research Center of the University of Michigan for the Federal Reserve Board and reported in the *Federal Reserve Bulletin*. See also 8 and a forthcoming publication of the Survey Research Center on consumer buying and inflation during 1950–52.

[11] It should not be implied that the concepts of utility and maximization are of no value for empirical research. Comparison between maximum

utility as determined from the vantage point of an observer with the pattern of goals actually chosen (the "subjective maximum"), which is based on insufficient information, may be useful. Similar considerations apply to such newer concepts as "minimizing regrets" and the "minimax."

[12] This principle of diminishing utility was called a "fundamental tendency of human nature" by the great nineteenth century economist, Alfred Marshall.

and these funds were highly concentrated among relatively few families; most individual families held no liquid assets at all (except for small amounts of currency). By the end of the year 1945, however, the personal liquid-asset holdings had risen to about 140 billion dollars and four out of every five families owned some bank deposits or war bonds. What is the effect of this great change on spending and saving? This question has been answered by several leading economists in terms of the saturation principle presented above. "The rate of saving is . . . a diminishing function of the wealth the individual holds" (5, p. 499) because "the availability of liquid assets raises consumption generally by reducing the impulse to save." [13] More specifically: a person who owns nothing or very little will exert himself greatly to acquire some reserve funds, while a person who owns much will have much smaller incentives to save. Similarly, incentives to increase one's income are said to weaken with the amount of income. In other words, the strength of motivation is inversely correlated with the level of achievement.

In view of the lack of contact between economists and psychologists, it is hardly surprising that economists failed to see the relevance for their postulates of the extensive experimental work performed by psychologists on the problem of levels of aspiration. It is not necessary in this paper to describe these studies in detail. It may suffice to formulate three generalizations as established in numerous studies of goal-striving behavior (see, for example, 12):

1. Aspirations are not static, they are not established once for all time.

2. Aspirations tend to grow with achievement and decline with failure.

3. Aspirations are influenced by the performance of other members of the group to which one belongs and by that of reference groups.

From these generalizations hypotheses were derived about the influence of assets on saving which differed from the postulates of the saturation theory. This is not the place to describe the extensive empirical work undertaken to test the hypotheses. But it may be reported that the saturation theory was not confirmed;

the level-of-aspiration theory likewise did not suffice to explain the findings. In addition to the variable "size of liquid-asset holdings," the studies had to consider such variables as income level, income change, and savings habits. (Holders of large liquid assets are primarily people who have saved a high proportion of their income in the past!) [14]

The necessity of studying the interaction of a great number of variables and the change of choices over time leads to doubts regarding the universal validity of a one-dimensional ordering of all alternatives. The theory of measurement of utilities remains an empty frame unless people's established preferences of A over B and of B over C provide indications about their probable future behavior. Under what conditions do people's preferences give us such clues, and under what conditions do they not? If at different times A and B are seen in different contexts—because of changed external conditions or the acquisition of new experiences—we may have to distinguish among several dimensions.

The problem may be illustrated by an analogy. Classic economic theory postulates a one-dimensional ordering of all alternatives; Gallup asserts that answers to questions of choice can always be ordered on a yes-uncertain (don't know)—no continuum; are both arguments subject to the same reservations? Specifically, if two persons give the same answer to a poll question (e.g., both say "Yes, I am for sending American troops to Europe" or "Yes, I am for the Taft-Hartley Act") may they mean different things so that their identical answers do not permit any conclusions about the similarity of their other attitudes and their behavior? Methodologically it follows from the last argument that yes-no questions need to be supplemented by open-ended questions to discern differences in people's level of information and motivation. It also follows that attitudes and preferences should be ascertained through a multi-question approach (or scaling) which serves to determine whether one or several dimensions prevail.

## ON THEORY CONSTRUCTION

In attempting to summarize our conclusions about the respective merits of different scien-

---

[13] The last quotation is from the publication of the U.S. Department of Commerce, *Survey of Current Business,* May 1950, p. 10. This quotation and several similar ones are discussed in 8, pp. 186 ff.

[14] The empirical work was part of the economic behavior program of the Survey Research Center under the direction of the author. See (8) and also (10) and (11).

tific approaches, we might quote the conclusions of Arrow which he formulated for social science in general rather than for economics:

To the extent that formal theoretical structures in the social sciences have not been based on the hypothesis of rational behavior, their postulates have been developed in a manner which we may term *ad hoc*. Such propositions . . . depend, of course, on the investigator's intuition and common sense (1, p. 137).

The last sentence seems strange indeed. One may argue the other way around and point out that such propositions as "the purpose of business is to make profits" or "the best businessman is the one who maximizes profits" are based on intuition or supposed common sense, rather than on controlled observation. The main problem raised by the quotation concerns the function of empirical research. There exists an alternative to developing an axiomatic system into a full-fledged theoretical model in advance of testing the theory through observations. Controlled observations should be based on hypotheses, and the formulation of an integrated theory need not be delayed until all observations are completed. Yet theory construction is part of the process of hypothesis-observation-revised hypothesis and prediction-observation, and systematization should rely on some empirical research. The proximate aim of scientific research is a body of empirically validated generalizations and not a theory that is valid under any and all circumstances.

The dictum that "theoretical structures in the social sciences must be based on the hypothesis of rational behavior" presupposes that it is established what rational behavior is. Yet, instead of establishing the characteristics of rational behavior a priori, we must first determine the conditions $a_1$, $b_1$, $c_1$ under which behavior of the type $x_1$, $y_1$, $z_1$ and the conditions $a_2$, $b_2$, $c_2$ under which behavior of the type $x_2$, $y_2$, $z_2$ is likely to occur. Then, if we wish, we may designate one of the forms of behavior as rational. The contributions of psychology to this process are not solely methodological; findings and principles about noneconomic behavior provide hypotheses for the study of economic behavior. Likewise, psychology can profit from the study of economic behavior because many aspects of behavior, and among them the problems of rationality, may be studied most fruitfully in the economic field.

This paper was meant to indicate some promising leads for a study of rationality, not to carry such study to its completion. Among the problems that were not considered adequately were the philosophical ones (rationality viewed as a value concept), the psychoanalytic ones (the relationships between rational and conscious, and between irrational and unconscious), and those relating to personality theory and the roots of rationality. The emphasis was placed here on the possibility and fruitfulness of studying forms of rational behavior, rather than the characteristics of *the* rational man. Motives and goals that change with and are adapted to circumstances, and the relatively rare but highly significant cases of our becoming aware of problems and attempting to solve them, were found to be related to behavior that may be called truly rational.

## REFERENCES

1. ARROW, K. J. Mathematical models in the social sciences. In D. Lerner, & H. D. Lasswell (Eds.), *The policy sciences.* Stanford: Stanford Univer. Press, 1951. Pp. 129–155.

2. ARROW, K. J. *Social choice and individual values.* New York: Wiley, 1951.

3. FRENCH, T. M. *The integration of behavior.* Vol. I. Chicago: Univer. of Chicago Press, 1952.

4. GUTHRIE, E. R. *Psychology of learning.* New York: Harper, 1935.

5. HABERLER, G. *Prosperity and depression.* (3rd Ed.) Geneva: League of Nations, 1941.

6. KATONA, G. *Organizing and memorizing.* New York: Columbia Univer. Press, 1940.

7. KATONA, G. Psychological analysis of business decisions and expectations. *Amer. economic Rev.,* 1946, 36, 44–63.

8. KATONA, G. *Psychological analysis of economic behavior.* New York: McGraw-Hill, 1951.

9. KEYNES, J. M. *The general theory of employment, interest and money.* New York: Harcourt, Brace, 1936.

10. KLEIN, L. R. Assets, debts, and economic behavior. In *Studies in income and wealth,* Vol. 14. New York: National Bureau of Economic Research, 1951.

11. KLEIN, L. R. Estimating patterns of savings behavior from sample survey data. *Econometrica,* 1951, **19**, 438–454.

12. LEWIN, K., *et al.* Level of aspiration. In J. McV. Hunt (Ed.), *Personality and the behavior disorders.* New York: Ronald, 1944.

13. MACHLUP, F. Marginal analysis and empirical research. *Amer. economic Rev.*, 1946, 36, 519–555.

14. MOSTELLER, F., and NOGEE, P. An experimental measurement of utility. *J. political Economy*, 1951, 59, 371–405.

15. PARSONS, T., and SHILS, E. A. (Eds.). *Toward a general theory of action.* Cambridge, Mass.: Harvard Univer. Press, 1951.

16. STIGLER, G. J. Rev. of P. A. Samuelson's *Foundations of economic analysis. J. Amer. statist. Ass.*, 1948, 43, 603–605.

17. WERTHEIMER, M. *Productive thinking.* New York: Harper, 1945.

# 15. A Moderate Family Living Standard —What It Is and What It Costs Today

GENE E. FARNSWORTH AND
JOHN W. LEHMAN

How much income does it take for a four person family to maintain an adequate but modest standard of living in St. Louis or Kansas City? What would this family have to have in Chicago or New York City? Would the budget change if there were four children rather than two, and how much? These frequently asked questions involve a wide range of individual, business, labor, and public policy decisions about income needs, changes in levels of living, measures of adequacy of economic growth, and variations in regional economic levels and practices.

## NEW MEASURING DEVICE

The latest tool to help policy-makers and researchers provide some of the answers is the new City Worker's Family Budget, a study developed by the Bureau of Labor Statistics of the U.S. Department of Labor.

Results of this study, completed in late 1967, show that the annual cost of a "moderate" living standard for a "well established" family of four—a 38 year old employed husband, a wife, a son age 13, and a daughter age 8—averaged $9,191 in urban areas in autumn 1966 (see Table 1). Separate Budget cost estimates and comparative indexes are provided for 39 metropolitan areas and four broad regional groupings of nonmetropolitan areas. The yearly costs for the family ranged from $7,855 in the small Southern cities to

◆ SOURCE: Reprinted by permission from *Business and Government Review* (University of Missouri), Vol. IX, No. 3, May-June 1968, pp. 5–12.

$11,190 in Honolulu. Kansas City's $9,189 and St. Louis's $9,241 fall close to the middle in the ranking of the 39 cities.

Of the total costs, about 80 per cent are allocated to family consumption items—food, housing, transportation, clothing, personal care, medical care, and other items of goods and services. The other 20 per cent represents allowances for gifts and contributions, basic life insurance, personal income and social security taxes, and occupational expenses.

Of all the major items in the Budget, housing costs show widest differentials and account in large part for the variations in total family consumption among metropolitan areas. Total housing costs ranged from $2,732 in Boston to $1,676 in Austin. Significantly, St. Louis at $2,202 and Kansas City at $2,083 were close to the U.S. median of $2,170 recorded for Cincinnati.

The survey results also provide insight into the homeowner vs. renter costs question; the homeowner averaging better than $600 a year more in costs than the comparable renter family. Shelter costs for homeowners, however, include regular monthly payments on the mortgage principal in addition to other expenses and charges, so there is an element of savings. Nevertheless, when these principal payments were excluded, homeowner costs were still 15 per cent above renters' costs.

Differentials in food costs are second to housing in accounting for variations in total family consumption expenditures between areas. These differences in food costs reflect both price variations and regional food prefer-

TABLE 1.   City Family Budget
(Annual by Major Components)*

| Item | Urban U.S. | St. Louis | Kansas City |
|---|---|---|---|
| Food | $2143 | $2199 | $2140 |
| at home | 1824 | 1865 | 1827 |
| away | 319 | 334 | 313 |
| Housing | 2214 | 2202 | 2083 |
| Renters | 1736 | 1719 | 1738 |
| Homeowners | 2374 | 2363 | 2199 |
| Shelter—Total | 1733 | 1709 | 1583 |
| Renters | 1255 | 1226 | 1236 |
| Homeowners | 1893 | 1870 | 1698 |
| Housefurnishings | 265 | 265 | 277 |
| Household oper. | 216 | 228 | 225 |
| Transportation | 815 | 839 | 871 |
| Auto owners | 860 | 872 | 871 |
| Nonowners | 151 | 225 | 198 |
| Clothing | 756 | 761 | 762 |
| Husband | 174 | 170 | 175 |
| Wife | 187 | 189 | 190 |
| Boy | 168 | 165 | 173 |
| Girl | 154 | 162 | 155 |
| Materials, etc. | 73 | 75 | 69 |
| Personal care | 214 | 222 | 234 |
| Medical care | 468 | 443 | 441 |
| Insurance | 219 | 217 | 207 |
| Physicians | 89 | 85 | 80 |
| Other | 284 | 264 | 272 |
| Other consump. | 719 | 710 | 741 |
| Reading | 65 | 67 | 67 |
| Recreation | 306 | 303 | 319 |
| Education | 55 | 60 | 60 |
| Tobacco | 134 | 131 | 142 |
| Alcoholic bev. | 72 | 62 | 67 |
| Miscellaneous | 87 | 87 | 86 |
| Total cons. | 7329 | 7376 | 7272 |
| Renters | 6850 | 6894 | 6926 |
| Homeowners | 7488 | 7537 | 7387 |
| Other costs | 413 | 415 | 412 |
| Gifts and contrib. | 253 | 255 | 252 |
| Life insurance | 160 | 160 | 160 |
| Occupa. exp. | 80 | 80 | 80 |
| Social Sec., etc. | 289 | 277 | 277 |
| Personal taxes | 1080 | 1093 | 1148 |
| Renters | 961 | 979 | 1008 |
| Homeowners | 1119 | 1130 | 1195 |
| Total Budget | 9191 | 9241 | 9189 |
| Renters | 8594 | 8645 | 8703 |
| Homeowners | 9390 | 9440 | 9351 |

* Group totals in Housing, Transportation and Medical Care are not equal to the sum of their components because of different weighting proportions assigned the various items in computing the group totals.

ence patterns, such as the importance given to chicken in Southern diets and to beef in the Northeast. Costs were almost $300 higher in the Northeast for a nutritionally comparable food plan.

TYPICAL BUDGET FAMILY

The estimates of living costs for all items, as we have noted, are based on a specific family situation. The City Worker's Family Budget is for a particular family of four persons. The man is employed and is an experienced worker assumed to be well advanced in his trade or profession. His wife of 15 years or more is not employed outside the home. Their family group is well established and has average inventories of clothing, house furnishings, major durables and other equipment.

While it is a specified family, as distinguished from the "average" family which may vary in composition and size from place to place and time to time, this is still a reasonably typical family. The buying habits of a family with two adults and two children range over a wide variety of goods and services common to family life. Also, this family represents a stage through which almost half of the families pass at one time or another. A wage that would support such a group of four at the described "moderate" level of living obviously would support a smaller family at a higher level, and a larger family at a lower level.

*Level of Living*

The level of living described by the Budget is one which is "determined by prevailing standards of what is needed for health, efficiency, nurture of children, social participation, and the maintenance of self-respect and the respect of others."[1] The standard can be visualized as a point on a scale of living patterns that ranges from a mere existence to levels of luxury living. It is essentially the point where the struggle for more and more things gives way to the desire for better and better quality of what is purchased. This "moderate" living standard on a scale of all living patterns may remain fixed in relation to what is high and low at any given time; but what makes up the overall pattern may change, with the result that the standard will continually change.

---

[1] Workers' Budgets in the United States, 1946–47; BLS Bulletin No. 927, p. 6.

Advances in educational levels, cultural developments, mobility of workers, and growth of purchasing power affect ideas of a "moderate" standard. New types of consumer goods and services are constantly being developed and made available with refined production and distribution techniques, and the consumer stimulated through mass communication and advertising. Marketing experts have often told us that—in the form they are currently presented—30 per cent of the items on the shelves of the local supermarket did not even exist just 10 years before. Items considered out of reach a short time ago are now taken for granted as part of the American way of life and have become part of our regular budgets.

## BUDGET DETERMINED

Quantities of goods and services for the Budget were compiled from basically two kinds of data—recognized scientific standards, where they exist, and statistical analysis of the ways in which people actually spend their money.

Where scientific standards of adequacy were available, they were used to specify the quantities and qualities of goods and services meeting Budget standards. For example:

1. The Food and Nutrition Board of the National Research Council has developed scientific standards for what constitutes adequate diets for various sex-age groups.

2. The American Public Health Association and the U.S. Public Housing Administration have established measures for housing adequacy by size of family.

3. The Department of Health, Education and Welfare has determined, with the help of the National Health Survey, the amount and kind of medical and other health services a family needs for adequate care.

Measures of this kind were available for almost half of the family consumption items.

For the other half of family consumption, the quantities and qualities for the pricing list were derived from actual choices of goods and services as determined by the Bureau of Labor Statistics Consumer Expenditures Survey.[2] It was the data from this survey which provided the basis for saying exactly where

the struggle for *quantity* gives way to the desire for *quality*. Purchases were examined at successive income levels to determine the income level at which the rate of increase in quantities purchased began to decline in relation to the rate of change in income. The method used is known as the expenditure-income elasticity technique and the point is referred to as the "point of maximum elasticity."

### Quantities Obtained

The kind of budget quantities this method yields are interesting and carry an identifiable sense of reality. The Budget family replaces its basic living room suite once every 25 years, TV set every 8 years, and auto every 4 years. If the Budget family lives in a nonmetropolitan area, it will replace the family auto in 3 years, reflecting greater usage and perhaps more frequent driving on less-improved roads.

The resistance of teen-age boys to wearing galoshes or rubbers is evidenced in the boy being credited with one pair every 4 years. This may also explain in part why he requires the greatest number of pairs of shoes of anyone in the family (more than four per year). Perhaps feeling guilty about the shoes he goes through, the boy fights his normal bent toward neatness and only gets about half as many haircuts as his father—a phenomenon that may be confirmed in the halls of the local junior high school.

While the nonmetropolitan family uses 144 medium-sized bars of toilet soap per year, the metropolitan area family uses 110. On the other hand, city dwellers buy 51 ounces of hair shampoo as opposed to the nonmetropolitan family's 32. Small towners may get their hands dirtier more often, but the pollutants in the city may make shampoos more necessary.

Knowing how the Budget family's dollar is divided among the various expenditure groups also adds to our better understanding. While 24.1 cents of every dollar is used for housing, 23.3 cents is spent for food. These are the greatest single outlays. Personal taxes, clothing and personal care, and transportation account for 11.8, 10.6, and 8.9 cents each. The balance of items consume the remaining 21 plus cents as shown in Fig. 1.

In preparing costs estimates for the Budget, once the items and quantities are determined, it is necessary to obtain prices for the kinds of

---

[2] Made in 1960-61 to determine the weighting patterns for the national and city Consumer Price Indexes.

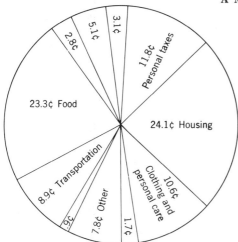

FIG. 1. The budget dollar. *Key:* 5.1¢, medical care; 3.1¢, Social Security and disability payments; 2.8¢, gifts and contributions; 1.7¢, personal life insurance; .9¢, occupational expenses.

commodities and services families buy.[3] These prices must be real; they must represent the average price level of the actual items and the quality of such family purchases. Items must be precisely defined and of specified quality to insure that intercity difference computations are accurate.

## EVOLUTION OF CONCEPTS

The development of a budget based on scientific standards and reflecting the combined judgments derived from the experience of all consumers as to what constitutes a "moderate" level of living has largely taken place since 1947. The interest in family budgets as a policy tool, however, goes back as far as the late 1800's. At that time, attention was beginning to be focused on the poor in the population. Many of the poor were emigrants attracted to large cities, who came ill-equipped for city life and work. Much of the nonmoney income, such as home-grown food and free fuel, available to rural and semirural workers was not available to these new city dwellers. Economists, struggling with questions of production and capital formation, and sociologists, struggling with the problems of caring for the poor and improving slum living conditions, were interested in only a subsistence level of income adequacy.

After the turn of the century, the subsistence or breakeven concept had evolved to what was termed the "living wage" concept. Agitation for health and labor legislation brought interest in a budget that would describe a level of living that was "minimum for health and decency." So these budgets, which were the first in this country expressed in quantities of goods and services to which prices were actually applied and costs determined, were described as representing: a "minimum standard of living"

. . . the smallest amount upon which families were living and apparently maintaining physical efficiency . . . it excluded everything except the bare necessities of life . . . a standard of living so low that one would expect few families to live on it.

There was also some interest in a "fair standard," that provides "not only physical efficiency but allows for the satisfaction and development of human attributes. . . ."[4]

### Welfare Benefits

By 1919 the Bureau of Labor Statistics was preparing quantity budgets defining a "standard of health and decency" significantly higher than the "fair" standard of the 1908-09 budgets. Long-run as well as short-run needs and more generous concepts of income adequacy for self-sustaining families were recognized.

The September 1924 issue of the Annals of the American Academy of Political and Social Science, which was devoted to "modern selling," pointed out the "interdependence of modern specialized industry," and contended that the "health and prosperity of a community is determined by the ability of the individual to take his part in the economic structure of his day." Recognition of the consumer's importance in the new era of production and marketing was growing fast. But family budgets were still primarily a tool for use by welfare agencies or as a means of evaluating incomes of self-supporting families at very low economic levels.

The 1936 Works Progress Administration *Quantity Budgets for Basic Maintenance and Emergency Standards of Living* provided a maintenance budget describing a "minimum

---

[3] The current Budget figures are from prices compiled in autumn 1966. It is planned to update these prices approximately once a year beginning in 1968.

[4] Family Budgets of Typical Cotton-Mill Workers, 61st Congress, Second Session, Senate Document No. 645, Washington, 1911.

subsistence level," but one which did not approach "the content of what may be considered a satisfactory American standard of living." [5] Since the middle thirties, however, theories of economics placing increasing importance on the relation of income and consumption to a healthy national economy have generated a revival of the social concept of income adequacy. The concept has become more important and more widely accepted while at the same time more complex and difficult to define precisely.

### Adequate Budgets

Immediately after World War II interest in a City Worker's Family Budget as we now know it was stimulated as a result of Congressional need for information on the cost of an adequate standard of living for use in appraising income tax exemptions. The BLS was directed "to find out what it costs a worker's family to live in large cities of the United States." [6] The 1946-47 Budget, developed by a panel of experts to meet this question, provided for the first time a standard determined by objective methods, made possible by improved statistical techniques; scientific knowledge of health, housing and nutrition; and a wealth of data on consumer expenditures. What the level of such a budget would be, could not be foretold. The data, not the investigators, shaped the budget of goods that people strive for.

Estimates of these objective budgets were published for 34 large cities as of March 1946, June 1947, October 1949, and October 1951. The basic concepts and methods designed for the 1946-47 Budget were again utilized in providing the Interim City Worker's Family Budget of autumn 1959.[7] The Budget discussed in this article is the latest in the series but the basic concepts and techniques are still those developed to answer the Congress in 1947, although the list of cities covered in each study varied somewhat.

Common to the 1951, 1959, and 1966 Budget reports (see Fig. 2) were 18 cities in which the total Budget cost averaged about $4,200 in 1951 and $6,100 in 1959, 45 per

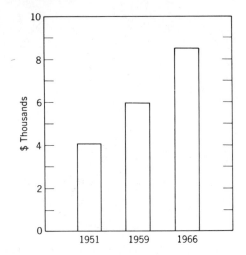

FIG. 2. City family budgets. 1966 budget is for renter families only to provide comparability with earlier studies which did not include owner families.

cent higher. The cost of the current "moderate" standard in the same cities in 1966 averaged $8,700, 43 per cent more than in 1959. The changes in total costs reflect increases in personal income and social security taxes and prices, but even more important the rise in the standard of living represented in these Budgets.

Over the 15 year period, improvements in the "moderate" standard of living account for a rise in costs of an average of 3.5 to 4 per cent a year. This is over and above the average annual increase of 1.5 per cent which results from price changes. Three factors account for the major contributions to the rising standard. One is an upgrading of the food component. This reflects changes in preference patterns which provide the nutritional standard and the increase in number of meals purchased away from home. Apparently the plea, "Let's go out to eat," is being heeded more often. The obvious increase in auto ownership and inherent greater car usage required by the extension of suburbs is a second factor in the rising standard. The third factor is better health care including a substantially higher standard of dental care.

[5] Works Progress Administration, Division of Social Research, Research Bulletin, Series I, No. 21, Washington, 1936.
[6] Congressional Record, 79th Congress, First Session, Volume 91, Part 2, pp. 2, 442–9.

[7] Because the revision was limited to changing the list of goods and services to reflect buying patterns in the 1950's and did not include a reappraisal of the concept, definitions, and general procedures, it was considered an "interim revision."

TABLE 2.   Cities Ranked by Budget

| | |
|---|---|
| 1. Honolulu | $11,190 |
| 2. New York City | 10,195 |
| 3. Boston | 10,141 |
| 4. Hartford | 10,000 |
| 5. San Francisco | 9,886 |
| 6. Milwaukee | 9,740 |
| 7. Buffalo | 9,724 |
| 8. Seattle | 9,665 |
| 9. Chicago | 9,506 |
| 10. Minneapolis | 9,495 |
| 11. Los Angeles | 9,445 |
| 12. Cedar Rapids | 9,421 |
| 13. Indianapolis | 9,394 |
| 14. Washington, D. C. | 9,381 |
| 15. Champaign-Urbana | 9,350 |
| 16. San Diego | 9,307 |
| 17. Cleveland | 9,297 |
| 18. Portland, Me. | 9,257 |
| 19. ST. LOUIS | 9,241 |
| 20. Denver | 9,235 |
| 21. Philadelphia | 9,193 |
| 22. KANSAS CITY | 9,189 |
| 23. Green Bay | 9,080 |
| 24. WICHITA | 9,052 |
| 25. Detroit | 8,981 |
| 26. Cincinnati | 8,976 |
| 27. Bakersfield | 8,921 |
| 28. Pittsburgh | 8,919 |
| 29. Lancaster | 8,890 |
| 30. Baltimore | 8,798 |
| 31. Dayton | 8,711 |
| 32. Durham, N. C. | 8,707 |
| 33. Nashville | 8,552 |
| 34. Baton Rouge | 8,538 |
| 35. Dallas | 8,472 |
| 36. Atlanta | 8,434 |
| 37. Orlando | 8,416 |
| 38. Houston | 8,387 |
| 39. Austin | 8,028 |

### Limitations

One continuing problem with the standard budget approach is, of course, that a single budget cannot represent the requirements of all family types, nor of one family throughout

its life span. A series of budgets would be required, starting with the couple newly married and ending with them again in late middle and old age. Different budgets are needed at any one time to show costs for different size families.

One way of shedding some light on these differences is to develop, from some of the data, an equivalence scale which estimates family consumption costs for families differing in size, age and composition. The cost of maintaining a family at a given level of living does not increase in direct proportion to its size. Successive additions result in smaller and smaller additions to the cost.

Although it is not true that "two can live as cheaply as one," or that "two can live as cheaply as one but only half as long," it is quite clear that it does not cost twice as much. Some items of living costs, such as food, clothing, personal and medical care, and even recreation, vary quite directly with the number and ages of family members. On the other hand, much of home furnishings, household equipment and even, in part, the cost of housing itself, can be considered "overhead," and will not vary much with family size.

The equivalence scales provide a means of estimating the total costs of goods and services needed to provide the same level of living for families of different size, age and composition. The values are expressed as a per cent of spendable income for the four-person Budget family, and must be applied to the total cost for goods and services.[8] They are not suitable for application to individual items of the Budget.

### POINT OF REFERENCE

In using the standard budget cost estimates being discussed, it must be remembered that they are primarily benchmark statistics providing a valuable research device for dealing with problems of family finance. When analyzed in connection with income distributions, they can help set useful guides for social and

---

[8] The equivalence scales show that while it took $7,272 to purchase these items (80 per cent of the total budget) for the four person Kansas City family, a young couple with one small child would need only $4,510 to provide the same level of living. For the four person family, if the age of the boy is increased from 13 to 16 or 17, the cost climbs to $8,217 (documenting the axiom that as

youngsters get older they cost more). A husband, wife, and four children with the oldest still under 16 require $9,599. Since taxes, insurance, occupational expenses, social security payments, etc., vary by family type, these items must be calculated separately and added to the estimated cost to get the total.

legislative programs dealing with wages, prices, credit, public assistance and taxation. They can be helpful, too, in planning individual family spending, but largely as a general reference against which a family can evaluate its spending in the light of its own characteristics and preferences.

The kinds of items and the quantities used provide guides for appraising the content of living and establishing needs in various situations. Budgets derived in the manner of this one reflect replacement rates based on the average inventories of budget-type families at the time of the basic expenditure study. While this is a valid assumption on which to base the annual rate of purchase in a standard budget, the resulting quantities may not be a good estimate of the purchases required by a particular family if its inventory of household items is substantially different from the average of the families from which the Budget quantities were derived. For many administrative purposes, also, the content and cost of component parts of the Budget probably are more useful than the total Budget cost estimates.

### Comparing Cities

It should be recalled, too, that the Budget provides a measure of living costs between cities, which includes more than just the differences in prices. It reflects both the affect of climate and regional preferences in the kinds and amounts of items required to provide the specified "moderate" standard of living in any particular city, and it also identifies differences due to varying state and local taxes (see Table 2).

The Budget does not include all possible costs which would face a person moving from one city to another. The housing component demonstrates this problem area particularly well since the Budget provides for occupancy of specifically defined dwellings for the Budget family which is well established in the community. But dwellings available to new residents may vary considerably from those available over a longer period.[9]

## CONCLUSION

Finally, the Budget does not attempt to show how an *average family* actually spends its money, nor does it in itself try to show how families should spend their money. It is a highly useful estimate of the total cost of goods and services considered necessary by four person families to maintain a "moderate" level of living according to today's standards. Because the Budget is based on typical experiences growing out of the way people actually behave, it sheds important light on current American values—how we spend our money, and what we think is important in our way of living.

Clearly, this Budget is not an absolute and unchanging thing. "The prevailing judgment of the 'necessary' will vary with the changing values of the community, with the advance of scientific knowledge of human needs, with the productive power of the community, and therefore (with) what people commonly enjoy and see others enjoy."[10] As subsequent studies are made, we will learn more about how those values vary as reflected in changing living standards.

---

[9] The standard budget provides living cost differentials from place to place, and by use of the equivalence table, between types of families. The BLS also publishes the Consumer Price Index—frequently, though incorrectly, referred to as the "cost of living" index, which measures the change in consumer prices from time to time but not the other factors which affect family living expenses. The Consumer Price Index is used too, as a meas-ure of change in the purchasing power of the consumer dollar; and wages or pensions are often adjusted by it. The Index is published monthly for the nation and five large metropolitan areas, and every 3 months for 18 other cities, including Kansas City and St. Louis.

[10] Workers' Budgets in the U. S., 1946–47, op. cit., p. 7.

# 16. Consumer Practices of the Poor

## LOUISE G. RICHARDS

To the economist, being poor means having an income below a certain figure—a figure that represents the minimum amount necessary for a decent life in America today. To the behavioral scientist, being poor means a number of characteristics found to be associated with low income: patterns of family life, health care, education, and general outlook on life. To the poor person himself, however, being poor may mean different things depending on how his money is spent. This report is a summary of research findings on those consumer practices. The report covers not only how money is spent by the poor, but also what kinds of behavior—shopping, methods of payments, and the like—go along with income disbursement.

Few would quarrel with the judgment that an income of $3000 is too low for a family to live on today. Hardly anyone would suggest that even the best consumer practices would solve the problem of poverty. Many would agree, however, that good consumer practices might alleviate some of the worst aspects. Knowledge of actual practices of the poor can suggest new areas for education and action.

One writer on the topic of consumer practices of the poor has concluded that they are irrational in their buying behavior. Some of the evidence for that conclusion is included in this report. To indict poor consumers as irrational is too simple an explanation, however. Moreover, it provides no handles for

action. Much of the evidence for irrationality should be considered in the light of other explanations that make equally good sense. The particular social and demographic characteristics of the poor must be taken into account. The inflexibility of low income per se must be kept in mind. And, finally, the possibility that apparent irrationality may stem from the very conditions of poverty must be dealt with. These explanations will be discussed more fully in a later section.

For practices to be labeled as irrational there must be a standard for judging their rationality. Many people would subscribe to the idea that there are good, common-sense rules for stretching income. Many of those who knew poverty during the Thirties, and those who have known severe reverses since then, would avow that such rules helped them keep their heads above water in difficult times.

Most common-sense rules of financial management are applications of the idea that everyone naturally tries to get the best living for the least money. Recent thinking on the topic includes the idea that psychological satisfactions can be added to material ones in arriving at a calculus of values. It is probably true, however, that low-income consumers can seldom afford outlays for emotional satisfactions, except perhaps in choices of low-cost items. Thus, the traditional rules are probably more pertinent today to the low-income consumer's situation than to that of higher income groups with their larger margins for discretionary purchases.

Very simply, the traditional rules for good consumership can be stated as follows:

1. Spend first for necessities and last for luxuries. Although many individuals disagree

◆ SOURCE: Louise G. Richards, "Consumer Practices of the Poor," *Low-Income Life Styles*, edited by Lola M. Irelan, United States Department of Health Education and Welfare (Wash., D.C.: U.S. Government Printing Office, 1966), pp. 67–84.

on how to classify specific goods, few would dispute that food, shelter, basic articles of clothing, and health should have priority over recreation and other categories of expenditure.

2. Buy the best quality of goods for the lowest price. This means that costly extra features—high styles, non-seasonal treats, store services, and above all, the cost of installment buying—should be avoided. In order to follow this rule, a person needs to shop widely and keep up with information about goods, prices, and sources.

3. Another rule stems from recognition of the fact that it is not easy to suppress desires for luxury goods and extra features: Budget small incomes carefully and plan purchases in advance. If possible, one should save for (or insure against) future emergencies to prevent insolvency.

4. Another rule covers the thousand-and-one suggestions for home production of needed goods: Try to get what is needed or wanted without spending money, or by spending only for raw materials. Home preservation of food, home sewing, self-building and self-repairing of homes, are a few of many recommended money saving practices.

5. Take advantage of certain benefits available to persons with limited incomes. Surplus food (and Food Stamps), legal aid, scholarships, day care for children, public housing, and medical and dental clinics are examples of such benefits provided through legislation or private funds.

Most detailed advice to consumers could be put under one of these five rules. Together they provide a backdrop for viewing actual consumer practices of the poor. In reporting the findings, these five rules will be referred to specifically. Before turning to those findings, we need to review what is known about the different kinds of people that constitute the poor population today, and the different kinds of studies that provide the facts.

## POPULATION CHARACTERISTICS OF THE POOR

Several writers have pointed out that the poor as a group are neither homogeneous nor strictly representative of the population as a whole. The *majority* of low income families are white, non-farm, and headed by a male between twenty-five and sixty-five years old.

Compared with the general population, however, poor families tend to include more non-whites, fewer earners, more families with female heads, larger families, and more old or young persons. The poor more often reside in rural farm areas or in cities (and less often in rural non-farm or suburban areas). Above all, poor people have completed fewer years of schooling than the rest of the population. Almost every family or individual below the poverty line can be characterized by at least one of these facts. These differences between the poor and the general population are important in interpreting research findings about their consumer habits.

## SOURCES OF FINDINGS

Two broad areas of research were drawn upon in this report. One area includes the economic surveys of consumer expenditures, savings, and debt made by government agencies and by business—a relatively old and well-established research activity. One continuing survey of this type, the Survey of Consumer Finances has been concerned also with certain attitudes and expectations of consumers.

The second research area includes those studies that examine specific consumer practices, the why's and wherefore's of consumption. The most recent comprehensive study in this area is Caplovitz' *The Poor Pay More*. Caplovitz' study provides information on types of stores used, methods of payment for goods, attitudes toward merchants and installment buying, and aspirations for future purchases on the part of a group of low-income families in New York City. Other studies provide facts about the decision making process, the different sources of consumers' knowledge, and the participation of husbands and wives in financial planning. Also included is a summary of findings from studies of the working-class wife. (Although many working-class families are by no means poor—and vice versa—this summary is the only recent one available on social class differences in taste.)

When possible, we report the practices of families whose incomes are less than $3000, and indicate how their practices differ from families with higher incomes. When available figures were not broken at the poverty line, we report merely the differences between lower and higher income groups.

## CONSUMER PRACTICES

Turning now to consumer practices in the framework of the above-mentioned rules for good consumership, here is the evidence:

### 1. Do Low-Income Families Buy Necessities First, and Luxuries Last?

For the most part, "Yes." When consumer goods and services are classified according to their survival value (beginning with Food and ending with Recreation), the poor spend more of their income than others do on the basic needs. When goods are classified as durables (automobiles, equipment, furniture, and the like) and non-durables, we find that the poor, on the average, do not buy durables as frequently as higher income families do. When we look at the poor who do purchase one or more durable goods in a given year, however, we find that a startlingly high proportion of their income is spent for those goods.

One weak spot in the poor family's purchasing behavior appears to be this overspending on durable goods. Since most durable goods are relatively expensive items, it is not hard to see why the purchase of a durable good makes heavy inroads on a small income. Moreover, it is difficult to judge whether or not a given durable good should be considered a luxury for a poor family. (One could argue that an automatic washing machine is not a luxury for a large family in which the mother's time is at a premium.) However, when purchasing families with incomes less than $2,000 spend almost half of their income on durable goods, we need to look for an explanation.

The durable goods that take the largest bites from poor families' incomes are large household appliances and radios, television sets, and phonographs. These are household items that can be considered part of the standard package of American consumption. According to one writer, these home items are especially significant to working-class wives who aspire to the role of the modern, efficient American housewife. Also, of course, much effort and money are devoted to the advertisement of these and other items in the standard package. The poor are no less vulnerable than others are to persuasive selling. Such pressure may be particularly hard for the Negro poor to resist, since traditionally they have been denied access to other forms of social status. There are other, less subjective factors in

the purchase of durable goods than role image and vulnerability to advertising. Young families and those with large numbers of children spend more on durables, regardless of income. Since the poor include proportionately larger numbers of young, large families, we can attribute some over-spending to heavier need in newly formed households with more demand for labor-saving devices. Another factor in some poor neighborhoods is the incidence of merchandizing practices that result in higher prices than those found for the same goods in middle-income shopping areas.

We have made some general statements about how the poor spend their incomes, and have provided some brief explanations of the patterns found. Some of the findings that support those statements are given below.

**A. Categories of Spending.** Food, shelter, and medical care take larger shares of the poor family's consumer dollar than they do in families with higher incomes, on the average. Clothing and transportation take smaller shares, on the average. Household operation (including furnishings and equipment) and other expenses (recreation, personal care, and education) take about the same share as in higher income families.

The above findings compare average proportions spent annually by different income groups, whether all families in a group made purchases in the category or not. In a given year, most families do buy food, shelter, and at least a few articles of clothing. They probably also pay at least one medical fee. We know from other data that in a given year fewer low-income families make purchases of automobiles, furniture, and household appliances. What is the share of income spent by poor families who do purchase a major durable in a given year?

Among those in the lowest income group (under $2,000) who bought a major durable in 1962, an average of 48% of their income was spent on such purchases. In the next higher income group ($2,000 to $4,999), the share was 28%. These percentages are high compared with the shares of income spent by the poor on "needs", and startlingly high compared with the shares spent on durables by families in other income groups. (In the category that included median family income ($6,000 to $7,499) in 1962, the share spent for durables was only 14%.) The durables that take the largest shares of poor families' income are large household appliances and radios, television sets, and phonographs. High consumption of these same items, and furniture, is reported in Caplovitz' study of low-income families in New York: 95% owned television sets, 63% owned phonographs, and 41% owned automatic washers.

**B. Effects of Class and Ethnic Values.** The special importance of household appliances, television, and furniture to the working class was discussed in some detail in Rainwater's analysis of the working-class wife. According to that author, appliances and furniture mean something different to working-class wives from what they mean to middle-class wives. The difference in values is a subtle one, but may be an important contribution to over-spending.

Working-class wives' lives revolve around home and housework to a greater extent than the lives of middle-class wives. The working-class wife knows that housework is inevitable, and she dreams of a home (especially a kitchen) that symbolizes the role of the modern, efficient American housewife. She also tends to associate the new with the beautiful. The middle-class wife, on the other hand, is interested in labor-saving appliances that free her as much as possible from the role of housewife so that she may enjoy the social, intellectual, and aesthetic pleasures of upper-middle-class life. These differences suggest that the working-class wife sees household durables as an end in themselves, rather than merely as means to other ends.

One sociologist describes another pattern of spending in terms of the symbolic value of certain products. Negroes underspend in four major areas—housing, automobile transportation, food, and medical care. On the other hand, a number of Negro women are more interested than white women in "high fashion," even in the Under-$3,000 income group. And Negro families report buying Scotch whiskey, a high-status drink, twice as often as white families do. One theorist writing on the subject of "conditions for irrational choices" suggests an explanation: Irrational choice making occurs when "something . . . [is] . . . repressed among a large number of individuals in a specific segment of our society with a distinctive sub-culture."

**C. The Effect of Youth and Size of Families.** In one analysis of frequency of purchase of selected durables, it was found that the rate for young married couples with incomes under $3,000 increases after the birth of their first child, whereas the rate for couples with incomes over $3,000 decreases Caplovitz' study also showed that family size among his low-income public housing tenants affects durable goods' ownership (or aspirations for ownership) regardless of the size of income.

These facts and the much cited findings by Caplovitz about high-priced durables in poor neighborhoods provide the evidence for our answer, "Yes, but . . ." to the question on whether the poor spend their incomes on basic needs. We do not want to leave the impression that the poor are profligate spenders on special goods, however.

There is some evidence that they do not have much desire for all kinds of special purchases. In one nationwide study, their desires for "special expenditures" were found to be less frequent than those expressed by middle and upper income families. Although poor families may not dream of as many new purchases as other families do, they do appear to be eager to acquire the standard package.

## 2. Do Low-Income Shoppers Try to Get the Best Quality for the Lowest Price?

Available evidence indicates that the answer is "No." Lower income consumers are not more deliberate in their shopping, more wide-ranging in their search for good buys, more price conscious, nor more informed on the characteristics of products than families with higher incomes. If anything, they are less apt to carry out those practices than others. Neither are low-income consumers more apt to buy used articles, to buy "separate items," nor to pay cash for their purchases.

On three counts, poor people do exhibit more economical practices. They tend more often to negotiate special deals on durables, especially through relatives or friends. The *very* poor tend to buy goods on sale more often than others. And, although there is just as much use of credit by low-income families as by others, fewer of the poor have installment or mortgage debt. Among those who do have installment debt, however, the effect on family solvency may be ruinous.

On the basis of strict rationality, one would expect low-income consumers to be more deliberate, searching, price-conscious, and informed than high-income consumers. The low level of education of many poor people goes a long way in explaining why they are not, and indeed, why they fall below other income groups in the frequency of some of these activities. Knowledge of the immense variety of goods on the American market is not easily acquired. Especially in the case of appliances, knowledge of technical features is highly specialized. Knowledge of the intricacies of credit agreements or consumer rights is not easy to acquire, either. The best that a poorly educated person can do, perhaps, is to rely on a known dealer, buy what a relative has bought, or try to negotiate a special deal. These are the very practices that many poor families follow.

Research findings also suggest that shopping practices are affected by length of exposure to urban American ways. The Puerto Ricans are an example of a newly arrived group that prefers traditional, personal stores rather than more bureaucratic, price-competitive outlets, and so do Negro migrants from the rural South. It is reasonable to expect that the longer people live in proximity to modern, depersonalized outlets, and the more they are exposed to knowledge about the urban world (through education or experience), the more often they will conduct wide-ranging searches of stores, and be price-conscious.

One reason for lower frequency of installment or mortgage debt among the poor is their ineligibility for loans under legal credit requirements. It is also possible that some poor families actually prefer not to be in debt. Among those families who are in debt for installment purchases, however, there is a large percentage of young, large families. Again, the pressing needs of this group probably account for some of the extremes of insolvency found among the poor.

The findings that support these views are:

**A. Deliberation in Buying.** In a nationwide sample of families, the poor were found to be neither higher nor lower than others on a scale of deliberation in durable goods purchases. On three deliberation activities in the scale, however, they were less active than others: They were less circumspect in seeking information, less concerned about the several features of the item and somewhat more dependent on brands. The poor families were no different from others in the extent of their enjoyment of "shopping around," an attitude found to be positively related to high deliberation.

Extent of formal education was more strongly associated with deliberation in buying durables than was income, in the study described above. The higher a person's level of education, the more he or she tended to score high on the deliberation scale. An interesting exception was in buying sport shirts, however: The less well-educated were more deliberate. Thus, the extent of deliberation may be influenced in some groups by the type of purchase.

**B. Shopping Scope.** Several findings point to the tendency of the poor to use nearby stores rather than distant ones, and to prefer personal buying situations (the peddler as an extreme form), rather than "bureaucratic," impersonal ones. The poorest housing tenants in the New York Study used independent neighborhood stores, chain stores, and peddlers more frequently than department stores or discount houses, for buying durable goods. Among these low-income families, it was the poorest who had the narrowest shopping scope. And it was those who bought from the neighborhood stores or peddlers who paid more for the goods, especially for television sets. In a Chicago study, the personal buying situation also was found to be more appealing to the upper-lower-class than to the lower-middle and upper-middle classes.

In a study of urban families in Wisconsin, the preference for independent and neighborhood stores (rather than chain stores) was related to motives concerning the store and its personnel, rather than to motives concerning price, and was more typical of rural migrants to the city than of natives or urban migrants. Caplovitz also found narrow shopping scope more typical of those who had been a short time in New York or any other city, and more typical of those with less education. He found, for example, that the Puerto Ricans in the study were narrower in shopping scope than Negroes or whites.

Another factor in shopping scope, according to Rainwater, is the discomfort felt by working-class women in "downtown" stores: ". . . [Clerks] . . . try to make you feel awful if you don't like something they have told you is nice and they would certainly think it was terrible if you told them you didn't have enough money to buy something."

**C. Information About Products.** According to several studies, formal education appears to be the key characteristic of the informed consumer. Income is slightly related to use of consumer rating magazines (the poor use them less often), but education is strongly related. Education is also clearly related to consultation of any kind of reading material (including advertisements) as a source of information about products.

These are formal channels of communication about products, and it is not surprising that those with skills and experience in formal communication are more active. Those with little education do make more use of relatives (though not necessarily more use of all other people) as a source of information about durable goods. Relatives were found to be a fruitful source of information for poorly-educated people in decisions on a model for a subsequent purchase of a durable. Other interesting differences between those with lower and higher levels of education have been found. In one study, the latter tended to buy a different model from the one seen at someone's house, whereas the former more often bought the same model. In another study, high-income persons were found to be more critical of features of goods, including obsolescence. Education apparently induces a more critical attitude and less reliance on reference groups in the choice of consumer goods.

D. *Purchase of Used Goods and Separate Items.* The tendency of low-income families in New York to buy new appliances and furniture (especially sets) was mentioned by Caplovitz, but no nationwide data are available to confirm this finding. The only nationwide figures found on the purchase of new vs. used items concern automobiles; the evidence is clear that the poor tend less often to buy new autos and more often to buy used ones.

On the topic of buying sets of furniture and other items sold as pre-selected groupings, one unpublished study indicates that low-income households purchase living room suites less often than higher income households. No difference was found in frequency of purchase of other kinds of sets by income group. There was a slight tendency for low-income respondents in that study to *prefer* suites, and some other types of sets, however, compared with respondents in higher-income households.

If lower-class consumers do tend consistently to prefer sets of furniture to separate pieces, two factors may be at work; one cultural, and one economic. There may be a true class difference in taste for the strictly harmonious room: More interest on the part of the working class. It is possible also that low-priced sets may be more numerous than separate items in furniture outlets located in poor neighborhoods.

E. *Use of Credit and Installment Buying.* Half or more of the poor families over the nation use consumer credit of some kind. (81 percent of the New York City tenants in Caplo-

vitz' study used it.) Poor families nationwide who had installment debt in 1962, however, were a smaller proportion—between one-fourth and one-third of all families below the poverty line. This proportion can be compared with half or more families with higher income who had installment debt in 1962.

Mortgage debt is also carried by a smaller proportion of the poor than of higher income families over the nation—only about one-fourth of the former owed on mortgages in 1962, compared with half or more of families in higher income brackets. Another kind of debt—money owed to doctors, dentists, and hospitals—was owed by a small proportion of poor families (about 17 percent), and this proportion is similar to that reported for families with higher incomes. It is not so much whether poor people buy on credit, however, as what it does to their financial situation that interests us. The ratio of debt to annual income is considerably higher for the poor than for others—about twice as high as the ratio among better-off families. (Also, debt is clearly responsible for a shaky financial status in many poor families, as described in the section below.)

There is conflicting evidence on whether the poor actually prefer buying on credit. On the one hand, findings from a nationwide study show that in general low-income consumers do approve of installment buying. On the other hand, the majority of Caplovitz' respondents said they thought that credit is a bad idea, although some felt that buying on time is easier than trying to save cash for larger purchases.

Only persons with high income or a college education are well informed on the real cost of credit, according to one nationwide study. Added to this fact are two others reported in the New York City study: (1) Credit costs were higher for goods bought in the very sources that many poor families use—peddlers and neighborhood dealers; and (2) A majority of the families did not know where to go if they should be cheated by a merchant. Thus, many factors seem to converge in making installment debt an especially pressing problem for the poor.

### 3. *Do Low-Income Families Budget their Incomes and Plan their Purchases?*

One proof of good financial management in families—whether or not they manage to stay solvent—suggests that poor families do not score very well. Few have many assets, and a sizable minority have negative net worth. (In other words, these families' debts exceed their assets.) Poor families who are insolvent are not complacent about it, however.

As a group, the poor save very little and are not often covered by insurance. Moreover, when they do save or invest, they tend to be less "modern" in their pattern of saving than higher income groups. Also, their views on the value of life insurance are more traditional.

The central place of installment debt in many poor families' insolvency was described earlier. Regardless of kind of debt, cultural factors may affect this proclivity to be in debt. Solvency as a moral obligation is not strong in all cultures. Thus, we might expect differences among ethnic groups in tightness of control over family finances. We might also expect changes in ethnic groups' state of solvency as they acquire education and higher-status occupations in the American setting.

Again, education is an important factor in explaining low efficiency of planning among the poor. Education can affect not only the amount of knowledge one has about financial matters, but also one's mode of thinking about money. The ability to think of money as a long-range, abstract value, rather than as concrete visible amounts, may allow educated consumers to weigh purchases and income more effectively. For the concrete thinker, it is easy to "Buy now" with a small portion of the weekly paycheck, and hard to see in advance how difficult it will be to "Pay later."

Hardly anyone would expect families on $3,000 or less income to save or buy insurance. Furthermore, since there are high proportions of families with no major earners among the poor (as high as 72 percent in the Under-$1,000 group), savings and insurance plans supported by employers or unions are often out of reach.

**A. Insolvency.** In 1962, 17 percent of those in the lowest income quintile had negative net worth. In these families, debts exceeded assets, whether those assets were savings or merely the value of their own houses and autos.

Negroes and Puerto Ricans in the New York City study were more often insolvent than whites, regardless of age and family size and good or poor consumer practices. Among Negroes, the debt component of the debt-income ratio was greater in the highest income group, while the opposite was the case for whites and Puerto Ricans. When those same groups were classified according to occupational groups, however, the racial difference decreased in importance. Negroes in white collar jobs or in business were more likely to be out of the red than those in unskilled or semiskilled jobs.

Low income families are not unconcerned about money or about the state of the family's finances, however. In the New York City study those families who were relatively insolvent were much more likely to mention financial worries than solvent families, and more likely to mention financial worries than other types.

**B. Efficiency of Planning.** In a Minneapolis study of planning, income per se was found to be less important than education in predicting "planfulness of actions" and efficiency in decision-making, in eight areas of family life. Also related to these qualities of consumership were certain attitudes characterized as developmental, modern, manipulative, prudential, and optimistic. On this basis, we would expect persons who are non-developmental (i.e., more material, traditional, fatalistic, impulsive, and pessimistic) in viewpoint to be less efficient. Among those same families, successful consumership was also related to good family agreement on roles, and good communication in the family.

A certain kind of efficiency is practiced by many workingclass wives, but it may not be the best method in the long run. According to Rainwater, the wife in the working-class family tries very hard to exert control over the outgo of cash income. Her style of control often resembles the old "sugar bowl" method, in which small amounts are doled out until the cache is gone. One workingman's wife described the process as follows:

"... if I have a little extra money then I buy something. If I don't have any money, I just don't buy any clothes for that time, or nothing extra. I like it that way. I always know where I am."

**C. Savings and Insurance.** The nationwide figures on extent of saving show that nearly 50 percent of those in the Under-$3,000 income group had no savings in 1962, compared with 28 percent or less of those in higher income groups. In the New York City study, 68 percent were found to have no savings. Low-income persons in general are also less often covered by insurance, either medical, hospital, or life insurance.

The kind of saving most often preferred by low-income families is the low-risk, non-investment type that can be easily liquidated. Those who think of investing at all think of real estate, farms, or business, rather than stocks, bonds, or insurance. Low-income persons who consider life insurance think of it as a source of funds for terminal medical and burial expenses, in addition to support for dependents in case of death.

The avowed purposes in saving differ for low-income families. Their reasons resemble the traditional view that one should try to secure the future against emergencies. Poor families who save, or would like to save, usually mention one reason—they want to save for old age or retirement. Although middle-income families mention this reason too, they also say that they want to save for purchases such as vacations or autos.

#### 4. Do Low-Income Families Meet Some Needs Through Home Production?

Evidence on home production by the poor is sparse, but what there is points to less, not more, production in two areas: food growing, and home repairs. However, since these types of home production are also affected by the extent of home ownership (known to be lower among the poor), these facts about the effect of income must be considered tentative.

In the one study consulted, it was interesting to note that those with the highest average amount saved through home production had training beyond high school (though not a college degree). Those with twelve grades of school or less, and those with a bachelor's degree or more, were below average in amounts saved through home production.

Those findings bear out our hunch that many home production activities will not be attempted, nor be successful, unless someone in the family has had special training or experience in these skills. Often, expensive tools and understanding of technical instructions are necessary for the success of a home project. This means that the poor, and the poorly educated, may be unable to improve their situation very much through this means.

#### 5. Do Low-Income Families Take Advantage of Consumer Benefits Available to The Poor?

The existence of many successful programs in legal aid, medical and dental clinics, and similar facilities, testifies to the variety of ways the poor could cut their cost of living if they took advantage of them. A summary of evaluations of so many diverse programs cannot be included in this report. Many experienced workers would agree, however, that there is need for greater coverage or utilization. The unmet health needs, the legal predicaments of the poor, and the great educational losses of poor children, are cases in point.

Whether coverage is adequate or not, the lack of full success by established programs often is justifiably attributed to apathy on the part of the people who need them most. Apparently, it is not enough to offer the service. It has to be carefully planned to conform to attitudes, schedules, and locales of potential recipients. Also, the availability of the service has to be communicated directly and simply, and the preliminaries have to be carried out quickly and smoothly. Thus, we must conclude that the poor do not use these resources to the full for easing their income situation.

### ADDING THE SCORE

How do consumer practices of the poor compare with the recommended rules of financial management? On almost every count, we have found that the poor fail to use what many would call the rational solution:

1. Although they spend most of their income on basic needs, those who buy durable goods make serious inroads on their incomes.

2. Most do not use more deliberation, consult more sources, or shop more widely, to get the best buys. Instead, many depend on known merchants or relatives for judgments of what to buy.

3. Few have savings of any size; most do not have life insurance; and only about half are covered by medical insurance.

4. It is doubtful whether many carry out home production activities to supplement cash purchases.

5. Many probably do not make full use of the programs established to provide services and goods free or at reduced rates.

Explanations of some of these apparently irrational consumer practices can be found in the special needs and characteristics of concentrated sub-groups of the poor. We have mentioned the concentration of young, large families, in connection with the problems of durable goods purchases, heavy installment debt, and insolvency. We have also mentioned the concentration of recent migrants (from within or outside the United States), in connection with findings about narrow shopping scope and preference for personal treatment in stores. A third group, one that undoubtedly includes many more of the poor, consists of those with little formal education. The lack of education shows up as an important factor in low level of knowledge about the market and the economy, and in inadequate conceptual tools for planning and making decisions.

Other kinds of explanations point to objective conditions (in sociological terms, to the social structure) that account for existing consumer practices by the poor. Three examples of such conditions are: the credit system, with its risk-cost formula and inexorable penalties that work against the poor; merchandising practices in some low-income area stores; and the fluctuating nature of employment in occupations followed by many low-income earners.

One purely economic explanation also deserves attention: the effect produced by low income, per se. The size of an income determines to some extent whether any "economies of scale" can be employed by a family. A small income has to be disbursed in smaller amounts than a large income, regardless of the different ways families now spend incomes. Thus, low-income families can less often take advantage of low prices for quantity purchases. On the other hand, some products and services are available in standard units that cannot be divided into smaller ones. Thus, large outlays (such as one month's rent in advance) are greater disturbances to a small than to a large income. Since there is less possibility for flexibility in the disbursement of a small income, there is more possibility of imbalance.

Finally, we come to the psychological explanations proposed by a number of writers for explaining consumer practices of the poor. Among the traits or values that are said to dispose the poor to behavior different from the middle and upper classes are: an attitude of fatalism; a preference for immediate gratification of impulses; a low level of aspiration and low need to achieve; an unclear view of the higher social structure; a concrete style of thinking; and over-concern with security.

Often the psychological differences attributed to the poor are discussed as if they were "givens," in much the same way as the idea of irrationality seems like a "given." However, these same differences are discussed by other writers as possible outcomes of objective social and economic conditions of the lower class.

One set of research findings indicates, for example, that a child's preference for immediate gratification is related to the absence of a father in the home. Another finding indicates that continued delay in reward can induce this same preference in children. In a like vein, it has been said that "splurges" by lower-class people are natural reactions to past deprivation and insecurity about the future. Still another writer argues that low ambition in the lower class is more apparent than real: Lower-class people have ambition, but since it is unrealistic for the poor to aspire to the same goals as the middle class, their goals only seem less ambitious. Thus, we have explanations that range from the social characteristics of the poor, through purely economic and purely psychological factors, and finally back to the environment of the poor. What does all this mean for planners of programs to improve their consumer practices?

At first glance, the problem seems to be so severe, and the explanations so deeply rooted in far-reaching social problems that it may seem futile to attack it at all. It is instructive, however, to look at some consumer programs that have been successful, and at some recommended programs based on the New York study. Examples of recent successful programs are described in some detail in the 1965 report of the President's Committee on Consumer Interest, "The Most For Their Money." Recommendations based on the New York study are found in the final chapter of Caplovitz' book.

In general, the successful programs and the recommended actions employ unorthodox, "backdoor" methods that capitalize on the very differences in the poor that we have described. They may use informal methods of education carried out locally in poor neighborhoods. They may attack problems of financial management indirectly through appeals to material interests rather than by teaching abstract principles. They may provide for intervention at the top in dealing with problems that stem from rigidities in the market itself. Finally, they may concentrate efforts on special groups of the poor who seem particularly vulnerable to buying mistakes or insolvency.

If the apparent irrationality of poor consumers can be dealt with in these realistic ways, we have some hope of softening the worst effects of a hand-to-mouth existence.

ADDENDUM

For the interested reader, Table 1 reveals some of the sharp contrasts in spending behavior by the several selected income levels. This also may be helpful in generating discussion or as a starting place for the reader to develop additional data.

TABLE 1. Survey of Consumer Expenditures, 1960–61: Average Annual Expenditures, Income, and Savings of Nonfarm Families of Two or More Persons by Annual Money Income after Taxes

| Item | All Families of 2 or More Persons | Annual Money Income After Taxes | | | | | |
|---|---|---|---|---|---|---|---|
| | | Under $2,000 | $2,000-$2,999 | $3,000-$5,999 | $6,000-$9,999 | $10,000-$14,999 | $15,000 and over |
| Number of families in sample | 9,930 | 664 | 872 | 3,829 | 3,437 | 873 | 255 |
| Estimated number of families in universe (000's) | 43,626 | 3,115 | 4,039 | 17,226 | 14,670 | 3,539 | 1,039 |
| Percent of families | 100.0 | 7.1 | 9.3 | 39.5 | 33.6 | 8.1 | 2.4 |
| Expenditures for current consumption | $5,654 | $1,878 | $2,809 | $4,608 | $6,852 | $9,704 | $14,661 |
| Food and beverages | 1,470 | 599 | 846 | 1,257 | 1,759 | 2,332 | 3,044 |
| Tobacco | 103 | 46 | 68 | 98 | 123 | 124 | 143 |
| Housing, total | 1,622 | 592 | 879 | 1,345 | 1,931 | 2,636 | 4,381 |
| Shelter, fuel, light, refrigeration and water | 992 | 411 | 601 | 851 | 1,169 | 1,510 | 2,311 |
| Household operations | 321 | 103 | 151 | 249 | 374 | 579 | 1,227 |
| Housefurnishings and equipment | 303 | 78 | 126 | 242 | 380 | 531 | 790 |
| Clothing, clothing materials, and services | 585 | 123 | 220 | 431 | 742 | 1,148 | 1,795 |
| Personal care | 163 | 57 | 91 | 139 | 196 | 261 | 347 |
| Medical care | 376 | 178 | 229 | 313 | 440 | 605 | 906 |
| Recreation | 229 | 39 | 75 | 164 | 294 | 481 | 686 |
| Reading and education | 112 | 23 | 33 | 69 | 132 | 282 | 540 |
| Automobile purchase and operation | 785 | 125 | 271 | 658 | 1,006 | 1,405 | 1,609 |
| Other transportation | 84 | 27 | 39 | 56 | 91 | 181 | 480 |
| Other expenditures | 125 | 69 | 58 | 78 | 138 | 249 | 730 |
| Gifts and contributions | 289 | 50 | 91 | 183 | 338 | 610 | 1,723 |
| Personal insurance | 343 | 47 | 89 | 239 | 449 | 705 | 1,228 |
| Money income before taxes | 6,957 | 1,444 | 2,593 | 4,983 | 8,565 | 13,598 | 27,820 |
| Money income after taxes | 6,177 | 1,425 | 2,521 | 4,597 | 7,594 | 11,716 | 21,933 |
| Other money receipts | 85 | 102 | 42 | 96 | 57 | 98 | 352 |
| Net change in assets and liabilities | 207 | -322 | -254 | -82 | 286 | 943 | 4,738 |
| Accounting balancing difference | -231 | -126 | -172 | -255 | -274 | -148 | -65 |
| Average family size | 3.6 | 2.7 | 3.1 | 3.5 | 3.8 | 4.1 | 3.8 |
| Percent nonwhite families | 11 | 27 | 20 | 12 | 5 | 4 | 1 |
| Percent homeowners | 60 | 48 | 46 | 50 | 70 | 79 | 88 |
| Percent auto owners | 82 | 38 | 55 | 83 | 93 | 96 | 96 |

◆ SOURCE: "Levels of Living Among the Poor," Survey of Consumer Expenditures, 1960–61, BLS (U.S. Dept. of Labor), Report No. 238-12, August 1965.

# D. Fashion and Culture

## 17. The Significance of Fashion

PAUL H. NYSTROM

The general interest in fashion has increased enormously during recent years. This interest, formerly believed to have been the result of rising incomes and standards of living, is apparently unaffected by business adversity. It continued as strong after 1929 as before. It will undoubtedly continue to grow in years to come.

### THE IMPORTANCE OF FASHION IN MODERN BUSINESS

Fashion, once the pursuit of the wealthy and aristocratic few, is now followed by the masses. In the past fashion was considered solely as a quality of goods at the highest price. It is now a necessary factor of goods at every price. It is as essential to the merchandise in a 5 and 10 cent store as to the wares of the most exclusive specialty shop. Excellence of material and the highest quality of workmanship mean little in present-day demand unless also clearly marked with current fashion.

Fashion is one of the greatest forces in present-day life. It determines both the character and the direction of consumption. Fashion makes men shave every day, grow moustaches, cut their hair in certain ways, wear certain colors in hats, clothing and shoes, certain shapes in collars, four-in-hand neckties, trousers creased, and low shoes all the year round. For women it changes the tint of the face powder, the odor of the perfume, the wave of the hair,

the position of the waist line, the length of the skirt, the color of the clothes, and the height of the heels. Fashion sometimes makes people wear more clothes and sometimes less. Fashion is a more important factor than wear and tear in displacing furniture, kitchen utensils, radio instruments, and automobiles. Fashion causes all of these changes and, at the same time, makes people like it. To be out of fashion is, indeed, to be out of the world.

Business succeeds when it goes with fashion but fails when it goes against the tide. Millions of dollars are wasted yearly by manufacturers and retailers who try to stem the trends of fashion by offering goods that are not in fashion and have not the slightest chance of becoming the fashion. Even during the depths of business depressions, goods that are in fashion are in demand. The only goods that sell during such periods, as we have recently seen, are the goods that are decidedly in fashion. When the purchasing power declines, the desire to secure the utmost of good fashion follows prices downward. Goods that are not in fashion cannot be sold in either good or bad times. Indeed, such goods cannot be given away.

Fashion is the result of powerful forces in human nature. Foolish and shallow-minded people have laughed at fashion but the wiser ones have tried to find explanations and to understand. The influence of fashion over all of us is such as to make certain designs in goods of common use seem beautiful at one time and hideous at others. It is hard to believe now that the hoop skirt, the bustle, and the leg-of-mutton sleeve were once considered very charming and highly appropriate. No doubt the

‡‡ SOURCE: Reprinted by permission from *Fashion Merchandising* by Paul H. Nystrom (New York: The Ronald Press Company, 1932), pp. 31–39.

present fashions will in time seem just as ridiculous and even as hideous as these past styles seem to us now.

The subject of fashion is therefore of utmost importance, not only from the standpoint of the consumer who follows it, not only from the standpoint of designers and business organizations that cater to it, but also from the standpoint of the student of human nature.

## DEFINITIONS

The first step to clear thinking about any subject is clear definition of the terms used. There is an unusually special need for such definition when dealing with the subject of fashion, for fashion, style, and design are terms that are constantly confused by most people. There is a world of difference in meaning among these three terms, but even the dictionaries have not, so far, made adequate distinctions. Our first step in the understanding of fashion and how it works will be taken by distinguishing between it and style.

*A Style is a Characteristic or Distinctive, Artistic Expression or Presentation.* A style is a fact of art. Thus we have styles of architecture, of sculpture, of painting, of literature, of drama, or of music. Similarly we have characteristic or distinctive conceptions, that is, styles, in the applied arts such as· in textiles, in dress, in interior decoration, and in advertising. There are styles in millinery and in automobiles, in dancing and in playing golf. There are styles in conversation, in gesturing, in pronunciation, and in penmanship.

*A Fashion, on the Other Hand, is a Style Accepted and Used by People.* A fashion is always based on some particular style. But not every style is a fashion. A fashion is a fact of social psychology. A style is a creation of an artist or a designer. A fashion is a result of social emulation and esthetic imitation. A style may be new or old. It may be beautiful or ugly. It may be good or bad. A style is still a style even if it never receives the slightest acceptance or even approval. A style does not become a fashion until it gains some popular use, and it remains a fashion only so long as it is so accepted.

*A Design is a Particular or Individual Interpretation or Version of a Style.* A style may be expressed in a great many designs, all different, yet all related because they are in the same style.

It is clearly possible, then, for a style to become a fashion repeatedly. Thus every important historic style such as the Greek, the Roman, the Renaissance, the Louis XV, or the Empire, has at one time or another been a fashion. There are in every field of both pure and applied art countless possible styles. There are large textbooks and enormous encyclopaedias describing the styles in such limited fields as interior decoration, furniture, architecture, and dress. Every library and museum is a repository of the records of styles.

Obviously, you and I as consumers, and the business people who supply us, must of necessity be interested in fashions rather than in styles. As consumers we confine most of our purchases to goods that approximate current fashions. Not to do so would brand us as being queer, and social interrelationships are today so interlaced that not only our friendships but our very jobs depend upon our being and looking normal and not queer. Yet we preserve our individuality because that invaluable quality of good taste helps us at every stage to bridge what is in fashion with what is individually beautiful and becoming.

Let us try to define two or three other terms in common use related to the subject of fashion. One of these is mode and another is vogue. These words, *mode and vogue, are synonyms of fashion.* Both imply a wave-like social acceptance of some manner of action, some design or style. A *fad is a miniature fashion* usually running for a shorter time and usually applying to some unimportant matter or detail in style of apparel, home furnishings, or other articles of use in which the quality of art is present and important.

From henceforth let us think of styles as products of art and of fashions as social acceptances of styles. This distinction will help us tremendously in understanding what fashion really is and how it works. We shall be able to see at once that current fashions are styles that for the time being have obtained public acceptance. We shall also see that there are at any given time but a few fashions. Finally, we will be able to agree that these fashions are constantly changing.

## CHARACTER OF FASHION MOVEMENTS

In this constant change of fashions, however, there is a definite orderliness of rise, of culmination and decline, a wave-like movement so regular, in fact, that it may be readily traced and even predicted with a fair degree of accuracy. There are already a few successful business concerns, those who have learned to distinguish between style as such and fashion, who are concentrating all of their efforts on fashions, who are able to forecast the coming fashions in their lines of business with marked success and with great profit to themselves as well as satisfaction to their customers.

## DIFFICULTY OF CHANGING OR INFLUENCING THE DIRECTION OF FASHIONS

It was formerly believed, and the view is still common, that any style, if launched with enough prestige and promoted intensively by advertising and display, could be made a successful fashion. There is no business fallacy which has wasted so much energy and money as this one. We now know that while styles may be created by the thousands, the final acceptance which determines the fashion rests with the consumer who has in recent years shown remarkably strong tendencies to follow certain fashion trends rather than others and to resist all prestige sales promotion, no matter how forcefully applied, to trends in other directions. If there were any kings or dictators of fashion in the past, there are certainly not any that are making a success of it today, except those who are able to forecast what consumers are going to want and then give it to them.

Success in design or style creation today requires a great deal more than merely artistic ability and the prestige of great names. Style creation, to stand any chance of fashion acceptance, must not only offer beautiful designs but must also mold its designs to a proper expression of the spirit of the times. A keen and sensitive appreciation of this spirit is a necessary foundation for fashion merchandising. The style that is most likely to become a fashion is one that expresses what the people most desire, that touches the sympathies and moves the imaginations of the public. To do this the style must be timely or modern as well as artistic.

There is undoubtedly a great deal of current dissatisfaction with the artistic qualities of goods now on our markets. Much of this dissatisfaction is largely due to a lack of clear comprehension on the part of designers and dealers of the importance and power of current trends in consumer taste. In other words, a great many artists as well as those who make and sell their creations are failing to meet the requirements of current fashion. They still apparently have the faith that a fashion can be made out of any style.

## WIDESPREAD MODERN INTEREST IN FASHION

There is a fundamental reason for the widespread consumer interest in fashion. It may be explained by reference to the part it plays in your and in my life. We are all members of society. We all participate in greater or less degrees in the material and artistic advantages provided by this age. We not only participate but we must also cooperate or at least go along with the major movements of our time. Our surroundings, our equipment, and our furnishings in some measure represent our contacts with the artistic conceptions and the tempo of our age. Since fashion is essentially the current, artistic expression of this spirit, we accept it just as we accept the automobile, the airplane, and the radio for their utilities. Fashion is the social, esthetic representation of present life. Fashion is the expression of mass taste, just as law and its administration is the expression of the mass desire for order.

## FASHION AND INDIVIDUALITY

This does not mean that people must or do slavishly accept specific current designs and styles, either in apparel, home furnishings, or in domestic architecture, without exception or without modification. Even a deep interest in fashion does not, of course, exclude the expression of individuality or the opportunity for the development of individual taste. Indeed, the very essence of the philosophy underlying modern fashion movements is the scope that it gives to individuality. There is nothing so tiresome to modern taste as the unimaginative, literal, mass use of certain styles under any or all circumstances by enormous numbers of people.

There is, indeed, both the need and the opportunity for the development of individuality within the more or less generalized but constantly changing molds set by fashion. In every item of merchandise affected by style there are elements that must of necessity conform to current standards of good taste, and that means fashion. But there are likewise the individual artistic adaptations which, while they do not carry the user beyond the parallels of fashion, produce the ever-changing interest that is individuality.

## BUSINESS EXECUTIVES WHO NEED TO KNOW HOW TO WORK WITH FASHION

It is for these reasons that a correct understanding of fashion and how to work with it is obviously of importance to every business owner, executive, and employee who has any constructive activity to carry on in the production or marketing of fashion goods. The artist or designer who combines beauty and individuality with current fashions in the creation of styles also needs the facts concerning fashions and their trends. In this group may be mentioned the factory manager who executes the designs in such detail as to convey the precise feeling of the fashions; the salesman of the firm who must be able to discuss the fashionableness as well as other qualities of their merchandise in intelligent terms; the retail store buyer who wants to be assured that the stock purchased and carried in his store shall be what his customers will want; and, finally, the salespeople of the store, who should have at least a rudimentary acquaintance with the nature of fashion and the way it works.

Every one who sells fashion goods needs to be able to describe the fashion features of his or her goods accurately. Every salesperson should be properly equipped with the current vocabulary of style and fashion terms. Every salesperson needs sufficient knowledge of present fashions to be able to make his or her statements about the goods to customers with confidence and authority. It would also be helpful if salespeople had sufficient knowledge of the technique of observing fashion changes so as to make satisfactory observations and reports to their employers and store heads on precisely what styles their customers seem most interested in and thereby help to carry on the store's necessary fashion analysis.

The advertising manager, his assistants, the copywriters and those who make the illustrations for use in advertising, as well as the display men who prepare window and interior store displays, need continuously authoritative information on present fashions and their trends. Nothing could be more harmful either to a manufacturing or to a retail organization than advertising or display which presents inaccurate information on current fashions. Errors made by advertising writers in such a simple matter as the names of specific styles are laughable to a sophisticated outside world and pathetic to business. In a recent advertisement of a well-known department store a chair was described as "Queen Anne," but the illustration accompanying clearly showed "Chippendale" characteristics. A lady called at a metropolitan store and asked for a Queen Anne mirror. The salesman replied, "Queen Anne is a leg, not a mirror!"

Statements purporting to be true as to current fashions when not in accord with actual facts are, of course, as dishonest as misstatements in the descriptions of other qualities of the goods. Most progressive, reputable business concerns have long held to the principle that a fabric made of a mixture of wool and cotton may not be described as "all wool," but must be described as a mixture and preferably in exact percentages of each kind of fibre. Similarly, all reputable businesses now insist that advertising statements should accurately state whether colors are fast or not, and, if possible, what degree of fastness may be expected. Any departures from this principle of truth in statement as applied to such points as materials, construction, or fastness of dye would not now be countenanced for a moment, but many concerns otherwise proud of their integrity frequently permit statements that articles of style are leading fashions when they are not, and in some cases have not the slightest chance of ever becoming fashions.

Accuracy of statement as applied to fashions is as necessary to modern business as accuracy in other respects and will come when it is recognized that there is not only no excuse for misstatement but great harm in such dishonesty. Fashion is, as we shall see, objective. There need be no guesswork as to what is in fashion. Consumers who are fooled by retailers' or manufacturers' statements are as likely to resent this as any dishonesty in statement about materials of construction.

# 18. How Predictable Are Fashion and Other Product Life Cycles?

## CHESTER R. WASSON

No aspect of marketing is so uncertain as the acceptance of new products, particularly those with a fashion element. Yet product introduction and fashion itself are such basic necessities for continued success that the gamble must be taken repeatedly. Clearly, a sound means of forecasting the onset of any popularity wave is needed, of predicting its course, and of recognizing the earliest symptoms of a forthcoming decline. Market planning needs a fundamental explanatory theory of the fashion cycle which would explain the clearly observable, ceaseless fluctuations and their subsequent course. The explanation can be sound only if based on known tendencies of human behavior and on the way human motives, both innate and socially conditioned, cause people to react to the kind of stimulus called a new product. To be useful the theory also must indicate at the minimum the general direction of the next fluctuation and detect the timing of at least the first signs of a new swing.

The thesis of this paper is that already a suitable framework exists for such a theory. It can be drawn from the documented results of product acceptance research when interpreted in the light of human reaction to product offerings and the social psychology of perception and motivation. Furthermore, the theory is at least testable for some kinds of products and corresponds with the results of some proprietary research, unfortunately not published. If

valid, this theory is the direct antithesis of the popular myth of "created" fashion.

## THE MYTH OF CREATED FASHION

That fashion is a synthetic creation of the seller is an idea so entrenched that even marketing professionals are often blind to the observably low batting average of those who attempt such "creation." Even within the area of women's apparel, the fact most obvious to those who follow the news of new offerings is the diversity of their direction and the large numbers of "dictated" designs which fall by the wayside after every Paris showing. However, fashion is not limited to women's apparel, nor confined to matters of commercial exploitation.

There are fashions in politics and in business decision methods as marked as the documented cycles in styles of clothing and architecture.[1] A colleague once demonstrated similar cycles in religious interest in a study of church publications, and followers of the stock market are aware of the constantly changing identity of the "glamor" stocks. Whether on the dance floor, in the dress shop, or in the business conference room, the "in" thing changes with the calendar.

No seller can afford to ignore the state of the fashion cycle. Chrysler's misreading of the trend in taste caused real trouble for the firm on at least three occasions: with the 1934 Air-

◆ SOURCE: Reprinted by permission from the *Journal of Marketing*, (National Quarterly Publication of the American Marketing Association) Vol. 32, July 1968, pp. 36–43.

[1] Chester R. Wasson, *The Strategy of Marketing Research* (New York: Appleton-Century-Crofts, 1964), pp. 67–77.

flow Chrysler and DeSoto, with the unpopular early 1950s designs, and with the "lean look" models of 1962. Ford's later correct reading of the trend gave the firm the well-publicized triumph of the Mustang introduction. In fact, even a superficial knowledge of the successes and failures of design introduction which dot the history of every major auto maker should long ago have convinced everyone that human behavior is not subject to the easy manipulation assumed by the created-fashions myth. The acceptance of a fashion is but one aspect of the process of new product acceptance and rests on the same principles of individual and social behavior.

## FASHION, PRODUCT ACCEPTANCE, AND HUMAN BEHAVIOR

Both fashions and fads are, of course, successful new product introductions. The distinction between the two is generally defined on an *ex post facto* basis—on the nature of their acceptance cycle. Fashions are generally thought to have an initially slower rise to popularity, a plateau of continuing popularity lacking in most fads, and a slow, rather than abrupt decline typical of the fad. (See Figures 1*a* and 1*b*.) The acceptance cycle of a fashion is thus considered the same as the accepted theoretical course of the normal product life cycle (Figure 1*a*). Such an empirical after-the-fact basis for distinction, however, deprives any theory of most of its potential utility. It cannot be used for rational market planning. To be useful the theory must distinguish fads from other new products *in advance* on the basis of measurable product attributes, which explain why a market development period might be unnecessary and why acceptance disappears at the very peak of the market. If such an explanation is possible, it should be possible to identify and predict in advance another class of products: a class which requires little or nothing in the way of early market development, but rises in an active growth market from the moment of introduction and then remains popular for long periods. (See Figure 1*c*.) Those who have observed any fashion-oriented market will also recognize the need to explain another related

phenomenon with the same theory—the *classic* —the style which is never out of style for its market segment and is rarely the "rage."

To be really useful for product planning, a product acceptance theory should be based on known tendencies of individual and social behavior and encompass in a single model an explanation of:

1. Why and how any new product gains acceptance, and why about half of the seemingly well-screened and well-researched products fail.[2]

2. Why some products must pass through a slowly accelerating period of market development of some length before sales catch fire whereas others zoom to early popularity from the start.

3. Why some products succeed in attainment of a relatively solid niche in the culture, why the popularity of others tends to fluctuate, and why the popularity of fads collapses at their very sales peak.

4. How and why classics exist in a fashion environment.

The behavioral basis for such an explanation starts with the managerial economics view of a product as a compromise bundle of attributes perceived by buyers as an inseparable set of sources of satisfaction and also of some offsetting dissatisfactions for times for a set of desires.[3] To gain the satisfactions, the buyer must pay some price—he must sacrifice some measure of time, money, and/or effort. Whether he moves toward possession of this offering depends on his personal evaluation of the net gain in satisfaction its possession will bring.

Expressed in these terms, an operant psychologist would recognize the purchase as an *approach-avoidance* reaction. Satisfactions sought cause the buyer to approach the offering and seek its possession. The offering, however, includes a repelling force—the avoidance factors of the various prices exacted to obtain those satisfactions. Part of the price is monetary, part is search effort, and an important part can be the compromise enforced by the nature of product design—the denial of satisfaction for some of the elements in the desire-set whose appeasement is sought.

[2] *Management of New Products* (Chicago: Booz, Allen & Hamilton, 1960).

[3] Edward H. Chamberlin, *Theory of Monopolistic Competition*, 8th edition (Cambridge, Mass.: Harvard University Press, 1962), Appendix F, pp. 275–281; Chester R. Wasson, *The Economics of Man-* *agerial Decision* (New York: Appleton-Century-Crofts, 1965), pp. 55–87; and Chester R. Wasson, Frederick D. Sturdivant, and David McConaughy, *Competition and Human Behavior* (New York: Appleton-Century-Crofts, 1968), pp. 4–25.

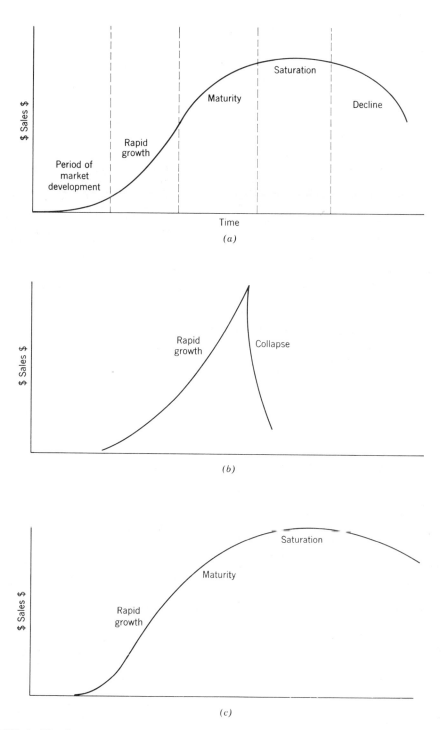

FIG. 1. The three types of product cycles. (a) The theoretical normal life cycle of a fashion or other new product. (b) Usual trajectory of a fad. (c) Apparent life cycle pattern of some new products for which the market seemed to be waiting.

### Product Compromise and the Hierarchy of Motives

The buyer usually seeks the simultaneous satisfaction of a set of several motivating desires in making a purchase. In practice, the product offering can seldom satisfy all at the same time and must strike some compromise in the kind and degree of satisfactions offered. Any offering will thus satisfy some buyers well, others partially; and some, perhaps not all, may even yield negative satisfaction for still others. The dress may be bought for physical warmth, figure enhancement, and freedom from restriction at the same time—attributes which cannot be equally well satisfied in the same design. The successful physician may long for the qualities of a prestige car but desire something sufficiently inconspicuous to avoid offending patients at billing time. Thus, the buyer must normally compromise between the ideal set of satisfactions sought and the reality of product design potentials. Nearly every purchase involves some compromise. This is evidenced by the fact that few, if any, products are immune to the inroads of differentiated offerings. Motivational compromise holds the key to an understanding of fashion oscillation when

viewed as an extension of the knowledge of the hierarchical nature of motives and their dynamic character.

The intensity of any one desire varies over time within an individual, and, at any given moment, some motives gain priority over others. Even such basic motives as hunger and appetite dominate only until satisfied. As the meal is consumed, the drive to eat is extinguished and some other drive assumes top priority. This second drive was already inherently present before the meal but was not evoked until the hunger was appeased. The hierarchical nature of the motivating drives has long been recognized.[4] Individuals respond most actively to those stimuli that promise satisfaction of those most highly valued drives which are at the moment least well satisfied and at the same time felt to be important. Every satisfactory purchase thus becomes in time the initiator of a search for a somewhat different offering to satisfy newly felt drives. Thus, this continual restructuring of the motivational hierarchy gives the basis for a model

[4] A. H. Maslow, "A Dynamic Theory of Human Motivation," *Psychological Review*, Vol. 50 (March, 1963), pp. 370–396.

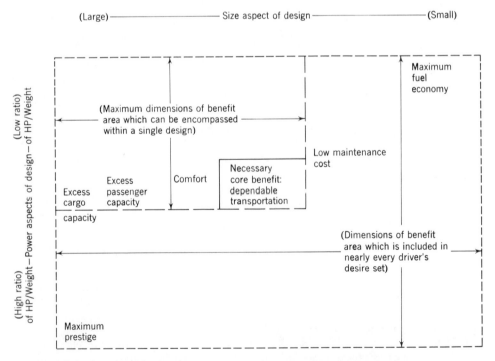

FIG. 2. The automobile design puzzle: How to get as much of what the driver wants in a single design?

explaining fashion oscillation and furnishes a framework for prediction of its new direction:

The popularity of design attributes in a given utility-bundle will oscillate because no one design can encompass in full measure all of the attributes in the desire-set. The oscillation will tend to be polar, swinging from one extreme to the opposite, because the satisfaction-yield span of any one design will extinguish the very drives which led to its adoption and bring to the fore those drives least well fulfilled by the design.

Consider the example of the automobile design problem (Figure 2) and the oscillations of popular approval between the large and massive and the compact, relatively economical. The 1955 designs fulfilled all of the drives associated with massive appearance and power. In developing these designs, the automobile industry had to leave some other drives less well satisfied—for example, low cost of ownership and maintenance and such ease-of-use aspects as parking and roadability. Once most drivers had acquired the highly ornamented mammoths they desired, attention began to focus on the drives whose satisfaction had been neglected, and size became an avoidance factor for many. Buyers became attracted by models offering high gasoline mileage, low physical and temporal depreciation, and ease of parking and handling. The sales of foreign makes which offered such attributes in abundance began a climb, and slowed down only when Detroit developed its own compacts in 1960. But the fickle customer, having a free choice of offerings giving most of what he desired, began to yearn again for the attributes associated with size, and the cycle restarted. By 1965, he was buying "compact" models almost as large as the 1955 "big" cars.

However, the composition of the desire-set varies so much from one person to another that the explanation needs one further element to account for the completeness of most new-fashion adoption and the rapidity of its spread. That element is furnished by that human drive for social approval—the desire to be "in the swim." The result is an almost universal tendency toward overadoption. Overadoption is painfully apparent with every extreme swing in the feminine fashion silhouette—the bandy-legged adopted mini-skirts which could only reveal physical deficiencies of the wearer. Overadoption became quite obvious in business management when organizations replaced an effective $300-a-month clerk with a $3,000-per-month computer which often did the clerk's job less efficiently. Overadoption has been documented in the studies of rural sociologists who found farmers adopting machinery which was uneconomic for their scale of operation.[5] The desire for social approval thus speeds adoption, but at the price of leading many to overadoption—to adoption of offerings which do not satisfy their desires well. The result is a considerable market segment which quickly develops an avoidance reaction to the fashion and triggers a decline from the peak.

The three principles of product acceptance—inherent purchase compromise, the changing hierarchy of motivation, and the tendency toward overadoption—furnish a necessary and sufficient explanation of the swings of fashion. However, they leave unexplained the existence of the classic—the style whose changes are minimal, but which remains always in the range of the acceptable. No theory of fashion can be adequate which omits an explanation of the classic and its appeal to a minority market which does not conform to major swings of fashion.

## THE CLASSIC

The changeless, always acceptable classic is found in every recognized area of fashion. A woman can always feel comfortable in a tailored suit with a skirt line close to the knees. In automobiles, designs similar to the postwar Loewy-designed Studebaker still find a ready market around the world. The values placed by buyers on some security issues respond little to the gyrations of the bulk of those listed on the Big Board. Beige and off-white colors always sell well in automobiles and house paints. Such classics occasionally become the reigning fashion, but seldom are they "the rage."

What makes a classic? Observation seems to indicate that all classics are midpoint compromises and their buyers either have a special kind of personality or are prospects seeking only a few of the core attributes in the bundle for sale. The classic automobile design is neither starkly spartan nor highly ornamented; it is roomy but not gargantuan. The classic color is not found in the "hot" red end of the spectrum nor at the icy blue extreme; it is moderately pleasing but not conspicuous. The

---

[5] Everett Rogers, *The Diffusion of Innovations* (New York: The Free Press, 1962), pp. 142–145.

classic gives some measure of satisfaction to nearly all of the desire-set of drives, and probably does so at the expense of complete satisfaction of any drives except those at the core of product's physical functions. The classic buyer, then, has to be a person seeking only the core function attributes (such as convenient transportation in a Volkswagen) or one who recognizes that compromise is necessary in any case and who has chosen a compromise least likely to develop over time. He most certainly must be an individual who does not value highly the satisfaction of the drive for new experience. Such a consumer is a poor prospect for any fad, but may well be an excellent early-market customer for innovations of major functional import which others would be slow to accept, since he feels little need for complete conformity. If so, he is important in the early adoption of those products which are slow to catch on at first. Certainly, the differences in the speed of acceptance of various kinds of offerings is one of the most obvious puzzles of new product introduction which must be explained.

## DIFFERENCES IN THE EARLY ACCEPTANCE PATTERN AND THEIR EXPLANATION

As already indicated, some products follow the standard conceptual curve of the product life cycle, but others, particularly fads, leapfrog the early market development phase of this curve with a rocket-like ascent to popularity. Clearly, the marketing mix must differ with the kind of sales acceleration likely to be experienced. Also, different levels of resource commitment are needed for the product which undergoes an extended period of slowly developing sales and those which attain their market potential early. When black-and-white television became a commercial reality, even fly-by-night electronic firms could get a profitable market share, and those who knew how to build on their early success could and did carve out a permanent market niche. Waiting out the ten long years until color television sales hit the growth phase, however, required the resources of an RCA.

A great many pairs of seeming anomalies can be cited from every kind of marketing operation. Soluble coffee existed for over a generation before World War II; and even when wartime developments brought its price down, six years were needed to develop the

market potential. Frozen orange juice, another wartime beneficiary, rose from scratch to peak market in three years, as fast as facilities could be developed. The astonishing benefits of hybrid corn yields were not sufficient to get more than 6% of the farmers interested during the first six years on the market, although little else is planted today. However, another farm improvement—2-4-D and related insecticides were so avidly sought by farmers upon their release after the war that they became a real threat to health. Some textbooks take years to gain acceptance of the approach championed, yet Samuelson's *Economics* rose to quick dominance of the elementary course in colleges.

The anomaly disappears when we examine the value an adopter perceives in any product new or otherwise. To the purchaser, a product is only one element in the use-system which is the real source of the satisfaction of the desire-set. Products deliver their potential satisfactions only in the context of some established set of procedural habits organized around their use. Seed corn yields the sought-after crop only when procured, planted, cultivated, harvested and stored in a carefully planned and well-learned system of habitual practices. Television yields entertainment only when manipulated and viewed in another set of habit patterns.

The development of most habit patterns is a painful—or at least annoying—process for most of us. The extinction of one habit system leading to a satisfactory result and its replacement of another is even more so, as anyone who has gone from a three-speed manual automobile shift to a four-speed can testify. The degree to which a product offering involves habit pattern relearning will thus slow down its adoption. Conversely, innovative products which can simply replace old ones using the same set of procedures, or the same set simplified, should gain ready acceptance.

Good examples of products fitting neatly into existing procedures are the new insecticides, black-and-white television, and frozen orange juice. The new insecticides were applied by the same spray methods, with a similar timing, as the ones they displaced. They simply delivered a noticeably higher level of satisfaction—greater kill over a broader spectrum of pests. Black-and-white television entertained in the same way the movies did, by sitting and viewing a picture, but it avoided many nuisance steps—additional cost for every show, problems of travel, parking and getting tickets, and finding a desired seat position. Black-and-white television, too, simply delivered more value in the same system. (Eventually, of course, adoption of TV changed family living patterns. But such pattern changes were not a pre-condition for adoption.) Frozen orange juice fitted into kitchens long used to canned goods; the fact that it was frozen fitted into established perceptions of frozen foods being the equivalents of fresh ones. These products required no substantial learning of new habits or relearning of old. By contrast, hybrid seed corn, color television, and instant coffee all involved learning of some sort.

Any new offering can pose the problem of one or more of three kinds of learning:

1. Learning of a new sequence of motor habits (as in changing over from a three-speed shift to a four-speed, or from a wringer to an automatic washer);

2. Learning to perceive new benefits as valuable and thus worth paying for (as in learning to appreciate the cornering qualities offered by the small sports car);

3. Learning to perceive one's role in the use of the product as of less importance (as in the acceptance of an automatic transmission).

The acceptance of the use of hybrid seed required the learning of both a new sequential element and of the perception of relative value. Before its adoption, the farmer usually saved some of the better quality of the previous year's crop and replanted it. The use of hybrid seed meant the complete disposal of the crop and the repurchase of seed each year. (The farm journals of the period ran many an article warning farmers not to replant seed from hybrid crops.) Moreover, the seed he bought cost several times as much per bushel as the farmer received for the crop he sold. This resulted in a real value-perception problem.

The acceptance of color television in 1955 required no change in motor or other use-habits, but did involve a substantial change in value perception. It required seeing that the mere addition of color to the picture was worth hundreds of dollars—at a time when Technicolor movies had never achieved use in more than a minority of films. Color also deprived the viewer of the satisfaction of closure—the supplying of missing details himself. Psychologically, successful closure heightened the satisfaction gained, and has probably always been an elements of successful enter-

tainment. The double-meaning joke gets its whole point from the use of closure.

Soluble coffee certainly simplified the brewing process and required little in the way of motor learning. Once wartime experience had reduced its cost, any problem disappeared. But soluble coffee downgraded the homemaker's role; it required her to see her role in relation to mealmaking as less important. Coffee brewing is susceptible to individual skill, and many housewives pride themselves on their coffee. Acceptance of soluble coffee required admission that the housewife's kitchen role was less vital to family happiness than it had been. Is it any coincidence that the use of soluble increased with the growing acceptance of the housewife as a major contributor to the family's *outside* income?

The overnight successes of radically new products like Samuelson's *Economics* are explainable as examples of products filling a missing link in an already developed system. They are products for which the market has been waiting. Economists began to pay increasing attention to the macro aspect of economic theory in the early 1930s. By 1946, when Samuelson's first edition was published, many economists were orienting their courses entirely in this direction. Since no satisfactory texts were available, a well-done text, as Samuelson's was, could hardly help but succeed. Rubber tractor tires provide a similar example. Mechanized farming became well established on the better-managed farms, but the steel-tired tractors compacted the soil, could not be run over paved roads, and did not always furnish the desired traction. Once a satisfactory tire was developed, the steel-wheeled tractor disappeared overnight. The supermarket was also a missing link in a developing food shopping and storing system. The automobile had widened the shopping range of the family; the need to park it called for a single stop. In addition, ownership of mechanical refrigerators was wide enough to eliminate the daily shopping trip. All that was needed was the foresight of a few independent entrepreneurs. Even though such missing link products do require learning of elements not required by the products they displace, the learning process is complete by the time of their introduction.

The rate of early-adoption acceleration is thus seen as contingent on the degree of learning required to accept and properly use any new offering. Both learning-content and attribute-compromise analyses are feasible, rendering the proposed model of product adoption speed and of fashion fluctuation subject to test and confirmation.

## THE EVIDENCE OF TESTABILITY

A model is valid if it has utility for prediction. The main recommendation for the proposed model is its testability—parts of it rather easily—and the fact that it is in harmony with some known successful proprietary unpublished private research predictions. Three kinds of evidence as to its validity can be cited:

1. Such known proprietary research clearly demonstrates that taste and fashion are predictable ahead of promotion and sales, and even in advance of design, on the basis of analysis of consumer reaction.
2. It is possible to cite at least a few examples of situations in which a simple learning-content analysis would have greatly improved otherwise extensive research on product acceptance.
3. Some limited observation and research has proved successful in prediction of a fashion cycle.

### Sensing the Trend in Taste Ahead of Introduction

A sizable body of proprietary research has established the fact that rather simple, carefully administered checks of consumer reaction can reveal in advance which of an equally-promoted group of designs will succeed and which will fail. Dilman M. K. Smith[6] has sketched some of the results of successful Opinion Research studies in this area, some going back over three decades. The author of this article himself was able to develop a very simple ahead-of-the-season measure of relative demand in a line of dresses over 20 years ago —a test still in routine use by the employer for whom he developed it. A research director for a maker of permanent waves was able to alert his firm to a change in hair style tastes months before the change began to show up in beauty parlors and thus permitted a successful effort to buttress the firm's market position. Even more relevant was an unpublished Opinion Research triumph: the development of a new, instantly successful rug weave based on a revelation of an unsatisfactory consumer

compromise. When research showed that housewives liked the texture of velvet rugs but were repelled by such a weave's tendency to show tracks, the firm advised a client to find a velvet weave which was trackless. After considerable prodding, designers came up with the sculptured wilton, which took off on a typical fast growth curve when introduced.

Unfortunately, understanding of consumer product acceptance has not gained much from this private research, since only fragments of a minor part could land in footnotable publications. The rest remains hidden in the files of those who pay for it and confined to conversations among a few research analysts. Confirmation of the learning content aspect of the proposed model, fortunately, does not always require access to any confidential data.

### Learning Content and Prediction

The author has shown at length[7] elsewhere that use-systems learning requirements can be determined easily by means of simple comparison of flow diagrams—one diagram for the current means of obtaining the satisfaction desired and one for the system which would be the setting for use of the new product. Such a comparison quickly reveals both the advantages and the avoidance factors involved in adoption of the new. One need read only the preparation instructions on a pouch of dehydrated soup to discover why this thoroughly-researched product was a market failure which cost Campbell's alone some $10,000,000 in unsuccessful promotion,[8] according to news stories. The flow diagrams reveal a tremendous time-and-effort price disadvantage for the dehydrated product relative to the canned concentrate. It should have been clear that the housewife would not pay such a price for the kinds of satisfactions expected from soup in the American diet pattern. It may well be much of the failure of carefully investigated new products traces to the failure to investigate the learning-content requirements and the preparation-time price.

Perceptual-learning and value-learning requirements do not yield to as simple an analytical device as the flow chart, of course, but they are certainly possible to discover with

---

[6] Dilman M. K. Smith, *How to Avoid Mistakes When Introducing New Products* (New York: Vantage Press, 1964).

[7] Chester R. Wasson, Frederick D. Sturdivant, and David McConaughy, *Competition and Human Behavior* (New York: Appleton-Century-Crofts, 1968), pp. 83–91.
[8] "Campbell's Drops Red Kettle Line," *Advertising Age* (August 29, 1966), p. 3.

currently available research techniques. And this singular aspect of the proposed model is manifestly testable against past history. Prediction of fashion oscillations is not so clearly testable against the past.

### Checking Fashion Oscillation Predictability

Almost any hypothetical model must start with some classification and observation of past experience. But any model involving as many complex factors as the one proposed for fashion oscillation cannot be safely checked against history alone. This is true particularly when few observations from that past contain any substantial evidence of the psychological motives that buyers hope to appease with their adoptions. Most such observations have to be limited to studies in the fluctuations among physically measurable attributes which may or may not be the relevant items involved. The result can be a number of plausible but different explanations, each of which can be rationalized as fitting if the classifications and other data are carefully chosen. An acceptable theory must give more than a plausible explanation of past events: it must have pragmatic validity, be capable of predicting the future in some meaningful manner.

In this respect, the author can cite only a single documented successful prediction although he has attempted several others, unpublished, which have borne or are bearing fruit. As noted earlier, the author, writing in 1961 (for publication in 1964), traced the history of the swings in research fashion and noted that the current wave was at the peak of the recurrent mathematical emphasis. A swing to behavioral models and techniques was predicted. At the time of the analysis, the *Business Periodicals Index*[9] listed only two articles under "Innovation," neither of them in marketing journals and neither of them on research into the process. Concurrently, one of the marketing publications turned down Lionberger's *Adoption of New Ideas and Practices* as "not germane to the interests of" its readers. By 1965, both the Detroit and New York chapters of the AMA were holding New Products conferences, and "diffusion theory" is now the current shibboleth.

One such prediction success, or any number of them, does not constitute the final test of validity, however. A sound theory in any

[9] *Business Periodicals Index* (Nw eYork: The H. W. Wilson Co., July, 1961-June, 1962), p. 378.

field must dig beneath any coincidence between its predictions and subsequent events to explain why the events can be expected to occur in the manner observed. A sound theory must have construct validity, be based on behavioral constructs which themselves are capable of test and confirmation or modification. The theory offered above is just such a theory. It is possible to test it pragmatically— to make predictions as to the next direction of a fashion swing or as to the speed of adoption of a projected new product and then to observe the objective events. But this theory also postulates a specific behavioral mechanism as responsible for the observed patterns, a mechanism fairly well established in behavioral knowledge and subject to test itself. What is being proposed is thus no mere attempt to invent plausible behavioral labels to explain known observations. Rather, it starts from a series of established behavioral constructs derived independently of the kind of data to which they are being applied, and attempts to see if their implications fit the phenomena of fashion and product acceptance. This theory thus offers a framework for research into product acceptance in general as well as formulating an improvement for the practical problem of new product screening and testing.

### CONCLUSION

Not only fashion, but product acceptance in general is far more predictable than is generally thought, providing we make full use of the basic concepts of a product as a compromise bundle of desire attributes, demand as a desire set based on social conditioning, and motives as existing in a dynamic hierarchy and constantly restructured in the very process of their appeasement. These concepts alone are adequate to explain both the existence of a constant oscillation in fashions and the directions these oscillations take. Fads are explainable within the framework of this model as products which satisfy solely a single utility-drive for new experience; thus they pose neither a learning requirement nor have much value once their newness has gone. The speed of adoption of products of any kind depends on the amount of required learning of three types: use-systems learning, value perception learning, and role-perception learning. All are researchable and describable in objective terms in advance.

# 19. Audience Characteristics—The Performing Arts

## WILLIAM J. BAUMOL and W. G. BOWEN

The relevance of an analysis of audience characteristics to a study of the economics of the performing arts may not be immediately apparent. After all, one might argue that, from a purely pecuniary point of view, the only pertinent factor is box office receipts, and not the identity of the individual who buys the tickets. If the box office does a sufficiently brisk business, a performing company's finances will be in satisfactory condition, no matter who purchases its tickets. Why, then, do we care about the make-up of the audience?

In fact, there are many reasons for our concern. First and perhaps most important, though not from an economic point of view, we care who attends because we believe participation in an audience contributes to the welfare of the individual. If the arts are a "good thing," we must concern ourselves with those who are deprived of the experience.

Second, we must know the characteristics of the audience if we are to evaluate ticket pricing and distribution policies. The complaints one hears about high ticket prices discouraging certain groups of people from attending can be evaluated ultimately only in terms of audience composition.

A third reason for concern with the nature of the audience is associated with the issue of government support. Both the desirability and the political feasibility of government support may depend, at least in part, on the composition of the audience.

Fourth, even if we consider the performing arts dispassionately as a product and nothing more, effective marketing policy requires that we know something about those who demand the commodity, just as an automobile manufacturer needs to know who buys his cars. This information helps the manufacturer to merchandise his product and to plan his physical facilities: by giving him a better idea of his future market potential, it enables him to reach more rational decisions on investment policy and on the size and direction of his future activities.

❅  ❅  ❅

## SURVEY METHODS

Most of this discussion is based on our own data—on figures compiled from direct questioning of a sizable sample of audiences throughout the country—because, by and large, detailed statistics on the audience for the performing arts throughout the country are unavailable. There do exist a number of earlier studies treating particular sectors of the arts, especially the theater. We shall refer to some of these later, but their structure and specialized character restrict the extent to which they can be related to our findings.[1]

◆ SOURCE: Reprinted by permission from *Performing Arts: The Economic Dilemma* by William J. Baumol and W. G. Bowen (New York: Twentieth Century Fund, 1960), pp. 71–97.
[1] For a few other audience survey results see: Moore; survey of the Tyrone Guthrie Theatre audience (Minneapolis); survey of the Charles Playhouse audience (Boston); *Playbill* surveys; survey of the Sadler's Wells audience (London); survey of the UCLA Theater Group audience (Los Angeles); survey of Baltimore Symphony subscribers; survey of the national FM radio audience by *Broadcasting* magazine and two Carnegie Hall surveys. Full references to all of these will be found in the Bibliography.

Some explanation of the nature of our survey and the procedures used in conducting it is necessary. Our general procedure involved the use of questionnaires which were distributed to a predetermined sample of the audience (usually 50 per cent) at performances of various kinds, by inserting copies into the programs. Recipients were requested to complete the forms and return them to us before they left the hall. The respondent was asked about his age, education, occupation, income, distance traveled to the performance, the amount he spent on tickets, transportation, restaurant and other expenses associated with his attendance, his frequency of attendance at other types of live performance, his inclination to contribute, and so on. Critical to the success of our survey was the truly extraordinary cooperation we received from the organizations involved. A request for permission to conduct a survey was rarely refused, and once it was granted we were usually offered all possible assistance.

The surveys were conducted from September of 1963 through March of 1965. In order to determine who should be surveyed, we first compiled a roster of professional organizations for each of the art forms, and then developed a sample which, though not random in a technical sense, gave us wide coverage in terms of art form, region and night of the week. In all, we surveyed 153 performances (88 theatrical, 30 orchestral, 8 operatic, 9 dance, 5 chamber music and 13 free open-air performances) and obtained 29,413 usable replies. The distribution of usable responses by art form corresponded closely to the distribution of estimated audience sizes. Only the Broadway audience was relatively underrepresented by our survey, and this was deliberate, for we already had a great deal of information about the New York City audience from other sources.

As a direct consequence of the geographic distribution of the nation's professional performing organizations, most of our surveys took place in cities of substantial size. The geographic scope of our investigation is best indicated by the list of cities in which surveys were conducted. The list includes Los Angeles, San Francisco, Portland (Oregon), Seattle, Oklahoma City, Dallas, Houston, Chicago, Ann Arbor, Minneapolis, Cleveland, Cincinnati, Pittsburgh, Atlanta, Abingdon (Virginia), Washington, Baltimore, Philadelphia, Brooklyn and Boston.

On the average, our response rate—the proportion of persons who returned the questionnaires they had been given—was almost exactly 50 per cent. This rate is high for a survey requesting information about income and other personal matters. Broadway and opera audiences produced the lowest rate of response—about 25 per cent in each case. While the low rate of return on Broadway is fairly easily accounted for by the special nature of its audience, which will be described later, our results for opera are less easily explained. The response rate is important not just because it affects the number of usable questionnaires, but also because it may have significant implications for the degree of bias in our results. For example, if bachelors were more willing than married men to provide the information requested, the tabulated results of the survey would report a proportion of married people in the audience much smaller than the true figure.

In order to determine whether, in fact, our results were seriously biased, we undertook several tests. In general, the results are reassuring. There were no marked differences in rates of return from various classes of seats; that is, holders of expensive tickets did not reply at a significantly different rate from holders of less expensive tickets. There was a very slight relationship between response rate and median income, with a small increase in rate of response associated with increases in the median income of audiences; and there was also a slight relationship between response rate and proportion of males in professional occupations—the higher the number of professionals, the higher the number of returns. However, most of these relations were very weak and, in technical terms, did not satisfy the requirements of "statistical significance." From a more general point of view, what is most comforting is the great consistency of our results. The fact that they show the same pattern at performances differing widely in type and geographic location suggests very strongly that they are not the consequences of accidental biases imparted by the nature of particular audiences.

## CHARACTERISTICS OF THE AUDIENCE: AGE

Before presenting the results of our survey we shall comment briefly on one important audience characteristic which, for a variety of reasons, we did not investigate directly— ethnic composition. Several persons experienced in the management of performing organizations emphasized that this is a crucial characteristic. As one commented, musical performances are often in trouble in a city without a large German, Italian or Jewish population. A Jewish holiday can decimate the audience even in a Midwestern city. Several managers noted that Negroes, on the other hand, attend infrequently, even where there is no overt discrimination, except perhaps when Negro themes and performers are pre-

**TABLE 1. Profile of the U. S. Performing Arts Audience, Compared with the Total Urban Population**

| | Performing Arts Audience[a] | Urban Population[b] (1960) |
|---|---|---|
| *Sex* | | |
| Male | 52.8% | 48.4% |
| | | |
| *Age* | | |
| Under 20 | 6.9% | 37.1% |
| Over 60 | 9.0 | 13.1 |
| Median age | 38 yrs. | 30.3 yrs. |
| | | |
| *Occupational category* | | |
| Males: | | |
| Employed persons:[c] | | |
| Professional | 63.0% | 12.7% |
| Teachers | 10.3 | 1.1 |
| Managerial | 21.4 | 12.6 |
| Clerical and sales | 13.0 | 17.2 |
| Blue collar | 2.6 | 57.5 |
| Students[d] | 13.9 | |
| | | |
| Females: | | |
| Employed persons:[c] | | |
| Professional | 63.2% | 14.0% |
| Teachers | 25.4 | 5.6 |

[a] Based on Twentieth Century Fund audience survey; 24,425 respondents. The figures given here are weighted averages of the results for individual art forms. The weights are based on estimated attendance in 1963–64 and are as follows (on a 100 point scale): Broadway = 38, off-Broadway = 5, regional repertory theater = 9, major orchestras = 38, opera = 6, dance = 4. See Appendix Tables IV–A and IV–J for the derivation of these weights and a comparison of this profile with the profile which uses numbers of questionnaires completed as implicit weights.

**TABLE 1. (*Continued*)**

| | Performing Arts Audience[a] | Urban Population[b] (1960) |
|---|---|---|
| Managerial | 7.2 | 3.9 |
| Clerical | 24.9 | 34.3 |
| Sales | 2.8 | 8.5 |
| Blue collar | 1.9 | 39.3 |
| Students[d] | 15.1 | |
| Housewives[d] | 35.2 | |
| | | |
| *Education* | | |
| Males (age 25 and over): | | |
| Grade school and less than | | |
| 4 yrs. high school | 2.2% | 56.6% |
| 4 yrs. high school | 6.5 | 22.1 |
| 1-3 yrs. college | 12.8 | 9.8 |
| 4 yrs. college | 23.1 | 6.2 |
| Graduate school | 55.4 | 5.3 |
| Median category | Grad. work | 2 yrs. h.s. |
| | | |
| Females (age 25 and over): | | |
| Grade school and less than | | |
| 4 yrs. high school | 2.8% | 55.1% |
| 4 yrs. high school | 15.3 | 28.9 |
| 1-3 yrs. college | 23.6 | 9.5 |
| 4 yrs. college | 26.7 | 4.5 |
| Graduate school | 31.6 | 2.0 |
| Median category | 4 yrs. college | 3 yrs. h.s. |
| | | |
| *Income* | | |
| Over $5,000 | 91.3% | 64.8% |
| Over $15,000 | 39.5 | 5.4 |
| Over $25,000 | 17.4 | 1.5 |
| Median income | $12,804 | $6,166 |

*Frequency of attendance*
Average number of performances attended in last 12 months:

| | Number |
|---|---|
| Theater | 8.4 |
| Symphony | 5.1 |
| Opera | 1.7 |
| Dance | 1.2 |
| Other serious music | 2.2 |

[b] Data from *U. S. Census of Population, 1960: Detailed Characteristics, U. S. Summary*, Tables 158, 173, 185, 194, 203, 224. A composite profile could have been built for just those cities where we conducted surveys, but some experimentation indicated that this refinement would have made little difference.
[c] The number of employed persons is the base for the following percentages. The percentage of teachers is a component of the "Professional" category.
[d] The base for these percentages is the total number of respondents.

sented. Of course, these are only casual observations, and we have no way of substanti-
ating them—let alone any way of separating
out the effect on attendance of ethnic characteristics *per se* from the effect of income.

What does our survey tell us about differences between the typical audience and the
population as a whole? A succinct summary
of our principal findings is given in Table 1,
where we present a composite profile of the
audiences at the various art forms, each
weighted by estimated attendance in 1963-64,
and a corresponding profile for the urban
population of the United States as of 1960.

The first thing these data suggest is that
the performing arts audience, contrary to what
many people believe, seems to be somewhat
more heavily male than the population as a
whole. Nearly 53 per cent of our respondents
were male, whereas only a little more than
48 per cent of the urban population is male.
However, this probably should not be taken

too seriously. It may simply reflect a male
prerogative: if a husband and wife were present and the questionnaire was contained in the
wife's program, it is very possible that the
husband would have filled it out.

Though the median age for the U.S. population is 8 years below that of the arts audience, this indicates simply that children do
not often attend the theater although they are
included in the Census. The rest of the data
on age indicate that the audience is relatively
young. This is shown most easily with the
aid of Figure 1. In that graph, the dark bars
represent the proportion of the audience in
different age groups and the light bars the
proportion of the urban population as a whole
in these age groups. We see that relative to
total population the arts audience is greatest
in the interval 20 to 24 years of age. Twice
as high a percentage of the arts audience
(12.2 per cent) lies in that age interval as is
the case for the total urban population (6.1

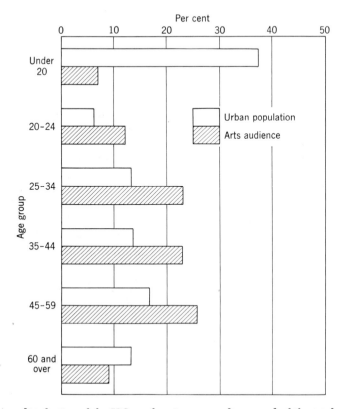

FIG. 1. Age distribution of the U.S. performing arts audience and of the total urban population. (See Table 1 for the data on which this graph and others in this selection are
based.)

per cent). This ratio of 2.00 is what we call the *relative frequency*; it is equal to the proportion of the audience within a given category divided by the proportion of the total urban population in that same category. Calculation of such figures for each of our other age group categories shows very clearly that relative frequency declines steadily with age once we get beyond the interval under 20 years of age. These figures tell us that the audience at a typical performance is far younger than the urban population as a whole, and that the older the age group, the smaller is its relative representation in a typical audience. Consequently, older people (those over 60) are the scarcest members of the audience in relation to their numbers in the urban population of the United States. In a word, audiences are young. With the proportion of the nation's population in the younger age brackets growing rather rapidly, this fact may be quite significant.

Two alternative hypotheses can explain the relative youthfulness of the arts audience. If the same age patterns have always characterized the audience, it means that people attend performances when they are young and then gradually drop out of the audience as they grow older. They may become less interested, or attendance may become more difficult for them, or other interests and responsibilities may keep them from the theater. The second hypothesis is more sanguine. It may be that the performing arts are now attracting a younger audience than ever before. If young people did not attend very frequently in the past, this would account for the smaller number of older patrons today, the absentees never having developed an interest in live performance. If this is so and younger Americans are attending in far higher relative numbers than they did in the past, then we may be building a base for a great future expansion.

\* \* \*

### Occupation, Education and Income

Turning next to the distribution of audiences by occupation, we see that roughly 15 per cent of all our respondents were students, and that among *employed males* only 2 to 3 per cent of the total audience included in the survey was composed of blue collar workers, as compared to a figure of nearly 60 per cent for the urban population as a whole. We conclude that the audience for the arts is made up

preponderantly—indeed, almost entirely—of people from the white collar occupations. In the typical arts audience all of the white collar groups are over-represented (in comparison with the urban population), with two exceptions, clerical and sales persons. The degree of over-representation is by no means the same, however. Among males there are roughly nine times as many teachers in the audience as in the urban population of the United States, and nearly five times as many professionals of all sorts (see Figure 2). The arts' share of professionals is also much greater than their share of managerial personnel. In general, the very high proportion of members of the professions in the arts audience is characteristic of both sexes. However, the proportion of teachers in the audience is much higher for men than for women. As a possible explanation one might surmise that a high rate of theater-going is characteristic of teachers at more advanced professional levels, and that female teachers are more heavily distributed in the lower grades of the schools.

Two numbers not shown on the table or the chart are of interest. Three per cent of our employed male respondents were themselves performing artists or performers and 5 per cent of the females were in this category. These proportions are surely significantly higher than those for the population as a whole, but the unavailability of related Census data prevents a direct comparison.

Next we turn to the educational attainment level of the audiences, reported in Table 1 and shown graphically in Figure 3. All of these results refer only to persons 25 years of age and over, in order to avoid the biases introduced by including persons who are still in school. We conclude that the audience is composed of *exceedingly* well-educated persons. Less than 3 per cent of the males and females did not graduate from high school, as compared to the more than 50 per cent of the U.S. urban population 25 years and over who did not do so. At the other end of the spectrum, over 55 per cent of the males attending performances did some work beyond college—an educational level attained by only 5 per cent of the urban population. Almost one third of the women in the audience did some graduate work, as compared with 2 per cent of the female urban population who did so. In Figure 3 the sharp decline in the length of the light bars as we move from top to bottom means that the proportion of the urban population

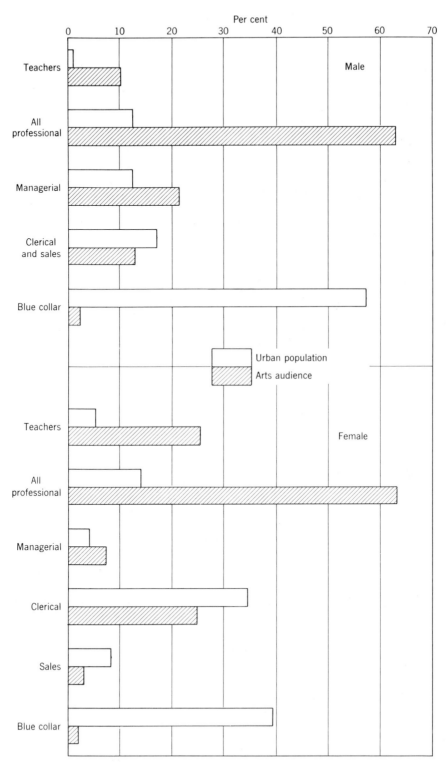

FIG. 2. Occupational distribution of the U.S. performing arts audience and of the total urban population.

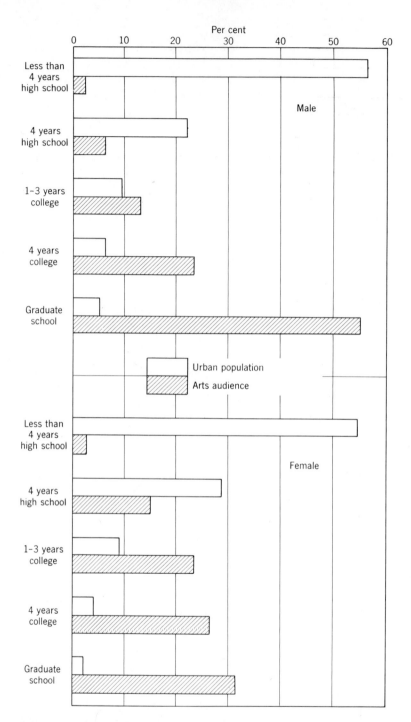

FIG. 3. Educational attainment of the U.S. performing arts audience and of the total urban population.

at each educational level falls very rapidly as the level of educational attainment increases; the reverse is true of the arts audience.[2]

The last socio-economic characteristic re-ported in Table 1, audience income, is de-scribed in more detail in Figure 4. Once more the results are clear-cut and extreme. They show that the median family income among

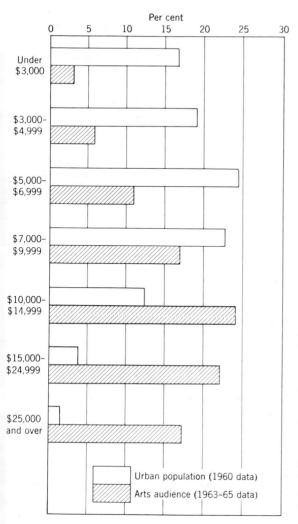

FIG. 4. Income distribution of the U.S. performing arts audience and of the total urban population.

a typical arts audience is roughly *twice* as high as that for the total urban population. Forty per cent of our arts audience had incomes of $15,000 or more, and 17 per cent had incomes of $25,000 or more. The proportion of the arts audience in the category $15,000 to $24,999 is nearly six times as high as that of the urban population as a whole; and about 11½ times as large a proportion of the audience earned over $25,000 as is true of the urban population generally.[3]

## DIFFERENCES IN PROFILES AMONG ART FORMS

What variations in audience characteristics can be observed when the several art forms are examined separately?

The most remarkable finding is that audiences from art form to art form are *very* similar. They all show a median age in the middle 30's; over 60 per cent of the audience for each art form consists of people in the professions (and this finding holds for both sexes); all exhibit an extremely high level of education, with 50 per cent of the males having gone to graduate school and 50 per cent of the females having at least completed college; and there is a consistently high level of income, in no case involving a median under $11,000.

Some moderate differences by type of performance are worth pointing out. For instance, there are differences in attendance by sex among art forms. Women tend to predominate in the audiences of symphonies and the dance, whereas men constitute the majority attending the theater, opera and programs of chamber music. There is also a slight difference in age among the various audiences, with symphonies

[2] The only serious disagreement between the results of other surveys and our own relates to the quantitative effect of level of education. While other investigations also report that the audience is very highly educated, their conclusions are not quite as extreme as ours. In general they show a plurality of persons with college degrees rather than a plurality of persons who have attended graduate school. Examples are the Baltimore Symphony audience survey: college graduate 41 per cent, graduate school 21 per cent; the UCLA Theater Group audience survey: college 55 per cent, post-graduate 13 per cent; the 1964 *Playbill* survey (males): college 50.3 per cent, graduate school 28 per cent; the Guthrie Theater audience survey (males): college graduate 25.4 per cent, post-graduate 45 per cent. These figures suggest

that our questionnaires, perhaps because of their length, were answered more readily by highly educated persons. But, despite some disagreement on the magnitudes involved, all of these results confirm fully our qualitative conclusion: that the audience for the arts is *very* highly educated.

[3] Since the income figures for the urban population of the United States are based on the 1960 Census, and income in 1963–1965, when our survey results were obtained, was undoubtedly somewhat higher, the true differential between the income of the audience and that of the general public is a bit smaller than our results suggest. Nevertheless, the differential is so substantial that a correction for this discrepancy would alter our numerical comparisons only slightly.

having a higher percentage of persons over 60. However, we must point out that symphonies, perhaps more than other art forms, frequently have special young people's concerts, none of which were surveyed by us. The existence of these concerts must surely bias our estimate of the age distribution of symphony audiences, because many of the young people who attend such special concerts might otherwise have been found in audiences attending other performances.

As to occupations, we find that a relatively small number of students attend ballet, opera and the theater, but that chamber music audiences are heavily peopled by students, teachers and professionals in general. While the number of blue collar workers is low for all art forms, the highest proportion is found at the opera. This finding could reflect the effect of the culture of Europe, where opera is a popular art form, and may, therefore, report what is primarily an immigrant group. On the other hand, because of the small number of operatic organizations surveyed, it may simply represent the influence of the New York City Opera with its low admission prices.

The number of blue collar workers remained consistently low throughout the survey. Their share of the total male audience reached 6 per cent in only 5 of our 35 theaters, never reached 5 per cent in any of the 12 major orchestras surveyed, constituted 5 per cent of the audience at the Brooklyn Opera, and 7 to 9 per cent of the audience for non-contemporary opera at the New York City Center. In dance, the proportion of blue collar workers was 7 per cent of the total at a performance of the Alvin Ailey Dance Theatre (a Negro company with a considerable Negro following), while in three of the other audiences surveyed there were no blue collar workers. In chamber music audiences the number of blue collar workers never reached 2 per cent.

Educational level was the most consistent element of all, with chamber music drawing the most highly educated audience—over 75 per cent of the males and 52 per cent of the females having attended graduate school.

Incomes also were consistently high, though theater patrons had an income about $1,500 higher, on the average, than members of the audiences of other art forms. In only 2 of the 35 theaters surveyed did median audience income fall below $10,000. The highest median income was not found on Broadway, but at a West Coast theater, where it was over $18,000.

A Broadway theater did, however, come in a close second. In 29 of our 35 theater audiences, median income was between $11,000 and $15,000. The top figure for any *single* performance was almost certainly higher, because these figures represent the average of all the surveys taken at each organization (there was more than one in almost every case). All 12 major orchestras surveyed showed median audience incomes above $10,000, the highest being $15,000. Again, the results varied little; 8 of the 12 exhibited median incomes between $11,000 and $13,000. Audience incomes at dance and chamber orchestra performances were slightly lower than those of audiences in general. Two of our five dance surveys reported median incomes under $10,000. Three of the five chamber group audiences were in this category, but one of the string quartet audiences had a median income over $16,500.

A distinct pattern emerges from the responses to questions about frequency of attendance. Theater is shown to be the most popular art form. With one exception, the patrons at *all* types of performance—members of dance, opera or chamber music audiences—indicated that the theater was the art form which they attended most frequently. Even in the exceptional case, the symphony, theater came in a very close second in frequency of attendance; that is to say, members of the symphony audience indicated that they attended theaters almost as frequently as they went to orchestral concerts.

## THE NEW YORK AUDIENCE

We also investigated the audience in New York City by itself. This enabled us to deal with a constant basic population, one drawn primarily from a single region. It also permitted us to make a direct comparison between off-Broadway and Broadway audiences, casting some light on differences between audiences for more and for less experimental theater groups.

In general, the off-Broadway audience resembles more closely that of the other art forms than it does the audience of the Broadway theater. On Broadway the age distribution is concentrated in the middle range—comparatively few persons under 20 and over 60 attend. Similarly, the Broadway theater audience includes fewer members of the professions than does any of the other art forms in New

York, both among males and females. But even there, professionals constitute more than 50 per cent of the audience. Broadway seems to draw a larger proportion of its audience from among the managerial group than do the other art forms. More housewives are represented in the Broadway surveys and, incidentally, in the orchestral audiences, than at other art forms. The educational level is slightly lower on Broadway, though even there it is remarkably high, with nearly 50 per cent of the men having done some post-graduate work. While income levels are highest in the orchestral audiences, they are not very much higher than median incomes of attendees on *and* off Broadway, and the off-Broadway incomes are surprisingly close to the incomes of the Broadway audience. In terms of socioeconomic characteristics there is no evidence to support the notion that off-Broadway attracts a clientele significantly different from that of any other art form.

The only reasonably comparable series of historical data on audiences which we have been able to find applies to the New York theater. The *Playbill* survey of the audience for the commercial theater on Broadway has been conducted for more than a decade, though at some point there was a change in procedure so that the data are not strictly comparable.[4] What is most noteworthy in the figures for the six years that are usable is how little change in audience composition has occurred during the decade. One can only say that today's audience is about the same as that of a decade earlier except that it earns more money now than it did then. Even this is a misleading observation, for incomes per capita in the United States have also been rising. Indeed, the figures suggest that in this respect, too, the theater audience has remained about the same in relation to the rest of the

population.[5] Thus, if there was a "cultural boom"—a movement toward "mass culture"—there is little sign of it in the composition of the audience of the commercial theater.

## AUDIENCES OUTSIDE NEW YORK

Since our investigation of the audience outside New York City showed the same patterns reported for the New York audience, a few brief comments on the subject will suffice. Three differences stand out. We found a relatively high proportion of students in the theater audience outside New York, a group which was comparatively poorly represented on Broadway. About 21 per cent of the theater audience was composed of students, as compared with figures of 8 per cent for Broadway and 11 per cent for off-Broadway. The same general pattern was evident in the orchestral and operatic audiences. Members of the professions made up a slightly larger proportion of the audiences outside New York City, and, if anything, the educational level was higher in other parts of the country. Income, however, was slightly higher in New York, though the median outside New York City was over $11,-000. Frequency of attendance was somewhat greater inside the city, but not nearly as much greater as one might have expected, given the availability of performance in New York. Indeed, attendance at chamber music concerts was, if anything, somewhat higher outside the city.

The main point, then, is that the general features of our over-all audience profile are by no means due solely to the characteristics of New York audiences—as a matter of fact many of its most noteworthy elements are even more apparent outside New York City.

*    *    *

---

[4] Unfortunately, we have been unable to locate a complete set of survey reports either from *Playbill* or any of the library theater collections. In fact, we have not seen the original report on the 1955–56 survey; our data for that year had to be reconstructed from figures quoted in an article by Max Frankel in the *New York Times* (May 20, 1956, Theater Section, p. 1).

[5] This can be seen as follows. The median income of the audience in 1959–60, the first year for which this statistic was calculated, was $9,650, whereas the figure for 1963 was $11,011. (As already indicated, the 1964 jump to $16,700 should probably be ascribed to the influx of World's Fair visitors

and so is irrelevant for a calculation of the basic trend.) This represents a rise of a little over 14 per cent during the three year period. Now, according to the U. S. Census, median family income in the United States rose about 9.5 per cent over the same time interval. (*U. S. Census of Population, 1960: Occupational Characteristics*, Final Report PC[2]–7A.) Since incomes of people in the professions have recently been rising more rapidly than those of the population as a whole, one suspects that the incomes of members of the audience of the commercial theater were perhaps just about keeping up with the incomes of others in the same socio-economic classes.

## THE FREQUENT AND INFREQUENT ATTENDERS

It should be clear by now that "the common man" is fairly uncommon among those who attend live professional performances. But one may well ask whether he is much better represented among those who go only very occasionally. To some extent this turns out to be the case. A breakdown of our data by frequency of attendance shows that people who are well educated, well-to-do, and who are engaged in professional occupations constitute a particularly large proportion of those who attend performances frequently. Conversely, those who attend only rarely have lower incomes, are a bit more frequently blue collar workers and have a slightly lower level of educational attainment. This relationship, the fact that the infrequent attenders more closely approximate "average citizens," was first observed by Moore among the members of the Broadway audience.

Our regional theater surveys show that among males who attended only once during the year of our survey 59 per cent were professionals, 8 per cent were blue collar workers, the median educational level was four years of college, and the audience's median family income was $9,500. But for those who attended at least 10 other performances that year the corresponding figures were 67 per cent professional, 3 per cent blue collar, the median educational level was graduate school and the median annual income was $14,500. Similar differences between frequent and infrequent attenders hold (but to a smaller degree) for the major orchestras and (much more markedly) for the Broadway theater. Moreover, with few exceptions, the relationship between these variables and frequency of attendance is perfectly regular. For example, among the audiences of the major orchestras one observes the following pattern:

| Number of performances attended per year | 1 | 2–5 | 6–10 | over 10 |
|---|---|---|---|---|
| Family income | $9,500 | $10,500 | $12,500 | $13,000 |

Curiously, students are generally better represented among the infrequent attenders, perhaps because their studies or their social activities keep them too busy or because they cannot afford to attend very often, though the availability of reduced rate student tickets may cast doubt on the latter explanation.

On the whole it appears that the group that attends performances very rarely is more similar to the general population in its composition than is the audience as a whole. Yet even the infrequent attender is no "common man." His (median) family income is over $9,500, his (median) educational level is at least four years of college, and, if he is an adult, there is a better than even chance that he is engaged in a professional occupation. This is still a highly select group.

## THE SIZE OF THE ARTS AUDIENCE

The data we have just discussed permit us to estimate the size of the audience for the live performing arts. In 1963-64 approximately 20 million tickets were sold by Broadway, off-Broadway and regional theaters, major and metropolitan orchestras, opera groups and (American) professional dance companies. But since most of the individuals who purchased these tickets attended more than one performance, we can be sure that the number of different persons purchasing tickets was considerably under 20 million. Table 2 summarizes our estimates of the number of different individuals who attended each of these art forms.

How large, then, is the number of Americans attending some type of live performance? That number must be considerably smaller than the total of the corresponding figures for the individual art forms because of the overlap in the audiences for different types of performance. If 50 persons attend only theater, 50 attend only opera and 50 attend both, then the theater and opera will each have 100 patrons even though, in all, only 150 individuals are involved. An intense examination of our data has led us to estimate that (excluding "the road" and summer stock) the audience of the live professional performing arts in the United States totaled 2½ to 3 million persons in 1963-64. We suspect that this figure and the estimates for the individual art forms in Table 2 are a little low since, as any student of survey techniques would affirm, respondents tend, perhaps unconsciously, to exaggerate the frequency with which they attend performances. In addition, the frequency figures are inflated by our inability to

TABLE 2.  Average Estimated Attendance, by Art Form

| | Average Estimated Attendance[a] | Average Number of Times Attended in Last 12 Months[b] | Number of Individuals Attending (col. 1 ÷ col. 2) |
|---|---|---|---|
| | (1) | (2) | (3) |
| Broadway | 7,000,000 | 4.5 | 1,555,556 |
| Off-Broadway | 900,000 | 6.5 | 138,462 |
| Regional theaters | 1,500,000 | 4.5 | 333,333 |
| Major orchestras | 6,600,000 | 4.8 | 1,375,000 |
| Opera | 1,700,000 | 2.6 | 653,846 |
| Dance | 750,000 | 2.3 | 326,087 |

[a] Taken from Table III–1.

[b] An average weighted inversely by frequency of attendance to correct for over-representation of frequent attenders in our sample (if individual A attends twice as often as B, he is twice as likely as B to be included in our sample). Specifically, let $i$ represent any one of our frequency of attendance categories (once, 2-5, 6-10, over 10), let $f$ be the average frequency of attendance for the given art form and category, and let $N_i$ be the number of individuals in the category. Then our weighted average figure in column 2 is obtained from the expression $\Sigma f_i (N_i/f_i)/\Sigma (N_i/f_i)$ or, more simply, $\Sigma N_i/\Sigma (N_i/f_i)$.

remove from them attendance at non-professional performances. If average frequency of attendance is lower than our figures indicate, then the 20 million tickets sold in 1963-64 must have been distributed among a correspondingly larger group of people. Nevertheless, it seems to us quite unlikely that the audience comprises more than 5 million individuals, a figure which would be 4 per cent of all residents of this country 18 years of age and older.

We have tried to provide an extensive profile of the audience of the live professional performing arts in the United States. Two of its features are especially significant.

The first is the remarkable consistency of the composition of audiences from art form to art form, from city to city and from one performance to another.

Second, the audience is drawn from an extremely narrow segment of the American population. In the main, it consists of persons who are extraordinarily well educated, whose incomes are very high, who are predominantly in the professions, and who are in their late youth or early middle age. This finding has important implications for the nature of whatever growth has occurred in audience demand

for the arts. Even if there has been a significant rise in the size of audiences in recent years, it has certainly not yet encompassed the general public. If the sociological base of the audience has in fact expanded, it must surely have been incredibly narrow before the boom got under way. This result indicates also, in a larger sense, that attempts to reach a wider and more representative audience, to interest the less educated or the less affluent, have so far had limited effects.

Yet there is also evidence that something can be done to broaden the audience base. As will be shown later, when professional performances are given free of charge or with carefully set low prices, the audience is drawn from a consistently wider cross section of the population. But even here there are no easy and overwhelming victories—in these audiences the number of blue collar workers is almost always under 10 per cent and the number of professionals is always well over 50 per cent; over 50 per cent of the males have completed college; and median incomes are almost always well over $9,000. Obviously, much still remains to be done before the professional performing arts can truly be said to belong to the people.

# E. The Legal Framework

## 20. Impact of Government upon the Market System

E. T. GRETHER and ROBERT J. HOLLOWAY

The maintenance of a strong, widespread and varied private enterprise base in a society requires that the myriads of private choices and decisions mesh into and through an effective market system. In the United States, the highest judicial tribunals have insisted on the maintenance of the "rule of competition" through the market system by reiterating that the alternatives are direct governmental operation and regulation or private cartelization.

An acceptably effective general market system must have the capacities to:

1. Respond to the free choices of buyers at all levels.

2. Respond to general and specific *external* environment influences, forces, and conditions (that is, the system must be open ended).

3. Interact among the elements of the system *internally*, including particularly the adjustment of resources from lesser advantaged uses to products, services, or geographical areas of greater advantage.

4. "Regulate" in the sense of placing the participants in the marketing processes under strong compulsions for both (a) the efficient use of resources in production and in marketing and (b) the effective fulfillment of the wants

◆ SOURCE: Reprinted by permission from the *Journal of Marketing*, (National Quarterly Publication of the American Marketing Association), Vol. 31, April 1967, pp. 1–7.

and desires of the members of the society.

The market system as a whole and its specific subsystems are under the continuing and increasing intervention of governmental policies and programs; that is, the market system, while "regulating," is also being "regulated." Most likely, the interventions by government at all levels (especially by the federal government) and the high rate of scientific and technological change are the two most significant external environmental forces affecting the market system. It is proposed, therefore, that both empirical and normative research studies be encouraged on the effects of governmental policies and programs on the functioning of the market system as a whole and on specific subsystems. Such studies should focus sharply upon the impacts of public policies and intervention upon the capacities of the market system as a whole to fulfill its basic functions of communication, coordination and organization, adjustment to strategic environmental forces and conditions, and internal interaction and regulation.

Obviously many thousands of helpful studies could be made with this general orientation and from its vantage points. Such studies, regardless of their number or whether they were essentially empirical or normative, would have accumulative value if focused as proposed. But since research resources are not infinite and there is high urgency for basic knowledge and wisdom to guide public policies, the following topical areas are highlighted:

I. Quantitative and qualitative analyses of the extent to which the economy is under the aegis of the competitive market system.

II. The influence of governmental policies and programs upon the leading classes of managerial decision making in marketing in the perspective of the requirements of an acceptable competitive general market system.

III. Special strategic topical issues in the context of current public policies affecting the functioning of the market system in the United States.

## EMPIRICAL AND NORMATIVE STUDIES

The traditional, classical models of the market system as a whole are derived from assumptions under which the market system and the economy are synonymous. There is a complete lack of quantitative measures of the extent to which the economy of the United States or other countries is, in fact, under the regulation of the market system. There are those who believe that even in the United States with its avowed policies in favor of regulation under the market system, the drift is inexorably away from the market system and hence away from a society with a private enterprise base. No systematic endeavors have been made to measure quantitatively or even to judge qualitatively the extent to which our economy is regulated by the market system. It is difficult to conceive of a study of greater potential significance for public policy than a careful quantitative and qualitative interpretive analysis of the extent to which the market system is operationally effective. A general or holistic approach, of course, would have to be considered only as tentative or preliminary. But it could have an enormous influence in guiding and stimulating research into special topics and areas and subsystems.

A possible approach would be through a breakdown of the components of the GNP in terms of the derivative relationship to or removal from the market system. A very difficult problem of appraisal arises in the areas of shared rule as between competition through the market system and governmental direct regulation. It would be most helpful to have such areas highlighted with some indications of the quantitative nature of the sharing. Ideally, a general approach should be under the direction of a task force composed of persons with varied backgrounds and interests. Useful, preliminary studies, however, could be done under a single aegis by persons of broad background and experience. It is inconceivable, however, that definitive measures or judgments could be developed, since the bewildering labyrinths of governmental intervention now probably defy full charting and appraisal.

## THE INFLUENCE OF GOVERNMENTAL POLICIES AND PROGRAMS

The influence of governmental policies and programs is to be considered in the dual perspective of the requirements of effective private decision making and the requirements of an acceptable, competitive general market system. Under this approach some orderly trails would be blazed through a few of the labyrinths of public regulations from the point of view of business enterprises in making strategic decisions. Five broad areas of research are proposed.

### Vertical Marketing Organization and Relationships (the Market Channels)

It is almost universally agreed that vertical organization and relations are uniquely the central area of the field or discipline of marketing. It is agreed also that it is a field of high and overlooked importance both in terms of private managerial decision making and of public policies affecting marketing. It has become increasingly evident that in modern complex industrial societies, competitive forces operate vertically as well as horizontally. But there is a great dearth of systematic knowledge and insight into the patterns and significance of vertical organization and relationships.

In the meantime, governmental policies and programs have intervened into this complex of relationships more or less haphazardly under antitrust enforcement, the Robinson-Patman Act, laws governing resale price maintenance ("fair trade"), special laws and actions affecting relationships between manufacturers and their dealers, actions affecting vertical integration and semi-integration, exclusive and selective dealer arrangements, franchising, and so on. But such legislative, judicial, or other interventions have not been investigated systematically in terms of the functioning of the market system. Thus, for example, regulation under the Robinson-Patman Act has never been examined in this framework and context. The Robinson-Patman cases and actions provide an almost ideal opportunity for research along these lines because of the focus upon primary, secondary and tertiary levels in the perspective of broad conflicting conflicts between types of enterprises. Yet the Act is couched and enforced in terms of a specific-commodity type of regulation of pricing almost guaranteed to avoid the most important issues. The effect of the Robinson-Patman Act is merely one example of fruitful areas awaiting research in terms of this approach. For example, there are the enormously important problems in numerous industries such as the automotive industries, involving not only the dealer structures and arrangements of manufacturers, but relations with suppliers. A very important area, of course, would be vertical integration upstream and downstream, in which there are great bodies of law, action, and judicial interpretation.

### Geographical Marketing Organization and Relationships

A primary test of the marketing system is its ability to support the geographical adjustment of market forces and conditions. This horizontal expression is the corollary of vertical organization and relationships. Involved here are governmental policies affecting sales territories, especially territorial confinement, laws and regulations affecting geographical pricing (as the basing point and other delivered price systems), interstate trade barriers (as through licensing and differential tax treatment), the favoritism of state and local governmental jurisdictions toward local industry, especially through subsidies, and other forms of differential treatment, and so on.

### Product Policies, Including Innovation, Diversification, Differentiation, and the "Product Mix"

In many ways, the area of product decisions is the most important of all. Possibly, too, it is the brightest spot of all in terms of the impacts of governmental policies and programs, except, perhaps, in a small number of industries under special legislation (as food and drug legislation). It would appear, however, that the enormous impacts of governmentally supported and encouraged research and development in relation to private efforts and programs, have fostered rapid technological advances and changes with respect to product innovation.

But there are conflicting interests and unsettled problems in connection with the patent system. And there are continuing problems in the endeavors to trademark, brand, package, and promote the *differentiated* products of particular enterprises. Antitrust implications and applications are becoming increasingly important in this area. Furthermore, product line diversification by the processes of acquisition are being questioned, increasingly, under antitrust. There is no doubt that the area of product policies in all of its expressions is basic and lends itself to a wide variety of research studies.

### Promotion

Promotion is of the essence in marketing, and particularly in an environment of (1) rapid product development and (2) antitrust enforcement intended to optimize the rule of competition and to forbid cartelization. Hence, the character and impacts of the governmental policies and regulations affecting personal selling, advertising, trademarking, branding, packaging, labeling, the use of credit, etc., are basic. Research could be focused upon the impact of the enforcement of specific statutes (as food and drug legislation, or alcoholic beverages legislation), or as affecting functional areas (as advertising), or specific practices (as packaging, labeling, credit terms and practices). Important also would be the impact of public mores, standards and attitudes in general and upon specific regulations.

Research in this area could become a testing ground for relating the functioning of the market system broadly and specifically to ethical standards and precepts by reference to the host of common law or other more specific statutory and judicial constraints upon market behavior and practices. Research in this area could test product differentiation and brand promotion empirically in relation to the prevalent conceptualization under much of economical analysis derived from the theory of monopolistic competition and assumptions as to effects upon entry. It is likely that, in the main, in the United States, governmental regulations affecting promotion do not now inhibit managerial decision making and implementation in a strategic manner. One of the purposes of the research would be to check this generalization in general and in specific situations.

## Pricing

Pricing is the "holy of holies" of both economic analysis and of antitrust enforcement in the United States. Consequently, there is a large literature of economic analysis and of public policy. From this standpoint, research needs are not as high as in other areas. What is needed, however, is empirical research into the exact nature of pricing and of its relationship to other aspects of decision-making and behavior in marketing. Many, perhaps most, economic analyses, make prices, pricing, and price structures and the price system the central aspects of the functioning of the market system and of the economy. Such emphasis, of course, is appropriate for the production and marketing of the great staple homogeneous products. This approach, however, is less appropriate for the modern, diversified business enterprise with rapid product innovation, which stresses product differentiation and promotion. Under these conditions, the totality of market offerings, practices, services, facilities, and relations affect market results—not merely the determination of the *basic price* of specific products. Obviously pricing and the "price system" in the case of well-known homogeneous commodities has one set of connotations for the functioning of the market system, whereas a broader, more flexible conceptualization and analysis are required for firms in other situations. Research studies focused upon pricing in this latter context could be exceedingly illuminating in terms of the actual functioning of the market system in areas other than staple, homogeneous commodities.

## SPECIAL, STRATEGIC TOPICAL AREAS AND ISSUES

### The Definition of the Market and Industry Under Various Types of Regulation

In many types of governmental regulation a basic aspect of regulation is the definition or determination of the "market" or "industry" or "product" or "line of commerce" or "area of effective competition," and so on. Such determinations have been and are being made unilaterally, statute by statute and in individual cases and situations. There has been no full endeavor to investigate such determinations for consistency and significance in relation to the impacts upon the regulation of the market system as a whole or upon specific subsystems. Thus, for example, under the Robinson-Patman Act the various provisions apply to commodities of "like grade and quality," and a physical characteristics test has been used for the most part instead of the economic test of market behavior.

All statutes governing specific industries require the delimitation of the areas of coverage —an increasingly difficult matter under our changing technologies and tendencies toward product and functional diversification. It would be exceedingly helpful to examine all governmental regulations involving such determinations (as tariff regulations, internal revenue definitions, the various antitrust statutes, Robinson-Patman, and the host of special statutes) in the dual contexts of consistency and significance in relation to the maintenance of a flexible, acceptable market system.

It is possible that the market system is being fragmented into segments by contradictory and arbitrary determinations and special regulations that run counter to the requirements of both effective, flexible adjustments and the inherent forces of modern technology which are tending increasingly to obliterate or break down traditional boundaries.

### Character and Impacts of Governmental Subsidies and of Subsidy-like Differential Treatment

Very likely, the most general, most insidious, and least understood of the various types of intrusions into the market system, as a whole and into specific subsystems, arise through governmental subsidies and subsidy-like differential treatment. The use of subsidies goes back deeply into American history, for the federal and state and local governments have engaged in a wide variety of such programs, intended often to expand local industry and to encourage foreign trade or to foster the provision of basic facilities. Thus, the railroads were the beneficiaries of land grants from 1850 to 1871 intended to encourage and speed railroad construction. Thus, too, the agricultural industries have received and still receive a wide variety of direct and indirect subsidies that have had and continue to have an enormous impact upon these industries. Currently, almost all major and minor sectors and segments of our economy are receiving or are under the impacts of various open or disguised forms of subsidies and differential, favored treatment. The worth of a congressman is often measured in terms of his ability to obtain federal assistance for his district. State and local governmental bodies are also deeply involved in similar programs. Thus many states and local governmental units try to influence the location of industry by tax exemptions and tax favoritism, financial assistance in building plants, tax exempt bonds, the provision of special facilities without cost or below cost, and so on.

The market system in general and specific sub-systems are affected by a broad variety of impacts, influences, and interventions intended to serve special interests or areas. The number, character, and variety of such interventions are too great to allow simple generalizations. Subsidies and differential treatment might actually strengthen the market system. There is no guarantee or likelihood that this is so—in fact, to the contrary. There is a challenging opportunity here for special studies as well as for general analysis and interpretation. It is difficult to conceive of any other area so widely open for productive research.

### Governmental Policies and Regulations Affecting the Growth of Individual Business Enterprises

In a society with a private enterprise base, it is of highest importance whether the total net effects of governmental policies and programs affect the growth of business enterprises favorably or adversely. All regulations intruding into the market system (such as subsidies and subsidy-like differential treatment) or affecting decision making in marketing by individual enterprises may affect their growth—one way or another. In general, there are strong positive endeavors to foster the growth of small business and to circumscribe or constrain the growth of large, powerful enterprises. Thus, there is the special Small Business Administration in the federal government dedicated to the interests of small business. Thus, too, the Supreme Court of the United States in recent decisions, especially *Brown Shoe,* has made the preservation of viable small business a

standard of action superior both to efficiency and the maintenance of competition in an abstract sense. Conversely, powerful well-established corporations find it increasingly difficult to grow by the simple processes of acquisition or merger.

The enforcement of the revised 1950 Section 7 of the Clayton Act is increasingly affecting the opportunities of growth by acquisition. Consequently, large enterprises are forced increasingly to plan growth through internal expansion—horizontally, vertically, functionally, and through conglomerate diversification. Possibly in the near future such avenues of internal growth may be under increasing questioning. Finally, the weight and specific character of taxes affect growth plans and opportunities.

### Public Policies and Programs Affecting Consumer-buyer Decision Making and Behavior

The character and relative effectiveness of the free choices of consumer-buyers are the most basic factors in the functioning of the market system in general and throughout its myriad of subsystems. Hence it is of highest importance to investigate the impacts of the host of governmental regulations, facilities, aids, and interventions upon the quality and efficiency of consumer-buyer decision making. Of course, all forms of marketing regulations will have some influence upon consumers' choices by affecting the relative qualities, availabilities, and competitiveness of market supplies and offers. In addition, there are the specific laws and regulations governing weights and measures, packaging, labeling, deceit and misrepresentation, credit terms, and so on.

There is a common generalization that we are moving steadily away from the ancient doctrine of *caveat emptor* to an emerging *caveat venditor.* Regardless of the exact nature of our drift, there is no doubt that abundant basic research opportunities and needs exist in this general area both in general terms and in sharp focus upon specific industries (as foods, drugs, and alcoholic beverages).

In a sense, research studies in the general area of consumer-buyer behavior and decision making could be means of summing up the effects of the other areas of research.

# Commentary on "Impact of Government upon the Market System"

SEYMOUR BANKS

This is an extremely well-written and interesting paper, directing attention to issues of undoubted importance. However, its very clarity, scope, and depth of perception raise questions of value judgment as much as research information and, perhaps, this is all to the good. It seems to this reviewer that Grether and Holloway are clearly on the side of private enterprise operating through what seems like the classical competitive system. Their phraseology makes their philosophy quite clear: governmental operations are "interventions." Are governmental actions "interventions"?

The value of Grether and Holloway's extremely lucid presentation is that it permits the reader with an opposing point of view to come to grips immediately with the concepts and facts at issue.

Grether and Holloway make the claim that the American market system, as a whole, as well as specific subsystems, is under the continuing and increasing intervention of governmental policies and programs. Thus this point takes for granted the very question under research. What indeed are the "facts"? First of all, one must decide on the nature of what is taken as facts—are the facts legal documents or responses to them? One can raise the question whether a feeling of confinement and intervention arises less from actual governmental legal and administrative regulatory framework and more from the frame of mind of any entrepreneur, as he sees the "rules of the game" under which he operates. Typically, one accepts the rules of the game and does not regard them as inhibiting performance or freedom of choice. What may be regarded as intervention by one generation may be accepted as part of the rules of the game by the next generation.

## POSSIBLE RESEARCH INTO INTERVENTION: HISTORICAL AND CROSS-SECTIONAL

Perhaps several different research studies are required. Basic are the documentary facts; there is opportunity for historical analysis of the scope—both in broad coverage and detailed application within industries—of actual governmental regulations or inhibition of business practices.

# 21. Are Planning and Regulation Replacing Competition in the New Industrial State?

JOHN KENNETH GALBRAITH, WALTER ADAMS,
WILLARD F. MUELLER, and DONALD F. TURNER

*Editor's note:* The Select Committee on Small Business, United States Senate, invited four eminent scholars to appear before it on the question: "Are Planning and Regulation Replacing Competition in the New Industrial State?" The seminar discussion included statements by each of the noted scholars. This Senate Committee and its several sub-committees have been conducting hearings for several years on questions of distribution, marketing practices, monopoly, and competition. Each of these issues raises important questions about the antitrust laws, their enforcement and effectiveness. The statements of each scholar present diversity of views and particularly raise questions about Dr. Galbraith's thesis presented in his book, *The New Industrial State.*

## STATEMENT OF
## DR. JOHN KENNETH GALBRAITH[*]

I am very happy to be here this morning. And while all of us take a natural pleasure in debate, I trust that no one will consider these to be adversary proceedings. I have long been a close and admiring student of Attorney General Turner's writings, as equally those of Professor Adams. I regard, as all of us do, Professor Mueller as one of the most distinguished of our colleagues in the Federal Service. As will become evident, Mr. Turner's position, fully explored, provides comprehensive and much appreciated support for mine.

This is perhaps especially true of his position before he became subject, however slightly, to the intellectual constraints of high public office. I would like to begin by defining this area of agreement, as I venture to see it. Then I will proceed to the, by comparison, much smaller area of argument.

In the lectures that precipitated this discussion and the book I have just published,[1] I took it for granted that American business has become very big.

The element of surprise in this conclusion is very small; I doubt that this conclusion will be much disputed. There are still a large number of small firms and small farms in the United States. They are, however, no longer characteristic of the American economy. In 1962, the five largest industrial corporations in the United States, with combined assets in excess

♦ SOURCE: Reprinted from, "Planning, Regulation and Competition." Hearings before Subcommittees of the Select Committee on Small Business, U.S. Senate, Ninetieth Congress, First Session, June 29, 1967, (U.S. Government Printing Office, Washington, D.C.).

[*] Paul M. Warburg Professor of Economics, Harvard University, Cambridge, Mass.
[1] *The New Industrial State* (Boston: Houghton Mifflin, 1967).

of $36 billion, possessed over 12 percent of all assets used in manufacturing. The 50 largest corporations had over a third of all manufacturing assets. The 500 largest corporations had well over two-thirds. Corporations with assets in excess of $10 million, some 2,000 in all, accounted for about 80 percent of all the resources used in manufacturing in the United States.[2]

In the mid-1950's, 28 corporations provided approximately 10 percent of all employment in manufacturing, mining, and retail and wholesale trade. Twenty-three corporations provided 15 percent of all the employment in manufacturing. In the first half of that decade —June 1950-June 1956—a hundred firms received two-thirds by value of all defense contracts; 10 firms received one-third.[3] In 1960 four corporations accounted for an estimated 22 percent of all industrial research and development expenditure. Three hundred and eighty-four corporations employing 5,000 or more workers accounted for 85 percent of these research and development expenditures; 260,000 firms employing fewer than 1,000 accounted for only 7 percent.[4]

If I might continue this somewhat exaggerated dose of statistics for just a minute, in 1965, three industrial corporations, General Motors, Standard Oil of New Jersey, and Ford Motor Co., had more gross income than all of the farms in the country. This is relevant to my statement that these are the typical, characteristic parts of the economy. The income of General Motors, of $20.7 billion, about equalled that of the 3 million smallest farms in the country—around 90 percent of all farms. The gross revenues of each of the three corporations just mentioned far exceed those of any single State. The revenues of General Motors in 1963 were 50 times those of Nevada, eight times those of New York, and slightly less than one-fifth those of the Federal Government.[5]

These figures, like all statistics, are subject to minor query on matters of detail. As orders of magnitude they are not, I believe, subject to any serious question. Nor are the consequences.

The large firms that dominate the nonservice and nonagricultural sector of the economy have extensive power over their prices. They have large influence over the prices that they pay—at least those costs that are important to their operations. And also the wages they pay. They supply themselves with capital; some three-quarters of all savings now come from the retained earnings of corporations, which is to say that the latter have largely exempted themselves from dependence on the capital market. And, with varying degrees of success firms with the resources to do so go beyond the prices that they set to persuade their customers as to what they should buy. This is a persuasion that, in various and subtle ways, extends to the State. There is great room for difference of opinion, and accordingly for debate, on how decisive are these several manifestations of power. But nearly all will agree that "There is a large correlation between the concentration of output in the hands of a small number of large producers and the existence of firms with significant degrees of market power." The observation just cited is that of Mr. Carl Kaysen and Mr. Donald F. Turner in their authoritative volume, "A Policy for Antitrust Law." [6]

They add, as would I, that a policy that deals with "the existence and significance of market power is not aimed at *merely marginal or special phenomena, but at phenomena spread widely through the economy*." [7] Still quoting Professor Kaysen and Mr. Turner.

---

[2] Hearings before the Subcommittee on Antitrust and Monopoly of the Committee of the Judiciary, U.S. Senate, 88th Cong., 2d sess., pursuant to S. Res. 262. Pt. I. "Economic Concentration. Overall and Conglomerate Aspects" (1964), p. 113. Data on the concentration of industrial activity in the hands of large firms, and especially any that show an increase in concentration, sustain a controversy in the United States that, at times, reaches mildly pathological proportions. The reason is that much of the argument between those who see the market as a viable institution and those who feel that it is succumbing to monopolistic influences has long turned on these figures. These figures are thus defended or attacked according to predilection. However, the general orders of magnitude given here are not subject to serious question.

[3] Carl Kaysen, "The Corporation: How Much Power? What Scope?" in *The Corporation in Modern Society*, Edward S. Mason, ed. (Cambridge: Harvard University Press, 1959), pp. 86–87.

[4] M. A. Adelman, hearings before the Subcommittee on Antitrust and Monopoly of the Committee on the Judiciary, U.S. Senate, 89th Cong., 1st sess., pursuant to S. Res. 70, pt. III. "Economic Concentration. Concentration, Invention and Innovation" (1965), pp. 1139–1140.

[5] Data from Fortune, U.S. Department of Agriculture and Statistical Abstract of the United States.

[6] Harvard University Press, 1959, pp. 8–9.

[7] *Ibid.*, p. 41. (Emphasis is Dr. Galbraith's.)

In my own volume I have gone on, at no slight length, to argue that this trend to the large corporation and this resulting exercise of substantial power over the prices, costs, wages, capital sources, and consumers is part of the broad sweep of economic development. Technology; the extensive use of capital; affluent and hence malleable customers; the imperatives of organization; the role of the union; the requirements imposed by public tasks, including arms development and space exploration, have all weakened the authority of the market. At the same time, these developments have both enabled and required firms to substitute planning with its management of markets for a simple response to the market. Bigness and market power, in other words, are but one part of a much larger current of change. To see them in isolation from other change is artificial. In part it is what results when a social discipline passes however partially from the custody of scholars to that of specialists and mechanics.

I have also been concerned in this book with the problem of how we are to survive, and in civilized fashion, in a world of great organizations which, not surprisingly, impose both their values and their needs on the society they are assumed to serve. But these further matters are not directly at issue this morning. In any case they do not directly involve the question of the antitrust laws.

The issue of the antitrust laws arises in response to a prior question. That question is whether we can escape the concentration and the attendant market control and planning which I have outlined and whether the antitrust laws, as now used, are an effective instrument for this escape. The present hearings materialized when I urged the contrary—when I said that the trend to great size and associated control was immutable, given our desire for economic development, and that the present antitrust efforts to deal with size and market power were a charade. I noted that the antitrust laws legitimatize the real exercise of market power on the part of the large firms by a rather diligent harassment of those who have less of it. Thus, they serve to reassure us on the condition they are assumed to correct.

The facts which lead to the foregoing conclusions are not at all obscure. Nor are they matters of great subtlety. They are accepted by most competent economists and lawyers including the very distinguished men here this morning. Only the rather obvious conclusions to be drawn from these facts encounter a measure of resistance. This, no doubt, is purely temporary, but while it persists it does cause a measure of confusion.

The most effective manifestation of economic power, all must agree, is simply the big firm. To be big in general and big in an industry[8] is by far the best way of influencing prices and costs, commanding capital, having access to advertising, and selling resources, and possessing the other requisites of market power. And, as we have seen, by common agreement the heartland of the industrial economy is now dominated by large firms. The great bulk of American business is transacted by very large corporations.

And here enters the element of charade in the antitrust laws. If a firm is already large it is substantially immune under the antitrust laws. If you already have the basic requisite of market power, you are safe. The Assistant Attorney General in Charge of the Antitrust Laws in the distinguished book to which I have already adverted argues that the market power of the large firm should now be made subject to the antitrust laws. This indeed is the main thrust of Mr. Turner's and Mr. Kaysen's book. If something needs to be done, he would not, of course, argue that it has been done. And in responding to the questions of this committee on May 2 of this year he affirmed the point, if in slightly more cautious language:

It is more difficult under present law to bring a case attacking *existing* concentration in an industry than to prevent further concentrations which firms attempt to realize through merger.[9]

But this we see is no minor qualification. If firms are already large—if concentration is already great—if the resulting power to use Mr. Turner's own words, is not "merely marginal" but is "spread widely through the economy" as he says, then it means that all so favored have won immunity or virtual immunity from the antitrust laws. And this, of course, is the case.

Meanwhile, the antitrust laws are effective in two instances where the firms do not have

---

[8] The two go together although some economists, in a desire to exculpate size while indicting monopoly, have, curiously enough, asserted the contrary.

[9] Letter to the Honorable Wayne Morse, May 2, 1967 (his emphasis).

market power but are seeking to achieve it. Where firms are few and large they can, without overt collusion, establish and maintain a price that is generally satisfactory to all participants. Nor is this an especially difficult calculation, this exercise of power. This is what we economists with our genius for the neat phrase have come to call oliogopolistic rationality. And this market power is legally immune or very nearly so. It is everyday practice in autos, steel, rubber, and virtually every other industry shared or dominated by, relatively, a few large firms. But if there are 20 or 30 or more significant firms in the industry, this kind of tacit pricemaking—this calculation as to what is mutually advantageous but without overt communication—becomes more difficult, maybe very difficult. The same result can only be achieved by having a meeting or by exchanging information on prices and costs and price intentions. But this is illegal. It is also legally vulnerable. And it is, in fact, an everyday object of prosecution as the Department of Justice will confirm. What the big firm in the concentrated industry can accomplish legally and effortlessly because of its size, the small firm in the unconcentrated industry does at the pain of civil and even criminal prosecution. Moreover, with this my colleagues will, I believe, agree.

The second manifestation of the charade has to do with mergers. If a firm is already large, it has as a practical matter nothing to fear under antimerger provisions of the Clayton Act. It will not be demerged. It can continue to grow from its own earnings; if discreet, it can even, from time to time, pick up a small and impecunious competitor, for it can reasonably claim that this does little to alter the pattern of competition in the industry. But if two medium-sized firms unite in order to deal more effectively with this giant, the law will be on them like a tiger. Again if large, you are exempt. If you seek to become as large, or even if you seek to become somewhat larger, although still much smaller, you are in trouble. And again I doubt that the committee will encounter a great deal of dissent.

Here we have the nature of modern antitrust activity. It conducts a fairly effective war on small firms which seek the same market power that the big firms already, by their nature, possess. Behind this impressive facade the big participants who have the most power bask in nearly total immunity. And since the competitive market, like God and a sound family life, is something that no sound businessman can actively oppose, even the smaller entrepreneurs who are the natural victims of this arrangement do not actively protest. It is possible that they do not know how they are being used.

As I say all of this is agreed—or at least is supported by the past writings and speeches of participants in this discussion. All I have done —I wish I could lay claim to greater novelty— is to state the rather disagreeable conclusion flowing from this agreement. The antitrust laws give the impression of protecting the market and competition by attacking those who exercise it most effectively. I wonder if the committee thinks that charade is an unjust word?

Now let me clear up two or three secondary matters which may seem to affect this discussion but really do not. The first requires me, I think for the first time—in substance as distinct from terminology—to quit company with Attorney General Turner. Mr. Turner, while conceding that the law is largely helpless in attacking achieved as distinct from aspired-to power, holds that it is important to act preventatively to keep smaller firms from getting larger. This he has emphasized in his responses to this committee. It will surely have occurred to the committee, as it must have occurred to Mr. Turner, that this does not meet the issue of gross discrimination as between those who already have and those who aspire to market power. Nor, one imagines, can a major law officer of the Government be entirely happy about such discrimination. It condones professional and accomplished wrongdoing, as it were, but stresses the importance of cracking down on amateur wickedness. Surely this is bad law. Also, given the size and market power that has already been achieved, and given its immunity, it will be evident that this justification amounts to locking the stable door not alone after the horse has been stolen but after the entire stud has been galloped away.

Next, I must correct a misapprehension of Attorney General Turner. His responses to the committee and his extremely interesting lecture attacking my general position in London convey the impression that I am concerned with making the economic case for the large corporation. I am, he suggests, especially concerned to defend its efficiency and technical virtuosity. To this he responds by arguing that, while the big corporation is more efficient than the small firm, there is no great difference between the big corporation and the giant corporation. He doesn't make altogether clear, incidentally, how big a big as distinct from a giant corporation is. All would, I imagine, be among the five hundred or thousand firms that dominate industrial activity. But I have a more fundamental objection. He attacks me on a point that concerns me little and which is of no importance for my case.

I am not concerned with making the case for big business. Nor am I especially concerned about its efficiency or inefficiency. Doubtless efficiency is worth having. But, like truth, regular bathing and better traffic regulation, it has an adequate number of exponents. I have always thought it unwise to compete with the commonplace. Mr. Turner may be correct in his conclusions about the giants. I am content to argue that we have big business, and that the antitrust laws notwithstanding, we will continue to have it, and that they give an impression of alternative possibilities that do not exist.

I conclude also that while big business and giant business may not be more efficient, their market power as manifested only on what they sell and what they buy and over buyers does give them advantages in planning their own future and insuring their own survival. Since big business in inevitable and will not be affected by the antitrust laws, I naturally go on to consider how we may come to terms with it. Much of my book is concerned with that. If my colleagues this morning disagree, as is their right, they must tell you how the antitrust laws are to be brought effectively to bear on the large corporation. Otherwise—and here let me interpolate an important point—there is no escape from the conclusion that the antitrust laws, so far from being a threat to big business are a facade behind which it operates with yet greater impunity. They create the impression, the antitrust laws, that the market is a viable control. Then, if a drug firm has exorbitant profits, it can say this is what the market allows. Or if an automobile firm does not want to install safety appliances, it can say that the market does not demand it. Or if there is resistance to Government price guideposts to prevent inflation, it can be said that these interfere with the market.

In each case, the antitrust laws effectively protect the large business from social pressure or regulation by maintaining the myth that the market does the regulating instead.

Finally, I agree that the antitrust laws have purposes other than those related to the structure of industry and the resulting power and planning. I agree in particular they are a code of what is deemed fair and decent as between

seller and buyers. They exclude the resort to activities—naked aggression, as in the case of the old Standard Oil Co. in the last century—based on superior economic resources, favoritism, surreptitious and unfair discounts, numerous other practices which the civilized commercial community holds in disesteem. I have no complaint about these aspects of the antitrust laws. On the contrary, I consider them serviceable. But only in the most marginal fashion do they thus affect the structure of industry. They are, in large part, a separate matter and do not affect the discussion here.

To what then does this all lead? It is possible that my distinguished colleagues here this morning will call for an all-out attack on achieved market power along the lines which Attorney General Turner has adumbrated in his book, which Prof. Walter Adams has long favored, and which I have just said would be necessary if they disagree with my conclusions on the inevitability of market power. This means action, including enabling legislation leading to all-out dissolution proceedings against General Motors, Ford, the oil majors, United States Steel, General Electric, IBM, Western Electric, Du Pont, Swift, Bethlehem, International Harvester, North American Aviation, Goodyear, Boeing, National Dairy Products, Procter & Gamble, Eastman Kodak, and all of comparable size and scope. For there can be no doubt: All are giants. All have market power. All enjoy an immunity not accorded to those who merely aspire to their power. Such an onslaught, tantamount, given the role of the big firms in the economy as I described it, to declaring the heartland of the modern economy illegal, would go far to make legitimate the objections to my position. It would mean that achieved market power was subject to the same legal attack as that which is only a matter of aspiration.

But I will be a trifle surprised if my distinguished colleagues from the Government are willing to proclaim such a crusade. I am frank to say I would not favor it myself; as I indicated at the outset, I do not think that the growth of the modern corporation can be isolated from other and intricately related changes in modern economic development. I doubt that one can operate on one part of this fabric. The political problems in proclaiming much of the modern economy illegal will also strike many as impressive.

If this crusade is not to be launched, then my good friends have no alternative but to agree with me. They are good men; they cannot acquiesce in a policy which by their own admission attacks the small man for seeking what the big firm enjoys with impunity. I readily concede that it would be quixotic to ask the repeal of the antitrust laws although other industrial countries function quite competently without them. But the antitrust laws are part of the American folklore. They receive strong support from the legal profession and vice versa. They have a reserve value for dealing with extreme and sanguinary abuse of power as occasionally occurs. I would be content were we simply to withdraw our faith from the antitrust laws—were we to cease to imagine that there is any chance that they will affect the structure of American industry or its market power and, having in mind the present discrimination in their application, were we then to allow them quietly to atrophy. Then we would face the real problem, which is how to live with the vast organizations—and the values they impose—that we have and will continue to have. This being so, nostalgia will no longer be a disguise for that necessity.

## STATEMENT OF DR. WALTER ADAMS*

Time precludes more than a cursory tribute to an eminently civilized and literate political economist—a leader in that small but brave army of men who "prefer to see the truth imperfectly and obscurely rather than to maintain error, reached indeed with clearness and consistency and by easy logic, but based on hypotheses inappropriate to the facts." It is Galbraith's cardinal virtue to focus on real problems and vital issues. His questions are invariably to the point. Regrettably, his answers are sometimes wrong.

In the "New Industrial State," Galbraith once again examines the reality of corporate giantism and corporate power, and outlines the implications for public policy. He finds that the giant corporation has achieved such dominance of American industry, that it can control its environment and immunize itself from the discipline of all exogenous control mechanisms—especially the competitive market. Through separation of ownership from management it has emancipated itself from the control of stockholders. By reinvestment of profits (internal financing), it has eliminated

the influence of the financier and the capital market. By brainwashing its clientele, it has insulated itself from consumer sovereignty. By possession of market power, it has come to dominate both suppliers and customers. By judicious identification with, and manipulation of the state, it has achieved autonomy from government control. Whatever it cannot do for itself to assure survival and growth, a compliant government does on its behalf—assuring the maintenance of full employment; eliminating the risk of, and subsidizing the investment in, research and development; and assuring the supply of scientific and technical skills required by the modern technostructure.

In return for this privileged autonomy, the industrial giant performs society's planning function. And this, according to Galbraith, is not only inevitable (because technological imperatives dictate it); it is also good. The market is dead, we are told; and there is no need to regret its passing. The only remaining task, it seems, is to recognize the trend, to accept it as inexorable necessity, and, presumably, not to stand in its way.

Mr. Chairman, here is a blueprint for technocracy, private socialism, and the corporate state. The keystone of the new power structure is the giant corporation, freed from all traditional checks and balances, and subject only to the countervailing power of the intellectual in politics—those Platonic philosopher-kings who stand guard over the interests of the Republic. Happily, this blueprint need not cause undue alarm: first, because Galbraith's analysis rests on an impirically unsubstantiated premise; and second, even if this analysis were correct, there would be more attractive public policy alternatives than Galbraith suggests.

Galbraith's contention that corporate giantism dominates American industry requires no abumbration. On that there is consensus. But Galbraith fails to prove that this dominance is the inevitable response to technological imperatives, and hence beyond our control. Specifically, he offers little evidence to demonstrate that Brobdingnagian size is the prerequisite for, and the guarantor of:

(1) Operational efficiency;
(2) Invention, innovation, and technological progress; and
(3) Effective planning in the public interest.

Let me comment briefly on each of these points, and in so doing indicate that the com-

---

* Professor of Economics, Michigan State University, East Lansing, Mich.

petitive market need not be condemned to the euthanasia which Galbraith thinks is inexorable, and perhaps even desirable.

## Efficiency

In the mass-production industries, firms must undoubtedly be large, but do they need to assume the dinosaur proportions of some present-day giants? The unit of technological efficiency is the plant, not the firm. This means that there are undisputed advantages to large-scale integrated operations at a single steel plant, for example, but there is little technological justification for combining these functionally separate plants into a single administrative unit. United States Steel is nothing more than several Inland Steels strewn about the country, and no one has yet suggested that Inland is not big enough to be efficient. A firm producing such divergent lines as rubber boots, chain saws, motorboats, and chicken feed may be seeking conglomerate size and power; it is certainly not responding to technological necessity. In short, one can favor technological bigness and oppose administrative bigness without inconsistency.

Two major empirical studies document this generalization. The first, by Dr. John M. Blair, indicated a significant divergence between plant and company concentration in major industries dominated by oligopoly. It indicates, moreover, that between 1947 and 1958, there was a general tendency for plant concentration to decline, which means that in many industries technology may actually militate toward optimal efficiency in plants of "smaller" size.[1]

The second study, by Prof. Joe Bain, presents engineering estimates of scale economies and capital requirements in 20 industries of above-average concentration. Bain finds that:

. . . Concentration by firms is in every case but one greater than required by single-plant economies, and in more than half of the cases very substantially greater.

In less precise language, many multiplant industrial giants have gone beyond the optimal size required for efficiency. Galbraith acknowledges the validity of Bain's findings, but dismisses them by saying:

The size of General Motors is in the service

not of monopoly or the economies of scale, but of planning. And for this planning . . . there is no clear upper limit to the desirable size. It could be that the bigger the better.[2]

If size is to be justified, then, this must be done on grounds other than efficiency. I shall return to this point in a moment.

## Technological Progress

As in the case of efficiency, there is no strict correlation between giantism and progressiveness. In a study of the 60 most important inventions of recent years, it was found that more than half came from independent inventors, less than half from corporate research, and even less from the research done by large concerns.[3] Moreover, while some highly concentrated industries spend a large share of their income on research, others do not; within the same industry, some smaller firms spend as high a *percentage* as their larger rivals. As Wilcox points out:

The big concern has the ability to finance innovation; it does not necessarily do so. There is no clear relationship between size and investment in research.[4]

Finally, as this committee well knows, roughly two-thirds of the research done in the United States is financed by the Federal Government, and in many cases the research contractor gets the patent rights on inventions paid for with public funds. The inventive genius which ostensibly goes with size would seem to involve socialization of risk and privatization of profit and power.

The U.S. steel industry, which ranks among the largest, most basic, and most concentrated of American industries, certainly part of the industrial state that Professor Galbraith speaks of, affords a dramatic case in point. It spends only 0.7 percent of its revenues on research and, in technological progressiveness, the giants which dominate this industry lag behind their smaller domestic rivals as well as their smaller foreign competitors. Thus, the basic oxygen furnace—considered the "only major breakthrough at the ingot level since before the turn of the century" was invented in 1950 by a miniscule Austrian *firm* which was less than one-third the size of a single *plant* of

---

[1] U.S. Senate Antitrust and Monopoly Subcommittee, Economic Concentration, pp. 1541–1551.
[2] Id., p. 76.

[3] Jewkes, Sawers, and Stillerman, *The Sources of Invention*, chapter IV.
[4] *Public Policies Toward Business*, 3d ed., p. 258.

the United States Steel Corp. The innovation was introduced in the United States in 1954 by McLouth Steel which at the time had about 1 percent of domestic steel capacity—to be followed some 10 years later by the steel giants: United States Steel in December 1963, Bethlehem in 1964, and Republic in 1965. Despite the fact that this revolutionary invention involved an average operating cost saving of $5 per ton and an investment cost saving of $20 per ton of installed capacity, the steel giants during the 1950's according to *Business Week*, "bought 40 million tons of the wrong capacity—the open-hearth furnace" which was obsolete almost the moment it was put in place.[5]

Only after they were subjected to actual and threatened competition from domestic and foreign steelmakers in the 1960's did the steel giants decide to accommodate themselves to the oxygen revolution. Thus, it was the cold wind of competition, and not the catatonia induced by industrial concentration, which proved conducive to innovation and technological progress.[6]

### Planning in the Public Interest

Modern technology, says Galbraith, makes planning essential, and the giant corporation is its chosen instrument. This planning, in turn, requires the corporation to eliminate risk and uncertainty, to create for itself an environment of stability and security, and to free itself from all outside interference with its planning function. Thus, it must have enough size and power not only to produce a "mauve and cerise, air-conditioned, power-steered, and power-braked automobile"[7]—unsafe at any speed—but also enough power to brainwash customers to buy it. In the interest of planning, producers must be able to sell what they make—be it automobiles or missiles—and at prices which the technostructure deems remunerative.

Aside from the unproved premise—and I keep coming back to this: technological necessity—on which this argument rests, it raises crucial questions of responsibility and accountability. By what standards do the industrial giants plan, and is there an automatic convergence between private and public advantage? Must we, as a matter of inexorable inevitability, accept the proposition that what is good for General Motors is good for the country? What are the safeguards other than the intellectual in politics—against arbitrary abuse of power, capricious or faulty decision making? Must society legitimatize a self-sustaining, self-serving, self-justifying, and self-perpetuating industrial oligarchy as the price for industrial efficiency and progress?

This high price need not and should not be paid. The competitive market is a far more efficacious instrument for serving society—and far more viable—than Galbraith would have us believe. Let me illustrate:

(1) In the electric power industry, a network of local monopolies, under Government regulation and protection, was long addicted to the belief that the demand for electric power was inelastic—that rates had little to do with the quantity of electricity used. It was not industrial planning, carried on by private monopolists under public supervision, but the yardstick competition of TVA which demonstrated the financial feasibility of aggressive rate reductions. It was this competitive experiment which proved that lower electric rates were not only possible but also profitable—both to the private monopolists and to the customers they served.

(2) In the airline oligopoly, also operating under the umbrella of Government protectionism, the dominant firms long suffered from the same addiction. They refused to institute coach service on the grounds that it would eliminate first-class service and—through a reduction in the rate structure—bring financial ruin to the industry. Again it was the force and discipline of competition—from the small, nonscheduled carriers, operating at the margin of the industry—which proved that the giants and their overprotective public regulators were wrong. As this committee observed, it was the pioneering and competition of the nonskeds which "shattered the concept of the fixed, limited market for civil aviation. As a result, the question is no longer what portion of a fixed pie any company will get, but rather how much the entire pie can grow."[8]

Again, a bureaucracy-ridden, conservative, overcautious, overprotected industry was shown to have engaged in defective planning—

---

[5] *Business Week*, Nov. 16, 1963, pp. 144–146.

[6] Adams and Dirlam, "Big Steel, Invention, and Innovation," *Quarterly Journal of Economics*, May 1966.

[7] *The Affluent Society*, p. 253.

[8] Senate Report No. 540, 82d Cong., first sess., 1951.

to its own detriment as well as the public's.

(3) In the steel industry, after World War II, oligopoly planning resulted in truly shabby performance. There was an almost unbroken climb in steel prices, in good times and bad, in the face of rising or falling demand, increasing or declining unit costs. Prices rose even when only 50 percent of the industry's capacity was utilized. Technological change was resisted and obsolete capacity installed. Domestic markets were eroded by substitute materials and burgeoning imports. Steel's export-import balance deteriorated both in absolute and relative terms; whereas the industry once exported about five times as much as it imported, the ratio today is almost exactly reversed, and steel exports are confined almost exclusively to AID-financed sales guaranteed by "Buy American" provisos. We may be confident that if this deplorable performance is to be improved, it will come about through the disciplining force of domestic and foreign competition, and not through additional planning or an escalation of giant size. It will come about through an accommodation to the exigencies of the world market, and not by insensitive monopolistic pricing, practiced under the protectionist shelter of the tariffs which the industry now seeks.

Without multiplying such examples, it is safe to say that monopoloid planning is done in the interest of monopoly power. Seldom, if ever, is society the beneficiary.

In conclusion, I would note that industrial giantism in America is not the product of spontaneous generation, natural selection, or technological inevitability. In this era of "Big Government," it is often the end result of unwise, manmade, discriminatory, privilege-creating governmental action. Defense contracts, R. & D. support, patent policy, tax privileges, stockpiling arrangements, tariffs, subsidies, etc., have far from a neutral effect on our industrial structure. Especially in the regulated industries—in air and surface transportation, in broadcasting and communications—the writ of the State is decisive. In controlling these variables the policymaker has greater freedom and flexibility than is commonly supposed; the potential for promoting competition and dispersing industrial power is both real and practicable.[9]

It seems to me that Professor Galbraith

keeps coming back to the charade of antitrust, but a competitive society is the product not simply of negative enforcement of the antitrust laws; it is the product of a total integrated approach on all levels of government —legislative, administrative, and regulatory. An integrated national policy of promoting competition—and this means more than mere enforcement of the antitrust laws—and is not only feasible but desirable. No economy can function without built-in checks and balances which tend to break down the bureaucratic preference for letting well enough alone—forces which erode, subvert, or render obsolete the conservative bias inherent in any organization devoid of competition. Be it the dictates of the competitive market, the pressure from imports or substitutes, or the discipline of yardstick competition, it is these forces which the policymaker must try to reinforce where they exist and to *build into* the economic system where they are lacking or moribund. The policy objective throughout must be to promote market *structures* which will *compel* the conduct and performance which is in the public interest.

The disciplining force of competition is superior to industrial planning—by the private or public monopolist, the benevolent or authoritarian bureaucrat. It alone provides the incentives and compulsions to pioneer untried trails, to explore paths which may lead to dead ends, to take risks which may not pay off, and to try to make tomorrow better than the best.

## STATEMENT OF
## DR. WILLARD F. MUELLER[*]

It is, indeed, an awesome challenge to cope with the ideas of the Goliath of the economics profession, one who gracefully moves from a high post in that most criticized of Government wartime agencies, the OPA, to the editorial desk of *Fortune* magazine and the halls of Harvard; one who is as much at home with the problems of the underdeveloped nations as with his so-called "new industrial state." Few in the fraternity of economists can match Professor Galbraith in his facility of expression and capacity to create provocative insights into the great issues of the day.

His recent Reith lectures on "The New Industrial State" caused a mild sensation in some

[9] Adams and Gray, *Monopoly in America*, (New York: Macmillan, 1955).

[*] Chief Economist and Director, Bureau of Economics, Federal Trade Commission, Washington, D.C.

circles.[1] I understand that among some segments of the European industrial community Galbraith's ideas fell like new rain on seeds already sprouted. But I suspect American economists will be less receptive to his ideas.

The heart of his thesis is that over the past 75 years certain "technological imperatives" have wrought great changes in the basic arrangement of modern economic life, the ultimate consequence of which is the "diminished effectiveness of the market." As a result, "the market is replaced by planning."

He argues that modern technological imperatives make the vast, "mature" industrial enterprise a perfect mechanism for planning the invention, innovation, and production process. But market power is not only an end result, it is prerequisite to the success of the system. The requirements of large-scale production, heavy capital commitments, and sophisticated technology demand elaborate planning. Successful planning, in turn, requires management of consumer wants to suit the needs of the business enterprise. The planning process is carried on by what Galbraith labels "the technostructure," which encompasses all the technicians and professionals required for effective group decision-making.

Additionally, modern technology requires increasing participation by the state in the planning process, for many jobs are too big even for the largest private industrial complex. Finally, Galbraith believes that public policy aimed at maintaining competition is based on a 19th-century conception of the economy. He, therefore, would abandon our traditional policy of relying on market forces to limit and discipline the use of private economic market power.

Where is the new industrial state taking us? Galbraith predicts that the mature corporation is increasingly becoming a part of the administrative complex of the state and that there will be a gradual convergence of capitalistic and communistic societies.[2] What will be the quality of life in the new industrial state? Should we continue to subordinate all to material welfare, that is what we will get. On the other hand, should we raise our sights to more es-

thetic goals, the industrial system will become "responsive to the larger purposes of society." He has shown us, in his words, "wherein the chance for salvation lies."[3] So, in the end, it will be up to us to choose. (This is a surprise ending in view of the irrespressible economic determinism which led to all his earlier conclusions.)

Although I shall emphasize points of difference, there is much in Galbraith's "new industrial state" with which I agree. In fact, much of what he says has become a part of the conventional economic wisdom—Berle and Means articulated in 1934 the thesis of separation of business ownership and control.[4] But Galbraith has put together these and other old ideas—some accepted and some rejected by economists—into a new and bigger package. And as always when Galbraith goes over even familiar ground, he discovers new things and paints a different and grander landscape than his forbears. But as one not so friendly reviewer observed, "novelty isn't everything: one can make a decent case for the proposition that it is more important to be right than different."

At the outset, let there be no mistake about it: Although Galbraith has articulated a provocative thesis concerning the causes and implications of "the new industrial state," he has not borne the burden of mustering the evidence to validate this thesis.

Time permits joining issues on only his key points. I shall challenge three of his major contentions:

1. Technological imperatives dictate vast industrial concerns and high levels of market concentration and, hence, the death of the market.

2. Public policy aimed at maintaining a market economy has failed in the past and is doomed to fail in the future.

3. The necessity for State planning in certain areas further diminishes the need for reliance on the market as a regulating and planning agent.

### The Technological Imperatives

Most fundamental to Galbraith's thesis are the so-called technological imperatives which

[1] John Kenneth Galbraith capsuled his views of "The New Industrial State" in six Reith lectures delivered over the British Broadcasting Corporation. These lectures, delivered during November and December 1966, appeared in "The Listener," published by BBC. A fuller exposition of his views appears in his book, *The New Industrial State,* published June 26, 1967, by Houghton Mifflin Co.

[2] *The New Industrial State,* pp. 389 ff.

[3] *Ibid.,* p. 399.

[4] Adolf A. Berle and Gardiner C. Means, *The Modern Corporation and Private Property,* 1934.

he views as the root causes of modern industrial organization. He asserts that we must have very large industrial complexes and high market concentration because of the requirements of large-scale production, invention, and innovation. As he puts it, "The enemy of the market is not ideology but technology." But what are the facts on this point?

Recent studies of this subject are almost unanimous in concluding that productive efficiency dictates high concentration in only a small and declining share of all manufacturing industries. On this point, there seems to be little disagreement.

There is a growing body of research into the extent to which economies of large scale dictate large business enterprise and high market concentration. The evidence is sharpest in the area of productive efficiency. This is an especially crucial area because of the public policy dilemma posed by industries with increasing returns to large scale. In clear-cut cases where large-scale production dictates monopoly, as with telephone and electric power, the American answer has been either regulation or Government ownership. But, if such industries prove the rule rather than the exception, this raises a basic question as to the compatability of productive efficiency and a competitively structured economy. It is, therefore, extremely significant that recent studies are unanimous in concluding that productive efficiency dictates high concentration in only a small—and declining—share of all manufacturing industries.[5]

But Galbraith does not rest his case on the requirement of large-scale production. He further argues that economies of scale in research and innovation make high concentration and near monopoly an inevitable outcome of modern capitalism. Since Joseph Schumpeter first set forth this doctrine in 1942[6] and Galbraith expanded upon it in 1952,[7] it has been subjected to extensive empirical testing. There has been a virtual flood of studies in recent years. All students of the subject are not in complete agreement. But as a minimum, a careful reading of the evidence shows that the theory has no general validity in explaining inventive and innovative activity in Amercan experience. Indeed, recent studies indicate that the thesis is on the verge of collapse. One of Schumpter's disciples recently discovered no systematic relationship between the degree of market power and inventive success. He concluded:

These findings among other things raise doubts whether the big, monopolistic conglomerate corporation is as efficient an engine of technological change as disciples of Schumpeter (including myself) have supposed it to be. Perhaps a bevy of fact-mechanics can still rescue the Schumpeter engine from disgrace, but at present the outlook seems pessimistic.[8]

Students of the problem owe a debt of gratitude to the Senate Subcommittee on Antitrust and Monopoly, chaired by Senator Philip A. Hart, for the exhaustive hearings it has held on the subject of the role of technology and industrial organization.[9] Over the past 3 years these hearings have reviewed systematically nearly all of the recent authoritative work on this subject. I shall not review this evidence here, but it is must reading for anyone genuinely interested in getting at the facts in this area. Regrettably, Professor Galbraith apparently has failed to explore this and other authoritative

---

[5] Some of the key studies on this subject are the following: Joe S. Bain, "Barriers to New Competition," 1956, John M. Blair, "Analysis of Divergence Between Plant and Firm Concentration." Hearings on Economic Concentration. Senate Subcommittee on Antitrust and Monopoly, Sept. 12, 1966. The FTC staff study, "The Structure of Food Manufacturing," Technical Study No. 8, National Commission on Food Marketing, June 1966, 83–99, summarizes the studies done on this subject in the food industries. Also, see various statements in hearings cited in footnote 9.

[6] Joseph Schumpeter, *Capitalism, Socialism, and Democracy,* 1942.

[7] John Kenneth Galbraith, *American Capitalism, The Concept of Countervailing Power,* 1952, p. 91. There are important differences, however, between the arguments of Schumpeter and Galbraith. Whereas Galbraith argues that technological imperatives make great market power inevitable, thereby destroying the market, Schumpeter thought "the process of creative distinction" would continually erode market power of those holding it.

[8] F. M. Scherer, "Firm Size, Market Structure, Opportunity and the Output of Patented Inventions," *American Economic Review,* December 1965, 1121–22.

[9] Hearings before the Subcommittee on Antitrust and Monopoly of the Committee on the Judiciary. U.S. Senate, 89th Cong., first sess., Economic Concentration, pt. 3. Concentration, Invention, and Innovation, 1965; pt. 4, Concentration and Efficiency, 1965.

work on the subject. Until he, or others, can come up with contrary evidence, the chief pillar of his thesis lacks an empirical foundation.

I think his use of illustration betrays his case. He illustrates, as you will recall from his Reith lectures and also his books, the matchless capability of the vast enterprise in planning inventive and innovative activity by a hypothetical example of how General Electric would go about the conception and birth of a new popup toaster.[10] But insight into this process is better revealed by experience than by hypothetical example. What support in experience is there for predicting that vast size is prerequisite to the development and introduction of new products and processes? Let's consider the electrical home appliances sold by General Electric. Perhaps the past is prolog to the future.

To begin, the electric toaster was not invented or introduced by a great corporation such as General Electric, which would fit so nicely Galbraith's invention-innovation-planning framework. On the contrary, according to the late T. K. Quinn, former vice president of General Electric, it was developed and brought into the market by a relatively small firm, the McGraw Co. And, according to Mr. Quinn, "for many years none of the giant companies were able to come near to matching [McGraw's] toaster." [11] This is no exception. Mr. Quinn credited small companies with discovery and initial production of electric ranges, electric refrigerators, electric dryers, electric dishwashers, the hermetically sealed compressor, vacuum cleaners, clothes-washing machines, deep freezers, electric hot irons, and electric steam irons.[12] Indeed, Mr. Quinn summarized his own experience with GE in this way:

I know of no original product invention, not even electric shavers or hearing aids, made by any of the giant laboratories or corporations, with the possible exception of the household garbage grinder, developed not by the research laboratory but by the engineering department of General Electric. But the basic idea of this machine came from a small concern producing commercial grinders.[13]

He concluded:

The record of the giants is one of moving in, buying out, and absorbing the smaller concerns.

Nor is this record unique to household appliances. In many other industries smaller companies generate at least their proportionate share of inventions and innovations, and frequently they do a good deal better than the industrial giants.[14]

Perhaps Galbraith's "technological imperatives" assumption has greater validity in areas where invention and innovation costs are higher and the planning horizons are more distinct than they are in consumer goods products. But here, too, Galbraith's premises are based more on sands of fancy than rocks of evidence. Perhaps no industry fits as snugly the Galbraith model for ideal planning as the American steel industry. Since the creation of United States Steel in 1901, the American steel industry has been highly concentrated and dominated by big enterprises. Presumably this market structure provided what Galbraith views as the "prime requirement" of planning: "control over decision."

There can be no doubt but that the market structure of the industry gave big steel considerable discretion in planning. But the relevant question is whether this discretion was used as Galbraith's theory predicts. Fortunately in this case we need not rely on speculation. The leading steel companies clearly had a lackluster record as inventive and innovative forces in this most basic industry. The accomplishments

---

[10] "The central characteristics of modern industry are illustrated by this culturally exciting invention. It would require a large organization, embracing many specialists, to get this product to consumers. Considerable capital would be required. While it is conceivably open to an individual entrepreneur, such as myself, to have an inspiration, no one would expect a one-man firm to produce such a product. It could be floated only by a big firm. All decisions on the toaster—those involving initiation, development, and ultimate acceptance or rejection—are the work of teams of specialists and are exercised deep down in the company. And no one would think of leaving price or demand to the market. The price would be subject to careful advance calculation * * *." (Second Reith lecture, p. 754.) He also uses this illustration in his book at pp. 68–69.

[11] T. K. Quinn, *Giant Business*, 1953, p. 117.

[12] *Ibid.*, pp. 116–117.

[13] *Ibid.*, p. 177.

[14] See especially summary of literature by Prof. Daniel Hamburg in "Economic Concentration," pt. 3, op. cit., pp. 1281–92. Also see Jewkes, Sawers and Stillerman, *Sources of Invention*, 1958; and W. S. Comanor, "Research and Technical Change in the Pharmaceutical Industry," *Rev. of Econ. and Stat.*, May 1965, p. 190.

of United States Steel have been especially disappointing. After an exhaustive study of the corporation, an engineering consulting firm reported to United States Steel in 1939 that it was lagging badly in many respects.[15] Nor have United States Steel or other large steel companies performed much better since 1939. A study of the 13 major innovations in the American steel industry between 1940 and 1955 reveals none was the outgrowth of American steel companies.[16] Four were based on inventions of European steel companies (generally small by American standards) and seven came from independent inventors.

Especially instructive is the postwar record concerning the introduction of the oxygen steelmaking process by dominant American steel firms. The basic oxygen process has been called the only major technological breakthrough at the ingot level of steelmaking since before 1900.[17]

Not only did the largest steel companies play no role in the discovery and initial development of this important innovation, but they lagged badly in introducing it.[18] A small Austrian steel company (which was one-third the size of a single plant of United States Steel) perfected and introduced the oxygen process. The first American company to adopt the new process was McLouth Steel, which had less than 1 percent of industry capacity. Although other smaller companies followed McLouth's lead, not until 1964 did United States Steel and Bethlehem introduce the process. This was fully 10 years after McLouth and 14 years after the small pioneering Austrian firm had introduced this revolutionary process.

Does Galbraith really want more industries structured like the American steel industry? Would he have permitted this industry to become even more concentrated through mergers among small enterprises (e.g., Bethlehem and Youngstown, which you will recall was one of the first merger cases) so that they could better emulate the performance of U.S. Steel?

## Is the Market Dead?

As a corollary of his assumptions concerning technology, Galbraith argues that we can no longer rely on market forces to allocate resources. Because of this, he continues, the struggle to maintain competition alive "has obviously been a losing one. Indeed, it has been lost." These assertions go to the heart of Galbraith's thesis, for it is because the market has perished that we must be saved by extensive extra market planning. Should this premise prove faulty, Galbraith's thesis comes tumbling down.

We have already seen that the evidence does not support his thesis that as a general rule technological imperatives require high levels of industrial concentration. It should therefore come as no surprise that in many industries competitive forces are considerably stronger than Galbraith suggests and that in many industries where concentration is highest, the market position of industry leaders is being eroded. I recently presented to this committee a rather comprehensive summary of postwar concentration trends.[19] Very briefly, during the post-war years—between 1947 and 1963—market concentration tended to decline across a broad front in the producer goods sector of manufacturing. While this is in direct conflict with the predictions of Galbraith's thesis, it is entirely consistent with the empirical evidence referred to earlier and which Professor Adams has mentioned. While in some industries technology may make it impossible for very small companies to operate efficiently, it does not dictate mammoth size and high levels of market concentration. Most American markets have become so large that they can sustain a rather considerable number of efficient-size enterprises.

Surprisingly, it is in consumer goods manufacturing industries where concentration has been on the rise in the postwar years. Surprisingly, I say, because the technological require-

[15] George W. Stocking, *Basing Point Pricing and Regional Development*, The University of North Carolina Press, 1954, p. 140.

[16] A study by Edwin Mansfield found that the leading steel companies also lagged in the innovation process. Edwin Mansfield, "Size of Firm, Market Structure, and Innovation," *Jr. of Pol. Econ.*, December 1963, pp. 556–76.

[17] Walter Adams and Joel B. Dirlam, "Big Steel,

Invention and Innovation," *Quarterly Journal of Economics*, May 1966, p. 169. The following discussion of the introduction of the basic oxygen process is based on the highly important study by Adams and Dirlam, *Ibid*.

[18] *Ibid.*

[19] Willard F. Mueller, statement before the Select Committee on Small Business, U.S. Senate, March 15, 1967.

ments in these industries demand relatively smaller enterprises than in producer goods manufacturing. Of course, the reasons for increasing concentration in consumer goods manufacturing are to be found in the requirements of product differentiation (especially the costs of large-scale promotion) and distribution, not in the technological imperatives that Galbraith assumes to be the kingpins of market power.

When postwar concentration trends are viewed together with the recent findings concerning the relationship between technology and industrial organization, we have a valuable insight into the future viability of the market as a regulator and planner of economic activity. Modern technology has not made obsolete our competitive, market-oriented economy. For it is precisely in the producer goods manufacturing industries where economies of large-scale invention, innovation, and production are most pronounced. Yet these industries have experienced a significant drop in market concentration. This has occurred because many industrial markets have grown more rapidly than have the requirements of large-scale business organization.

These trends in market concentration may yet be irrelevant if Galbraith's concept of market power is correct. Throughout his discussion he implies that, "characteristically," American industries are concentrated "oligopolies," and that the firms operating in them have great discretionary pricing power independent of the market.[20] But like Gertrude Stein, Galbraith has difficulties with shades of difference. Fortunately, however, all oligopolies are not alike and there are important differences in the degree of market power conferred by varying market structures. The accumulating evidence of the relationship between an industry's structure[21] and its performance leaves little room for agnosticism concerning the powerful role played by the market in limiting discretionary pricing power.[22] And, importantly, there is now persuasive evidence demonstrating that in the larger part of American manufacturing industry market forces limit quite severely the discretionary pricing power of firms.[23] But, again, Galbraith has ignored the mounting evidence which runs counter to one of his central premises.[24]

This isn't to imply that there are no strong positions of entrenched power in our economy

---

[20] Galbraith not only wrongly implies that market concentration is increasing, but also overstates the levels of market concentration. He says, ". . . in the characteristic market of the industrial system there are only a handful of sellers." He then lists the automobile and 17 other industries, and says that there are a "host" of others. *The New Industrial State*, pp. 180–181. Galbraith has not selected "characteristic" industries. In each industry cited the top 4 did two-thirds or more of the business. But of the "host" of other industries not cited, more than 3 out of 4 had lower levels of concentration. Also, 13 of the 18 high concentration industries which he cites experienced declines in concentration in recent years. The big exceptions were consumer goods items—most notably, automobiles, a favorite example of Galbraith.

[21] The key structural elements are market concentration, ease with which new competitors can enter the market, and the degree to which the products of individual sellers are "differentiated."

[22] See, for example, Joe S. Bain, "Relation of Profit Rate of Industry Concentration: American Manufacturing, 1936–40," *Quarterly Journal of Economics*, August 1951: L. W. Weiss, "Average Concentration Ratios and Industrial Performance," *Journal of Industrial Economics*, July 1963. Norman R. Collins and Lee Preston, "Concentration and Price Margins in Food Manufacturing Industries," *The Journal of Industrial Economics*, July 1966, 226. A report by the staff of the Federal Trade Commis-

sion, "The Structure of Food Manufacturing," Technical Study No. 8, National Commission on Food Marketing, June 1966, pp. 202–210. H. Michael Mann, "Seller Concentration, Barriers to Entry, and Rates of Return in Thirty Industries, 1950–1960," *Review of Economics and Statistics*, August 1966, pp. 296–307. Unpublished study by Norman R. Collins and Lee Preston, "Concentration and Price-Cost Margins in Manufacturing Industries," April 1, 1966.

[23] Empirical evidence indicates that discretionary pricing power becomes quite severely limited when the top 4 firms in an industry control less than half and the top 8 less than 70 percent of industry output. See Bain, op. cit., "FTC Staff Study," op. cit., Mann, op. cit. The greater part of all manufacturing occurs in industries where the top 4 firms control less than 50 percent of industry output. See Mueller, Statement before Senate Small Business Committee, op. cit., p. 63. Kaysen and Turner estimated that 23 percent of manufacturing industry shipments were made in industries where the top 8 firms controlled 40 percent or more of industry shipments. Kaysen and Turner, "Antitrust Policy," 1959. These authors used rather broad definitions of industries and therefore understate somewhat the level of market concentration.

[24] In his two chapters on "Prices in the Industrial System," Galbraith does not cite a single empirical study to support his assertions *The New Industrial State*, pp. 178–197.

—there are. Again, however, Galbraith greatly overstates his case. But, importantly, whereas he pays tribute to the firms with substantial market power—indeed, he believes such power is essential—the evidence indicates that firms with great power perform less admirably than he assumes. Hence, the facts support a precisely opposite public policy than that advocated by Galbraith—we need more competition, not less.

The rising concentration in consumer-goods industries at first blush seems to bear out Galbraith's thesis of managing consumer wants to suit the needs of the business enterprise. But the causes of developments here are not rooted in Galbraith's technological imperatives. As noted earlier, the requirements of large-scale production, invention, and innovation are less demanding in the manufacture of consumer goods than in other areas of manufacturing. It is true that many sellers try to manage consumer wants. But this is because of the form which competition takes where opportunities for product differentiation exist. True, the market operates less perfectly as a result—though I suspect it operates better than Galbraith assumes. If Americans really are strongly dissatisfied, however, they can do something about this problem; though they probably won't. Nor will Galbraith's "new industrial state" change things on this score.

Despite its shortcomings, particularly in the area of some consumer goods, the market clearly has not disappeared as the key coordinating and integrating force in allocating resources in most of the economy. The picture that emerges when one studies the entire industrial landscape is not that painted by Galbraith. Whereas he concedes his thesis does not encompass the entire economy, close inspection shows it captures only a small part of the real world.[25]

### Is Antitrust a Charade?

But the mere absence of factors requiring high market concentration does not guarantee that excessive concentration will not arise or that it will decline in industries where it already is too high. Simply put, effective competition is not a flower that thrives unattended. Powerful firms may engage in competitive strategies which counteract the forces working toward deconcentration. Specifically, until the passage of the Celler-Kefauver Act in 1950, horizontal and vertical mergers often had the effect of offsetting these forces, with the result that in many industries concentration remained unchanged or even increased.

Again, I feel that Professor Galbraith has neglected his homework. He has not kept abreast of contemporary antitrust policy or its effects. He asserts that it is a "charade" acted out, "not to prevent exploitation of the public," but, "to persuade people in general and British Socialists and American liberals in particular, that the market is still extant."[26] He sums up his views of current antitrust policy as follows (he has already mentioned them this morning):

A great corporation wielding vast power over its markets is substantially immune. . . . But if two small firms seek to unite, this corporate matrimony will be meticulously scrutinized. And, very possibly, it will be forbidden.[27]

These assertions simply do not square with the facts. Antimerger effort has been directed almost exclusively against the largest indus-

---

[25] Galbraith says that he is not concerned with "the world of the independent shopkeeper, farmer, shoe repairman, bookmaker, narcotics peddler, pizza merchant, streetwalker, and the car and dog laundries." He feels obliged to emphasize this point, he says, because, "One should always cherish his critics and protect them where possible from foolish error. The tendency of the mature corporation in the modern industrial system to become part of the administrative complex of the state cannot be refuted by appeal to contrary tendencies elsewhere in the economy." Sixth lecture, p. 916. But as I explained earlier, his thesis explains only a small part of the manufacturing sector of the economy. Moreover, his technological imperatives obviously are even less important in wholesale and

retail trade, in the services industry and in agriculture, which today comprise about 35 percent of national income outside the Government sector. Nothing drastically new has occurred in the other segments of the economy which suggests a trend toward decreasing importance of market forces. Competition in transportation and finance, etc.—which generate another 13 percent of national income—is probably as effective today as in prewar years. This leaves communications and public utilities, which provide 5 percent of national income. But they, of course, have been subject to a degree of regulation since at least the 1930's.
[26] Third lecture, p. 794.
[27] *Ibid.*

trial concerns.[28] It has not, as he suggested, been an attack on industrial midgets. Over 60 percent of the largest, those with over a billion dollars, and merely a third of the top 200 have been subjects of antimerger complaints. Practically all of these complaints have not involved the challenging of miniscule mergers, but rather have involved an attack upon mergers by large concerns. I have discussed this at greater length elsewhere.[29] My major conclusion, however, is that there has been an enormous effort. Perhaps Professor Galbraith would say that my intellectual outlook has been affected somewhat by the techno-structure within which I now operate. But even if I were back at the University of Wisconsin—or even at Harvard—I would still come to the same conclusion, as I am sure he will when he reads my other statement. In my opinion, this enforcement effort represents a great victory for competition, as well as a clear demonstration that antitrust policy can be an effective instrument of public policy in the last half of the 20th century.

It is true that antitrust policy cannot easily —and certainly not quickly—solve problems of deeply entrenched power. Fifty years of ineffective public policy toward mergers resulted in unnecessarily high concentration in many industries. But recent developments show that much can be accomplished. I say categorically: Whether or not the market survives in the greater part of our economy, or is destroyed by vast aggregations of market power, will not be determined by technological imperatives but by public policy toward the achievement and retention of power. The market may well be destroyed in the next generation as Galbraith predicts, but not for his reasons. It will be a matter of public will or neglect, not technology.

---

[28] The great bulk of merger complaints challenged mergers by the country's 500 largest concerns. Fully 62 percent of the 52 $1 billion industrial corporations have been subjects of complaints as have 35 percent of the top 200. Mueller, "The Celler-Kefauver Act," *op. cit.*

[29] *Ibid.*

[30] He also is incorrect in implying that the great role of the state as a customer of goods and services is mainly related to technological imperatives. It is true that the state buys nearly a fifth of our economic output. But what are these purchases? In 1967 expenditures related to our military and international commitments and the cost of past wars accounted for fully 79 percent of the Federal budget: National defense (54 percent),

## Planning and the State

In the "new industrial state" the Government plays a central role in economic planning with a concomitant diminution in reliance upon the market. Specifically, it stabilizes aggregate demand, underwrites expensive technology, restrains wages and prices in limiting inflation, provides technical and educational manpower, and buys upwards of a fifth of our economic output.

It is true that the Government does these things, and more. But Galbraith exaggerates the role of the state (as opposed to the market) in the planning process.[30] He points out correctly that one of the main responsibilities of the modern state is to sustain aggregate demand and stimulate economic growth. He fails to perceive, however, that the state's planning in this respect is neither in competition with, nor a substitute for, planning by business enterprise, and it certainly does not require abandonment of the market. On the contrary, the basic philosophy of the Employment Act of 1946 is that the state create a general economic environment within which private enterprise can generate economic growth.[31] Within this environment the basic "planning" decisions of what and how much of each product to produce are left to private enterprise responding to aggregate demand.

Experience increasingly demonstrates the heavy role played by the market in implementing or frustrating monetary and fiscal policy aimed at full employment. Only if competition is effective are extensive price controls not a necessary adjunct to planning for rapid economic growth without inflation.

The wage and price guideposts of the Council of Economic Advisers are a symptom of the absence of effective competition in some seg-

space research and technology (5 percent), international affairs and finance (4 percent), veterans' benefits (5 percent), and interest on the national debt (11 percent). Thus the growing size of the Federal budget is not the outcome of technological imperatives but of international imperatives of being the world's leading power.

[31] The Employment Act of 1946 states in its "Declaration of Policy" that the Federal Government shall "coordinate and utilize all its plans, functions, and resources for the purpose of creating and maintaining, in a manner calculated to foster and promote free competitive enterprise and the general welfare * * *." Employment Act of 1946, As Amended, with Related Laws, 60 Stat. 23, Public Law 304—79th Cong.

ments of the economy.[32] But, happily, these segments are in the minority. Were it otherwise, it probably would be impossible to push toward full employment without implementing extensive wage and price controls.

None appreciate these facts of life so keenly as those economists responsible for public policy in this area. Dr. Walter Heller, the former Chairman of the Council of Economic Advisers and prime mover in gaining public acceptance for the "new economics," has emphasized the importance of keeping competition alive. He does not believe that planning for rapid economic growth requires abandonment of the market. Rather, he argues forcibly in his recent book that we must make competition more, not less, effective. As he puts it:

There are substantial differences among economists on how far the government should go in protecting consumers or setting guideposts for wages and prices. But there is little difference—at least among the vast majority of economists—in supporting strong measures to protect the free play of market forces against monopoly and price-fixing, and in strongly opposing direct wage and price controls as inefficient and inequitable substitutes for market forces, to be considered only as a last resort in a war economy.[33]

In a similar vein, the Joint Economic Committee of the Congress has repeatedly emphasized the importance of maintaining effectively competitive markets, and I do not think they are merely playing charades. Its most recent report on the Economic Report of the President concluded, "Antitrust must be assigned a central role in national economic policy of no less significance than monetary and fiscal policy."[34]

Do not misunderstand me. Certainly, many of the most pressing problems of the day—water and air pollution, job retraining, urban and rural poverty, preservation of our natural resources, promotion of basic research, to name a few—require action and planning by the state. But it is wrong to infer that the failure of the market to solve these kinds of problems represents a fatal flaw in the system. Unfortunately, many persons are inclined to damn the market—which to them means the businesses

operating within it—for failing to do jobs better left to the state. And, unfortunately, the defensively hostile responses of some business leaders to every social welfare proposal lend credence to the argument that the real issue at stake is the market system. Actually, however, the real issue usually is whether or not a particular job should be done at all, and who is going to pay for it. Once it is agreed that there is nothing inherently un-American or antimarket in admitting that some things are best left to the state, the state and the market can live in happy coexistence. In truth, they are indispensable complements of one another, rather than rivals or substitutes. But this has little to do with economic imperatives and the abandonment of the market.

## STATEMENT OF
## HON. DONALD F. TURNER[*]

I do not believe that Professor Galbraith's evaluation of our economy's market structure is accurate. I subscribe almost in toto to the points that have been made previously by Dr. Mueller and Dr. Adams. They have spared me the task of dealing in detail with those aspects of the argument.

But in any event, I think it would be more suitable for me to discuss the charges that have been made against antitrust law and the characterization that has been put upon it.

On the impact of antitrust law, I think it is undeniable that it has been more vigorous and more effective in attacking price fixing, other restrictive agreements and mergers than in dealing directly with existing market power. I suppose that may even be characterized as a massive understatement. But, on the failure of antitrust law to deal adequately with undue existing market power, I do have a few comments.

The first is that to some extent this failure to deal with existing market power makes sense. I think it clearly makes sense to the extent that size and whatever market power that happen to go with it truly reflects economies of scale. I think it may also make some sense, although in my opinion perhaps less, where market power was acquired by initial competitive

[32] Walter W. Heller, *New Dimensions of Political Economy,* 1966, p. 43.
[33] *Ibid,* pp. 8–9.
[34] Report of the Joint Economic Committee, Congress of the United States, on the January 1967

Economic Report of the President, 90th Cong., 1st sess., Rept. No. 73, Mar. 17, 1967, p. 25.

[*] Assistant Attorney General, Antitrust Division, Department of Justice, Washington, D.C.

superiority and has been maintained without exclusionary behavior of any kind.

We have here, at least arguably, a problem of incentive. The fundamental purpose of the antitrust laws is to encourage competitive striving. It would be a little paradoxical, to say the least, to turn on the winner when he wins. If that were regular practice, one might anticipate some disincentive problems which may reach serious proportions.

I do now know the answer to that argument, but I just suggest, as I said, that it may make some sense to permit some conditions of market power which may be acquired and maintained in unexceptionable ways. Beyond this, I agree it would be desirable to increase the effectiveness of antitrust in dealing directly with existing market power. Of course, in saying so, I am proceeding on the premise that my friends Mueller and Adams more accurately access the current validity of the competition than Professor Galbraith has. There may be some ways of expanding the scope of antitrust within the confines of existing legislation. That is worth probing, and it is being probed.

I would also add that I still subscribe to the views Professor Kaysen and I set forth, now some 8 years ago, in which we urged additional legislation which would make it easier to deal with monopoly and oligopoly problems. However, I suppose it is highly likely that if I sent such a proposal forward to the administration, it would not be rushed over to the Hill the following morning.

Even assuming, however—and I will make that assumption for the purposes of the balance of my remarks—that our present relative inactivity in dealing with existing undue market power shall continue for the indefinite future, I do not agree that it is bad public policy or bad law or bad anything to continue to attack price fixing and other restrictive agreements and mergers likely to increase market power in those areas where we still have hope.

To put it somewhat differently, the fact that for historical reasons of one sort or another we have had to accept a measure of unfortunate development in one or more areas of our economy does not mean, it seems to me, that we are compelled to make things worse by permitting more.

It seems to me that to describe the kind of policy we have have been carrying on as "discrimination" is to apply a most inappropriate term. In antitrust or in any other area of public policy it has always been true that even

though we cannot undo the past we can try to do better for the future, and we cannot rationally measure prospective public policy by past mistakes. Past mistakes by no means compel repetition.

In this regard, while monopoly and oligopoly are, indeed, a problem, I think we should be careful not to overstate it, as I believe Mr. Galbraith has. To quote from his book, "Oligopoly is not a special but a general case. It is the market structure of the industrial system."

Now, unaccustomed as I am to calling attention to the nonoligopolistic sector of our economy, I do feel compelled to put Professor Galbraith's remarks in perspective. Taking mining and manufacturing together with transportation and public utilities, Professor Kaysen, a man whom we both view with high regard, estimates that the oligopolistic sectors produce around 20 percent or probably 25 percent of national income. Concededly, this is not a trivial figure. But neither does it amount to the domination that Professor Galbraith's remarks suggest.

That being so, we have wide areas of economy which have not been afflicted or badly afflicted, and it seems clear to me that it makes good public policy sense to endeavor to preserve competition where it can be preserved in those areas. I see no reason why we should not continue to attack outright price-fixing agreements, even though, in some industries, concentration is so high and the nature of the product is such that the sellers, as Mr. Galbraith indicates, can achieve close to the kind of price determination that an outright agreement would.

I have already given some general reasons for this. I would add a particular one. That is that price-fixing agreements involving a rather large number of firms in a way is the worse of all possible worlds. You get all of the disadvantages of price fixing and the kind of interference with competition and allocation of resources that gives you without any of the economies of size that come from growth of firms—except, I should say, perhaps some planning advantage. But I doubt very much the episodic kind of price fixing that we have seen really makes any significant contribution to this.

Now, turning to mergers, where industries are currently relatively unconcentrated, why permit further concentration by merger? There may, indeed, be some economic changes taking place in some industries which tend to indicate that the current size of firms is below that which would be necessary for the achievement of economies. But typically, substantial economies will be developed by internal growth, and without having any figures, I would guess that internal growth has been the means by which most economies of scale have been achieved in the past.

Where there is already a fair degree of concentration in an industry, even where there may be one or two or three dominant firms, the problem posed by merger involving firms other than the largest is indeed a somewhat more difficult problem than it appears to be in the unconcentrated industry. But it is also, I suggest, much more complicated than Professor Galbraith suggests by using the term "discrimination."

Let me give you a specific example: In the steel industry, several years ago, Bethlehem, the No. 2 firm, and Youngstown—I forget which, No. 5 or No. 6—proposed to merge. Both were substantially smaller than the United States Steel Corp. and the merged company was still considerably smaller. Indeed, the argument was made that we should have permitted those two companies to merge in order that they could more adequately deal with United States Steel. It seems perfectly plain to me that apart from any moral reason, which I reject, there was no persuasive economic reason to permit this merger and, the decision was eminently correct. I will only give a couple of reasons.

Even assuming that the merger would have increased the competitive ability of the merged firms, which was disputable, there was no reason to suppose that the merger would have made the industry in fact any more competitive than it was or, to put it somewhat differently, that a merged Bethlehem-Youngstown would have embarked upon a competitive pricing spree or any kind of other competitive spree as a consequence of the merger. Moreover, to have permitted the merger would have made it much less likely that future technological changes, if they came, that would have lowered the size of firm necessary for economies of scale, would have led to an appropriate deconcentration of that industry.

Now, in all of these activities, as in attacks on patent licensing restrictions and the like, the purpose of the antitrust laws, even assuming that we can do nothing about existing concentration, is to preserve the opportunity for declining concentration in the future as new developments take place—new entry, new products, and the like. And I would cite in this connection, lest there be doubt that any such happy developments will ever take place, that Dr. Mueller's figures over the past 15 years show more often than not, many more oftentimes than not, there has been declining concentration in the producer-goods industries.

To sum up, even if we did nothing more than we now do in directly attacking undue market power, I am firmly convinced that a strong antitrust preventive policy makes economic sense and, on the basis of evidence now available to us, would still appear to promote longrun benefits for the economy.

# 22. *What Management Can Learn From the Borden Case—*

THOMAS F. SCHUTTE, VICTOR J. COOK, JR.,
and RICHARD HEMSLEY

In 1959, Professor W. David Robbins stated that the Robinson-Patman Act is ". . . one of the most complicated and controversial of antitrust laws. Twenty-three years of enforcement have produced crystal-clear confusion regarding some of its provisions. . . ."[1] For example, Section 2 (a) of the Robinson-Patman Act reads in part:

It shall be unlawful for any person engaged in commerce, in the course of such commerce, either directly or indirectly, to discriminate in price between different purchasers of commodities of *like grade and quality.* . . .[2] [Italics inserted]

The phrase "like grade and quality" is of central importance to management because commodities must be of the same grade and quality before the Federal Trade Commission can establish *any* price discrimination violation under the Robinson-Patman Act.

The basic question for both the commission and management on this aspect of the act is whether only physical and chemical attributes of products are pertinent in determining grade and quality, or whether consumer preference for a brand should also be considered. This question comes into sharp focus when considered in the light of the growing amount of private branding done by major manufacturers. Because of the economics of private label business, manufacturers tend to produce closely similar products for both their own and private labels. These products often differ physically only in external facade or in minor ingredient variation, but they are often sold at considerable price differentials. It is in the area of private branding that business and government have experienced the greatest difficulty in reconciling the meaning and interpretation of "like grade and quality."

## HISTORICAL BACKGROUND

During the 1936 congressional hearings on Representative Patman's bill, some concern developed that the effect of Section 2 (a) would be to restrict or even eliminate private brand ing. It was suggested that the section read: ". . . commodities of like grade, quality *and brand.*" [Emphasis added] It was argued that, without the added word "brand," private labels ". . . would thus be put out of business by the nationally advertised brands."[3] But supporters of the bill feared that the courts would construe "like grade, quality and brand" to mean that the sale of products differing only as to label would be outside the reach of the

---

♦ SOURCE: Reprinted by permission from *Business Horizons*, Vol. 9, No. 4, Winter 1966, pp. 23–30.
[1] W. David Robbins, "A Marketing Appraisal of the Robinson-Patman Act," *Journal of Marketing,* XXIV, July 1959, p. 15.

[2] The Clayton Act, 38 Stat. 730 (1914), as amended by the Robinson-Patman Act, 15 U.S.C. Section 13 (a).

[3] Hearings on H. R. 4995 before the House Committee on the Judiciary, 74th Cong., 2nd Sess., p. 335.

statute. The proposed amendment was rejected in committee.

Prior to the final passage of the Robinson-Patman Act, the FTC took action, based on the Clayton Act, against the private label activities of Goodyear Tire and Rubber Company.[4] The commission charged Goodyear with price discrimination in the sale of tires to Sears, Roebuck and Company under the Allstate label at much lower prices than the prices charged to its own dealers for tires of similar quality sold under the Goodyear label. The company *admitted* that the quality of the Allstate private label tires was comparable to that of the Goodyear brand. The FTC ruled that Goodyear had violated Section 2 of the Clayton Act because "at no time did it offer to its own dealers prices on Goodyear brands of tires which were comparable to prices at which respondent was selling tires of equal or comparable quality to Sears, Roebuck & Company."[5]

The important effect of the Goodyear decision was the rejection of differences in consumer preferences between the established products as a basic criterion for determining product grade and quality. The Goodyear case set the tone for subsequent proceedings under the Robinson-Patman Act. Although every FTC proceeding in this area has implied *some* legal definition of "like grade and quality," the commission has not been consistent in applying physical product characteristics in judging "like grade and quality" for purposes of Section 2 (a) of the act. Despite twenty-three years and the plethora of cases involving price discrimination between purchasers of "like grade and quality" products, it was not until 1958 that a manufacturer forcefully challenged the inconsistencies among the commission, the courts, and the Department of Justice, and sought an answer to whether or not significant brand distinction constituted a basis for disproving "like grade and quality" of otherwise physically similar products for purposes of the Robinson-Patman Act. "Like grade and quality" was finally specifically interpreted by the Supreme Court in March, 1966, in a decision involving the private branding practices of the Borden Company.

## THE BORDEN CASE

### Initial Investigations and Decisions

In April, 1958, the FTC charged that the Borden Company violated Section 2 (a) of the Robinson-Patman Act and discriminated in price between buyers of evaporated milk of "like grade and quality." The Borden Company engaged in "dual branding": it produced both a manufacturers' brand (under the Borden label) and private brands (under the labels of several retailers) of evaporated milk. Both the manufacturers' and private brand milk were physically and chemically the same. The containers were the same. Although only the labels were different, Borden charged a higher price for its manufacturers' branded milk than for the private brand product.

The FTC's hearing examiner rendered a decision in December, 1961. He found that the evaporated milk under the Borden brand and private label were commodities of like grade and quality for purposes of the Robinson-Patman Act. However, the hearing examiner held that no price discrimination in violation of the act was established because it could not be shown that competition had been substantially lessened or that a reasonable probability existed of such changes to competition in the future. Also, the hearing examiner found that Borden had sufficiently cost justified the price differences shown.

Both parties appealed the decision to the full commission. Government attorneys supporting the complaint challenged the hearing examiner's findings that there was lack of competitive injury and that the price differences had been cost justified. Borden primarily challenged the finding that both the Borden brand and private label milk were of like grade and quality.

The full FTC reviewed the case and set aside the hearing examiner's decision. A cease-and-desist order was entered against Borden in November, 1962. The commission based its decision on four salient points.[6] *First,* the Borden brand and the private label evaporated milk were of like grade and quality for purposes of the Robinson-Patman Act. *Second,* the price differential was discriminatory within

---

[4] 22 F.T.C. 232 (1936).
[5] H. R. Report No. 2287, 74th Cong., 2nd Sess.
(Washington: U.S. Gov't Prtg. Office, 1935), p. 4.
[6] F.T.C. Dkt. 7129.

the meaning of Section 2 (a); that is to say, a price discrimination is merely a price difference. *Third,* the commission held that the required competitive injury had been shown, that some smaller packers of private label evaporated milk lost some accounts to Borden after Borden expanded private label business to two of its southern plants.[7] In addition, several smaller producers had left the industry as Borden gained a share of the private label market. *Fourth,* the commission rejected the cost justification defense in which Borden had used average prices and costs. The commission held that, for purposes of this case, broad averaging camouflaged the economic effect of actual prices in specific situations.[8]

In addition, the commission rejected the cost analysis on the basis of Borden's failure to classify costs by type of customers (such as retailers, wholesalers, and cooperatives). "It was incorrect for the purpose of cost study to average all such costs together without distinctions as to the customer groups." [9]

### Appeals to Higher Courts

Upon receiving the FTC cease-and-desist order, the Borden Company appealed the case to the Fifth District Court of Appeals. In December, 1964, this court set aside the decision of the commission, maintaining that determination of product grade and quality ". . . may not be based solely on the physical properties of the products without regard to the brand names they bear and the relative acceptance these brands enjoy. . . ." [10] Furthermore, the court maintained that although a brand name per se may not be sufficient for demonstrating differentiation in grade, it was the consumer's preference for one brand over another *and* his willingness to pay a higher price for a well-known brand that placed the price differential beyond the reach of Section 2 (a). Thus, this court concluded that the private label evaporated milk was not of the same grade and quality as the milk sold under the Borden brand, and that Section 2 (a) of the Robinson-Patman Act did not apply.

The FTC appealed the Court of Appeals de-

cision to the Supreme Court. On March 23, 1966, the Supreme Court issued a 7-2 decision that reversed the position of the Court of Appeals. Thus, the Supreme Court held that, for purposes of the Robinson-Patman Act, a well-known label alone does not make a product different from one sold under a private label. In issuing the opinion of the Supreme Court, Justice White stated that: ". . . labels do not differentiate products for the purpose of determining grade or quality, even though the one label may have more customer appeal and command a higher price in the marketplace from a substantial segment of the public." [11]

Two justices strongly dissented. They believed that there was a difference in grade and quality between the manufacturer's brand and private label milk that should be recognized in the law. Laboratory analysis alone ignored a crucial factor—whether the products were different in the eyes of the consumer. Moreover, the dissenting justices did not find the precedent of the Goodyear case compelling in the Borden situation.

Contrary to the belief of many marketers, the Borden case has *not* been terminated with the recent Supreme Court decision. Borden has neither won nor lost the case. The Supreme Court examined one argument—whether or not differences in labels can result in different grade and quality for purposes of the Robinson-Patman Act. Upon *denying* the marketer the privilege to justify differences in like grade and quality on the basis of branding distinctions, the Supreme Court returned the case to the Federal District Court to examine the validity of Borden's defenses: (1) the absence of injury to competition and (2) cost justification.

## IMPLICATIONS FOR THE MARKETER

The Borden case has the greatest impact upon those companies that produce both manufacturers' brand and private labels (mixed brand policy), and those firms that produce only manufacturers' brands but are considering a mixed brand policy.

---

[7] "Borden Co. Wins Fight Against FTC Decision on Antitrust Charge," *Wall Street Journal,* Dec. 7, 1964, p. 13.

[8] Evidence at the hearing showed that the Borden brand milk was sold for as much as $6.00 per case and the private brand milk for as low as $4.89. In its cost defense, Borden used an average manufac-

turers' brand price of $6.4046 per case and an average private label price of $5.1743 per case.

[9] "Borden Company," *Trade Regulation Reports,* Dkt. 7129, paragraph 16, 191 (1962).

[10] *The United States Law Week,* XXIV (March 22, 1966), p. 4288.

[11] *The United States Law Week,* p. 4288.

The Supreme Court ruling does not mean the inevitable death or even restraint of private brands as some Jeremiahs have suggested. However, the ruling has made it clearer than ever that the mixed brand producer must recognize and reappraise the legal aspects of the private brand segment of his business. If it is true that the mixed brand producer's private brands generally sell for lower prices than the manufacturers' brands, four alternatives are available to legally justify the dual brand program. The first two alternatives *remove* the producer's mixed brand program from reach of Section 2 (a) of the Robinson-Patman Act; the last two alternatives are legal justifications for acknowledged price discrimination.

### Physical Variance in Quality

The essential question that the producer must raise under this alternative is "To what extent must the physical characteristics of products differ in order to escape the jurisdiction of Section 2 (a)?" Despite his realization that substantial differentiation is necessary, the mixed brand producer may be forced by the exigencies of marketing and production to hold differences between the manufacturer's and private label to a minimum.

On the basis of legal precedent, there is some evidence of what might constitute sufficient product variation. Perhaps the most positive and encouraging evidence for the mixed brand producer comes from recent precedents established by the FTC's 1953 Champion Spark Plug case, the 1955 attorney general's committee report, and the Atalanta Trading Corporation 1958 circuit court decision.

In the Champion case, the company sold spark plugs to Montgomery Ward under the Riverside label at a price 8¢ lower than the Champion brand sold to dealers.[12] Physical product differentiation, obvious only in the insulators and ribs, was minimal. The FTC, however, ruled that the two brands of plugs were not of like grade and quality.

In a study of antitrust laws, the attorney general's committee examined the prevailing law of like grade and quality as found in Section 2 (a). Although quite general, one section of their report is meaningful to the private brander: "Actual and genuine physical differentiations between two different products adapted to the several buyers' uses, and not merely a decorative or fanciful feature, probably removed differential pricing of the two from the reach of the Robinson-Patman Act."[13]

While it is difficult to interpret the exact meaning of actual and genuine product differentiations, the mixed brand manufacturer must exert special effort toward tailoring his private brand products to meet the needs of the customer. For example, a mixed brand manufacturer of automatic washers will vary the instrument panels, chromium pulls, color, and possibly the interior lining of his private brand product. Such efforts are very clearly attempts to differentiate a product to meet the needs of the private brand customer.[14]

Unlike either the Champion case or the attorney general's report, the 1958 Atalanta decision indicated the importance of packaging as a differentiating device for producers of mixed brands. The Atalanta Trading Corporation discriminated in promotion allowances between buyers of its packaged meat products. The allowances were made available only to those who purchased special, holiday-packaged canned pork products.

The commission held that, since the meat was derived from a common source and sold under a single trade name, the products should be considered of like grade and quality regardless of the special packaging. The Court of Appeals set this doctrine aside, holding that "artificial distinctions" do not escape the reach of the Robinson-Patman Act, but that "this does not mean that all distinctions are to be disregarded."[15]

A well-known commentator said of this decision:

While "artificial distinctions" in a product will not dispel its 'like grade and quality' if otherwise physically the same, substantial brand or packaging variations may suffice to overcome the purely physical analogy of products which do not sell "in the same price

[12] 50 F.T.C. 30, 47 (1953).

[13] U.S. Department of Justice, *Report of Attorney General's National Committee to Study the Antitrust Laws* (Washington: U.S. Gov't. Printing Office, 1955), p. 158.

[14] A minority of the members of the Attorney general committee argued that packaging was an important element in product differentiating a firm's private brands from its manufacturers' brands. For further discussion, see p. 158 of the Attorney General's Report.

[15] 258 F. 2d 365, 371 n. 5.

range," appeal to distinct customer classes, or 'price-wise are not competitive.' [16]

The Atalanta decision seems to make a strong case for the importance of packaging as a device for accomplishing product differentiation. In doing so, the case suggests an important managerial sideline: packaging distinctions *must not* be superficial. Rather, packaging must represent a serious attempt of the producer to differentiate his product from all others.

In using the strategy of product differentiation as a means for removing a mixed brand manufacturer's pricing policies from Section 2 (a) of the act, it should be recognized that the commission has not been consistent in ascertaining product grade and quality. An example is the General Foods case. General Foods packaged an institutional grade of coffee with an additional kind of bean for longer freshness, distinct coloration, and aroma, and sold it to distributors who specialized in serving public food service establishments. The FTC ruled in 1956 that the company's institutional coffee product and its Maxwell House brand coffee packed for grocery store distribution were of like grade and quality. The commission, in effect, did not believe that the addition of a variety of bean changed the product's grade and quality.

### Availability of Private Brands

A mixed brand manufacturer may avoid price discrimination charges if the private branded product is available to all its customers. For some firms, this is easier said than done. A successful mixed brand manufacturer generally restricts his private brand to those buyers who meet requirements based on volume of order, credit, or contract time period. Thus, the private brand product may not be available to all customers. Small private brand accounts may not be profitable for the supplier.

Some mixed brand manufacturers, however, could make all private brand products available to all customers. Perhaps rigorous account selection criteria are immaterial to the success of the supplier's private brand business. In addition, in light of the product similarity between the manufacturers' brand and private label, the producer may be able to combine the physical distribution activities of warehousing, inventory control, transportation, and over-all logistics systems planning for both brands.[17] One astute observer of the grocery industry has pointed out the good sense of making the private brand product available to all customers:

With the food business operating as it does today, it would seem rather pointless for an advertised brand/private label packer—whose products move through grocery warehouses—not to offer to pack private label for *all* of his customers—i.e. 'old line,' wholesalers, voluntary groups, retailer cooperatives, and chains.[18] [Italics inserted.]

### Cost Justification

Unlike the first two alternatives or strategies, the cost justification defense does not remove the firm's price discrimination from the jurisdiction of Section 2 (a) of the act. Rather, the firm is able to discriminate legally in price if it can be shown that there are differences in production and marketing costs between the two brands.

To employ this defense successfully, the mixed brand manufacturer must maintain an accurate cost accounting record system, and he must be able to justify completely its price differentials in terms of permissible cost savings. Unfortunately, many mixed brand manufacturers practice self-deception in their private brand cost accounting. They allocate only incremental or directly applicable variable costs to the private brand segment of their business. As a result, costs are generally understated. Hence, it would appear that pricing differences between the firm's manufacturers' brand and the private label products can be cost justified. Under an incremental costing and pricing practice, the risk of incurring an FTC complaint is great.

Inclusion of some costs is not permitted by the government. For example, in the Borden

---

[16] Frederick M. Rowe, *Price Discrimination Under the Robinson-Patman Act* (Boston: Little, Brown, 1962), p. 72. This is Rowe's interpretation of the court's Atalanta decision.

[17] John B. Matthews, Jr. and others, *Marketing: An Introductory Analysis* (New York: McGraw-Hill,

1964), p. 311.

[18] Roy Harrison, "Will You Bring Me Up to Date on That Borden Case?" *The Food Institute: Weekly Digest*, LXXII (New York: American Institute of Food Distribution, Inc., April 16, 1966), p. 1.

case, the FTC ruled that Borden could not include investment cost or cost savings resulting from the elimination of brokerage commissions. Investment cost is not a cash expense. It is often an arbitrary percentage of inventory value. In an opportunity cost sense, this percentage would be equal to the rate of return possible if the inventory funds were used instead in the most profitable alternative investment.[19]

### Absence of Injury to Competition

The absence of injury to competition defense is more difficult for the mixed brand firm to use successfully than the cost justification defense. Legal precedent indicates that absence of injury to competition refers to both *probable* as well as *actual* injury. Thus, the commission does not have to prove that a mixed brand manufacturer's private brand program injured competition. The commission can rule on the probable impact of a manufacturer's private brand program upon other suppliers in the future. In addition, damage to competition under the act is not limited to a manufacturer's private label competitors. Damage to competition can occur among competing wholesalers, chains, or independent retailers.

Some small business bias exists among governmental agencies and courts. This bias was most apparent in the Borden case. The commission was deeply concerned about the two small private brand suppliers who lost a share of market when the Borden Company expanded its private program. Whether or not absence of injury to competition is a dependable defense against a price discrimination charge, politically and legally astute companies should be aware of the effect of their private brand programs upon competition. This information might provide management with additional information with which to assess legal risks.

Not until the Supreme Court decision of

March, 1966 was a clearer interpretation made of the "like grade and quality" clause of Section 2 (a) of the Robinson-Patman Act. Before this decision, manufacturers and distributors hoped that differences in brands would provide an important basis for product differentiation.

The Supreme Court decision does not mean an end to private branding. Rather, the decision has made it more necessary than ever for the mixed brand manufacturer to develop specific legal justification for the private brand segment of his business. It is clear that the mixed brand manufacturer has two major alternatives. *First,* the firm can develop a private brand product that is physically differentiated from the manufacturers' brand. Hence, the producer removes himself from the jurisdiction of Section 2 (a). *Second,* the firm may develop a private brand product that is physically similar to its own brand. It is here that the court decision forces the firm to justify its pricing differences between the private and manufacturers' brand. Rather than justify pricing differences of products of like grade and quality on the basis of one possible defense, the manufacturer must examine and develop a minimum of two defenses in order to increase the probability of escaping a Section 2 (a) violation. He should have a clear and reconcilable cost justification defense. Furthermore, it behooves the firm to back up this defense with packaging variations between the two brands.

The concept and philosophy of private branding have become deeply enmeshed in the marketing system. Private branding will probably continue to be an important force in nearly every consumer product category—creating opportunities for manufacturers and suppliers to produce and develop private brands in their marketing programs. However, no manufacturer can afford the risks of producing and marketing private brand without first reconciling the legal justification for its pricing policies.

---

[19] For a detailed presentation and evaluation of Borden's costing analysis, see Daniel Jay Baum, *The Robinson-Patman Act: Summary and Com-* *ment* (Syracuse, N.Y.: Syracuse University Press, 1964), pp. 23–25.

# 23. Consumers' Protection and Interest Program

JOHN F. KENNEDY

*To the Congress of the United States:*

Consumers, by definition, include us all. They are the largest economic group in the economy, affecting and affected by almost every public and private economic decision. Two-thirds of all spending in the economy is by consumers. But they are the only important group in the economy who are not effectively organized, whose views are often not heard.

The Federal Government—by nature the highest spokesman for all the people—has a special obligation to be alert to the consumer's needs and to advance the consumer's interests. Ever since legislation was enacted in 1872 to protect the consumer from frauds involving use of the U.S. mail, the Congress and executive branch have been increasingly aware of their responsibility to make certain that our Nation's economy fairly and adequately serves consumers' interests.

In the main, it has served them extremely well. Each succeeding generation has enjoyed both higher income and a greater variety of goods and services. As a result our standard of living is the highest in the world—and, in less than 20 years, it should rise an additional 50 percent.

Fortunate as we are, we nevertheless cannot afford waste in consumption any more than we can afford inefficiency in business or Government. If consumers are offered inferior prod-

◆ SOURCE: Message from *The President of the United States* Relative to Consumers' Protection and Interest Program, Document No. 364, House of Representatives, 87th Congress, 2d Session, March 15, 1962.

ucts, if prices are exorbitant, if drugs are unsafe or worthless, if the consumer is unable to choose on an informed basis, then his dollar is wasted, his health and safety may be threatened, and the national interest suffers. On the other hand, increased efforts to make the best possible use of their incomes can contribute more to the well-being of most families than equivalent efforts to raise their incomes.

The march of technology—affecting, for example, the foods we eat, the medicines we take, and the many appliances we use in our homes —has increased the difficulties of the consumer along with his opportunities; and it has outmoded many of the old laws and regulations and made new legislation necessary. The typical supermarket before World War II stocked about 1,500 separate food items—an impressive figure by any standard. But today it carries over 6,000. Ninety percent of the prescriptions written today are for drugs that were unknown 20 years ago. Many of the new products used every day in the home are highly complex. The housewife is called upon to be an amateur electrician, mechanic, chemist, toxicologist, dietician, and mathematician—but she is rarely furnished the information she needs to perform these tasks proficiently.

Marketing is increasingly impersonal. Consumer choice is influenced by mass advertising utilizing highly developed arts of persuasion. The consumer typically cannot know whether drug preparations meet minimum standards of safety, quality, and efficacy. He usually does not know how much he pays for consumer credit; whether one prepared food has more nutritional value than another; whether the performance of a product will in fact meet his needs; or whether the "large economy size" is really a bargain.

Nearly all of the programs offered by this administration—e.g., the expansion of world trade, the improvement of medical care, the reduction of passenger taxes, the strengthening of mass transit, the development of conservation and recreation areas and low-cost power—are of direct or inherent importance to consumers. Additional legislative and administrative action is required, however, if the Federal Government is to meet its responsibility to consumers in the exercise of their rights. These rights include:

(1) The right to safety—to be protected against the marketing of goods which are hazardous to health or life.

(2) The right to be informed—to be protected against fraudulent, deceitful, or grossly misleading information, advertising, labeling, or other practices, and to be given the facts he needs to make an informed choice.

(3) The right to choose—to be assured, wherever possible, access to a variety of products and services at competitive prices; and in those industries in which competition is not workable and Government regulation is substituted, an assurance of satisfactory quality and service at fair prices.

(4) The right to be heard—to be assured that consumer interests will receive full and sympathetic consideration in the formulation of Government policy, and fair and expeditious treatment in its administrative tribunals.

To promote the fuller realization of these consumer rights, it is necessary that existing Government programs be strengthened, that Government organization be improved, and, in certain areas, that new legislation be enacted.

## I. STRENGTHENING OF EXISTING PROGRAMS

This administration has sponsored a wide range of specific actions to strengthen existing programs. Major progress has already been achieved or is in prospect in several important areas. And the 1963 budget includes recommendations to improve the effectiveness of almost every major program of consumer protection.

### (1) Food and Drug Protection

Thousands of common household items now available to consumers contain potentially harmful substances. Hundreds of new uses for such products as food additives, food colorings, and pesticides are found every year, adding new potential hazards. To provide better protection and law enforcement in this vital area, I have recommended a 25-percent increase in staff for the Food and Drug Administration in the budget now pending before the Congress, the largest single increase in the agency's history. In addition, to assure more effective registration of pesticides, a new division has been established in the Department of Agriculture; and increased appropriations have been requested for pesticide regulation and for meat and poultry inspection activities.

### (2) Safer Transportation

As Americans make more use of highway and air transportation than any other nation, increased speed and congestion have required us to take special safety measures.

(a) The Federal Aviation Agency has reexamined the Nation's air traffic control requirements and is designing an improved system to enhance the safety and efficiency of future air traffic.

(b) The Secretary of Commerce has established an Office of Highway Safety in the Bureau of Public Road to promote public support of highway safety standards, coordinate use of highway safety research findings, and encourage cooperation of State and local governments, industry, and allied groups—the Department of Health, Education, and Welfare is likewise strengthening its accident prevention work—and the Interstate Commerce Commission is strengthening its enforcement of safety requirements for motor carriers.

(c) In addition, I am requesting the Departments of Commerce and of Health, Education, and Welfare, to review, with representatives of the automobile industry, those changes in automobile design and equipment which will help reduce the unconscionable toll of human life on the highways and the pollution of the air we breathe. Additional legislation does not appear required at this time in view of the automobile industry's action to incorporate in the new model design changes which will reduce air pollution.

### (3) Financial Protection

Important steps are being taken to help assure more adequate protection for the savings that prudent consumers lay aside for the future purchase of costly items, for the rainy day, for their children's education, or to meet their retirement needs.

(a) Legislation enacted last year has strengthened the insurance program of the Federal Savings and Loan Insurance Corporation.

(b) The Securities and Exchange Commission has undertaken at the request of the Congress a major investigation of the securities market which should provide the basis for later legislation and administrative measures.

(c) The Postmaster General and the Department of Justice have stepped up enforcement of the mail fraud statutes. Arrests for mail fraud last year set an alltime record; and convictions increased by 35 percent over the previous year.

### (4) More Effective Regulation

The independent regulatory agencies also report increased emphasis on programs directly helpful to consumers.

(a) The Interstate Commerce Commission has instituted proceedings designed to prevent excessive charges for moving household goods in interstate commerce.

(b) The Civil Aeronautics Board has recently taken action to protect air travelers from abuses of overbooking.

(c) The Federal Trade Commission has intensified its actions against deceptive trade practices and false advertising affecting a variety of goods, including refrigerators, house paint, sewing machines, vacuum cleaners, kitchen utensils, food wrapping, and carpets.

(d) The Federal Power Commission is initiating a vigorous program to assure consumers of reasonable natural gas prices while assuring them of adequate supplies—revitalizing all of its regulatory programs in the electric power field—and undertaking a national power survey designed to identify ways of bringing down power costs in the decades ahead by making the best possible use of our capital and energy resources; and I recommend that the Congress enact legislation and make available funds to enable the Commission to provide for 34 million natural gas consumers the information similar to that now provided electrical consumers on typical bills in various areas, thus spotlighting abnormally high rates and stimulating better industry performance.

(e) The Federal Communications Commission is actively reviewing the television network program selection process and encouraging the expanded development of educational television stations; and it will also step up in fiscal year 1963 its enforcement program to prevent interference with air navigation signals, distress calls, and other uses of radio important to public safety.

(f) For all of the major regulatory agencies, I am recommending increased appropriations for 1963 to provide the increased staff necessary for more effective protection of the consumer and public interest.

(g) Of the important changes in agency organizational procedure recommended last year to eliminate delays and strengthen decisionmaking, the great majority have been authorized by reorganization plans or legislation and are being put into practice by agency heads; and, to permit similar improvements in the operations of the Securities and Exchange Commission and the Federal Power Commission through greater delegation of assignments, I recommend enactment this year of legislation along the lines of S. 2135 for the SEC and S. 1605 and H.R. 6956 for the FPC.

### (5) Housing Costs and Quality

The largest purchase most consumers make in their lifetimes is a home. In the past year, significant steps have been taken to reduce the cost of financing housing and to improve housing quality. The level of interest rates and other charges on mortgage loans has been reduced by a variety of Federal actions. Under authority provided by the Housing Act of 1961, new programs have been started (a) to encourage experimental construction methods likely to develop better housing at lower cost, (b) to provide lower interest rates and longer maturities on loans for rehabilitation of existing housing, (c) to provide especially low cost rental housing for moderate income families, and (d) to provide housing for domestic farm labor. The same legislation also authorized demonstration grants to develop better methods of providing housing for low income families.

### (6) Consumer Information and Research— and Consumer Representation in Government

Government can help consumers to help themselves by developing and making available reliable information.

(a) The Housing and Home Finance Agency will undertake, under the budget proposed for fiscal 1963, new studies to discover ways of reducing monthly housing expenses, lowering the cost of land for homebuilding, and minimizing financing charges.

(b) The Department of Agriculture is undertaking similar research designed to help raise rural housing standards and reduce costs.

(c) The Food and Drug Administration will expand its consumer consultant program which, together with the home demonstration program of the Agriculture Extension Service, now provides valuable information directly to consumers on product trends, food standards, and protection guides.

(d) The Bureau of Labor Statistics is now conducting a nationwide survey of consumer expenditures, income, and savings, which will be used to update the widely used Consumer Price Index and to prepare model family budgets.

Too little has been done to make available to consumers the results of pertinent Government research. In addition to the types of studies mentioned above, many agencies are engaged— as aids to those principally concerned with their activities, in cooperation with industry or for Federal procurement purposes—in testing the performance of certain products, developing standards and specifications, and assembling a wide range of related information which would be of immense use to consumers and consumer organizations. The beneficial results of these efforts—in the Departments of Agriculture, Commerce, Defense, and Health, Education, and Welfare, and in the General Services Administration and other agencies—should be more widely published. This is but one part of a wider problem: the failure of governmental machinery to assure specific consideration of the consumer's needs and point of view. With this in mind, I am directing:

First, that the Council of Economic Advisers create a Consumers' Advisory Council, to examine and provide advice to the Government on issues of broad economic policy, on governmental programs protecting consumer needs, and on needed improvements in the flow of consumer research material to the public; this Consumers' Council will also give interested individuals and organizations a voice in these matters;

Second, that the head of each Federal agency whose activities bear significantly on consumer welfare designate a special assistant in his office to advise and assist him in assuring adequate and effective attention to consumer interests in the work of the agency, to act as liaison with consumer and related organizations, and to place increased emphasis on preparing and making available pertinent research findings for consumers in clear and usable form; and

Third, that the Postmaster General undertake a pilot program by displaying in at least 100 selected post offices, samples of publications useful to consumers and by providing facilities for the easier purchase of such publications.

## II. NEW LEGISLATIVE AUTHORITY FOR ADDED CONSUMER PROTECTION

In addition to the foregoing measures, new legislative authority is also essential to advance and protect the consumer interest.

### (A) Strengthen Regulatory Authority Over Foods and Drugs

The successful development of more than 9,000 new drugs in the last 25 years has saved countless lives and relieved millions of victims of acute and chronic illnesses. However, new drugs are being placed on the market with no requirement that there be either advance proof that they will be effective in treating the diseases and conditions for which they are recommended or the prompt reporting of adverse reactions. These new drugs present greater hazards as well as greater potential benefits than ever before—for they are widely used, they are often very potent, and they are promoted by aggressive sales campaigns that may tend to overstate their merits and fail to indicate the risks involved in their use. For example, over 20 percent of the new drugs listed since 1956 in the publication "New and Non-Official Drugs" were found, upon being tested, to be incapable of sustaining one or more of their sponsor's claims regarding their therapeutic effect. There is no way of measuring the needless suffering, the money innocently squandered, and the protraction of illnesses resulting from the use of such ineffective drugs.

The physician and consumer should have the assurance, from an impartial scientific source, that any drug or therapeutic device on the market today is safe and effective for its intended use; that it has the strength and quality represented; and that the accompanying promotional material tells the full story—its bad effects as well as its good. They should be able to identify the drug by a simple, common name in order to avoid confusion and to enable the purchaser to buy the quality drugs he actually needs at the lowest competitive price.

Existing law gives no such assurance to the consumer—a fact highlighted by the thoroughgoing investigation led by Senator Kefauver. It is time to give American men, women, and children the same protection we have been giving hogs, sheep, and cattle since 1913, under an act forbidding the marketing of worthless serums and other drugs for the treatment of these animals.

There are other problems to meet in this area:

(1) An extensive underground traffic exists in habit-forming barbiturates (sedatives) and amphetamines (stimulants). Because of inadequate supervision over distribution, these drugs are contributing to accidents, to juvenile delinquency and to crime.

(2) Two billion dollars worth of cosmetics are marketed yearly, many without adequate safety testing. Thousands of women have suffered burns and other injuries to the eyes, skin, and hair by untested or inadequately tested beauty aids.

(3) Factory inspections now authorized by the pure food and drug laws are seriously hampered by the fact that the law does not clearly require the manufacturer to allow inspection of certain records. An uncooperative small minority of manufacturers can engage in a game of hide-and-seek with the Government in order to avoid adequate inspection. But protection of the public health is not a game. It is of vital importance to each and every citizen.

(4) A fifth of all the meat slaughtered in the United States is not now inspected by the Department of Agriculture, because the coverage of the Meat Inspection Act is restricted to meat products moving across State lines. This incomplete coverage contributes to the diversion of unhealthy animals to processing channels where the products are uninspected and can, therefore, be a threat to human health.

In short, existing laws in the food, drug, and cosmetic area are inadequate to assure the necessary protection the American consumer deserves. To overcome these serious statutory gaps, I recommend:

(1) First, legislation to strengthen and broaden existing laws in the food-and-drug field to provide consumers with better, safer, and less expensive drugs, by authorizing the Department of Health, Education, and Welfare to:

(a) Require a showing that new drugs and therapeutic devices are effective for their intended use—as well as safe—before they are placed on the market;

(b) Withdraw approval of any such drug or device when there is substantial doubt as to its safety or efficacy, and require manufacturers to report any information bearing on its safety or efficacy;

(c) Require drug and therapeutic device manufacturers to maintain facilities and controls that will assure the reliability of their product;

(d) Require batch-by-batch testing and certification of all antibiotics;

(e) Assign simple common names to drugs;

(f) Establish an enforceable system of preventing the illicit distribution of habit-forming barbiturates and amphetamines;

(g) Require cosmetics to be tested and proved safe before they are marketed; and

(h) Institute more effective inspection to determine whether food, drug, cosmetics, and therapeutic devices are being manufactured and marketed in accordance with the law;

(2) Second, legislation to authorize the Federal Trade Commission to require that advertising of prescription drugs directed to physicians disclose the ingredients, the efficacy, and the adverse effects of such drugs; and

(3) Third, legislation to broaden the coverage of the Meat Inspection Act administered by the Department of Agriculture, to promote adequate inspection—in cooperation with the States and industry—of all meat slaughtered in the United States.

### (B) Require "Truth in Lending"

Consumer debt outstanding, including mortgage credit, has almost tripled in the last decade and now totals well over $200 billion. Its widespread availability has given consumers more flexibility in the timing of their purchases. But, in many instances, serious abuses have occurred. Under the chairmanship of Senator Douglas, a subcommittee of the Senate Banking and Currency Committee has been conducting a detailed examination of such abuses. The testimony received shows a clear need for protection of consumers against changes of interest rates and fees far higher than apparent without any real knowledge on the part of the borrowers of the true amounts they are being charged. Purchasers of used cars in one study, for example, paid interest charges averaging 25 percent a year, and ranging well above this; yet very few were aware of how much they were actually paying for credit.

Excessive and untimely use of credit arising out of ignorance of its true cost is harmful both to the stability of the economy and to the welfare of the public. Legislation should therefore be enacted requiring lenders and vendors to disclose to borrowers in advance the actual amounts and rates which they will be paying for credit. Such legislation, similar in this sense to the truth-in-securities laws of 1933-34, would not control prices or charges. But it would require full disclosure to install-ment buyers and other prospective credit users, and thus permit consumers to make informed decisions before signing on the dotted line. Inasmuch as the specific credit practices which such a bill would be designed to correct are closely related to and often combined with other types of misleading trade practices which the Federal Trade Commission is al-ready regulating, I recommend that enforce-ment of the new authority be assigned to the Commission. The Government agencies most concerned in this area have been cooperating with the subcommittee in developing the in-formation necessary to prepare a workable and effective bill; and in view of the exhaustive hearings already held, I hope that the Congress can complete action on this important matter before it adjourns.

### (C) Manufacture of All-Channel Television Sets

Five out of six home television receivers today are equipped to receive programs on only the 12 very-high frequency (VHF) chan-nels. As a result, in most areas, stations de-siring to operate on any of the 70 ultra-high frequency (UHF) channels would usually have such small audiences that there is little incentive to make the substantial initial in-vestment and continuing expenditures that

effective broadcasting requires. The result is a sharply restricted choice for consumers.

After extensive study, the Federal Com-munications Commission has concluded that an effective and genuinely competitive nation-wide television service, with adequate provi-sion for local outlets and educational stations, is not possible within the narrow confines of 12 VHF channels. Legislation now before the Congress would authorize the Commission to prescribe the performance characteristics of all new television receivers shipped in inter-state commerce to assure that they can receive both VHF and UHF signals. I strongly urge its passage as the most economical and prac-tical method of broadening the range of pro-grams available. This step, together with the Federal aid for construction of educational television stations which is nearing final pas-sage by the Congress, will speed the full realization of television's great potential.

### (D) Strengthen Laws Promoting Competition and Prohibiting Monopoly

The most basic and longstanding protections for the right of consumers, to a choice at a competitive price, are the various laws de-signed to assure effective competition and to prevent monopoly. The Sherman Act of 1890, the Clayton Act of 1914, and many related laws are the strongest shields the consumer possesses against the growth of unchecked monopoly power. In addition to the measure now nearing final passage which would pro-vide subpena powers for civil as well as criminal antitrust investigations, several other improvements are needed:

(1) The Federal Trade Commission should be empowered to issue temporary cease-and-desist orders against the continuance of unfair competitive practices while cases concerned with permanent relief from such practices are pending before the Commission. Under the present law, smaller competitors may be driven into bankruptcy or forced to accept merger on adverse terms long before present remedies become effective, thus reducing the competitive safeguards vital for the consumer. Similarly, deceptive trade practices in con-sumer goods may do their damage long before the Commission can "lock the barn door." I, therefore, reiterate my previous recommen-dation that the Congress give prompt consid-eration to effective legislation to accomplish this purpose.

(2) The consumer's right to a reasonable price can also be adversely affected by mergers of two business firms which substantially reduce effective competition. As in the case of unfair methods of competition, damage once done is often irreparable, and the Government, acting through the courts, cannot readily restore the degree of competition existing prior to the merger. Accordingly, I strongly recommend enactment of legislation to require reasonable advance notice to the Department of Justice and to the appropriate commission or board of any merger expected to result in a firm of substantial size. This will enable the businessman to obtain advice in advance, without litigation, as to whether a proposed merger would be regarded as contrary to the public interest. In addition, along with the recommended authority for the FTC to issue cease-and-desist orders, it is an essential safeguard against combinations which might cause unwarranted increases in consumer prices.

(3) In view of the potentially anticompetitive abuses to which the use of patents and trademarks are by nature subject, I recommend:

(a) Enactment of legislation requiring publication of the terms of all settlement agreements between different persons applying for patent rights on the same invention—for recent hearings have shown that such agreements may include features designed to weaken future competition at the expense of the consumer; and

(b) Enactment of legislation authorizing the FTC to apply for the cancellation of any trademark which is, or becomes, the common descriptive name of an article and thus should be in the public domain.

While a competitor has such a right today, it is important—if the FTC is to have clear authority to halt this kind of unfair commercial advantage—that the Senate insert this provision in its review of trademark legislation (H.R. 4333) already approved by the House.

### (E) "Truth in Packaging"

Just as consumers have the right to know what is in their credit contract, so also do they have the right to know what is in the package they buy. Senator Hart and his subcommittee are to be commended for the important investigation they are now conducting into packaging and labeling practices.

In our modern society good packaging meets many consumer needs, among them convenience, freshness, safety, and attractive appearance. But often in recent years, as the hearings have demonstrated, these benefits have been accompanied by practices which frustrate the consumer's efforts to get the best value for his dollar. In many cases the label seems designed to conceal rather than to reveal the true contents of the package. Sometimes the consumer cannot readily ascertain the net amount of the product, or the ratio of solid contents to air. Frequently he cannot readily compute the comparative costs per unit of different brands packed in odd sizes, or of the same brand in large, giant, kingsize, or jumbo packages. And he may not realize that changes in the customary size or shape of the package may account for apparent bargains, or that "cents-off" promotions are often not real savings.

Misleading, fraudulent, or unhelpful practices such as these are clearly incompatible with the efficient and equitable functioning of our free competitive economy. Under our system, consumers have a right to expect that packages will carry reliable and readily useable information about their contents. And those manufacturers whose products are sold in such packages have a right to expect that their competitors will be required to adhere to the same standards. Upon completion of our own survey of these packaging and labeling abuses, in full cooperation with the Senate subcommittee, I shall make recommendations as to the appropriate roles of private business and the Federal Government in improving packaging standards and achieving more specific disclosure of the quantity and ingredients of the product inside the package in a form convenient to and useable by the consumer.

As all of us are consumers, these actions and proposals in the interest of consumers are in the interest of us all. The budgetary investment required by these programs is very modest—but they can yield rich dividends in strengthening our free competitive economy, our standard of living and health, and our traditionally high ethical patterns of business conduct. Fair competition aids both business and consumer.

It is my hope that this message, and the

recommendations and requests it contains, can help alert every agency and branch of Government to the needs of our consumers. Their voice is not always as loudly heard in Washington as the voices of smaller and better organized groups—nor is their point of view always defined and presented. But under our economic as well as our political form of democracy, we share an obligation to protect the common interest in every decision we make. I ask the Congress, and every department and agency, to help in the fulfillment of that obligation.

# F. Ethical Considerations

## 24. Is Advertising Morally Defensible?

ARNOLD TOYNBEE

"It is argued that marketing—including the kinds of new products introduced, the design of those products, and advertising—reflects public wants and tastes rather than shapes them." I have been asked whether I believe this to be true. I do not believe that. If advertising were just an echo of desires that were already in the housewife's mind, it would be a superfluous expense of time, ingenuity and money. It would be nothing more than a carbon copy of a house-wife's own shopping list. I believe that advertising does have an effect. I believe it stimulates consumption, as is suggested in the second point put to me:

"It is argued that personal consumption, stimulated by advertising, is essential for growth and full employment in an economy of abun-dance." If this were demonstrated to be true, it would also demonstrate, to my mind that an economy of abundance is a spiritually unhealthy way of life, and that the sooner we reform it the better. This may sound paradoxical to mod-ern Western ears. But if it is a paradox, it is one that has always been preached by all the great religions. In an article published in *Print-ers' Ink* on October 20, 1961, Mr. James Webb Young dismisses the example set by St. Francis of Assisi. "Americans today," Mr. James Webb Young writes, "see little merit in these medieval hairshirt ideas." St. Francis got his ideas from a premedieval teacher, Jesus. These ideas can-not be dismissed without rejecting Christianity and all the other great religions, too.

‡‡ SOURCE: Reprinted by permission from *Yale Daily News*, Special Issue 1963, p. 2.

WILLIAM BERENBACH

Mr. Toynbee's real hate is not advertising. It's the economy of abundance or, as we have all come to know it, capitalism. This is per-fectly all right if only he would make clear the real target he is shooting at. There are many things about capitalism that need correcting, and Mr. Toynbee would be doing the world a great service if he could persuade us to make these corrections. But he's never going to do that if he throws up smoke screens with tirades against a tool that happens to be used by big business in its efforts to sell more goods.

Advertising, like so many techniques avail-able to man, is neither moral nor immoral. Is eloquence immoral because it persuades? Is music immoral because it awakens emotions? Is the gift of writing immoral because it can arouse people to action? No. Yet eloquence, music and writing have been used for evil purpose.

Only recently we were asked to prepare an advertisement by the National Committee for a Sane Nuclear Policy. We conceived an ad featuring Dr. Spock. Its purpose was to dis-courage nuclear testing. If Mr. Toynbee will agree that this is a good purpose, then he must also agree that in this case at least, advertising was not an instrument of "moral mis-educa-tion." He would also be happy to learn that here was an advertisement so persuasive that it prompted one of the chairmen of SANE to telegraph his congratulations for "by all odds the most powerful single statement I have seen over the imprint of SANE."

For the past two years we have run advertis-

181

The moral that I draw is that a way of life based on personal consumption, stimulated by advertising, needs changing—and there are dozens of possible alternatives to it. For instance, we could still have full employment in the economically advanced countries if we gave up advertising and restricted our personal consumption to, say, the limits that present-day American monks and nuns voluntarily set for themselves, and if we then diverted our production to supply the elementary needs of the poverty-stricken three-quarters of the human race. Working for this obviously worthwhile purpose would bring us much greater personal satisfaction than working, under the stimulus of advertising, in order to consume goods that we do not need and do not genuinely want.

But suppose the whole human race eventually became affluent; what then? Well, I cannot think of any circumstances in which advertising would not be an evil. There are at least three bad things intrinsic to it:

Advertising deliberately stimulates our desires, whereas experience, embodied in the teaching of the religions, tells us that we cannot be good or happy unless we limit our desires and keep them in check.

Advertising makes statements, not in order to tell the truth, but in order to sell goods. Even when its statements are not false, truth is not their object. This is intellectually demoralizing.

Advertising is an instrument of moral, as well as intellectual, mis-education. Insofar as it succeeds in influencing people's minds, it conditions them not to think for themselves and not to choose for themselves. It is intentionally hypnotic in effect. It makes people suggestible and docile. In fact, it prepares them for submitting to a totalitarian regime.

Therefore, let us reform a way of life that cannot be lived without advertising.

ing for Volkswagen cars with the purpose of persuading Americans that simplicity, craftsmanship and low price were available to them in an automobile. These were ads that conveyed facts simply and honestly to the customer. They seemed to sell the country on filling their automotive needs modestly and with good taste. Would Mr. Toynbee call this effort evil merely because advertising was involved? The Volkswagen was built to give the buyer the greatest value in automotive transportation. Isn't advertising performing a valuable function by making that fact clear to the buyer?

No, advertising is not moral or immoral. Only people are. I can cite many instances in commercial advertising that would prove Mr. Toynbee's point of view. I can cite just as many that would disprove it.

If Mr. Toynbee believes a materialistic society is a bad one (and I am not saying he is wrong in that belief), then he owes it to mankind to speak to the point. He owes it to mankind to speak out against such a society and not merely against one of the tools that is available to any society. He may even find that nothing will "sell" his point as effectively as advertising.

# 25. Some Thoughts on the Nature of Ethics in Marketing

JOHN H. WESTING*

The remarks are based on the assumption that in our increasingly secular society we either have lost, or are in process of losing, our historical foundation for a system of ethics in business. The presentation attempts to find an alternative foundation and to relate ethical practice to such a foundation.

Business is having trouble with its ethics today. But, then, business has always had trouble with its ethics. As far as one may care to go back into history he will find intellectuals castigating businessmen for their bad ethics. It appears that, for the most part, the criticism went unheard, or unheeded. It is true that during much of human history businessmen lived on the very fringe of "good" society and that this semi-ostracism may well have resulted in part from the bad ethics imputed to businessmen. During most of this time the businessman, while he may have deplored his social alienation, did not seem to care enough to pay the price for social respectability.

Today, at least in the sense of caring, the situation seems to have changed. This is not to say that the businessman today is willing to pay a *high* price for moral respectability, but he is sufficiently concerned to want to know the price. The concern of the businessmen is evident in a variety of ways: in the increasing flow of brochures and pamphlets published by companies on the social responsibilities of business; by the willingness to question whether business may have goals other than profit maximization; by the concern being exhibited over racial equality, slum clearance, and pollution control; and, most of all, by an amazing eagerness to discuss the subject of morality and ethics. I well recall about ten years ago organizing a seminar for executives on business ethics and being told by our business advisors that

executives not only would not come, but would resent the implications implicit in a session on ethics. On that occasion we toned down the title somewhat and got an adequate, but disappointing, turnout. More recently we have held a number of undisguised seminars on ethics and have had an enthusiastic response, both in numbers and participation. I believe that anyone who has had the temerity to talk on this subject will bear me out in the statement that if one is willing to discuss this "hairy" subject he will soon have more opportunities than he cares to accept.

If it is true that there has been a notable change in the attitude of businessmen toward ethics, how does one explain it? Let me offer this hypothesis. The executive today is no more nor less concerned about ethics than was his counterpart a century ago. The man has not changed, but his environment has. In a subsistence economy, ethics get short shrift. This is not only true over time, but is equally true geographically at a point in time. I think it can be said that there is a direct relation between per capita income and the ethical standards of a country—and, incidentally, this variation in standards poses one of the knottiest ethical problems possible for a company engaged in trade with developing countries. But, to get back to the point, when one is destitute he is less likely to indulge his ethical impulses when he is comfortable or satiated. Since, in the United States today, we are materially more

◆ SOURCE: Reprinted by permission from *Changing Marketing Systems*, (Chicago: American Marketing Association, 1967), pp. 161–163.

* Chairman, Department of Marketing, University of Wisconsin.

183

comfortable than we have ever been before, our concerns naturally tend to turn from further satisfaction of our physical needs to the satisfaction of needs in higher categories of the need hierarchy—and ethics fall into one of those categories. If this line of reasoning is correct, I think it leads to the conclusion that, in the future, businessmen are likely to become still more concerned with ethical consideration. And, as professors of business subjects, we should be anticipating this concern or once again we may find ourselves rationalizing business practice rather than moulding it.

A tremendous amount of time and effort can be spent on the argument over whether ethics in business are worse than in such fields as law, medicine, politics, or education. Personally, I think a good case can be made for the likelihood that, at a given time, the level of ethics in all major occupational groups of a society are very nearly the same. With no social barriers and few economic barriers to the entry into the various occupational fields it is unlikely that they would attract people with widely varying ethical standards. One could, of course, argue that the professions attract those with a high sense of humanitarianism and worldly renunciation, and such people might have higher ethical ideals. However, this position is somewhat hard to defend if one notes the level and trend of income prevailing in the professional fields and the rush to the highly specialized fields where income is likely to be maximized and the service element minimized. It seems more likely to me that any differences which exist result, not from intrinsic differences in the moral standards of individuals or groups, but from the fact that moral temptations and pressures may be greater in some fields than others. Quite obviously, if one is attempting to assess the moral stamina of two individuals, he must either measure their performance under similar conditions or make allowances for the differences in the environments where they are tested. Perhaps it is the failure to make such allowances that causes the businessman to come off badly when ethical comparisons are made between him and members of other occupational groups. If the corroding effects of the "love of money" are recognized—as they have been throughout history—it must be admitted that the businessman is subject to more frequent and more extreme ethical temptations than most other men. Thus, he may not be ethically weaker, just more sorely tried.

The above issue is an interesting one and, I believe, one that deserves more thought than it has received. However, in one sense it is irrelevant, and in another sense it might even be harmful. It would seem to me to be positively harmful if it led any substantial number of businessmen to conclude that complacency was warranted. Society today, as well as the businessman himself, is uneasy about the state of ethics in business. Under these conditions, complacency may cost the businessman a further loss of his rapidly vanishing freedom. This, of course, is a pragmatic rather than a philosophical argument. The issue of whether the ethics of the businessman are better or worse than those of others is irrelevant because it involves a measurement against the wrong standard. There will be argument on this point, but I maintain that the issue should not be whether the ethics of the businessman are *relatively* as good as those of others but whether they are *absolutely* good enough to sustain the good life in a highly complex society.

This point goes to the very heart of the issue of ethics, and unless it can be resolved, I doubt that there is much chance of any real progress of the ethics front. The absolute position identifies, and at times almost equates, ethics with religion. This has been the traditional position, and it was a viable position so long as religion held real or nominal authority over a majority of the people. It seems to me there was a time, within my memory, when most people—non-church members as well as members—acknowledged the *rightness* of a code of ethics based upon the second table of the Decalogue. Many may not have complied with the code in practice, but an admission of its rightness at least gave society a point of reference—a north star—for guidance.

Today, in his quest for scientific verification of everything, man has to a large extent discarded normative standards such as the ethical component of the Decalogue. In most areas even scientific man does not discard conventional wisdom until he has found it wrong and has discovered something better to replace it. In the field of ethics, unfortunately, modern man has been too impatient for this. Ethical principles were so clearly not based on empirical research that he discarded them without having even begun a search for anything to replace them. Someone might argue that relativism or situational ethics has replaced the more formalized code, but I would contend that as a replacement relativism is an illusion. In an economic order, in which the central motivating principle is based on selfish advancement, ethical performance can only decline unless there is some countervailing force to offset the drive to better one's self at the cost of others.

One could easily move from the position that if the traditional standards are not working and relativism will not work we are in a perilous, and, perhaps hopeless, position. I suspect that not a few people may be close to this point without having bothered to take their bearings and define their position. May we not, however, be able to reason our way to an intermediate position—one that establishes ethics as a normative standard without making it a part of religion.

To do this one must make the assumption that our world is an orderly world—not only the physical environment but the social environment as well. More specifically, the assumption about the social environment of man must be that living together in society is possible over the long term only if we recognize and comply with inherent social laws which are as inviolable as the physical laws of the universe. Just as we can defy, but not break, physical laws, we can defy, but not break, social laws. This does not seem to me to be an unreasonable assumption. Could not our rising concern over ethics be an implicit recognition of the fact that our increasingly intimate social relationships demand that we regulate our associations by better ethical norms?

If one wonders why we have made so much progress in discovering the physical laws of our universe and so little in finding the ethical laws, he might note that physical cause and effect relationships are mostly short term whereas social cause and effect rleationships may not come to light in less than generations or centuries. We do know that societies rise and fall but we have never done much more than speculate idly about the reasons. Admittedly, the difficulty of discovering such ethical verities will be difficult, but with man in possession of something approximating ultimate power the penalty for not discovering these hidden relationships may well be extinction. If the issue is this stark we certainly ought to get on with the job.

Let us look at the matter for a moment from the point of view of the religionists, of which group I consider myself to be a member. We have always tended to be a bit hazy and uncertain about the *other* worldly and the *this* worldly aspects of religion. When one considers

that traditional religion traces its antecedents back to a time when society was ruled as a theocracy, it can be seen that the man-to-God and man-to-man relationships would not be clearly distinguished. We have tended to carry this full set of religious rules over into a society that is now sharply divided into spiritual and secular segments. The second table of the Decalogue is in substance a prescription for how man must live with man in ethical terms if communal life is to succeed. In this connection it is interesting to note that, while all major religions differ significantly in their man-to-God prescriptions, they all agree quite well in their ethical prescriptions. As a matter of fact, in this universality of ethical norms we might find a promising approach to the development of a set of secular ethical standards. If we would disregard the question of how these norms came into being, translate them into modern phraseology, and begin to check them against human history we might well have a start toward our difficult goal. Essentially, in terms of broad principles, the universal religious code of ethics demands respect for truth, respect for persons, respect for human institutions, and respect for property. These principles would seem to be sufficiently non-controversial so that they could be accepted as secular norms.

Now, how does one get from this high plain of lofty principles, to the more mundane level of operational ethics. It seems to me that one must make the transition in a series of steps.

First of all, there is the law, which is or ought to be the lowest common denominator of ethical practice. I do not by any means subscribe to the facile but faulty maxim that says, "If it's legal, it's ethical." To say this, I think, exhibits a misunderstanding of both law and ethics. Law codifies only that part of ethics which society feels so strongly about that it is willing to support it with physical force. The common misunderstanding also frequently gets us into the dilemma of passing laws that are unenforceable because society does not feel certain enough about them to apply the force which is implicit in law. So, the man who thinks he is ethical because he is not knowingly violating civil laws is, in fact, only practicing ethics at its lowest level. Furthermore, if no one did any *better* than that, society could degenerate morally, but could never regenerate.

Probably in the field of business the next level of ethical performance is measured by company policy. Of course, not all company policy has an ethical dimension, but when it does deal with it, policy must transcend the ethical level of law. If it were lower than the law, the policy would be illegal, if it were equal to the law it would be pointless, so it must transcend the law. It might be observed that we enforce ethical principles at this level, not with physical force, but with economic force. We fire, demote, reduce pay, etc. These are powerful sanctions and this avenue represents an approach that has not been explored very far. With the present tendency of companies to assume social responsibilities there could be substantial achievements in the ethical realm that would probably benefit business as well as society.

There are ethical problems that cannot be reached through company policy and are not appropriate for law. These concern matters in which an industry's competitive environment exerts a depressing effect on ethical conduct and the competitive situation does not allow the individual companies to practice the ethics they would like. The only way we have found to deal with such issues is through industry codes of ethics and they have had a spotty, and not very inspiring, history. Part of the trouble here has been that industries have so frequently tended to confuse bad ethics with hard competition. Many groups have tried to write hard competition out of their industries through the vehicle of ethical codes and have found that it did not work for long. Then they have concluded that codes of ethics will not work. I believe, that with better understanding of what they are supposed to do, industry codes deserve another chance and stronger support. It might be noted that the force behind ethical codes is strictly a social kind of sanction. Such sanctions may not have much raw power, but in a prosperous economy with people striving to satisfy acceptance goals, the force is not inconsiderable.

Finally, we arrive at the epitome of ethics, where a man is face-to-face with an ethical issue and must decide it in a way that will satisfy his personal standards. This is the touchstone of ethics in a free society. In the end the other levels of ethics all derive their substance from the performance of each individual as he wrestles with ethical issues. If he does not have adequate standards and is not willing to pay an economic price to satisfy his standards our economic society is inevitably going to suffer from degenerating ethics.

As I see it, then, our task is two-fold: to define ethics in a way that will gain intellectual acceptance for it, and to induce its practice by the business community. The business educator is of critical importance to both.

# 26. Controlling Marketing Behavior in the Large Firm

EARL A. CLASEN

If you had a good upbringing; if you went to Sunday School and attended church regularly; if you learned the Ten Commandments and in your adult life have attempted to apply these precepts, along with the golden rule. . . .

If, in short, you have absorbed the formal expressions of our moral tradition and strive to exemplify them in your daily life—and if, solely on this basis, you assume the job of controlling marketing behavior in a large corporation —then God help you!

My subject is "Controlling Marketing Behavior in the Large Firm," and it was through prolonged struggle with this subject that I reached the conclusion I have stated.

Do not think that my deliberations led me into agreement with those contemporary critics who see a fundamental conflict between social morality and business purpose. This is not the case. There is no conflict.

Given the situation I have described, you would not find yourself forced to violate your principles in order to succeed. Rather, you would find that these principles simply are not adequate to  guide your decisions. You would find them almost everywhere applicable, and almost nowhere sufficient in themselves *to resolve the ethical* problems you face.

If this sounds like an anomaly, let me say that it was just one of many I encountered as I explored the sources of ethical decision making

◆ SOURCE: Reprinted by permission from *Ethics and Marketing*, Lectures from a symposium sponsored by The Merrill Cohen Memorial Fund and The Graduate School of Business Administration, University of Minnesota, April, 1966.

in a large, consumer marketing company. In this exploration I was ably assisted by a number of my co-workers who must make ethically relevant decisions every day of their business lives.

In the course of our discussions, we probed, I am sure, most of the traditional wellsprings from which business ethics are supposed to originate and in which the public welfare is supposed to find its protection. In no case could we identify a single basis for making ethical business decisions which was totally adequate. To be more specific, we could find no one source of those principles which, if consistently applied, would ensure that all of our marketing decisions would be ethical and would, in fact, contribute to the public welfare.

## TRADITIONAL SOURCES OF ETHICAL GUIDANCE

Let me review some of these traditional sources. The first I have already touched on. It is the personal conscience, molded and formed by the ethical traditions of our society. The personal conscience and high personal standards were quickly singled out as playing a major role in the control of marketing behavior in a large business organization. But as I shall later demonstrate, they are not in themselves adequate to do the job.

Another source which we examined is the law and its corollary, an articulated corporate philosophy and explicit statements of policy.

A third source is organizational structure and procedures which ensure the interjection of the ethical component of decision making through a system of checks and balances.

A fourth is the marketplace which, in the terms of Adam Smith, exerts its own ethic upon buyer and seller alike.

A fifth is knowledge—that professional and technical expertise which allows one to know what is good for someone else, even when the other is unaware of the factors and the ethics involved.

A sixth is full and free and open communication between buyer and seller which in itself represents a kind of ethic.

My purpose is to deal with each of these sources today, examining their adequacies and their limitations for controlling marketing behavior in a large corporation. Out of this examination, hopefully, may come an approach to business ethics which can serve as a working hypothesis for those of us who must continue to pursue the goal, even as we apply it in our daily lives.

### Conscience

Let us consider the adequacy of conscience in business decision making. The personal conscience is a wonderful and sacred thing. But not all personal consciences are alike. Prelates and theologians, representing many groups of consciences, have in our time caught the popular imagination with their attempts to reconcile differences of conscience. The businessman must act.

Recently my company purchased a Sunday morning network television show for children. Are we commercially encouraging that element of our population which prefers to stay home rather than go to church on Sunday? A raft of consumer letters will tell us so. Their writers will solemnly affirm that they will not again purchase our products until the offending show is dropped.

Do you enjoy a cocktail at day's end? We are currently test-marketing a citric, noncaloric, presweetened drink mix in three flavors. The product was conceived to satisfy adult and teen-age tastes. It mixes well with gin or vodka to make an unusually good summer cooler. For ten cents you can have four glasses. There is no other product on the market which compares in quality or economics with this mix as an alcoholic mixer. Yet we are preventing any reference in our advertising, publicity, or promotion to use of the product with alcoholic beverages. The policy is set. Our marketing de-

partment, our advertising agencies, and our publicity people know it. But we will miss a large sales volume as a result of our decision.

Now to the cynical these decisions may seem capricious. They may appear to be inconsistent. They are perhaps frivolous and arbitrary. Would the alternate decisions have been unethical? My point is not to ask you to judge them, although you are indeed free to do so. What I would like you to do is to consider the fact that the individual conscience is a sacred but individual thing. The individual conscience is absolutely essential to ethics in marketing behavior but is by no means adequate to serve as a guide. For which individual conscience would you follow? And how would you sustain it against all of the individual consciences in the marketplace?

One answer, of course, is for the marketing manager to explore the range of differences of conscience on a particular decision with his colleagues. For this technique to be effective, several conditions must be present. First, he must have serious, dedicated people who have high personal standards of ethics. Second, he must create an atmosphere of openness in which people feel free to express their commitments and ethical viewpoints. Third, he must create a situation in which they can interact with one another in healthy conflict. Out of the clashings and collisions of individual consciences, a group consensus can emerge which cuts broader and deeper in its search for truth than would any individual conscience working in isolation.

In our company we have found this interaction a most effective way to engage the individual conscience in our decision making. As a means of controlling marketing behavior it substitutes personal involvement for coercion; individual commitment for external control.

### Law

Let us turn now to law as a source of ethical decision making and as a means for controlling marketing behavior in a large corporation. Law in this sense may be either public or private. The private law of the corporation is articulated in statements of philosophy and policy. Many writers on business ethics have viewed this private law of the corporation as the primary source of ethical decision making. We view it as a valuable but not totally adequate contributor.

When you set out to control marketing behavior in the large corporation, you are dealing with every business law of the land from anti-trust laws to the regulations of the post office. Law and corporate policy represent the fences which people must stay within. You need a working knowledge of the law deep down in your organization, and with this knowledge, a feel for potential problems; a sixth sense. You need proper interpretation of the law and prop-er execution of its intent. Where the law is clear, there is no problem. Where the law can be interpreted—and competitors interpret it differently than you do—the pressure can be severe. Ironically, it is in this continuing gray area of interpretation that you most have need of a set of ethical touchstones.

We market a pancake mix which contains 9.3 percent buttermilk solids. This is approxi-mately equivalent to a pint of buttermilk in each one pound package. It is so rich a mix that the housewife needs only to add water to prepare it. The product competes directly with a product that contains only half as much but-termilk, to which the housewife must add whole milk. Our product obviously costs more to manufacture. And obviously, the pressure is great to cheapen it. Neither law nor corporate policy tells us whether the product should con-tain 5 percent, 8 percent, or 15 percent butter-milk. But our expertise as an experienced mix manufacturer tells us that the 9.3 percent for-mulation is in a range which produces opti-mum consumer acceptance. Figuratively, this is a case where we have taken our ethics from a test tube rather than from law or policy.

Let me give you another example. We mar-ket a nutbread mix. Our market research indi-cates that consumer acceptance of the product is optimum when it contains 50 percent fil-bers and 50 percent almonds. Recently the price of filberts increased sharply. We were under pressure to convert to a 100 percent al-mond product thus protecting our margins. But we decided not to do this. We also made a de-cision not to pass on the increased cost to the consumer despite pressure from our account-ing, procurement, and marketing functions—proper pressures, I might add, based on sound technical judgements.

### Organizational Structure

Decisions like these must be made at the top, and this brings us to another source of ethical control—organizational structure. Our company operates on the principle that no man should be forced to act as both executor and judge on the same issues. Our plant managers, for ex-ample, do not establish our quality standards nor audit our performance against them. The quality of our grocery products is subjected to the continuing scrutiny and review of a free au-ditor who reports to no one but me. Our con-sumer service kitchens, which provide an ex-tremely important auditing function, report to the president of the company.

Not all decisions can flow through the top office, but ethical decisions must be shared up-wards. Problems arise when a man puts em-phasis on just one of his job objectives—say, maintaining a margin on a particular product. He must be able to get relief from above if his alternative is to sacrifice product quality.

In blunt terms, when the choice is between shrinking margins and ethics, which is going to give? Choices of this kind must be forced upward in the corporation, for profit itself rep-resents an ethical standard as one assumes in-creased obligations toward employees and stockholders.

But what of the general manager who must make ethical decisions which balance profit and product quality? To what set of ethical guideposts does he turn? Organizational struc-ture, with its system of checks and balances and built-in auditing functions, becomes a less effective control device as you move up the ladder of responsibility. Like personal con-science and personal standards, and like the law and corporate policy, it is an important but not totally adequate source of ethical control for the corporate manager. It doesn't supply all of the answers to all of the questions he must face.

### Technical Knowledge and Expertise

Another source of ethical decision making is your own technical knowledge and expertise as a manufacturer. In this sense you apply for the consumer the kinds of tests and standards which she can not apply for herself. Let me il-lustrate with an example. We manufacture an apricot nutbread mix. The product enjoyed a high level of consumer acceptance and was moving well in the market. But we continued to experiment with its formulation and saw that it would be improved by the addition of more apricots. We moved to this new formula-tion, which cost us more to produce, and were gratified to find that sales of the product in-creased.

This is not always the case with product improvements. Many improvements which affect a product's total performance go unnoticed by the consumer. The temptation to label these products as "new and improved" is very great. But we have decided to limit such an appellation to those instances where the improvement is perceived as such by the consumer. Not all manufacturers follow this practice. A pancake mix currently on the market is referred to by its manufacturer as a "new" product, when all that has been changed is its package and label.

### Consumer Preference

This brings us to a consideration of the marketplace itself and the role played by consumer wants and preferences in determining marketing behavior. What does the consumer want? What does the consumer expect; what kinds of values and at what price? The ethical control of marketing behavior requires a deep understanding of the demographic changes which are occurring in our society. It means maintaining a contemporary view of market segmentations which are developing at an ever-increasing rate.

To rely solely on one's own standards of quality and value may be tantamount to serving an ever-decreasing slice of a growing and changing market. Let me illustrate this point with an example. For many years we have produced an angel food cake mix of extraordinarily high quality. Very few housewives can prepare as good a cake from their own ingredients as they can from our mix. But its two-step preparation proved a stumbling block to that growing segment of the market which places a tremendous premium on ease, speed, and convenience. To meet the needs of these modern housewives, we developed a one-step angel food cake mix which requires just one minute from package to baking pan. Our tests show that it does not equal the old-fashioned quality of our regular angel food mix. Yet for millions of American housewives it is the preferred product. We made a judgment that, were we to insist on maintaining the old quality standard at the expense of ease and convenience, we would not satisfy those millions who find that the new mix better suits their needs.

The people who are in charge of marketing our brownie mix wanted to use the phrase "loaded with nuts" in their advertising. Consumer research showed that 50 percent of all consumers would agree with this claim; 25 percent thought the product contained too many nuts. But a significant 25 percent thought that there were not enough nuts in the product. On this basis, we eliminated the claim from our promotional copy.

There are many types of consumers in the marketplace. There is the weights-and-measures type, represented by Consumers Union, to whom the most important fact about a product label is the net weight, preferably evened off to avoid fractional ounces. There is the harried husband, left at home with three kids, to whom the most important fact is how many servings he can expect to get from a can of beef stew. He could care less about net weight or fractions of ounces.

What consumer standard do you follow? Our one-step angel food cake mix fits the standards of one customer group, exactly, but offends the standards of another. You have to have data on the market. You have to know what consumers want, for example, in the matter of servings. You can't put out a product that meets every standard in the marketplace. Nor can every package direction fit every user.

The need to meet consumer wants exerts a powerful control on marketing behavior. But as we become more adept at defining consumer wants through market research, our ethical problems become increasingly complex. With so many audiences to serve, how is it possible to suit one group without offending another? For example, we are now dealing with a new generation which has created a different frame of reference in which to judge product quality. To them the "home-made" standard of quality no longer applies. This is a generation which has never eaten a home-made cake or tasted fresh orange juice.

Can we use consumer acceptance as an ethical standard? Would not the relativity of consumer standards imply a relativity of ethics? And what is to prevent a kind of Gresham's law from operating in the marketplace to bring about a continuing erosion of product quality? I think that if our ethical standards are based on consumer acceptance, we can not escape from relativity.

## AN ETHICAL DILEMMA

This, then, seems to lead us to the horns of our dilemma; or perhaps I should say, stretches us upon the antlers of a polylemma. We have examined the individual conscience and the role played by high personal standards in the control of marketing behavior in the large corporation. But the dictates of personal conscience, even in a society informed by a common ethical tradition, are relative and individual.

We have examined the law and the role of corporate policy in the control of marketing behavior. But the law and policy merely push back the frontiers of ethical decision to new, gray areas of interpretation. We have looked at organizational structure and procedures which can function as a system of checks and balances, analogous to those of our political institutions. But as critical issues ascend through this system, it ultimately evolves upon one man to make final decisions without further recourse.

We have considered knowledge—the state of the art—as a source of ethical dicta, as indeed it is. But the standards of the craftsman must be continually checked and modified to conform with the real needs of a fast-changing marketplace. We have looked to the marketplace itself—to consumer wants and needs—as a source of ethical decisions. But consumer wants and consumer acceptance yield the most relative of variables.

Where, then, do we look for our ethical system? System aside, where even do we look for some source of those touchstones which can supply a working basis for ethical decision making?

I would like now to break off this search for what ought to be the case and turn to a description of what I believe is the case in most large marketing organizations, including my own. After careful consideration, I have concluded that we do, in fact, rely on each of these ethical sources in our day-to-day decision making. Depending on situation and circumstance, we may rely more heavily on one than on the others in a particular instance.

I can not recall, however, a single instance—and this, I think, is important—I can not recall a single instance in which the entire ethical content of a decision derived solely from one of these sources. In every instance in which I have been personally involved, we have had recourse to two or more of our sources in framing what we hope is an ethical decision.

Conscience, policy, organizational procedure, consumer acceptability, technical expertise—each contributes its standards, its demands, and its responsibilities to the marketing decision maker.

## CONCLUSIONS

In considering our multi-ethical circumstance, I have been tempted to single out those sources which seem particularly pertinent to the marketing man. This is a risky business, but I do think there are two sources of ethical standards which predominate in all marketing situations. That is, they are always present, regardless of whichever sources also contribute their moral imperatives. Furthermore, they seem to me to be interrelated in a way which gives rise to another, and underlying, ethical principle.

The first of these is knowledge, which I have variously defined as the state of the art; craftsmanship; that professional and technical expertise which allows one to know what is good for someone else, even when the other is unaware of the factors and the ethics involved. If you think about the foods which you personally will consume today, you will realize the degree to which you are staking your welfare on the professional expertise of persons totally unknown to you. We who control the marketing behavior of a national foods company are dealing with massive trust. Our attitude has to be one of love and of service. Of course, this is also true of the airline, of the manufacturer of drugs and medicines, and in varying degrees of a host of other producers of products.

Now this massive trust implies an interdependence between buyer and seller which demands that they engage in a dialogue. How does this dialogue come about? In simpler times, it was a rudimentary dialogue literally carried on through the medium of the marketplace. The baker produced his bread or cake and put it up for sale in the marketplace. If the consumer purchased it, he or she in effect gave an assent to the question asked by its manufacturer.

This rudimentary dialogue is still at the basis of all marketing transactions in a free economy. But it has become vastly more complex as a result of mass production, mass communication, and mass consumption. We who deliver our promotional messages daily, in what are literally millions of impressions, must assure ourselves that the consumer believes what we say about our products; that our claims are perceived as accurate and truthful.

How do we get this assurance? By a careful testing of consumer attitudes and responses. By listening to and heeding those consumer voices which tell us, for example, that the claim "loaded with nuts" will be disbelieved by 25 percent of all housewives, even though another 25 percent think we put too many nuts in the brownies.

Thus, consumer wants and consumer acceptance become the second predominant source of ethical standards in all marketing situations. In my view, professional expertise and consumer acceptance are the two poles of a vast ethical dialogue, carried on between buyer and seller.

It is our responsibility to bring to the marketplace an expert point of view. Our decisions must, in fact, constitute what the consumer would do or choose if she had the best technical education available, if she had the most modern tools for testing and evaluating. We must apply, for the consumer, the kinds of tests and standards she can not apply for herself.

Then we must continually check back and forth with her. We must create an interchange of our special knowledge, our technical resources, with her expression of her wants and needs. In the course of this interchange, we must never forget that we control the media of its expression. We produce, label, and advertise the product. This is a one-way street. The consumer's response is limited to a decision to buy or not to buy. Such distortions as occur in our channels of communication are of our own making.

But there is another channel, also within our control, which allows the consumer to respond more adequately and fully with respect to her wants and needs and unformed wishes. This is the channel of consumer research—of attitudinal and market analysis. Through the application of consumer research we are able to pinpoint and define, for example, consumer interest in a simpler, easier-to-make, angel food cake mix. We are able to confirm the levels of ingredients—be they buttermilk solids, apricots, or filberts—which most nearly suit the consumer's taste.

Such distortions as occur in this channel of communications are not the result of ethical lapse but of technical inadequacy—the state of the art. In the realm of practical ethics, our mandate is clear—continuing refinement of technique.

Obviously, both we and the consumer have a major stake in the adequacy of our channels of communication. And the requirements of adequate communication, in fact, impose their own ethic. Granted the ethical dialogue I have proposed—between professional expertise on the one hand and consumer wants on the other—the purity and efficacy and efficiency of our channels of communication become all important. To the extent that we in marketing control these channels—and we, alone, control them—a major source of our ethic is clear. We have a moral responsibility to cherish them, to develop and improve them, and above all, to guard and protect their integrity. Our goal is in view, although we may but imperfectly realize it—full and free and open communication between buyer and seller.

# G. Competition and Economic Environment

## 27. What is Competition?

JOHN MAURICE CLARK

Competition is an indispensable mainstay of a system in which the character of products and their development, the amount and evolving efficiency of production, and the prices and profit margins charged are left to the operation of private enterprise.[1] In our conception of a tenable system of private enterprise, it is a crucial feature that the customer should be in a position (as Adam Smith put it) to exert effective discipline over the producer in these respects. Otherwise, government would feel constrained to undertake discipline over these matters—as it does in the field of public-service industries. It is competition that puts the customer in this strategic position, hence its crucial character. It is the form of discipline that business units exercise over one another, under pressure of the discipline customers can exercise over the business units by virtue of their power of choosing between the offerings of rival suppliers. Competition presupposes that businesses pursue their own self-interest, and it harnesses this force by their need of securing the customer's favor. By reason of this discipline, business, which is profit minded,

has to become production minded as a means of earning profits dependably.[2]

This has its seamy side, as when the pressures of competition toward reducing money costs of production lead to substandard wages and working conditions, which increase the human costs of industry or lead to deterioration of the quality of products. These defects arise from a variety of causes: handicapped or relatively inefficient employers may be forced to make up for their disadvantages by lower money wages and may be able to do so because the competition they face as hirers of labor is less compelling than their competition as sellers of products; or customers may be poor judges of products, or certain qualities of products may be inscrutable. These are defects of a serviceable institution. In an impossibly perfect, omnipresent, and equal competition, they would presumably not arise; but that is an unattainable ideal. In the actual market place they have to be dealt with, and mitigated, by a variety of public and private measures adapted to the causes at work, including the "countervailing power" of orga-

◆ SOURCE: Reprinted by permission from *Competition as a Dynamic Process,* by John Maurice Clark, (The Brookings Institution, 1961), pp. 9–18.

[1] The reader need hardly be reminded that this system includes many public controls to protect such values as safety, health, conservation, and truth in advertising.

[2] The phrase "profit minded" is used deliberately, to avoid the implication that business is solely and uniquely governed by an unrealistically precise "maximization" of profits.

nized labor, which uses anticompetitive pressures and has its own seamy side. Many of the remedies are themselves subject to abuse.

These defects are responsible for the view held in some quarters that it is the inherent tendency of competition to sacrifice serviceability to "vendibility" and to debase or impair the human values it touches. These things can happen; but if they were the whole story, the system of private business would not exhibit the strength it does today. Remedies that sustain the "level" of competition are in the interest of the business community, as well as the broader community of citizens. This is a more generally applicable course of action than the one envisioned a half-century ago by Gerald Stanley Lee, in a small volume entitled *Inspired Millionaires,* based on the idea that there existed men of wealth whose dominant motive was to use it to benefit humanity. To such a person, his first prescription was: "get a monopoly." Free yourself from the competitive compulsions that force you to squeeze down costs and prevent you from putting human values first.

The attraction of this procedure might have been somewhat dimmed by a hard-headed contemplation of the methods by which monopolies are established and defended. The element of truth in the prescription might better have been expressed in terms of organizing one's processes of production efficiently enough to give a margin of superiority affording leeway for experiments in promoting human values, not all of which need justify themselves by increasing profits. This, being consistent with competitive checks, would have been more clearly defensible.

A secure monopoly—if such a thing exists or can exist in industry or trade—might be able to save some of the wastes of competitive marketing. After spending part of the savings on public-relations advertising, it might choose to give the public some share of the resulting net economy. Indeed, there are quite cogent reasons why it might do this, or at least might refrain from exploiting to the utmost its immediate power over profits. Nevertheless, we would oppose such a monopoly, regardless of its good performance, because this performance would rest on its arbitrary choice. It would have power, if it chose, to make larger profits by giving the customer less for his money rather than more. The choice to give him more would depend too much on its enlightenment and good will.

While the good performance of our economy is more dependent on such qualities than many of us realize, our resources in this direction are limited. They are already heavily taxed or overtaxed by the requirements of good faith and responsibility in many relationships essential to the economic process and concerned with maintaining the level of competition. They would surely be overtaxed by laying upon them the whole burden of making economically correct decisions in the central matter of amounts produced and prices charged. In such decisions the opposition between private and community interest, is direct and powerful. Hence we do well to seek to keep these decisions subject to forces that are visibly and tangibly cogent, after the fashion of impersonal and competitive "economic law." So we are unwilling to leave in uncontrolled private hands the kind of power that goes with monopoly.

The patent system, with its grant of temporary legal monopoly, is less of an exception than might seem on the surface, as will appear later when we discuss innovation. Innovations are first selected and their value tested by their success in competition with existing practice. If innovation is to be stimulated by public policy, it is hard to devise a totally different system that would not depend more on arbitrary or bureaucratic judgment. Imperfections in the operation of the system present difficult problems, as we shall see, but do not destroy this general principle.

When an industry is recognized as a "natural monopoly," controls of the public utility kind are resorted to, imposing an enforceable obligation to render adequate service at reasonable charges. But we would quite rightly shrink from extending this system to the whole of industry and trade. And where effective competition exists, the customer does not need this sort of protection. Given a chance to choose between the offers of rival producers, his protection rests with his own ability to make an intelligent choice, plus his willingness to take the trouble involved. As to his ability, when he is faced with the inscrutable qualities of many products of modern applied science, there are difficulties, as we shall see, and there are various things that can be done about them, starting with various ways of giving the customer the most appropriate kinds of information. Minimum standards of quality may be set, publicly or privately, and some harmful products may be prohibited. But public control of output and price is not called for to meet this kind of need.

The customer can put pressure on the producer to create a supply corresponding to demand, produced at economical cost and sold at a price reasonably related to cost. "Consumer sovereignty" may be effective in this primarily quantitative sense; but it should be noted with some emphasis that this is not all there is to serviceability. Serviceability depends on how well the customer's patronage reflects those needs and interests that are properly identified with his welfare—using the term in its generally accepted meaning. This is more than an economic problem—a fact which is often used as a pretext for ignoring its economic aspects. The forces shaping our wants include the arts of salesmanship, at a time when our increased consuming power makes it disturbingly easy to become so preoccupied with the *mélange* of trifles or worse that salesmanship offers that we lose something really indispensable—a sense of worthwhile purpose in life.[3] At the utilitarian level, we shall accept consumer sovereignty as an agency that is demonstrably limited and fallible, in need of practical aids to getting what is wanted—aids that can be furnished. Yet with all its defects this agency is indispensable in a society in which the task of shaping worthwhile lives is basically voluntary, rather than dictated by central authority.[4]

So far we have been speaking of the effect of competition, from the standpoint of the alternative choices it offers to the customer, but without trying to define competition as an activity of the producers. For the present purpose, the most useful kind of definition is one that is full enough to suggest some of the important differences in degree and kind of situation, objective, and activity that the realistic student should be prepared to encounter. This kind of definition might also help to explain why competition is so many things to so many different people. They may take hold of it at different points and encounter

different aspects, like the blind men and the elephant. Our elephant should have legs, tail, trunk, tusks, and ears. The following definition is framed with this in mind.

Competition between business units in the production and sale of goods is the effort of such units, acting independently of one another (without concerted action), each trying to make a profitable volume of sales in the face of the offers of other sellers of identical or closely similar products. The pursuit of profits includes attempting to minimize losses if that is the best the situation permits. The process normally involves rivalry, though this may or may not be direct and conscious. In perhaps the chief example, the case of staple farm products sold on organized exchanges, the rivalry of the growers is indirect and for the most part unconscious. In contrast, business units consciously attempt to get customers away from their rivals by the relative attractiveness of their offers. To the extent that the customer does his choosing effectively, the way to secure his business is to offer him good value for his money, backed by dependable information about the product. To the extent that he is incompetent or otherwise unable to choose effectively, specious selling appeals and scamped products have their opportunity. Business firms as buyers are better equipped and more competent than most consumers, and the methods of selling to them reflect this. But even with business buyers, the seller must bring his product to their attention. There may be rivalry between products not closely similar—this is ordinarily called "substitution" rather than "competition."

Rivalry may be active or latent. In the latter case it has its most visible effect when it becomes active; but if this possibility influences the conduct of active competitors without waiting for the latent rivalry to become active, then latent competition as such has some effectiveness. It may come from the potential entry of new firms, but it is nowadays often a matter of an existing producer branching out

<hr>

[3] Cf. Barbara Ward, *New York Times Magazine*, May 8, 1960. She said that in the frivolous and ridiculous choices we make, "the modern moralists see . . . more than the virtuosity of the ad man . . . a society corrupted . . . by a scale of choice that . . . finally extinguishes all sense of the proper ends of man." Here the economic goal of affluence is indicated, jointly with the failure of individuals to meet the moral challenge that arises as material necessities are conquered and marginal striving

moves on to things of less and less human importance.

[4] Cf. the symposium on our national purpose, Life, *The National Purpose* (1960). Here, because our society is of the sort indicated above, the problem of individual purpose is largely bypassed, and with it the problem of national purpose relative to the individual citizen. As J. K. Galbraith has indicated, the affluent society presents its own special problems and is not an unambiguous gain.

into a new type of product or a new market. Much of the most formidable competition takes this form.

Where profits are attainable, competitors may aim at the largest feasible short-run profit, or at a profit thought of as reasonable and probably the best attainable in the long run. The point in either case is that the feasible profit and the methods of pursuing it are limited by the return for which other competitors are willing and able to produce goods and offer them to buyers. The aim may be to excel the attractiveness of their offerings, or to equal it, or to come as near equaling it as possible, in cases in which the rival has something that is, at least for the time being, inescapably superior as a sales appeal. In the latter case, the first firm is under pressure to find ways of improving the appeal of its offerings. Or the aim may be merely to secure enough business to survive.

The attempt to excel may be called aggressive competition, in effect if not in intent; it may or may not be aimed at a particular rival's business. The attempt to equal a competitor's offer or minimize a rival's advantage is clearly defensive. Under competition the one implies the other, and it takes both kinds to make an effectively competitive situation—certainly in industry and trade and probably in agriculture. A proper understanding of the processes of competition in industry and trade requires a recognition of the different and complementary roles of aggressive and defensive actions. This distinction has been recognized, but its basic importance does not appear to have been developed.

Overlapping this, but not coextensive with it, is the distinction between moves of an initiatory character, including moves responding merely to the general situation in which a competitor finds himself, and responses precipitated by specific moves of a rival or rivals —responses of the nature of parries or ripostes. They may imitate the rivals' moves, or may be countermoves of a different sort. Initiatory moves may be aggressive, as defined above; or they may be made by a competitor who is in a defensive situation, in an attempt to improve his position by trying something fresh. This distinction between initiation and response has been more fully recognized than the distinction between aggression and defense. In fact, it is the basis of that theory which claims that effective competition occurs only when firms making initiatory moves disregard the responses their rivals will make. Where competi-

tors are few and a competitive action by one has a substantial impact on his rivals, they are virtually certain to make some kind of response. If the initiator of the move does not have foresight enough to anticipate this, experience will soon drive it home to him. To assume that he ignores it requires him to be far more stupid than businessmen are. If competition really depends on this kind of stupidity on the part of businessmen, its prospects are not good.

Fortunately, this pessimistic view contains only part of the truth, and a part that is seldom fully controlling. Businessmen are not only able to anticipate that rivals will respond, but to devise moves of sorts that cannot be easily and quickly neutralized by rivals' responses. And it is not necessary that all should initiate such moves; if some do, resulting competitive pressures will spread, not instantly or in precisely predictable forms, but, in general, effectively. For this purpose, it is important that firms differ in situations and perspectives. Fewness does not eliminate the incentive to improve productive efficiency or to increase the attractiveness of the product; and the resulting differences tend to spill over into price competition, often of irregular sorts. Anticipation that rivals will respond does not carry certainty as to how prompt or effective the responses will be. This uncertainty allows some firms to hope that, as the outcome of initiating a competitive move, they may end with an improved relative market position, which will mean increased profits for them, after profits in the industry as a whole have reached a normal competitive state. There are a variety of conditions that may lead some firms to this kind of an expectation, including the hope of avoiding a worsening of the firm's market position if it fails to make competitive moves when other firms are doing so. At the best, gains may be progressive over time. This, in nonmathematical language, is a rudimentary explanation of the paradox of competition, whereby single firms see an advantage in actions that tend to eventuate in reduced profits for the entire industry. This explanation supplies some essential elements that are left out of the simplified theoretical model that runs in terms of an "individual demand function" substantially more elastic than the industry function.

The forms which this condition may take hinge on the different means competitors may use in making their offerings attractive to customers. These include the selection and design of a product, selling effort to bring it to the favorable notice of potential customers, and price. The appeal of a seller's offer is a joint resultant of all three. Nevertheless, it has meaning to distinguish "competition in price" from competition in selling effort or product design. Any one of the three may change while the others do not. Indeed, estimates of the probable effects of such single variations are implied in the attempt to devise the most effective joint combination. But all three are tied together by the fact that they all need to be appropriate to one another and to the type and level of market demand the seller is aiming to reach.

The attempt to attract the customer's trade, in this three-sided appeal, costs money, whether it takes the shape of a high-quality product, an expensive selling campaign, or a low price. To make a profit on this money outlay or sacrifice, efficient and economical production is needed; and the more economical the production, the more effective the selling inducements can be made, consistently with profits. Therefore, though low-cost production is not a direct act of rivalry (a producer *may* reduce his costs and pass none of the benefit on to his customers), it is an essential enabling factor and as such is part of the whole process. A struggling competitor may have to reduce his costs if he is to stay in business at all. So it may be added as a fourth means of competitive appeal.

Most of these responses take time and involve uncertainty, starting with the responses of the customers that determine how effective the initial move is, after which rivals' responses take further time. The outstanding exception is an openly quoted reduction in the price of a standardized product. Here response can be prompt and precise; and the expectation of such responses can interfere with the competitive incentive to reduce prices and tends to shift price action to the more irregular forms, which create problems of their own, or to increase competitive emphasis on moves in the field of product and selling effort, which present a different array of problems as to the conditions of effective and serviceable competition. Competition over distance also presents its special problems in identifying serviceable forms of competitive price behavior. All in all, the conditions of serviceable competitive behavior in price, product, or selling effort leave much to be defined.

For example, does competition improve or deteriorate quality? Actually, it can do either or both. How can we judge the conditions determining whether the range of quality offered corresponds to the range desired or misrepresents it? By what criteria can we appraise the productiveness or wastefulness of the indispensable function of advertising or balance its informative and perverting effects on the guidance of demand? Would genuine competition drive prices down to marginal cost? Whose marginal cost, and short-run or long-run? The simplified formulas of abstract theory have too-often bypassed such questions. Or would genuine competition cause prices to fluctuate continually with every change in the relation of "demand and supply" (or rather, of demand and productive capacity)? If a given price remains unchanged for weeks or months, is price competition non-existent during those intervals?

To answer the last question first, the decisive fact seems to be that the purpose of a firm in setting a price on its goods is to sell the goods at the price that has been set. If a price is set competitively, it would be absurd to claim that the price competition ended with the setting of the price and before any goods had been sold. The selling of the goods is part of the price competition. What remains is an arguable question how often prices should change, and such questions do not belong in a definition. The same applies to the other controversial questions about how competitive prices should behave. A definition should facilitate the study of such questions, not foreclose it by purporting to give a final answer.

Perhaps some of the difficulties can be reduced by accepting the consequences of the proposition that effective competition requires both aggressive and defensive actions. A second saving consideration is that price competition must, in reason, include some way in which prices can rise, on occasion, without concerted action. Some conceptions appear to leave room only for price reductions except when demand exceeds capacity. As to specific behavior, it is clear that price competition is something different for a wheat grower, a cement manufacturer, an automobile producer, or Macy's department store.

For the competition to be effective, the crucial thing seems to be that prices be independently made under conditions that give some competitors an incentive to aggressive action that others will have to meet, whenever prices are materially above the minimum necessary supply prices at which the industry would supply the amounts demanded of the various grades and types of products it produces. What profit or loss a given competitor will individually make will depend on whether he is a high-cost or a low-cost producer, and on whether the industry is shrinking or expanding.

It may be worth while calling attention to certain things that this definition does *not* set up as essential characteristics of competition. It does not limit it to cases in which the seller merely accepts a going price, which he has no power to influence. It does not define competition as a struggle to excel, after the simile of a race, in which there can be only one winner. It does not incorporate the effort to maximize profits—still less their actual maximization—as part of the definition of competition. The definition needs to leave room for competing firms that may conceive their aims in ways not necessarily inconsistent with the attempt to maximize profits, but including elements that are formulated in different terms. Perhaps the chief trouble with the conception of maximization is its implication of a precision which is unattainable and can be misleading. Secondarily, the meaning of profit maximization is ambiguous unless the time perspective that controls the firm's policy is carefully specified. Incidentally, and paradoxically, the producer who is likely to be trying hardest to maximize his profits is the one who is not making any—he is struggling for survival.

Finally, the definition does not require that each form of competition should be active at every moment, in the sense of new technical methods, new products, new selling tactics, or changed prices. All these may remain unchanged between active moves and may still embody the resultant of active and effective competitive forces. If so, this implies that preparedness is under way for further moves as occasion may present the need or the opportunity. Of course, this preparedness may lapse into ineffectiveness; but the producer who allows this to happen in his own establishment is likely to find himself fatally outclassed. And if preparedness is active, it is likely to eventuate in action.

# 28. *Competition as Seen by the Businessman and by the Economist*

JOEL DEAN

## RESEARCH METHODS

The two people who ought to know most about competition are the economist, whose profession it is to study it, and the businessman, whose profession it is to practice it. The purpose of this little disquisition is to contrast the views of these two experts.

Economists, of course, differ greatly among themselves, and their views on this subject range over a broad continuum. Any attempt to lump together the opinions of such a notoriously discordant group of people must, therefore, be at best a bold simplification, and more probably a foolhardy caricature. Business executives also cover a wide spectrum of attitudes toward competition and differ strikingly in their penchant for looking at the economic mechanism as a whole. Hence, any attempt to speak about the views of "the businessman" necessarily abstracts from the great variation among individual executives, and runs the risk of merely reflecting the prejudices of the generalizer.

Instead of attempting to mitigate these hazards, I have accentuated them. No effort has been made to survey systematically a wide range of businessmen's opinions on the subject, and no effort has been made to present a central tendency of the views of the typical executive. Dr. Kinsey has established that statistics can make anything dull. So I have steered

‡‡ SOURCE: Reprinted by permission from *The Role and Nature of Competition in Our Marketing Economy* edited by Harvey W. Huegy (Bureau of Economic and Business Research, University of Illinois, 1954, pp. 8–15.)

clear of statistics and confined my inquiries to businessmen whose views intrigued me.

I have maintained the same high standards of statistical thoroughness and Olympian objectivity in summarizing my dinner table findings with respect to economists. Observing that the inner soul of the academician is seldom bared in the learned journals, I have religiously abstained from any examination of the literature on the subject and instead have gone out into the byways and the unbeaten paths of casual conversation and taking my cocktail in hand, have coaxed cozy confidences from my cloistered colleagues.

Economists, doubtless as a consequence of the rigor of the scientific method and the broad factual foundation for their science, vary in their views on competition over a vast range. One can move along this continuum from the managerial economist with intimate participation in the highest policy decisions of huge corporations (like myself) along a trajectory of marginal futility down through the geologic strata of sophistication to the neoclassical, welfare economist who still takes the model of atomistic competition seriously.

A simple, scientific, and completely satisfactory solution for the annoying individuality of economists has been found. It consists of classifying them into two groups: (a) sophisticated industrial economists and (b) foolish cloistered economists. Following the pattern of our scientific treatment of the businessman, we shall ignore altogether the views of the sophisticated economists and confine ourselves to the foolish ones.

### What Competition Is

By these research methods we obtained impressions about the economist's and the businessman's view of the characteristics of a competitive situation.

### Hallmarks of Competition Listed by Businessman

Generally speaking, competition, to the businessman, is whatever he has to do to get business away from his rivals and whatever they do to take sales away from him. To be more specific let us look at nine hallmarks of an intensely competitive situation, as seen through the eyes of our businessman:

1. *Price uniformity.* Close similarity of quoted prices of rivals, usually accompanied by undercover price shading.
2. *Price differentiation.* A structure of price discounts characterized by wide spreads between the lowest and the highest net price, e.g., the discount structure that is usual for suppliers of fairly standardized products to the automobile industry.
3. *Selling activities.* Substantial promotional outlays, i.e., much advertising, point-of-sale merchandising, and direct personal salesmanship.
4. *Product differentiation.* Preoccupation with the modernity, quality, and style of the company's products as compared with rivals' products and with "good service."
5. *Product research.* Large outlays on product research that is focused on creation of new products and continuous improvement in the firm's existing products.
6. *Selective distribution.* A strong dealer organization, i.e., rivalry through and for sponsored, franchised (and often exclusive) distributors.
7. *Market share.* Acute consciousness of the activities and position of competitors, and preoccupation with the company's market share and with the market occupancy of individual rivals.
8. *Market raiding.* Uninhibited efforts to detach big customers from rivals, often by price shading, or special concessions, business patronage, and "services." Sporadic penetration of the market by distant rivals, who frequently dump, so that their net-back is much lower than from sales in their own backyard territory. The converse is customer-freezing, i.e., the use of sewing-up devices such as requirements contracts, reciprocity, and lavish gifts, which make good customers hard to alienate.
9. *Customer sharing.* Widespread acceptance of the strike-born doctrine that for each important material or component the buyer needs the protection of having at least two suppliers.

### Economist's View — Appraisal

Influenced by fashionable doctrines of "imperfect competition" and "monopolistic competition" many neoclassical economists have taken the view that only atomistic competition is the real thing; that any form of rivalry that departs from the paragon of perfect competition falls from grace, i.e., is monopoly. Classifying all departures from the purity of atomistic rivalry as monopolistic is a simplifying analytical device of proven pedagogical value. The inference drawn by many students and, unfortunately, by some of their teachers is that all aspects of rivalry among sellers which deviate from "perfect" competition are "monopolistic," and therefore, are not competition at all.

The result of this doctrinaire dissection of the geometry of competition is the unconscious conviction on the part of many young economists that monopoly, rather than competition, is now the dominant characteristic of American capitalism. The impression that competition has been "declining" is a frequent, though not necessary, corollary.

A weird consequence is that the same behavior traits which the businessman sees as hallmarks of competition are viewed by many economists as indicia of monopoly.

*Price Uniformity.* To many economists close similarity of prices quoted or bid by rivals is an almost classic indication of a monopoloid situation. Some economists view "price matching" as conclusive proof of culpable collusion. Undercover price concessions have been regarded not only as buttressing the evidence of collusion but also as pernicious in themselves because they are a particularly insidious kind of price discrimination.

The businessman sees uniformity of official prices as evidence that rivals' products are such close substitutes that competition is driven underground, where dark and terrible subterranean struggles produce differences in quality, service, and terms which work out to differences in real prices.

The businessman sees no practical competitive alternative to similarity of quoted prices where products are standardized and competitors are few. Each seller knows that official price cuts will be promptly met. Overt price reduction is, therefore, a futile device for extending a firm's market share. And since open price reductions are not easily reversible undercover concessions provide the necessary mechanism for flexible adjustment to rapid changes in economic and competitive environment.

*Price Differentiation.* Charging different prices to different people makes the economist suspect price discrimination, roughly defined as price differences that are not "justified" by cost differences. Price discrimination is an indication of monopoly power, since it is unthinkable under atomistic competition. Price discrimination may also be employed to acquire, perpetuate, or abuse market power. Accordingly, most economists have been "agin" it. But few have recognized that under modern technology it is very difficult to define price discrimination, and almost impossible to measure, detect, or avoid it. (See *Managerial Economics*, pp. 504-10.)

The businessman sees his structure of price discounts as an instrument of competitive strategy in fighting for position in different sectors of the market. Aware of the furious consequences of failing to meet rivals' net prices as they differ among market sectors and aware of the impossibility of finding the full cost of serving different sectors he sees the sort of cost-price disparity (price discrimination) that distresses the economist as an everyday unavoidable and not particularly culpable practice. He is amazed that price differentiation that is so directly geared to market conquest and defense should be viewed as a symptom of monopoly and is even more puzzled that it should be viewed as culpable or as avoidable.

*Selling Activities.* By our economist, all sales effort has characteristically been viewed with serious misgivings. His ire has been concentrated on the purest forms of selling cost, such as advertising, but it has slopped over into every aspect of promotional effort. Economists, particularly of the more dedicated neoclassical persuasion, have seen in selling efforts a device for enhancing the monopoly power of the firm by differentiating the product in the minds of the prospective buyers. According to this view, the resulting "consumer franchise" is an island of monopoly power largely created by selling efforts.

To the businessman, selling activities seem the essence of competition. Pained by the unfamiliarity and indifference of consumers to the virtues of his product and service, he sees sales effort as dissolving the rigidities of ignorance and inertia that block access to substitutes. Thus it converts the incipient rivalry of substitutes into effective competition.

*Product Differentiation.* Physical differences among sellers' products have come under opprobrium similar to psychological differentiation. These economists consider that commercially successful product competition which develops a distinctive product that people want creates a monopoly power. This power is limited, to be sure, by the adequacy of substitutes, but nevertheless product innovation and adaptation to consumers' desires bears the opprobrium of monopoly. Thus these economists see in each new product and each improvement of an existing product an effort to escape from the competitive struggle into a stronghold of monopoly. In contrast, the businessman, in industries where product innovation and improvement is a dominant aspect of rivalry, would look upon it as the very core of competition. (Witness the workings of real-world rivalry in the automobile industry.)

*Product Research.* Many neoclassical economists have looked on the outlays of large corporations for technological research with apprehension. The results of research are patented; patents constitute legalized monopolies, and patents build barriers to entry. Hence research expands and perpetuates a firm's monopoly power in the view of some economists.

The businessman sees whatever monopoly power he succeeds in building up by technological research as being transient. It is eternally threatened by the competitive inroads of rivals. His experience indicates that perpetuation of his power to compete can be achieved only by research which creates new products and which keeps existing products abreast of the technological innovations of his rivals. He properly sees his existing products and methods threatened, to an extent never experienced before, by inborn substitutes that may provide dramatically cheaper solutions for his customers' problems. He sees patents as poor protection in today's dynamic, fluid technology.

*Selective Distribution.* Flowing the product to consumers through an organization of sponsored, franchised (and sometimes exclusive) dealers has been viewed by some economists not only as evidence of monopoly power but also as an unwarranted extension and consolidation of the market power of product differentiation. The businessman, in contrast, sees an effective dealer organization as a major weapon of competition. In some industries a dealer organization appears essential to make the manufacturer's competition operational at the point where competition counts, namely, in the decisions of the ultimate consumer.

Economists have not only feared the distributive power conferred by a strong dealer organization, they have also looked upon exclusive dealerships as a grant of locational monopoly and as a monopolistic denial of access to rival sellers. To the businessman, exclusive dealerships are a means of assuring single-minded and dedicated effort to compete with dealers of rival manufacturers.

*Market Share.* Preoccupation with the company's market share has ominous monopolistic overtones to the neoclassical economist. For a firm to have market occupancy big enough to make its market share perceptible is in itself a significant departure from the standard of perfect competition. Making market-share goals pivotal for pricing and promotional policy is, to these economists, a sure sign of a monopoloid situation. Similarly, when the very awareness of rivals as individuals is a sinful slip from atomistic competition, overt study of rivals' reactions to the firm's market thrusts is to these economists clear litmus of "monopoly power." To the businessman who watches his market share apprehensively and at considerable cost and who frequently sacrifices immediate profits for long-run strengthening of his sinews for market-share rivalry, it is incredible that his concern about his "competitive position" should be damned as monopolistic.

Even more culpable in the eyes of the economist is industry-wide cohesion in the face of threatened encroachment by rival industries (for example, the movie industry's battle with television and radio for consumer attention and for the amusement dollar). The businessman, more painfully impressed with the realities of substitute competition, sees industry solidarity as improving his competitive effectiveness in this wider arena and hence as intensifying rather than diminishing competition.

*Market Raiding.* Muscling in on stable and satisfied (established) customers is to the businessman proof of voracious competition. To the neoclassical economists, however, the very existence of long-lived, uninterrupted commer-

cial relationships with individual large customers is an indication of monopoly power, since it is unthinkable under perfect competition. And the subterranean efforts to dislodge the favored supplier smack of discriminatory tactics.

Similarly, raiding by suppliers who are geographically (or in other ways) distant strikes the businessman as indicating that the arena of competition has been widened and hence intensified. Also, the hit-and-run tactics of the raider disturb the price peace and may force a substantial realignment of market occupancy. To the neoclassical economist, in contrast, raiding demonstrates the existence of a private preserve to raid, and raiding tactics produce disparity in the net revenue between backyard and distant sales which have discriminatory results, presumably possible only with the substantial degree of monopoly power.

Customer freezing is in a sense the converse of market raiding. To the businessman it indicates the length to which he must go to keep his established customer relationships intact and protect them against the heartless and ceaseless competitive efforts of his rivals. To some economists these sewing-up devices look like the creation of noncompetitive nooks which impose barriers to the access of rivals.

*Customer Sharing.* Customer sharing is to many economists proof that rivalry is imperfect. Predetermined sharing of the business even of an individual customer is a departure from the essentially anonymous and happenstance division of patronage that is assumed under perfect competition.

To the businessman, who is forced by the growing acceptance of the dual-supplier doctrine to share his established customers with rival suppliers, customer sharing shows the essential equivalence of their products and services and often sales volume, thereby intensifying competition.

### Sad Conclusion

No plaudits had been expected by our businessman for his little foray into economics. But it is downright discouraging to find that his nine telltales of a tough competitive setup are to our economist sure symptoms of monopoly. Recognizing that competition is clearly just the opposite of what it seems, our business friend sadly climbs back through the looking glass.

# H. Technological Developments and Marketing

## 29. *Management and the Challenge of Change*

FRANK K. SHALLENBERGER

The greatest fact of life in the next 20-30-40 years—the remaining years of the twentieth century—will be the fact of change, rapid, accelerating technological, social and economic change. And nowhere will change have greater impact than on business and the management job.

❊   ❊   ❊

Scientists tell us that the world is five billion years old. The mammal we call man has been on the earth for about 250,000 years. Recorded history dates back only about 5,000 years. All but a very few of the products that we buy and sell and use today had their origins less than 50 years ago. Items of major current interest and discussion—automation, the computer, management sciences, guided missiles, antibiotics, executive development, electronic data processing, television and the Common Market—these are post-war developments of the last 20 years. Eighty per cent of the prescriptions filled today at the corner drugstore could not have been filled ten years ago. Sputnik was launched only eight years ago—yet already we are sending probes to the moon and to Mars and to Venus, and are orbiting man around the earth and building hardware

◆ SOURCE: Reprinted from the Stanford Graduate School of Business *Bulletin*, Vol. 34, No. 3, Winter 1966, pp. 2–7 and 27–30. © 1966 by the Board of Trustees of the Leland Stanford Junior University. All rights reserved.

for his trip to the moon. In *eight* years out of *five billion* years!

If the earth's history is equated to the distance around the world, the last fifty years, the period of our lifetimes, the period of most rapid development, would be *one foot!*

Consider the earth's history as a book of 100,000,000 pages, a book 25,000 feet (or almost five miles) thick. The period of technological discovery and development would be the *last page!*

Or compress the earth's history into one calendar year. From January to August there was no life. Between August and November there was only single-celled life, elementary virus, primitive bacteria, jelly-fish. Mammals first came into the world December 15. Man arrived December 31, 11:45 P.M. Written history dates back only to December 31, 11:59 P.M. The last 100 years, in which period practically all modern science has developed, occupies only the last one-half second of the year. The post-war period is the last one-tenth second!

Now ask yourselves what is going to happen on the next page, in the next one-fifth second, the next 30-40 years of our time, the remainder of the twentieth century, the period of your business careers. By any measure you wish, virtually all the technological progress of mankind has been crowded into a mere instant of time. And the acceleration is continuing. The next few years will see the creation of more new knowledge, new technology, new change, than the world has ever seen.

## THE IMPACT OF CHANGE

Technological and social and economic changes have, in the past, revolutionized or destroyed industries, cultures, mores, living standards, religions, empires and even civilizations. Will the increasingly rapid change of the immediate future have any less impact? No. Change will be just as disrupting, just as revolutionizing, just as destructive to our present way of life and to our industries and business as the more leisurely change of the past—in all probability, much more so.

Does it not follow, therefore, that a major responsibility, perhaps *the* major responsibility, of top executives, into whose hands has been placed responsibility for the success and preservation of the corporation, will be that of sensing change, of predicting it, of adapting to it, of taking advantage of it, and—for the true executive—*creating* change, to his own company's advantage and his competitor's disadvantage, using change itself as a major competitive weapon?

What areas of change can best dramatize our prediction of rapid technology in the next few years? Technology advances on extremely broad and varied fronts; we have space to discuss only a few out of very many.

### Atomic Energy

First developed and used only twenty years ago for destructive military purpose, *atomic energy* is now widely used for peaceful power generation, analysis and detection, propulsion, medical purposes and research. Its potential for power or heat generation, anywhere in the world, with complete freedom from dependence on hydroelectric or fuel resources, is almost unlimited.

A fascinating proposed use of atomic energy has been termed "geographical engineering," the massive changing of the face of the earth —creating a harbor or an island where none existed before, building canals and tunnels, creating valleys or removing mountains. Currently under serious consideration are a new canal across Central America paralleling the Panama Canal, one across the foot of the Aleutian Chain, and the so-called Kra Canal across the Malay Peninsula.

The use of atomic energy to blast a series of tunnels or valleys through the Andes to bring water from the rain forests to the arid coast would revolutionize the economy of Peru. Underground blasts could be used to create vast storage reservoirs in areas of high evaporation and low rainfall, such as North Africa, the Middle East, Central Australia. Atomic energy may enable us to convert sea water to fresh water in unlimited amounts, doubling or tripling the food-producing capacity of the world. Or through the heat and pressure of atomic energy we may be able to exploit the 700 billion barrels of oil in the Athabasca tar fields of western Canada and oil shale deposits throughout the world. Mining as done today differs little from that of ancient times. We burrow like moles under the ground to extract minute bits of metal from the earth. Could atomic energy be used to break up the ore so we might leach out the minerals? Could we even smelt some ores underground and bring only concentrates to the surface?

### The Oceans

One of the truly great industrial frontiers, an untapped treasure house of wealth and knowledge, is the *ocean*, "the bountiful sea." No single area of technology, including space, offers greater opportunities for research and industrial exploitation by man.

The oceans cover three-fourths of the earth's surface to an average depth of two miles. They have unknown and virtually inexhaustible food resources—fish, animal and plant life. They are the only feasible source of protein to feed the world's exploding population. Since time began, the rivers of the land world have been carrying the chemicals and minerals of the land to the sea. Now, dissolved in its waters, or lying on its floor, is more mineral wealth than we have ever mined—probably more than exists on or under all the land areas. We are already starting to mine the ocean for gold, tin, diamonds, manganese, coal, phosphorites, iron ore and oil. Every cubic mile of the ocean holds over 6 million tons of valuable minerals, salts and chemicals. And there are 390 *million cubic miles!* There is reason to believe we may find in the minute plankton, in fish and in the plants of the sea, the mechanisms and the secrets of extracting and concentrating these chemicals and minerals.

The oceans have currents equal to thousands of Mississippis. They have temperature differentials, tides and waves which produce more energy than all the power of the winds, coal, oil and natural fuels. They have all the water necessary for any conceivable human or agricultural consumption and perhaps within themselves the energy to break it free.

Yet we know almost less about the bottom of the sea than we know about the surface of the moon. We can instantly detect a missile thousands of miles away in the atmosphere—it took us months to find a submarine lost at 8,000 feet. We fish the sea like the hunters of old—with crude weapons, ancient hit-or-miss methods, steeped in tradition and superstition. We don't produce—we hunt. We use none of the techniques of modern agriculture or animal husbandry—planting, cultivation, fertilization, feeding, selective breeding.

We spend less than one-twelfth as much on ocean sciences as we do on space. When industry and government awake to the danger and opportunity in the ocean and start investing substantial sums in marine research, the knowledge that will come from the sea will stagger us. And the new knowledge will create an impact on the economy far greater than has the space program, for the wealth of the oceans is at our doorstep. There is threat and promise here for transportation, food products, communications, metals, chemicals, drugs, power, electronics and many other industries.

### Bionics

Bionics is one of the most exciting of the new technologies. In the past, engineering and design problems have been tackled as problems in physics or chemistry or mechanics. Now we have suddenly awakened to the fact that Nature has solved many of these problems long before we even knew they existed. She has, for the last billion years or so, in the vast laboratory of the evolutionary world, been carrying on an untold number of trial and error experiments, keeping solutions that worked, rejecting those that failed. In this way she has developed practical answers to many technical problems we are only now facing.

If you want to know how to live in the hostile environment of other planets we will visit, study the ecology of mammal life in the Arctic, or the desert, or the tropics, or the sea, and observe nature's adaptation to life in such environments.

Do you want to know how to develop better sonar for underwater detection or to develop electronic "eyes" for the blind? Study the porpoise and determine how while blindfolded it can detect an object an eighth inch in diameter 50 feet away, distinguish between a square object and a round object, a smooth object and a rough object, a soft object and a hard object. Or study the bat and its amazing ability to fly blindfolded at high speed through a maze of closely spaced wires.

Do you want to know how to propel a ship or a submarine faster with less power? Again, study the porpoise. Why can it swim 40 per cent faster than it size and energy theoretically should permit?

Do you want to learn how to build a miniature computer? Study the brain and its fantastic storage and logic capacity. Do you want a machine to read printing or writing or movement for computer or radar input? Study the frog's or pigeon's eye to determine how they preprocess information and filter out all except the limited critical information their tiny brains can handle. All this priceless knowledge is there for the taking, if and when. we learn how to read and understand it.

### Population

The advance of technology is deeply intertwined with social and economic change, much of which technology creates. One of the most important and interesting changes, one whose genesis lies largely in technology, and a great "tide in the affairs of men," is the popularly-called population explosion. What will be the impact on business of a doubling of the population every 35 years? Of 7,000 births every hour? Of 10,000 births during the reading time of this article? Of adding *every two months* another New York City to feed, to clothe, to house, to sell to, to find jobs for?

The world's population today is slightly over 3 billion. Before the end of the century it will be 6 billion. A hundred years from now it will be 25 billion, eight times the present population! What will this mean in terms of a drain on our already largely depleted resources? Many basic resources already face the need for substitution, secondary working of reserves, increased recycling, improved recovery techniques if we are to avoid exhaustion in the next 10-20 years. At the end of this century we will consume as much power in one year as has been consumed to date in all the history of mankind. Will the "have" nations become the "have nots"?

Can technology, which created the population explosion, also support it? Economic welfare is a fraction—output over population. In spite of the millions India has invested in economic development her people have less to eat today than twenty years ago—their numbers have grown faster than the production of food. Egypt's great new Aswan dam will add 2 million acres of new farmland by 1972—yet the Egyptians will not eat any better, for the population growth will have added 13 million new mouths to feed. Little wonder a report of the National Science Foundation states, "Other than the search for lasting peace, no problem is more urgent than the control of population growth."

### Some Others

To be conservative is dangerous, because all but the wildest dreamers tend to far underestimate the future. Who, in light of an anticipated rate of change far greater than anything we have experienced in the past, can possibly put *any* limitations on what we may see in our lifetimes or our children's lifetimes?

Supersonic jets promise within the next ten years flights from South America to Europe or the United States in two to three hours. Who can say what is beyond? One hour? One-half hour? Then what happens to our concepts of administration, decentralization, branch plants, markets, free trade areas, lines of communication, span of control? We are also promised world-wide video communication as realistic as face-to-face contact. Why travel, when you can hold a world-wide conference in your office?

Who can say that within our children's lifetime we won't have a cure for all diseases, fully replaceable body organs, control of aging and death only by accident? Until several years ago we could transplant only corneas. Now we have transplanted kidneys, and in animals—hearts, lungs, and other organs. We have successfully constructed artificial arteries, heart valves, and heart pacers, and thousands of lives are today extended by such devices. How far away are artificial or transplanted lungs, stomachs, eyes, hearts, even brains? A Stanford scientist describes the transplant of hearts as only a matter of "simple plumbing," and asks what are the economics of a market in which many people want to buy, at any price, and no one wants to sell? To how many hearts is a man entitled? Having worn out his own, and a replacement, should he, if he has the wealth, be allowed to purchase a third? Or a fourth?

Medical science has successfully conquered most of the communicable diseases of childhood. Assume then that it attacks and overcomes with equal success the diseases of old age, and where it cannot overcome the disease it replaces the diseased or worn-out organ with a transplant or artificial device. Assume we successfully conquer aging itself? Suppose life expectancy is extended by these means to 100, 150, 200 years, and useful working life proportionately?

What then of your retirement and pension and social security plans? Will industry still relegate people to the scrap heap at 65? Who will support them for the remaining half of their lives? What will happen to our tax bills, insurance rates, pension funds? In what security markets could we conceivably invest enough money to support a third or more of our population in retirement and another third in childhood and college? To what level must the remaining work force raise its output to support such a non-working population? What new markets will be created for airlines, railroads, oil companies, pharmaceuticals or leisure products.

Assume we do not retire them at 65. Suppose we keep managers, engineers, scientists working productively until they reach 80. What if you don't tap this reservoir of experience and maturity and judgment and your competitor does? How can we provide challenge and opportunity and experience for our younger employees? How will we maintain the necessary influx of imagination, daring, willingness to try new approaches, to challenge tradition, dogma, the old way of doing things? Can adequate managerial opportunities and challenge and experience for the younger executives be created through growth and expansion and diversification and decentralization?

What effect would a doubling of life expectancy have upon the world's accumulated wisdom and culture and ethics? What would be the impact on the pattern and rate and direction of change itself if a Galileo, or Newton, or Einstein could live and work productively for 150 years?

### The Mind

The *human mind,* like the oceans, is a virtually untapped frontier, of whose ultimate potential we have absolutely no concept. The mind weighs only a few pounds and yet, in many ways, its capacity exceeds that of the largest and most complex computer. It can do many things a computer can never do. Like the computer, it can think, it can remember, it can reason. But it can also create, it can invent, it can dream, it can feel, and it can love. Who can say that it cannot also communicate freely with other minds? Who can say we will not someday, perhaps even in our own lifetime, have effective and widely used thought transmission? Then what of your newspapers, periodicals, telephone, telegraph, radio, television, transportation industries? What will be the impact on education, company organization, advertising, collective bargaining, business morality, and a thousand and one other areas? Who can say—with certainty—that we will not someday have useable, effective, planned clairvoyance, the ability to foresee the future? What effect on planning, inventories, markets, economic, military affairs? Impossible? The airplane, in its infancy, was "proven" impossible by competent scientists.

Can anyone say we will not someday, perhaps soon, and through some force of whose existence we may not even know, develop control of mind over matter, psychokinetics? Who can say we might not someday transfer intelligence and learning from one being to another—by injection, by drugs, perhaps by brain transplants or genetic manipulation? Attempts are now under way to transplant the brains of mice, to determine whether training or intelligence can be transferred from one body to another. Experiments with planaria, or flatworms, indicate possible transfer of knowledge and learning by other means.

We have pills that induce sleep, relax, tranquilize, stimulate, anesthetize. We have drugs that slow metabolism, drugs that kill pain, drugs that expand consciousness, induce dreams, hallucinations and euphoria. How far away are drugs that improve concentration, expand memory, speed up the thinking process by a factor of 2, or 10, or 100? Education is a distressingly inefficient process, why not learning pills? We spend a third of our lives asleep—can we learn during sleep? Or can we eliminate or reduce the need for sleep? Could a drug, or perhaps hypnosis, substitute for sleep?

### Other Planets?

Now, a little farther out, who can say that we may not soon communicate with intelligent beings on other planets? Impossible? Intelligent life on other planets appears to be a virtual certainty. At least 600 million other planets are said to be capable of supporting life. By what stretch of imagination and probability can we presume that the particular combination of pressure, chemicals, and temperature that generated the first spark of life on this planet occurred here and on no other planet?

Assume that on at least *one* other planet, life began a mere forty years before that on earth, one-fifth second on our condensed time scale. If we assume also that evolution proceeded there at the same rate that it has on earth, that planet would be forty years ahead of us, and all the technological development which we have just predicted for our own immediate future on earth, plus much more, would already have taken place. Suppose we could communicate with the beings on this other planet and draw from them today the details of our next forty years' achievements! Is such speculation only wild dreaming? Is it any more impossible than atomic fission was fifty years ago?

You might argue that the speed of light, the speed of electromagnetic waves, places an insurmountable time barrier against practicable communication with any but the nearest planets. What is the speed of thought transmission?

If it is agreed that even some of what has been suggested may come to pass, then we must face the hard and practical questions of how we as citizens and as businessmen live with, adapt to, make the most of changing technology.

A basic decision for any individual, any manager, any corporation, is whether to participate in the rat race or not. It can't be avoided completely. You can't "Stop the world, I want to get off." But you can choose for yourself or for your company those industries least subject to change. Thus you can obtain lower than average risk—and must thereby reconcile yourself to lower than average gains.

Within any industry, even the most technical, there are both leaders and followers. You can let the others do the pioneering, break with the past, take the risks, while you ride their coattails. Again you "play it safe," but for more modest stakes. (The long-run risks may of course be even greater than those taken by the leaders. You may fall off the coattails, may be lost by the wayside in the competitive race.)

You can attempt to protect yourself by diversification—by spreading your risks, by placing your bets on all the horses in the race. (Here again you may risk more—by dividing your attention, by averaging your organization to a level of mediocrity unable to compete in a changing world.)

But these are defensive actions, taken to protect *against* change. The great excitement and big rewards will go to those who welcome and capitalize on change, those who themselves lead and create, rather than accept, technological advance. How does one organize to join this club? How does one foster alertness, pioneering, imagination, receptivity to change? How do you overcome the normal pressures toward stability, mediocrity, caution, playing it safe, the red tape, the checks and balances, that characterize so many organizations? How do you attract, encourage, appraise, and reward daring creativity, vision?

One leader in the technological race has developed an organization structure, procedures and policies specifically geared to the challenge of changing times and changing technologies. It has tried to create an environment which encourages the flow of new ideas, and waters and cultivates and protects and helps new ideas grow. It has encouraged vision and wide-ranging thinking and imagination by spreading individual responsibility throughout the organization, right down to the lowest supervisory authority. It has tried to capture the initiative, the motivation, the creativity of the small firm. It has tried to attract truly entrepreneurial executives and to encourage them at all levels to function as managers in business for themselves. It gives them full responsibility for their own area and for its profits and growth. It provides opportunity for individual growth and self-expression. And it offers commensurate rewards, big rewards—"you can't catch a tiger with a worm on a hook." (Note the difference between this environment and that in which other writers describe the one most likely to succeed as the dedicated, loyal, deferential, adaptable, well-bred, well-poised conformist—the "grade A corporation creep.")

This company has been outstandingly successful. Thirteen years ago it didn't exist; today it has 140 plants, located throughout the world. Its average annual growth rate has been over 50 per cent, and profits have kept pace. It is presently operating at a sales level of over one billion dollars per year.

The problem seems to be that in the years ahead, "the future will come sooner." The future will be no easier to predict but it will be far more important to predict. The time for evaluation and appraisal of developments in the marketplace and in the laboratory, as well as for taking corrective action, will be drastically shortened. The problem will be not just one of keeping up with current technology, but rather one of keeping well *ahead* of technology, of developing a corporate foresight or vision, a sense of direction or movement and corporate destiny, an ability to know what's ahead and to plan and prepare in the same manner that a gunner leads his target.

This is far different from random jumping on the technological bandwagon *after* the trends become apparent. It implies making goals, plans and decisions *in anticipation of trends.* It implies a continuous, objective, and at the same time intuitive, analysis of where the profit opportunities lie, not today, but tomorrow and the day after tomorrow. It means even more than before planning and organizing, not in generalities but in specifics, with consistent, realistic, integrated research, investment and marketing goals, programs and timetables, fully communicated and accepted throughout the organization. And it means continuous follow-up, evaluation and control of performance against the plan.

How can we resolve the conflict between planning and flexibility? How can we plan and organize and invest against anticipated trends and at the same time retain our ability to adjust to the unpredictable? Can we choose our research and development projects so well, even before the trends become clear, that we are consistently in the winning circle? Can we maintain bridges behind us to allow for a fast retreat or adjustment? How can we maintain profits and growth, and write off costs of development and capital investment and promotion when product lives are measured in months or years rather than decades?

What changes in organization, recruitment, training, appraisal, and rewards are ahead? A recent study by *Scientific American* indicates that among top U.S. corporation executives the proportion having degrees or equivalent experience in science or engineering rose from 6.8 per cent in 1900 to 13.5 per cent in 1925, 20 per cent in 1950, and 36 per cent in 1963. Among managers in the age group 35-45, the pool from which tomorrow's top managers will be drawn, *51 per cent* have such background!

How, in the technological age, will small business fare in competition with the magnificent laboratories, the generous development and promotional budgets of large industry? Hold no fear for the smaller firm; it seems well able, if it utilizes its natural advantages of flexibility, specialization, resourcefulness, creativity, enthusiasm and high motivation, to succeed. One can better fear for the future of many larger firms "too paralyzed by their own bureaucratic structures to survive in the swift cross-currents of contemporary affairs."

## THE DEVELOPING WORLD

The problems created by technological change are even more challenging in the newly developing countries than in the more advanced countries. We of the industrialized world face merely an *adjustment* in the rate of change—the developing countries face a complete *revolution* in their way of life.

Technology is highly transportable. It is at least theoretically possible to impose on a primitive agrarian economy, virtually overnight, the highest level of industrial sophistication—to leap from handcrafts to full automation, from the canoe to jets, from the wooden plow to the bulldozer, from the witch doctor to antibiotics, from drums to television. The Manu tribe of Papua and New Guinea has in one generation literally come from the Stone Age to the 20th Century! Think of it! People who spent their youth in an age which did not even know metals, now spending their adult years in the age of jets, nuclear power and space exploration!

In another generation or two the developing countries will make the transition from a world where the greatest problems are hunger, disease and ignorance, to a world where their greatest problems may be affluence and the constructive use of leisure time. How do peoples or countries adjust to such change? How much change—in his environment, his culture, his ambitions, his problems—can man stand?

Every resource of the developing countries is threatened by obsolescence—cheap labor by automation, fiber and food products by synthetics, hydroelectric power by nuclear power, minerals by new materials. How does a country which competes in world markets with cheap labor defend itself against modernized plants which produce with *no* labor? Nothing is safe from obsolescence.

Countries, like companies, must look ahead, must anticipate unfolding technology, must "lead the target," must act now in anticipation of the technology of the future. Peru has an ambitious and exciting program under way for the colonization of its vast jungle area. Highways are the primary and most costly element in this program. How far should Peru lead the target? How soon will it be cheaper to fly fruits and meat and lumber and livestock and oil and grain and cement over the Andes and jungle by cargo plane than to make the long and difficult haul by truck or rail? Should Peru be building highways? Or airports?

The proposed railroad across Tanzania to haul Zambian copper to the coast raises the same question. Will the railroad be obsolete before it is completed? Reportedly, a politician insisted 200 years ago that unless a mammoth program of planting oak trees were undertaken to provide oak for ships, England's dominance of the seas would end. How far should you lead the target?

What are the economic, social, political consequences of bringing *three-fourths* of the world's population from a level only slightly above animal existence to one of material comfort and nourishment and education? This is a Pandora's box of problems and possibilities. It implies fantastic changes in the world's economy, a quadrupling of the world's markets, an upsetting of all the present economic and political and social relationships. Coupled with the population explosion and its demands for food, fibers, minerals, transportation, jobs, power, products, capital investment, markets, competition, it promises economic changes of a magnitude never before seen.

At the individual company level it brings many new opportunities, but also extremely difficult short-term uncertainties stemming from continually changing governmental policy on planning, controls, protection, ownership, taxes, labor, fiscal affairs, economic cooperation.

## THE COST

Unfortunately, technological and scientific advance does not always benefit mankind. In all the glamour and excitement of "the brave new world," we must recognize that in return for all that science offers us in freedom from disease, relief from heavy physical labor, longer life, plentiful food, we pay a terrible price.

We pay in jammed freeways, highway slaughter, slums, urban sprawl, sleazy, cheap, unimaginative subdivisions. We pay through the loss of human individuality in every phase of life. We pay in the loss of pride and challenge and meaning in work. We pay in ulcers, neuroses, coronary disease, emphysema, lung cancer. We pay in synthetic, bland, canned, frozen, dehydrated, premixed foods. We pay in a flood of equally synthetic television and radio programs, magazines and paperbacks geared to the lowest intellectual level. We pay in distorted and confused mass education, stifling the excellent, the dissenter, the protester, and emphasizing academic performance rather than learning and understanding, and science at the expense of the humanities.

We submit willingly to outrageous intrusions on our personal lives by Madison Avenue, motivating us to purchase things we neither want nor need. We pay in the wastage of sound values through planned obsolescence. We tolerate the widespread destruction of our natural heritage—the hills, the fields, the streams—by billboards, highways, dams, mines, factories, powerlines. We accept the slaughter of our wildlife through obliteration of grazing lands, forests and streams. We are suffocating ourselves in our own wastes—smog, stream pollution, pesticides, detergents, sewage.

We pay through technological unemployment and obsolescence of individual skills that took lifetimes to build. We tolerate tragic poverty in the midst of plenty. We are enmeshed in an economic-political system so complex that we can't find a way to distribute our disgraceful food surpluses to a starving world —instead we continue exhausting our land resources to produce even greater surpluses. It sometimes doesn't seem to matter where we're going so long as we get there quickly. Our materialistic orientation, our worship of the god of efficiency and productivity, distorts or destroys our more fundamental human values. We live in fear of a technology that could destroy the world.

Some observers think we pay much too high a price, and who can say they are wrong? Many express deep concern with the direction and emphasis of technology:

"Technique, efficiency, management, results! But what does the poor man in these countries live for? . . . . Nobody asks the fundamental question as to what is the whole blooming thing for. Nobody cares to find out what spirit pervades the whole thing. Nobody has the time to ascertain whether Man, in his freedom and in his fullness, exists at all."

"Just because we can do something, does this mean we should do it? Technology develops to answer human needs, but what human needs does the supersonic transport answer?

What is growth? Is it getting bigger or getting better? What is a good standard of living? More things to consume or better things to appreciate and discriminate? What is a better use of the moon? To hit it with a rocket or just to look at it? What are the frontiers of human enterprise? Should people build and pioneer always outwards, or sometimes inwards?

At a fantastic cost—$30 billion—mankind puts a man on the moon—to impress mankind. Where is our sense of priorities?

With $30 billion we could give a 10 per cent raise in salary over a ten-year period to every teacher in the U.S. from kindergarten through universities (about $9.8 billion); give $10 million each to 200 of the best smaller colleges ($2 billion); finance seven-year fellowships (freshman through Ph.D.) at $4,000 per person per year for 50,000 new scientists and engineers ($1.4 billion); contribute $200 million each toward the creation of ten new medical schools ($2 billion); build and largely endow complete universities with medical, engineering and agricultural faculties for—fifty-three of the nations which have been added to the United Nations since its original founding ($13.2 billion); create three more permanent Rockefeller Foundations ($1.5 billion); and still have $100 million left over to popularize science.

## IN CONCLUSION

We cannot stop the advance of technology. We can do very little to slow it. As citizens— and managers—of the twentieth century we cannot escape its impact. But we can guide it, we can direct and control it with wisdom and understanding to maximize the social gain and minimize the social cost. We have been given the unique and boundless blessing of the human mind. We were given it not to destroy ourselves but to develop and use for the greater understanding and improvement of ourselves and our surroundings. Surely this gift promises mankind a much higher destiny than to wallow in problems he has created himself, to drown himself in his own stupidity, to blow himself off the face of the earth, and to destroy all that a billion years of evolution and labor and thought have thus far accomplished. Surely we are more than links in a grand experiment about to come to an end.

What a paradox! Technology has given us the technique—the threat—and the promise. Military technology provided us with a new and powerful research capability. This in turn has brought us to an unstable truce enforced by the threat of mutual annihilation, by "equal fear equally shared." And now the truce gives us the opportunity to turn our immense new problem-solving capability to the *right* questions, to the search for new sources of food, water, and energy, to the exploration of the oceans, to the threat of nuclear war, to the conquering of disease—and beyond these to the human mind, man's relationship with his fellow man.

These problems are far too important to leave to politicians. Nor can they be left to the scientists who create the new technology. Society and business, the exploiters of technology, must choose whether it will be used for the benefit or detriment of mankind.

If private enterprise is to survive as a viable, independent, self-directed force, business executives must accept responsibility for leadership, not only in directing the use of science and technology to constructive ends, but also in seeking solutions to problems of poverty, old age, population, leisure time, diminishing resources and to those relating to spiritual and moral values. These are *your* problems, *your* responsibility. You are executives in your companies, in your jobs—you are also executives in the progress of the universe.

The journey of mankind is a wonderful journey, an "immense journey," out of darkness. Since mankind first emerged, his first preoccupation has been the fight against hunger, disease, and physical want. Now for the first time in history he holds the technology necessary to erase these problems—or himself—from the face of the earth. We have come to the fork in the road—one branch leads back to darkness, the other to the elimination of human want and ignorance. What a wonderful choice! What a wonderfully exciting thrill to stand as travelers at the crossroad, to stand where no man has stood before—to hold such power for good or evil—and as business executives to have both the responsibility and the opportunity of directing and continuing the journey to understanding and man's destiny.

# 30. *Marketing Myopia*

THEODORE LEVITT

Every major industry was once a growth industry. But some that are now riding a wave of growth enthusiasm are very much in the shadow of decline. Others which are thought of as seasoned growth industries have actually stopped growing. In every case the reason growth is threatened, slowed, or stopped is *not* because the market is saturated. It is because there has been a failure of management.

## FATEFUL PURPOSES

The failure is at the top. The executives responsible for it, in the last analysis, are those who deal with broad aims and policies. Thus:

¶ The railroads did not stop growing because the need for passenger and freight transportation declined. That grew. The railroads are in trouble today not because the need was filled by others (cars, trucks, airplanes, even telephones), but because it was *not* filled by the railroads themselves. They let others take customers away from them because they assumed themselves to be in the railroad business rather than in the transportation business. The reason they defined their industry wrong was because they were railroad-oriented instead of transportation-oriented; they were product-oriented instead of customer-oriented.

¶ Hollywood barely escaped being totally ravished by television. Actually, all the established film companies went through drastic reorganizations. Some simply disappeared. All of them got into trouble not because of TV's

‡ SOURCE: Reprinted by permission from *Modern Marketing Strategy,* edited by Edward C. Bursk and John F. Chapman (Harvard University Press, 1964, by the President and Fellows of Harvard College): pp. 24–48.

inroads but because of their own myopia. As with the railroads, Hollywood defined its business incorrectly. It thought it was in the movie business when it was actually in the entertainment business. "Movies" implied a specific, limited product. This produced a fatuous contentment which from the beginning led producers to view TV as a threat. Hollywood scorned and rejected TV when it should have welcomed it as an opportunity—an opportunity to expand the entertainment business.

Today TV is a bigger business than the old narrowly defined movie business ever was. Had Hollywood been customer-oriented (providing entertainment), rather than product-oriented (making movies), would it have gone through the fiscal purgatory that it did? I doubt it. What ultimately saved Hollywood and accounted for its recent resurgence was the wave of new young writers, producers, and directors whose previous successes in television had decimated the old movie companies and toppled the big movie moguls.

There are other less obvious examples of industries that have been and are now endangering their futures by improperly defining their purposes. I shall discuss some in detail later and analyze the kind of policies that lead to trouble. Right now it may help to show what a thoroughly customer-oriented management *can* do to keep a growth industry growing, even after the obvious opportunities have been exhausted; and here there are two examples that have been around for a long time. They are nylon and glass—specifically, E. I. duPont de Nemours & Company and Corning Glass Works:

¶ Both companies have great technical competence. Their product orientation is unquestioned. But this alone does not explain their success. After all, who was more pridefully product-oriented and product-conscious than the erstwhile New England textile companies that have been so thoroughly massacred? The DuPonts and the Cornings have succeeded not primarily because of their product or research orientation but because they have been thoroughly customer-oriented also. It is constant watchfulness for opportunities to apply their technical know-how to the creation of customer-satisfying uses which accounts for their prodigious output of successful new products. Without a very sophisticated eye on the customer, most of their new products might have been wrong, their sales methods useless.

Aluminum has also continued to be a growth industry, thanks to the efforts of two wartime-created companies which deliberately set about creating new customer-satisfying uses. Without Kaiser Aluminum & Chemical Corporation and Reynolds Metals Company, the total demand for aluminum today would be vastly less than it is.

### Error of Analysis

Some may argue that it is foolish to set the railroads off against aluminum or the movies off against glass. Are not aluminum and glass naturally so versatile that the industries are bound to have more growth opportunities than the railroads and movies? This view commits precisely the error I have been talking about. It defines an industry, or a product, or a cluster of knowhow so narrowly as to guarantee its premature senescence. When we mention "railroads," we should make sure we mean "transportation." As transporters, the railroads still have a good chance for very considerable growth. They are not limited to the railroad business as such (though in my opinion rail transportation is potentially a much stronger transportation medium than is generally believed).

What the railroads lack is not opportunity, but some of the same managerial imaginativeness and audacity that made them great. Even an amateur like Jacques Barzun can see what is lacking when he says:

I grieve to see the most advanced physical and social organization of the last century go down in shabby disgrace for lack of the same comprehensive imagination that built it up. [What is lacking is] the will of the companies

to survive and to satisfy the public by inventiveness and skill.[1]

### SHADOW OF OBSOLESCENCE

It is impossible to mention a single major industry that did not at one time qualify for the magic appellation of "growth industry." In each case its assumed strength lay in the apparently unchallenged superiority of its product. There appeared to be no effective substitute for it. It was itself a runaway substitute for the product it so triumphantly replaced. Yet one after another of these celebrated industries has come under a shadow. Let us look briefly at a few more of them, this time taking examples that have so far received a little less attention:

¶ *Dry cleaning*—This was once a growth industry with lavish prospects. In an age of wool garments, imagine being finally able to get them safely and easily clean. The boom was on.

Yet here we are 30 years after the boom started and the industry is in trouble. Where has the competition come from? From a better way of cleaning? No. It has come from synthetic fibers and chemical additives that have cut the need for dry cleaning. But this is only the beginning. Lurking in the wings and ready to make chemical dry cleaning totally obsolescent is that powerful magician, ultrasonics.

¶ *Electric utilities*—This is another one of those supposedly "no-substitute" products that has been enthroned on a pedestal of invincible growth. When the incandescent lamp came along, kerosene lights were finished. Later the water wheel and the steam engine were cut to ribbons by the flexibility, reliability, simplicity, and just plain easy availability of electric motors. The prosperity of electric utilities continues to wax extravagant as the home is converted into a museum of electric gadgetry. How can anybody miss by investing in utilities, with no competition, nothing but growth ahead?

But a second look is not quite so comforting. A score of nonutility companies are well advanced toward developing a powerful chemical fuel cell which could sit in some hidden closet of every home silently ticking off electric power. The electric lines that vulgarize so many neighborhoods will be eliminated. So will the endless demolition of streets and service interruptions during storms. Also on the horizon is solar energy, again pioneered by nonutility companies.

Who says that the utilities have no competition? They may be natural monopolies now, but tomorrow they may be natural deaths. To avoid

---

[1] Jacques Barzun, "Trains and the Mind of Man," *Holiday*, February 1960, p. 21.

this prospect, they too will have to develop fuel cells, solar energy, and other power sources. To survive, they themselves will have to plot the obsolescence of what now produces their livelihood.

¶ *Grocery stores*—Many people find it hard to realize that there ever was a thriving establishment known as the "corner grocery store." The supermarket has taken over with a powerful effectiveness. Yet the big food chains of the 1930's narrowly escaped being completely wiped out by the aggressive expansion of independent supermarkets. The first genuine supermarket was opened in 1930, in Jamaica, Long Island. By 1933 supermarkets were thriving in California, Ohio, Pennsylvania, and elsewhere. Yet the established chains pompously ignored them. When they chose to notice them, it was with such derisive descriptions as "cheapy," "horse-and-buggy," "cracker-barrel storekeeping," and "unethical opportunists."

The executive of one big chain announced at the time that he found it "hard to believe that people will drive for miles to shop for foods and sacrifice the personal service chains have perfected and to which Mrs. Consumer is accustomed." [2] As late as 1936, the National Wholesale Grocers convention and the New Jersey Retail Grocers Association said there was nothing to fear. They said that the supers' narrow appeal to the price buyer limited the size of their market. They had to draw from miles around. When imitators came, there would be wholesale liquidations as volume fell. The current high sales of the supers was said to be partly due to their novelty. Basically people wanted convenient neighborhood grocers. If the neighborhood stores "cooperate with their suppliers, pay attention to their costs, and improve their service," they would be able to weather the competition until it blew over. [3]

It never blew over. The chains discovered that survival required going into the supermarket business. This meant the wholesale destruction of their huge investments in corner store sites and in established distribution and merchandising methods. The companies with "the courage of their convictions" resolutely stuck to the corner store philosophy. They kept their pride but lost their shirts.

### Self-Deceiving Cycle

But memories are short. For example, it is hard for people who today confidently hail the twin messiahs of electronics and chemicals to see how things could possibly go wrong with these galloping industries. They probably also cannot see how a reasonably sensible businessman could have been as myopic as the famous Boston millionaire who 50 years ago unintentionally sentenced his heirs to poverty by stipulating that his entire estate be forever invested exclusively in electric streetcar securities. His posthumous declaration, "There will always be a big demand for efficient urban transportation," is no consolation to his heirs who sustain life by pumping gasoline at automobile filling stations.

Yet, in a casual survey I recently took among a group of intelligent business executives, nearly half agreed that it would be hard to hurt their heirs by tying their estates forever to the electronics industry. When I then confronted them with the Boston streetcar example, they chorused unanimously, "That's different!" But is it? Is not the basic situation identical?

In truth, *there is no such thing* as a growth industry, I believe. There are only companies organized and operated to create and capitalize on growth opportunities. Industries that assume themselves to be riding some automatic growth escalator invariably descend into stagnation. The history of every dead and dying "growth" industry shows a self-deceiving cycle of bountiful expansion and undetected decay. There are four conditions which usually guarantee this cycle:

1. The belief that growth is assured by an expanding and more affluent population.
2. The belief that there is no competitive substitute for the industry's major product.
3. Too much faith in mass production and in the advantages of rapidly declining unit costs as output rises.
4. Preoccupation with a product that lends itself to carefully controlled scientific experimentation, improvement, and manufacturing cost reduction.

I should like now to begin examining each of these conditions in some detail. To build my case as boldly as possible, I shall illustrate the points with reference to three industries—petroleum, automobiles, and electronics—particularly petroleum, because it spans more years and more vicissitudes. Not only do these three have excellent reputations with the general public and also enjoy the confidence of sophisticated investors, but their managements have become known for progressive thinking in areas like

---

[2] For more details see M. M. Zimmerman, *The Super Market: A Revolution in Distribution* (New York: McGraw-Hill, 1955), p. 48.

[3] *Ibid.*, pp. 45–47.

financial control, product research, and management training. If obsolescence can cripple even these industries, it can happen anywhere.

## POPULATION MYTH

The belief that profits are assured by an expanding and more affluent population is dear to the heart of every industry. It takes the edge off the apprehensions everybody understandably feels about the future. If consumers are multiplying and also buying more of your product or service, you can face the future with considerably more comfort than if the market is shrinking. An expanding market keeps the manufacturer from having to think very hard or imaginatively. If thinking is an intellectual response to a problem, then the absence of a problem leads to the absence of thinking. If your product has an automatically expanding market, then you will not give much thought to how to expand it.

One of the most interesting examples of this is provided by the petroleum industry. Probably our oldest growth industry, it has an enviable record. While there are some current apprehensions about its growth rate, the industry itself tends to be optimistic. But I believe it can be demonstrated that it is undergoing a fundamental yet typical change. It is not only ceasing to be a growth industry, but may actually be a declining one, relative to other business. Although there is widespread unawareness of it, I believe that within 25 years the oil industry may find itself in much the same position of retrospective glory that the railroads are now in. Despite its pioneering work in developing and applying the present-value method of investment evaluation, in employee relations, and in working with backward countries, the petroleum business is a distressing example of how complacency and wrongheadedness can stubbornly convert opportunity into near disaster.

One of the characteristics of this and other industries that have believed very strongly in the beneficial consequences of an expanding population, while at the same time being industries with a generic product for which there has appeared to be no competitive substitute, is that the individual companies have sought to outdo their competitors by improving on what they are already doing. This makes sense, of course, if one assumes that sales are tied to the country's population strings, because the customer can compare products only on a feature-by-feature basis. I believe it is significant, for example,

that not since John D. Rockefeller sent free kerosene lamps to China has the oil industry done anything really outstanding to create a demand for its product. Not even in product improvement has it showered itself with eminence. The greatest single improvement, namely, the development of tetraethyl lead, came from outside the industry, specifically from General Motors and DuPont. The big contributions made by the industry itself are confined to the technology of oil exploration, production, and refining.

### Asking for Trouble

In other words, the industry's efforts have focused on improving the *efficiency* of getting and making its product, not really on improving the generic product or its marketing. Moreover, its chief product has continuously been defined in the narrowest possible terms, namely, gasoline, not energy, fuel, or transportation. This attitude has helped assure that:

1. Major improvements in gasoline quality tend not to originate in the oil industry. Also, the development of superior alternative fuels comes from outside the oil industry, as will be shown later.

2. Major innovations in automobile fuel marketing are originated by small new oil companies that are not primarily preoccupied with production or refining. These are the companies that have been responsible for the rapidly expanding multipump gasoline stations, with their successful emphasis on large and clean layouts, rapid and efficient driveway service, and quality gasoline at low prices.

Thus, the oil industry is asking for trouble from outsiders. Sooner or later, in this land of hungry inventors and entrepreneurs, a threat is sure to come. The possibilities of this will become more apparent when we turn to the next dangerous belief of many managements. For the sake of continuity, because this second belief is tied closely to the first, I shall continue with the same example.

### Idea of Indispensability

The petroleum industry is pretty much persuaded that there is no competitive substitute for its major product, gasoline—or if there is, that it will continue to be a derivative of crude oil, such as diesel fuel or kerosene jet fuel.

There is a lot of automatic wishful thinking in this assumption. The trouble is that most refining companies own huge amounts of crude oil reserves. These have value only if there is a market for products into which oil can be converted—hence the tenacious belief in the continuing competitive superiority of automobile fuels made from crude oil.

This idea persists despite all historic evidence against it. The evidence not only shows that oil has never been a superior product for any purpose for very long, but it also shows that the oil industry has never really been a growth industry. It has been a succession of different businesses that have gone through the usual historic cycles of growth, maturity, and decay. Its over-all survival is owed to a series of miraculous escapes from total obsolescence, of last-minute and unexpected reprieves from total disaster reminiscent of the Perils of Pauline.

### Perils of Petroleum

I shall sketch in only the main episodes:

¶ First, crude oil was largely a patent medicine. But even before that fad ran out, demand was greatly expanded by the use of oil in kerosene lamps. The prospect of lighting the world's lamps gave rise to an extravagant promise of growth. The prospects were similar to those the industry now holds for gasoline in other parts of the world. It can hardly wait for the underdeveloped nations to get a car in every garage.

In the days of the kerosene lamp, the oil companies competed with each other and against gaslight by trying to improve the illuminating characteristics of kerosene. Then suddenly the impossible happened. Edison invented a light which was totally nondependent on crude oil. Had it not been for the growing use of kerosene in space heaters, the incandescent lamp would have completely finished oil as a growth industry at that time. Oil would have been good for little else than axle grease.

¶ Then disaster and reprieve struck again. Two great innovations occurred, neither originating in the oil industry. The successful development of coal-burning domestic central-heating systems made the space heater obsolescent. While the industry reeled, along came its most magnificent boost yet—the internal combustion engine, also invented by outsiders. Then when the prodigious expansion for gasoline finally began to level off in the 1920's, along came the miraculous escape of a central oil heater. Once again, the escape was provided by an outsider's invention and development. And when that market weakened, wartime demand for aviation fuel came to the rescue. After the war the expansion of civilian aviation, the

diancelization of railroads, and the explosive demand for cars and trucks kept the industry's growth in high gear.

¶ Meanwhile centralized oil heating—whose boom potential had only recently been proclaimed—ran into severe competition from natural gas. While the oil companies themselves owned the gas that now competed with their oil, the industry did not originate the natural gas revolution, nor has it to this day greatly profited from its gas ownership. The gas revolution was made by newly formed transmission companies that marketed the product with an aggressive ardor. They started a magnificent new industry, first against the advice and then against the resistance of the oil companies.

By all the logic of the situation, the oil companies themselves should have made the gas revolution. They not only owned the gas; they also were the only people experienced in handling, scrubbing, and using it, the only people experienced in pipeline technology and transmission, and they understood heating problems. But, partly because they knew that natural gas would compete with their own sale of heating oil, the oil companies pooh-poohed the potentials of gas.

The revolution was finally started by oil pipeline executives who, unable to persuade their own companies to go into gas, quit and organized the spectacularly successful gas transmission companies. Even after their success became painfully evident to the oil companies, the latter did not go into gas transmission. The multibillion dollar business which should have been theirs went to others. As in the past, the industry was blinded by its narrow preoccupation with a specific product and the value of its reserves. It paid little or no attention to its customers' basic needs and preferences.

¶ The postwar years have not witnessed any change. Immediately after World War II the oil industry was greatly encouraged about its future by the rapid expansion of demand for its traditional line of products. In 1950 most companies projected annual rates of domestic expansion of around 6% through at least 1975. Though the ratio of crude oil reserves to demand in the Free World was about 20 to 1, with 10 to 1 being usually considered a reasonable working ratio in the United States, booming demand sent oil men searching for more without sufficient regard to what the future really promised. In 1952 they "hit" in the Middle East; the ratio skyrocketed to 42 to 1. If gross additions to reserves continue at the average rate of the past five years (37 billion barrels annually), then by 1970 the reserve ratio will be up to 45 to 1. This abundance of oil has weakened crude and product prices all over the world.

### Uncertain Future

Management cannot find much consolation today in the rapidly expanding petrochemical industry, another oil-using idea that did not originate in the leading firms. The total United States production of petrochemicals is equivalent to about 2% (by volume) of the demand for all petroleum products. Although the petrochemical industry is now expected to grow by about 10% per year, this will not offset other drains on the growth of crude oil consumption. Furthermore, while petrochemical products are many and growing, it is well to remember that there are nonpetroleum sources of the basic raw material, such as coal. Besides, a lot of plastics can be produced with relatively little oil. A 50,000-barrel-per-day oil refinery is now considered the absolute minimum size for efficiency. But a 5,000-barrel-per-day chemical plant is a giant operation.

Oil has never been a continuously strong growth industry. It has grown by fits and starts, always miraculously saved by innovations and developments not of its own making. The reason it has not grown in a smooth progression is that each time it thought it had a superior product safe from the possibility of competitive substitutes, the product turned out to be inferior and notoriously subject to obsolescence. Until now, gasoline (for motor fuel, anyhow) has escaped this fate. But, as we shall see later, it too may be on its last legs.

The point of all this is that there is no guarantee against product obsolescence. If a company's own research does not make it obsolete, another's will. Unless an industry is especially lucky, as oil has been until now, it can easily go down in a sea of red figures—just as the railroads have, as the buggy whip manufacturers have, as the corner grocery chains have, as most of the big movie companies have, and indeed as many other industries have.

The best way for a firm to be lucky is to make its own luck. That requires knowing what makes a business successful. One of the greatest enemies of this knowledge is mass production.

### PRODUCTION PRESSURES

Mass-production industries are impelled by a great drive to produce all they can. The prospect of steeply declining unit costs as output rises is more than most companies can usually resist. The profit possibilities look spectacular. All effort focuses on production. The result is that marketing gets neglected.

John Kenneth Galbraith contends that just the opposite occurs.[4] Output is so prodigious that all effort concentrates on trying to get rid of it. He says this accounts for singing commercials, desecration of the countryside with advertising signs, and other wasteful and vulgar practices. Galbraith has a finger on something real, but he misses the strategic point. Mass production does indeed generate great pressure to "move" the product. But what usually gets emphasized is selling, not marketing. Marketing, being a more sophisticated and complex process, gets ignored.

The difference between marketing and selling is more than semantic. Selling focuses on the needs of the seller, marketing on the needs of the buyer. Selling is preoccupied with the seller's need to convert his product into cash; marketing with the idea of satisfying the needs of the customer by means of the product and the whole cluster of things associated with creating, delivering, and finally consuming it.

In some industries the enticements of full mass production have been so powerful that for many years top management in effect has told the sales departments, "You get rid of it; we'll worry about profits." By contrast, a truly marketing-minded firm tries to create value-satisfying goods and services that consumers will want to buy. What it offers for sale includes not only the generic product or service, but also how it is made available to the customer, in what form, when, under what conditions, and at what terms of trade. Most important, what it offers for sale is determined not by the seller but by the buyer. The seller takes his cues from the buyer in such a way that the product becomes a consequence of the marketing effort, not vice versa.

### Lag in Detroit

This may sound like an elementary rule of business, but that does not keep it from being violated wholesale. It is certainly more violated than honored. Take the automobile industry:

Here mass production is most famous, most honored, and has the greatest impact on the entire society. The industry has hitched its fortune to the relentless requirements of the annual model change, a policy that makes customer orientation an especially urgent necessity.

---

[4] *The Affluent Society* (Boston: Houghton Mifflin, 1958), pp. 152–160.

Consequently the auto companies annually spend millions of dollars on consumer research. But the fact that the new compact cars are selling so well in their first year indicates that Detroit's vast researches have for a long time failed to reveal what the customer really wanted. Detroit was not persuaded that he wanted anything different from what he had been getting until it lost millions of customers to other small car manufacturers.

How could this unbelievable lag behind consumer wants have been perpetuated so long? Why did not research reveal consumer preferences before consumers' buying decisions themselves revealed the facts? Is that not what consumer research is for—to find out before the fact what is going to happen? The answer is that Detroit never really researched the customer's wants. It only researched his preferences between the kinds of things which it had already decided to offer him. For Detroit is mainly product-oriented, not customer-oriented. To the extent that the customer is recognized as having needs that the manufacturer should try to satisfy, Detroit usually acts as if the job can be done entirely by product changes. Occasionally attention gets paid to financing, too, but that is done more in order to sell than to enable the customer to buy.

As for taking care of other customer needs, there is not enough being done to write about. The areas of the greatest unsatisfied needs are ignored, or at best get stepchild attention. These are at the point of sale and on the matter of automotive repair and maintenance. Detroit views these problem areas as being of secondary importance. That is underscored by the fact that the retailing and servicing ends of this industry are neither owned and operated nor controlled by the manufacturers. Once the car is produced, things are pretty much in the dealer's inadequate hands. Illustrative of Detroit's arm's-length attitude is the fact that, while servicing holds enormous sales-stimulating, profit-building opportunities, only 57 of Chevrolet's 7,000 dealers provide night maintenance service.

Motorists repeatedly express their dissatisfaction with servicing and their apprehensions about buying cars under the present selling setup. The anxieties and problems they encounter during the auto buying and maintenance processes are probably more intense and widespread today than 30 years ago. Yet the automobile companies do not *seem* to listen to or take their cues from the anguished consumer.

If they do listen, it must be through the filter of their own preoccupation with production. The marketing effort is still viewed as a necessary consequence of the product, not vice versa, as it should be. That is the legacy of mass production, with its parochial view that profit resides essentially in low-cost full production.

### What Ford Put First

The profit lure of mass production obviously has a place in the plans and strategy of business management, but it must always *follow* hard thinking about the customer. This is one of the most important lessons that we can learn from the contradictory behavior of Henry Ford. In a sense Ford was both the most brilliant and the most senseless marketer in American history. He was senseless because he refused to give the customer anything but a black car. He was brilliant because he fashioned a production system designed to fit market needs. We habitually celebrate him for the wrong reason, his production genius. His real genius was marketing. We think he was able to cut his selling price and therefore sell millions of $500 cars because his invention of the assembly line had reduced the costs. Actually he invented the assembly line because he had concluded that at $500 he could sell millions of cars. Mass production was the *result* not the cause of his low prices.

Ford repeatedly emphasized this point, but a nation of production-oriented business managers refuses to hear the great lesson he taught. Here is his operating philosophy as he expressed it succinctly:

Our policy is to reduce the price, extend the operations, and improve the article. You will notice that the reduction of price comes first. We have never considered any costs as fixed. Therefore we first reduce the price to the point where we believe more sales will result. Then we go ahead and try to make the prices. We do not bother about the costs. The new price forces the costs down. The more usual way is to take the costs and then determine the price, and although that method may be scientific in the narrow sense; it is not scientific in the broad sense, because what earthly use is it to know the cost if it tells you that you cannot manufacture at a price at which the article can be sold? But more to the point is the fact that, although one may calculate what a cost is, and of course all of our costs are carefully calculated, no one knows what a cost ought to be. One of the ways of discovering . . . is to name a price so low as to force everybody in the place to the highest point of efficiency. The low price makes everybody dig for profits. We make more discoveries concerning manufacturing and selling under this forced method than by any method of leisurely investigation." [5]

### Product Provincialism

The tantalizing profit possibilities of low unit production costs may be the most seriously self-deceiving attitude that can afflict a company, particularly a "growth" company where an apparently assured expansion of demand already tends to undermine a proper concern for the importance of marketing and the customer.

The usual result of this narrow preoccupation with so-called concrete matters is that instead of growing, the industry declines. It usually means that the product fails to adapt to the constantly changing patterns of consumer needs and tastes, to new and modified marketing institutions and practices, or to product developments in competing or complementary industries. The industry has its eyes so firmly on its own specific product that it does not see how it is being made obsolete.

The classical example of this is the buggy whip industry. No amount of product improvement could stave off its death sentence. But had the industry defined itself as being in the transportation business rather than the buggy whip business, it might have survived. It would have done what survival always entails, that is, changing. Even if it had only defined its business as providing a stimulant or catalyst to an energy source, it might have survived by becoming a manufacturer of, say, fanbelts or air cleaners.

What may some day be a still more classical example is, again, the oil industry. Having let others steal marvelous opportunities from it (e.g., natural gas, as already mentioned, missile fuels, and jet engine lubricants), one would expect it to have taken steps never to let that happen again. But this is not the case. We are now getting extraordinary new developments in fuel systems specifically designed to power automobiles. Not only are these developments concentrated in firms outside the petroleum industry, but petroleum is almost systematically ignoring them, securely content in its wedded bliss to oil. It is the story of the kerosene lamp versus the incandescent lamp all over again.

---

[5] Henry Ford, *My Life and Work* (New York: Doubleday, Page, 1923), pp. 146–147.

Oil is trying to improve hydrocarbon fuels rather than to develop *any* fuels best suited to the needs of their users, whether or not made in different ways and with different raw materials from oil.

Here are some of the things which nonpetroleum companies are working on:

¶ Over a dozen such firms now have advanced working models of energy systems which, when perfected, will replace the internal combustion engine and eliminate the demand for gasoline. The superior merit of each of these systems is their elimination of frequent, time-consuming, and irritating refueling stops. Most of these systems are fuel cells designed to create electrical energy directly from chemicals without combustion. Most of them use chemicals that are not derived from oil, generally hydrogen and oxygen.

¶ Several other companies have advanced models of electric storage batteries designed to power automobiles. One of these is an aircraft producer that is working jointly with several electric utility companies. The latter hope to use off-peak generating capacity to supply overnight plug-in battery regeneration. Another company, also using the battery approach, is a medium-size electronics firm with extensive small-battery experience that it developed in connection with its work on hearing aids. It is collaborating with an automobile manufacturer. Recent improvements arising from the need for high-powered miniature power storage plants in rockets have put us within reach of a relatively small battery capable of withstanding great overloads or surges of power. Germanium diode applications and batteries using sintered-plate and nickel-cadmium techniques promise to make a revolution in our energy sources.

¶ Solar energy conversion systems are also getting increasing attention. One usually cautious Detroit auto executive recently ventured that solar-powered cars might be common by 1980.

As for the oil companies, they are more or less "watching developments," as one research director put it to me. A few are doing a bit of research on fuel cells, but almost always confined to developing cells powered by hydrocarbon chemicals. None of them are enthusiastically researching fuel cells, batteries, or solar power plants. None of them are spending a fraction as much on research in these profoundly important areas as they are on the usual run-of-the-mill things like reducing combustion chamber deposit in gasoline engines. One major integrated petroleum company recently took a tentative look at the fuel cell and concluded that although "the companies actively working on it indicate a belief in ultimate success . . . the timing and magnitude of its impact are too remote to warrant recognition in our forecasts."

One might, of course, ask: Why should the oil companies do anything different? Would not chemical fuel cells, batteries, or solar energy kill the present product lines? The answer is that they would indeed, and that is precisely the reason for the oil firms having to develop these power units before their competitors, so they will not be companies without an industry.

Management might be more likely to do what is needed for its own preservation, if it thought of itself as being in the energy business. But even that would not be enough if it persists in imprisoning itself in the narrow grip of its tight product orientation. It has to think of itself as taking care of customer needs, not finding, refining, or even selling oil. Once it genuinely thinks of its business as taking care of people's transportation needs, nothing can stop it from creating its own extravagantly profitable growth.

### Creative Destruction

Since words are cheap and deeds are dear it may be appropriate to indicate what this kind of thinking involves and leads to. Let us start at the beginning—the customer. It can be shown that motorists strongly dislike the bother, delay, and experience of buying gasoline. People actually do not buy gasoline. They cannot see it, taste it, feel it, appreciate it, or really test it. What they buy is the right to continue driving their cars. The gas station is like a tax collector to whom people are compelled to pay a periodic toll as the price of using their cars. This makes the gas station a basically unpopular institution. It can ever be made popular or pleasant, only less unpopular, less unpleasant.

To reduce its unpopularity completely means eliminating it. Nobody likes a tax collector, not even a pleasantly cheerful one. Nobody likes to interrupt a trip to buy a phantom product, not even from a handsome Adonis or a seductive Venus. Hence, companies that are working on exotic fuel substitutes which will eliminate the need for frequent refueling are heading directly into the outstretched arms of the irritated motorist. They are riding a wave of inevitability, not because they are creating something which is technologically superior or more sophisti-

cated, but because they are satisfying a powerful customer need. They are also eliminating noxious odors and air pollution.

Once the petroleum companies recognize the customer-satisfying logic of what another power system can do, they will see that they have no more choice about working on an efficient, long-lasting fuel (or some way of delivering present fuels without bothering the motorist) than the big food chains had a choice about going into the supermarket business, or the vacuum tube companies had a choice about making semiconductors. For their own good the oil firms will have to destroy their own highly profitable assets. No amount of wishful thinking can save them from the necessity of engaging in this form of "creative destruction."

I phrase the need as strongly as this because I think management must make quite an effort to break itself loose from conventional ways. It is all too easy in this day and age for a company or industry to let its sense of purpose become dominated by the economies of full production and to develop a dangerously lopsided product orientation. In short, if management lets itself drift, it invariably drifts in the direction of thinking of itself as producing goods and services, not customer satisfactions. While it probably will not descend to the depths of telling its salesmen, "You get rid of it; we'll worry about profits," it can, without knowing it, be practicing precisely that formula for withering decay. The historic fate of one growth industry after another has been its suicidal product provincialism.

## DANGERS OF R & D

Another big danger to a firm's continued growth arises when top management is wholly transfixed by the profit possibilities of technical research and development. To illustrate I shall turn first to a new industry—electronics—and then return once more to the oil companies. By comparing a fresh example with a familiar one, I hope to emphasize the prevalence and insidiousness of a hazardous way of thinking.

### Marketing Shortchanged

In the case of electronics, the greatest danger which faces the glamorous new companies in this field is not that they do not pay enough attention to research and development, but that the pay *too much* attention to it. And the fact that the fastest growing electronics firms owe their eminence to their heavy emphasis on technical research is completely beside the point. They have vaulted to affluence on a sudden crest of unusually strong general receptiveness to new technical ideas. Also, their success has been shaped in the virtually guaranteed market of military subsidies and by military orders that in many cases actually preceded the existence of facilities to make the products. Their expansion has, in other words, been almost totally devoid of marketing effort.

Thus, they are growing up under conditions that come dangerously close to creating the illusion that a superior product will sell itself. Having created a successful company by making a superior product, it is not surprising that management continues to be oriented toward the product rather than the people who consume it. It develops the philosophy that continued growth is a matter of continued product innovation and improvement.

A number of other factors tend to strengthen and sustain this belief:

1. Because electronic products are highly complex and sophisticated, managements become topheavy with engineers and scientists. This creates a selective bias in favor of research and production at the expense of marketing. The organization tends to view itself as making things rather than satisfying customer needs. Marketing gets treated as a residual activity, "something else" that must be done once the vital job of product creation and production is completed.

2. To this bias in favor of product research, development, and production is added the bias in favor of dealing with controllable variables. Engineers and scientists are at home in the world of concrete things like machines, test tubes, production lines, and even balance sheets. The abstractions to which they feel kindly are those which are testable or manipulatable in the laboratory, or, if not testable, then functional, such as Euclid's axioms. In short, the managements of the new glamour-growth companies tend to favor those business activities which lend themselves to careful study, experimentation, and control—the hard, practical, realities of the lab, the shop, the books.

What gets shortchanged are the realities of the *market*. Consumers are unpredictable, varied, fickle, stupid, shortsighted, stubborn, and generally bothersome. This is not what the engineer-managers say, but deep down in their consciousness it is what they believe. And this accounts for their concentrating on what they know and what they can control, namely, product research, engineering, and production. The emphasis on production becomes particularly attractive when the product can be made at declining unit costs. There is no more inviting way of making money than by running the plant full blast.

Today the top-heavy science-engineering-production orientation of so many electronics companies works reasonably well because they are pushing into new frontiers in which the armed services have pioneered virtually assured markets. The companies are in the felicitous position of having to fill, not find markets; of not having to discover what the customer needs and wants, but of having the customer voluntarily come forward with specific new product demands. If a team of consultants had been assigned specifically to design a business situation calculated to prevent the emergence and development of a customer-oriented marketing viewpoint, it could not have produced anything better than the conditions just described.

### Stepchild Treatment

The oil industry is a stunning example of how science, technology, and mass production can divert an entire group of companies from their main task. To the extent the consumer is studied at all (which is not much), the focus is forever on getting information which is designed to help the oil companies improve what they are now doing. They try to discover more convincing advertising themes, more effective sales promotional drives, what the market shares of the various companies are, what people like or dislike about service station dealers and oil companies, and so forth. Nobody seems as interested in probing deeply into the basic human needs that the industry might be trying to satisfy as in probing into the basic properties of the raw material that the companies work with in trying to deliver customer satisfactions.

Basic questions about customers and markets seldom get asked. The latter occupy a stepchild status. They are recognized as existing, as having to be taken care of, but not worth very much real thought or dedicated attention. Nobody gets as excited about the customers in his own backyard as about the oil in the Sahara Desert.

Nothing illustrates better the neglect of marketing than its treatment in the industry press.

The centennial issue of the *American Petroleum Institute Quarterly*, published in 1959 to celebrate the discovery of oil in Titusville, Pennsylvania, contained 21 feature articles proclaiming the industry's greatness. Only one of these talked about its achievements in marketing, and that was only a pictorial record of how service station architecture has changed. The issue also contained a special section on "New Horizons," which was devoted to showing the magnificent role oil would play in America's future. Every reference was ebulliently optimistic, never implying once that oil might have some hard competition. Even the reference to atomic energy was a cheerful catalogue of how oil would help make atomic energy a success. There was not a single apprehension that the oil industry's affluence might be threatened or a suggestion that one "new horizon" might include new and better ways of serving oil's present customers.

But the most revealing example of the stepchild treatment that marketing gets was still another special series of short articles on "The Revolutionary Potential of Electronics." Under that heading this list of articles appeared in the table of contents: "In the Search for Oil," "In Production Operations," "In Refinery Processes," "In Pipeline Operations."

Significantly, every one of the industry's major functional areas is listed, *except* marketing. Why? Either it is believed that electronics holds no revolutionary potential for petroleum marketing (which is palpably wrong), or the editors forgot to discuss marketing (which is more likely, and illustrates its stepchild status).

The order in which the four functional areas are listed also betrays the alienation of the oil industry from the consumer. The industry is implicitly defined as beginning with the search for oil and ending with its distribution from the refinery. But the truth is, it seems to me, that the industry begins with the needs of the customer for its products. From the primal position its definition moves steadily backstream to areas of progressively lesser importance, until it finally comes to rest at the "search for oil."

### Beginning and End

The view that an industry is a customer-satisfying process, not a goods-producing process, is vital for all businessmen to understand. An industry begins with the customer and his needs, not with a patent, a raw material, or a selling skill. Given the customer's needs, the industry develops backwards, first concerning itself with the physical *delivery* of customer satisfactions. Then it moves back further to *creating* the things by which these satisfactions are in part achieved. How these materials are created is a matter of indifference to the customer, hence the particular form of manufacturing, processing, or what-have-you cannot be considered as a vital aspect of the industry. Finally, the industry moves back still further to *finding* the raw materials necessary for making its products.

The irony of some industries oriented toward technical research and development is that the scientists who occupy the high executive positions are totally unscientific when it comes to defining their companies' over-all needs and purposes. They violate the first two rules of the scientific method—being aware of and defining their companies' problems, and then developing testable hypotheses about solving them. They are scientific only about the convenient things, such as laboratory and product experiments. The reason that the customer (and the satisfaction of his deepest needs) is not considered as being "the problem" is not because there is any certain belief that no such problem exists, but because an organizational lifetime has conditioned management to look in the opposite direction. Marketing is a stepchild.

I do not mean that selling is ignored. Far from it. But selling, again, is not marketing. As already pointed out, selling concerns itself with the tricks and techniques of getting people to exchange their cash for your product. It is not concerned with the values that the exchange is all about. And it does not, as marketing invariably does, view the entire business process as consisting of a tightly integrated effort to discover, create, arouse, and satisfy customer needs. The customer is somebody "out there" who, with proper cunning, can be separated from his loose change.

Actually, not even selling gets much attention in some technologically minded firms. Because there is a virtually guaranteed market for the abundant flow of their new products, they do not actually know what a real market is. It is as if they lived in a planned economy, moving their products routinely from factory to retail outlet. Their successful concentration on products tends to convince them of the soundness of what they have been doing, and they fail to see the gathering clouds over the market.

## CONCLUSION

Less than 75 years ago American railroads enjoyed a fierce loyalty among astute Wall Streeters. European monarchs invested in them heavily. Eternal wealth was thought to be the benediction for anybody who could scrape a few thousand dollars together to put into rail stocks. No other form of transportation could compete with the railroads in speed, flexibility, durability, economy, and growth potentials. As Jacques Barzun put it, "By the turn of the century it was an institution, an image of man, a tradition, a code of honor, a source of poetry, a nursery of boyhood desires, a sublimest of toys, and the most solemn machine—next to the funeral hearse—that marks the epochs in man's life." [6]

Even after the advent of automobiles, trucks, and airplanes, the railroad tycoons remained imperturbably self-confident. If you had told them 60 years ago that in 30 years they would be flat on their backs, broke, and pleading for government subsidies, they would have thought you totally demented. Such a future was simply not considered possible. It was not even a discussable subject, or an askable question, or a matter which any sane person would consider worth speculating about. The very thought was insane. Yet a lot of insane notions now have matter-of-fact acceptance—for example, the idea of 100-ton tubes of metal moving smoothly through the air 20,000 feet above the earth, loaded with 100 sane and solid citizens casually drinking martinis—and they have dealt cruel blows to the railroads.

What specifically must other companies do to avoid this fate? What does customer orientation involve? These questions have in part been answered by the preceding examples and analysis. It would take another article to show in detail what is required for specific industries. In any case, it should be obvious that building an effective customer-oriented company involves far more than good intentions or promotional tricks; it involves profound matters of human organization and leadership. For the present, let me merely suggest what appear to be some general requirements.

_____
[6] Op cit., p. 20.

## Visceral Feel of Greatness

Obviously the company has to do what survival demands. It has to adapt to the requirements of the market, and it has to do it sooner rather than later. But mere survival is a so-so aspiration. Anybody can survive in some way or other, even the skid-row bum. The trick is to survive gallantly, to feel the surging impulse of commercial mastery; not just to experience the sweet smell of success, but to have the visceral feel of entrepreneurial greatness.

No organization can achieve greatness without a vigorous leader who is driven onward by his own pulsating _will to succeed_. He has to have a vision of grandeur, a vision that can produce eager followers in vast numbers. In business, the followers are the customers. To produce these customers, the entire corporation must be viewed as a customer-creating and customer-satisfying organism. Management must think of itself not as producing products but as providing customer-creating value satisfactions. It must push this idea (and everything it means and requires) into every nook and cranny of the organization. It has to do this continuously and with the kind of flair that excites and stimulates the people in it. Otherwise, the company will be merely a series of pigeonholed parts, with no consolidating sense of purpose or direction.

In short, the organization must learn to think of itself not as producing goods or services but as _buying customers_, as doing the things that will make people _want_ to do business with it. And the chief executive himself has the inescapable responsibility for creating this environment, this viewpoint, this attitude, this aspiration. He himself must set the company's style, its direction, and its goals. This means he has to know precisely where he himself wants to go, and to make sure the whole organization is enthusiastically aware of where that is. This is a first requisite of leadership, for _unless he knows where he is going, any road will take him there_.

If any road is okay, the chief executive might as well pack his attaché case and go fishing. If an organization does not know or care where it is going, it does not need to advertise that fact with a ceremonial figurehead. Everybody will notice it soon enough.

# 31. Research and the Marketing Concept

## W. B. REYNOLDS

Marketing literature has for some time devoted space to the so-called total marketing concept in American business and has developed a substantial rationale for the benefits which potentially can be derived through the intelligent application of the concept. I emphasize the words "intelligent application of the concept" since a few marketing experts seem to feel that total marketing concept means turning over management of all aspects of the company's business to them. These people are delighted by articles such as that by Theodore Levitt entitled "Marketing Myopia" which appeared in the *Harvard Business Review* of July-August, 1960. That this article is filled with sweeping generalizations based upon factual distortion seems to escape them.

If the total marketing concept is an opportunity to reappraise marketing thinking, it at the same time makes demands upon marketing organizations which they must realistically face. One of the most important of these demands is the understanding of the proper relationship between the total marketing concept and the intelligent use of research and development.

A successful manufacturing corporation today rests upon three essential bases— (1) an informed, aggressive and intelligent executive management, (2) sound marketing concepts administered by superior marketing management, and (3) sound technology developed

‡‡ SOURCE: Reprinted by permission from *Marketing Innovations*, Proceedings of the 8th Biennial Marketing Institute, American Marketing Association, Minnesota Chapter, November 1961, pp. II: 14–21.

by superior scientific and technological personnel. Enlightened executive management will see to it that a proper partnership develops between marketing and technology and that neither becomes subservient to the other. Each has an important and easily defined area of basic contribution requiring a high degree of creativity and innovation. Creativity thrives best when free of undue pressure and domination.

Since authors like Mr. Levitt are reaching unwarranted conclusions based upon irrelevant or incorrect facts, I should like to reexamine the general area of the Marketing-Research relationship.

At the outset I want to make it clear that I agree thoroughly with Mr. Levitt's thesis that marketing has been frequently neglected and that many companies and even a few industries have declined because of what Levitt terms "marketing myopia." Levitt's basic fallacy is not that he emphasizes the marketing concept but that he suffers from acute technological myopia.

Permit me to illustrate by referring to the petroleum industry which seems to be Mr. Levitt's favorite whipping boy. Although Levitt's "Perils of Pauline" analogy is clever journalism, it completely begs the question of the greatness of today's industry. What happened during the first 50 years after Col. Drake spudded in his first well at Titusville is rather academic at this stage. Any new industry in a nineteenth-century environment was likely to experience growing pains. But the petroleum industry was never in any real danger of demise as Levitt implies because petroleum was then and still is inherently the cheapest practical source of energy and it will continue to be so in the forseeable future. And modern civilization, friend Levitt, is based upon cheap energy. The petroleum industry has developed to its present enormous strength and virility because it has used sound technology to provide a better product at lower prices. And it has never lost sight of its basic mission of finding and exploiting the cheapest sources of fossil carbonaceous deposits.

To assert that the petroleum industry is in the energy business and should, therefore, quickly jump into atomic energy, fuel cell technology or any other energy producing or converting innovation that happens along without regard for the technological "fitness" for so doing is an error as grave as marketing myopia. Take the fuel cell.

Mr. Levitt castigates the petroleum industry for its "watch and wait" attitude on fuel cell technology. To quote: "We are now getting extraordinary new developments in fuel systems specifically designed to power automobiles. . . . Over a dozen firms now have advanced working models of energy systems which, when perfected, will replace the internal combustion engine and eliminate the demand for gasoline." end quote. Specifically this weird generalization seems to be based upon the fuel cell, storage batteries, and solar energy converters. And Mr. Levitt complains that none of the oil companies are enthusiastically researching fuel cells, batteries, or solar power plants. Here his technological myopia is quite evident.

In the first place, none of these represents a serious immediate threat to gasoline as the prime fuel for automobiles. A moment's reflection should make this obvious. The only presently developed practical fuel for the fuel cell is hydrogen. Can you imagine an automobile powered with hydrogen? Hydrogen is a light gas which cannot be liquified under any practical conditions for use in automobiles. Even under very high pressures which would require enormously heavy cylinders a practical amount of hydrogen could not be carried in an automobile. And to cap it all, hydrogen is one of the most highly explosive substances known, when mixed with air. A hydrogen cylinder leak in a home garage could blow a whole neighborhood apart. In short, hydrogen will not be used to power automobiles. If it is ever used to power stationary engines or generate electrical power, it will doubtless be obtained from methane, a petroleum product.

Because of these considerations the oil companies have worked with hydrocarbons as fuel for cells. This is the only practical approach for moving power plant use and was motivated by sound technical considerations, not an obsession with their basic raw material as Levitt contends.

The use of batteries and solar cells to power automobiles is equally impractical. The last time I used a battery-powered golf cart both the battery and my patience gave out on the fourteenth fairway. The new gasoline-powered golf carts are rapidly taking over. Even assuming great technical progress in batteries and solar cells, they cannot be regarded as more than very long-range technical possibilities. The petroleum industry has quite correctly adopted a wait-and-see attitude. In the first place, the odds are strongly in favor of petroleum fuels, and in the second place the technology involved in batteries and solar cells doesn't fit. A company should move into an entirely new field of technology only when there are compelling reasons such as unusual profit opportunities or a dire and imminent threat to present lines. Finally, the timing of potential obsolescence of motor fuel by *anything* is such that the oil industry will have at least ten years warning of a serious threat. To dilute its efforts today by moving away from established technology into an entirely new technology (in this instance electronics and electrical equipment) because of a minor and long-range threat just doesn't represent sound business judgment for the petroleum industry.

The petroleum industry is basically engaged in finding, producing and upgrading fossil deposits. In this they have had preeminent success. Mr. Levitt is quite incorrect in his statement that ". . . major improvements in gasoline quality tend not to originate in the oil industry." On the contrary, *all* major improvements in gasoline quality, with the possible exception of tetra ethyl lead, have originated in the oil industry, e.g., thermal cracking, catalytic cracking, catalytic reforming, alkylation, etc., etc. The octane rating and other performance characteristics of unleaded gasolines have consistently improved from year to year. Tetra ethyl lead was discovered by Thomas Midgeley, who took it to DuPont for production because DuPont was technologically qualified to produce it. It remained in the chemical industry because that was where it belonged technologically. On the other hand, petrochemical technology does fit the petroleum industry and many petroleum companies now derive a substantial percentage of their profit from petrochemicals. Levitt feels that petroleum management cannot find much consolation today in the rapidly expanding petrochemical industry since petrochemicals represent only 2% of the volume of oil processed. But, in fact, petrochemicals represent a much higher percentage of the *value* of hydrocarbons processed. It is not unusual for a petrochemical to sell for 50 to 100 times the value of the hydrocarbon from which it was made. The oil companies have moved rapidly into petrochemicals because the technology is right.

To emphasize the marketing myopia of the oil industry Levitt points out that gasoline users strongly dislike the bother, delay and experience of buying gasoline. Hence, the industry must quickly develop an efficient, long-lasting fuel to eliminate filling-station stops. I might point out to Mr. Levitt that there is also great popular demand for a safe, economical magic carpet and a really workable Aladdin's lamp. Where does Mr. Levitt suggest we look for this magic fuel? Atomic energy? Fuel cell? Solar devices? The petroleum companies are in the business of producing and upgrading *oil*. A company must put its research dollars into technological areas with the maximum chance of success. Otherwise like Ponce de Leon, they will die withered and frustrated. In connection with the utility of that great American institution, the filling station, I might parenthetically ask Mr. Levitt if he has ever taken a motor vacation with a carload of youngsters.

I have dwelt upon Levitt's treatment of the petroleum industry for the purpose of making a single point, namely, that the total marketing concept cannot be successful unless it is administered wisely in the light of sound technological considerations. As marketing men you have not only an opportunity but a compelling responsibility to know and understand important aspects of the technology underlying your field of interest and to benefit by what that technology can bring to your company in the way of new product opportunities.

Levitt says that an industry begins with the customer and his needs, not with a patent, a raw material or a selling skill. But I submit, on the contrary, that most new industries have grown out of technological progress leading to the development of new products which fulfill basic human needs. Dr. Wallace Carothers developed nylon, not because marketing people were clamoring for a synthetic fiber, but because his fundamental research on polyamide resins revealed that these resins had interesting fiber-forming characteristics. The great, modern plastics industry has grown from exploratory research on high polymers which, for the most part, was not slanted toward any particular market needs. Once these new products were developed, effort was then directed toward their place in the market and, if no need was apparent, extensive applications research and market development soon found many customers, frequently in unexpected places.

For some time after polyethylene was discovered there was little demand for it. Little by little, new uses were found and, most important, the price was brought down through intensive research until today sales of this product approach half a billion dollars annually. This achievement was brought about by a successful marriage of marketing and technology. And the flow was fundamental research, new products, applications research, new end product, marketing and sales to the customer, not the Levittized or backward process. The customer demand for most polyethylene products did not exist until it was created by creative applications research and marketing. And I might say parenthetically that most of the creative marketing in polyethylene and polypropylene has been carried out by the petroleum industry, whose development of low-cost olefins has made the whole thing possible.

Please do not interpret my strong disagreement with Mr. Levitt's version of the marketing concept as a lack of appreciation for the value of an enlightened total marketing concept. Whereas Levitt castigates technology and scientists in management and downgrades unreasonably the position of technology in the profit picture, an enlightened marketing concept will exploit to the utmost the contributions of technology.

In my discussion today I have been asked to emphasize the decision-making process in new product development. One of the most basic decisions executive management and marketing management must make relative to new products is whether or not *all* research projects should arise from consumer studies and marketing research. If this decision is affirmative, I submit that executive and marketing management suffer from technological myopia and have, per se, cut themselves away from tremendous profit possibilities. As I have pointed out, many of the most highly profitable new products have resulted from unexpected discoveries made during the course of fundamental and exploratory research. These products would never have been developed as an answer to consumer wants arising from marketing research for the twofold reason that the consumer want often was not recognized *a priori* and usually the product grew out of developing technology which would not have developed in response to a defined product need.

On the other hand, many profitable new products *have* developed as a result of clearly-defined consumer needs. Frequently, but by no means always, these consumer needs have received corporate notice as a result of marketing research. Others, such as synthetic rubber, have been so obviously needed that they became prime objectives of technology, itself.

The point to be emphasized is that new products arise in *two* ways; one, in response to clearly-defined consumer needs and, two, from fundamental and exploratory research, i.e., developing technology. The first and most important management decision relative to new products is to take full advantage of both sources of new products and to organize so that products and concepts from each source can and will be fully evaluated as to both marketing and technological appropriateness. This will avoid the pitfalls of (a) trying to sell a new product out of technology for which no basic need exists or (b) senselessly spending research money to develop a product which might satisfy a need but for which the technological chances of success are nil or very small.

Once a product has been placed on the market it must be supported continuously thereafter by aggressive research to improve quality and lower cost. This is the technological input that keeps a product on the market long after it otherwise would have become obsolete. But simultaneously, vigorous exploratory research must be carried out to develop new products and processes which will make the old ones obsolete. This is a continuing responsibility of research and development and here, at least, it seems that Mr. Levitt and I are on common ground. Except, and the exception is very important, I would emphasize that the limited research dollar be aimed toward programs that make technological sense both from the standpoint of technical feasibility and proper fit with the company's established technology and marketing capabilities.

If I have managed to make the point that technology, itself, has a major contribution to make to the product development function, the question naturally arises as to how this can be accomplished in a consumer, marketing oriented company. Assuming that executive and marketing management are aware of this gold in the technological rainbow, its exploitation becomes an easy organizational matter. Fundamental and exploratory research from which these products arise is set up as a corporate function, financed by the corporation and responsible only to executive corporate management. Here we are dealing with the creative talents of skilled scientists and, in the words of Mr. James F. Bell, "We must follow where research leads."

This is the kind of research that led to nylon, to the transistor, to polyethylene and to a host of other new products. True, these products were successful only because they fulfilled basic needs, but the scientists who developed them were not consciously slanting their efforts toward the fulfillment of those needs. They were pushing forward the frontiers of science simply to find out what was there. Since no one knows *a priori* what is there, it is a bit ridiculous to say that this aspect of the research program should be market directed or even strongly influenced by market considerations.

On the other hand, once the outline of a definable product begins to emerge from this black box of technology, an enlightened market research becomes as important as the product itself. The decision to perfect the product through further applied research should be made only in the light of basic marketing considerations. Through this stage of the development marketing plays an important supporting role. Once the product is perfected, the final decision to manufacture and sell becomes a dominant marketing function. The important factor in the decision making process relating to these technology-nurtured products is proper liaison between research, marketing, and executive management. It is important that this liaison be at the highest research and division management level.

As already noted, the other prime source of new product concepts comes directly from studies of consumer wants and needs. Usually the product can be reasonably well visualized and its development becomes a matter of short-term, applied research. This type of product-development may be carried out by the operating department, itself, or it may be carried out by the corporate research function under conditions assuring the satisfaction of marketing needs. Decisions regarding new products arising in this way are straightforward and relatively easy to make. If the economics are right and the original marketing input was right, the product should make money.

However, not all consumer wants and needs can be met by easily defined products. For example, it doesn't require a very erudite marketing study to know that one of the most urgent human needs is a cure for cancer. This does not at all mean that the chemical and pharmaceutical industry should (on the basis of business judgment) devote their major research efforts toward chemotherapy agents for cancer. A mature scientific evaluation of the difficulty of the problem and hence the chances for success requires prudence in research expenditures in this field. In fact, the technology is so difficult, even though the potential rewards are great, that most cancer research has been carried out with government or non-profit foundation funds. The point here is that a compelling market need is not per se an adequate reason for an extensive product development program. This is the point missed by Theodore Levitt in his castigation of the petroleum industry for not developing a "permanent" motor fuel to eliminate filling station stops. Technical considerations practically eliminate this idea as something to be taken seriously. Thus another of the basic decisions regarding new product research must be that purely marketing considerations must be fully evaluated 'in the light of sound technology.

This again emphasizes the corporate tripod of sound management, sound marketing and sound technology. My marketing friends tell me there is little consumer interest in a two-legged stool. And my corporate experience tells me that there are few if any successful companies balancing on a bipod. Strong marketing doesn't offset weak technology, and strong technology cannot offset marketing myopia.

Since product decisions are based in substantial part upon market research and since in a short run research and development manpower and budgets are relatively fixed, marketing managements have an increasing responsibility to be sure that the wants and needs which they are communicating to research and development personnel are more real than imagined. These must be supplemented with a rigorous examination of factors such as competition, trends in the industry, investment requirements, advertising appropriations necessary, channels of distribution, and a host of other critical factors. For despite the wants and needs of the consumer, and they are many and varied, corporate managements are asking for a more realistic assessment of the total risk.

In its final form the identification and interpretations of consumer wants lead ultimately to a prediction problem; and the information which managements are really asking of marketing management is prediction of consumer behavior at some future point in time. Under these conditions, and if research and development effort is not to be misdirected, it would appear that the tools and techniques to be applied in predicting consumer behavior now need the same kind of scrutiny that predictive mechanisms in the physical sciences have undergone for a hundred years.

The question becomes one of maximizing the corporation's opportunity for being right, since once the decision has been made to move in any given product area with the research and development program, valuable manpower and time is committed. If this commitment is made, and if it later develops that the commitment was improperly made, then not only has the research and development time and manpower been used unwisely but valuable time has been lost which could have been devoted to more adequately thought-through projects.

Both marketing and research managements are sensitive, to greater or lesser degrees, to the action of competitors. To a reasonable extent, this is necessary. However, the most desirable situation would be one in which the consumer's wants were being interpreted on a constant and rolling basis with an applied development program closely geared to these wants and the capacity of the individual corporation. Research and development programs cannot be all things to all men and there must come a point at which management makes a series of judgments as to what will and will not be researched. These decisions are critical to the well being of the organization and demand more complete evaluative techniques.

Even assuming that the ability to predict future consumer behavior becomes more sensitive as we learn to live with the marketing concept, the responsibilities of marketing managements do not end here. The reason for this is that the purpose of predicting and interpreting is to provide intelligent outlines for research and development programs which, if successful, will find acceptance with the consumer. The consumer, however, is not the only governing factor. Research managements must at the same time evaluate their applied projects in view of a total evaluation of the future climate in which the proposed products will find themselves competing. Research and development departments have a real responsibility in technological forecasting just as marketing managements have a responsibility in demand and business forecasting. The rate at which technology is growing has accelerated to the point where decisions must be made today on the possible impact of tomorrow's technology. The rate at which our decisions can be made obsolete is truly staggering.

An enlightened total marketing concept requires three major technical programs. These are a fundamental research program engaged in a search for new knowledge, an exploratory research program which becomes more immediate than the fundamental program, and an applied product development program aimed specifically at introducing new products in time and with particular characteristics which will satisfy consumer wants as interpreted through marketing managements. With these three programs, it is possible to work not only from the consumer back toward development, but also to work from a developing technology toward the consumer.

It is important for marketing people to understand what the research and development process is. Accustomed as they are to dealing with the uncertainties of human nature, they frequently fail to understand the uncertainties of technology. A new product should not be ordered from research as one would order a toothbrush from the drug store. There are many difficult uncertainties in product development both as to timing and quality. Frequently undue pressure from marketing leads to hastily conceived products of questionable quality. It takes a great deal of time and painstaking effort to develop good products, and requests from marketing to research should be most carefully considered and documented. Otherwise there is tremendous spinning of wheels and little forward motion.

Marketing is in the van of corporate thinking and action. The responsibility is very great as are the potential rewards. An enlightened marketing management will seek neither to direct the methodology of product development nor to dominate the conception of new products. Rather will it recognize the joint responsibility of marketing and research and seek to make its corporate contribution through supporting and promoting exploratory research and constructive guidance and mature understanding of the problems of applied research.

As one of my colleagues puts it, research is not sheer adrenalin. It is a mechanism through which the corporation can satisfy consumer wants at a profit.

# I. The Institutional Framework of Marketing

## 32. The Personality of the Retail Store

¶ One of the leading retail grocery chains in Chicago has been exceptionally successful in the newer communities and particularly in the suburbs. In one neighborhood after another, stores of this chain far outsell competing stores offering the same services, the same merchandise, the same prices, the same parking capacity, the same amount of advertising. Why such an overwhelming preference?

¶ One midwestern dealer has become a leading seller of foreign sports cars without advertising either special "deals" or the engineering superiority of his cars. How does he manage to do it?

¶ One Chicago quality department store has tremendous customer draw for the middle-class Negro, far more than all the other department stores put together. Some actual research on the underlying causes of this consumer behavior stresses the absence of any classical price considerations or functional factors. Again, why the preference?

What is it that draws the shopper to one store or agency rather than another? Clearly there is a force operative in the determination of a store's customer body besides the obvious functional factors of location, price ranges, and merchandise offerings. I shall show that this force is the store personality or image—the way in which the store is defined in the shopper's mind, partly by its functional qualities and partly by an aura of psychological attributes. Whereas the retailer thinks of himself as a merchant concerned with value and quality,

there is a wide range of intangibles which also play a critical role in the success or failure of his store.

### POWER OF THE IMAGE

What kinds of intangibles are important? What is the effect of a retail store's personality? For answers, let us turn to the customers themselves—and, to make it specific, to the customers of the three retailers cited at the beginning of the article.

In the case of the grocery chain, for instance, one new unit developed over twice the sales of a new competing store of the same size and description. Research showed that the women of the community characterize the store as "clean and white," "the store where you see your friends," "the store with helpful personnel." This chain unit conveys a pleasant feeling of independence to the shopper. The aisles are spacious and not cluttered. In short, shopping in this store is a pleasurable experience instead of a routine duty. It is significant that not once did any of the shoppers interviewed mention lower prices, better bargains, or greater savings.

The tip-off to the automobile dealer's success is in the agency personality he has created.

This dealer is a former yacht captain, so that he developed outside the rituals and mythology of automobile retailing. Instead of belaboring "deals" and carburetors, economics and functions, he has imbued his establishment with the symbolic appeal of the foreign sports car.

All the salesmen are British—no matter what they know about car mechanics, as long as they are recognizably British. Reinforcing their ac-

‡‡ SOURCE: Reprinted by permission from *Harvard Business Review*, Vol. 36, No. 1, January-February 1958, pp. 47–55.

cents, they wear slacks and blazers with "Sports Car Club of America" emblems.

Also, the dealer energetically promotes sports car clubs for different age groups, and he writes a column on sports cars in the classified advertising. In short, he has built and is constantly reinforcing a symbolic image congenial to a particular customer group.

In the example of the department store, the consumer group ascribe their preference to an atmosphere of acceptance for them. "I get a warm feeling of acceptance," "It makes you feel good to go shopping there," "I like it because it seems to have a warm atmosphere," and similar comments typified most of the customers' explanations. By contrast, Negroes dislike other stores in the neighborhood because of the feelings of rejection they have—even though the managements have been trying to serve them.

### Retailers vs. Shoppers

Despite all of this, the typical retailer's promotions and advertising proclaim price cuts and huge savings to the shopper, as if that were the only consideration in a buying decision. Tire store advertising, liquor store advertising, furniture advertising, appliance advertising—all have the same monotonous chant. Chain drugstore advertising is typically a bargain potpourri of nondrug items such as alarm clocks, salad bowls, TV tables, flashlight batteries. A grocer builds a beautiful store in a modern shopping center and promptly plasters his windows with gaudy signs giving it a fire-sale atmosphere.

Yet research indicates that women do not believe there is any substantial difference between the pricing of various supermarkets. They are all competitive in price, customers think, and it is impossible to make any material savings by shopping at one chain instead of another. A woman's primary reason for reading a particular advertisement is "this is my store." If she glances at other advertising, it is largely to reassure herself that her favorite store *is* competitive in price. Instead of comparing prices, she evaluates the supermarket from a different set of criteria: variety of goods, orderliness of the store, services and nonservices, personnel, other shoppers, and goals of the owner or manager.

When our researchers talk to women about department stores, their comments invariably cover a wide range of elements which bear on whether they will or will not shop in a particular store. They are quite vocal about the physical plant itself, the elevator banks, the washrooms, the location; about the attitudes of the clerks and the other people in the store; about service facilities such as credit policies and returns; about whether the styling is extreme, conservative, smart, ageless, or in poor taste; about the displays and windows; about such intangibles as odors and colors—all these in addition to price considerations.

### Personality Identification

When the shopper looks at a store's particular advertising, she unconsciously asks herself these questions: "What is the status of the store? Is it high-class or low-class or what?" "What can I expect of it in over-all atmosphere, product quality, and personal treatment?" "How interestingly does it fulfill its role?" "How does this image match my own desires and expectations?"

Of course, she is not oblivious to price; in fact, she may be proud of what she *thinks* is price-conscious in order to justify her choice of a store. But plumb her mind—go beneath any pat answers—and you will find that she is not the "economic woman" that American businessmen have so long and glibly assumed.

### The Typological Approach

The shopper seeks the store whose image is most congruent with the image she has of herself. Some stores may intimidate her; others may seem beneath her. A store may be acceptable for one type of goods and not for others. A shopper may go to one department store for bargains, children's clothes, or housewares, and to another one for gifts or personal items. Thus, when the question was asked in a city-wide study about the preferred store for an everyday dress, two mass-appeal department stores were overwhelmingly chosen by the wage earners' wives. But when asked where they would buy a good dress, most of the women selected different stores. In fact, one store clearly stood out as the luxury store for the lower-income families.

Economic factors will always be important. But unless the store image is acceptable to the shopper, price announcements are meaningless. The upper-status woman cannot conceive of herself shopping in the subway store of a large department store. Regardless of bargains, she is repelled by the thought of odors, milling crowds, poorly educated clerks. Conversely, the wage earner's wife is not going to expose herself to the possibility of humiliation by shopping in the quality store, whether it be Bonwit Teller or Nieman Marcus or Lord and Taylor—even if she has the money to buy something there. In other words, regardless of ability to pay, all shoppers seek stores whose total image is acceptable and appealing to them individually.

This concept of the store image goes hand-in-glove with a growing realization that retailing generally must take a typological approach to marketing. As Virgil Martin, general manager of Carson, Pirie, Scott, has stated:

It is high time we retailers recognize that we cannot be all things to all people. When we try to do that, we end up with no particular appeal for anybody. Each of us has his own individual niche in the market place. It is up to us to determine where we fit, who comprises our customer body, and then to fulfill as completely and satisfactorily as possible the expectations of our particular group and our logical market.[1]

### Illusion of Mass Appeal

As a researcher with some crude tools for describing customer groups along both sociological and psychological dimensions, I am continually confronted with amazing disparities be-

[1] From a speech, "The Dynamics of the Present," 1957 National Conference, American Marketing Association.

tween the retailer's concept of his customer draw and the actuality. For example:

¶ One Chicago retailer believes that his store does the largest volume in its product category in the market. When we discussed his marketing philosophy and future goals, I asked him about the character of his customer body. He did not hesitate to state that the entire market was his oyster—people from all income brackets, all surrounding areas, and all social groups.

But an analysis of his sales tickets reveals that nothing could be further from reality. An extremely disproportionate share of his customers is concentrated in the lowest economic third. Although his store is located in the Chicago central shopping district and should attract traffic flow from all parts of the area, his customers are coming in a statistically significant ratio from the south part of the city and the southern suburbs.

¶ In making a social class analysis of the customers of Chicago retail organizations, we asked this question: "If you were going to buy new livingroom furniture for your home, at which store would you be most likely to find what you want?" Fig. 1 summarizes the answers in profile form for two leading stores. If the customer body of each store had been truly representative of the social classes in the metropolitan area—or, more precisely, if it had corresponded with the chance expectancy of choice based on the numbers of people in these classes —the result would have shown up as the hori-

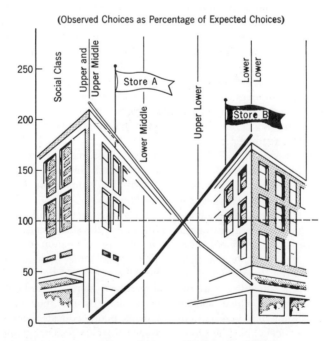

FIG. 1.   Customer profiles: store choices of people in different social classes.

zontal broken line opposite the figure 100. But in neither case did it turn out this way, as the thick lines show. Store A appealed strongly to people in the upper and middle classes, and Store B appealed strongly to shoppers from the lower social classes.

Yet the advertising director of Store A, a leading department store with a broad range of price lines and a basement store, was astonished to learn that not every person read his stores' advertising. And the executive vice president of Store B, one of a chain of retail furniture stores, was on record as saying: "We sell everybody. We have stores throughout the area, we advertise in all the mass media, we have furniture in all price ranges."

Not by any stretch of the imagination do these stores have universal appeal. Each organization is successful, yet each is attracting out of the market a distinctive customer group.

### Stores of Distinction

The foregoing examples are not unusual ones. A lengthy list of customer profiles in many categories and along several dimensions makes it perfectly clear there is no such thing as a store image with equal appeal for all income groups, all social classes, all ages, all types. The store that is successful in the new communities and suburbs has competitive difficulties in the mill districts and the lower economic areas, and vice versa. The competitive pricing structure may be the same, but the elements of the store image which are so attractive to one group of shoppers are not attractive to another group.

It has to be this way. Different classes and different types of shoppers have different psychological outlooks on the world and different ways of life. Each segment of the market looks for a different emphasis. In general, the lower-status shopper looks at goods in a functional sense; she wants the store image to reflect her values of concreteness, practicality, and economy. She is concerned with quality of the merchandise and dependability of the store. The upper-status shopper, by contrast, is interested in whether the symbolic meaning of the store reflects her status and her style of life.

Take, for instance, the Marshall Field store in Chicago. It is much admired by perceptive competitors because all of the organization's activities are consistent and reinforce its strong symbolic character. The advertising, windows, merchandising events, restaurants, architecture, store policies, and attitudes of the sales personnel—all say the same thing symbolically. A shopper may feel she cannot afford to buy there, she may feel more comfortable in the atmosphere of another store. but she knows precisely what to expect. Marshall Field epitomizes elegance and sophistication. It creates a mood that helps to transform the shopping trip into an exotic adventure. It is described by shoppers as a "little world in itself" where the shopper can browse and enjoy her fantasies.

But just as the Marshall Field store represents so much to one kind of shopper, so does Sears, Roebuck & Co. have tremendous appeal to another kind. It is considered the friendliest and most comfortable department store in Chicago, with outstanding strength in all kinds of appliances, household staples, paint, tires, and children's wear. The type of woman considered typical of Sears' customers is pictured as hard-working, careful, practical, and home-minded. Sears has created a public image of itself as a family store, both in the type of merchandise it carries and in such intangible meanings as warmth, comfort, friendliness, honesty, dependability, and even unselfishness. Whereas the wife is more apt to go shopping alone at Marshall Field, it is not uncommon for the Sears shopping trip to be a safari for the entire family.

Sears, Roebuck and Marshall Field are the two largest department stores in Chicago, yet their store images are entirely different. The very merchandising strategies and personality aspects which are so successful for Sears are not uppermost for the Marshall Field audience, and vice versa. The upper-status woman expects a respect and a restrain from the salesclerk that would be interpreted by the wage earner's wife as formal and forbidding. On the other hand, the family atmosphere and the great emphasis on savings which attract the Sears customer are distasteful to the Marshall Field shopper.

### The Dull Personality

What happens to the retail store that lacks a sharp character, that does not stand for something special to any class of shoppers? It ends up as an alternative store in the customer's mind. The shopper does not head for such a store as the primary place to find what she wants. Without certain oustanding departments and lines of merchandise, without a clear-cut attraction for some group, it is like a dull person.

When we asked Chicago women to characterize a department store on a range of qualities, the one attribute most applied to the alternative store was, "You don't hear much about it." It may spend many millions annually for advertising and promotion events, yet many, many shoppers will characterize it this way. Here is an interesting story of what happened to a store that lost its personality and then regained it:

A leading southern department store originally possessed a distinctive image emphasizing the traditionalist values of its city. The lighting and the fixtures were old-fashioned, and the total store atmosphere was congruent with the city-wide interest in antiques, old families, old homes, old restaurants, and historical monuments.

Then the women's apparel merchandiser modernized his department. He introduced new fixtures and lighting, more high-fashion styling, and a promotional flavor similar to any aggressive chain store in this field. The fortunes of the store declined in definite progression—first women's apparel, then children's, then men's, and finally all the hard-line departments.

A management consultant determined that the store had dissipated the strongest component in its image, the key to which lay in the women's apparel department. It had become indistinguishable from any other store. On his advice, the store set about restoring its traditionalist, distinctively period personality. The old-fashioned lights and fixtures and the ultra-conservative styling were brought back. As management reformulated the symbolic meaning which had given the store distinction and character, its fortunes changed sharply for the better in the same progression as they had declined—first women's apparel and ultimately the hard lines.

## PERSONALITY FACTORS

What makes up a store's image in the minds of customers? There are many elements—architecture, color schemes, advertising, salespeople, and others. Let us look at the most important ones.

### Layout and Architecture

The layout and architecture of the store itself invariably come in for comment. Women in modest-income suburbs are likely to describe changes in department stores over the years in terms of the modernization of the physical plant

itself: "Modernization in the better stores is the big item nowadays." "They are all modernized inside now and are much better than they were ten years ago—in appearance and comfort for the customer."

Sometimes when elevators and escalators are set too deep in the store, women experience a panicky feeling of being lost. A shopper in such a store complained, "One day I thought I never would find my way out." Some shoppers are overwhelmed by counters and displays which are built too high. "They build up the display way over eye level so that things are staring at you and it bears down on you," they may comment; or, "On entering that store, the whole place gives you the feeling of crushing you."

Especially when comparing the advantages and disadvantages of the department store with those of the specialty shop, a very sizable proportion of women express feelings of confusion, of being overwhelmed by the crowds and size of the department store. Very possibly, the same reaction may be created by huge supermarkets.

The fixtures of a store add in a subtle but potent way to the general décor and atmosphere management wants to create—or subtract from it. They affect the success of promotions and can be used to transmit any elegant, exotic, or unusual emphasis in store policy. Thus:

¶ J. L. Hudson's new Eastland Center in Detroit, while located in a higher-income area than the same firm's fabulously successful Northland Center, is designed to be more colorful and lively while still reflecting highest quality. The entire décor of the first floor presents a subdued effect of dark woods, cherry showcases in center islands, but with a greater use of color on wall panels and in various metal displays running from floor to ceiling. Hardware finish is bronze, of the richest type of finish available. Besides the effect of various woods and colors to create personality, the type of fixture is significant. A quality store such as this uses a large number of showcases and center islands which lend a rich feeling to the store, as compared to a table-top presentation.

¶ T. A. Chapman's new Capitol Court in Milwaukee uses bronze profusely throughout, including bronze displays, plus many species of wood, to express a modern but high-fashion character.

¶ Julius Garfinkel's which is an outstanding carriage trade department store in Washington, made two fixture changes in its new lower-level store in Fairfax County, Virginia, in deference to the modern age. While the design is similar to the fixtures in the downtown Washington store that express conservatism and fashion, the new store uses a light ash wood plus more open selling to create greater accessibility of merchandise.

¶ Harvey's in Nashville, created a lively Victorian personality by buying an old carousel and placing the animals throughout the store and on the marquee. The store restaurant is in the form of a carousel, and the cashier's booth resembles a ticket seller's booth.

### Symbols and Colors

In a psychological study which was conducted for us on gasoline brands and companies,[2] by far the most distinctions and meanings were created by the emblems and the color schemes used on the retail stations, rather than by any product differences or verbalized claims of the companies. Sometimes these meanings were positive, sometimes negative. But whereas the differences between individual companies and brands were mostly blurred in the motorist's mind, rich meanings were conveyed to him by the symbols and colors.

A similar study, conducted by a New York industrial designer,[3] took the symbols of midwestern gasoline companies to eastern motorists who presumably were not familiar with them. Their evaluations of the companies were based therefore entirely on the shape and color of the symbols. Wherever this study examined the same symbols as our study did, the respondents' evaluations were in almost complete agreement. For example, the company using an oval-shaped symbol and a red, white, and blue color scheme was accorded by far the most positive evaluations. The company using a triangle was rated lowest on every scale. A dark color scheme used by another company cast an aura of dirtiness over its stations. Still another design and color created a company image that was "old-fashioned" and "inadequate" in motorists' minds.

What applies to gasoline stations applies with equal force to many other types of retailers. In

the customer's mind color schemes and designs have an intrinsic meaning. They tell him something about the company as surely as the architecture, fixtures, and other visual factors. The association may not be logical, but it is real.

### Advertising

The retailer's advertising is an especially important factor in expressing the character of the store. But while the retailer thinks mostly of the factual *content* of his advertising—item, price, timeliness, quality of merchandise—the shopper is impressed by the physical appearance, general tone, and style of the advertising as well as by the words. Just as we instinctively make judgments about another person from his clothing and his mannerisms, so does the shopper believe she can abstract symbolic cues from the advertisement. To illustrate: This year, in a study of retail grocery advertising, we took characteristic advertisements of several Chicago chains to different parts of the country where the shoppers were totally unfamiliar with the stores. When the judgments of women who knew nothing whatever about the stores were compared with the opinions of Chicago women familiar with the stores, they were in remarkably close agreement.

Retail advertising has become a language unto itself. It accurately conveys to the shopper whether the store is exotic and high-style, a dependable family store, or a promotion store hammering at bargains and pennies saved. She decides which atmosphere is most appealing and where she fits. Certain elements of the advertising lend themselves by logical extension to the store itself and to the goals of the owner. High-style art and restraint of tone and typography convey that the store is expensive and formal. The advertisements which are overly black and filled with typographical tricks indicate that the store is disorderly, with cluttered aisles and a strictly volume-turnover philosophy.

Obviously, there is no one advertising style which is best for all stores because each is trying—or should be trying—to convey different meanings about itself. The promotion store and the predominantly mass-appeal store would be mistaken to run the beautiful advertising of the exclusive shop and the quality department store; for a grocery in one neighborhood it might be mandatory to promote trading stamps, but for a grocery in another section of town, very unwise; and so on. In other words, the

---

[2] William E. Henry, *Gasoline, Gasoline Companies and Their Symbols* (Chicago: *The Tribune*, 1957).
[3] *A Study of Consumer Response to Oil Company Gas Station Signs* (New York: Lippincott and Margulies, 1957).

symbolic meaning of the advertising has to be consistent with the character of the store itself.

### Sales Personnel

Perhaps the biggest single factor in the store image is the character of the sales personnel, in spite of the fact that so much discussion of retailing in recent years has virtually disposed of the salesclerk. The success of the supermarket and the extension of self-service into other fields has led some to assume that personnel will someday disappear from the retailing scene. We talk about robot retailing and the necessity for preselling; we say the store clerk performs only a wrap-up function in the typical store; we detail how the automobile salesman is now only a sharp-pencil operator instead of an aggressive outside salesman.

Moreover, many department-store executives to whom I have talked appear resigned to a steady downgrading in the quality of their sales help. They feel they cannot compete in the labor market with other industries and are therefore forced to take whatever is available.

Yet the fact remains that shoppers almost invariably evaluate the personnel in discussion of specific stores. Even in the grocery chains that have no salesclerks, women will talk about the checkers and the stock boys, whether they are friendly or indifferent, cooperative or brusque. As the shopper tries to imagine how her family would like some new dish or some unfamiliar brand, she naturally is anxious for support and information from some source. She is unhappy when the stock boys are so engrossed in their tasks of refilling shelves that she feels her questions would interrupt them and be resented.

In the case of department stores, clerks are mentioned more often than any other image-creating factor. Here are typical comments: "A salesperson's personality makes the store." "If the clerks are courteous and friendly and act as if they enjoy their work and their merchandise, I enjoy shopping." "The employees make you feel at home or uncomfortable in a store by their attitude when they wait on you. Sometimes if you decide not to buy, they can make you feel like you'll never go back." "I was just browsing in the millinery department of the store when a snippy saleswoman asked me not to handle the merchandise. That was enough for me. I would never return there again."

In contrast to the impersonality of the downtown-store salesperson, the relationship between clerk and customer in the outlying center can be more personalized. The fact that both usually live in the same community or general area makes the clerk more perceptive to the shopper's attitudes and wants. As one shopper said; "You get to know the same salespeople in the local stores, and they know just what size and style and price you want."

I believe that the courtesy and adequacy of sales personnel is one of the decisive factors in the growth of the outlying and suburban store. In the words of another woman, "Why shop downtown when the local stores are so much friendlier?"

It is ironical that at the very time when a better educated and discriminating shopper expects more from the store and the clerk, management is dragging its feet in upgrading salespeople. The stores are more beautiful and interesting; they have escalators, air conditioning, and improved fixtures; they have buyers ranging far and wide to offer the broadest merchandising selection. But what about the salespeople.

## TRENDS IN BEHAVIOR

Perhaps a great many retailers will consider this concept of the store image as vague and inexact. While they may find it pleasant to know that there is such a thing, they are far too much concerned with the operational problems of being good merchants to devote any mental energy to it. But I believe that somebody in top management should think about these intangibles of store reputation and public attitudes. Somebody high up should ponder whether the over-all store image is positive and appealing or negative and dull, and whether it is in tune with what shoppers want today. The image plays an increasingly vital part in the fortunes of business.

Some of the reasons for this are economic— for instance, the increase in discretionary spending power, or the rise of new types of competition. Such trends make the subjective element of choice more important at the same time that the consumer is presented with more alternative ways of spending his money. But there are other reasons why top management should give more attention to the company image—reasons that are not so obvious. Some of them apply with particular force to department stores; some are of interest primarily to other types of retailers. Let us see what they are.

## Suburban Shopping

Today with the customer flow in most great cities moving outward toward the periphery and the beautiful new shopping centers, with so much of the population moving away from the heart of the city, the retail executive is concerned with placing stores in various strategic outlying locations. Just as the manufacturer is weighing the risks of product diversification, so is the retailer studying the uncertainties of geographical diversification. In the central shopping district of the past, he did not have to concern himself with store personality so much because all roads figuratively led to Rome. All shoppers found their way to the downtown area.

Now the situation is quite different. The executive has to take his store image into fairly stratified communities whose shopping expectations and style of life may be totally out of keeping with the traditional image of his store. In one instance, when a promotional bargain store was located in a community of ambitious, mobile, well-educated young families, these people took the store as almost an insult to their set of values. In another situation, a high-status and a low-status store both entered a middle-class community, and both were rejected because shoppers said, in effect, "I don't trust them."

The problem is far more difficult than merely locating a store where there are population concentrations and doing research to learn what kind of a personality to give the new store so that it will "fit in." The branch store and the suburban store partake of the personality and character of the big downtown store. Even though management may build very attractive branch stores which in themselves would be congruent with the new community, these stores cannot dissociate themselves from the core meanings of the main store image, which are deeply etched into the shopper's consciousness. If, for example, merchandising techniques and promotional approaches have made the downtown store successful with lower-income families, a branch will operate under a cloud in a smart new suburb. And, conversely, when the high-status store locates a branch in a fairly prosperous mill district, the advertising which is building an image of sophisticated modernity for the main store's customers is also visible to shoppers in the mill district, who shy away from such a store image.

The spectacular growth of the outlying shopping center has created another problem. Very often this center has included whatever stores the real estate promoter could interest, quite without regard to how their images fitted together. As a result, the stores in many centers are pulling against each other. The smart high-fashion department stores and apparel stores find themselves in centers with drugstores, grocery stores, and a miscellaneous assortment of small shops negating their image, so that the center becomes a hodgepodge to the shopper.

If the opposite is true—if most of the store images *do* reinforce each other—a "shopping-center mood" will result that will make these stores more successful than they could have been operating by themselves. But any stores that are out of character with the over-all image will have a harder time than they would otherwise. As an illustration, one grocery chain is having difficulty in a very successful center which is dominated by stores that create a mood of elegance, ornateness, formality, and sheer luxury throughout. The shopper coming to this center is dressed for the occasion and not likely to be attracted to a routine grocery store.

Earlier I stated that the question of the image was one for top management. It should now be easy to see why this is so whenever store location is the issue. It makes no sense to ask a group of executives to operate a branch in a new location until careful attention is first given to the store personality they will be working with. It can bless their efforts or plague them! Either way it is a factor of tremendous importance.

## The New Customer

In a study of the new community shopper, based on four rising communities which I felt were typical of different social classes and income groups, I noticed two large-scale trends:

¶ A new set of family values is developing. There has been a shift from the philosophy of security and saving to a philosophy of spending and immediate satisfaction, to rise of the child-centered family, more self-indulgent spending, a tendency to equate standard of living with possession of material goods, and great emphasis upon community values.

¶ The influence of the store image is increasing. People place great stress upon their interaction with other people—talking and socializing with others. How do they react to the growing impersonality of metropolitan life? Cutting all her ties with friends and family to move to a new city or new suburb, shopping in stores where she cannot know the owner or the clerks or where there may be no clerks, the shopper compensates for less personal contact by personalizing the store. She behaves in considerable measure toward this inanimate object as if it were a person. It becomes a symbol to which she can form deep attachments or dislikes. A department store, like a person, is characterized as "modern, practical, casual, and exciting." A grocery chain is characterized as "young, progressive, growing, friendly." Another store is called "dull," and still another is described as if it were somebody she did not like.

The National Association of Retail Grocers has conducted seminars for its member stores whose sole theme was the importance of developing an appealing and distinctive store personality. Throughout the country there are countless instances of imaginative independents successfully competing with the chains because they have created their own character in many and diverse ways. One Chicago grocer recently opened a "kiddy theater" which adults cannot enter without crawling on hands and knees. The youngsters sit entranced on benches watching cartoons while mother enjoys her shopping.

### Brand Products

Much of what applies to stores also applies to products and packages. Package designers startle our moral sense when they say that today's consumer is more interestd in the package than in what is inside; she takes the contents for granted. Styling and décor are the key to the automobile sales picture today, not engineering. Refrigerators present the "sheer look." Today even the most prosaic products are offered in a choice of many colors.

All of these are externals which have nothing to do with economics or function, yet which are demonstrably important in the sales fortunes of the brand.

### Service Organizations

Company image and personality are also important to the success of service organizations. Here the primary differences between competing companies are generally not matters of price and service so much as they are stereotyped attitudes in the public mind. Whether true or not, they exercise tremendous influence upon buyer choice. For example: Airlines offer the same

rates and much the same services. Yet a Chicago *Tribune* study of the airlines serving Chicago shows very wide differences in their company images. In fact, no two of the seven airlines studied have anything like the same profile.

United Airlines is accredited with a broad range of rich meanings: safe, up-to-date, good for traveling with children, efficient stewardesses, extremely dependable, excellent food, comfortable, excellent personal attention, luxurious service, and attractive interiors in the planes.

Capital Airlines has a very different image, stemming largely from its use of Viscounts: fast, quiet, smooth, good views, comfortable seats, an ultramodern, progressive line.

Interestingly enough, the same feelings were expressed by those who had flown in Viscounts and those who had only heard about them. This confirms findings of other studies that the attitudes toward a company image are not necessarily formed from experience. Rather, they may be shared ideas relayed by word of mouth.

### A POINT OF VIEW

Management is accustomed to look at shopping in an atomistic way—in terms of how many items were bought in what stores and at what prices. It should and must analyze retailing in this way. But it must not forget that statistics on sales provide only a partial basis for intelligent decision making. It must not be so captivated by the logic of figures that it overlooks the nonlogical basis of shopping behavior. Whether the customer is buying airline tickets, gasoline, hardware goods, or department store merchandise, his actions defy analysis in terms of after-the-sale statistics alone. To understand "why," management must look for deeper insights on customer behavior.

I have focused much of this article on department store customers not because they are different (they are, after all, the same people who buy automobiles, life insurance, and so on), but because studies of them offer some of the most dramatic evidence to support my points. We have found that the customer generally thinks of shopping as a total experience which runs through a number of departments in a number of stores and ends when she (or he) returns home. This is particularly true when she shops downtown or in a major shopping center requiring some travel and time. She faces many extraneous problems: How does she get there? If she drives, where does she park? Which store does she go to first? Is it the store where she plans to buy, or will it be the comparison point? If she expects to be gone for long, what about the restroom and restaurant facilities?

Curiously, the lowest-income shoppers mentioned the holiday aspects of such a trip more than any other group, probably because their routine lives are closer to humdrum practicality.

The shopping situation must therefore include many things not directly associated with specific items but closely connected with various patterns of consumer behavior. As the shopper fits the stores into her planning, she manipulates store images in her mind—not images of this counter or that department but impressions or pictures of entire stores. In large part, where she goes and what she buys depends on the subjective attributes that are part of these store images—atmosphere, status, personnel, other customers. Consciously or unconsciously, they sway her expectations and direct her steps.

# 33. Social Pressures and Retail Competition

STANLEY C. HOLLANDER

The most ambiguous, the most accommodating and changeable, and yet the most pervasive and potent forces that control retail competition are custom, consumer expectations, and social pressure. Suppliers frequently try to direct their dealers' behavior. Retail unions and other worker groups have sought, sometimes successfully, to influence store hours, services, and operating methods. The market in many ways limits what retailers can do. The wares that merchants offer must be adjusted to customer needs and tastes: the sale of antifreeze at the equator and of bathing suits at the Arctic Circle usually are not viable merchandising alternatives. Similarly, price policies must be adapted to the incomes and spending habits of the market. But in some sense even more fundamental than the market is the set of ideas that both merchants and the public share as to what is the proper way for a retail business to be conducted.

In some cases the public's concept of what is appropriate retail action becomes crystallized in legislation. Legislative action may result when the behavior of some retailers differs substantially from what an influential segment of the public believes to be fitting and proper conduct. Aside and apart from formal legislative codes, however, custom and expectations create very real, even if somewhat vague, limits on the competitive alternatives that the retailers can successfully adopt.

The relationship between retailing and its

environment is complex. It is difficult for us to perceive that relationship as it operates within our own culture, since our questions and expectations of retailing are very largely determined by that same culture. A sort of cross-cultural anthropological economic analysis is needed to discover the social determinants of retailing. In the past few years marketing specialists and anthropologists alike have become increasingly interested in that sort of analysis; and so we have recently had, for example, some fascinating studies of the social forces that determine trading relationships, the use of credit, and merchandising practices in Indonesian villages. British economists have tried to establish statistical relationships between socio-economic variables, on one hand, and, on the other, the number and kind of stores that will operate within a given community. Many other interesting studies are becoming available,[1] and while they are still exploratory rather than definitive, they do much to suggest society's role in shaping the limits of competition.

## SOCIETAL CONTROLS

Most merchants are even unlikely to conceive or consider alternatives outside those limits, a fact that in turn reinforces the original impact of the social controls. Few merchants in Ameri-

◆ SOURCE: Reprinted by permission of the publisher, the Bureau of Business and Financial Research, Division of Research, Graduate School of Business Administration, Michigan State University, from Business Topics, Vol. 13, No. 1, Winter 1965, pp. 7–14.

[1] See the sources cited in Stanley C. Hollander "Retailing: Cause or Effect," in William S. Decker (ed.), Emerging Concepts in Marketing (Chicago: American Marketing Association, 1962), pp. 220–32. Also see Robert Bartels, Comparative Marketing (Homewood, Illinois: Richard D. Irwin, Inc., for the American Marketing Association, 1963), pp. 1–6, 283–308, for a discussion of comparative analysis in wholesaling.

today, for example, would consider as a competitive tool the use of a "puller-in," that is, a man stationed at the doorway to coax window shoppers into the store. The use of these men was once a common competitive tactic, yet today it is simply outside the average merchant's frame of reference.

The August fur sale illustrates the self-reinforcing nature of many retail customs. At one time very few furs were sold in August, which is what one would expect to have been the case in the days before air-conditioning. Apparently some furriers tried offering drastic price inducements to offset this normal seasonal slump in business. Their competitors followed suit, and eventually a large, price-conscious segment of the market began to do its fur shopping in August. Consequently, the merchants who wanted to attract this segment had to offer their more attractive specials that month, before the customers purchased elsewhere. The concentration of specials, in turn, tended to strengthen the consumers' belief that August was the time to buy, and so on in circular fashion.

A similar illustration of self-reinforcement appears in the recommendations that the American Newspaper Publishers' Association offered to the retail trade for many years. Although the Association's Bureau of Advertising has recently modified its position somewhat, it used to suggest that retailers concentrate their advertising of each type of merchandise in those months when the consumer purchases of that merchandise were greatest.

Of course, societal forces shape all businesses, not merely retailing alone. As one economist has put it:

No less important is the unconscious influence provided by the mores, folklore, customs, institutions, social ideals, and myths of a society which lay the foundation for formal organization. More immediately relevant to any one firm's behavior are the standards and values of the groups with which it comes into contact as an organization, as well as the groups, communities and organizations to which its members belong. It should be clear that the preference system of the firm, as well as the attitudes of the participants in the firm's organization toward such things as co-operation, efficiency, innovation, etc. must be profoundly affected by the broader community within which the firm operates.[2]

The totally public nature of retailing and of some of the service trades does nevertheless create some special problems for businessmen in those fields. Often a factory or a wholesale establishment in an isolated or unfrequented location, for example, may operate at full force on Sunday subject to possible resentment only among its own employees and their families. The storekeeper who opens on Sunday, however, is more likely to come to the attention of, and to irritate, segments of the general public that may include both voters and potential customers. Local sentiments, which vary from place to place, determine whether clothing merchants must cover their windows when changing the garments on the display dummies.

In an entirely different sense as well, dealing with the ultimate consumer probably leaves the retailer more susceptible to the influence of custom and tradition than most other businessmen. For over two hundred years economists, marketing specialists, and psychologists have debated whether habit and past practice are more important in guiding the purchases of consumer buyers than those of the supposedly more rational industrial and commercial buyers. This debate has often centered around the supposedly more crucial role of customary prices in consumer markets than in commercial ones. The argument is by no means settled, but the only question in all the debate has been whether consumer dependence on tradition is greater than or only equal to that of business buyers. No one has ever seriously urged that it is less. The retailer's problem is that his public is indeed *the* public.

Caplow has argued that the prevailing customs and expectations influence the retailer's entire relationship to his customers and, to a considerable extent, even his behavior outside the store. In contrasting the occupation of shopkeeper with that of factory worker, he says:

The control of occupational behavior is entirely different, being at once much wider and much more diffuse. Indeed, it is the popular belief that self employment in a small business carries with it freedom from personal coercion which constitutes the principal appeal of retail trade, just as it is often the impact of

---

[2] Andreas G. Papandreou, "Some Basic Problems in the Theory of the Firm," in Bernard F. Haley (ed.), *A Survey of Contemporary Economics* (Homewood, Illinois: Richard D. Irwin, Inc., 1952), II, 192.

impersonal coercion which subsequently disillusions the neophyte proprietor.

He describes the coercion as orginating with suppliers, creditors, and customers. Then he goes on to say:

[Compared to the rigid system of control exercised by suppliers and other creditors], the control which the customer exerts upon the occupational comportment of the merchants is very informal. It is none the less important. Particularly since the restrictions of price and quality competition, personal relations with customers are often the decisive factor in the history of a retail business.

The "rules" are essentially these:

1. The merchant is expected to minimize his status and exaggerate that of the customer by exaggerated forms of deference, by yielding in minor arguments, by expressing more interest in the customer's personal affairs than the customer is expected to show in his, and by small personal services.

2. Under this ritual, it becomes essential that the habits of the customer be identified and protected. A strain is thus produced on the merchant to maintain nearly absolute consistency in his manners, his purchasing routines, and his hours of work. . . .

The norms of deference imposed on the shopkeeper prevent him from displaying a distinctly higher status than his customers [in life style], while his aspirations toward the role of businessman impel him to do so.[3]

This picture is somewhat overdrawn, particularly if it is used to depict all retailer-customer relations. Certainly many of the most successful mass-retailers exhibit little of the deference suggested by the first "rule" cited above. And the smaller merchants who have succeeded without much servility are also numerous. But in spite of these and other criticisms of Caplow's picture, we must grant that a retailer in the typical American community today cannot long behave like the operator of a trading post on the Navaho reservation who says: "The important thing is to show the Indians who is boss."[4] Nor can he expect to take on the general role of social, economic, financial, and technical advisor to the community, as did so many pioneer merchants of the Western frontier. In short, society has dictated the general limits of the retailer's role. It also dictates many of the details of his operation.

## PRICING

As any one retailer faces his world, he finds that it tells him a number of things about what it considers appropriate pricing policies. Our society, for example, regards haggling and bargaining as permissible in some retail situations and improper in others. Automobile dealers are expected to bargain, haberdashers are not. Of course, the explanation can be offered that the size of the automobile transaction and the unstandardized condition of the trade-in are conducive to bargaining in the car dealership, while different conditions obtain in the haberdashery. This is perfectly reasonable, and true. But the point is that in other times, and at other places, haberdashers have been expected to bargain, while in our society they definitely are not expected to do so. Also, we generally feel that such professional men as architects and physicians, whose output is also unstandardized and sometimes of substantial size, should not bargain, although under some conditions they may discriminate between patrons.

Some patterns of discriminatory prices have become so widely accepted in the sale of some, *but not all,* goods and services that it requires a conscious effort of mind to appreciate that these patterns do, in fact, discriminate between customers. These conventional discriminations are often based upon age, and occasionally upon sex. Children's rates, lower than those for adults, are frequently offered in the sale of transportation, amusement, and other services. In cases such as the provision of restaurant meals and haircuts, it can properly be argued that the child receives a different, albeit perhaps more troublesome, service than the adult. This is not so in the case of many amusement and transportation services in which the child,

[3] Theodore Caplow, *The Sociology of Work* (Minneapolis: University of Minnesota Press, 1954), pp. 118–19, 128–29. Caplow, it should be made clear, directs his remarks specifically to small shopkeepers.

[4] William Y. Adams, *Shonto: A Study of the Role of the Trader in a Modern Navaho Community,* Smithsonian Institution, Bureau of American Ethnology, Bulletin 188 (Washington: U.S. Government Printing Office, 1963), pp. 210–12, 287–90. The traders cited by Adams reverse every one of the rules of deference indicated above, and in order to discourage automobile ownership among the Indians, go so far as to deliberately create disorder and uncertainty in the marketing of gasoline.

charged the lower rate, receives exactly the same privileges as the higher rated adult. Some aspects of family-plan airline and railroad fares, and the free admission of women to baseball parks on Ladies' Day are examples of similar discriminations based upon sex.

Some discriminatory practices based on the patronage status of the purchaser seem to be of general acceptability. Special introductory rates for new subscribers are very frequently used in building magazine subscription lists. Department store private sales for the benefit of old customers cast the discriminatory advantage in the opposite direction. While magazine introductory rates usually are actually restricted to new subscribers, many so-called private sales are much less impregnable. In many stores the term is used to describe the practice of giving charge customers notice of approaching sales before the advertisements appear in the newspaper. Rational justifications can be offered for each of these discriminations. But again the point is that each of these sets of price differentials seems to be regarded as acceptable only within a particular context. Clothing merchants usually find that extra alteration charges are more readily accepted in the sale of women's clothing than in menswear. Generally however, commodity retailers, unlike service trade operators usually do not think in terms of age or sex-based price differentials and the public doesn't seem to expect them to do so, although there is as much social justification for a child's discount on toothpaste as on movie admissions. A department store sale that was confined to non-customers would engender waves of ill will, and no department store executive would dream of such a sale. Yet magazine publishers do it every day, with apparently very little criticism.

Another curious way in which public expectations, reinforced by retail practice, limit the retailer's freedom to select among competitive pricing alternatives is in the matter of "customary prices." This is the popular belief that only certain prices or price endings are appropriate for certain types of goods. The use of these prices has been condemned as a mechanism that forces price increases into unnecessarily large steps, and praised as a device that facilitates consumer comparisons. Whether desirable or not, most retailers feel

that the public's expectation that these traditional price endings should be used is a very real force that must be considered in setting prices. Very few studies attempting to measure the strength of consumer attachment to customary prices have been reported. The best known one started with a hypothesis on the part of the researcher and his mail-order house sponsors that the whole thing was a myth. The only conclusion was that the dangers of testing outweighed the possible benefits of the test.[5] And finally the public often seems to have some vague sense of what it considers as unfair or fair prices. An experienced retailer puts it this way:

It is generally accepted as poor policy to charge what the traffic will bear. Whenever an article is priced higher than eye-value would seem to justify, the retailer is at pains to explain that the fault is not his, but the high price of the manufacturer. Indeed, he may often shade his mark-on in order to avoid criticism.[6]

## MERCHANDISE

The public also has some expectations as to the type and nature of the merchandise that each type of retailer will carry. Such expectations are in fact necessary, if shopping is not to be a matter of haphazard searching. The importance of these traditional expectations about merchandise offerings is denied to some extent by recent developments of "scrambled merchandising," i.e., the sale of many types of goods in non-traditional outlets —for example, the introduction of non-foods into grocery supermarkets. Yet it is interesting to note that some commodity lines, which the public apparently considers too different from the usual grocery stock, such as clothing accessories, have encountered considerable customer resistance in many supermarkets. On the other hand, soap is considered so traditional a grocery line that no one ever refers to it as a "non-food," even though it is hardly edible; and consequently, no grocer would dare exclude it from his stocks.

A very different sort of public pressure arises if the retailer handles goods that come from sources that are objectionable to some portion of his public. The reaction may take the form of picketing, boycotts, or attempts to

[5] Eli Ginzberg, "Customary Prices," *American Economic Review*, XXVI (June 1936), 296.
[6] *Oswald Knauth*, "Considerations in the Setting of Retail Prices," *Journal of Marketing*, XIV (July 1949), 7.

secure some type of controlling legislation. Most recently this sort of reaction has occurred in connection with the sale of goods originating in the communist-bloc countries. At various times, similar responses have been evoked by the sale of low-priced Japanese textiles, products made by firms that practice racial discrimination, prison-made and non-union-made goods, and items from Nazi Germany and elsewhere.

And, of course, the public or a segment may protest if it considers the merchandise itself objectionable. Again, apparently, the reaction will often be directed with different strength against different types of retailers. At least one book distributor reports that the public seems to tolerate more lurid paperbacks in drugstores than it will in supermarkets.

## SERVICES

When the Twentieth Century Fund sponsored its classic study of distribution costs a number of years ago, it also asked a distinguished panel to prepare recommendations on ways of reducing those costs. Among other things, the panel recommended that retailers separate the charge for each service rendered the customer from the basic price of the merchandise itself.[7] This suggestion was based upon the belief that the general practice of quoting a single price for the item and the attendant services leads many consumers to use more services than they really want or would be willing to pay for in a free market. The panel felt that many consumers would like the option of choosing between service and price savings. Also charging for services in proportion to use would be more equitable than the prevailing practice. The idea seems thoroughly reasonable. Yet many merchants, and especially the ones to whom this suggestion was particularly addressed, were, and to a great extent still are, extremely reluctant to adopt it.

Their reluctance has been based upon a strong feeling that the public associates a particular bundle of services with each type of store, and that any attempt to reduce those bundles will create a sense of outrage. Again, the public expectations seem to have a differential impact. As a very perceptive analyst points out, what is considered appropriate will vary with the store's price-policy and with the socio-economic class it seeks to attract.[8] Department store operators claim that their comparatively long history as operators of full service institutions makes them subject to consumer expectations of expensive delivery, credit, exchange, return, and miscellaneous other privileges. Yet, they allege, the same consumers will patronize such competitive outlets as discount houses, chain stores, and mail-order house retail shops without demanding any of the services whose discontinuance by department stores would be vigorously resented. Undoubtedly the harshness of the situation is sometimes exaggerated by department store people as an excuse for poor profit performance, but nevertheless the problem does exist.

One aspect of retail services about which many people, including both customers and non-customers, have strong feelings is the matter of store hours, and particularly the question of Sunday openings. In many areas local pharmacists' associations have detected some public dissatisfaction with the hours observed by drug stores and have formulated plans under which there will always be at least one pharmacy open in the community at any hour to handle emergency needs. In contrast, an increasing trend toward Sunday sales on the part of roadside clothing, hardware, furniture, general merchandise stores, and automobile dealers has induced a call for some type of control in many parts of the country. The issue is complicated by the varying economic interests of the retailers and the communities involved, the diverse desires of retail workers, and the thorny question of the proper position of government in matters that have religious overtones. But it is clear that a number of people in this country do believe that at least some types of stores should close on Sunday.

## IMPACT OF SOCIAL PRESSURE

The strength of the social forces that we have just looked at can easily be overestimated. The merchants who are affected by these forces may be particularly likely to see more power than is actually there. Customs may persist, not because of any inherent vitality, but because of inertia and the absence of any strong incentive for change. Department store

---

[7] Paul W. Stewart and J. Frederick Dewhurst, *Does Distribution Cost Too Much?* (New York: Twentieth Century Fund, 1939), pp. 351–52.

[8] W. T. Tucker, *The Social Context of Economic Behavior* (New York: Holt, Rinehart & Winston, Inc., 1964), pp. 73–81.

merchants who have been beset by discount house competition have found that they could, in many cases, move to self-service, to the elimination of some frills, and to separation of commodity and service charges. Possibly this increased freedom to compete has been due to changes in the consumer between 1935 and 1950 and 1964. Some of it probably is. But at least some of the change probably is a correction of an erroneous impression as to the amount of service the consumer really wanted. Katona mentions another instance of failure to judge what was permissible among the many apparel merchants who offered totally unnecessary seasonal reductions during the wartime shortage years of 1942 and early 1943.[9] Other such examples could be cited.

Yet in spite of all such instances, the fact remains that the retailer is in the business of dealing with the public, and so he must be responsive to the public's demands upon him. Frequently, as in the case of the mail-order firm that wanted to question the strength of customary pricing, attempts to test those demands involve risks of lost sales or of customer alienation. The risks are greatest, although sometimes the rewards also may be greatest, when an individual retailer tries to move independently, counter to the practices of his competitors. Thus, for example, two authors who generally favor independence and competitiveness in retailing, urge group action to reduce the returned goods rate:

Although the individual store can do much to reduce its returns, group action of the retailers within a given shopping area is often necessary for best results. The group can afford to do many things which the individual store cannot do. Also, some of the steps the individual retailer might take would merely drive his customers to competitors, where they would still return as much merchandise, so that the returned-goods problem of the community would be as important as before. Group action, therefore, has the major advantage of making it easier to establish a sound educational program on the costliness of returns and of making it less difficult for individual stores to refuse returns because of the established "law" in the community governing such matters.

Realizing the advantages of group action, merchants in such cities as Dallas, Los Angeles, Kansas City and Milwaukee have joined together to reduce returns. Such action usually involves agreement on one or more of the following points: establishing uniform time limits, setting up a standard policy of refusing to pick up certain merchandise for return, standardizing extra charges for return pickups, framing sanitary provisions and obtaining local ordinances involving sanitary considerations, activating educational campaigns and providing material for publicity drives, exchanging information about customers with records of excessive returns, and exchanging return-ratio data.[10]

Anyone who is dedicated to a classical "hard-core" antitrust position might question the propriety of some of the actions outlined above, although several of them are similar to recommendations of the Twentieth Century Fund's distribution cost panel. But they do also illustrate the difficulty of making individual changes in the established way of dealing with the public.

[9] George Katona, *Psychological Analysis of Economic Behavior* (New York: McGraw-Hill Book Company, Inc., 1951), p. 51. See also John K. Galbraith, *The Theory of Price Control* (Cambridge: Harvard University Press, 1952), p. 12.

[10] Delbert J. Duncan and Charles F. Phillips, *Retailing: Principles and Methods* (6th ed.; Homewood, Illinois: Richard D. Irwin, Inc., 1963), pp. 591–92.

# 34. Designing the Distribution System

## THOMAS L. BERG

The marketing executive needs some model of his distribution system to guide day-to-day trading operations. Organization theory might be used in constructing the model, for trade channels and internal company organizations are similar in important respects. Both deal with economic functions performed by interdependent human agents requiring motivation and coordination. Both involve continuous personal relationships, routinized tasks, and stable expectations of reciprocal performance. Despite the analogies, the idea that all distribution systems might be designed as organizational models has not been widely recognized nor warmly embraced. This study shows the idea to be technically feasible in the hope that one barrier to its acceptance will thus be removed. The complex process of channel model-building is depicted as unfolding in five separate but related phases. In demonstrating the feasibility of this approach, insights into the more intractable issues of practicality and morality are also revealed.

## INTRODUCTION

Marketing management suffers from schizophrenia. Students of the firm are encouraging corporate psychoses identified by the classic syndrome: (1) loss of contact with company environments and (2) disintegration of the whole-properties of corporate organisms. The disease is amenable to treatment. This study is intended as a partial prescription, although it is not to be construed as any sort of a panacea.

To see the nature and origin of the malady in more concrete terms, it is necessary to understand how the total company is linked to its environment.

### The Firm as an Operating System

Any manufacturing enterprise can be viewed as an input-output system consisting of three parts: (1) the *internal organization* of the firm, (2) the company *environment*, and (3) various kinds of *external organizations* serving to link the internal organization with its economic milieu for the interorganizational transmission and processing of inputs and outputs.

Connections with suppliers, networks of financial intermediaries, and trade channels are examples of external organizations. Although they may not appear on company charts or in manuals, these should be regarded as logical extensions to the internal organization of the firm. Internal and external organizations are similar in that both deal with economic functions performed by interdependent human agents requiring motivation and coordination through communication. Both involve continuous personal relationships, routinized tasks, and stable expectations of reciprocal performance.

◆ SOURCE: Reprinted by permission from *The Social Responsibilities of Marketing* (Chicago: American Marketing Association, 1962) pp. 981–90.

Failure to pay due respect to the systemic nature of the enterprise and to the fundamental similarities between internal and external organizations has resulted in schizoid thinking in management and marketing. Management theorists have been preoccupied with problems of *internal organization* and have failed to show how the firm is connected to its environment via externally organized linkages. An unnatural cleavage between internal and external aspects of structure has developed in the management literature.

Administrative and organizational theories seem to have concentrated upon the administration of single organizations and have not specifically recognized that a system of separate organizations requires administration also. It is suggested . . . that that body of theory and research which contributes to an understanding of the administrative process in single organizations is pertinent to the administration of primary and secondary organizations.[1]

Over the years, a handful of people have come to suggest that the full development of organization theory awaits the day when management theorists explicitly bring environmental entities and external organizations into their analyses. The sire of this thought appears to be Chester Barnard.

The conception of organization at which I arrived in writing *The Functions of the Executive* was that of an integrated aggregate of actions and interactions having a continuity in time. Thus I rejected the concept of organization as comprising a rather definite group of people whose behavior is coordinated with reference to some explicit goal or goals. On the contrary, I included in organization the actions of investors, suppliers, and customers or clients. Thus the material of organization is personal services, i.e., actions contributing to its purposes.[2]

Barnard's words have apparently fallen on deaf ears. Administrative theorists are concentrating more on refining theories of internal organization and less on extending and testing their notions in external realms. But the student of marketing is equally responsible for the observable symptoms of schizophrenia.

In contrast to the management theorists' focus on internal aspects of business systems, marketers have been preoccupied with environmental forces and external trading channels without clarifying how these tie in to problems of internal administration and organization. Marketing academicians seem to appreciate the need of some model for building and operating trade channels, but few have recognized the potential role of organization theory in its design. Businessmen in marketing seem to know intuitively that channel-building is an organizational problem, although few acknowledge the need for a model to guide them in their organizing.

As a result, trends in management and marketing thinking become more and more divergent. To bring about some convergence, and to assure that both disciplines reverse the trend to schizophrenia, it is necessary to (a) persuade the internally-oriented administrative theorists to consider the application of their ideas to external-environmentals entities and (b) convince marketers to draw more heavily on internally-oriented theories for insights into building and operating external marketing systems. This study takes the distributive subsystem of the firm as an example of the applicability of organization theory to external systems.

### The Distribution Subsystem

The term "trade channel" is often reserved to the network of external entities in a company's distribution setup. In this study, the term "distribution system" embraces all elements of the internal-external-environmental triad. Corporate marketing staffs and field salesforces are elements of internal organization, segments of ultimate consumer markets are the key environmental sectors, and retail merchants and other trade intermediaries make up the external organization. This study attempts to show that useful models of distribution systems can be designed with the help of organization theory.

Today, distribution systems are developed more by intuition than design. In part, this accounts for widespread cases of ineffective performance of trade management functions. Actual channel formation, budgeting for distribution, the setting of distributor's margins, the appraisal of dealer performance and similar management tasks could be performed more effectively if marketing managers had distribu-

---

[1] Valentine F. Ridgway, "Administration of Manufacturer-Dealer Systems, *Administrative Science Quarterly*, Vol. 1, March, 1957, pp. 466–67.

[2] Chester I. Barnard, *Organization and Management*, Cambridge, Mass., Harvard University Press, 1948, pp. 112–13.

tive models to guide them in the day-to-day administration of trading functions and trading relationships.

For many reasons, the basic idea that distribution models might be designed by drawing upon organization theory has not been widely recognized nor warmly embraced. The notion is still a relatively new one accepted by a fairly small group of people. Those who have heard of the idea often seem not to have grasped its full significance. The understanding of some has been barred by the persistence of traditional perspectives on trade channels. Those congenial to the basic idea may not know how to push it to the level of operational reality. Lack of know-how simply prevents others from seeing that the approach is feasible. Those that agree to its feasibility may be reluctant to devote the time, energy, and cash to what inevitably is a difficult design job. Some apparently see the feasibility of the notion but do not regard the approach as useful on pragmatic grounds. Still others may object on philosophical bases, for when organization theory is pushed far enough into market relationships difficult questions concerning prevailing concepts of competition are bound to arise.

The purpose of this study is simply to overcome a few of these barriers to acceptance of the fundamental proposition. The chief test applied in the study is the test of feasibility. As a purely technical matter, organization theory *can* be meaningfully applied to external distribution systems, and not only to direct manufacturer-dealer organizations. In the process of demonstrating feasibility, insights into the more intractable pragmatic and philosophical issues are also revealed.

## NATURE OF THE STUDY

This study focuses on the contactual, or trading, aspects of distribution as opposed to the logistics, or physical distribution, dimensions of the problem. It is nonsituational, i.e., the study is not restricted in scope to a particular product, institution, or historical period. It is addressed to marketers in manufacturing firms, although the ideas may also be of interest to others.

Few businessmen can yet verbalize their opinions and attitudes toward the application of organization theory to the design of distributive models. Therefore, personal interviews could not be used as a sole method of research. Information had to be gleaned piecemeal from a variety of sources—including protracted informal interviews with some 150 marketing executives and teachers, widely scattered secondary sources, and pure cogitation.

In effect, the study attempts to present elements of prudent practice within the unifying framework of organization theory. It does not describe any approach taken by a known manufacturer.

### Elements in the Design Process

The process of designing a distributive model for a producer is envisaged as unfolding in five interrelated stages: (1) factoring the company-wide strategic situation, (2) converting key factors into functional prerequisites for the system, (3) grouping individual tasks into work units, (4) allocating tasks to appropriate functionaries, and (5) designing a structure of relationships to provide loci of distributive authority and responsibility within the work structure erected in the previous stages.

In the study, separate chapters are devoted to each of these elements and an integrating case is used to help synthesize the materials as the process unfolds.

***Step One—Factoring the Strategic Situation.*** Early in the research, comparative studies of existing systems were undertaken with the aim of accounting for the sometimes marked inter-firm differences in distribution practices observable in many industries. Those variables were then abstracted which seemed to serve as decision-making constraints for a wide variety of the firms studied. These fell into two broad classes: (a) the nature and interests of various environmental entities as interpreted by top management, and (b) factors relating to the company's resource base. Environmental entities and company resources are related through broad marketing strategy to the functional necessities and structural features of distribution systems. Environmental entities include stockholders, employees and their unions, supplier interests, trade associations, governments, competitors, and ultimate consumers. The resource base refers especially to finances and manpower but also includes material, spatial, temporal, and other resources. In the study, these factors are arranged and presented in meaningful sequence, and illustrations are provided to suggest the possible impact of each variable on channel function or structure. The goal was to help the manager conduct a comprehensive position audit for his own particular firm in its unique competitive market setting in order to isolate key bits of information which might provide clues as to appropriate distributive structure in the specific case. The study thus offers a method of attack for factoring a firm's strategic situation as well as illustrating the potentialities for interfirm differences in distribution systems.

*Step Two—Converting Key Factors into Activity Requirements.* The research revealed that surprisingly few producers can meaningfully reply to the question, "What do you want your distribution setup to do for you?" It may be suggested here that until managers can verbalize the nature of the *work* they want performed by distribution systems, there can be little hope for real application of organization theory to trading networks.

Yet, the study offers guides for developing the inferential value of key factors uncovered in step one in sufficient detail to permit the generation of a fairly clear-cut list of activities to be performed by the yet-to-be-designed distribution system. At this point in the study, the integrating case is also introduced to illustrate how one firm actually posited its channel tasks in a simplified situation.

*Step Three—Grouping Tasks into Work Units.* This step involves a straightforward adaptation of organization theory, which alternatively depicts the process as one of a *division of labor* or of *grouping tasks* together in a meaningful fashion. No real problems of applying organization theory were encountered. However, there is clear evidence that the channel analyst might profit from taking this step very seriously. Traditional channel discourses, for example, have tended to stress specialization solely on the basis of function. Organization theory demands adequate attention to alternative modes of specialization, i.e., by product, by customer, by time, by location, by process, and by composite patterns of these basic varieties. All of the alternatives are relevant to distribution systems as well as to internal organization. Furthermore, channel planners perhaps stress short-term efficiency considerations too much in deciding what kind of task-split might be effected with the trade. Organizational theorists call attention to the needs for structural coordination, for promoting co-operation and reducing conflict, for recognizing the vagaries of local conditions, and other criteria for picking proper kinds and degrees of work specialization.

There is reason to assume that managers would uncover a much wider range of distribution alternatives and would probably end up by delegating more of the overall distributive job to tradesmen if they self-consciously applied the broader perspectives of organization theory to this step in the design of distribution systems. Finally, some varieties of organization theory focus first on the work and secondly on the worker. Classical institutional and commodity approaches to trade channels seem to have reversed the order of analysis.

*Step Four—Allocating Tasks to Middlemen.* In matching work and worker, the best procedural approach seems to be to begin with segmenting the end markets to be served and then to progress upward through a process of sequential segmentation in intermediate markets until the intervening work structure can be made to tie together with the producer's internal organization.

At each stage of this process of closing gaps separating the producer from his ultimate markets, a set of interrelated issues must be resolved.

All alternative middlemen must first be *recognized* as alternatives. This is less obvious and more difficult than it appears. Semantic traps, statistical fictions, informational gaps, trained incapacities, managerial impatience and other barriers to creativity befog and bury alternatives from view. Brainstorming and other alternative-producing techniques, of course, are relevant in overcoming this problem.

With the alternatives before him, the manager must sort out ineligible types of outlets, drawing upon earlier key factors, activity requirements, and preliminary grouping analysis for screening criteria. Next, the remaining eligible outlet-types can often be arrayed meaningfully in order of their apparent suitability to the producer, using the same criteria.

At this juncture, several additional types of questions often need to be answered before proceeding to another stage of the vertical channel stretch, e.g., whether there are economies of scale for each outlet-type, how many of each type will be required, and what areal coverage pattern should be used. Since many of the variables used to resolve the latter issues lend themselves to quantification, some companies have been able to program them for computer solutions.

This set of decisions, made at successive stages in bridging the vertical gap between customers and the producer, completes the steps involved in planning the structure of distributive *work*. Before going further, however, the study discusses principles and procedures which serve as possible checks on the adequacy of the activity structure erected thus far on paper. The final step is to define desired relationships between individuals and institutions in the distribution system to provide loci of authority and responsibility as a basis for cooperative action.

*Step Five—Designating Appropriate Structural Relationships.* As a starting point in performing this step, the producer must know specifically what kinds of activities need to be controlled in order to comply with law, to ensure adequate profits, to generate goodwill and repeat business for his brands, to keep risk within limits, and to provide for effective coordination of his overall marketing program. Next, the producer must identify the sources of his capacity for influencing power-patterns in the distribution system. These sources are rooted in governmental sanctions, specific laws, the strength of the consumer franchise held by the producer, and similar factors.

Basically, he now faces two alternatives for structural action. He can either try to accumulate market power which will then be exercised unilaterally to exact the compliance of middlemen or he can undertake to create conditions under which authority may safely be dispensed in the system. In short, the alternatives are either to reserve authority from tradesmen, or to delegate distributive authority to them. There are an infinite number of possible ways to mix these two basic alternatives. In this study, the outright ownership of facilities, existence of concubine outlets, pre-retailing practices, widespread consumer deals, and fair-trade arrangements are viewed as manifestations of the "reservation of authority" phenomenon. The delegation alternatives involve outright contractual or other specification of intended delegations, and these steps may be supplemented by the provision of facilitating and auxiliary service units (e.g., distributor training groups and dealer advisory councils) which help all parties to hold the exercise of authority within responsible bounds. The specific pattern of reservation-delegation devices chosen by the producer will depend on the way in which power has come to be institutionalized in the particular work structure he has put together, on the relative size and bargaining strength of producer and middlemen, on the past history of cooperation and conflict with similar patterns of tradesmen, and related factors.

When the five steps of the model-building process have been completed, the overall structure can then be described in charts and manuals. Job descriptions and man-specifications for middlemen may also prove useful as guides to implementation of the model.

## CONCLUSION

In very skeletal fashion, these five steps to the organizational design of distribution systems represent the ground covered in this study. Chester Barnard's basic idea is shown to be operationally meaningful; as a technical proposition, organization theory can usefully be extended to the design of external systems. But the task is just as difficult, frustrating, and time-consuming as it is in internal analyses—perhaps more so.

Yet the approach is practical for most firms. Organization theory provides a systematic and rational basis for superseding many of today's intuitive approaches to channel-building. It is a body of doctrine that respects the inherent uniqueness of companies while providing guidelines for both orthodox and unconventional distribution systems. And it allows us to deal with both the *work* to be done in the system and the human *relationships* important to that performance.

Step-by-step application of concepts from organizational theory helps in the discovery of gaps in traditional ways of thinking about distribution. At the same time, it aids in uncovering more distributive alternatives and in providing criterial for choosing between them, it encourages the challenging of old concepts which may have outlived their usefulness, and it leads to a fuller understanding of the implications of past, present, and future trading actions.

There are many additional ways in which administrative theory can be effectively used to improve the management of distribution systems. Knowledge of institutional leadership and control in internal realms needs to be further extended, and perhaps modified, to apply in all external systems. By breaking down the walls tending to separate marketing from the field of general administration, marketers can also find themselves testing and improving administrative theory. The problem of choosing from alternative theories of organization still exists today. Perhaps further attempts to apply these theories to external systems could contribute to the unification of divergent threads.

This study was one test of organization theory in an external setting. The conclusion is that organization theory stands up better under analysis than does the marketer's concepts of distribution.

Increased awareness of the general applicability of administrative and organization theory to external systems may encourage further inter-disciplinary contributions to marketing and management. Industrial relations specialists could collaborate with marketers, for instance, in exploring points of similarity and difference between employee-union relationships within the firm and the extra-firm relationships between merchants and their trade associations. Something akin to collective bargaining is said to take place in some trades with respect to the setting of distributor margins and other issues. It would be interesting to pursue this further.

Sociologists are now attempting to apply insights from general studies of bureaucracy to manufacturer-dealer relations. The concept of reference group behavior could perhaps be investigated more thoroughly for its relevance to trade channels. The anthropologist's idea of tangent relations and tangent institutions might provide further insights into the design and operation of distribution systems.

In short, recognition of the fact that organization theory offers immediate and practical help to manufacturers in the design of all distribution systems should open many doors for further research and remedy present tendencies toward schizophrenia in understanding business needs and company practices.

# Directing the Marketing Effort

Marketers' efforts are carried on within the environmental framework developed in Part II. Marketing effort should match the firm's resources with segments of the market. More specifically, these efforts are concerned with the development of the markets. The development of markets involves planning. Planning encompasses the price, design, promotion of the product, and the utilization of efficient channels of distribution.

The success with which marketing strategies are derived and later implemented is due in some measure to the use of marketing information. For this reason the readings in Part III begin with marketing research and then proceed to the important marketing efforts. These efforts, though described one by one, are integral parts of the total marketing program.

# A. Introduction

## 35. *The Marketing Revolution*

ROBERT J. KEITH

The consumer, not the company, is in the middle.

In today's economy the consumer, the man or women who buys the product, is at the absolute dead center of the business universe. Companies revolve around the customer, not the other way around.

Growing acceptance of this consumer concept has had, and will have, far-reaching implications for business, achieving a virtual revolution in economic thinking. As the concept gains ever greater acceptance, marketing is emerging as the most important single function in business.

### A REVOLUTION IN SCIENCE

A very apt analogy can be drawn with another revolution, one that goes back to the sixteenth century. At that time astronomers had great difficulty predicting the movements of the heavenly bodies. Their charts and computations and celestial calendars enabled them to estimate the approximate positions of the planets on any given date. But their calculations were never exact—there was always a variance.

Then a Polish scientist named Nicolaus Copernicus proposed a very simple answer to the problem. If, he proposed, we assume that the sun, and not the earth, is at the center of our system, and that the earth moves around the

‡‡ SOURCE: Reprinted by permission from the *Journal of Marketing* (National Quarterly Publication of the American Marketing Association), Vol. 24, No. 3, January 1960, pp. 35–38.

sun instead of the sun moving around the earth, all our calculations will prove correct.

The Pole's idea raised a storm of controversy. The earth, everyone knew, was at the center of the universe. But another scientist named Galileo put the theory to test—and it worked. The result was a complete upheaval in scientific and philosophic thought. The effects of Copernicus' revolutionary idea are still being felt today.

### A REVOLUTION IN MARKETING

In much the same way American business in general—and Pillsbury in particular—is undergoing a revolution of its own today: a marketing revolution.

This revolution stems from the same idea stated in the opening sentence of this article. No longer is the company at the center of the business universe. Today the customer is at the center.

Our attention has shifted from problems of production to problems of marketing, from the product we *can* make to the product the consumer *wants* us to make, from the company itself to the market place.

The marketing revolution has only begun. It is reasonable to expect that its implications will grow in the years to come, and that lingering effects will be felt a century, or more than one century, from today.

So far the theory has only been advanced, tested, and generally proved correct. As more and more businessmen grasp the concept, and put it to work, our economy will become more truly marketing oriented.

## PILLSBURY'S PATTERN: FOUR ERAS

Here is the way the marketing revolution came about at Pillsbury. The experience of this company has followed a typical pattern. There has been nothing unique, and each step in the evolution of the marketing concept has been taken in a way that is more meaningful because the steps are, in fact, typical.

Today in our company the marketing concept finds expression in the simple statement, "Nothing happens at Pillsbury until a sale is made." This statement represents basic reorientation on the part of our management. For, not too many years ago, the ordering of functions in our business placed finance first, production second, and sales last.

How did we arrive at our present point of view? Pillsbury's progress in the marketing revolution divides neatly into four separate eras —eras which parallel rather closely the classic pattern of development in the marketing revolution.

### FIRST ERA—PRODUCTION ORIENTED

First came the era of manufacturing. It began with the formation of the company in 1869 and continued into the 1930's. It is significant that the *idea* for the formation of our company came from the *availability* of high-quality wheat and the *proximity* of water power—and not from the availability and proximity of growing major market areas, or the demand for better, less expensive, more convenient flour products.

Of course, these elements were potentially present. But the two major elements which fused in the mind of Charles A. Pillsbury and prompted him to invest his modest capital in a flour mill were, on the one hand, wheat, and, on the other hand, water power. His principal concern was with production, not marketing.

His thought and judgment were typical of the business thinking of his day. And such thinking was adequate and proper for the times. Our company philosophy in this era might have been stated this way: "We are professional flour millers. Blessed with a supply of the finest North American wheat, plenty of water power, and excellent milling machinery, we produce flour of the highest quality. Our basic function is to mill high-quality flour, and of course (and almost incidentally) we must hire salesmen to sell it, just as we hire accountants to keep our books."

The young company's first new product reveals an interesting example of the thinking of this era. The product was middlings, the bran left over after milling. Millfeed, as the product came to be known, proved a valuable product because it was an excellent nutrient for cattle. But the impetus to launch the new product came not from a consideration of the nutritional needs of cattle or a marketing analysis. It came primarily from the desire to dispose of a by-product! The new product decision was production oriented, not marketing oriented.

### SECOND ERA—SALES ORIENTED

In the 1930's Pillsbury moved into its second era of development as a marketing company. This was the era of sales. For the first time we began to be highly conscious of the consumer, her wants, and her prejudices, as a key factor in the business equation. We established a commercial research department to provide us with facts about the market.

We also became more aware of the importance of our dealers, the wholesale and retail grocers who provided a vital link in our chain of distribution from the mill to the home. Knowing that consumers and dealers as well were vital to the company's success, we could no longer simply mark them down as unknowns in our figuring. With this realization, we took the first step along the road to becoming a marketing company.

Pillsbury's thinking in this second era could be summed up like this: "We are a flour-milling company, manufacturing a number of products for the consumer market. We must have a first-rate sales organization which can dispose of all the products we can make at a favorable price. We must back up this sales force with consumer advertising and market intelligence. We want our salesmen and our dealers to have all the tools they need for moving the output of our plants to the consumer."

Still not a marketing philosophy, but we were getting closer.

### THIRD ERA—MARKETING ORIENTED

It was at the start of the present decade that Pillsbury entered the marketing era. The amazing growth of our consumer business as the result of introducing baking mixes provided the immediate impetus. But the groundwork had been laid by key men who developed our sales concepts in the middle forties.

With the new cake mixes, products of our research program, ringing up sales on the cash register, and with the realization that research and production could produce literally hundreds of new and different products, we faced for the first time the necessity for selecting the best new products. We needed a set of criteria for selecting the kind of products we would manufacture. We needed an organization to establish and maintain these criteria, and for attaining maximum sale of the products we did select.

We needed, in fact, to build into our company a new management function which would direct and control all the other corporate functions from procurement to production to advertising to sales. This function was marketing. Our solution was to establish the present marketing department.

This department developed the criteria which we would use in determining which products to market. *And these criteria were, and are, nothing more nor less than those of the consumer herself.* We moved the mountain out to find out what Mahomet, and Mrs. Mahomet, wanted. The company's purpose was no longer to mill flour, nor to manufacture a wide variety of products, but to satisfy the needs and desires, both actual and potential, of our customers.

If we were to restate our philosophy during the past decade as simply as possible, it would read: "We make and sell products for consumers."

The business universe, we realized, did not have room at the center for Pillsbury or any other company or groups of companies. It was already occupied by the customers.

This is the concept at the core of the marketing revolution. How did we put it to work for Pillsbury?

### The Brand-Manager Concept

The first move was to transform our small advertising department into a marketing department. The move involved far more than changing the name on organizational charts. It required the introduction of a new, and vitally important, organizational concept—the brand-manager concept.

The brand-manager idea is the very backbone of marketing at Pillsbury. The man who bears the title, brand manager, has total accountability for results. He directs the marketing of his product as if it were his own business. Production does its job, and finance keeps the profit figures. Otherwise, the brand manager has total responsibility for marketing his prod-

uct. This responsibility encompasses pricing, commercial research, competitive activity, home service and publicity coordination, legal details, budgets, advertising plans, sales promotion, and execution of plans. The brand manager must think first, last, and always of his sales target, the consumer.

Marketing permeates the entire organization. Marketing plans and executes the sale—all the way from the inception of the product idea, through its development and distribution, to the customer purchase. Marketing begins and ends with the consumer. New product ideas are conceived after careful study of her wants and needs, her likes and dislikes. Then marketing takes the idea and marshals all the forces of the corporation to translate the idea into product and the product into sales.

In the early days of the company, consumer orientation did not seem so important. The company made flour, and flour was a staple—no one would question the availability of a market. Today we must determine whether the American housewife will buy lemon pudding cake in preference to orange angel food. The variables in the equation have multiplied, just as the number of products on the grocers' shelves have multiplied from a hundred or so into many thousands.

When we first began operating under this new marketing concept, we encountered the problems which always accompany any major reorientation. Our people were young and frankly immature in some areas of business; but they were men possessed of an idea and they fought for it. The idea was almost too powerful. The marketing concept proved its worth in sales, but it upset many of the internal balances of the corporation. Marketing-oriented decisions resulted in peaks and valleys in production, schedules, labor, and inventories. But the system worked. It worked better and better as maverick marketing men became motivated toward tonnage and profit.

## FOURTH ERA—MARKETING CONTROL

Today marketing is coming into its own. Pillsbury stands on the brink of its fourth major era in the marketing revolution.

Basically, the philosophy of this fourth era can be summarized this way: "We are moving from a company which has the marketing concept to a marketing company."

Marketing today sets company operating policy short-term. It will come to influence long-range policy more and more. Where today consumer research, technical research, procurement, production, advertising, and sales swing into action under the broad canopy established by marketing, tomorrow capital and financial planning, ten-year volume and profit goals will also come under the aegis of marketing. More than any other function, marketing must be tied to top management.

Today our marketing people know more about inventories than anyone in top management. Tomorrow's marketing man must know capital financing and the implications of marketing planning on long-range profit forecasting.

Today technical research receives almost all of its guidance and direction from marketing. Tomorrow marketing will assume a more creative function in the advertising area, both in terms of ideas and media selection.

### Changes in the Future

The marketing revolution has only begun. There are still those who resist its basic idea, just as there are always those who will resist change in business, government, or any other form of human institution.

As the marketing revolution gains momentum, there will be more changes. The concept of the customer at the center will remain valid; but business must adjust to the shifting tastes and likes and desires and needs which have always characterized the American consumer.

For many years the geographical center of the United States lay in a small Kansas town. Then a new state, Alaska, came along, and the center shifted to the north and west. Hawaii was admitted to the Union and the geographical mid-point took another jump to the west. In very much the same way, modern business must anticipate the restless shifting of buying attitudes, as customer preferences move north, south, east, or west from a liquid center. There is nothing static about the marketing revolution, and that is part of its fascination. The old order has changed, yielding place to the new—but the new order will have its quota of changes, too.

At Pillsbury, as our fourth era progresses, marketing will become the basic motivating force for the entire corporation. Soon it will be true that every activity of the corporation—from finance to sales to production—is aimed at satisfying the needs and desires of the consumer. When that stage of development is reached, the marketing revolution will be complete.

# ADDENDUM: The New Management and The Changing Role of the Corporation

ROBERT J. KEITH

I saw an article recently that suggested the times in which we live should be labeled, "Subject to change without notice."

The same thing could be said about business. Indeed, it is almost redundant to use the words "change" and "business" in the same sentence. Change is of the essence of business; it is occurring at an accelerating pace, fueled by our expanding technologies, whipped along and channeled by the growing demands of the consumer.

As a matter of fact, the biggest single change that I have observed in business has concerned change itself: It is the evolvement of the need to create and not follow change. To be sure, companies continue to have change thrust upon them by technological advances and the pressures of competition. But they have learned that it is possible to reach out and create change instead of waiting for change to come to them.

The changes in business, whether thrust upon it or created by it, are too many to be catalogued. And they are not easily summarized. In an effort to gather my observations into some kind of organized framework, however, I will discuss them:

*First* in terms of the changing corporate structure, and

*Second* in terms of the people we need to deal with and be a part of change.

## MANAGEMENT CHANGES

Corporations, like people, have experienced a population explosion. There are a lot more of them than there used to be, and of course, they are quite different. The men who run them have changed considerably, too.

The chief executive has evolved from a man

◆ SOURCE: Reprinted by permission from the School of Business Administration, University of Minnesota. (A talk delivered before Annual Meeting, Mid-Continent East Region, American Association Collegiate Schools of Business, Oct. 19–20, 1967, Minneapolis, Minn.) pp. 1–9.

who made all the decisions to a man who sees that all the decisions are made. He is no longer able to accomplish his goals through the use of raw power. He must now get the job done with a new set of management tools: information, prediction and persuasion.

The first two of those—information and prediction—are made possible in great measure by the computer. The third—persuasion—has not yet been computerized; it's still up to the executive, and if he had the foresight to get himself a degree in psychology, he finds that it comes in handy.

The computer, a device that does mysterious things routinely and routine things mysteriously, has contributed in a major way to the changing shape of the corporation.

While saving industry from suffocation in its own paperwork, it has—among other things—made industry a much more exciting place for a young businessman to work.

Young men joining the Pillsbury Company today, for example, are likely to find themselves making important decisions—or at least helping to make important decisions—almost as soon as they start receiving their paychecks. Within a few days or weeks they may find themselves on project-teams working on more or less equal footing with vice-presidents and others of stature and long experience.

It used to be—and not very long ago, either —that a man had to work his way up to the rank of department head before he got to decide anything more important than where to eat lunch. Not so anymore. Now he must be equipped to make business decisions when he completes his graduate education, because his apprenticeship will be brief.

## ORGANIZATIONAL CHANGES

What has happened is this: The computer has made possible an information system that has largely dissolved the traditional box-and-line organizational structure of our company. The old organizational charts no longer illustrate the actual working relationships of our managers. They no longer trace the actual flow of information, reports and authority.

The information that used to filter to the Executive Office through layer after organizational layer, arriving in distorted and out-dated form, is now available swiftly, almost instantaneously. The computer draws the information directly from the points of origin in production, sales, marketing and distribution. It classifies, organizes, analyzes and reports simultaneously to every level of management in the company—in as much detail as desired.

This does not mean that the Executive Office is likely to use this abundance of current operating data to totally dominate operations. On the contrary: In the days when the Executive Office got 30-to-45-day-old data, it had to get a feel of the business through involvement. Now that current information is available to give us readings on how things are going, the executive officers are able to withdraw from operations to a degree not possible in the past. It has, to be frank about it, removed us as bottlenecks in the decision-making process.

### NEED FOR SPECIALIST AND GENERALIST

It is not uncommon today for three, four or even five levels of management to come together in one meeting to bring to bear on a problem their various talents and perspectives. That's the way the project-team system works.

The project-team requires, of course, that we have two kinds of men: the specialist who can focus his particular expertise on the problem at hand, and the generalist who can see enough of the whole picture to quarterback the specialists.

It isn't enough for the generalist to know what the specialists are talking about, however. They must know what he's talking about, too. He must know how to use the English language —both in person and on paper. Face-to-face communication is what makes the team work. And he will have reports to write that must be concise to be effective.

### UNDERSTANDING GOVERNMENT IMPORTANT

We need men trained early in life to understand business *and* government. The relationship grows ever closer. There was a time when business ignored government. But as Thomas Gates, chairman of Morgan Guaranty Trust Co., has observed, "It's safe to say that business-government relations have come out of their Ice Age."

On the government side, former Secretary of Commerce Alexander Trowbridge has said: "Business and government today jointly serve America in many ways . . . By focusing on 'public problem-solving,' business is expanding its service to the nation that yields several types of profit. Across the whole broad range of national life, nothing is more essential to continued growth and progress than a sound, balanced relationship between business and government."

It seems clear to me that we need young men trained to the thought that government will influence business and that business, through capable people, will influence government.

### CREATIVITY AND APPROPRIATE REWARDS

I realize that creativity is a pretty nebulous subject to talk about, but nebulous or not I think business has established more avenues for its expression than ever before. We need men who can travel those avenues, for how can we create change without creative people?

I know there's an old saying that poverty is the step-mother of genius. But I happen to think genius should be rewarded handsomely; big salaries should go with big imaginations. In fact, it's not hard to imagine a creator making more money than his boss—in the fashion of a star baseball player who commands a bigger salary than his manager.

I have a closing thought about the attitudes of the young business school graduate: We find too many who are interested in tours of duty rather than a career. They have been encouraged in school, I'm told, to test themselves in several companies.

Viewing changes in business is a little like looking at the world from the observation car of a passenger train: You have a better idea of where you have been than where you are going. I have presented some of the changes as I see them—past, present and future—in terms of the anatomy of the corporation and in terms of the men business needs.

My conclusion is that business now has more to offer a man with a degree than ever—and needs him more than ever. Our hope is that the degree-holder has more to offer, too.

# 36. A Marketing View of Business Policy

WROE ALDERSON

The American economy is a market-oriented economy. It is essential that the top management of successful companies consist of market-oriented executives.

Top management executives who accept the marketing concept must rely on marketing executives who are knowing and skillful users of the techniques of analysis and planning which are still being pioneered by the membership of this association.

What does it mean to assert that the American economy is a market-oriented economy? A market-oriented economy, to begin with, is one in which consumers obtain most goods and services through the market and in which the dynamics of the economy are governed essentially by consumer sovereignty.

Our economy today is surely not the subsistence economy of colonial times which we were still fighting our way out of when Lincoln spoke at Gettysburg. Increasingly our wives are skilled buyers, as in sharp contrast with their great-grandmothers who were primarily skilled operators of household industries.

Our economy is surely a long way from the state capitalism of Russia under which the flow of consumer goods is inadequate in quantity and dreadfully dull in character. Here we seek to maximize the production and use of consumer goods, and, incidentally, to broaden the economic base which can support essential government expenditures for civil or military requirements.

Ours is not the raw materials economy of

◆ SOURCE: Reprinted by permission from *Advancing Marketing Efficiency*, Proceedings of the Winter Conference of the American Marketing Association, December 1958, pp. 114–119.

some underdeveloped countries in which natural resources which might support a good life for all are being steadily depleted to provide luxury for a few. It is true that these raw-materials producers are dependent upon markets, but that is not market orientation.

Ours is not the economy of some European countries dominated by market-sharing cartels and by caste-bound petty tradesmen. We not only welcome change in our society but reserve our greatest rewards for the innovator. Profits in our system are for those who develop products which expand the range of consumer choice or who find better ways of bringing products to market.

Finally, ours is not the economy of classical economic theory. The theorist here typically assumes that the demand follows production rather than the reverse. In marketing we know that investment in specialized and automated capacity, to achieve greater productivity, must follow from a careful assessment of potential demand. The theorist usually assumes that exchange transactions are costless, but one of the essential tasks of the marketing practitioner is to reduce transactional costs which might otherwise be prohibitive. Another economic postulate is that perfect knowledge of markets is a prerequisite for perfect competition. Fortunately, perfect knowledge is not essential to workable competition since the quest for perfect knowledge would bankrupt any firm which adopted it as a fixed goal.

What does it mean to say that top management must consist of market-oriented executives? Certainly, nothing is more significant to the top executive than his sales expectations. In critical situations I have even seen top management pacing the floor waiting for a report on yesterday's sales, but market orientation is more than that. If a man without a marketing background or understanding of the marketing concept is suddenly catapulted into top management responsibility and comes to realize that all of his crucial decisions are now inherently marketing decisions, he has some cause for worry.

Many top executives are star salesmen, even though they have never served in a full time sales capacity. One of their greatest values to their firms may be as charming hosts for leading customers or as shrewd negotiators of major contracts. A company president who is not consciously exerting any sale effort at all may be the ideal symbol for the corporate image the firm wishes to project as part of its effort to maximize sales. But personal selling, however effective, is only one aspect of marketing.

The highest function of the top executive is to think in terms of a system of action, to control or influence the behavior of the system in ways that are favorable to maximizing its output, and to remodel or rebuild the system should changing conditions render it obsolete. The system of action which he must try to understand and direct embraces not only the resources and employees of his firm but the actual and potential customers for its products and the distribution channels by which the firm reaches its customers. The greatest uncertainties within this system of action are those which lie beyond the limits of corporate ownership and control. The problems which will offer the greatest challenge to his creative imagination and objective judgment are problems which arise in the market place.

As he works his way into the all-embracing task of top management, the top executive may remember with some embarrassment the more limited perspective which he reflected in the past. If he comes out of production management, it would be surprising indeed if he had never censured the marketing department for not providing the firm figures on expected requirements which would facilitate his operations. If he will search his memory, he may recollect some statement to the effect that he could scarcely be expected to avoid fluctuations in production unless marketing was willing to specify the monthly or weekly quantities required for each product in the line. Similarly, when chided for swollen inventories, he may have replied that scientific inventory control was impossible unless marketing was ready to set cost figures against lost sales.

If the top executive comes out of research and development, he may now for the first time see some of his most cherished technical projects in the cold light of market acceptance and expected sales and profits. Faced with the urgencies of potential competitive developments, he may be forced to take some risks in the market introduction of products not yet fully perfected, which would have previously seemed intolerable to his scientific spirit.

If he comes out of accounting and finance, he may wonder how he could have ever been so stiff-necked in resisting pleas for functional cost analysis or statistical analysis of sales records to guide management decision. He will undoubtedly acquire a new vision as to the place of long range market forecasts in an investment program and as to degree of flexibility requisite to sound marketing in operating under an expenditure budget.

Even if the top executive comes out of sales and advertising, he will find that he now needs a greater depth of understanding of marketing rather than less. He may have interpreted his past role in terms of unwavering loyalty to his sales force in order that they in turn might be loyal to him. He may have acted as an advocate for a constantly increasing advertising budget on the assumption that the adverse forces were so strong that any budget approved would never be quite enough. As a top executive, the key issue lands squarely in his lap, namely—what is the right amount to spend for sales and advertising?—neither too little nor too much.

More and more, executive preferment will come to those production managers, controllers, research directors, sales and advertising managers who manifest some understanding of the broader marketing concept even while filling subordinate roles. More and more, training for the ultimate responsibilities of top management will include a substantial marketing component in the mix.

\* \* \*

What does it mean to say that we need marketing executives who are knowing and skillful users of techniques pioneered by members of this association?

On the one hand, he should appreciate both the potentialities and the limitations of the analytical techniques now available in solving marketing problems. On the other hand, he should recognize that the greatest pioneering in systematic decision-making still lies ahead and that these advances cannot happen without his collaboration. I am referring particularly to the discipline of marketing planning, currently a backward art compared to the progress which has been achieved in marketing research and analysis.

The stereotype of the self-sufficient executive making one quick decision after another is no longer appropriate in complex and dynamic markets. It is characteristic of marketing decisions to be linked together in interdependent groups. Marketing decisions are linked from customer to customer, from product to product, and in time. A major decision, made in isolation, will almost inevitably make other decisions doubly difficult. Planning is the process of weighing the net effect of a group of interdependent decisions. The planning process provides a framework for strategic decision, a framework that is continuously adjusted to the state of the action system.

A systematic discipline of marketing planning will provide the future pattern of collaboration between an analytical staff and the decision-maker in marketing. This pattern will embrace all of the tested procedures of research and analysis which are now established in marketing. It will use analytical models and electronic simulation of marketing systems which we are only beginning to explore. The difference is that when this approach to planning is fully developed, our present conception of a sequential attack on one problem after another will be largely superseded.

In one sense, effective planning is the stockpiling of prefabricated or semi-fabricated decisions. By determining what should be done in a specified type of repetitious situation, a plan provides in advance for hundreds of such occasions. In another sense, planning is like a tool factory turning out the instruments of more detailed decision-making.

To summarize, a fully developed discipline of marketing planning would accomplish three things:

a. The mass production of decisions concerning repetitive situations.

b. The design of decision rules for handling less frequent and more diverse situations.

c. The maintenance of a comprehensive and up-to-date framework for guiding strategic decisions.

I am really talking here about something that is broader even than planning. I began by asserting that we live in a market-oriented economy which must be guided by market-oriented executives and then attempted to suggest how planning can and must contribute to systematic decision-making. I am attempting to speak today in prophetic mood rather than in didactic tones, to picture what can be done rather than to describe current practice.

Let us now look briefly at one more question which may have come to your minds in the course of this talk. What does all of this have to do with the American Marketing Association and its program for attracting and serving marketing management? Simply, that the subject of greatest moment for the marketing executive as well as for the marketing teacher or the market analyst is the structure of the decision-making process. The marketing executive who can see beyond the limits of his particular company or product field will find much in common with the two groups which now constitute our membership. They need his help in preparing marketing students for executive responsibility and in educating themselves to the changing needs of marketing management. He will obtain in return an enriched understanding of the marketing concept which is now in the forefront of advanced management thinking.

# B. Marketing Research

## 37  The Place of Marketing Research in Economic Activity

### D. MAYNARD PHELPS

Marketing research is concerned with getting the best possible answers to certain major questions of business; namely, what to produce or handle, when and how much to produce, where to place the product over the market, where to direct sales effort, and what price to charge. Questions such as these are never permanently answered, rather they are constantly recurring ones. Frequently—in many cases each season—decisions must be made anew. Therefore, the marketing research task is never completed. Although these questions are simple and easily understood, they are most difficult to answer with any degree of assurance that error is avoided. Undoubtedly the simplicity of the questions belies the difficulty of arriving at correct answers. Yet they must be answered with a considerable degree of effectiveness if an enterprise is to be successful, and, furthermore, if the economic system under which we live is to operate effectively. In a capitalistic economy, responsibility for decisions on these questions may be taken by consumers directly, by producers, or by market intermediaries. As a matter of fact, it is taken partially by each of these groups. But regardless of which group takes responsibility, there must be anticipation of demand, and this leads to observation of the market. First, each of the questions previously enumerated will be considered briefly by way of introduction to the general problem, and the importance of the questions will be discussed. Later, attention will be given to the direction of productive effort—the extent to which the re-

‡‡ SOURCE: Reprinted by permission from *Marketing Research* (Bureau of Business Research, Graduate School of Business Administration, University of Michigan, 1937) pp. 69–74.

sponsibility for answering these questions is assumed by consumers, producers, and market intermediaries. Finally, the difficulties of market observation and the results of faulty decisions will be considered in some detail.

## QUESTIONS OF MARKETING POLICY

### What to Produce

Deciding what to produce is obviously the initial step toward production activity. Agriculture furnishes an illustration in which the individual in charge of a production unit must make a decision at the beginning of each crop year. Yet the farmer's decision is a relatively simple one. Climate and soil conditions narrow the range of product choice appreciably. Moreover, there is in farming, as compared with manufacturing, little opportunity for choice regarding variations in such characteristics of the product as size, quality, and color. Many of the variations in the product as harvested depend not upon independent choice but upon the vagaries of nature during the production period. The manufacturer's problem is essentially more difficult because there is a greater range of possible variations in the finished product and because an independent choice must be made in regard to those variations. When we consider the great variety of products even within narrow classifications, including differences in size, shape, color, and other distinguishing characteristics, likewise the tendency to change products frequently from period to period, the difficulty involved in deciding just what to produce becomes fully apparent.

263

### When and How Much to Produce

We now come to questions concerning the quantity which the market will take and the correct timing of productive effort. Obviously these questions are closely connected. They are not of great importance if the product is one for which the production period is relatively short, for then adjustments to demand can be made without difficulty and errors in judgment are not costly. But when, because of the duration of the production process, a manufacturer must start production many months prior to sale, these questions assume major significance. Moreover, demand for most products has pronounced cyclical and seasonal variations, and if similar fluctuations in production are to be avoided, the manufacturer must be able to produce in advance and store his product. But advance production necessitates the forecasting of demand over a still longer period than the duration of the production process, and thus the problem is further complicated. Nor are problems of cyclical and seasonal demand particularly easy to solve. Moreover, in the usual situation the extent of total demand is not immediately apparent, nor the part of total demand which a company can expect to secure in competition with others. Yet, in order to operate profitably, business executives must arrive at reasonably accurate decisions. Shortage of goods when demand appears, too heavy inventories, perhaps waste through obsolescence, may result from ineffectiveness in determining the correct time at which to produce varying quantities of product.

### Where to Place Products Over the Market

A business enterprise must determine where to place its products geographically in order to meet demand as it appears. Since demand often needs to be satisfied immediately, stocks must be placed in various parts of the country. By a correct placement of stocks it is possible to avoid a shortage at one place and a surplus elsewhere at the same time. If, for example, immediate delivery is wanted for certain units of equipment in one of the southern states and supplies are lacking, heavy supplies in Chicago are of very little value. Particularly is this true in an active competitive situation. Another company with supplies in the South which the buyer can purchase for immediate delivery is likely to secure the order.

In another sense it is likewise necessary to have the product spread correctly over the market. Here we are thinking not of the physical product but of knowledge of the product. Those individuals or institutions who are potential buyers must know of the existence of the product, its qualities and distinguishing characteristics, and the utility which it will give. Although questions of expediency may temporarily dictate otherwise, in general, knowledge of the product should be disseminated over the market in accordance with potential demand. This involves the determination of what type of people or institutions will be likely to purchase the product, and of where they are located.

### What Price to Charge

Most manufacturers enjoy some measure of independence in price determination. The unusual features which differentiate one product from those manufactured by competitors create for the manufacturer a semi-monopolistic situation. While too high a price will lessen demand by causing substitution, it will probably fail to stop purchases completely. A lower price will induce greater purchases. Therefore, an executive must think of varying demands in relation to a range of prices and decide what combination of sales volume and profit per unit sold will result in the highest net profit. Thus it appears that the question of what price to charge often resolves itself into three subordinate questions: (1) How distinctive is the product in question when compared with others of its class? (2) How important are the distinguishing features of the product to consumers? (3) How much extra will consumers be willing to pay for a product embodying these characteristics?

### Importance of Questions Enumerated

Admittedly these questions are not the only important ones which those in charge of business activity are called upon to answer. Still it must be conceded that they are questions of "first degree." The fact of their basic importance does not depend for its demonstration merely upon logical reasoning. It is attested by the heavy expenditures of many large corporations for the designing and perfecting of new products which they hope will be acceptable from the market standpoint, and by the increase in statistical and commercial research departments which attempt to answer the *how much, when,* and *where* questions. Moreover, many business failures can be directly traced to the omission of careful and painstaking study of these questions. In any type of economic system, whether it be socialistic, communistic, or capitalistic, these questions, with the possible exception of that regarding price, must be answered.

Perhaps the comment might be made that the previous remarks assert the obvious, that no one doubts the importance of the questions discussed. But it is all too evident that business concerns frequently blunder along and do not produce the right products, in the correct quantities, at the right time, and that both stocks and sales effort are *not* placed strategically over the market. This indicates one of two things: either those in charge of production do not realize the importance of these questions and consequently neglect them, or, although realizing their importance, they have been unable to answer them effectively. It may likewise indicate the essential difficulty of the problems involved. More will be said of this later. First, it is our task to consider the broad bases upon which the individual business man arrives at conclusions regarding these questions, and the part which he actually plays in directing production.

## THE DIRECTION OF PRODUCTION

Immediately, of course, certain individuals in each concern decide whether a product shall be manufactured. If their decision is in the affirmative, production schedules are arranged, and sooner or later units of product are ready for the market. But in a broader sense the selection of what shall be produced is not in the hands of producers but in those of consumers. In a regime of free enterprise, a capitalistic economy, production is guided by consumers' choices acting through the price system. Individuals receive money incomes as a result of their separate contributions to the productive process, and they are largely free to apportion their incomes among various goods and services as they desire. Whether a person uses a part of his income to buy this or that article depends upon the utility which he thinks it will give him, and upon its cost in relation to the cost and utility of other articles. In a situation where all wants cannot be satisfied, each expenditure is necessarily an alternative one. One product, or perhaps additional units of it, can be had only at the sacrifice of other products. Each individual, therefore, within the limits of his own income and the products and services which are available, determines his own demand schedule. When one product is chosen rather than another, its total demand is thereby increased and the total demand for some other product is necessarily less than it otherwise would be. Increased price is likely to follow increased demand; at any rate, the producer is encouraged to increase output, perhaps through higher prices and therefore greater profits, perhaps through decreased production costs as a result of greater volume at the same prices. Thus it appears that, through the price system, the extent of demand for various products, which is simply an agglomeration of many individual choices, determines what shall be produced, and that, in a very real sense, consumers as a group direct production.[1]

While economists largely agree on the conclusions of this analysis—that consumer choice is the final determinant of what shall be produced—we must recognize that consumers are influenced by producers in their selections of product and that, in many instances, demand does not appear prior to the time that production is started. When an entirely new product is designed and ready for manufacture, or when a well-known product is greatly changed, consumer choice has not had an opportunity to "direct" production and is therefore of little immediate aid to the business man in determining whether the new product should be placed in manufacture, or whether the old product should have been changed. Consumer choice will tell the business executive *later* whether more or less should be produced. But whether it is a good venture to go ahead in the first place is a question that must be decided independently of consumers, or at least without any definite act on their part. Unless a manufacturer has orders in advance, he must *anticipate* what consumer wants and choices will be. Thus, in many cases, production is directed, not by consumers' choices in the first instance, but by *anticipation* on the part of producers of what consumers' choices will be. The tool which the business man must then use is *observation* of the market. Thus we see that, in determining what and how much to produce, the business man follows one of two guides—either orders in advance or observation of the market.

---

[1] See F. M. Taylor, *Principles of Economics* (New York: The Ronald Press, 1925), chap. 45; also R. T. Bye and W. H. Hewett, *Applied Economics* (New York: Alfred A. Knopf, 1928), chap. 3.

# 38. Market Measurement in a Free Society

RALPH CASSADY, JR.

In a free society, some knowledge of consumer demand is not merely desirable but an absolute necessity if vendors are to be successful.[1] Those offering goods and services must know not only the type of merchandise desired by consumer-buyers, but also the style of item preferred, the amount consumers will take, the nature of service desired, where consumers can expect to buy the product, the particular time the item is required, and how much prospective buyers will pay for it. It is only after knowing these things that vendors can safely attempt to promote the sale of their merchandise offerings without incurring losses due to consumer resistance.

The key to intelligent competitive activity is market research which seeks information about consumer wants and behavior patterns to serve as a basis for effective marketing activity.

## HOW THE MARKET IS INVESTIGATED

There are, of course, various methods of obtaining market information available to those who undertake the responsibility of providing for consumer wants. It is the main purpose of this paper to consider such procedures and to relate them to various specific marketing problems.

Before examining the several market research methods in detail, a number of preliminary points should be made about market research as compared with other types of scientific investigation.

## BASIC RESEARCH METHODS

As in every other field of knowledge, only a limited number of basic research methods are available to the investigator who is interested in probing markets. This is not to say that there are not innumerable research techniques available for use in our investigatory activity, but only that various devices possess basic characteristics which permit classification into only one of a very few categories.

While hypothesis-testing[2] is used as a research device in economic (including market) analyses, its use is not as extensive as in some other areas. One reason for this, perhaps, is that the state of knowledge in the marketing field is such that research has been confined largely to exploratory investigation, and less emphasis has been placed on precise explanations for various developments.

It is in this latter phase of research activity that hypotheses are most useful. One might add

---

[1] The only exception to this is in a sellers' market when the competition for supplies of goods is much more intensive than the competition for customers, e.g., in wartime.

‡‡ SOURCE: Reprinted by permission from the *California Management Review*, Vol. 2, No. 2, Winter 1960, Copyright 1960 by The Regents of the University of California.

[2] According to Webster's (*Webster's New International Dictionary*, 2nd ed., Unabridged) a hypothesis is "2. A proposition, condition, or principle which is assumed, perhaps without belief, in order to draw out its logical consequences and by this method to test its accord with facts which are known or may be determined."

that those engaged in economic investigations often appear to confuse hypotheses (tentative explanations) with theory (confirmed generalizations).

In economic investigations, heavy reliance is placed on inference for conclusions. This is due, in part at least, to the difficulty of employing experimentation in this field. For example, if in an analysis of market data a marked change appears in the statistical pattern, which upon further analysis is found to coincide with a particular development that reasonably could have had an effect on the results, an inference is apt to be drawn that it did indeed have such an effect.

But research which leads to inferential conclusions is not unique to economic analysis. It will be recalled that the cigarette-lung cancer researches have thus far been mostly statistical, with inferential conclusions being based upon the apparent relationship between heavy smoking and the incidence of this disease.

While statistical studies may result in a strong inference toward a cause and effect relationship between cigarette smoking and lung cancer, the heavy smoking and the cancer might conceivably both stem from a common cause. Hence experimentation must be employed to confirm or invalidate the hypothetical conclusion that heavy smoking is the causal factor.[3]

Market researchers must, in large part (as in some other new areas of investigation) devise their own apparatus for market-measurement purposes. The mark of a good research man in this field is his ability to design effective methods of measuring various market phenomena, such as buying habits, brand preferences, market potentials, etc. Thus, over the years, there have been contrived all kinds of ingenious devices for measuring market behavior, including pantry surveys (which serve as the basis for drawing inferences concerning consumer brand preferences), mechanical recorder attachments for radios and television sets (which reveal the listening and viewing habits of householders), retail-store brand-preference audits (which reflect consumer buying habits),

consumer diaries (which provide invaluable information concerning buyer preferences and practices), and automobile license number studies (which reveal much information about consumer patronage habits in relation to various retail institutions).[4]

Research methods in the marketing field as in other disciplines may be classified as deductive (seeking answers by the application of logic to a problem) and inductive (seeking answers by empirical study of the problem).

## DEDUCTIVE ANALYSIS

Although stress in market research is laid on inductive investigation, those who are well versed in research methodology do not "look down their noses" at deductive analysis. Deduction is an extremely effective supplementary research tool. Indeed, inductive research would lose much of its effectiveness without the aid of deductive analysis.

Some deductive activity is merely hypothesizing,[5] designed either to provide tentative explanations of certain phenomena or to suggest a possible behavior pattern, say, which might be subject to test later on. However, deductive investigation may extend knowledge at least in the sense of making clear the full implications of inductively-established conclusions.

Thus deductive analysis may serve at least three purposes in market investigation:

1. It may suggest hypothetical relationships whose actual existence may be later subject to test through inductive means.

2. It may provide tentative explanations of phenomena which may later be confirmed or vitiated through inductive study.

3. It may make possible the extrapolation of knowledge gained from inductive investigations by providing inferential conclusions based on fact-founded premises.

There has been considerable advancement in our thinking concerning buyer attitudes and competitive behavior at the abstract level during the past 25 years as a result of investigative effort which might reasonably be classed as market research. Thus, the work of Prof. Edward H. Chamberlin and Mrs. Joan Robinson

---

[3] A difficulty here might be the devising of experimental methods which would not endanger the health of human "guinea pigs." This does not mean, however, that investigations that endanger health are precluded. It will be recalled that Dr. Walter Reed made use of volunteers in his famous yellowjack investigations of sixty years ago which were designed to test the hypothesis that mosquitos were carriers from which infection resulted.

[4] See Ralph Cassady, Jr. and Harold M. Haas, "Analyzing the Market of Mail Order House Retail Stores," *Harvard Business Review*, Summer 1935, pp. 493–502.

[5] See footnote 2.

is based almost entirely on deductive analysis and, while still largely hypothetical, has led to the development of the area of nonperfect competition with its classification based on variation in numbers, differentiation of product, and amount of market information in possession of buyers and sellers.

The author's own studies have been in part deductive in nature also. For example, some years ago, J. M. Clark published a trail-blazing article on what he called "workable competition." [6] In this presentation Prof. Clark suggested the possibility (or perhaps better, the probability) that elasticity of demand was substantially conditioned by the passage of time.[7] This led to a great deal of reflection by this author on the time element as it affects consumer demand, and ultimately to a publication of his views.[8]

While these hypotheses are still subject to confirmation, some headway has been made by isolating the issues and thus simplifying the task for the inductive investigator and indeed in informing practical marketing executives about probable consumer behavior patterns.

To take another example, this author was a participant in a recent international roundtable on fisheries and fishery products. The discussion included the nature of the demand for fish by American consumers. One part of the analysis was concerned with cross-elasticity of demand between fish and meat (i.e., the impact on the sale of one product resulting from a change in the price of another).

Ordinarily, a high degree of cross-elasticity between two competing products would mean that when the price of one goes up the amount taken of the other increases and vice versa. Fish, however, is considered by Americans to be a second-class food and hence—according to this hypothesis—cross-elasticity would appear to be much lower when a change in price favors fish than when a change in price favors meat.[9]

While this hypothesis still remains to be tested, the formulation of the hypothetical proposition is a definite step toward the solution of the problem because it isolates the question which needs to be answered and prevents wasted investigatory effort. Although no suggestion is being made at this time regarding a scheme which one might use to test this hypothesis, there is little doubt that a testing device can be devised in time.

It is this writer's opinion that even without confirmation deductive analysis may be valuable because of the fact that it provides the practitioner with a suggestion as to possible behavior patterns that might alert him to potential dangers and opportunities. The possibility for instance that the impact of a price change will be greater over time than it is at the moment the change is made may be of great significance to those engaged in actual market operations.

Similarly, practitioners stand to gain greatly from a hypothetical finding that consumer demand for various products and services may vary greatly during a day or week and that greater response can be expected to the offerings of vendors if consideration is given to the place where consumers are when they feel the need of the item most keenly.[10]

## INDUCTIVE ANALYSIS

Despite the valuable contributions of deductive analysis, the large bulk of market research activity is inductive in nature. That is, findings are the result of actual market investigation. While the methods utilized in field study differ greatly in details, basically there are only three inductive approaches available to market researchers.[11] These will be discussed briefly in following paragraphs.

## OBSERVATIONAL METHOD

Under this scheme (which is, of course, relied on very heavily by astronomers) information is derived either directly or indirectly by observing and recording the phenomena under study, for example, the behavior of people who are going about their normal daily tasks—pre-

[6] J. M. Clark, "Toward a Concept of Workable Competition," *The American Economic Review*, June 1940, pp. 241–256.

[7] See p. 247 of footnote 6.

[8] See Ralph Cassady, Jr., "The Time Element and Demand Analysis," Cox and Alderson (eds.), *Theory in Marketing* (Chicago: Richard D. Irwin, 1950), pp. 193–207.

[9] Ralph Cassady, Jr., "The Marketing of Fishery Products in the United States," Turvey and Wiseman, (eds.), *The Economics of Fisheries* (Rome: Food and Agriculture Organization of the United Nations, 1958), p. 201.

[10] E.g., ice-cold "Coke" in service stations and places of work.

[11] The author is indebted to Professor D. M. Phelps for his extremely able analysis of marketing research methodology as described in *Marketing Research* (Ann Arbor: University of Michigan Press, 1937).

paring meals, keeping house, listening to the television, moving about the community, shopping, performing marketing functions, etc. As was suggested immediately above, observation may be performed directly in a first-hand manner or it may have been performed by someone else at an earlier time and only later reported by the observer as a result of second-hand investigation.

## DIRECT OBSERVATION

In the use of this approach, observations are made at the time the event is taking place. For example, an observer at some carefully selected vantage point is able to tell a great deal about consumer acceptance of a particular style (e.g., the number of men out of every hundred wearing Homburg hats). The author participated in a foot-traffic study for a certain location on Market Street in San Francisco some years ago in order to determine, by actual count, the types of persons passing by the place under study and the time of passing. This information then could be utilized as a basis for deciding the most effective use of the retail location under study.

Similarly, a tabulation of automobile license numbers found in parking lots of two Midwestern retail establishments yielded vast amounts of useful market information, such as the number of patrons at different times of the day and week, the distances traveled by customers from home to the store, and (determined from the location of the home of each car owner) the estimated income bracket of the patrons.[12]

One recently reported application of the direct observational method in American business is the use of a one-way mirror (so-called) to permit a study of the reactions of children to various types of toys with which they have been invited to play, without awareness on their part that they are being observed.

Diary studies, based on detail records of consumer purchases and commonly used by market researchers to derive information about family living and purchasing habits, are basically similar to the schemes just discussed except that the diarist is often both the observer and the observed.

## INDIRECT OBSERVATION

Under this scheme, observations are made after the event has taken place (although some

recording of events might have taken place earlier) and reliance is placed on existing evidence of what has occurred in the past rather than on personal observation of the event as it occurred. Essentially, this is feasible because past developments usually leave in their wake some evidence in the form of records or reports by participants or primary observers which may be utilized as a basis for determining what took place at an earlier time.[13]

The indirect observational method may be classed either as qualitative or quantitative.

## QUALITATIVE INVESTIGATION

In this type of investigation the information the researcher is attempting to obtain concerning past events is essentially subjective rather than statistical in nature. Some of our historical studies are essentially taxonomic—that is, their contribution to understanding is based largely on the systematizing of the information gathered so as to make such data more comprehensible and thus applicable in planning market strategy.[14]

A qualitative study of the Los Angeles wholesale grocery trade several years ago revealed the evolutionary change from the full-service type of operation to the limited-function method of food distribution which, of course, is a reflection of changing consumer patronage habits.[15] Similarly, the writer has been working recently on a study of price warfare (including consumer behavior patterns found therein) in which he relies to some extent on records of past events. These records may in turn be in the form of second-hand observations rather than reports by direct observers at an earlier time.[16]

---

[13] It should be noted that the indirect observational method is so designated because the researcher does not observe phenomena directly but reports on the observations that someone else has made.

[14] See, for example, Ralph Cassady, Jr., "Techniques and Purposes of Price Discrimination," *The Journal of Marketing*, October 1946, pp. 135–150, which is essentially a classification of price discrimination methods employed by various types of individuals and firms in the business and professional world.

[15] See Ralph Cassady, Jr. and Wylie L. Jones, *The Changing Competitive Structure in the Wholesale Grocery Trade* (Berkeley: University of California Press, 1949).

[16] See, for example, a description of the Santa Fe–Southern Pacific rate wars of the mid-eighties found in Glenn S. Dumke, *The Boom of the Eighties in Southern California* (San Marino: Huntington Library, 1944), pp. 17–27.

---

[12] On a basis of the relationship between income and housing cost. See footnote 4.

It is sometimes possible to interview direct observers simultaneously with the unfolding of the event observed (e.g., interrogating those actively engaged in a price war). However, there is a question as to whether participants in particular economic behavior situations (such as price warfare) should be interviewed *during* such altercations or after they are concluded.

Some argue that the former is the correct approach because the events are fresh in the minds of the participants and the researcher is therefore likely to get a more accurate appraisal of conditions and motivations. However, a major objection to this approach is that participants' views may be distorted by emotional reactions and, indeed, such individuals may be reluctant to tell the whole truth when the outcome of the struggle might be affected by such a revelation.

Qualitative historical research results may have commercial as well as pure research value. For example, some business concerns have made use of analytical studies of certain types of existing legal restrictions on selling activities, with the purpose of establishing a basis for planning future market strategy. By knowing the nature of the legislative restrictions which condition a firm's activities in relation to consumer-behavior patterns, management may be able to make a more intelligent decision as to whether it should attempt to meet consumer needs through its own method of operation or to withdraw from the particular field. Indeed, the firm may actually choose to remain in the field and seek some easing of the restrictions through the legislative process.

## QUANTITATIVE INVESTIGATION

The market information sought by quantitative studies is essentially statistical in nature. One interesting application of this type of investigation to market-measurement problems is an analysis which was made of the shift of retail trade of a large metropolitan area from the central shopping district to outlying areas. This investigation was conducted by recasting Census of Business data from political subdivisions to economic subregions, thus providing a basis for measuring the movement of trade from one time to another.[17]

Similarly, some years ago a study was conducted of the seasonal behavior of apple prices to serve as a basis for a top-level executive decision in a large food chain organization. This analysis, which was predicated on published auction price statistics, had the specific purpose of providing an answer to the question as to whether a large food firm might find it more profitable to acquire title to supplies of this type of product early in the season rather than to continue purchasing the goods as needed on a hand-to-mouth basis.

It should be obvious that if conclusions are to be drawn regarding general behavior patterns which are to be considered generally applicable to other similar situations, the historical data chosen for observation must be properly representative of the whole universe under study.

## INTERROGATION METHOD

This approach is relied on very heavily by researchers who inquire into human behavior and motivation (e.g., psychologists). Some types of market information cannot readily be acquired except by the use of such techniques. For example, a person's income (and hence his purchasing power) may not be accurately obtainable by observation (although, of course, certain inferences might be drawn regarding this matter on a basis of one's occupation or place of residence). Thus investigators must resort to interrogation if adequate information is to be obtained.[18]

The survey method of research (as it is sometimes called) relies not on observing what people do but on gathering information which reposes in people's minds and which must be acquired by questioning individual respondents. A large part of market research, of course, is based on the use of this general method of investigation.

---

[17] See William K. Bowden and Ralph Cassady, Jr., "Decentralization of Retail Trade in the Metropolitan Market Area," *The Journal of Marketing*, January 1941, pp. 270–275, and Ralph Cassady, Jr. and W. K. Bowden, "Shifting Retail Trade Within the Los Angeles Metropolitan Market," *The Journal of Marketing*, April 1944, pp. 398–404.

[18] It must be admitted that there is a danger of upward bias in attempting to gain information about incomes through interrogation, due to the element of prestige which is connected with high incomes, although this would depend to some extent at least on the agency collecting the data. (Some companies no longer require job applicants to list salaries earned on former jobs, since it has been found that these are frequently overstated by a $1,000 a year or more.) The U. S. Bureau of Census can undoubtedly obtain income data in its sample studies with a certain degree of accuracy.

Information which may be obtained by survey techniques includes the number of persons in various age groups. For example, the number of youngsters between 10 and 14 years of age might serve as a basis for estimating the market for some proposed children's magazine. Information may be obtained concerning individuals' reading habits, brand preferences, patronage habits, motivational influences, and future purchasing plans by survey also.

Just as in the observational approach, great care must be taken to obtain scientifically selected samples in survey studies. This is a highly technical procedure and requires a great amount of skill if sound results are to be obtained. In addition, however, it is necessary to prepare properly constructed questionnaires and to select and train skilled field personnel.

## SIMPLE INTERVIEWING

In this type of procedure the questions to be asked are predetermined and precisely stated and the interviewer is not permitted to depart from the schedule of queries previously prepared. Care must be taken to ask questions which will elicit from the respondent the desired information with the least amount of bias or distortion.

A simple question in a gasoline patronage study, asking for the brand of gasoline purchased most recently and in which station it was purchased, should yield sound and valuable market information. Likewise, questions concerning the brand of shortening the housewife has on hand should produce equally successful results. Questions concerning the television program which one watched at a specified recent time should also result in the required information. (It is interesting, incidentally, that the latter type of information might be obtained through observational methods (i.e., a recording device can be attached to the television chassis.)

The interrogation method was utilized several years ago in a study of consumer meat-purchasing habits in a Midwestern community to determine to what extent consumer buyers shift their patronage from one institution to another in accordance with lower prices offered, as a basis for a defense against a charge of violation of a "cost floor" act.[19]

## DEPTH INTERVIEWING

It is well recognized by competent market researchers that motivation cannot be accurately determined by ordinary questioning, either because respondents do not know why they behave as they do or because they do know but are reluctant to tell. Motivational research techniques are those which are designed to determine why who does what when. The depth interviewing technique, undoubtedly borrowed from the psychoanalyst (who in turn borrowed it from the anthropologist), is designed to overcome the limitations inherent in simple (closed-end) interrogation. In this technique, questions to be asked are only generally outlined with the expectation that the subtle aspects of the respondent's behavior will be discovered by intensive discussion. Thus, by skillful probing, reluctance of respondents is overcome and memories refreshed.

Deep-seated information concerning preferences for certain brands of a particular food item may be discovered by means of depth-interviewing techniques.[20] A survey of Palm Springs pay-television subscribers several years ago elicited interesting and extremely valuable information concerning consumer attitudes on subscription television service which may be applicable generally. Thus, depth interviewing makes possible the substitution of basically sound responses for "top-of-the-mind" answers.

## EXPERIMENTAL METHOD

Experimentation which is employed so extensively in certain of the physical sciences (e.g., chemistry), also may be advantageously employed by investigators into market phenomena. Experimentation—in a broad sense at least—may under certain circumstances be clas-

[19] The point here was that such legislation typically permits the meeting of competitors' lower prices for comparable merchandise, but the question in this instance was whether consumers might not shift patronage in response to lower prices for an inferior product, and hence the firm selling the superior product might have to protect its position by offering its product at lower prices.

[20] The results of one such study are given in an article by William F. Brown, "The Determination of Factors Influencing Brand Choice," *The Journal of Marketing*, April 1950, pp. 699–706. For additional information on depth interviewing see the American Marketing Association's Research Committee report, "Depth Interviewing," in the same issue of *The Journal of Marketing*, pp. 721–724, and L. M. Paradise and A. B. Blankenship, "Depth Questioning," *The Journal of Marketing*, January 1951, pp. 274–288.

sified as an observational type of investigation, but is distinguished from the first-named approach by the fact that in the experimental scheme test conditions are prearranged. Thus, people are observed not as they go about their normal tasks but in an artificial situation devised for the particular purpose. This procedure may be classified as either simple or controlled.

## SIMPLE EXPERIMENTATION

This term suggests that the experiment is not controlled—that is—no attempt is made to provide a bench mark of normal expectation against which results may be measured. For example, a firm might simply wish to find out whether a certain demand manipulative scheme is likely to be successful. By the use of a consumer jury technique, it is possible to determine which of a number of different sales appeals is most attractive to consumer buyers. Or a firm, in bringing out a new brand of shaving cream, may desire to test the item simply by providing a sample of the proposed product to a panel of consumers and probing their reactions to the new item.

There are innumerable other applications of simple experimentation in market research. For example, a large retail concern may wish to test the efficacy of telephone selling by store employees. Such a test can be conducted by selecting the names of a certain segment of its charge list to whom the phone calls might be made announcing certain special offerings. Purchases of all such individuals then may be recorded and, on a basis of sales results, the promotional device evaluated. An interesting application of the technique has been employed also in the entertainment field in probing audience response to a presentation by instructing panel members to express their reactions to a test performance through the use of a recording device.[21]

Simple experimentation may be used in pricing studies also. The head of an outstanding American market research organization devised a scheme some years ago which was designed to aid in the pricing of a new brand or make of product. This scheme called for a panel of consumer jurors to evaluate the new brand

against competitive offerings.[22] The new article, unpriced, was available for examination by the jurors along with the products with which this item might be expected to compete.[23] Thus each consumer juror "priced" the product in comparison with the standard composed of all competitive items in the field.

While a control in the usual sense was absent in this experiment, a standard was provided against which consumers could evaluate the new item. It is interesting, as a side-point, that the results of such an experiment might provide the vendor with an approximation of a miniature demand curve for his product.

Each of these schemes, it should be noted, is based on some sort of prearrangement of conditions but is uncontrolled. While some types of experimental investigations may not require controls for sound research results (see above), some do. The *sine qua non* of some investigations is an evaluation of the impact of a particular stimulus on market results. In such investigations, the absence of some sort of control is a serious flaw because without it, it is impossible to isolate the stimulus under study from other stimuli which may have a simultaneous effect on market results.

## CONTROLLED EXPERIMENTATION

The aim of controlled experimentation is to keep all stimuli precisely the same in the experimental as well as in the control group, except the one whose effect is being studied, so that the results from the one stimulus can be distinguished from those of others. Referring to the telephone sales study mentioned above: How is one to tell that sales made to those telephoned *resulted* from such calls when some of the individuals might have visited the store and purchased the merchandise even in the absence of the specific stimulus under study?

It is not enough to know what the sales were in a pretest period, and to assume that any increase in the test-period sales resulted from the stimulus under test, because other

---

[21] For further information on this method see Ralph Cassady, Jr., "Statistical Sampling Techniques and Marketing Research," *The Journal of Marketing*, April 1945, p. 339.

[22] See Wroe Alderson, "New Applications for Market Research," *Sales Management*, February 1, 1947, p. 46.

[23] It is not clear from Alderson's brief description of the experiment (See footnote 22) whether the prices of the competing products were indicated to panel members, but the present author would be inclined to believe that best results would be obtained if such prices were available to the test group.

stimuli (such as seasonal or industrial changes) might have occurred simultaneously and these may have caused *all* sales to increase at this time. As a basis of measuring the results of a specific stimulus (telephone calls to test group), one must compare results with the purchasing behavior of a control group made up of individuals of the same type in all respects except that they have not been subjected to the specific stimulus under study (i.e., telephone solicitation).

To take another example: A company might wish to test a formula of a proposed product by providing panel members with supplies of the item under consideration along with supplies of the leading brand in the field in masked containers as a sort of "control,"[24] after which panel members may be questioned concerning preferences, and observations can be made of remaining amounts of product.[25]

And still another: A firm might wish to determine to what extent (if at all) a counter display rack would enhance sales for a particular brand of product, for example, razor blades. To determine effectiveness of the rack, sales might be recorded in a store selected for the purpose during a pretest period and then be compared with sales of the store during the test period. But the use of another store (similar in all respects to the first except that no display rack is utilized) would serve as a control which would make possible the isolation of the sales resulting from the use of the display rack from those resulting from other existing stimuli.[26]

Controlled experimentation also lends itself to studies of the effectiveness of alternative prices and pricing arrangements.[27] For example, a chain store organization may wish to know the most effective price to charge for a single unit of a specific item or for a multiple offering of the same item.

The question of a multiple offering may involve subquestions regarding the effectiveness of a multiple offering *per se* (where the price charged for the group as a whole is the same as the price of the individual unit times the number of units making up the group) as compared with multiple-unit offerings where the total price of the group reflects discounts for quantity. If the regular price of the item were 10 cents, the problem might indeed be to determine what sales results might be expected from offering the item at two for 20 cents, at 9 cents per unit, at two for 18 cents, or at two for 19 cents.

In order to obtain a definitive answer to this problem, several cooperating stores must be used, including the control store (at which the regular price is charged).[28]

This method might also be used in solving other market-measurement problems. These could include packaging problems (consumer preferences for tin versus glass containers, or mesh sacks versus paper bags, etc.), and shelving of merchandise (position in relation to eye-level, location of goods in relation to a family of related items, amount of shelf frontage for each item, etc.). It might, in addition, be used to study the effect of the introduction of new products (impact on any competing items already in stock as well as on related items), and improvements in store equipment (effectiveness in serving consumers resulting from mechanized check-out stands). Undoubtedly, controlled experimentation techniques may be utilized in other studies of consumer behavior and response.[29]

Controlled experimentation in market research is not confined to sales-test studies. The

---

[24] This type of experimentation has certain limitations. For example, its use is greatly restricted if not actually precluded in some fields (such as drugs) by legislative circumscriptions. However, this type of test may have applications in certain lines which do not appear to be promising (appliances, say), although experimental conditions must be adapted to the peculiar circumstances of the product under study.

[25] It should be noted that what panel members may say about their preferences may not jibe with the consumption habits as evidenced by residual amounts of product. When such a correlation is absent, it may reveal certain very subtle preference patterns (such as liking ease of preparation but disliking the flavor) of the product under consideration.

[26] The difficulty, of course, is to find stores which are sufficiently similar to one another (in sales, location, type of patronage, etc.) to be used as a basis of comparison.

[27] William Applebaum and Richard F. Spears, "Controlled Experimentation in Marketing Research," *The Journal of Marketing*, January 1950, p. 513.

[28] The result must, of course, be measured by the percentage change in sales between the pretest and test periods. Generally speaking, if a change in the number sold is no greater in test stores than in the control store, it indicates that the change in prices was not the causal factor.

[29] Applebaum and Spears, *op. cit.*, pp. 512–515.

projective technique (which is designed to elicit uninhibited judgments from those under study) might be considered an example of controlled experimentation. In this scheme, the respondent is asked to project himself or herself into situations which are different in only one respect, and to interpret given phenomena, thereby disclosing deep-seated attitudes or motives of such individuals.

For example, if one wishes to determine secret or subconscious consumer attitudes toward instant coffee, he might (as one researcher did)[30] prepare two lists of food items precisely the same in every respect except for the inclusion of instant coffee in one and regular coffee in the other, and ask respondents to characterize the persons who purchased each group of food items. From the respondents' attitudes toward the purchaser of a certain type of item one can infer attitudes toward the item itself.

The scheme makes possible the discovery of biases which might not be readily revealed otherwise because ostensibly the respondent is not making a self-analysis but rather an evaluation of others, and, moreover, it isolates the respondent's attitude toward the item under test by controlling all conditioning stimuli except this one. A similar scheme has been used to test the inner attitudes of housewives toward trading stamps.[31]

One final point might be made *re* the use of controlled experimentation in market research: While the concept of control is very simple, the effective application of this scheme to market research problems is extremely difficult. The main reason for this is that controlling all factors except the one under study, while easy enough in medical research,[32] is difficult

in market research because of the existence of innumerable variables between test and control situations which may alter results in one but not in the other, hence vitiating conclusions. However, with all of its limitations, we can look for greater and greater use of controlled experimentation in market research because of the promise of more precise solutions to demand-analysis problems.

## CONCLUSIONS

The author has attempted to present an overview picture of the methods which may be employed in determining the market for firm and industry offerings. While it is true that the consumer in the free-enterprise system may choose as he pleases, hence complicating the job of the vendor, there is little excuse for ignorance on the part of sellers concerning the markets they are serving at this stage of our knowledge of research methodology. Actually, methods of investigation are available which may provide vendors with needed market knowledge.

It should be noted, however, that the various methods are not alternative schemes of investigation to be chosen as one chooses the color of a jacket to be worn on a certain day. Rather, the method should be selected as an expert chooses a golf club for a specific task to be performed. Usually only one scheme will precisely produce the results one wishes to achieve, although some studies must be based on a combination of methods because of the limitations of any one method in providing all of the information required. The trouble in golf *and* research is that one must be skilled enough to be able to choose the most effective implement to use.

One final word: Information concerning markets, no matter how complete and accurate, is no substitute for intelligent executive action. That is, the results of market investigations do not automatically provide answers to the best course to take, given all the circumstances of the problem with which the firm is faced. Moreover, decisions have to be made concerning hundreds of different questions which cannot economically be studied or which are beyond the purview of the investigator. It must be kept in mind, further, that even assuming information is available, intelligent use must be made of it. The point is, however, the market research findings should be extremely helpful tools to those who are responsible for making wise managerial decisions.

[30] The results of such an experiment, Mason Haire, "Projective Techniques in Marketing Research," *The Journal of Marketing*, April 1950, pp. 649–656, indicate that (a) instant coffee on food lists is viewed by certain respondents as evidence of laziness on the part of the housewife (p. 653), and (b) this attitude is fairly deep-seated because respondents having such views do not purchase the product themselves (p. 655).

[31] Bertrand Klass, "The Controversies Surrounding Motivation Research," *Proceedings of the Fourth Annual Meeting—Social Science for Industry* (Menlo Park: Stanford Research Institute, April 4, 1956), pp. 46–47.

[32] Giving a serum to every other patient, applying a medicament to burns on only one side of the face, etc.

# 39. Psychology in Market Research

ERNEST DICHTER

The fact that the businessman must market his products means that he must deal with people—his customers, the users of his services. The psychologist too deals with people. Both businessman and psychologist are interested in what makes people tick, what motivates them, and how they can be molded and influenced. This article, then, is an exploration of how businessmen can work together with modern psychologists and make use of their fund of special knowledge, particularly in the marketing of consumers' goods.

## CONSUMER MOTIVATIONS

American industry has been fairly successful with machinery and technical processes, and there have also been some attempts to control the more obvious human factors like safety, labor relations, aptitudes, and morale. Likewise definite beginnings have been made in the measurement of markets: We know how to determine sales potentials, we can make product tests, we can measure attitudes, and we know something about the effectiveness of advertising campaigns.

But by and large we are still using outmoded and inefficient methods to determine and understand consumer motivations. We are only scratching the surface. In making marketing decisions, we are relying on surveys based on what people say they think and feel. Yet even in the everyday aspects of modern life we have learned to distinguish between what a man

❁ SOURCE: Reprinted by permission from *Harvard Business Review*, Vol. 25, No. 4, Summer 1947, pp. 432–443.

says and what he really means deep down. We know that to deny jealousy, for example, is very frequently only an admission of the emotion. We know that often we do things because of inferiority feelings. We also know that we forget names and objects and tasks because of an unconscious desire not to remember. We know that constant denial of pleasure to a child will frustrate him and that frustration leads to aggression.

In these and many other ways we are, bit by bit, introducing modern scientific thinking into our everyday lives. It would seem to be time to take similar steps in industry and commerce, where an understanding of human nature is basic and where so much is at stake. For instance, we already know that fear and psychological depressions are more dangerous than economic setbacks; in fact, they often cause such setbacks. The interdependence of cold, sober business statistics and deeply seated human motivations is obvious even to the completely untrained. In marketing where we have no direct control over the factors with which we must contend and where we must make decisions on the basis of what is at best intangible evidence—here especially we need all the clear insight we can get.

Cooperation between the practical businessman and the psychologist is not just a nice or desirable state; rather it is an essential development if we are to progress from a medicine-man stage of selling and advertising to a scientifically controllable one. Of course the businessman will not and cannot apply to the psychologist for help with all his marketing problems. There are a number of clearly visible situations, however, when he can reasonably assume that normal research resources will not suffice. Questions like the following present real challenges:

*Do You Really Know Why Your Customers Like or Dislike Your Product?* Your customers tell you they bought a particular make of car because of its "performance," "economy," or "trade-in value." Are you sure these are the real reasons? Many surveys have shown that they are but pure rationalizations. They were mentioned in answer to the usual type of questioning because they sounded better, more logical. This becomes clear when you compare the motivating reasons for purchase given by Ford buyers, Plymouth buyers, and Chevrolet buyers; they are exactly the same for all three.

Deeper reasoning, then, must have been at work. Emotional factors such as loyalty, fear, and tradition are usually much more important than the actual quality differences which people are likely to offer as reasons. Obviously an advertising campaign which does not rely on the answers to "surface" questioning but which capitalizes on the actual motivating forces revealed by questioning that digs down into people's minds is much more likely to be effective.

*Do You Know What Kind of People Your Customers Are?* Although you may know the average age, income, educational level, and so on, of your customers—the factors usually sought for in market surveys—you may still not know the real factors that determine their acceptance or rejection of your product. For example, the degree of customer security or insecurity (in a psychological sense) may be the all-important variable which you have to ascertain before you can market your product intelligently. Suppose the product is a deodorant. The appeals which will influence persons who are desperately anxious to be socially acceptable may fall flat with persons who already feel satisfied with their position.

*Are You Sure You Do Not Insult Your Customers?* Suppose you are in the pipe tobacco business. Your advertising uses colorful language to describe the aroma of your tobaccos in order to make them sound more desirable than your competitors' products. Yet, unless you are careful, many of the words you use may arouse feminine associations of a nature unpleasant to the pipe smoker, intent as he is on convincing himself of his masculinity. A study showed "aromatic," which on the surface sounds like a perfectly good word, to be of this type. Many times manufacturers run up against other such obscure inhibitions, deep-seated

prejudices, hatreds, negative associations, and unconscious forms of resistance which, when uncontrolled, may play havoc with their sales.

These are just a few examples of the kinds of problem which a businessman selling consumer products may run into and which, when attacked by customary means, i.e., either by pure guess work or by inadequate, purely statistical market research, may lead to trouble. In a broad sense, any time a businessman is in doubt about why his customers act the way they do, or, in other words, any time he must deal with a *why* question, a truly scientific approach to his problem is indicated.

Of course there are many questions that can be answered by the customary type of market research department or outside research agency —as a matter of fact, all those questions where the answers are clear in the customer's mind. The consumer knows how many bottles of beer he consumes in one week, which brand of bread he buys, where he buys his motor oil, and so on. The reader can report that he read only parts of a certain book and which parts they were. The radio listener can reliably inform the researcher that he fell asleep during this program or laughed 14 times during that program.

But the moment the investigator attempts to get the answers to such *why* questions as what actually made respondents switch from one brand of soap to another, or to find out their *true* opinions about such matters as various brands of soft drinks, then he is in trouble. What he is doing is the same thing that the physician would be doing if he asked his patient for an explanation of his ills. The patient, looking for some causal relationship, as he saw it, might explain the pain in his right side as due to overwork and strain, whereas actually it might be the beginning of an appendicitis. Of course, the patient might also chance to be right, especially if he had picked up a smattering of physiological knowledge, but the odds are against him. Curiosity, unwillingness to accept superficial explanations, good common sense— all these may help to get the right answer. Nevertheless there are very few of us who, experiencing a bad pain, do not desire to consult the expert, in this case the doctor, because of the importance of having the best possible diagnosis.

## SIGNIFICANCE OF FINDINGS

While up to about ten or fifteen years ago businessmen were entitled to assume an attitude of regretful resignation, tinged with hope that their intuitions were right, at the very times when they wanted to be sure that they understood the basic function of their products and services, this is no longer true. It is not necessary now to face with perplexity, or even to dismiss as unanswerable, questions concerning the apparently mysterious forces that control the success or failure of a product, a magazine, a service, a motion picture, a radio program, or a Broadway show. For modern social psychology has undergone considerable changes over the last decade or so; it has become much more capable of producing practical findings.

Let us look now at some examples of the kind of thing the psychologist can find out for the businessman, thus adding strength to market research in its task of measuring and understanding the interrelation of human needs and their satisfactions. We shall then, in a subsequent section of the article, go on to discuss briefly the technical methods by which such findings are produced.

### The Customer's Inner Needs

The psychologist can be helpful in finding out the needs and innermost wishes the consumer expects to see fulfilled by a type of product. This is what might be called the functional approach.

In a study the author recently completed for *Time* magazine, direct questioning about why people read *Time* evoked such answers as "It condenses the news for me," or "It is written in a brilliant style," or other similar quality *descriptions* of the magazine. In the functional research approach, however, we are not so much interested in finding out what people think about the magazine, or what they think they think about it, as we are in finding out what the magazine actually *does* for them. In the case of *Time*, this approach showed that one of the major functions of the magazine was to provide what the psychologists call "ego-benefits." That is, it bolstered up the readers, because it made them *feel* like busy executives whose position demanded that they be well informed but whose schedule was so crowded that they needed to get their news quickly. As one reader actually said, in response to deeper questioning: "When I read *Time*, I like myself." Such a statement is quite different from a descriptive remark about the product itself; it depicts a real psychological effect produced on the reader.

Now such a functional finding permits action on the part of the publisher. For example, if he knows that some of his readers are looking for such ego-benefits, then he can make use of this knowledge. The more *Time* offers those readers the opportunity to experience this kind of feeling by the way the magazine is written and edited, the better they like the magazine and the more they are inclined to buy further copies at the newsstand or to renew their subscriptions. Furthermore it can be decided, and actually has been, to make a specific appeal to this feeling in *Time's* circulation promotion efforts, where a fraction of a percentage point improvement in the rate of returns will add up to a substantial dollars-and-cents savings. Presumably the appeal will be introduced subtly and in such a way as to re-enforce the description of the magazine's quality, features, and services.

It is worth noting, too, that in this way *Time* introduces an important new aspect into the whole field of education. For hundreds and possibly thousands of years our good-intentioned educators have attempted to convince us that it is not an easy job to increase our knowledge. *Time* encourages and produces the opposite conviction. While the academic archeologist tells you that it takes scores of years really to know the field, *Time* promises you a workable knowledge after only a comparatively few pages of reading.

For the Chrysler Corporation the application of modern functional research operated in the following way. The objective of the executives concerned was to use advertising to get more people to switch from other makes of cars to Chrysler cars. To do this they needed to know why about 75% of all car buyers purchase the same make of car year after year; they wanted to change that habit. Direct questioning uncovered the apparent reason: rational satisfaction with the quality of the previously owned car. The obvious advertising approach, dealing with such surface rationalization, would have been to stress the fact that the new make of car was startlingly different and better, that it was time to get rid of the old car with all its repair bills and troubles.

From the point of view of the psychological findings this was exactly the opposite of the correct approach. A psychological survey revealed that the real reasons for the high percentage of repeat purchases were based on unconscious fear of automobiles as dangerous, powerful instruments, taking the form of fear of the unfamiliarity of a new make of car, fear of disloyalty to the old car which had demonstrated its safety, emotional attachment to the old car, and similar factors. Instead of talking down the old car, the advertiser needed to compliment the prospective customer on his friendship and loyalty to the presently owned car and to promise him that the new car would permit him to feel the old familiarity within a few hours. The Chrysler executives decided to use this approach in all their advertising and to include it in their sales training courses. The result was a 100% rise in the Starch rating of Chrysler and Plymouth advertisements and a substantial increase in sales.

For the same reasons, the salesmen's usual habit of kicking the tires of old cars brought for trade-in was found to be psychologically detrimental to the transaction. Controlled tests showed that customers actually accepted lower trade-ins when the old car was complimented —"It's easy to see this car was well taken care of"—than when it was deprecated. Thus, functional research reveals the deeper-lying, real motivations for buying behavior and permits correct, effective sales methods to be substituted for others that are often dangerously wrong business-wise.

### Creative Programming

The same development of functional psychology can also be helpful in presentation of such a product as a radio program. Take the research for the CBS atomic bomb program, "Operations Crossroads," as an example. The ordinary approach would have been first at the content level—contemplating such considered questions of program format and presentation as whether it should be given in fictionalized form or as a round-table discussion or as a documentary. The functional approach, however, was to consider the desired effect of the program first, with the idea that the format and content should be subordinated to this all-important goal.

A study of polls and surveys had revealed that about 75% of the public were thoroughly scared by the atomic bomb but had largely chosen to dodge the issue. They wanted to keep the secret or build bigger battleships or have the bomb outlawed, or simply felt that things should be left to take care of themselves—all more or less inadequate solutions. It became clear that if this radio program was to have any effect at all it would have to be in the direction of cutting short all these forms of escapism.

By applying functional research techniques to the study of this problem, it was found that the main program aim should be to convince the listener that he had to face the real issue, which (it seemed to those responsible) concerned the necessity of a world government. Therefore it was necessary to demonstrate to the listener in a step-by-step, almost psychoanalytical procedure, descending from surface forms of escapism to deeper psychological mechanisms, that none of the escapist solutions could possibly work. The method decided on was to stage a series of interviews in which the people questioned began by advocating the escapist solutions and then were forced gradually to admit the illogic of their positions. Once the program had thus indirectly pushed the listener into a corner, so to speak, getting him to admit to himself that all the escapist solutions were inadequate, it then could lead him to positive suggestions. Even though it might enrage him in the course of getting him there, it could leave him at the end of the broadcast with a feeling of encouragement and clarity as to what decision he would have to make.

Once this clear concept of the psychological structure of the program had been worked out in detail, research had come very much closer to defining the job of the creative writer. While all the artistic intuition and sense of drama still had full play in the actual dramatic translation of this concept, the job of arriving at the finished product had been made a lot easier than if the nonfunctional type of research had been the only one applied to this program. Thus, the functional research approach provides a way to bridge the gap between purely descriptive research and creative work.

The same technique can be applied to any other problem in programming and advertising. (It has already been applied in studies of shoes, magazines, candy, chewing gum, and movies.) The first step is to ask what psychological function the message or product should fulfill and how it can be achieved. Then, like a medical practitioner systematically examining several hypotheses suggested by his knowledge of blood, lungs, heart, and so on, the researcher translates the clinical picture into a series of directly observable indices in a questionnaire and makes a quantitative check-up of the various buying, reading, or listening mechanisms which he has reason to think may be involved. Next comes the creative job of programming or advertising indicated by the research. The final step is a clearly focused test of whether or not the average listener has actually been induced to do what it was intended he should do. In the case of the "Operations Crossroads" program, psychological audience tests indicated the success of the methods used, and this was borne out by the many requests for rebroadcasts, the unusually large number of enthusiastic letters, and so on.

### Dynamic Behavior

Many research procedures concern themselves quite properly with critical judgments made by the audience, the ad reader, and so on. Often this approach has a static aspect, however. The inquiry is concerned, for instance, with whether a particular advertisement has been accepted or rejected, or how many people have read it—and many advertisers may have a pretty accurate answer to such questions. But much more important than this is a knowledge of what *happens* in the mind of the reader as he inspects the advertisement. What are his impressions? What is he thinking about? What associations does the advertisement create? What desires or blockages does it mobilize? Even when the advertiser knows the motivations determining purchase of his product, he still has to know whether he is correctly translating these appeals into copy in terms of present-day motivations and needs of buyers.

The dynamic effects produced by advertising and other selling techniques are particularly important now that people are so concerned with help in planning for the future and with guidance in finding their way again within the intricacies of peacetime economy and the transition to a free market. While a company's advertising and sales approach may be technically excellent, special emphasis should be given now to the actual help that sales representatives can give to customers. Several magazine studies showed that the readers were mainly interested in those features which helped them chart the future, which attempted to organize their thinking, and which gave them hope. It is obvious that if the same function were fulfilled by salesmen and advertising, the customer would just as eagerly reach to the product for gratification.

To avoid soliciting meaningless aesthetic judgments from ad readers, the author has developed a procedure whereby the attitude toward the product and its verbal and pictorial associations are matched with the associations and impressions created by an advertisement. Take oleomargarine for an example. Questioning revealed that one of the major prejudices against it stems from a feeling of artificiality,

low social acceptance, and general doubt about the composition and nutritive values of the product. It would seem logical, then, that a correctly conceived advertisement would serve the purpose and effect of combating these prejudices and of rendering reassuring information. Yet questioning further revealed that most women visualize margarine as a fatty white substance which is changed into an artificial yellow by mixing a powder into it, and those asked to react to margarine ads reported that the feeling of artificiality was heightened by the extreme brightness of the ad colors (and in some cases surrealist trees in the ad). There was also a general feeling that a special effort had been made to combat consumer suspicion. Because the readers thought it was done in an obvious, exaggerated fashion, a general feeling of insincerity was created, further increasing the feeling of artificiality.

Phonograph records, especially classical records, constitute another case. When you talk to people about their record collections, they connect records with such things as memorable events in their lives, demonstrate their pride of possession with a sweeping gesture indicating the size of their record collections, and make many other references to the meaning of records in the lives of their families. Today, with a much greater consciousness of being eye-witnesses to history-in-the-making, most people have a heightened desire to enjoy themselves while they can and to hold on to their fast-moving lives in tangible forms. In addition to stressing the quality of records as exemplified by the name of the conductor or singer, the technical processes used in recording, and so on, it simply is good selling psychology to make use of more personal appeals based on what records actually mean to buyers. Yet relatively few of these basic psychological appeals are translated into record advertisements.

If psychological investigation shows a consistent discrepancy between the presently existing product attitude and the effects and impressions created by an advertisement, it is obvious that the ad is not doing the job it could, even though the figures show it to be well read. Research on advertisement effectiveness is another example of the application of modern scientific thinking which can help the sales executive or market research man to gauge the success of his attempts to win and influence the consumer. This research, instead of relying on the erratic, subjective, and static likes and dislikes of ad readers, proceeds on the basis of analysis of basic human emotions, expressions, feelings, and associations, ascertained by objective, scientific, psychological means.

## Multiple Motivations

Most actions are motivated by a whole field of reasons. In other words, we speak of multiple motivations, all of them interlocking and acting together to produce the final result. Some of these reasons lie within ourselves; others, again, come from the environment. For example, you make love to a girl. Your motivations in doing so may be only partly related to a basic sex urge. You may want to feel powerful, or you may be in need of affection, or you may need to convince yourself of your manliness.

Modern motivational research has to employ methods which can investigate these multiple motivations in their natural structure and mutual relationship without tearing them apart or arranging them in the artificial atomistic order of a check list. A method which the author has tried to develop, taking into consideration the "personality" approach, is the psycho-panel. A psycho-panel is a representative group of several hundred families about which not only factors such as age, income, and marital status are known (as in the case of the consumer panels which have already proved so helpful in commercial market research), but also personality factors such as whether the individual families are governed by the authority of the father or the mother, whether the members are secure or insecure, resigned or ambitious, overspending or miserly, conspicuous or modest, emotional or rational, escapists or realists, and so on. The psychological needs of the panel members are known specifically, and they can be interviewed and questioned when needed. The continuing relations build mutual confidence between interviewer and panel members and add reliability to the responses secured.

The actual methods of interviewing and testing, such as are used in connection with the panel, will be discussed later. All we want to do here is to bring out the significance for businessmen of the personality factors which can be thus uncovered. For example, suppose two families are found to resemble each other in income, family size, education—in short, they belong to the same group according to the socio-economic criteria of typical consumer research. But the members of one family may have a strong sense of security, be well balanced, optimistic, and have reached a high saturation of their needs; they may be content with the life they can lead on their income. The family next door, however, may consider the same income just a temporary one; its members may be insecure, pessimistic, and overambitious. Advertisers who plan their campaigns efficiently must regard these families as two different units, must remember that the general market is made up of both kinds of family, and must decide which they wish to solicit, and then act accordingly.

Whenever a product attitude appears to be influenced by personality factors, which is the case very frequently, use of the psycho-panel provides an opportunity for confirmation or refutation of the existence of such a relationship, since the files of each family unit in the panel include a long list of personality information gathered by an array of psychological tests, detailed depth interviews, and frequent family contacts. The psycho-panel serves as a sort of X-ray laboratory by use of which we can discover obscure and subtle relationships. For example, if a businessman has a hunch that degree of security influences the buying habits of his particular customers, he can ask questions of the secure and insecure members of the panel and thus find out whether there does exist an actual relationship between this personality factor and buying habits. This turned out to be significant with the deodorant mentioned earlier.

## Rationalization vs. Real Motivations

The discovery of the existence of several levels of consciousness—the ego, superego, and unconscious—is the basis of another reason why modern psychological methods can help market research. People rationalize their actions and beliefs, try to justify them on moral and logical grounds. We are loath to admit that we sometimes act for completely irrational and possibly idiotic reasons. Almost automatically we construct a fool-proof system of explanations which is completely logical and, if possible, moral and ethical. Psychology, however, teaches us that many of our actions are guided by irrational and emotional reasoning. This is illustrated by many of the examples already cited, particularly that of the reasons for repeat purchases of cars.

Therefore, a research approach not capable of distinguishing between rationalizations and real reasons can go very far astray. The respondent in an interview is frequently unaware of his real motivations to action; they are unconscious.

This fact is extremely important. So-called "depth psychology" teaches us that unconscious reasons are usually more basic and powerful than are the conscious ones. Obviously, direct questioning runs no chance of success in uncovering unconscious motivations, so we are forced to introduce new and different methods for the investigation of *why* problems.

## RESEARCH METHODS

The approach the author uses in his work is often termed "depth interviewing." But this phrase does not represent the total picture. It is completely misleading to use the terms "depth interviewing" and "motivational research" interchangeably. Depth interviewing is only *one* of the methods used in modern motivational research. Other methods are content analysis, laboratory experiments, effectiveness tests, field observations, psycho-panels, and finally statistical methods. (The psychologist, by the way, uses statistical methods to the same extent as any other researcher; the only difference is that he considers statistics a technical tool, like all the other procedures we have just mentioned, and not something which can substitute for sound psychological thinking.) Rather than trying to define these various methods separately, let us try to see how they would all work together in solving a specific problem.

We might have a problem of how believability of the curative effect of a stomach remedy can be achieved: Should it be through *logical* arguments and testimonials, or through reference to some directly observable feature of the medicine such as its color and consistency—even if *illogical?* Or we might have a question of the real motivations for buying life insurance: Are they *fear* and *solicitude* for the man's family, or are they more in the nature of *pride* in being a good family man? Or we might want to know why individuals tend to buy ice cream in specific stores: Is it *convenience,* as they say, even though they will walk by a nearer store selling the same brand, or has it something to do with the *feeling of luxury* they experience in their favorite store? We might have any of these problems, or a thousand more. But suppose our assignment is to find out the major gratifications of a certain motion picture, that is, what the effects of its showing are on the movie-goers— an admittedly difficult job since there are so many conflicting factors to be taken into account, but for that very reason requiring added insight.

Our initial task would be to analyze the problem in a psychological sense, to investigate all the possible domains in psychology and sociology which this problem touches. We would thus become somewhat oriented and could see what general fields should be covered in our research—aesthetics, personality research, leisure time occupations, family organization, mechanisms of emotion, frustrations, and so on. From this general survey of topics, a systematic procedure evolves. We know we are dealing with communication and that in a psychological sense any form of communication represents a stimulus-response situation.

Suppose, further, that the motion picture is an MGM "Red" Skelton comedy. Because it is a comedy, we would know that we were dealing with the difference in attitudes of people toward reality and toward comedy. In one such film which was investigated by the author, there were a few initial scenes that gave the members of the test audience, although they knew they were watching what was supposed to be a comedy, the idea that all the scenes they were about to see would be realistic. As the story progressed, many of the comic scenes became completely unacceptable because they were seen through the filter of reality set up by the initial scenes, yet they probably would have been satisfactory if seen as parts of a purely comedy plot. In other words, the research had to concern itself with the domains of realism and comedy and with identification.

In such a case there are really three research jobs to do: (1) investigate the stimulus, i.e., the motion picture; (2) study the responding individual or audience member; and (3) study interactions taking place between the stimulus and the respondent, such as identification, emotional response, and so on. All three are aimed at achieving a complete psychological understanding of the problem.

### Psychological Understanding

Content analysis is used for the first research task. Scripts are taken apart, and we investigate possible psychological stimuli offered by the film, types of characters in the story, settings, and lessons which could possibly be taught by the drama. Here is where we might have become aware that the two contradictory frames of reference, reality and comedy, had become dangerously mixed in the film. In any event, having acquired a familiarity with the operating stimuli of the film, we could approach our second job, the movie-goer analysis, in a sound, direct way.

The movie-goer analysis is handled by the depth interview method (sometimes called "case study" method). This method cannot be explained by calling it a longer interview, an informal interview, or any similar name. It is simply a device which has been used by many clinical psychologists who have been confronted by the problem of finding out why their clients behave in a particular way. It might best be described as a procedure by which the respondent achieves an insight into his own motivations. In other words, for the respondent it is a sort of introspective method. Psychological laboratories have been using it for decades in the investigation of the complicated workings of the human mind.

In a depth interview the interviewer attempts to bring about a full and spontaneous expression of attitudes from the respondent. It is the proof of a good interview if at its end the respondent has the feeling that he himself has expressed his own reactions. After a satisfactory interview, some people remark, "I never knew that there was so much to going to the movies (or buying a pair of shoes). It just dawns upon me now why I do all these things." Such statements prove to us that we have succeeded in bringing about an understanding in the respondent which permitted him, and us, to perceive the true reasons, the basic motivations for his actions.

In our specific example, psychological interviews revealed a resentment against the comedian, who displayed an inane shirking of life's responsibilities and yet was rewarded with the girl, the job, and the money. The respondents, seeing themselves in the same kind of awkward dilemmas as "Red" Skelton, knew they would surely have to pay for their stupidity; and the fact that he "got away with it" unconsciously upset them.

The third step, investigation of the processes taking place between the stimuli and the respondents, uses another group of methods. It is necessary to study the processes of identification, catharsis, frustration, and other psychological concepts of a relatively complicated nature. Unfortunately they cannot be approached directly, but must be dissolved into their ascertainable components. Identification, for instance, has many ramifications: It must be clearly separated from admiration. There are different forms of identification—some harmful and some desirable. And different factors serve as the basis for identification. In our particular example, we would be concerned with how the men in the audience identified themselves with the film's supposed hero.

At the end of these three research tasks, we often have found sufficiently clear understanding of the problem we tackled to permit action —whether it be in the field of communications, advertising, merchandising, selling, or public relations. In many cases such a grasp of the basic psychological mechanism at work in the effect of a movie, in the acceptance or rejection of a product, and so on, will be the final step.

## Quantitative Data

In many other cases, however, we would still need more precise quantitative data. In such cases, the preceding psychological research helps in the forming of meaningful hypotheses. Then indicator or clue questions can be developed to test the hypotheses. And when answers have been collected, counted, and tabulated, we can come up with accurate and significant figures.

To make this clearer, let us take another example—the problem of finding out why one brand of chewing gum was preferred over another. Without the preliminary psychological research, we might have been inclined to compare the flavors of various brands and to conclude from the expressed preferences for one specific brand that it was better liked because it had a better flavor. Having conducted such research, however, we would know that there were other reasons why this brand was preferred, such as a suggestion of fun (bubble blowing) and a feeling of aggressiveness (tougher chewing). In the questionnaires, therefore, we would try to uncover the extent of such psychological associations, and we would not just ask for flavor preferences but would introduce such clue or indicator questions as: "Which one of these various brands makes you think of fun?" and "Which one makes you think of the feeling of getting your teeth into it?"

In this way, the preceding psychological research helps in developing the kind of questions we need to ask in order to find out the quantitative facts we are after. In the case of the film which we discussed, the questions might be: "Which one of the characters was most like yourself?" "Whom did you have a feeling of trying to help?" By analyzing the answers to such questions, we can begin to measure the strength of the psychological factors involved.

Getting the answers and tabulating the results can be handled in the usual way: by sending out a great number of interviewers or questionnaires to a correctly selected sample of people. Once the returns are in, however, we are able to go far beyond the usual type of cross tabulating of age groups, education, income, and so on, because of the thorough understanding of our hypotheses and the intimate structure of the problems given us by our previous research. We gather our information from apparently widely separated fields and fit it together into a meaningful structure. All the elements of our procedure, beginning with the case studies and ending with the mass treatment of indicator questions, can be molded into a complete and integrated unit.

Thus, it is possible to deliver a scientifically correct and adequate answer to the initial problem of people's motivations in a specific field; e.g., the film failed to make the audience laugh as much as the producer hoped it would (1) because of the confusion between reality and comedy, in the case of men and women alike, and (2) because of the resentment against "Red" Skelton caused by his getting away with being a "jerk," particularly in the case of the younger men.

What is more, once we understand the mechanism of these motivations, we can also indicate the ways by which improvements can be made. As for the motion picture discussed, the film had already been released to the public and nothing could be done. The practical thing to do with motion pictures, however, would be to test them psychologically before release. It would have been comparatively simple to cut a few feet of film and remove the realistic scenes from the beginning of the "Red" Skelton comedy, thus eliminating the sense of confusion, and also to add a scene at the end in which Skelton stumbled and fell flat on his face, thus sending out the audience with a more comfortable feeling. Both minor changes would have unquestionably enhanced the picture's commercial success. Similarly, in the case of

other types of product, psychological research should be conducted before outlays of possibly thousands of dollars have been wasted in ill-conceived advertising or selling effort.

In summary, then, social psychological research embraces problems which can be solved by merely counting noses, and it also includes problems which necessitate more complicated methods. Because in the last analysis all social psychology is concerned with the individual, his attitude, his motivations, and his behavior, it uses all those methods which help in better understanding of the individual. At the same time, every scientific procedure has to be capable of yielding generalized statements about groups and populations. The single individual can only be understood because of his membership in human society. Any true social psychological method has to be able to cover both these aspects in the most modern and advanced fashion science permits.

Although at first glance it may seem that this kind of psychological research would only add expenditures to already extended research and advertising budgets, the justification for it is similar to that for an X-ray needed to insure better care of a patient. Without the outlay for the X-ray, the treatment may remain ineffective and the cure unduly delayed. With the knowledge provided by real understanding of the causes of difficulties, however, a more concentrated and sharply focused attack on the problem is possible—and quite often at an ultimate dollars-and-cents savings. It is the wise man who knows the value of expert assistance.

Of course there are many problems not important enough to warrant psychological X-rays, and there are many problems where a sound, penetrating, common-sense approach will yield answers which are reliable for all practical purposes. Yet, even here a recognition of the principles discussed in this article can be helpful, if only in stimulating and directing the thinking of a company's regular research department. There still will remain, however, many problems that need and deserve expert assistance from trained psychologists, either on a consulting basis or, in the case of large companies, as a specialized part of the company's own staff.

# C. Promotion

## 40. The Propaganda Function in Marketing
### EDMUND D. McGARRY

The most controversial aspect of marketing is advertising. Ever since advertising began to appear, moralists and critics have complained that it distorted people's natural desires, misinformed them as to the products they needed, played upon their emotions, and led to waste of resources.

Proponents of advertising, on the other hand, have argued that it is an economical method of distributing goods, that it provides entertainment, and actually adds to the value of the goods advertised. The purpose here is not to discuss these issues directly, but rather to place the advertising process in its proper perspective as a function of marketing.

Advertising as used today is primarily a type of propaganda. The essence of propaganda is that it conditions people to act in a way favorable to or desired by the propagandist. It deliberately attempts to influence, persuade, and convince people to act in a way that they would not otherwise act. Propaganda had its birth in the attempt of the church to propagate the faith. It is used by leaders who seek a following in politics, in religion, and in all affairs which require action by large bodies of people.

In business it is used primarily by sellers to obtain a market by conditioning people in the market to accept the particular products offered. The growth of new techniques of communication has greatly extended the range of propaganda penetration, has expanded the number of products advertised, and has in-

creased the total amount of propaganda disseminated; but the aim of the messages carried is essentially unchanged since the beginning of civilization.

In fact, the use of force of argument instead of physical force marked the change from savagery to civilized living. "The creation of the world," said Plato, "is the victory of persuasion over force."

The use of persuasion is part of man's apparatus to adapt his way of life to change. Without some stimulus to action, man tends to be indifferent and apathetic to change, and unwilling to exert the effort which change necessitates. He prefers to follow his preconditioned routines rather than direct his effort in some different way. There must be some extra stimulus to action; and this stimulus is afforded either by compulsion of force or the threat of force, or by persuasion in the form of the written or spoken word.

### PROPAGANDA VERSUS EDUCATION

Propaganda differs from education in that education presumably is oriented toward the dissemination of "truth"—dispassionate, objective, and unbiased. Pure education takes an impartial non-partisan point of view. It is not prejudiced; it has no slant. Yet all of us know that education must persuade to get students to study; it must propagandize to get funds.

Propaganda, on the other hand, by definition is biased, partial, and one-sided. It has an axe to grind; therefore it is always controversial. But unlike education, in which there is no sponsor, the sponsor of propaganda, particularly

‡‡ SOURCE: Reprinted by permission from the *Journal of Marketing* (National Quarterly Publication of the American Marketing Association), Vol. 23, No. 2, October 1958, pp. 131–139.

advertising propaganda, is known. And everyone knows what the sponsor is trying to do, what his motives are, and how he would like others to act. The sponsor of commercial propaganda must identify himself and the product he advertises and he must take the responsibility for it; otherwise, his propaganda cannot be directed to his purpose.

Every advertisement is designed to predispose its readers to a favorable consideration of its sponsor and his product. It is deliberately planned to make its readers and listeners take sides—to affiliate and ally themselves under its banner and to ignore all others.

Advertising is the obtrusive display of the conflict of interests in the market place. It represents a parade of the contestants in the battle for market supremacy, each imploring the audience to follow him. By its very nature advertising must be prejudiced in order to be potent.

## THE BARRAGE EFFECT OF PROPAGANDA

Commercial propaganda is a social phenomenon, and its analysis must necessarily be in a social framework. It is, in fact, a part of our culture and at the same time exercises a considerable influence on that culture. Professor David M. Potter speaks of it "as an instrument of social control comparable to the school and the church in the extent of its influence upon society." [1]

Like other types of propaganda, advertising has a barrage effect. Although it is designed primarily to induce people who have the money and the need to buy the product, its effect cannot usually be confined to these. It creates a pattern of thought in a much larger population. Its results are diffuse and pervasive rather than selective. Because of this diffusion, many who are not in a position to buy, read, or listen to the advertisement, and many others who do not see or hear the message directly, learn of it from others by word of mouth.

Moreover, the pattern of thought created by advertising is likely to last for an indefinite period. If consecutive appeals are used, the effect tends to be cumulative both because of the widening group which sees it and because of the intensification of the impression it makes. This cumulative effect continues to a point of diminishing returns which is reached either

through saturation of the market, through the counteracting influence of competing messages, or through the saturation of receptivity.

There is another sense in which there is a spill-over of advertising effectiveness. This is what might be called the cross-product influence. It is said, for instance, that when vacuum cleaners were first advertised the demand for brooms increased; the inference is that the promotion of cleanliness in the home leads to the increased sales of any product that enhances cleanliness.

Still another type of spill-over effect is seen in the case of the firm selling a family of products in which the advertising of any one will increase to some extent the sales of other products in the same group. It seems probable also that the advertising of a particular brand influences the sales of all other products in the same use-class, even if they are marketed by competitors.

It would seem logical to assume that, when two competing advertisers attempt to promote their individual brands for a particular use, the impact will be greater than if only one is advertised; and, if the market can be expanded, the advertising of each will have a complementary effect on that of the other. If this is true, then there is a cumulative effect of advertising generally in the sense that, as more advertising is published, there is developed a greater propensity to purchase advertised goods of all kinds. The increase may be at the expense of non-advertised goods, it may be at the expense of savings, or it may result in greater effort on the part of consumers to secure more income.

### Advertising vs. Personal Selling

Advertising today has to take a large part of the responsibility for making sales. To a great extent salesmen, particularly at the retail level, have become anonymous persons—unknown either to the selling firm or to the buyer—who merely facilitate the sale by formally presenting the product and accepting payment. The real job of adjusting the consumer to the product is done by the mass propaganda called advertising.

In taking over the task formerly performed by the salesman, advertising must substitute symbolic language for the personal appeal of man-to-man at a point where the merchandise is itself present and the transaction takes place. The task of persuading the customer is pushed

[1] David M. Potter, *People of Plenty* (University of Chicago Press, 1954), p. 168.

back in time to a point where it can be planned and partly executed months before the product reaches the market. It is removed in space from the point of sale to the business office, where the entire selling technique is planned and developed without benefit of the presence of the buyer. The sale must thus consist of an impersonalized message to thousands of unidentified potential customers, who have no way of communicating their impressions.

Modern advertising has many tasks to perform, which do not arise when selling is done face-to-face at the point of sale:

1. It must create or point out a need by identifying the circumstances under which it arises.

2. It must link the need to the possibility of fulfilling it with a general product, so that when the need arises the respondent will think of the product that will fulfill it.

3. It must differentiate the particular brand and its sponsor from other products which might satisfy the need approximately as well.

4. It must connect the particular branded product with the place and the conditions under which it can be obtained.

5. It must show that the need is urgent and that the task of buying is easy.

6. It must give a rational basis for action, for people do not like to buy goods which they cannot justify to their own consciences.

7. It must stimulate the respondent to make a firm decision on which he will act at a later time.

In accomplishing these tasks, advertising acts under the kleiglights of publicity. Unlike personal selling, where the promotion is carried on in private between two or more people, the messages publicized in advertising are conspicuous and cannot escape observation. This is one of the reasons why advertising comes in for a great deal of criticism that is equally relevant to selling on a personal basis. The so-called abuses which are concealed and disguised in the personal sales transaction are flaunted in the face of the public when they are published on the printed page or appear on the television screen. There is little doubt that there is more misrepresentation, deceit, and fraud in person-to-person sales relationships than in advertising.

### The Purpose of Advertising

Commercial propaganda or advertising had its genesis in the need of the mass producer to sell goods in large quantities, and competition of other goods forced him to resort to an anonymous market: an aggregation of people scattered geographically, and unknown and unidentified as individuals. These conditions, and the growing separation of the locus of production in time and space from the locus of consumption, necessitated some means of making an individual manufacturer's product known and thus assuring it a continuous market.

Through the use of propaganda it was possible to create markets that were more stable than their component parts; for, although individual consumers are notoriously whimsical in changing their minds, their reactions in the market as a whole tend to cancel each other out.[2]

In order to accomplish these results the advertiser must use all the tools at his disposal. He must have an intimate understanding of the product advertised and be able to sense these characteristics whether inherent or inferred, which will fulfill the hopes and expectations of the potential owner and user. He must envisage the product in its use-setting. He must comprehend and appreciate the nature of human behavior. And he must be able to use the tricks of his trade—often the same as, and always closely akin to, those used on the rostrum and in the pulpit.

If the propaganda which the advertiser writes is to be effective, it must be expressed in terms in which the consumer thinks, with the same overtones and exaggerations of the product that the well-disposed consumer will attribute to it. It must recognize that the consumer to whom it appeals is but imperfectly rational, that he hates the labor of rational thinking, and that he is sometimes more impressed by what seems to others to be superficial than by the real merits of the product.

### RATIONAL VERSUS EMOTIONAL APPEALS

In a broad, general sense advertising appeals either to man's reason or to his emotion or to both. It is difficult, of course, to differentiate in any precise way between these; but generally speaking rational appeals seem more effective in deciding alternative means to ends rather than the ends themselves. Emotion, on the other hand, is usually the trigger to action, particu-

---

[2] Compare Neil H. Borden, *The Economic Effects of Advertising* (Chicago: Richard D. Irwin, 1942).

larly when the actions mean a change of attitude on the part of the person.

There are many road-blocks to actions based on rational appeals; for rational arguments tend to raise questions rather than to answer them. Emotional appeals, on the other hand, attempt to stimulate the individual to carry through impulses which he already has. Assuming that this is true, the rational appeal is likely to be more lasting and its secondary effect to be stronger, because people are more likely to repeat rationalizations than they are to communicate their emotional feelings.

Advertising is highly concentrated on marginal products, things that one can do without, things that can be purchased with free income after the more austere basic needs such as necessary food, housing, clothing, etc., are taken care of.[3] It is these marginal products that give the real satisfactions in life. Even in the case of basic products, it is the exotic, the unusual elements—the fringe benefits—that set one off from his fellow creatures and thus claim the attention of consumers.

### The Most Common Motives

Some years ago Victor Schwab suggested that there were ten leading motives or desires of the average consumer to which advertising must appeal in order to be effective:[4]

1. *Money and a better job.* "There must always be some kind of short-cut to getting ahead faster."

2. *Security in old age.* "When I get along in years, I want to be able to take it easy."

3. *Popularity.* "It's fun to be asked out all the time, to be wanted by everybody."

4. *Praise from others.* "Praise from others is a nice thing to get and I like to get it when I deserve it, and I often do."

5. *More comfort.* "A lot of people who are not as industrious or as capable as I am seem to have more comforts, so why shouldn't I spread myself once in a while?"

6. *Social advancement.* "Where would a person be if he never tried to better himself and to meet and associate with better people?"

7. *Improved appearance.* "It is awfully nice to have people tell you how attractive and well-dressed you are. If I had the time and money

some people spend on themselves, I would show them."

8. *Personal prestige.* "I am going to see to it that my children can prove that they have parents they need never be ashamed of."

9. *Better health.* "I don't feel any older than I did years ago, it's just that I don't seem to have the drive and energy I used to have."

10. *Increased enjoyment.* "I work hard, I do the best I can about things so why shouldn't I get as much enjoyment as I can?"

Advertisers have found by trial and error that these types of appeals are effective. It is evident that each appeal contains a bit of rationality with a large dose of sentimentality. The fact that these appeals are effective simply indicates that "the average human mind is a montage of hasty impressions, fuzzy generalities, bromidic wall-motto sentiments, self-justifications and sentimentalities."[5] It is out of this "jumble of ideas and feelings" that the advertiser must find a background for his appeals.

### More and Better Wants

"The chief thing which the common-sense individual actually wants," wrote Professor Frank H. Knight, "is not satisfactions for the wants which he has, but more and better wants. There is always really present and operative, though in the background of consciousness, the idea of, and desire for a new want to be striven for when the present objective is out of the way."[6] Advertising attempts to present goods which are new or additional in the consumers' inventory of wants, and to indicate how they can be realized. In doing this, it both creates a want and the means of satisfying it.

The fact that advertising concentrates its efforts on changing people's customary wants has given rise to the contention that it corrupts people's desires and stimulates so-called "artificial" consuming habits. But this argument is beside the point for, as Professor Knight has indicated, "there is no issue as between natural and artificial wants. All human wants are more artificial than natural, and the expression 'natural wants,' if it has any meaning, can only refer to those of beasts. By the same token, human wants are more sentimental than real."[7]

[3] F. P. Bishop, *The Ethics of Advertising* (London: Robert Hale, 1949), p. 48.

[4] Victor Schwab, "Ten Copy Appeals," *Printers' Ink*, December 17, 1943, pp. 17ff.

[5] *Ibid.*

[6] Frank H. Knight, *The Ethics of Competition* (New York: Harper, 1935), p. 22.

[7] *Ibid,* p. 103.

Most people have always lived rather drab and unimaginative lives. The so-called golden ages of history were golden only to the few. The great masses lived by drudgery, and thought in terms of only the elemental emotions such as hunger and comfort. The so-called "democratic way of life" rests simply on the idea that our present economy is oriented to change the thinking of these masses. Propaganda, if it is to be effective, must appeal to the masses in the terms of their own mental processes.

It is sometimes alleged also that, through advertising, businessmen foist on people goods they do not want. This, of course, is sheer nonsense. There are, in fact, few acts necessarily more deliberate than that of the consumer's action in response to advertising.

Picture the consumer in his living room reading a magazine advertisement. He has had to choose the particular magazine, and pay for it; he has had to select from among the hundreds of pages those he wishes to read, and he can either accept or reject the arguments presented. Assuming that he accepts them and resolves to make the purchase, he must still wait hours or even days before an opportune time arises to make the purchase. During the interval between the time he reads the advertisement and the time he undertakes the overt act of buying, he is entirely outside the influence of the message and may deliberate and search his soul to his heart's content either in private or in consultation with his friends. There is not even mass psychology to influence him. He is a free agent and there is no possibility of coercion, duress, or constraint of any kind.

But the impossibility of advertising to force consumers to buy what they do not want should not be confused with the fact that advertisers sometime overstep the bounds of propriety to make claims for their products which cannot be justified. In some product areas effective protection has been provided by law, but in general the chief defense of the consumer lies in his own discrimination of whom he will patronize or refuse to patronize.

## THE LARGER SYSTEM OF BELIEFS

In discussing propaganda generally, psychologists Krech and Crutchfield state that "suggestions which are accepted as a consequence of propaganda tend to be in harmony with some larger system of beliefs or some already existing predisposition, and therefore presumably with the major needs and interests of the subject." [8]

To put this another way, at any given time the subject of propaganda has many prejudices, beliefs, and attitudes of different intensities. Some are deeply entrenched, while others are at a superficial level. The more deeply entrenched these predispositions are, the more difficult it will be to change them, and some seem to be entrenched so deeply that they cannot be changed by propaganda at all.

Since it is easier and less expensive to modify existing predispositions than to oppose them, propagandists find it expedient to fit their messages into the current pattern of thinking rather than oppose it head on. It is for this reason that most changes in attitudes and wants achieved by advertising are almost imperceptible, and can be objectively observed only over a period of time.

Both in the selection of the characteristics of the product to promote and in the framing of appeals, the advertiser must give attention to consumers' preconceived ideas of what they want. He develops his product and its appeals to fit into these ideas and to project them further. If his advertising is successful in selling his product, competitors will find it necessary to discover other new products or new characteristics of old products, likewise in line with consumers' ideas, as a basis for their counterpropaganda. Thus, competition in advertising tends to develop a constantly increasing improvement of the product to fit consumers' wants, while at the same time it raises the standards of wants in the consumers' minds.

### Discounting the Message

The very mass of advertising and the great amount that comes to the attention of consumers is often open to criticism. Critics ask, for instance, "Is there no limit to the increasing din of the market place?" "Will it continue until all businesses are wasting their substance and crying their wares?" "Are there no antidotes for this infectious disease?" We suspect there are.

The editor of *Harper's Magazine*, puts it this way: "Perhaps, however, we will in the long run have reason to be grateful to the copy-

---

[8] D. K. Krech and R. S. Crutchfield, *Theory and Problems of Social Psychology* (New York: McGraw-Hill, 1948), p. 347.

writers and press agents, even the worst of them. It may turn out that thanks to advertising and public relations, the American people will become the first people in history to be impervious to propaganda. Maybe it isn't such a bad thing that the advertisers and other word-manipulators have got us to the point that we never take words quite at their face value. In all events, it is hard to imagine that the people inured to American advertising would whole-heartedly believe the kind of promises and assurances, whereby Hitler and Stalin have enslaved two great nations in our time." [9]

When two advertisers say approximately the same things about their product, the message of one tends to neutralize that of the other, and the public learns to discount what is said by both. In a free world the right to persuade and be persuaded is one of the essential freedoms. We assume that each of us has the mentality and the fortitude to choose—to accept or reject what he hears or what he reads.

Each has the right to act or to refuse to act on the basis of all the propaganda he absorbs, whether it is in the form of advertising or word-of-mouth gossip. That he often rejects propaganda is a matter of record. But we assume that, whether a person acts wisely or foolishly, he will take the responsibility for the act and that he himself will reap the benefits or the penalties of his action. For this reason he will eventually learn to listen more discriminatingly and act more wisely in the light of all the information available.

## EFFECT ON MEDIA CONTENT

It is sometimes alleged that advertising, because it pays most of the cost of magazines and newspapers, dominates and controls the information in these media. It is said that, since the advertiser pays the piper, he must call the tune.

Actually this is seldom true because the medium that publishes biased or slanted news tends to lose its circulation when its bias becomes known, and in this way it ceases to be an effective means of communication. Even the most severe critics of advertising admit that this type of direct and overt influence is pretty well eliminated by the intense competition among media themselves.

The effect of advertising on news content and editorial opinion is far more indirect and subtle.

Editors themselves are human and they live in the same environment as the rest of us. They, too, are subject to the propaganda which all of us read; and it would be too much to expect that they are not influenced in a general way by what they read. As a part of the total environment it tends to set a point of view which is not unfavorable to advertising.

### The Function of Media

From the advertiser's point of view, the function of the newspaper, the magazine, the broadcasting station, or any other medium of publication is to gather a crowd or furnish an audience. [10] Once the crowd has gathered, it must be entertained, amused, or at least interested enough to hold together while the advertiser's message is being delivered. The need for holding the audience arises from the fact that advertising is selective, in the sense that a specific message is likely to have an appeal only to a scattered few among the many in the crowd. As for the many others who have no need or interest in the particular product, they become bored and resentful that their attention has been disrupted.

The fact that advertising is selective in its expectations, though not in its aims, means that its impact on those to whom the message does not apply or who do not care to listen ranges from irritation to exasperation. From the listener's point of view, it is an unwarranted intrusion on their privacy, by some "jerk" who wants to sell something.

Therefore, the advertiser must use every art he can contrive to make his message palatable, even to those who do not want to listen; and at the same time he searches for a vehicle which will capture and hold his audience while he gives them "the works." In rare cases he is able to convert his message into news which is interesting and entertaining in itself; but often there is a trail of resentment left in the listener's mind, and he deliberately tries to develop some means of shutting out the message from his consciousness. The result is that a great deal of advertising never passes the threshold of the reader's or the listener's consciousness.

Although there is danger of exaggerating the importance of advertising in causing certain changes in our culture, it would be erroneous to conclude that its influence is negligible. Ad-

[9] Robert Amory, Jr., "Personal and Otherwise," *Harper's Magazine*, 1948, p. 6.

[10] See G. B. Hotchkiss, *Milestones of Marketing* (New York: Macmillan, 1938), p. 10.

vertising is so prevalent, so pervasive, so extensive, and so conspicuous that it would be absurd to argue that it does not affect our attitudes.

On the other hand, the fact that advertising, in order to be successful and economical, "must be in harmony with some larger system of beliefs or some already existing predisposition" indicates that its influence is tangential rather than direct, that it tends to fit in with and supplement other motivational influences rather than act as an independent force.

## EFFECT ON CONSUMER STANDARDS

Advertising, both for individual products and in the aggregate, appeals to the anticipatory aspirations of the group.[11] It offers goals of attainment that would not otherwise be thought of. It sets up ideals to be sought after. Its appeals are designed to stimulate action which will result in a more comfortable, congenial and satisfying life.

Thus, in the aggregate it creates an ever-expanding series of aspirations for the future. In doing this, it shapes the standards of living for the future; and, since man lives largely in a world of anticipation, it lays the basis for much of his enjoyment.

In American business, commercial propaganda is part and parcel of the mass-production process. Our present American business could no more operate without advertising than it could without the automatic machine or the assembly line. By means of this propaganda, the millions of people coming from many nations and races and diverse backgrounds are conditioned to want sufficient amounts of a given standardized product to make it possible to produce that product at a fraction of the cost which would otherwise be necessary.

If left without such propaganda as is found in advertising, people would not choose the same products they do choose. Whether they

would choose the same product at a later date is purely a matter of conjecture, but it seems unlikely. If it is assumed that without advertising they would choose something different, then no producer would be able to secure sufficient production to provide these diverse things at prices people could afford to pay. This is another way of saying that standardization of wants through advertising is in part the basis for the economies which come through mass production.

In spite of the necessity that people's wants be so standardized as to secure mass production, the enormous market and the high-level purchasing power available in America have enabled firms to proliferate these standards and to offer a wider variety of goods for sale than would be possible even under a handicraft system where goods are presumably made to fit the consumer's specifications.

Incidentally, the assumption sometimes made, that people would make wiser choices if there were no advertising, ignores the fact that preconceived notions of what they want have themselves been formed by other types of propaganda and other influences no less biased and no more rational than the propaganda used by sellers.

As people get more income, and as competition becomes stronger among sellers for a share of this income, adjustment of goods to the consumer becomes finer. More attention is given to the marginal aspects of goods. New quality standards are developed in terms of their psychological rather than their utilitarian values. For instance, people in buying shoes are often more interested in style and how they look to others than in comfort and durability, which are likely to be taken for granted.

These types of desires are often hidden and so subtle that sellers are faced with a continuously changing market, difficult to interpret and almost impossible to predict. They are thus forced to offer their products with infinite variations in characteristics and appeals. To the consumer, the opportunity to choose from this vast variety of products is itself a major element in his standard of living.

---

[11] See Wroe Alderson, *Marketing Behavior and Executive Action* (Homewood, Ill.: Richard D. Irwin, 1957), p. 276ff.

# 41. The Concept of the Marketing Mix

## NEIL H. BORDEN

> Marketing is still an art, and the marketing manager, as head
> chef, must creatively marshal *all* his marketing activities to ad-
> vance the short and long term interests of his firm.

I have always found it interesting to observe
how an apt or colorful term may catch on, gain
wide usage, and help to further understanding
of a concept that has already been expressed
in less appealing and communicative terms.
Such has been true of the phrase "marketing
mix," which I began to use in my teaching and
writing some 15 years ago. In a relatively short
time it has come to have wide usage. This note
tells of the evolution of the marketing mix
concept.

The phrase was suggested to me by a paragraph in a research bulletin on the management of marketing costs, written by my associate, Professor James Culliton (1948). In this
study of manufacturers' marketing costs he
described the business executive as a

> "decider," an "artist"—a "mixer of ingredi-
> ents," who sometimes follows a recipe
> prepared by others, sometimes prepares
> his own recipe as he goes along, some-
> times adapts a recipe to the ingredients
> immediately available, and sometimes ex-
> periments with or invents ingredients no
> one else has tried.

I liked his idea of calling a marketing executive a "mixer of ingredients," one who is constantly engaged in fashioning creatively a mix
of marketing procedures and policies in his
efforts to produce a profitable enterprise.

For many years previous to Culliton's cost
study the wide variations in the procedures
and policies employed by managements of

◆ SOURCE: Reprinted by permission from the
*Journal of Advertising Research*, Vol. 4, No. 2,
June 1964, pp. 2–7.

manufacturing firms in their marketing programs and the correspondingly wide variation
in the costs of these marketing functions, which
Culliton aptly ascribed to the varied "mixing of
ingredients," had become increasingly evident
as we had gathered marketing cases at the
Harvard Business School. The marked differences in the patterns or formulae of the marketing programs not only were evident through
facts disclosed in case histories, but also were
reflected clearly in the figures of a cost study
of food manufacturers made by the Harvard
Bureau of Business Research in 1929. The
primary objective of this study was to determine common figures of expenses for various
marketing functions among food manufacturing companies, similar to the common cost
figures which had been determined in previous
years for various kinds of retail and wholesale
businesses. In this manufacturer's study we
were unable, however, with the data gathered
to determine common expense figures that had
much significance as standards by which to
guide management, such as had been possible
in the studies of retail and wholesale trades,
where the methods of operation tended toward
uniformity. Instead, among food manufacturers the ratios of sales devoted to the various
functions of marketing such as advertising,
personal selling, packaging, and so on, were
found to be widely divergent, no matter how
we grouped our respondents. Each respondent
gave data that tended to uniqueness.

Culliton's study of marketing costs in 1947-
48 was a second effort to find out, among other
objectives, whether a bigger sample and a more
careful classification of companies would pro-

duce evidence of operating uniformities that would give helpful common expense figures. But the result was the same as in our early study: there was wide diversity in cost ratios among any classifications of firms which were set up, and no common figures were found that had much value. This was true whether companies were grouped according to similarity in product lines, amount of sales, territorial extent of operations, or other bases of classification.

Relatively early in my study of advertising, it had become evident that understanding of advertising usage by manufacturers in any case had to come from an analysis of advertising's place as one element in the total marketing program of the firm. I came to realize that it is essential always to ask: what overall marketing strategy has been or might be employed to bring about a profitable operation in light of the circumstances faced by the management? What combination of marketing procedures and policies has been or might be adopted to bring about desired behavior of trade and consumers at costs that will permit a profit? Specifically, how can advertising, personal selling, pricing, packaging, channels, warehousing, and the other elements of a marketing program be manipulated and fitted together in a way that will give a profitable operation? In short, I saw that every advertising management case called for a consideration of the strategy to be adopted for the total marketing program, with advertising recognized as only one element whose form and extent depended on its careful adjustment to the other parts of the program.

The soundness of this viewpoint was supported by case histories throughout my volume, *The Economic Effects of Advertising* (Borden, 1942). In the chapters devoted to the utilization of advertising by business, I had pointed out the innumerable combinations of marketing methods and policies that might be adopted by a manager in arriving at a marketing plan. For instance, in the area of branding, he might elect to adopt an individualized brand or a family brand. Or he might decide to sell his product unbranded or under private label. Any decision in the area of brand policy in turn has immediate implications that bear on his selection of channels of distribution, sales force methods, packaging, promotional procedure, and advertising. Throughout the volume the case materials cited show that the way in which any marketing function is designed and the burden placed upon the function are deter-

mined largely by the overall marketing strategy adopted by managements to meet the market conditions under which they operate. The forces met by different firms vary widely. Accordingly, the programs fashioned differ widely.

Regarding advertising, which was the function under focus in the economic effects volume, I said at one point:

> In all the above illustrative situations it should be recognized that advertising is not an operating method to be considered as something apart, as something whose profit value is to be judged alone. An able management does not ask, "Shall we use or not use advertising," without consideration of the product and of other management procedures to be employed. Rather the question is always one of finding a management formula giving advertising its due place in the combination of manufacturing methods, product form, pricing, promotion and selling methods, and distribution methods. As previously pointed out different formulae, i.e., different combinations of methods, may be profitably employed by competing manufacturers.

From the above it can be seen why Culliton's description of a marketing manager as a "mixer of ingredients" immediately appealed to me as an apt and easily understandable phrase, far better than my previous references to the marketing man as an empiricist seeking in any situation to devise a profitable "pattern" or "formula" of marketing operations from among the many procedures and policies that were open to him. If he was a "mixer of ingredients," what he designed was a "marketing mix."

It was logical to proceed from a realization of the existence of a variety of "marketing mixes" to the development of a concept that would comprehend not only this variety, but also the market forces that cause managements to produce a variety of mixes. It is the problems raised by these forces that lead marketing managers to exercise their wits in devising mixes or programs which they hope will give a profitable business operation.

To portray this broadened concept in a visual presentation requires merely:

1. a list of the important elements or ingredients that make up marketing programs;
2. a list of the forces that bear on the mar-

keting operation of a firm and to which the marketing manager must adjust in his search for a mix or program that can be successful.

The list of elements of the marketing mix in such a visual presentation can be long or short, depending on how far one wishes to go in his classification and subclassification of the marketing procedures and policies with which marketing managements deal when devising marketing programs. The list of elements which I have employed in my teaching and consulting work covers the principal areas of marketing activities which call for management decisions as revealed by case histories. I realize others might build a different list. Mine is as follows:

### Elements of the Marketing Mix for Manufacturers

1. *Product Planning*—policies and procedures relating to:

   (a) Product lines to be offered—qualities, design, etc.
   (b) Markets to sell: whom, where, when, and in what quantity.
   (c) New product policy—research and development program.

2. *Pricing*—policies and procedures relating to:

   (a) Price level to adopt.
   (b) Specific prices to adopt (odd-even, etc.).
   (c) Price policy, e.g., one-price or varying price, price maintenance, use of list prices, etc.
   (d) Margins to adopt—for company; for the trade.

3. *Branding*—policies and procedures relating to:

   (a) Selection of trade marks.
   (b) Brand policy—individualized or family brand.
   (c) Sale under private label or unbranded.

4. *Channels of Distribution*—policies and procedures relating to:

   (a) Channels to use between plant and consumer.
   (b) Degree of selectivity among wholesalers and retailers.
   (c) Efforts to gain cooperation of the trade.

5. *Personal Selling*—policies and procedures relating to:

   (a) Burden to be placed on personal selling and the methods to be employed in:

   (1) Manufacturer's organization.
   (2) Wholesale segment of the trade.
   (3) Retail segment of the trade.

6. *Advertising*—policies and procedures relating to:

   (a) Amount to spend—i.e., the burden to be placed on advertising.
   (b) Copy platform to adopt:
   (1) Product image desired.
   (2) Corporate image desired.
   (c) Mix of advertising: to the trade; through the trade; to consumers.

7. *Promotions*—policies and procedures relating to:

   (a) Burden to place on special selling plans or devices directed at or through the trade.
   (b) Form of these devices for consumer promotions, for trade promotions.

8. *Packaging*—policies and procedures relating to:

   (a) Formulation of package and label.

9. *Display*—policies and procedures relating to:

   (a) Burden to be put on display to help effect sale.
   (b) Methods to adopt to secure display.

10. *Servicing*—policies and procedures relating to:

    (a) Providing service needed.

11. *Physical Handling*—policies and procedures relating to:

    (a) Warehousing.
    (b) Transportation.
    (c) Inventories.

12. *Fact Finding and Analysis*—policies and procedures relating to:

    (a) Securing, analysis, and use of facts in marketing operations.

Also if one were to make a list of all the forces which managements weigh at one time or another when formulating their marketing mixes, it would be very long indeed, for the behavior of individuals and groups in all spheres of life have a bearing, first, on what goods and services are produced and consumed, and, second, on the procedures that may be employed in bringing about exchange of these goods and services. However, the important forces which bear on marketers, all arising from the behavior of individuals or groups, may readily be listed under four heads, namely the behavior of consumers, the trade, competitors, and government.

The outline below contains these four behavioral forces with notations of some of the important behavioral determinants within each force. These must be studied and understood by the marketer, if his marketing mix is to be successful. The great quest of marketing management is to understand the behavior of humans in response to the stimuli to which they are subjected. The skillful marketer is one who is a perceptive and practical psychologist and sociologist, who has keen insight into individual and group behavior, who can foresee changes in behavior that develop into a dynamic world, who has creative ability for building well knit programs because he has the capacity to visualize the probable response of consumers, trade, and competitors to his moves. His skill in forecasting response to his marketing moves should well be supplemented by a further skill in devising and using tests and measurements to check consumer or trade response to his program or parts thereof, for no marketer has so much prescience that he can proceed without empirical check.

Below, then, is the suggested outline of forces which govern the mixing of marketing elements. This list and that of the elements taken together provide a visual presentation of the concept of the marketing mix.

### Market Forces Bearing on the Marketing Mix

1. *Consumers' Buying Behavior*, as determined by their:

    (a) Motivation in purchasing.
    (b) Buying habits.
    (c) Living habits.
    (d) Environment (present and future, as revealed by trends, for environment influences consumers' attitudes toward products and their use of them).
    (e) Buying power.
    (f) Number (i.e., how many).

2. *The Trade's Behavior*—wholesalers' and retailers' behavior, as influenced by:

    (a) Their motivations.
    (b) Their structure, practices, and attitudes.
    (c) Trends in structure and procedures that portend change.

3. *Competitors' Position and Behavior*, as influenced by:

    (a) Industry structure and the firm's relation thereto.

        (1) Size and strength of competitors.
        (2) Number of competitors and degree of industry concentration.
        (3) Indirect competition—i.e., from other products.
    (b) Relation of supply to demand—oversupply or undersupply.
    (c) Product choices offered consumers by the industry—i.e., quality, price, service.
    (d) Degree to which competitors compete on price vs. nonprice bases.
    (e) Competitors' motivations and attitudes—their likely response to the actions of other firms.
    (f) Trends technological and social, portending change in supply and demand.

4. *Governmental Behavior—Controls over Marketing:*

    (a) Regulations over products.
    (b) Regulations over pricing.
    (c) Regulations over competitive practices.
    (d) Regulations over advertising and promotion.

When building a marketing program to fit the needs of his firm, the marketing manager has to weigh the behavioral forces and then juggle marketing elements in his mix with a keen eye on the resources with which he has to work. His firm is but one small organism in a large universe of complex forces. His firm is only a part of an industry that is competing with many other industries. What does the firm have in terms of money, product line, organization, and reputation with which to work? The manager must devise a mix of procedures that fit these resources. If his firm is small, he must judge the response of consumers, trade, and competition in light of his position and resources and the influence that he can exert in the market. He must look for special opportunities in product or method of operation. The small firm cannot employ the procedures of the big firm. Though he may sell the same kind of product as the big firm, his marketing strategy is likely to be widely different in many respects. Innumerable instances of this fact might be cited. For example, in the industrial goods field, small firms often seek to build sales on a limited and highly specialized line, whereas industry leaders seek patronage for full lines. Small firms often elect to go in for regional sales rather than attempt the national distribution practiced by larger companies. Again, the company of limited resources often elects to limit its production and sales to products whose potential is too small to attract the big fellows. Still again, companies with small resources in the cosmetic field not infrequently have set up introductory marketing programs employing aggressive personal selling and a "push" strategy with distribution limited to leading department stores. Their initially small advertising funds have been directed through these selected retail outlets, with the offering of the products and their story told over the signatures of the stores. The strategy has been to borrow kudos for their products from the leading stores' reputations and to gain a gradual radiation of distribution to smaller stores in all types of channels, such as often comes from the trade's follow-the-leader behavior. Only after resources have grown from mounting sales has a dense retail distribution been aggressively sought and a shift made to place the selling burden more and more on company-signed advertising.

The above strategy was employed for Toni products and Stoppette deodorant in their early marketing stages when the resources of their producers were limited (cf. case of Jules Montenier, Inc. in Borden and Marshall, 1959, pp. 498-518). In contrast, cosmetic manufacturers with large resources have generally followed a "pull" strategy for the introduction of new products, relying on heavy campaigns of advertising in a rapid succession of area introductions to induce a hoped-for, complete retail coverage from the start (cf. case of Bristol-Myers Company in Borden and Marshall, 1959, pp. 519-533). These introductory campaigns have been undertaken only after careful programs of product development and test marketing have given assurance that product and selling plans had high promise of success.

Many additional instances of the varying strategy employed by small versus large enterprises might be cited. But those given serve to illustrate the point that managements must fashion their mixes to fit their resources. Their objectives must be realistic.

## LONG VS. SHORT TERM ASPECTS OF MARKETING MIX

The marketing mix of a firm in large part is the product of the evolution that comes from day-to-day marketing. At any time the mix represents the program that a management has evolved to meet the problems with which it is constantly faced in an ever changing, ever challenging market. There are continuous tactical maneuvers: a new product, aggressive promotion, or price change initiated by a competitor must be considered and met; the failure of the trade to provide adequate market coverage or display must be remedied; a faltering sales force must be reorganized and stimulated; a decline in sales share must be diagnosed and remedied; an advertising approach that has lost effectiveness must be replaced; a general business decline must be countered. All such problems call for a management's maintaining effective channels of information relative to its own operations and to the day-to-day behavior of consumers, competitors, and the trade. Thus, we may observe that short range forces play a large part in the fashioning of the mix to be used at any time and in determining the allocation of expenditures among the various functional accounts of the operating statement.

But the overall strategy employed in a marketing mix is the product of longer range plans and procedures dictated in part by past empiricism and in part, if the management is a good one, by management foresight as to what needs to be done to keep the firm successful in a changing world. As the world has become more and more dynamic, blessed is that corporation which has managers who have foresight, who can study trends of all kinds—natural, economic, social, and technological—and, guided by these, devise long-range plans that give promise of keeping their corporations afloat and successful in the turbulent sea of market change. Accordingly, when we think of the marketing mix, we need to give particular heed today to devising a mix based on long-range planning that promises to fit the world of five or ten or more years hence. Provision for effective long-range planning in corporate organization and procedure has become more and more recognized as the earmark of good management in a world that has become increasingly subject to rapid change.

To cite an instance among American marketing organizations which has shown foresight in adjusting the marketing mix to meet social and economic change, I look upon Sears Roebuck and Company as an outstanding example. After building an unusually successful mail order business to meet the needs of a rural America, Sears management foresaw the need to depart from its marketing pattern as a mail order company catering primarily to farmers. The trend from a rural to an urban United States was going on apace. The automobile and good roads promised to make town and city stores increasingly available to those who continued to be farmers. Relatively early, Sears launched a chain of stores across the land, each easily accessible by highway to both farmer and city resident, and with adequate parking space for customers. In time there followed the remarkable telephone and mail order plan directed at urban residents to make buying easy for Americans when congested city streets and highways made shopping increasingly distasteful. Similarly, in the areas of planning products which would meet the desires of consumers in a fast changing world, of shaping its servicing to meet the needs of a wide variety of mechanical products, of pricing procedures to meet the challenging competition that came with the advent of discount retailers, the Sears organization has shown a foresight, adaptability, and creative ability worthy of emulation. The amazing growth and profitability of the company attest to the foresight and skill of its management. Its history shows the wisdom of careful attention to market forces and their impending change in devising marketing mixes that may assure growth.

## USE OF THE MARKETING MIX CONCEPT

Like many concepts, the marketing mix concept seems relatively simple, once it has been expressed. I know that before they were ever tagged with the nomenclature of "concept," the ideas involved were widely understood among marketers as a result of the growing knowledge about marketing and marketing procedures that came during the preceding half century. But I have found for myself that once the ideas were reduced to a formal statement with an accompanying visual presentation, the concept of the mix has proved a helpful devise in teaching, in business problem solving, and, generally, as an aid to thinking about marketing. First of all, it is helpful in giving an answer to the question often raised as to "what is marketing?" A chart which shows the elements of the mix and the forces that bear on the mix helps to bring understanding of what marketing is. It helps to explain why in our dynamic world the thinking of management in all its functional areas must be oriented to the market.

In recent years I have kept an abbreviated chart showing the elements and the forces of the marketing mix in front of my classes at all times. In case discussion it has proved a handy device by which to raise queries as to whether the student has recognized the implications of any recommendation he might have made in the areas of the several elements of the mix. Or,

referring to the forces, we can question whether all the pertinent market forces have been given due consideration. Continual reference to the mix chart leads me to feel that the students' understanding of "what marketing is" is strengthened. The constant presence and use of the chart leaves a deeper understanding that marketing is the devising of programs that successfully meet the forces of the market.

In problem solving the marketing mix chart is a constant reminder of:

1. The fact that a problem seemingly lying in one segment of the mix must be deliberated with constant thought regarding the effect of any change in that sector on the other areas of marketing operations. The necessity of integration in marketing thinking is ever present.

2. The need of careful study of the market forces as they might bear on problems in hand.

In short, the mix chart provides an ever ready checklist as to areas into which to guide thinking when considering marketing questions or dealing with marketing problems.

## MARKETING: SCIENCE OR ART?

The quest for a "science of marketing" is hard upon us. If science is in part a systematic formulation and arrangement of facts in a way to help understanding, then the concept of the marketing mix may possibly be considered a small contribution in the search for a science of marketing. If we think of a marketing science as involving the observation and classification of facts and the establishment of verifiable laws that can be used by the marketer as a guide to action with assurance that predicted results will ensue, then we cannot be said to have gotten far toward establishing a science. The concept of the mix lays out the areas in which facts should be assembled, these to serve as a guide to management judgment in building marketing mixes. In the last few decades American marketers have made substantial progress in adopting the scientific method in assembling facts. They have sharpened the tools of fact finding—both those arising within the business and those external to it. Aided by these facts and by the skills developed through careful observation and experience, marketers are better fitted to practice the art of designing marketing mixes than would be the case had not the techniques of gathering facts been advanced as they have been in recent decades. Moreover, marketers have made progress in the use of the scientific method in designing tests whereby the results from mixes or parts of mixes can be measured. Thereby marketers have been learning how to subject the hypotheses of their mix artists to empirical check.

With continued improvement in the search for and the recording of facts pertinent to marketing, with further application of the controlled experiment, and with an extension and careful recording of case histories, we may hope for a gradual formulation of clearly defined and helpful marketing laws. Until then, and even then, marketing and the building of marketing mixes will largely lie in the realm of art.

## REFERENCES

BORDEN, NEIL H. *The Economic Effects of Advertising.* Homewood, Ill.: Richard D. Irwin, 1942.

BORDEN, NEIL H., and M. V. MARSHALL. *Advertising Management: Text and Cases.* Homewood, Ill.: Richard D. Irwin, 1959.

CULLITON, JAMES W. *The Management of Marketing Costs.* Boston: Division of Research, Graduate School of Business Administration, Harvard University, 1948.

# 42. The Industrial Salesman as a Source of Market Information

FREDERICK E. WEBSTER, JR.

The central element in the promotional strategy of the majority of companies is the salesman—not advertising. Investigation suggests that few firms are using salesmen to the best advantage. By limiting, either explicitly or implicitly, the salesman's role to that of a promotional agent, the company minimizes his opportunity to function as a source of market information.

## VALUE OF MARKET INFORMATION

In the past decade especially, managers and educators have been exposed to a large quantity of literature expounding the so-called marketing concept. The various interpretations of the marketing concept have at least one common ingredient—emphasis on the importance of information about customers' needs and wants as an essential basis for management decisions. Under this concept, the marketing task is to direct the firm's operations toward the product and service requirements of customers. Marketing starts with the customer, not the product. In fact, the whole course of business starts with the customer by first learning what his needs are and then determining whether and how the company is able to provide a commodity that can contribute to the customer's satisfaction.

Gathering information and using it to make decisions are most visible in customer survey marketing research. A different kind of infor-

mation gathering is represented by the day-to-day reports of market information by the sales force. As compared with survey research, salesmen's information about customers, competitors, and other market factors offers the following advantages:

1. The incremental costs are low.
2. The salesman tends to have well-established relationships with customers and a familiarity with their needs and wants.
3. Customers, to the extent that they perceive the salesman and his company as a potential supplier of problem-solving products and services, will be more willing to provide information to salesmen than to an unknown questioner.
4. Salesmen can collect and report information with little additional effort, submitting it with their regular call reports.

Because the research for this article exclusively concerned technical industrial products, the following discussion pertains primarily to industrial companies characterized by:

1. Heavy reliance upon salesmen as opposed to advertising
2. A product line that changes continually as the result of technological developments
3. Flexibility in adapting product designs to fit customer requirements, which also change rapidly as the result of technological developments
4. Markets consisting of easily identified

◆ SOURCE: Reprinted by permission from *Business Horizons*, Spring 1965, Vol. 8, No. 1, pp. 77–82.

customers, actual and potential, in terms of numbers, size, and location.

It should be stressed that these are factual observations, not assumptions, about companies selling technical products to industrial producers. With the exception of the changing product line, these characteristics pertain to most firms selling in industrial markets. The industrial supplier probably needs more and better information about customer requirements than the consumer goods producer because of the relatively greater importance of the individual customer to the firm's operations. While the industrial salesman is still important as a promotional agent, he must operate within the constraints established by the customer's production requirements.

## USING SALESMEN'S INFORMATION

Use of the salesman for gathering information can be much more critical than his use for promotion. While this generalization obviously does not hold for every company and every industry, the practices of several electronics firms suggest that industrial marketing efficiency can be greatly improved through increased reliance upon the salesman as a source of market information. This article will focus upon four principal uses of information provided by salesmen: product planning, sales forecasting, competitive strategy, and pricing. These are not the only areas where the salesman can provide essential information, nor are they independent. For example, pricing and competitive strategy involve wide areas of interdependence. Also, the salesman is certainly an important source of information on matters relating to sales force management. In the following discussion, however, only these four functions will be considered.

### Product Planning

The company supplying industrial manufacturers must frequently adapt or modify its product line to fit customers' needs. To be effective each change must be based on sound information about what the customers require. While salesmen may have substantial bias with respect to product development needs, just as engineers do, the salesman gains information about the market more easily than does the development engineer. Thus, the salesman's bias

can provide a necessary offset for the engineer's bias.

For the industrial producer, product planning frequently involves anticipation of changing customer product requirements with a carefully planned technical development program. As one moves along the continuum of nontechnical to technical products, anticipating the changing customer requirements becomes more complex. The development process can only be efficient to the extent that it is based on current, complete, and correct information about customers' requirements and plans. Although prediction can never be entirely accurate, it is possible to develop a more direct approach if accurate information is available. Specific development targets can replace such generalized developmental research goals as "to advance the state-of-the-art," which are more appropriate for basic research. A rifle can be substituted for a shotgun in R&D efforts, with the payoff of increased results and lower costs.

Although this point of view seems obvious, the author's research suggests that it is not always obvious to engineering groups, to management in general, or even to marketing management in the companies that were studied. All too frequently, marketing has defined too narrowly its role in company operations. Technically-oriented firms in particular have been slow to recognize the need for defining marketing in terms broader than selling. One result has been inefficiency in the product development program; all companies studied could report at least one instance of developing a product for which there was virtually no market demand, and many marketing opportunities have been foregone because the company did not have a product to meet the new requirements of its customers.

To define the salesman as a selling agent exclusively is to ignore the opportunity for significant improvement in product planning efficiency. Salesmen in industrial companies are usually sufficiently well-trained (many have at least a bachelor's degree in engineering), to be able to perform an initial evaluation of the feasibility of a customer's requests for a product modification or development. The risk is not great, therefore, if salesmen are given the task of providing new product ideas, of generating too many irresponsible development ideas. Furthermore, the salesman is particularly sensitive to the adequacy of his company's product offerings in respect to market demands. He is sensitive to obsolescence and gaps in the company's product line because they make his selling job more difficult.

### Sales Forecasting

Information supplied by salesmen is more commonly used for sales forecasting that for product planning. They frequently provide estimates of the size of the market in their assigned territories and occasionally break down these estimates into product groupings. The estimates are used to compute sales forecasts, which in turn are used for sales force evaluation and control, sales budgeting, and production planning. Different forecasts are frequently used for each purpose.

A unique dimension of forecasting presents itself to companies that rely on competitive bidding for most of their sales volume. Here the problem is to estimate the likelihood of winning a particular contract, rather than the size of the market. This is the major forecasting problem for the defense contractor, although it is typical of any firm relying on competitive bidding. One approach to forecasting bidding success defines a unique role for the salesman.

A company asked its salesmen to assign probabilities to the event of winning contracts on which it had bid. The dollar value of the potential contract, multiplied by this probability, provided an expected value for the contract. By adding expected values for each outstanding bid, the company obtained a sales forecast they could use as the basis for production planning in the current period. (This will be recognized as a simple application of Bayesian decision theory.)

An example will make the procedure clear. Assume that the company has four outstanding bids to be opened during the current period, and that these bids are for $100,000; $200,000; $50,000; and $500,000. If the company were certain of success in each of these bidding competitions, the sales forecast would be $850,000. But because of competitive bidding the company cannot be certain of winning each contract award, so the sales forecast should be less than $850,000. Salesmen assigned to each of these four accounts provided the following estimates of the chance of winning each contract: 25 per cent, 50 per cent, 10 per cent, and 30 per cent respectively. The table summarizes the calculations necessary to arrive at a forecast.

| Contract | Bid Price | Probability of Winning Award | Expected Revenue from Each Award |
|---|---|---|---|
| A | $100,000 | .25 | $ 25,000 |
| B | 200,000 | .50 | 100,000 |
| C | 50,000 | .10 | 5,000 |
| D | 500,000 | .30 | 150,000 |
| Sales forecast = | | | |
| Total expected revenue= | | | $280,000 |

This example is somewhat unrealistic because the small number of contracts introduces a great deal of variability in estimates. When the number of outstanding bids is large, however, and salesmen do not exhibit consistent bias, very accurate estimates can result. The company using this method reported an enviable average variability of 1.5 per cent on a monthly basis.

The "probability of winning award" is really a very complex statistic surrounding the mation about the conditions surrounding the bidding competition, including: the strength of the company with the particular customer, compared with competition; an estimate of competitive bid prices; the acceptability of the company's bid in terms of product offering; and, if available, the salesman's evaluation of the effectiveness of the presentation. Each of these factors is likely to be significant in the customer's final award decision, especially if there are differences in the "technical proposals" or product offerings submitted by competing bidders. Of course, if the procurement is strictly a "nuts and bolts affair" and all products precisely meet rigorous specification requirements, then the decision is likely to be influenced solely by price. In many industrial procurement situations, however, bidders vary considerably in their product offerings and nonprice factors become important.

In these complex procurement situations, the salesman is in the best position to estimate the company's various strengths and weaknesses. The assignment of probabilities forces the salesman to think explicitly and to quantify his judgment of his company's competitive strength. The probability figure summarizes the influence of a host of competitive factors upon revenue expectations. Because of his familiarity with the customer and with the local competitive situation, the salesman can make this estimate with greater accuracy than a less well-informed observer.

The preceding discussion has concentrated

on one aspect of the salesman's potential contribution to sales forecasting; the competitive bidding situation defines a special role for the salesman. Extension of this basic approach to other estimates of market potential and market share, using probability notions, is fairly straightforward. The arguments in favor of using salesmen as sources of information for sales forecasting in general are well known and will not be repeated here.

### Competitive Strategy

It is somewhat unrealistic to separate competitive strategy from other marketing considerations since each decision, whether in the area of product, price, promotion, or marketing-channels policies, cannot be realistically separated from the over-all competitive strategy and marketing mix. Nonetheless, to explore competitive strategy as a separate area highlights the need for information about competitors' actions. Proximity to the market gives the salesman an opportunity to provide information about competitors' actions.

The industrial market is dynamic because of changing customer requirements and is made increasingly dynamic by the variability in competitors' reactions to changing customer requirements and to each other. Any marketing decision that does not take competitors' behavior into account is likely to lead up a blind alley.

The salesman once again has an important role to play in providing information on competitors' offerings and plans, not only in terms of products, but also such diverse elements of the marketing mix as pricing, delivery commitments, call frequency, credit terms, warranties, follow-up services, and trade relations. The salesman has access to two sources of information about competitors' plans and activities—competitors' salesmen and customers. Most certainly, customers represent the better source of information, since competitors will obviously try to keep important strategic activities confidential. Customers are frequently willing to talk about promises and commitments made by competitors, however, hoping for a more favorable commitment from the salesman.

Information about competitors can be used effectively by the company in planning competitive strategy and in modifying the marketing mix. Trade journals, trade shows, and the inevitable grapevine are all very useful supplements

—but the salesman has the best access to current and continuous information about competitors' behavior. He can provide it routinely as part of his reporting procedures, or he can provide specific information about a course of action being contemplated by the company. For example, he can solicit customers' reactions to a planned product modification, a change in billing procedures, or virtually any other element of the marketing program that is likely to affect the customer's decisions about suppliers. The salesman might find, for example, that competitors had recently begun promoting a new product similar to one being contemplated by his company. Thus, the salesman can be used to provide information about competitors' activities, customers' reactions to competitors' offerings, and customers' probable reaction to changes in company strategy. Each kind of information is significant in evaluating potential changes in the company's competitive strategy.

### Pricing Decisions

Nowhere is the need for information about competitors' practices and customer reaction made clearer than in the pricing decision. Salesmen are quite frequently asked to determine what the market will bear. In many industrial market segments, product offerings are diverse and there is no established market price for a product, although there may be many close substitutes. Often, the nub of the problem is to predict how much extra the market is willing to pay for a particular product feature. The salesman may be able to provide a good estimate of an appropriate selling price.

In the competitive bidding situation, the salesman's conversations with a buyer may reveal, within narrow limits, the prices being quoted by competitors. While several ethical issues are involved that we cannot explore here, many of our respondents reported that the critical function of the salesman in a competitive bidding procedure is to find out what the competition has bid. A common practice, often referred to as the Chinese auction, consists of the buyer telling each salesman that his company's bid is higher than another company's bid in an attempt to force the price as low as possible. The salesman must then estimate the truthfulness of the buyer's statement in order to determine what price quotation to recommend to his company.

In the more general pricing situation, the

salesman has access to three types of information that are necessary inputs to the pricing decision: the value of the product in the customer's planned application or end-use; the prices being quoted by competitors for similar products; and the customer's expectations about the price he will have to pay. Because each type of information is likely to be peculiar to the individual customer, and because the salesman is closest to the customer, the salesman is in the best position to estimate the price the customer is willing to pay for a given product.

## IMPLEMENTING THE SALESMAN'S INFORMATION RESPONSIBILITY

The task of holding the salesman responsible for supplying information is easier if it is carefully planned, has clearly defined objectives, and makes specific provision for evaluation and control. Many companies studied recognized the potential contribution of their sales force, but had been frustrated in their attempts to make the plan operational. The major problems appear to be training salesmen to provide information and making effective use of the information in company planning. Because the task places increased demands upon the salesman, he will probably not perform it unless he is specifically ordered to. And the information will be of little value unless the company has specific procedures for summarizing and evaluating it. One of the companies studied required that the salesman fill out a report on each call. This generated more than two hundred call reports per day, which the marketing manager's secretary screened. She filed the reports that were not of more than routine interest, and the company made no further use of the information in them.

The salesman must be informed as to what kinds of information are useful to, and required by, the company which will use it. The R&D group will want one kind of information, the production department another, and the sales manager yet a third kind. Information required and requested by each department should be evaluated to determine whether the potential contribution warrants the cost and effort of obtaining it. Specific procedures must then be established for collection, summarization, and evaluation. Finally, some method of evaluating the salesman's collection efforts must be established for control purposes. Most frequently, this evaluation is best performed by the person or group using the information, in conjunction with the sales manager.

Doesn't this informational role place a tremendous burden upon the salesman, a burden he will resist and resent? Unfortunately, the answer is affirmative unless the salesman sees results that increase his effectiveness. Whether or not he sees these results depends strongly upon the ability of the organization to use the information efficiently and intelligently. If the company is using the salesman's information to keep its product and marketing strategy optimally tuned to the ever-changing requirements of the market, selling the product will be a much easier job.

The customer contact function is useful as both a source and a use of information. In his contact with customers, the salesman obtains information that is used as an input for strategy decisions; the output of these decisions is a set of strategy directives designed to increase the promotional efficiency of the salesman in his contact with customers. If the company is making proper use of the salesman as a source of information, and is using that information effectively, product offerings will be optimally fitted to market requirements, as will the company's other services and terms of sale.

Furthermore, the salesman will find satisfaction in being asked to play a critical function in the company's planning efforts. If this contributes to his selling effectiveness, the salesman is going to see the importance of the information that he provided. Inherent in the intelligent use of salesmen as a source of market information, therefore, is a strong motivational element to stimulate salesmen to stronger selling effort.

# D. Distribution Planning

## 43. A Systems Approach to Transportation
WILLIAM LAZER

The transportation industry and its methods of operation are in the throes of a major transition.

A far-reaching and fundamental change in the philosophy of transportation management, in the methods of improving services, and in decision making is taking place. The major characteristics of the change may be summed up in one word—systems.

### SYSTEMS APPROACH

Executives in transportation are embracing the systems approach to transportation's role in company operations and as a solution to distribution problems. The approach interrelates the total complex of transportation and storage activities with other aspects of business operations. Thus it assures company stability, growth, and profit.

This approach, which is now evident in the operation of progressive companies, stresses the interrelationship and coordinacy of all activities in physical distribution. It perceives the transportation function as one segment of the complete system of business action.

The systems approach to transportation management emphasizes the impact of decisions made by this department on every segment of transportation, on all physical distribution activities, or other marketing operations, and on the total business system.

Too often traffic managers regard transportation narrowly. Many of them see it as a functional operation existing largely because

of and for itself. In this sense, the performance of transportation functions are viewed as major reasons for the existence of a traffic manager.

### SPECIALIZED ACTIVITY

From this viewpoint, transportation is considered a specialized operating activity. It falls within the domain of one department affecting one aspect of the organization. Transportation decisions are made and activities conducted largely in the light of transportation dimensions.

This functionalized approach to transportation has serious negative consequences. Companies adopting it are not likely to maximize their profits because:

There will exist a lack of planning and action designed to optimize the use of total company resources and to maximize over-all profits.

Numerous independent decisions will be formulated and implemented without recognizing the consequences for other elements of physical distribution and business operations.

Transportation policies and services will not be designed and adapted to better meet company and customer needs.

A lack of coordination of space and movement strategy will occur which may generate disfunctioning in the total system of business action.

For example, there is often a lack of integration of decisions concerning the types of

◆ SOURCE: Reprinted by permission from *Marketing Logistics*, N. E. Marks and R. M. Taylor (eds.), (New York: John Wiley & Sons, Inc.) 1967, pp. 197–202.

◆ SOURCE: Reprinted by permission from *Distribution Age*, Vol. 59, No. 9, (September 1960) pp. 33–35 and 64, 65.

carriers, warehouse location, inventory levels, storing, and packaging problems. Each may have an impact on the other. As a result, the transportation department may work towards achieving its own specific objectives. They may run counter to the major goals of the company. Profits drop.

In such cases transportation objectives can be achieved. But relatively high costs result for the firm as a whole. Thereby much of the true meaning and value of transportation management may be lost. In such a situation, the total contributions of the transportation department are not as great as they should be. Total profits realized are less than company action warrants.

To overcome these severe limitations, informed traffic managers are becoming adherents of the systems approach. They are viewing transportation problems in terms of operating wholes.

The systems approach does not defend or favor transportation at the expense of the total organization. By adopting a unified and integrated concept of distribution, decisions may be made which will maximize the total output received from all business inputs. It is this coordinated management approach which will lead to increasing efficiency.

### Implementation

What are the concrete evidences of the systems approach? Perhaps the most specific evidence is a shift in the organizational title and responsibility of the traffic manager. Several companies have broadened both the "label" and duties to include related activities other than those usually referred to in the field of "traffic."

The position is often referred to by a title such as distribution manager or physical distribution manager. This change recognizes the broader dimensions of responsibility included within the domain of the top transportation executive. It emphasizes the impact of transportation functions on other distribution activities within a company.

The second piece of evidence parallels the organizational evolvement of the position of

distribution manager. It is the development of a new concept—physical distribution.[1]

Physical distribution refers to the integration of all aspects of physically handling, storing, and transporting goods on their way to the market. According to this concept, transportation activities in the broadest sense, are regarded as comprising a whole—a system of physical distribution. Management should not think in terms of methods of transportation, warehousing, or handling separately. Management must think in terms of the impact of decisions on each of the other physical distribution segments and on the total company.

### Integrated Operations

Third, in recent transportation literature more emphasis is being given to the systems method. Clyde E. Phelps has written in *Distribution Age* that "The warehousing industry today is on the threshold of an entirely new pattern of distribution—distribution center warehousing. Only the beginning phase of a new concept, it encompasses the physical distribution of goods from plant to storage area to point of final consumer market via multi-plant transit stocks."

This transiting is a system by which the manufacturer can ship a complete order of his entire line of produce at one time, and, on one bill of lading on through rates from the producing point . . . to set up such a program, a sound basis of traffic research coordinated with the production and sales pattern is essential.[2]

Referring to airlines specifically, *Business Week*, March 14, 1959, reported that "The Airline's problem in selling air freight is that the lines have to make their pitch on the basis of distribution as a complete integrated system. . . . The moral is simply that approaching distribution as a total process—and not one made up of separate functions—will sometimes shake management out of long established practices."

In the March 1958 issue of *Distribution Age*, "Lift-On-Lift-Off On the Road to Total Transportation;" explains that "The day of total transportation may be closer than we think. Basically, total transportation is the integration

[1] For a definitive discussion of the physical distribution concept, see "Physical Distribution: A New Concept" by Edward W. Smykay and Frank H. Mossman, in *Managerial Marketing: Perspectives and Viewpoints,* by Eugene J. Kelley and

William Lazer (eds.) (Homewood, Ill.: Richard D. Irwin, Inc., 1958), p. 360.

[2] Clyde E. Phelps, "Transiting—Revolution in Warehousing," *Distribution Age;* February, 1958, p. 37.

of two or more modes of carriage to provide the shipper with a unified service."

It is evident that the concepts referred to advance systems thinking in distribution. They describe certain basic trends and practices in current transportation management which adopt an integrated, coordinated, and total approach to the solution of problems of physically distributing goods. The writers are expressing forward-looking and practical ideas of managerial significance to the transportation industry.

### Lack of Clarity

However, since the observations and writings have been offered by several thoughtful people, definitions and meanings are bound to overlap. The same terms are used to designate difference activities.

The materials which follow will present one viewpoint of a systems approach to transportation and warehousing activities. It will include a brief discussion of: The total transportation system, total warehousing system, physical distribution system, and physical distribution as a segment of the marketing and business system.

### Total Transportation

The total transportation system is shown in Chart 1. Essentially, it is the integration of two or more modes of transportation to provide shippers with more effective services. Under this concept, various alternative and complementary methods of transportation are coordinated to better meet the shipper's needs. The concept is not as broad in scope as the physical distribution concept. Instead it is one sub-system of the total system of physical distribution.

Specifically, the total transportation system

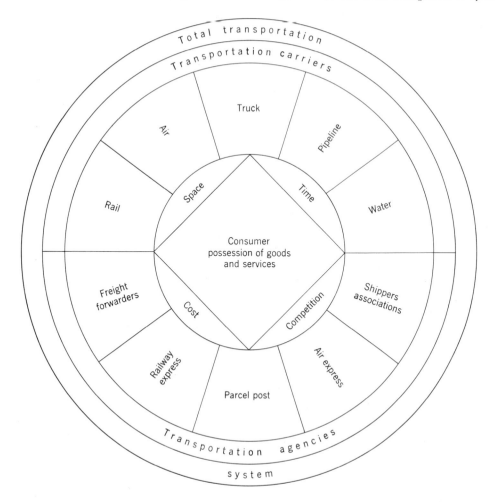

CHART 1. The total transportation system

combinates rail, air, truck, pipeline, and water carriers. It is concerned, too, with such facilitating transportation agencies as freight forwarders, railway express, parcel post, air express, and shipper's associations. Management faces the challenge of combining transportation elements in an optimal manner to obtain the most profit. Trailership and piggyback are examples of individual carriers combined to achieve more efficient handling and movement.

The total warehousing concept deals with integration of storing and handling. Under such a concept, the warehouse is no longer just a storage facility. It is an important component of the marketing channel. Its goal is moving goods in the most efficient manner possible.

In the total warehousing system, all the functions performed in storing and handling merchandise are coordinated. This overcomes barriers of space, time, and competition in get-

ting goods to consumers as effectively as possible. This coordinated approach to warehousing activities is resulting in new and more efficient distribution patterns. Chart 2 presents the elements of the total warehousing system.

The total warehousing system is comprised of two major groups of activities—handling and storage functions and merchandising functions. Included among the handling and storage responsibilities are warehouse location, storing, receiving, consolidation, breaking bulk, handling, packaging, marking, order processing, shipping and delivery, and billing. The merchandising aspects include display, selling, financing, credit, and grading.

Distribution executives are concerned with the integration of storage, handling, and merchandising functions to achieve the optimal warehousing combination. It is in this context

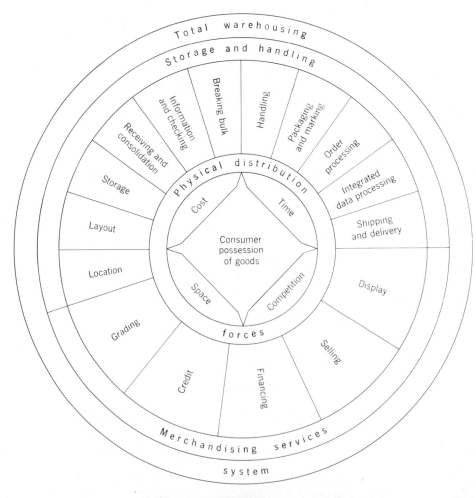

CHART 2.

or a planned and integrated facility that the warehouse is considered to be a distribution center. Through the use of mechanical equipment, automatic data processing, and by coordinating warehouse-related activities more effective systems of distribution are being achieved.

## DISTRIBUTION SYSTEM

To obtain optimal efficiency in physically distributing goods, it is necessary to coordinate all of the company's transportation and warehousing activities. These should be grouped under the authority and responsibility of a major executive. This is the domain of the executive in charge of physical distribution.

The physical distribution manager should be charged with the spatial arrangement of plant capacity and distribution facilities. These two aspects of company operations are linked by transportation systems. As a result the physical distribution manager is concerned with coordinating and combining all aspects of storing, handling, and transporting goods in the most profitable manner.

Essentially, physical distribution as a system has two major sub-systems—the total transportation system and the total warehousing system. This is shown by Chart 3.

Under the physical distribution concept, all of the elements of both systems are to be combined to achieve the most efficient over-all system of distribution. This is one of the primary

CHART 3. The physical distribution system

responsibilities of the distribution manager. Clearly the scope of these activities lies well beyond the boundaries suggested by the title "traffic manager."

What do these ideas mean to transportation management? What will the management consequences be for companies adopting the systems approach?

Essentially, these developments emphasize that transportation management has come to recognize that a hierarchy of systems exists in business. First, the company is regraded as a total system of business action—the primary management system. Its purpose is to integrate the production of men, materials, money, machines, and management—whether used for transportation, production, marketing, finance, or other functional purposes, to maximize company profits.

There exists an over-all business system within which transportation and other physical distribution functions take place. This system sets primary limits upon transportation decisions and objectives. It is within the system that the sub-system of physical distribution must operate.

The second implication is that physical distribution is but part of a larger marketing sub-system, which in turn is part of the broader business system. Other components of the company's marketing sub-system are: channels of distribution, pricing and credit, service and product policies, and advertising and selling programs. Decisions concerning physical distribution should be made in terms of their impact on other elements of the marketing system.

Third, the physical distribution sub-system in turn has two major components: the total transportation system and the total warehousing system.

Fourth, the company embracing the systems approach to the solution of distribution problems should benefit because:

Physical distribution assumes an integral position in contributing to the company's over-all profit and efficiency.

Various aspects of transportation and warehousing activities are coordinated for maximum efficiency.

Physical distribution decisions are brought into line with the major objectives and policies of the firm.

The scope and functions of "transportation" executives are broadened to include all of the major activities involved in physically distributed goods.

Physical distribution is recognized as an important company activity in the organization structure.

# 44. Information Systems for Logistics Management

ROBERT M. IVIE

## INTRODUCTION

Before discussing business logistics information systems it is important to define the business logistics concept. By re-assembling and rearranging many elements, techniques and problems of management studied in other functional areas of business, and by adding certain additional concepts to these elements, an entirely new approach is possible for the study of a subject that runs like a connecting thread through all other functions of business: logistics.

Recent recognition of the elements of business logistics as components of a single entity or area of management might lead one to overlook the fact that the elements themselves have been previously identified, studied and developed.

The military, as it has with so many other management concepts, provides a likely origin for the term "logistics." Logistics has long been considered as one of the three major functions of the military mission, along with tactics and strategics. In the business enterprise the strategists are those who plan manufacturing methods, designate products to be included in the product line and decide on the amounts of supplies needed to fulfill manufacturing requirements. The tacticians are those who purchase

necessary supplies and carry out the job of transforming them into usable finished products if this is necessary. The logistician is responsible for managing the physical placement of goods at the point and time that they are needed by the strategist and tactician.

There are important differences between logistics in the military and business sense. Military logistics can be described as the transport, quartering, and supply of troops and their materiel. The military logistician can and does set up priorities for demand that constantly exceeds supply.[1] Customer "control" is possible in the military but virtually impossible in business. This control or lack of control over the customer (user of goods) can be considered the major difference between military and business logistics.

Exhibit 1 illustrates how the various managerial and operational functions of business logistics are grouped or aligned within the firm. Demand-supply coordination includes order processing, information flow, inventory management, scheduling and allocation. Movement control includes warehousing and traffic and transportation; those activities concerned with the physical movement of the product.

No matter who manages or performs activities of physical supply and physical distribution within an individual organization, a set of activities exists which undeniably belong

◆ SOURCE: Reprinted by permission from *Marketing Logistics,* N. E. Marks and R. M. Taylor (eds.) (New York: John Wiley & Sons, Inc.), 1967, pp. 121–131.

◆ SOURCE: Reprinted by permission from *American Transportation Research Forum,* Third Annual Meeting, (December 1962) pp. 37–52.

[1] For an interesting discussion of a recently implemented military system, for the purpose of comparisons, see N. D. Chetlin, "The Navy's New Supply Priorities System," *National Defense Transportation Journal,* July–August 1960, pp. 38–39ff.

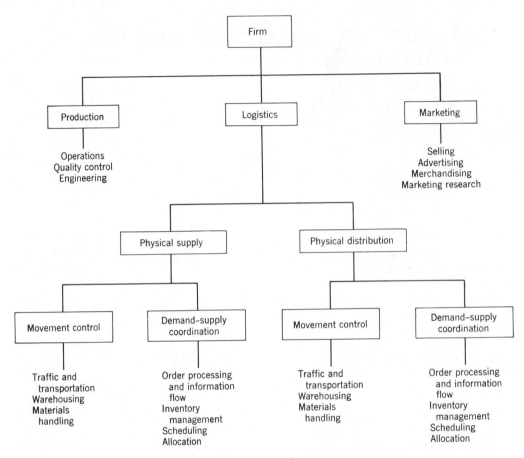

EXHIBIT 1. The business logistics concept.

within the same scope of managerial activity. It is in this sense that "business logistics" is defined as *the management of all activities which facilitate movement and the coordination of supply and demand in the creation of time and place utility in goods.*

In discussing logistic information systems we are concerned with that phase of demand-supply coordination which pertains to the processing of orders and the flow of logistics information inside and outside the firm. The fact that this paper deals almost exclusively with the physical distribution aspect of logistics management should not be construed as a de-emphasis of the physical supply element of business logistics. Time and space limitations of this paper make it necessary to restrict the discussion to physical distribution, that phase of business logistics with which managers and educators are most familiar.

## THE "NEED TO KNOW" CONCEPT

Information is valuable to a manager only if he "needs to know" about a particular aspect of the firm, its market, or the techniques that can be employed to improve the operations for which he is responsible. He may be curious about many phases of business activity with which he is not concerned, but he is probably well advised to become involved only with that information which is required for operation of his department, essential to effective communication with other departments within the firm, or necessary to maintain sound relations with customers and suppliers. This is not to suggest that the manager should bury his head in the sand of his own operational problems but it does suggest that he determine what he "needs to know" about the firm and its market, and what other parts of the firm "need to know" from him. For example, the logistics manager may be curious about special "deals" made with specific customers, the reasons for sales declines even with maintenance of standard customer service levels, or why production has so much scrap at the end of production line. None of these are his problem. Investigation of them (no matter how slight) can create managerial conflict and waste managerial time.

As an introduction to the detailed discussion of external and internal information systems it is important to document the nature and type of information that flows between the firm and its customer (external) and between the logistics department and other functional departments. The information that the functional managers "need to know" and must communicate to the customer is included in Exhibit 2. Exhibit 3 illustrates the type of information that flows, or should flow, between logistics and other functional departments within the firm. In this latter exhibit it should be noted that to cover the entire scope of information flow within a firm it would be necessary to diagram the types of information that move between each of the functional areas. These diagrams of information flow provide a general overview which will vary materially among firms as the relative importance of one or more functions is changed.

Before beginning the discussion of external and internal logistics information it is important to note the importance of personal communication between manager, supervisor and worker. The fact that organizations operate with people cannot be over-emphasized. People communicate more information than all of the forms and reports combined. Forms and reports do not provide any indication of the extent to which communication or information flow may be accomplished verbally in the conference room, on the telephone, or by other means. It is not my intention to discuss the psychology of personal communications except to emphasize that personal contact, and a proper attitude toward it, is perhaps the most important element of a sound information system.

## EXTERNAL AND INTERNAL INFORMATION SYSTEMS

External information flow refers to the communication of information between the firm and its customers and suppliers. Internal information flow systems provide for the exchange of information between functional departments within the firm. With respect to external information flow, this discussion will deal primarily with communication of information between the logistician and the customer. The fact that a similar information system must be maintained with suppliers should not be overlooked because we consider in this discussion only the communications system between the logistician and the customer. The discussion of internal information systems will be concerned primarily with the methods of processing customer orders.

## EXTERNAL INFORMATION SYSTEMS

The customer has a variety of demands all of which tend to improve the profitability of his operations. The customer will "demand the moon" if he believes that there is any chance that his supplier will arrange to send it to him. The determination of the level of customer service is a matter for which the sales manager is responsible. It is the function of the logistics manager to determine how the firm's and its customers' logistics systems can be made more compatible without changing the established standard of customer service.

Two of the keys to success in establishing a sound external logistics information system with customers are: (1) the ability to enlist the cooperation of customers, and (2) the degree to which proper information is provided for the advance planning, operation, and control of logistics activities. Their accomplishment requires coordination both outside and inside the organization. The necessary flow of information for planning and control of logistics and other functions of management is covered in the "need to know" diagrams referred to above. Types of customer cooperation, and ways in which they can be enlisted, are the subject of the following section.

### Customer Coordination

Various steps can be taken, with the customer's cooperation, which make it easier for a supplier to meet predetermined customer service levels, particularly from the standpoint of logistics. They include adjustment of customer: (1) order patterns, (2) materials handling systems, (3) reorder point on stock, and (4) order procedures. In this regard, the logistics manager must rely heavily upon marketing's "eyes" and "ears," the salesman, and work with

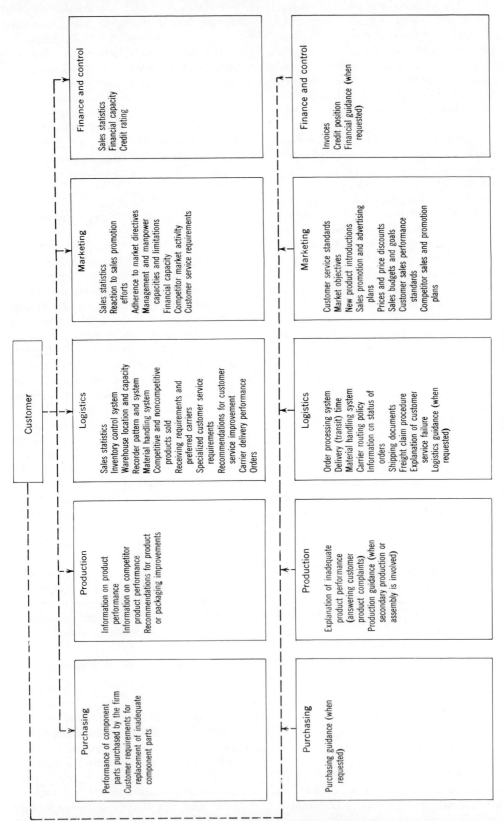

**EXHIBIT 2.** External information flow.

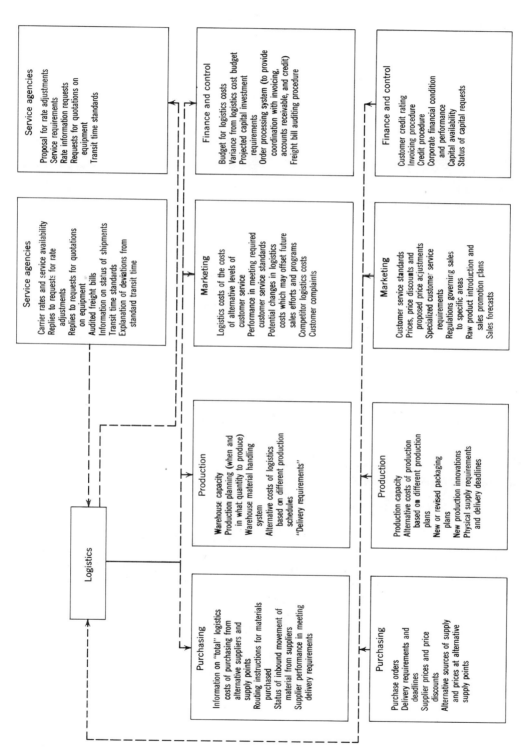

**EXHIBIT 3. Internal information flow.**

and through him. The logistics manager can review reports from sales representatives to obtain much valuable information about customer service performance and specialized requirements of customers but this method of communication has its limitations. For example, the sales representative may not be adequately qualified to determine how the firm can meet the specialized customer service requirements. In many firms the number or location of customers may make it impractical for the logistics manager or members of his staff to visit customer facilities to develop improved methods of customer service. However, when it is feasible, this type of inquiry can provide a completeness of information that is difficult if not impossible to obtain by other means. It is not reasonable to assume that the logistics manager can sit at his desk and determine what the optimum system will be for any customer or group of customers without direct contact with them. It goes without saying that this can only be accomplished with the support and cooperation of the marketing function.

### Customer Order Patterns

The timing of customer orders can affect the costs and speed required to serve them. If obtained concurrently, orders from adjacent customers can be consolidated to move in the same shipment, thereby reducing the transportation cost per unit required to serve each. Because vehicle-load shipments generally move faster than those of smaller quantity, consolidation of orders into a vehicle-load shipment can result in better transportation service at lower cost to the shipper. This may require the customer to adjust his procedures. If he has carefully planned his reorder pattern to comply with an individual inventory control system, adjustment may be a difficult, if not impossible, task for the logistician and sales representative to accomplish. When previous orders have not been placed according to a formalized plan, a customer may be unwilling to conform in any way to supplier suggestions without a price incentive to do so.

In the case of one company supplying many wholesale outlets over a multi-state region, the firm was able to obtain customer cooperation in ordering every two weeks (on a staggered basis for various territories) by reducing prices 5% under the new system. Unfortunately, all customers must either comply with the new order pattern, or those not complying must be given the discount uniformly with cooperating distributors. This is necessary to avoid a Robinson-Patman Act stipulation [Section 2(a)] prohibiting discrimination in price between different purchasers for commodities of like grade and quality, and in like quantity.

### Materials Handling Systems

Compatibility of materials handling and movement systems between supplier and customer can result in substantial savings. For example, palletization of product at a supplier's storage point, and in transportation equipment, is of no advantage to the customer not equipped to handle pallets in his warehouse. In such cases, supplier financing may be necessary to encourage the customer to adjust his system.

In a recent situation involving a West Coast processor of convenience grocery items and one of its distributors, the distributor was encouraged to move its main warehouse out of its traditional location and into the center of its major market area in order to obtain savings on subsequent delivery costs. The logistics manager of the supplying firm assisted the distributor in relocating his warehouse on a rail siding to obtain savings possible from receiving shipments at lower rates by rail rather than truck. Situations such as this point up the fact that a supplier, whether he be manufacturer or wholesaler, usually has more resources which he can bring to bear on problems of customer service involving logistics.

### Stock Reorder Levels

Customer stock reorder levels are considered in terms of the number of days of inventory (given anticipated sales) in stock at the time of reorder. Stockout situations (emergency customer logistics service problems) arise when the reorder cycle exceeds the customer stock reorder level in length of time. For example, a reorder cycle of four days would make a customer vulnerable to a stock-out where products are supplied on a five-day reorder period. A customer stock reorder cycle can be any quantity, positive or negtive. The customer who, for one reason or another, allows his stock to run out for seven days before reordering actually has a reorder level of minus seven days. A four-day reorder cycle for a supplier, when added to the customer's reorder cycle, would result in an eleven-day stock-out period.

Several types of techniques can be employed to avert the situation described above. First, a major part of the selling effort (which often comes under the category of sales service) often involves the appraisal of inventory and the stocking of shelves in retail and wholesale customer facilities. In addition to insuring the acceptable appearance of the product, such effort also makes certain that the customer realizes his stock situation and anticipates possible stock-outs. The logistician must place heavy reliance on the sales representative to accomplish results that can ease his problems.

In some situations, pre-punched data cards are enclosed with the supplier's shipments. These cards provide a rapid feedback of information on the proficiency of the logistics system in maintaining customer service standards and provide partial information on inventory levels at various wholesale or retail points. This type of system has several pitfalls. It relies upon: (1) the conscientiousness with which the wholesaler or retailer removes and mails the pre-punched data cards, and (2) the effectiveness of sales representatives in encouraging the customer to carry out the manufacturer's wishes. Because of human reluctance to cooperate or neglect to do so, information derived from these systems generally has to be adjusted to reflect the number of unreturned cards.

### Order Procedures

This is an area of external customer coordination most common to many firms. Implicit in a customer's agreement to adhere to a standard or uniform ordering procedure proposed by a supplier is a hope for better service.

In the past, uniformity in the physical nature of customer orders was achieved by: (1) assigning supplier salesmen the responsibility for personally filling out the orders, and (2) placing a supply of standard reorder forms in the hands of customers. Uniformity of order size and location of pertinent information has saved suppliers a great deal of clerical effort in the processing of incoming orders.

Many suppliers, particularly of industrial goods, are attempting to establish punched-card ordering processes with their customers. In this type of system, a customer need only select a pre-punched card supplied him previously and mail it to his supplier's order processing point. Here it is used to create the necessary order information on either paper or

tape for subsequent processing. Makers of aircraft parts and the various airline users are believed to be the first to have created a uniform ordering system such as this on an industry-wide basis. Because of the desirability of complete customer cooperation, this type of system appears more feasible for suppliers of industrial than ultimate consumer goods.

### Principles of Successful External Information Systems

The several elements of a successful adjustment of customer order patterns, materials handling systems, stock reorder levels, or order procedures have been implied in the previous discussion. Stated more explicitly, they are:

1. Adjustment should be undertaken to make customer-supplier procedures more compatible.

2. Any plan suggested should provide a mutual increase in the profitability of operation for customer and supplier if it is to be acceptable to both.

3. The sales representative is ultimately responsible for external coordination with customers; it is he who must enlist a customer's cooperation in procedural change. The logistician is likely to play the role of technical or expert adviser to his company's sales representatives and customers in these matters.

4. New ideas for changes in the supply procedures do not necessarily all come from the supplier; in fact, it may be necessary for the logistician to consult with larger customers (usually in the presence of his company's sales representative) in order to detect opportunities for change leading to a higher degree of customer-supplier system compatibility.

### INTERNAL INFORMATION SYSTEMS

Exhibit 3 illustrates the major forms of information which must be communicated between logistics and other functional areas of management. The customer order is the single document of physical distribution on which an overwhelming portion of internal information flow is based. The same relationship holds for the purchase order and physical supply activities. As indicated previously, this paper is necessarily limited to the discussion of the physical distribution aspect of business logistics.

The order that a customer sends to his supplier may appear to be only a piece of paper with a name, address, and series of digits written on it. Where the order came from, what it contains, and when it demands servicing structures and sets the entire logistics system in motion. When the customer order is properly anticipated and its demands are met, the logistics system is likely to function properly. When the order is not anticipated, or when it is over-anticipated, the logistics system moves out of phase. When it is not anticipated, customer service performance fails; when it is over-anticipated, logistics costs become excessive. For this reason, the order and the processing of it must be considered in relation to the over-all system for information flow which exists formally or informally in any firm.

The purposes of the following discussion are: (1) to define the elements of order processing, (2) to consider alternative methods of order processing, and (3) to assess the importance of the speed and accuracy with which orders are processed.

### Elements of Order Processing Systems

The "order cycle" is the period between the time of placement of a customer order and time of arrival of the order at the customer's place of business. The cycle is made up of order transmittal, processing, and shipment components. It is the second of these components, order processing, with which this discussion is mainly concerned.

Order processing can be designed as a routine activity, or it can be complicated by failure to systematize it. Common functions of order processing are to: (1) complete order forms and/or check customer or purchase orders for error, (2) keep customers, salesmen and/or manufacturing and purchasing executives informed of the status of orders in process, (3) make the order or copies of it available to promotion, finance, accounting, and purchasing for the extraction of necessary information from it, (4) coordinate with the credit department on the clearance of orders from customers with doubtful credit ratings, (5) communicate the order to the appropriate shipping point with a minimum of delay, and (6) up-date inventory control records and manufacturing or purchasing schedules.

### Order Collection

Problems of order collection primarily concern control over the manner in which orders are placed. Adherence to a pre-set form in the placement of order is a necessity if a mechanized order processing facility is to operate at peak efficiency; it is highly desirable for the manual system. Problems of internal control over the placement of orders by purchasing or manufacturing arise much less frequently than those placed by customers external to a firm's organization.

Control over the firm in which customer orders are placed may take many forms. Included among these are the provision of a supply of standard company order forms, offering a list of pre-printed items opposite which only quantities need to be entered. This might be termed the "laundry list" approach. A derivation of this technique made desirable by the adoption of electronic equipment or order processing is that of the pre-punched order card. Even standard order quantities, customer addresses and special instruction for processing may be punched into the cards, supplied in quantity to the customer.

A classic method of controlling the collection and completion of orders is to charge the sales representative with the job. It is a technique that has not been made obsolete by more modern methods because of the influence that personal contact may have on the size of the order when it is being made up.

Order discrepancies can be limited by reducing the number of transcriptions of information from one document to another. Where customers are allowed to use their own purchase order form, the supplier must transcribe the information to a form in which he can use it, thereby opening the door for error. In addition to the time (and cost) saved by eliminating order transcription, the order processing activity can be absolved of any responsibility for order errors if the customer is responsible for preparing the order form used throughout the processing system.

### Status Reporting

If the logistics system performs consistently (that is, consistently complies with customer service standards), the necessity of keeping others informed of the status of orders will be decreased. A customer, for example, might indicate on his order: "confirm order on receipt, advise car number and route on date shipped, trace and expedite shipment, and advise any delays—please communicate by wire." As calculated in Table 1, the cost to the supplier to meet this type of customer request could reach serious proportions. Consistent performance would eliminate the necessity for much reporting activity.

### Internal Order Transmission

Sales records, credit status reports, billing schedules, manufacturing and purchasing schedules, and many other types of records are derived from the order form. A basic question is that of the function with greatest priority for

TABLE 1. **Costs to Provide Order Status Reports: An Example**

| | Cost to Supplier |
|---|---|
| Confirmation of receipt of order (wire) | $1.50 |
| Car number & route on date of shipment (wire) | 1.50 |
| Tracing & expediting: 4 local phone calls @ 10¢ | .40 |
| Manpower: 10 minutes per call @ $2.50/hr. | 1.67 |
| Total without an order delay | $5.07 |
| Report of delay (wire) | 1.50 |
| Total with delay | $6.57 |

handling this much-demanded document first. Order processing systems which allow the inexpensive and accurate duplication of completed order forms allow all demands to be satisfied concurrently. Where the system either does not provide for duplicate documents or they are not thought necessary, it is likely that the most expeditious route for a customer order form to take is logistics to finance to accounting to sales to manufacturing or purchasing. All other operations and record up-dating can then be performed while the order is being readied for shipment. In the case of purchase orders (physical supply), a possible corresponding sequence is logistics to manufacturing to purchasing to accounting and/or to finance, to sales (for processing of reciprocal sales information). In either of these cases, the exact order may be debated. The question leading to the determination of a proper sequence to meet any situation is: "Which sequence least interrupts the flow of information resulting in a minimum order cycle?"

### Credit Checking

Credit clearance is another order processing activity which can be routinized or compli-

cated, depending on the situation given to it. Credit problems are handled best between the credit manager and the local sales representative. With prompt communication between them, the credit status of an order need not be a problem involving logistics. No orders would be received unless they were "credit cleared." Frequently, this is not the case. A sales representative often is interested in obtaining orders irrespective of credit status. In some cases he may even act contrary to credit policy and try to "get an order through" even when there is a known credit problem. In the absence of field credit control, credit clearance must be obtained quickly upon receipt of customer orders to prevent order processing delays, and credit "holds" must be resolved one way or the other without delay.

## INTERNAL ORDER COMMUNICATION

Internal order communication time can be as short as the 30-second period for the order to pass through an air chute from the order processing desk to the warehouse to as long as three or four days to mail an order from the order processing center to a distant warehouse facility. Efficient order transmittal and documentation can be negated by an ineffective internal communication system. The longer an order "rests" at any point in the order processing cycle the greater the opportunity the customer has to amend his order. These amendments may be the result of variations in customers' forecast sales patterns or errors by the customer in preparing his order. Changes in orders are expensive to the supplier because of the duplication of work and the increase in error possibility. Rapid internal communication is necessary to "keep the order moving." Each time an order comes to rest in a pile of orders, it means that it must be re-examined to determine its status and analyzed again to determine its relative priority.

There is no substitute for speed in internal order communication. The faster an order is processed, the more quickly things which depend upon order processing will occur. For the warehouse which has an optimum inventory (i.e., all items in stock in quantities necessary to meet demand) the receipt of the order triggers the shipment. The only warehouse delay would be the interval between the receipt of the order and the placing of the transportation vehicle at the shipper's loading dock. To a warehouse which has something less than optimum inventory (i.e., a stock-out situation) rapid communication of the order permits early recognition of an out-of-stock situation and may provide time for stock replenishment without delaying the shipment. The possibility of timely inventory replenishment or adjustment diminishes as the speed of the order system decreases.

Firms which manufacture to order (job shop operations) frequently maintain order backlogs. The question might be asked: If the order just goes into the order backlog file why is there a need for order system speed? The answer is that managers need to know their position relative to capacity and the demand placed upon that capacity. With prompt information on orders the production manager can schedule or reschedule production to make optimum use of machine time or can communicate material requirements in time to allow purchases in optimum quantities.

Rapid order communication may appear to be an expensive operation, but it is incorrect to regard it as expensive without comparing the cost if improvement with the effect that it will have on the entire logistics system.

## ALTERNATIVE ORDER PROCESSING SYSTEMS

### Manual Systems

It is most likely that no two firms process orders in the same way. In most firms, orders are processed manually, tha tis, without the aid of modern data processing equipment. Assuming a manual system of order processing, the most effective device for reducing order processing effort and cost is to use one form, with multiple copies for different purposes. The multi-copy order form reduces errors (by limiting the number of times that order information must be transcribed from one document to another) and manpower requirements (by reducing the number of transcriptions).

Little value would be obtained from a discussion of various types of manual order processing systems. Suffice it to say that they vary greatly. The design of order forms to be easily integrated into the system is a major task in the use of manual order processing procedures.

### Mechanical Systems[2]

The primary attribute of the mechanical system of order processing is its ability to routinize the creation of accurate records which stem from the customer order. In the absence of a mechanical system much duplication or repetition of the work related to a customer's order must be done by clerical workers.

A mechanical data processing system is not inherently "faster" or "better" than manual systems. In some cases, mechanical systems of order processing may be completely impractical because of a limited volume of sales, orders, or items.

A basic problem connected with all mechanical data processing systems is the tendency to concentrate on making the machine work correctly rather than effectively and accurately designing the system. As illustrated by McNerney, there is also a tendency to attribute system improvement to the mechanical equipment rather than the design of the system:

In an attempt to justify office machinery, whether it be punched card equipment or a computer, gains or improvement which are really due to the *design* of the system are often attributed to the equipment. In many cases, these same gains or improvements could be achieved with much less expense by modifying the existing system. One of the real needs in evaluating data processing proposals and equipment is to ascertain whether various operations can be performed only by the use of certain equipment, and to consider alternative (and less expensive) ways of handling the same operations.[3]

When the operations involved in order processing are subject to many exceptions, manual methods may be preferable. According to McNerney:

Clerks are extremely flexible; where many exceptions and special situations must be handled, manual methods may be quite desirable. Where operations are completely internal and highly routine, as they tend to be in accounting or payroll operations, punched card equipment can be quite satisfactory. But if mechanical means are used, many of the exceptions and special situations that are processed with no difficulty by the clerks cannot be handled by machine. In types of operations

---

[2] The material in this article relies heavily upon the work of John Peter McNerney, *Installing and Using an Automatic Data Processing System* (Boston: Division of Research, Harvard University Graduate School of Business, 1961).

[3] *Ibid.*, p. 64.

where more variations and exceptions occur, provision must still be made to handle these situations clerically. Clerks are more versatile and more flexible data processors than tabulating equipment; handling exceptions and varying situations by mechanical means is so inefficient and expensive that the variation must either be eliminated or handled by extra clerks.[4]

The fact that more separate steps may be required in the mechanical system should not, however, be interpreted as an indication of its comparative speed and cost. These elements must be separately computed, based on the characteristics of an individual situation.

Logistics, in common with other functions of the firm sometimes suffers from the fact that electronic data processing equipment for use in record-keeping and in analytical work is usually controlled within one function, most often that of accounting. Where they have been used most effectively, computers are considered as a company-wide resource which benefits all functions.

One of the most elaborate and sophisticated mechanical order processing systems in current use is that devised by the Westinghouse Electric Corporation for its apparatus products group. Orders are processed between the Company's 90 sales offices, 265 plants, and 85 warehouses within an average time span of 30 minutes.[5] The 30-minute order processing cycle starts when an order is sent by the regional sales offices to the Company's "Information Center" near Pittsburgh, Pennsylvania. As such, the 30-minute interval does not cover the time required for the transmittal of the order from the firm's 15,000 customers to a regional sales office. This could, of course, be as short as one minute for an order phoned in by the customer to a day or more when a salesman takes a written order and mails it into the regional sales office.

Using a Univac 490 as the core of the system, orders are teletyped from the sales office tele-computing center. The computer locates the stock which is in the most appropriate location to move to the customer, prepares the invoices, and up-dates the inventory records. According to a report on the system:

The speed of this operation—sales order to computer to warehouse—means immediate information on all inventory balances. It enables the company to have a report on the most active items on each salesman's desk every Monday morning, telling him how many of what products are in stock and where.[6]

This firm has reported a reduction of inventory costs on its apparatus products group by $2.3 million per year as a result of reducing its average order processing time from 6 days to 30 minutes.

### Principles of Successful Internal Information Systems

In the design of an internal logistics information system the following principles have been stressed:

1. Speed is the single most important element in obtaining market information through the flow of orders from customers.

2. The customer order is the document which triggers the subsequent flow of much internal information in an organization.

3. Where necessary, a priority on information availability must be established.

4. Priorities in the planning of an internal information system should be established on the basis of that priority ranking which least delays actions based on the information.

5. External and internal coordination is the key to the successful exchange of information necessary to meet performance objectives in the processing of customer orders.

[4] Ibid., pp. 64–65.
[5] For more complete discussions of this order processing system, see Joseph S. Coyle, "Commuter Speeds Distribution," Traffic Management, January, 1962, pp. 51–52, "At Westinghouse," Traffic &

Distribution Management, November 1961, pp. 8–13.
[6] Joseph S. Coyle, "Computer Speeds Distribution," Traffic Management, January 1962, pp. 51–52.

# E. Product Development

## 45. Behavioral Science Concepts for Analyzing the Consumer

### HERTA HERZOG

In earlier years, marketing, strongly influenced by economic theory, emphasized the objective factors in buying behavior although it was never unaware of the importance of "emotional" factors. It struggled with the problem but it had no systematic way of approaching the question as to the kind of psychological factors present in a given situation and as to the why and how of their importance. This was one of the main troubles with the application of the early "lists" of buying motives.

Psychological research, or what commonly goes under the name of "Motivation Research," has received new attention during the last decade when the post-war seller's market changed into a buyer's market. This economic change stimulated widespread recognition of the need to understand the consumer thoroughly. At the same time, the behavioral sciences had developed to a point where it seemed promising to attempt application of some of their concepts and methods to the specific problems of buying and consumption behavior.

The attempts so far have been quite encouraging but they represent only a beginning. Motivation researchers have been busy doing specific studies; we have not yet had enough time to think through what we are doing and what general findings emerge. We have made uneven use of the available behavioral science concepts, and for some of the marketer's problems the behavioral sciences do not yet offer concepts or methods.

‡‡ SOURCE: Reprinted by permission from *Proceedings of the Conference of Marketing Teachers from Far Western States* (Berkeley, California: September 1958), pp. 32–41.

Application of existing behavioral science material is further complicated by the fact that we are not yet dealing with a unified theoretical system. Interdisciplinary integration is far from complete and so is consensus within the various disciplines. Psychology, for instance, offers at least three major approaches to motivation.

There is the approach of the laboratory psychologists who in many instances use animals for their subjects and who have tended to focus on the physiological tensions or "body needs" as motivational forces.

There is the work of the clinical psychologists, and of dynamic psychology in particular, which has focused on the role of psychological factors. They see in the handling of the biological drives within the mores of society a key problem, and also a possibility for influencing behavior. Conflicts between basic drives or motives and social restrictions, they say, put great stresses on the individual. Since he cannot tolerate them, the motives become repressed, unconscious but not eliminated as driving forces. They continue to make themselves felt in a variety of ways.

A third approach to the study of motives is represented by the Gestalt psychologists and, particularly, the work of Kurt Lewin. This socio-psychological approach emphasizes the fact that people are reacting in an environment and that behavior must be understood as a function of the person and the environment in which he lives, with both of these being mutually dependent variables. Behavior, as these psychologists see it, is largely goal-directed and results from a person's motives as well as his perception of the environment at a given time.

In short, at this point the behavioral sciences

offer a variety of differing theories and approaches to the understanding of behavior. Thus you will find the application of behavioral science concepts to marketing varies with the theoretical orientation of the researchers, or that market researchers borrow eclectically depending on which theoretical concepts seem most applicable and fruitful in a particular case.

## WHAT IS A PRODUCT?

Let me begin with the question "What is a product?"—a question of concern to every marketer. From a strictly technical manufacturing standpoint, a product consists of a number of raw materials so put together that the end result, the product, serves a useful purpose of consumption, be it in feeding, clothing, housing, transporting the consumer, etc.

You need only to think about your car, however, to realize that it represents neither the sum total of its parts for you, nor merely an instrument of transportation. This has, of course, been long recognized and one of the concerns of marketing has been to determine just which product "features" are important to the consumer. Thus market research on a food product has tried to measure the relative appeal of such features as taste, color, consistency, quality of ingredients, price etc. Studying cars, we have tried to assess the interest in engineering features such as power steering, power brakes or automatic transmission as compared with appearance, comfort, up-keep, trade-in value, etc.

These familiar classifications are not fully satisfactory. Obviously, "trade-in value" is a feature of a rather different kind than some of the others I have mentioned. To know that a consumer values "comfort" does not tell us too much. What constitutes comfort to him, we want to know: is it the upholstery, leg room, head room, trunk space, good springs, or what? Is it correct to interpret a car owner's concern with power steering as an expression of interest in engineering features or, rather, does it mean "easy parking," another comfort item to the consumer? Will the consumer tell us what he wants when we ask him to compare looks with, let's say, economy or technical quality?

In short, the traditional methods of classification are somewhere inbetween a product definition in terms of the manufacturer and a product definition in terms of the consumer. Thus they tend to fall short of telling the manufacturer how and what the consumer sees in a car

so that he can build a car that will deliver these consumer benefits.

The application of behavioral science concepts, particularly the various psychological theories, has been useful in helping us toward a better understanding of the "product."

In pointing out the subjective component in perception, they suggested that we must go the whole way in determining how the consumer sees the product, not what it is technically. The concept of the "psychological environment" includes the notion that what people "see," depends on the stimulus characteristics as well as their personality—the type of person they are, the state they are in, and their ideology. It contains a strong social and cultural component: we "see" things in the way our culture and the particular social group in which we move have induced us to see them. And we see things in context, not as isolated elements or objects but as part of the "total situation," the inner and outer environment. It is useful to add here a key concept borrowed from psycho-analytic theory, namely, that the "inner environment" may contain repressed needs and wants as well as those the individual is aware of.

These theoretical concepts have led to the notion of the *product image and the exploration of the various meanings, rational and symbolic, which the product* may have to the consumer.

For example, getting at the product image of gasoline, we asked motorists, among a number of questions, what other purchases they consider "similar" to buying gasoline, and why they are similar. We found three main types of conceptions: gasoline was likened to other types of fuel such as electricity, water, etc., by a small percentage; gasoline purchases were likened to other purchases having to do with transportation such as bus tickets, railroad fares, by another small proportion. More than half of the respondents likened gasoline to personal consumption items: things which keep the human body fed such as bread or milk, which keep it protected such as hats or shoes, which keep it pepped up, such as beer or cigarettes.

This particular study was done before the first gasoline additive broke on the market, at a time when in convential questioning the large majority of consumers stressed that gasoline is rather an uninteresting product, all main gasolines are pretty much alike, and that in buying gasoline they look for station convenience and service rather than the particular product sold at the station. The findings on the product image suggested that via the car, viewed as an extension of the body, there was a good deal more potential interest in the product itself which should be catered to in product development and subsequent product promotion.

Or take another example—airplanes and air travel. In another type of so-called projective questioning, people who like plane travel and those who do not care for it were asked to draw their idea of an airplane and tell a story about their drawings. The responses revealed marked differences in product image among the two groups, which were confirmed by other data. The fan sees himself at the controls of a wonderful instrument, while the non-fan tends to see himself as a passenger, looking at a plane mainly as a perhaps time-saving vehicle of transportation.

The famous Mason Haire study is another example of exploration of the product image. As you know, Haire made up two "shopping lists" containing a series of everyday household purchase items such as a pound and a half of hamburger, two cans of Del Monte peaches, etc. One list contained Nescafe while the other, identical with the first, substituted Maxwell House regular for the instant coffee. When he asked a matched group of housewives to describe the type of woman who would purchase each list of products, he found that a considerable proportion mentioned "lazy" housewives, "women who don't plan well," for the list containing instant coffee. Direct questioning had given no indication that this was a connotation associated with the perception of the new product.

Since the meanings associated with a product are often quite varied, it is useful to employ a variety of questioning techniques which will uncover the rational as well as the emotional connotations: direct questions, open-end type questions and projective devices, some of which I mentioned. Also, the questioning must give the respondent a variety of opportunities to say what he or she has in mind about a product. In addition to asking what she likes about the product or how she rates specific features, one might ask about the "ideal" product in a given category. Or one might invite the respondent to describe how she uses the product, or have her report her thoughts as she actually uses it. One might ascertain memories of outstanding enjoyment of the product, ask the consumer how she would feel if she had to do without the product, and why, etc.

From such types of questioning one can document that an apparently simple product such as cigarettes had a variety of "meanings"—even before the days of health concern. Some smokers, for example, saw in a cigarette something to manipulate, a means of assertion; they were particularly interested in specific features such as firm packing. For others, a cigarette was a means of comfort—deep inhaling, the strength of a cigarette, were some of the things they particularly valued. Some saw in a cigarette an outlet of nervous tension; there were no particular features that interested them more than others. Some saw in a cigarette primarily an oral sensation; taste of course was one of the features they were interested in. In each case it could be shown that the product definition was strongly linked to basic tendencies on the part of the smoker and linked also to an interest in particular product attributes.

Studies relating to product image have also taught us that the same word used loosely by the consumer, may have very different meanings. Take "taste," for example. In a study of Kippers we found that a large proportion of respondents who in direct questioning said they didn't use the product because they didn't like its taste, actually had never tasted it. In depth interviewing, it turned out that dislike of "taste" in this case was merely a way of talking about something that was unfamiliar, foreign, unacceptable, unconventional. The average American housewife had a kind of mental image of barefoot dock workers slopping around in these slimy fish in some far away port. In the case of soda crackers, liking for "taste" stands primarily for texture characteristics. In the case of toothpastes, "taste" stands for the total sensation in the mouth, not just a particular flavor. And in the case of hard liquor, "taste" is a means to describe and to anticipate effect characteristics.

Product image studies need to be repeated. Consumer conceptions about a product do not stand still: technical developments, degree of market saturation, availability, are some of the environmental factors which may restructure the consumer image. There was a time when ammoniated toothpastes had a special health connotation attractive mainly to the hypochondriac. With the subsequent advent of chlorophyll and anti-enzyme ingredients, the image of a toothpaste changed; today the anti-decay feature is a part of a modern, up-to-date toothpaste that the majority of consumers would not want to do without.

## WHAT IS A BRAND?

You will have gathered from the preceding that brands, like product types, are perceived by the consumer in the form of "brand images." This is the sum total of impressions the consumer receives from many sources: from actual experience and hearsay about the brand itself as well as its packaging, its name, the company making it, the types of people the individual has seen using the brand, what was said in its advertising, as well as from the tone, format, type of advertising vehicle in which the product story was told.

All these impressions amount to a sort of brand personality which is similar for the consuming public at large, although different consumer groups may have different attitudes toward it. For instance, users generally interpret the brand image more favorably than non-users although both groups agree on its essential outline. The user may like a brand because it is "tried and true," the "first and best on the market," while the non-user may call the same brand "old-fashioned," with both agreeing that it is an old, well-established brand.

The brand image contains objective product qualities, particularly if there are observable product characteristics such as differences in strength or taste or shape or texture. These qualities themselves have rational as well as symbolic meanings which merge with the meanings created by all the other sources through which the public meets a brand.

In the gasoline study quoted before, it was found that motorists tended to think of Gulf, among other things, as a "friendly" gasoline—a notion that stemmed from associations with the name which reminded of "outdoor sports," the "Gulf of Mexico," etc. These notions were supported by the "sunny" yellow color used in its emblem, the "friendly" approach in its advertising copy (Go Gulf), and the nature of the advertising vehicle, a program called "We the People" which, although no longer on the air at the time of the study, had done its share in contributing to the brand image.

Interviews with smokers done by various motivation researchers, indicate that although they may not be able to tell brands apart in a blindfold test, they nevertheless have quite clear-cut images of various brands. Both Camels and Luckies, for example, are thought of as "strong" cigarettes as compared with Philip Morris which is associated with mildness. But there are further marked differences in the images of Camels and Luckies. This was measured, for example, by a set of questions in which people were asked to "match" each brand with a series of socio-economic and psychological characteristics, which presumably were "typical of the person likely to smoke the brand."

The concepts consumers have of a brand result from objective facts; at the same time, these concepts serve to shape sales patterns. For we find rather frequently that consumers tend to prefer the brand whose image is congenial to them. This brings me to a third point—the question "What is a consumer?"

## WHAT IS A CONSUMER?

Marketing has always thought of the consumer in terms of who buys what, for what purpose, at what price, where, etc. This kind of information, derived from observable consumer behavior data, is very important in locating a product or brand in the total market picture. But certain marketing needs, specifically those of the people concerned with the creative aspects in product development and brand promotion, require more qualitative dynamic knowledge about the consumer than his age, income or family status. They require an answer to the question why consumers buy a particular product and how current non-users can be switched to a specific brand.

This statement of the problem of consumer motivation is in itself different from the way in which it used to be stated, and strongly influenced by the application of behavioral science concepts.

From trying to apply a general list of buying motives to the purchase of a particular product or brand, market research proceeded to ask the user why he bought or preferred the brand, to find out from the former user why he switched to it, and from the non-user why he never used it. This was a step ahead because it attempted to trace the purchase decision for a particular brand, and included the user and the non-user.

As you can well imagine, the non-user in particular finds it difficult to explain why he doesn't use the brand. "I just never thought of it," "I don't need it," "I like my current brand," are rather typical answers. Even more specific ones such as "I don't like the color," and "It's too expensive" do not indicate with enough certainty what appeal would be effective in inducing purchase. If one were to take the an-

swers seriously and changed the color or reduced the price, two drastic changes on the
part of the manufacturer, would the non-user
really become a consumer, one wonders? And
what impact would these changes have on the
current consumer?

In today's third stage of development we are
mindful of the concept that the consumer acts
in a total situation and we also consider that
behavior results from the interplay of his personal make-up and his perception of the environment. Thus we tend to look upon a particular brand as one possible choice the consumer
might make among other brands in the category, and even among other kinds of products.
And allowing for external situational influences
which might have a bearing on buying behavior,
motivation research proper attempts to assess
the hold the brand has on its current consumers
(some of whom might switch away from it tomorrow), as well as the appeal it might offer to
its most likely prospects (not *all* non-users). It
does so by relating the perception of the brand
to the "needs" of the consumer.

In this analysis of needs one must provide
for the fact that consumer behavior serves physiological as well as psychological needs; needs
the person is aware of and needs he may not be
conscious of although they are "projected" into
his buying behavior; needs he is willing to tell
and those he doesn't want to admit, falling back
on "rationalization." The needs are patterned
by the culture and the social class to which
he belongs, his stage of development as well as
his "personality."

Therefore, a good motivation study must be
based on a thorough knowledge of the market
in terms of such background characteristics as
socio-economic status, age, city size, region; and
it employs the total arsenal of methods that the
behavioral sciences have at their command so
far to get at conscious as well as unconscious
needs. This means personality tests and depth
interviewing, as well as direct questioning.

One of the general findings that has emerged
from this type of research is the concept of
*psychological market segmentation* which cuts
across and refines the traditional concept of
market segmentation based on such characteristics as age or income. Consumers tend to buy
the brand whose image most closely corresponds to their own needs; the image selects
the type of consumer for whom the brand
promises particular satisfaction. This is true in
product categories where you would expect
it, such as in the cigarette field or the use of

hair tonics among men. It also holds for durable
goods such as cars, for foods down to peanut
butter, for household supplies down to dis-
infectants.

The main research task in finding out what
motivates the consumer toward product use
and brand preferences is to find the psychological dimension(s) which characterize the
user and differentiate him from the non-user.
These might have to do with the "self-image"
which the consumer acts out, as it were, in his
consumption behavior. The self-image is important, for example, in determining whether
or not a man (with enough hair on his head)
will use a hair tonic, and what type of hair
tonic he will use. The basic compulsivity of a
woman and the way she sees her role as a
housewife, have a marked bearing on the type
of household items she uses. People on comparable income levels handle the conflict between
the impulse for self-indulgence (buying) and
the demands for self-restraint (postponement
of buying) in ways which differentiate the saver
from the non-saver. In a study dealing with a
service from a "big" company, we found that
this key characteristic of the image had a positive attraction for at least two consumer groups.
Those who as personalities sought and needed
protection, bought the company's products because bigness provided assurance. At the other
end of the pole were the assertive, aggressive
people who also reacted positively because bigness provided a self-conscious gratifying identification with success.

However, there were also groups representative of many consumers who reacted negatively for a variety of reasons. In some instances
the resistance against a "big" brand was as
basic as its appeal to other consumer groups.
In other instances, the negative responses expressed merely a feeling that the company was
remote, aloof, efficient but not close enough
to the consumer.

The data not only indicated that these non-
users could be interested but the interviews
contained a number of important clues as to
just what the brand must do to hold its current
customers and come closer to these prospects.
The clues included changes in marketing strategy, media policy and selling arguments.

## WHAT IS AN AD?

I will be very brief on a fourth question,
"What is an ad?" because you are probably
least interested in this area of application.

Let me make one point on layout, the physical appearance of the ad, since the application of behavioral science concepts to advertising copy follows pretty much from what I have already said about findings on consumer motivations.

Thousands of readership checks in the past have served to indicate that on the average photographs or life-like drawings are in most product fields a means of obtaining attention. Borrowing some of the concepts developed particularly by scientists working on theory of instincts, we have come to understand what accounts for the occasional very high readership obtained by ads that do not use the photographic technique.

These scientists, working with animals, have come up with the concept of "perceptual releasers." These are attributes of the stimulus which are sufficient to activate memory traces which then produce the response. For example, studying the courtship behavior of the Stickleback fish, they found that the male will pursue the dummy of a female, held into the aquarium by the experimenter, as long as it has a swollen abdomen (even though it may be only a very crude model), in preference to a life-like reproduction of a normal female. He will court the dummy particularly if it is lowered into the aquarium in the typical position of the female Stickleback in the courting situation.

The perception of an ad apparently works similarly. For example, one successful campaign featured an insurance salesman, Mr. Friendly, who was drawn in almost cartoon fashion. It was certainly not a life-like portrayal but copy research indicated that this piece of artwork served indeed to catch and release the reader's ambivalence about insurance and insurance salesmen. It was real in the sense of touching a real experience.

In conclusion, I should like to apologize that I know little or nothing about your special area of interest, the teaching of marketing. If the behavioral science approach is not part of your curriculum, I should think it worthy of your consideration—even if its application to marketing problems is not yet fully developed.

# 46. What Is "New" about a New Product?

CHESTER R. WASSON

Consider the case of the soup-maker who, by freezing, was able to develop commercial production of soups which previously had to be fresh-prepared—an oyster stew among them. Estimating that the market potential might be approximated by the average relationship between frozen and canned foods, he tried his soups in a single test market. The oyster stew sold out so fast that he had to withdraw it from test until he could expand production facilities even for this one market.

Or take the case of the industrial manufacturer who developed a silo-like forage storer, capable of increasing livestock production profits substantially if properly used. Yet when put into distribution through experienced dealers in heavy farm equipment, it lay dormant for more than four years. In fact, no appreciable market headway was made until it was taken out of the hands of what had seemed to be a logical channel for any kind of farm equipment.

Then, consider the business executive with soap-and-cosmetic experience who acquired rights to a promising soil improver. Trade checks indicated that consumers liked it very much, and an impartial laboratory test indicated technical properties of substance. Put into a few test garden stores with no more than nominal advertising sales seemed satisfactory. Nevertheless, jobbers would not take it on, and when direct sales to a wider group of dealers was tried, none of the outlets developed any major volume. Even though both amateurs and

⁂ SOURCE: Reprinted by permission from the *Journal of Marketing* (National Quarterly Publication of the American Marketing Association), Vol. 25, No. 1, July 1960, pp. 52–56.

professionals who have tried it like it, and come back for more, and in spite of the fact that the economics of its use is reasonable and that theoretical demand seems attractive, the executive is about to write it off after four years of trying.

## THE DIFFERENCE LIES IN WHAT IS NEW

All three cases are simple examples of a too prevalent failure to analyze the "what's new?" in the new product, to make sure that marketing strategy, channels of distribution, and available resources are compatible with the elements of novelty in the new product. The ease or difficulty of introduction and the characteristics of the successful marketing strategy depend basically on the nature of the "new" in the new product—the new as the customer views the bundle of services he perceives in the newborn.

Take the oyster stew—what was really new, the stew itself? In "R" months, oyster stew has been traditional in homes and restaurants from Boston and San Francisco to What Cheer, Iowa, from the Waldorf-Astoria to Harry's Diner. Assuming adequate quality in the commercial product, oyster stew was an old and welcome dinner-table friend. Was the idea of commercial preparation new? For oyster stew, yes, of course, but not for soup. Just look at the facings in the gondolas of any supermarket, or at the empty cans in the trash of any restaurant.

Of course, the idea of a frozen soup was new, but not the concept of frozen prepared foods. Food-store freezer cases had indeed established the association of fresh-quality taste with freeze-processing. But to the consumer, the only "new" aspect about frozen oyster stew was the greater availability and convenience implied in "frozen." With this particular item, the probability of great development might have been anticipated and prepared for in advance.

The silo and the soil improver, by contrast, looked deceptively similar to known items. But actually both embodied, for the consumer, radically new ideas; and both required extreme changes in user habits and user ways of looking at familiar tasks.

The forage storer looked like the familiar silo from the outside, but really embodied a new principle of preservation whose major benefits would be realized only when livestock were taken off pasture and barn-fed harvested forage the year around. Adoption of the device meant, in effect, adoption of a radically new pattern of work organization, and even of farm buildings in some cases.

No matter how great the promised benefit, such a major turnabout of habits requires a great deal of personal selling to get even the more venturesome to try it. Traditional farm-equipment channels are not prepared to carry out the prolonged and intensive type of pioneering personal sales effort and demonstration required. A reasonable degree of success began to accrue only after the manufacturer realized these facts and made the necessary changes in his selling plan.

Likewise, the soil improver resembled other growth stimulants in that it was sold in large bags and had a granular appearance. But the method of use was entirely different from, and more difficult than, the methods of surface application common to most growth stimulants in garden use. It had to be dug in, to be physically intermixed with the soil. In addition, the benefit was an unfamiliar one, and perhaps not easily believable—simple soil aeration. True, in cultivation, all gardeners practice aeration; but they think of weed killing, not aeration, when they hoe their gardens.

With such a product, success can reasonably be expected only after a strong educational campaign based on intense advertising, wide publicity, and personal contacts with consumer groups such as garden clubs and women's clubs. The resources needed were far in excess of those available in a "bootstrap" operation.

### The Toni Example

Determination of the novel aspects of a new product is no simple mechanical process. What is new depends on what the prospective consumer perceives, or can be brought to perceive, in the new product.

Determining such potential aspects requires a high order of imagination, and spectacular successes such as the Toni Home Permanent are due in no small part to the introducer's skill in pinpointing the nature of the novel aspects of the product, and devising the kind of marketing strategy needed to fit the various types of "new" elements in his product.

When the Harrises first introduced Toni, they clearly perceived that their key problem was to gain credibility for the idea of a safe and satisfactory "permanent wave" done in the home. Home curling of hair was an old custom, but the home-produced curl had always been very temporary. Permanent waves had been available, and proved, for nearly thirty years, but only at the hand of a skilled hairdresser, and in a specially equipped beauty parlor. With the perfection of the cold-wave lotion, a true home permanent became possible, using a technique not very different from those already in use for temporary home curling. The principal benefit was one for which the times of the middle and late 1940's were ripe—a major saving in cost as compared with the professional job.

The problem was to gain credibility for the safety and the effectiveness of the product claiming the benefit (Toni)—a problem requiring intense selling effort. The Harris strategy consisted of: persuading the girl behind every cosmetic counter in town to use a kit herself before it went on sale; making sure that every cosmetic counter had a stock before the day of introduction; working one town at a time, putting the maximum advertising effort behind the introduction; plowing back all income into further advertising until market saturation was accomplished; and then using funds from established markets to open new ones.

If, on hindsight, this solution seems to have been the obvious, it should be noted that Toni was not the first cold-wave home permanent— merely the first successful one. The forgotten competitor, who was really first, never appreciated the intensity of consumer education that would be needed, and had so little success that his product is remembered by few.

### WAYS A PRODUCT CAN BE "NEW"

In how many ways can a product be new? Of course, each case should be analyzed on its own. Nevertheless, there are at least thirteen possibilities which should be considered:

A. Six novel attributes are positive, in the sense that they ease the job of introduction:

1. New cost—or, better yet, price—if lower.
2. New convenience in use—if greater.
3. New performance—if better, more dependable and in the range of experience of the prospect—if believable.
4. New availabiliy, in place, or time, or both (including antiseasonality).
5. Conspicuous—consumption (status symbol) possibilities.
6. Easy credibility of benefits.

B. At least four characteristics make the job more difficult, slow up market development, and usually make it costlier:

7. New methods of use (unless obviously simpler).
8. Unfamiliar patterns of use (any necessity for learning new habits in connection with performance of a task associated with the new product).
9. Unfamiliar benefit (in terms of the prospect's understanding).
10. Costliness, fancied or real, of a possible error in use.

C. Three others are ambivalent in their effect—that is, the effect on market development probably depends not only on their exact nature, but also on the cultural climate at the moment. However, extreme unfamiliarity would probably be negative in effect:

11. New appearance, or other sensed difference (style or texture, for example).
12. Different accompanying or implied services.
13. New market (including different channels of sale).

The oyster stew had four to six positive characteristics (only lower cost and conspicuous consumption omitted), and no negative ones. The silo and the soil improver had all of the negative attributes listed, and only performance among the positive. Toni had cost and performance in its favor, and marketing strategy involved an overwhelming attack on the negative aspects (fear of error and credibility of results).

The ambivalence of style should be obvious to those who have followed automobile history. The turtle-shaped DeSoto of the 1930's was one of the most spectacular design failures of history. The design was "too radical" for the motor-ists of that era. Twenty years later the very similar appearance of the Volkswagen "beetle" proved no deterrent to the initiation of a radical reorientation of the American automobile market. And while the Volkswagen brought into that market items of dependable performance, greater convenience in use, and a lower cost than had been available for some time, one element in its success was the recognition of the necessity for continuing the availability of an established implied service in the sale of the car —ready availability of parts and service. Volkswagen entered no area until it had made certain of a high-grade service network in that area.

### A Fourteenth Characteristic

Omission of a possible fourteenth characteristic—new construction or composition—is purposeful. This characteristic is neutral—that is, it has no consumer meaning except to the extent that it is identified with, or can be associated with, one or more of the consumer-oriented characteristics listed above.

All that is new in any product is the package of consumer-perceivable services embodied in it. The innovator leads himself astray who analyzes the novel in his newborn in terms of physical and engineering attributes.

### An Example in Television

The physical similarity of color TV to black-and-white TV probably led the electronic industry to expect, erroneously, that color-set introduction would parallel the "mushroom" market development experienced with black-and-white. Physically, the parallel was certainly there. Color adds a new dimension to the signal received, just as the picture added a new dimension to the radio signal. But black-and-white television was not, for the consumer, a simple extension of radio. To the family, and most especially to the children, it was a vastly more convenient theater—it was "movies in the parlor." In an era in which children were being granted almost everything they asked for, the pressure for ownership soon became overwhelming. And to add to that pressure, the black-and-white television set required an unmistakable and quite conspicuous symbol of possession—the distinctive aerial. Black-and-white television never had to be sold—it was bought.

Color television, however, to the consumer, *is* simply an extension of black-and-white, which he already owns, and to which he is thoroughly accustomed. The mere idea of an added color dimension has only potential interest to the adult, and probably little to the child. Programs, moreover, are fully compatible—the owner of the color TV set can talk about no program the black-and-white neighbor has not been able to see.

Color television's one positive characteristic is thus simply better performance—a degree of better performance which has not as yet acquired much value in the eyes of the consumer. Offsetting this are the factors of higher cost, questions as to perfection of color TV, and a benefit that is relatively unfamiliar, so far as the experience of most prospects is concerned.

If color television is to become dominant, it will have to gain acceptance the way most other home appliances have—by "hard" direct-to-customer personal selling, probably operating through selective retail distribution, backed up by strong advertising and shrewd publicity that will build up the latent added value of color reception into kinetic reality.

### The Old Can Be New

Even the well-established can be "new" so far as the buyer is concerned. The pharmaceutical industry is well aware that when its ethical formulations can be made available for over-the-counter sales, new sales vistas can be opened by a new sales effort. Ecko discovered that an invention of the 1890's could gain quick success when reintroduced to the modern market (the case of the one-hand egg-beater). And one of the most interesting research results the author ever had was the discovery that a minor product which a client had been making for over fifty years needed only a different kind of sales effort, including a new channel of sale, to turn it into a promising new major product in the industrial-component field.

### MARKET MANAGEMENT OF INNOVATION

Skilled management of the innovation phase of the enterprise is, increasingly, a prerequisite to business success. Today's fast-moving markets pay best profits to firms in the van of those with product improvements and new products. In some industries, even mere survival depends on constant, successful new-product introduction. New-product success follows only when the marketing plan is suited to the innovational characteristics of the individual product, as the customer views it, or can be brought to view it.

Really consistent success in the marketing of innovations requires an all too rare understanding that the extent and nature of the new is not measurable in terms of the physical specifications of the product nor in the logical blueprint of the service. The nature of the new is in what it does to and for the customer—to his habits, his tastes and his patterns of life.

Some aspects of the new product make familiar patterns of life easier, cheaper, more convenient, or otherwise more pleasant. These aspects aid speedy introduction and adoption. Other aspects of the innovation require new patterns of life, new habits, the understanding of new ideas or ways of looking at things, the acceptance of the difficult to believe, or the acquisition of new tastes. The latter require the maximum concentration of marketing energy, to add enough value to the strange service to counterbalance the pain of the new idea.

Finally, some characteristics can be positive, negative, or neutral, dependent on the trend of the cultural climate. The current valence of these must be carefully evaluated at the time of introduction, and the marketing plan, or even the product design, fitted to the value determined.

Skillful development of new-product marketing plans would thus seem to consist of three basic steps:

1. Careful analysis of the positive and negative aspects of the specific product.

2. Maximum exploitation of the improvements in the familiar embodied in the product, to gain added value necessary to overcome the negative aspects.

3. Application of the maximum promotional effort in countering the negative aspects and lending value to the new and unfamiliar.

# F. Pricing The Offering

## 47. Price Policies and Theory

EDWARD R. HAWKINS

Although the theory of monopolistic competition is now almost twenty years old it remains virtually unused by marketing students, even those who are attempting to develop theory in marketing. In particular, "marketing price policies" are still treated as though they have no relation to economic theory of any sort. In the leading marketing text books there are sections describing such pricing policies as "odd prices," "customary prices," "price lining," "psychological prices," etc.[1] These are presented as descriptions of market behavior, presumably discovered by marketing specialists and unknown to economists. Even the one marketing text that explains the basic pricing formula under conditions of monopolistic competition fails to use it in the discussion of price policies.[2] Since text book writers treat the subject in this way it is not surprising that practitioners writing on pricing do not attempt to relate their policies to economic theory.[3]

It is the purpose of this article to show that these price policies are special cases of the general theory of monopolistic competition. Perhaps clarification of this point will serve to narrow the gap between the economic and marketing conceptions of pricing, and to systematize the discussions of price policies in marketing literature.

The thesis is that each of the familiar price policies represents an estimate of the nature of the demand curve facing the seller. It is not possible, on the basis of available evidence, to generalize on the validity of these estimates in various situations. The point merely is that a seller using one of these policies is implicitly assuming a particular demand curve. In the following sections various price policies are discussed in these terms, after a brief review of the general theory of pricing which is basic to all of the policies discussed.

---

[1] R. S. Vaile, E. T. Grether, and Reavis Cox, *Marketing in the American Economy* (New York: Ronald Press, 1952), ch. 22; E. A. Duddy and D. A. Revzan, *Marketing* (New York: McGraw-Hill, 2nd ed. 1953), ch. 29; P. D. Converse, H. W. Huegy, and R. V. Mitchell, *Elements of Marketing* (New York: Prentice-Hall, 5th ed. 1952) ch. 10; H. H. Maynard and T. N. Beckman, *Principles of Marketing* (New York: Ronald Press, 5th ed. 1952) ch. 35, 36; R. S. Alexander, F. M. Surface, R. E. Elder, and Wroe Alderson, *Marketing* (Boston: Ginn, 1940) ch. 16. Since these policies are fully described in marketing texts the explanation of them in this article will be brief. The attempt, rather, is to express the policies in terms of demand curves in order that the relationship to the theory of monopolistic competition may be seen.

‡‡ SOURCE: Reprinted by permission from the *Journal of Marketing* (National Quarterly Publication of the American Marketing Association), Vol. 18, No. 3, January 1954, pp. 233–240.

[2] Charles F. Phillips and Delbert J. Duncan, *Marketing, Principles and Methods* (Chicago: Richard D. Irwin, rev. ed. 1952), ch. 29, 30, 31.

[3] For example, Oswald Knauth, "Considerations in the Setting of Retail Prices," *Journal of Marketing*, Vol. 14, No. 1, July 1949, pp. 1–12; Q. Forrest Walker, "Some Principles of Department Store Pricing," *Journal of Marketing*, Vol. 14, No. 4, April 1950, pp. 529–537.

## THE GENERAL THEORY OF PRICING

The theory of correct pricing under conditions of monopolistic competition, as developed by Chamberlin and Robinson is illustrated in Fig. 1. Each seller with some degree of monopoly created by product differentiation has his own negatively-inclined average revenue curve, AR. From this he derives the marginal revenue curve MR, and determines his price by the intersection of MR and MC, his marginal cost. Marginal cost can be derived from either average cost AC, or average variable cost AVC, since it would be the same in either case. In practical terms this means that for correct pricing the seller does not need to allocate over-

would result at various volumes at different prices. On each such TR curve a point can be estimated showing the sales volume that would actually be obtained at that price. If these points are connected a type of demand curve results (DD'), indicating total revenue rather than average revenue as in the usual demand curve.[4] The objective of correct pricing is to maximize the vertical distance between DD' and the TC (total cost) curve. This formulation has an advantage over the MC-MR one in that in addition to indicating the correct price and volume it also shows total cost, total revenue, and total net profit. It may also be more acceptable to business men and engineers who are accustomed to break-even charts.

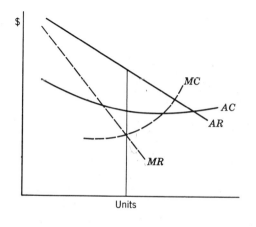

FIG. 1

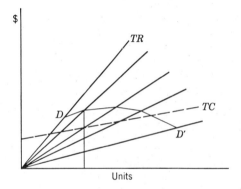

FIG. 2

head cost to individual items. For that matter, he does not even need to compute MR and MC, for the same correct price can be derived from AR and AVC by maximizing the total of the spread between them multiplied by the volume.

An alternative solution which may be more understandable to business men can be obtained from break-even charts. The customary break-even chart is deficient for pricing purposes because it is based on only one price and reveals nothing but the quantity that would have to be sold at that price in order to break even. A modification can be devised that remedies this shortcoming of the break-even chart, and even has some advantages over the MC-MR formula. Fig. 2 shows such a chart, in which a number of different total revenue (TR) curves are drawn, indicating the total revenue that

In the following discussion of marketing price policies, however, the AR curve will be used because it more clearly illustrates the points made.

### MARKETING PRICE POLICIES

#### Odd Prices

The term "odd prices" is used in two ways in marketing literature; one refers to a price ending in an odd number while the other means a price just under a round number. If a seller sets his prices according to the first concept it

---

[4] Cf. Joel Dean, *Managerial Economics* (New York: Prentice-Hall, 1951), p. 405. Dean shows a total revenue curve without, however, indicating its relationship to break-even charts.

means that he believes his *AR* curve is like the one shown in Fig. 3.[5] In this case each price ending in an odd number will produce a greater volume of sales than the next lower even-numbered price. Many sellers appear to believe this is true, although the only large-scale test ever reported was inconclusive.[6]

The second concept of odd-pricing implies an *AR* curve like the one shown in Fig. 4, with critical points at prices such as $1, $5, and $10.[7] The presumption is that sales will be substantially greater at prices just under these critical points, whether ending in an odd or even number.

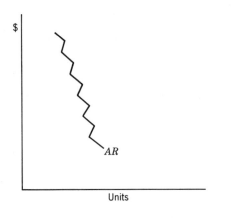

FIG. 3

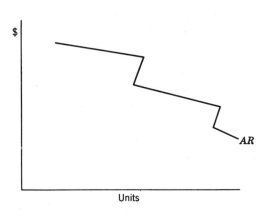

FIG. 4

---

[5] This curve might be regarded as discontinuous, especially since the difference between points is only one cent. But it is customary to draw demand curves as continuous even though, as Chamberlin has said, *any* demand curve could be split into segments. E. H. Chamberlin, "Comments," *Quarterly Journal of Economics*, Vol. 64, November 1934, p. 135; and A. J. Nichol, although drawing important conclusions from the supposed discontinuity of certain demand curves, states that the curves would be continuous if it were feasible to change prices by small amounts. A. J. Nichol, "The Influence of Marginal Buyers on Monopolistic Competition," *Quarterly Journal of Economics*, Vol. 64, November 1934, footnote 7, p. 126. Henry Smith believes that discontinuous demand curves might result from such heavy advertising of a certain price that the product would be unsalable at any other price. *Cf.* "Discontinuous Demand Curves and Monopolistic Competition: A Special Case," *Quarterly Journal of Economics*, Vol. 64, May 1935, pp. 542–550. This would not seem to be a very common case, however, since marketing literature reveals heavily advertised products selling at various prices.

[6] Eli Ginsberg, "Customary Prices," *American Economic Review*, Vol. 26, No. 2, 1936, p. 296. Some economists doubt the validity of positively-inclined segments of demand curves, believing either (a) that the case could happen only if consumers regard price as one of the qualities of the product, thus making it improper to show these "different" products on one demand curve, or (b) that it simply does not happen that consumers will buy more of a product at a higher price than they will at a

lower one. In regard to the first view, the important thing for purposes of the seller's pricing policy is the shape of the *AR* curve for what *he* knows is the same product. And while he may be interested in the psychology lying behind the consumer's demand curve he is not committed to the belief that it must be capable of explanation in terms of indifference curves. In regard to the second point, many marketing writers have commented on the view that a higher price will sometimes sell more than a lower one. For example, Phillips and Duncan say it may be possible to sell a greater number of a 15-cent item at 19 cents than at 15 cents (*op cit.*, p. 656). Q. Forrest Walker (*loc. cit.*), suggests that 98 cents may sell better than 89 cents. Maynard and Beckman state "It is said that more articles can be sold at 17 cents than at 14 cents." (*op. cit.*, p. 656). Converse and Huegy say "Some sellers feel that odd prices are better than even prices; others, that it makes little difference" (*op. cit.*, p. 209). A New England supermarket chain reports that their meat prices never end in the figure "1," because their price tests show they can sell more at a price ending in "3." And a U. S. Department of Commerce study reports a price of 79 cents selling more than a price of 75 cents, and a case where silk underwear sold more readily at $2 or $5 than at $1.95 or $4.95 respectively. *Cf.* F. M. Bernfield, "Time for Businessmen to Check Pricing Policies," *Domestic Commerce*, Vol. 35, March 1947, p. 20.
[7] This idea is applied even to very high prices. Thus, an automobile may be sold at $1995 rather than at $2,000.

### Psychological Prices

Some of the marketing text books give the name of "psychological pricing" to policies quite similar to the one just discussed. It has been found in some pricing experiments that a change of price over a certain range has little effect until some critical point is reached. If there are a number of such critical points for a given commodity the AR curve would look like the one in Fig. 5, resembling a series of steps. This differs from the concept of odd pricing in that the curve does not necessarily have any segments positively inclined, and the critical points are

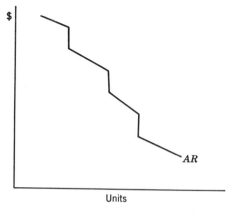

FIG. 5

not located at each round number but only at the prices psychologically important to buyers. Pricing tests at Macy's have disclosed such step-shaped AR curves.[8]

### Customary Prices

Another pricing policy usually described as though it has no relationship to theory is the one using "customary prices." This is most frequently associated with the five-cent candy bar, chewing gum, soft drink, or subway fare. The chain stores have experimented, apparently successfully, with combination cut prices on such

_____

[8] Oswald Knauth, "Some Reflections on Retail Prices," in _Economic Essays in Honor of Wesley Clair Mitchell_ (New York: Columbia University Press, 1935), pp. 203–4. Although these tests involved _changes_ in price, the important thing is that changes that reduced price below the critical points produced much greater increases in sales than changes that did not. In other words, the demand curve had very different elasticities at different points.

items, and inflation has brought about upward changes in others. In the main, however, the five-cent price on items for which it has been customary has persisted. To the extent that the policy is correct it merely means that the AR curve is like the one shown in Fig. 6, with a kink at the customary price.[9]

### Pricing at the Market

Fig. 6 also illustrates the estimate of the AR curve which results in a policy of "pricing at the market." A firm that adopts this policy believes that a price above those of competitors

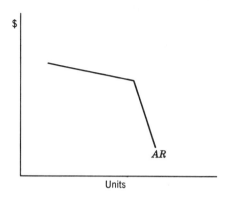

FIG. 6

would curtail sales sharply, while a lower price would not significantly increase them. This pricing policy is one of the most common, possibly because ignorance of the true shape of the AR curve suggests that the safest policy is to imitate competitors.

The policy of pricing at the market is also designed to avoid price competition and price wars. But a rule-of-thumb policy is not the correct solution to this problem, for the theory of monopolistic competition provides the basis for the proper calculation. What is required is an estimate of the AR curve after competitors have made whatever response they would make to the firm's pricing moves. In Fig. 7 this is indicated by $AR_2$, while AR is the customary curve based on an assumption of "all other things remaining the same." While it is very difficult for a seller to guess what competitors will do, the theory of correct oligopoly pricing along the

_____

[9] Of course where the policy of customary pricing is not correct, as may be true in some of the chain-store cases mentioned, the demand curve would be quite elastic below the customary price.

$AR_2$ curve is quite clear, and does not necessarily call for "pricing at the market."

### Prestige Pricing

It has often been pointed out in marketing literature that many customers judge quality by price. In such cases sales would be less at low prices than at high ones. This idea was the original legal basis for Fair Trade laws. While most manufacturers appear to be less impressed by this possibility than retailers are, there have been cases reported in which low prices led to reduced sales. The shape of the $AR$ curve illustrating this situation has already been indicated in economic literature.[10] See Fig. 8.

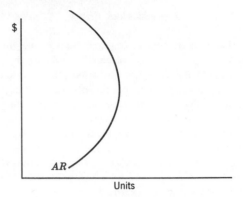

FIG. 8

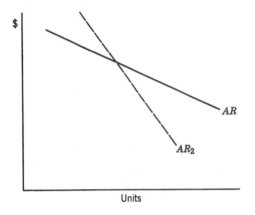

FIG. 7

### Price Lining

Many retailers when questioned about their pricing policies seem to feel they have avoided the problem entirely by adopting customary price "lines." Once the lines are decided upon, prices may be held constant over long periods of time; changes in market conditions are met by adjustments in the quality of the merchandise.

[10] F. R. Fairchild, E. S. Furniss, and N. S. Buck, *Elementary Economics* (New York: Macmillan, 1939), 4th ed., Vol. 1, p. 166. Converse and Huegy cite an instance of aspirin being tried out at different prices, 19¢, 29¢, 39¢, and 49¢, with the highest sales resulting at 49¢ (*op. cit.*, p. 207). And they comment on this reason for positively inclined demand curves, "Thus merchandise can be priced too low as well as too high. Customers may fear that at the low price it cannot be of good quality, and will actually buy more at a somewhat higher price than they would at a lower price" (p. 206).

While this policy does not require pricing decisions, except initially and in case of special sales, it does present the seller with exactly the same choice as a variable price policy does in respect to the question of whether to equate marginal cost and marginal revenue, or to use a customary per cent of markup. This decision is made with reference to the prices paid for merchandise rather than the prices at which it will be sold. Although manufacturers and wholesalers dealing in types of merchandise which is customarily price-lined at retail usually tailor their own prices to fit the retail prices, the retailer does have some choice in regard to the quality of goods he buys. Presumably, the more he pays the more he can sell, at any given price line. That is, the lower his per cent of markup the higher his sales volume should be. Fig. 9 illustrates this situation, where $P$ is the established price at retail, and $CG$ shows the various quantities that could be sold at different costs of goods to the retailer. The retailer should equate his marginal cost with marginal revenue

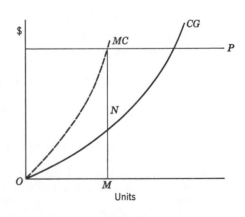

FIG. 9

(the price), paying *NM* for the goods and selling quantity *OM*. If instead he buys at a price that provides a customary or arbitrary per cent of markup it would be purely accidental if he would obtain the maximum gross margin.

Since there are few variable costs associated with the sale of most items at retail, except the cost of goods, the retailer's aim in general should be simply to maximize his gross margin dollars. If, however, other variable costs are significant they can be added to the cost of goods and a calculation made of the average variable costs, from which marginal cost can be computed. In Fig. 9 the curve *CG* would merely be replaced by an *AVC* curve.

### Resale Price Maintenance

Another situation in which the retailer feels he has no pricing problem is when the manufacturer maintains resale prices by means of Fair Trade contracts. Even here, however, the retailer may find it advantageous to sell above the Fair Trade price in some cases, in states where the Fair Trade laws call for minimum rather than specified prices. In any case the retailer must decide whether to equate marginal cost and marginal revenue or to insist upon a customary per cent of markup. If he selects the latter he may refuse to handle, or to push, many low markup items which would actually be very profitable to him.

The price policy appropriate for a manufacturer using resale price maintenance is illustrated in Fig. 10. At any given retail price *P*, which he may set, he will have an *AR* curve determined by the retailers' attitudes towards the amount of markup resulting from the price at which he sells to them. At low markups some dealers will refuse to handle the item, and oth-

ers will hide it under the counter. At relatively high markups dealers will push the item and will be able to sell more than consumers would otherwise take at the given retail price. The manufacturer should calculate his optimum price by computing *MR* from this *AR* curve and equating this with his *MC*. He should do this with the *AR* curve associated with each retail price and then select the combination of retail and wholesale prices that will result in maximum profit for him.[11]

### Quantity Discounts

Quantity discounts are usually described in marketing texts, and explained in terms of the lower unit cost of handling large orders, or simply the desire to increase sales volume. Economic analysis of the quantity discount policy would focus on the theory of price discrimination. With reference to this theory, a quantity discount schedule, open to all buyers, is a very rough device for price discrimination, and should not be used if the laws allowed freedom of discrimination. Instead, the seller should estimate the demand curve of each buyer, and offer each the price (or prices) that would maximize the seller's revenue in respect to that buyer.[12] This might well mean lower prices for some small buyers than for some large ones, depending on the elasticity of their demand curves.

Fig. 11 illustrates a case in which the large buyer's demand curve is inelastic in the significant range, while the small buyer's curve is quite elastic. It would therefore be foolish to offer them a quantity discount schedule that would give the large buyer lower prices than the small one. The large buyer would take almost as large a quantity at high prices as at low ones, while the small buyer will not. This may not be a usual situation, but it is a possible one, and indicates that the seller should consider the elasticities of demand rather than adopt an arbitrary discount schedule.

The correct theory of price discrimination, where each buyer is to be offered a different

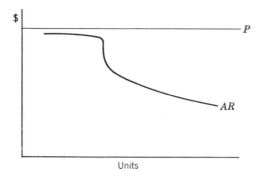

Units

FIG. 10

---

[11] For a fuller discussion see E. R. Hawkins, "Vertical Price Relationships," ch. 11 in Reavis Cox and Wroe Alderson (ed.), *Theory in Marketing* (Chicago: Richard D. Irwin, 1950).
[12] If the buyer is in a monopsonistic position he does not have a demand curve in the Marshallian sense, but it is possible to estimate how he will respond to various price offers.

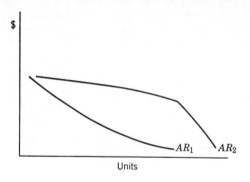

FIG. 11

price, has been outlined by Mrs. Robinson.[13] It indicates that the seller should equate the marginal revenue from each buyer with the marginal cost of the entire output.

Different costs of selling to different buyers can be taken into account by computing the AR curves as *net* average revenue curves, after deduction of the variable costs associated with the particular sales. And it would still be possible that the large buyer should be charged a higher price than the small one.

Some economists have used the term "quantity discount" to refer to a situation, unusual in marketing practice, in which each buyer is offered a quantity discount scale tailored to his own demand curve.[14] Of course a "quantity discount" of this kind would usually produce more net profit for the seller than a single price to each buyer, since it is an approach toward the maximum profit situation of perfect price discrimination, in which each buyer would be charged the highest price he would be willing to pay for each successive unit he bought. A seller may be attempting to gain some of the advantages of this type of pricing when he constructs a general quantity discount schedule with an eye to its effects on certain large buyers. In so doing, he would have to take care that the gain would not be cancelled by the adverse effect of the schedule of his net profits from other buyers.

### Geographic Pricing

While some economists have long been concerned with the geographic aspects of pricing, and this interest has recently been spreading,

on the whole marketing specialists and economic geographers have regarded the spatial aspects of economics as their own province. Unfortunately they have developed theories which do not include the essential economic aspects of the problem. Fig. 11 may be used to illustrate some of the problems of geographic pricing. If the AR curve of each buyer is taken as a *net* average revenue curve, after deduction of transportation costs, then it is clear that the nearer buyer should not necessarily be given the lower delivered price. The elasticity of each buyer's demand curve is the important factor which should be considered. As has been indicated by Mrs. Robinson, the correct net price to each buyer would equate the seller's marginal revenue with the marginal cost of his entire output.[15]

While the Robinson-Patman Act does not permit the free price discrimination that would maximize the seller's profit, it does allow some discretion in pricing. The seller is not permitted to employ price differentials greater than his cost differentials; but he is free to give discounts less than the amount of cost saving to him. Moreover, he is allowed some discretion to employ price differentials when the buyers are not in competition with each other, or where he himself is "meeting competition." He may also, of course, discriminate by selling slightly different products, under different brand names.

### CONCLUSION

The discrepancy between economic theory and actual pricing policies, as observed by marketing specialists, is more apparent than real. Most of the pricing behavior reported by marketing students is quite consistent with the general theory of monopolistic competition, and can be integrated with that theory. A considerable gain can be made on both sides if this integration is accomplished. Economists need to know more about the pricing policies actually used by businessmen. On the other hand, marketing students can understand these policies better if they appreciate the theoretical basis for them. Most of the "price policies" described by marketing specialists are merely special cases of the general theory of monopolistic competition. If so regarded, not only would clarification result, but perhaps additional insight would be gained regarding the advantages and disadvantages of each policy, and the situations to which they are appropriate.

[13] Joan Robinson, *The Economics of Imperfect Competition* (London: Macmillan, 1933), p. 182.

[14] James M. Buchanan, "The Theory of Monopolistic Quantity Discounts," *Review of Economic Studies*, Vol. 20, No. 3, 1952-1953.

[15] Joan Robinson, *loc. cit.*

# 48. Pricing a New Product

JOEL DEAN

New product pricing is important in two ways: it affects the amount of the product that will be sold; and it determines the amount of revenue that will be received for a given quantity of sales. If you set your price too high you will be likely to make too few sales to permit you to cover your overhead. If you set your price too low you may not be able to cover out-of-pocket costs and may face bankruptcy.

## WHAT IS DIFFERENT ABOUT NEW PRODUCTS?

New products that are novel require a different pricing treatment than old products because they are distinctive; no one else sells quite the same thing. This distinctiveness is usually only temporary, however. As your product catches on, your competitors will try to take away your market by bringing out imitative substitutes. The speed with which your product loses its uniqueness will depend on a number of factors. Among these factors are the total sales potential, the investment required for rivals to manufacture and distribute the product, the strength of patent protection, and the alertness and power of competitors.

Although this process of competitive imitation is almost inevitable, the company that introduces the new product can use price as a means of slowing the speed of competitive imitation. Finding the "right" price is not easy, however. New products are hard to price correctly. This is true both because past experience is no sure guide as to how the market will

✖ SOURCE: Reprinted by permission from *The Controller*, Vol. 23, No. 4, April 1955, pp. 163–165.

react to any given price, and because competing products are usually significantly different in nature or quality.

In setting a price on a new product you will want to have three objectives in mind: (1) getting the product accepted, (2) maintaining your market in the face of growing competition, (3) producing profits. Your pricing policy cannot be said to be successful unless you can achieve all three of these objectives.

## WHAT ARE YOUR CHOICES AS TO POLICY?

Broadly speaking, the strategy in pricing a new product comes down to a choice between (1) "skimming" pricing, and (2) "penetration" pricing. There are a number of intermediate positions, but the issues are made clearer when the two extremes are compared.

*Skimming Pricing.* For products that represent a drastic departure from accepted ways of performing a service or filling a demand, a strategy of high prices coupled with large promotional expenditures in the early stages of market development (and lower prices at later stages) has frequently proven successful. This is known as a skimming price policy.

There are four main reasons why this kind of skimming price policy is attractive for new and distinctive products: *First*, the quantity of the product that you can sell is likely to be less affected by price in the early stages than it will be when the product is full-grown and imitation has had time to take effect. This is the period when pure salesmanship can have the greatest effect on sales. *Second*, a skimming price policy takes the cream of the market at a high price before attempting to penetrate the more price-sensitive sections of the market. This means that you can get more money from those who don't care how much they pay, while building up experience to hit the big mass market with tempting prices. *Third,* this can be a way to feel out the demand. It is frequently easier to start out with a high "refusal" price and reduce it later on when the facts of product demand make themselves known than it is to set a low price initially and then boost the price to cover unforeseen costs or exploit a popular product. *Fourth,* high prices will frequently produce a greater dollar volume of sales in the early stages of market development than a policy of low initial prices. If this is the case, skimming pricing will provide you with funds for financing expansion into the big-volume sectors of your market.

A skimming-price policy is not always the answer to your problem, however. High initial prices may safeguard profits during the early stages of product introduction, but they may also prevent quick sales to the many buyers upon whom you must rely to give you a mass market. The alternative is to use low prices as an entering wedge to get into mass markets early. This is known as penetration pricing.

*Penetration Pricing.* This approach is likely to be desirable under the following conditions: *First,* when the quantity of product sold is highly sensitive to price, even in the early stages of introduction. *Second,* when you can achieve substantial economies in unit cost and effectiveness of manufacturing and distributing the product by operating at large volumes. *Third,* when your product is faced by threats of strong potential competition, very soon after introduction. *Fourth,* when there is no "elite" market—that is, a body of buyers who are willing to pay a much higher price in order to obtain the latest and best.

The decision to price so as to penetrate a broad market can be made at any stage in the product's life cycle, but you should be sure to examine this pricing strategy before your new product is marketed at all. This possibility certainly should be explored as soon as your product has established an elite market. Sometimes a product can be rescued from a premature death by adoption of a penetration price policy after the cream of the market has been skimmed.

The ease and speed with which competitors can bring out substitute products is probably the most important single consideration in your choice between skimming and penetration pricing at the time you introduce your new product. For products whose market potential looks big, a policy of low initial prices ("stay-out pricing") makes sense, because the big multiple-product manufacturers are attracted by mass markets. If you set your price low enough to begin with, your large competitor may not feel it worth his while to make a big production and distribution investment for slim profit margins. In any event, you should appraise the competitive situation very carefully for each new product before you decide on your pricing strategy.

## WHAT SHOULD YOU LOOK AT IN SETTING A PRICE?

When you have decided on your basic pricing strategy you can turn to the task of putting a dollars-and-cents price tag on your new product. In order to do this you should look at at least five important factors: (1) potential and probable demand for your product, (2) cost of making and selling the product, (3) market targets, (4) promotional strategy, and (5) suitable channels of distribution.

## DEMAND

The first step in estimating market demand is to find out whether or not the product will sell at all—assuming that the price is set within the competitive range. That is, you should find out whether or not this product fulfills a real need, and whether enough potential customers are dissatisfied with their present means of filling that need. To do this, you should make some estimate of the total potential market for the new product and all its competing substitutes and then estimate the portion of this potential that your product is likely to get.

Next, you should determine the competitive range of price. This will be easier when substitutes are relatively close or when customers are familiar with the cost and quality of substitutes and act rationally on the basis of performance.

The next step is to try to guess the probable sales volume at two or three possible prices within the price range. The best way to do this is by controlled experiments; next best is by a close estimation of buyers' alternatives in the light of market preference.

Finally, you should consider the possibility of retaliation by manufacturers of displaced substitutes. If your new product hits any one of your competitors hard enough, you may be faced with price retaliation. The limit to this price cutting is set by the out-of-pocket cost of the price-cutting competitors. Therefore, some knowledge of the out-of-pocket cost of making competing products will be helpful in estimating the probable effects of a particular price.

## COSTS

Before going ahead with your new product, you should estimate its effect on your investment, your costs, and your profits. First you should estimate the added investment necessary to manufacture and distribute the new product. This investment estimate should include estimates of increased working capital that will be required at various sales volumes. Then you should estimate the added costs of manufacturing and selling the product at various possible sales volumes. The way to estimate costs is to calculate what your total costs would be with and without the new product; the difference should be assigned to the new product. Allocations of overheads that you are already incurring should not be assigned to the new product because they will be the same whether or not you go ahead with the addition to your product line.

In building up your two sets of cost and investment figures—one showing the situation *without* the new product, and the other showing the contrasting situation *with* the new product added to your line—be sure to take into account *all* pertinent items. It often happens that companies which lose money on new products have run into trouble because of unanticipated costs or investment requirements which have absorbed most of or all the profits realizable from the new idea.

New product costs may be segregated into half a dozen main categories: direct labor, materials and supplies for production, components purchased outside, special equipment (such as jigs, dies, fixtures and other tools), plant overhead, and sales expenses.

*Direct Labor.* Methods of estimating direct labor may be built up in one of three ways: (1) You can compare each operation on each component with accumulated historical data, from your files, on similar operations for similar components, (2) you can develop a mockup of the proposed work-place layout and actually time an operator who performs a series of manufacturing operations, simulated as accurately as possible, (3) you can apply one of several systems of predetermined, basic-motion times which are currently available from private sources.

Make certain, however, that you include any added time used for setup work, or needed to take the item from its transportation container, perform the operations, and return the item again to its transportation container. When the total direct labor time is determined multiply it by the appropriate labor rates.

*Materials and Supplies for Production.* In developing reliable cost figures for materials and supplies make a methodical list of all requirements. Having listed everything in an organized fashion, you can enter the specifications and costs on a manufactured-component estimate form. Remember to include any extra costs which may be incurred as a result of requirements for particular length, widths, qualities, or degrees of finish. Allowances for scrap should also be made as accurately as possible and corrected by applying a salvage factor if the scrap can be sold or reused.

*Components Purchased Outside.* Place your specification for parts purchased from other concerns with more than one reliable supplier and get competitive bids for the work. But in addition to price considerations be sure to give proper weight to the reputation and qualification of each potential producer. Moreover, if you use a substantial volume of purchased parts you may want to use a "plus" factor above the cost of the components themselves to cover your expenses involved in receiving, storing, and handling the items.

*Special Equipment.* Take careful precautions against making a faulty analysis of your expense and investment in special jigs, dies, fixtures, and other tools which you will need to produce the new product. To avoid trouble in this area make a table showing all cases where special equipment will be needed. The actual estimating of the costs of such equipment is best done by a qualified tool shop—your own if you have one or an outside organization. Here again, competitive bidding is an excellent protection on price. Do not include costs of routine inspection, service, and repair; these are properly charged to plant overhead.

*Plant Overhead.* The overhead item may be estimated as a given percentage of direct labor, machine utilization, or some other factor determined by your accountants to be the most sensible basis. In this way you can allocate satisfactorily charges for administration and supervision, for occupancy, and for indirect service related to producing the new product. Overhead allocations may be set up for a department, a production center, or even, in some cases, for a particular machine. In calculating plant overhead make certain that in setting up your cost controls, your accountants have not overlooked any proper indirect special charges which will have to be incurred because of the new product.

*Sales Expenses.* Your estimates of sales revenue at various potential volumes can now be compared with your estimates of added costs at those volumes. The difference will be the added profits of introducing the new product. Although the costs themselves probably should not be used as a basis for setting price, you should not go into any venture that will not produce for you a rate-of-return on the added investment required that is adequate to compensate for the added risk and still be at least as high as the return you could get by investing your money elsewhere. If no price that you set will provide enough revenue to produce an adequate profit over your added costs, then you should either drop the venture, try to cut costs, or wait for a more favorable time to introduce the product.

## MARKETING TARGETS

Assuming that the estimates of market demand and of cost and investment have been made and that the profit picture looks sufficiently rosy, you are now in a position to set up some basic goals and programs. A decision must first be made about market targets—that is, what market share or sales volume should be aimed at? Among other factors, you should probably consider what effect it will have upon investment requirements, whether or not your existing organization can handle the new product, how it fits in with the rest of your present product line, and so forth. These decisions should be made after a cold-blooded survey of the nature of your new product and of your company's organization and manufacturing and distributive facilities.

## PROMOTION

Closely related to the question of market targets is the design of promotional strategy. As an innovator, you must not only sell your product, but frequently you must also make people recognize their need for this kind of product. Your problem here is to determine the best way of "creating a market." You must determine the nature of the market and the type of appeal that will sell the product and secure prompt acceptance by potential buyers. And you should also estimate how much it will cost you to achieve this goal.

## CHANNELS OF DISTRIBUTION

Frequently, there is some latitude in your choice of channels of distribution. This choice should be consistent with your strategy for initial pricing and for promotional outlays. Penetration pricing and explosive promotion calls for distribution channels that promptly make the product broadly available. Otherwise you waste advertising or stymie mass-market pricing. Distribution policy also concerns the role you wish the dealer to play in pushing your product, the margins you must pay him to introduce this action and the amount of protection of territory and of inventory required to do so.

## YOUR DECISION

These are the factors you should look at in setting a price. Estimating these factors shrewdly and objectively requires specialized training and experience. Good estimates will make your pricing more realistic and successful. But pricing cannot be established by formula. Combining these factors into a pricing policy requires judgment. In the last analysis you must pull all the estimates of the experts together and arrive at your own decision. You will want to make sure that the pricing analysis is guided by sound principles and that the activities of your specialists are all geared toward the same end—devising a sound, effective marketing and promotional program in conjunction with a price that will meet your objectives of market acceptance, competitive strength, and profits.

# 49. Price Sensitivity of the Consumer[1]

ANDRÉ GABOR and C. W. J. GRANGER*

The effect of advertising often depends partly on the price set for the product. Price-setters will do well, as the authors show, to learn how much consumers know about prices and how ready they are to buy at various price levels.

Even the best advertising campaign may fail if the price of the product is not appropriate, yet retail prices are still determined more by rules of thumb than systematic study.

As far as we know, there are three main methods of pricing. The first can quickly be dismissed, since it is just to copy the prices of the main competitor even though there is no actual compulsion to do so. The second method is to apply a standard mark-up to the cost of the article. This has rightly been described by the director of trading of an important retail organization as "the antithesis of good retail merchandising" (May, 1959). The third method has been called backward costing and is essentially the opposite of the "cost plus" procedure. Here the starting point is a list of standard prices, and a predetermined gross profit margin is taken off the selected retail price to determine the permissible cost. The article is built to fit this cost figure, the aim being to give the best value compatible with allowable net cost. In spite of its elaborate nature, this method also may result in a price which is not right for the market, since so much depends on the appropriateness of the list of standard prices.

Long before economic theory and consumer research penetrated the world of commerce, the compilers of these standard lists sensed that the subjective price scale of the consumer resembles a ratio (logarithmic) scale rather than the so-called natural scale. That is, a given price change should have a much greater effect for a low-priced product than for an

---

British Currency

12 pennies (12d.) = 1 shilling (1s.) = $0.14
20 shillings = 1 pound (L1.) = $2.80
21 shillings = 1 guinea = $2.94

On price labels it is customary to separate the shillings from the pennies by a stroke. Thus 16/11 means 16s.11d.

The guinea was coined in gold from 1663 to 1813. Its value was fixed at 21 shillings in 1717, or one shilling more than the pound. It is at present only a notional unit. Used in professional fees, certain subscriptions, and some prices, pricing in guineas appears to serve two purposes. First, it implies that in spite of its low cost the article is a high quality product (in the late 1930's, guinea and half-guinea dress shops were common in London and some provincial towns). Second, it conceals the fact that expressed in pounds, shillings, and pennies the price would be above some round figure. Hence the habit of pricing certain household durables, such as washing machines, refrigerators, and TV sets at, say, 59 guineas or 67 guineas.

---

expensive product. Relative rather than absolute change should better predict consumers' reactions. For example, say the price of an article is gradually reduced from $20.00 to $9.50. When the price drops from $20.00 to $19.00, a five per cent change, let us say that sales expand by eight per cent. Later, the price is reduced from $10.00 to $9.50, again a

---

[1] Some of the material on which this article is based emerged in the course of a collaborative study with members of Research Bureau Limited (Unilever).

* © Copyright 1964, André Gabor and C. W. J. Granger.

◆ SOURCE: Reprinted by permission from the *Journal of Advertising Research,* (December 1964), pp. 40–44.

five per cent change, and if the consumers' subjective valuation follows a ratio scale, then sales should again increase by eight per cent. Economists would describe this as constant elasticity of demand; psychologists would recognize it as analogous to the Weber-Fechner Law of subjective judgments of changes in light intensity and volume of sound.

The actual structure of prices in the market place further implies the belief that, besides this tendency to react to relative rather than absolute price changes, the consumer also shows a heightened price sensitivity at critical points, where a slight increase in price would result in a substantial drop in sales. For example, over a part of its price list one firm only has prices ending in 11 pennies, which implies the conviction that all the prices from, say 16/1 to 16/11 look alike to the consumer, but that 17/0 would appear to be significantly higher than 16/11.

Most compilers and users of such price lists would probably feel inclined to protest against this sort of theoretical generalization of what they regard simply as facts of experience. They would say that some prices have been found to be more effective in promoting sales than others, and there is nothing more to it. However, since the typical list of standard prices to which we referred above, bears the title, "Regulation prices to be used for all merchandise except food," it is clear that the generalization is theirs rather than ours. This generalization is precisely the issue which we propose to examine critically.

## MEASURING PRICE SENSITIVITY

An alternative and, we believe, superior approach to price determination is to gauge the price sensitivity of the potential consumer and, if this sensitivity is significant, to examine the ranges of price acceptability of each of the more important socio-economic subgroups. Following the lead of French researchers (Stoetzel, 1954; Adam, 1958) we have devised a method of exploring price acceptability which can reveal the extent to which customers judge the quality of an article by its price. In certain product fields, we have found that sales can just as easily be lost by having too low a price, thus implying poor quality, as by too high a price. But where price sensitivity is low, it would be a waste of effort to aim at high precision in pricing.

Some results of our research have been published elsewhere (Gabor and Granger, 1961). Here we shall only discuss two important points. The first is the established fact that price sensitivity appears to vary greatly from product to product. The second concerns the efficacy of fixing prices just below certain round figures.

High price sensitivity is inconceivable without correspondingly high price awareness, though the reverse may not necessarily be true. This last point is best illustrated by an example: until recently the price of a railway platform ticket was one penny. It was probably the best known of all prices, having been the same for many decades, yet it could safely be doubled to two pennies without risking any substantial sales resistance.

Price awareness can be measured by recall, i.e., by the percentage of regular purchasers who remember the price more or less correctly. We took the view that a housewife who cannot even recall what she last paid for eggs, could not possibly be very sensitive to a small change in price, or to a small difference in price between two shops. Very little published material is available on the problem, and as an American study (Progressive Grocer, 1964) noted:

There are several schools of opinion on price knowledge possessed by customers. Some maintain that they know little—others say they know a great deal. Some operate on the theory that customers know prices of 10, 50, or perhaps 100 items. Some contend that customers are aware of the competitive prices of only the specific items they buy, while others believe customers can closely know or can estimate prices of hundreds, even thousands of items.

In this American study, 59 different branded articles were set up on tables in stores, and customers were asked to state the price of each item. In our 1958 study we followed a different procedure. Investigators called on and questioned 422 housewives about their recent purchases of 15 selected products. Answers were recorded only if the housewife said she had purchased the commodity within the last week.

The importance of remembering the *exact* price is debatable and it seems that the significance attached to it must vary with the method of investigation. Since the Americans asked the subjects to state the price of each item, their response rate was probably near to 100 per cent, hence what mattered was the precision of the answers. They found that the proportion of customers who named the correct price varied with the article from two per cent to 86 per cent, or, if a five per cent error is allowed, from 12 to 91 per cent.

Of 15 product groups in our study, seven could be checked against actual prices, and the variation in the percentage correct ranged from 44 per cent to 80 per cent, with an average of 59 per cent. With a five per cent margin of error, the average was 65 per cent; with a ten per cent margin, it rose to 73 per cent. Table 1 shows the results for the seven product groups.

### Table 1.    Accuracy of Price Recall*

|  | Total | Correct | Wrong | Don't Know | No.of Base: Purchases |
|---|---|---|---|---|---|
| Tea | 100% | 79% | 16% | 5% | (357) |
| Coffee | 100 | 68 | 22 | 10 | (160) |
| Sugar | 100 | 67 | 13 | 20 | (397) |
| Jam and marmalade | 100 | 60 | 23 | 17 | (197) |
| Margarine | 100 | 46 | 44 | 10 | (252) |
| Flour | 100 | 36 | 29 | 35 | (281) |
| Breakfast cereal | 100 | 35 | 40 | 25 | (244) |

* SOURCE: Gabor and Granger (1961). Reproduced with permission of *Applied Statistics*.

Note the striking differences between the commodities. Comparing tea with breakfast cereal, we find that 95 per cent of the respondents gave a price for tea, the large majority of the answers being correct. For breakfast cereals, more than half of the 75 per cent who ventured to state the price misremembered it.

Owing to differences in method, the findings of the American study are not directly comparable with ours. What is common in the results is the wide variability in price recall. This cannot be explained simply by frequency of purchase because, to mention one example only, tea scored much better than sugar in our study and so did Coca Cola in America. In both cases, it is intriguing to note, the national beverage topped the list.

Variability in price recall implies similar variability in sensitivity to price changes and differences. Yet it does not necessarily follow that the customer who is fully aware of the price will always plump for the cheapest comparable brand or buy it at the lowest-priced retail outlet. In a recent British study (Bird, 1958), high proportions of housewives said they felt that their regular grocer charged more than others for bacon, eggs, cheese, etc. The main factor in choosing a regular grocer was found to be proximity to the person's home. This does not, however, affect the main issue, which is simply that the "right" price has a wide latitude for some commodities and practically none for others.

Finding the right price for a given brand is a different problem from predicting the probable effects of a change in the whole structure of prices of competing brands. Individual price setters are right in keeping an eye on competitors' price policy; they are wrong only if they think, as they often do, that this is all that matters. Aiming at the lowest possible price for a given product also is not the complete answer to the problem. There are recorded instances where a sharp increase in price had beneficial effects both on gross sales figures and profits.

## GOOD PRICES AND BAD

The second problem which we propose to discuss is the efficacy of the 19/11 (or one penny below 20/0) type of price. "Just-below-the-round-figure" prices are widespread at least throughout Western Europe and the United States, and in some cases have become almost a fetish. (A recent American advertisement said "Save $2.98." Clearly, to emphasize the amount saved by accepting the offer, the figure should have been $3.00!) If such prices have an important effect upon sales, it would imply irregularities in the customer's subjective price scale.

What we have to say here is based on certain implications of our latest survey, the full results of which will shortly be published. Unlike our 1958 study, which was conducted on a relatively small scale, in this survey we interviewed 3,200 housewives.

There can be little doubt that some people look upon 4/11, say, as "four shillings and something" and do not consider it appreciably different from 4/7, 4/9, or 4/10. But there certainly are others whose mind registers "five" or "almost five" shillings when confronted with 4/11, and it is regrettable that so little work has been done to establish the proportions of these two kinds of customers.

While our recent study was not specifically designed to investigate this issue, the results do throw some light on the public's attitude to the penny-below-the-round-figure type of pricing. We have concluded that the attitude depends largely on the price structure prevailing in the particular market. If setters in the market are obsessed with the idea that 4/11 is a "good" price, while 4/10 and 5/0 are "bad" prices, a certain proportion of the public will be induced to look upon 4/11 as a "real" price and 5/0 as "phoney," simply because no known brand happens to be available at this price. But where prices are fixed without attention to the "penny-below" doctrine, no such idea will take root in the consumer's mind.

This will be illustrated by two examples, one from each type of market. In order to safeguard commercial interests, we shall denote the products by A and B only. Both markets are keenly competitive, but the similarity ends here. Somehow or other, the price setters of practically all the Product A brands have argued themselves into a position where at least in the range below 10 shillings prices ending in 11 pennies are almost exclusively used, while the brands of Product B are being priced without much attention to this principle.

The data on which our conclusions are based were obtained by calling out selected prices to subjects who were asked to respond by saying either "Buy", or "No, too expensive", or "No, too cheap." Figures 1 and 2 show the percentages of customers who declared themselves ready to buy at the prices concerned. (Though the price ranges of the two figures are different, they refer to comparable sets of data.)

For Product A, Figure 1 appears to confirm the belief that 5/11 is a much better price than 6/0, and 6/11 than 7/0. But surprisingly, it also shows that customers prefer 5/11 to 5/10, and 6/11 to 6/10!

For Product B, Figure 2 presents an entirely different picture: there is an uninterrupted decline beyond 3/6, and the drop from 3/10 to 3/11 actually exceeds that from 3/11 to 4/0. In other words, the curve gives no support whatever to the tenet that a price ending in 11 pennies is the best price of its region.

The answer to this apparent contradiction can be found in the prevalent price structure in each market. Since leading brands of Product A in the price range shown are priced at 5/11 and 6/11, the implication is that prices such as 5/10 and 6/0 were regarded as something unreal by some subjects. What is surprising is not so much the relatively favorable response to prices ending in 11 pennies, but rather that most subjects attached so little importance to the difference between, say, 5/6,

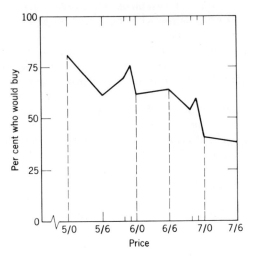

FIG. 1. Product A.

5/10, 5/11 and 6/0. Figure 2 shows that where the price setters are not obsessed by the penny-below-the-shilling idea, subjects do not display any particular preference for the "penny-below" price. Thus the dominance of the 11-penny price in certain markets may be largely, if not entirely, an artifact. Once introduced, it imprints itself on some customers' minds, and when this has happened the price setter can easily delude himself into believing that his hunch was correct.

The problems we have raised in this article are not simple and our conclusions are not final. But we do believe that two points are

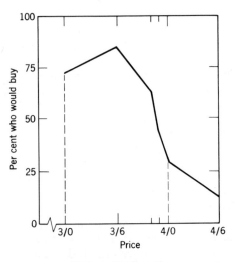

FIG. 2. Product B.

valid: price sensitivity varies considerably both with the nature of the product and with the dominating pricing policy in the market. Hence lists of regulation or standard prices may have administrative advantages, such as savings on price labels, but they should not be applied without proper regard to the factors mentioned. And since experience suggests that even the most expert advertising may not be capable of correcting a serious mistake in pricing, businessmen would be well advised not to trust the traditional rule-of-thumb methods of price determination but explore the attitude of their customers to the proposed price before embarking on an expensive campaign.

## REFERENCES

ADAM, DANIEL. *Les Réactions du Consommateur Devant le Prix.* Paris: Sedes, 1958.

BIRD, ALFRED & SONS, LTD. *Mrs. Housewife and Her Grocer.* Birmingham: published for private circulation by Alfred Bird and Sons Ltd., 1958.

GABOR, ANDRE AND C. W. J. GRANGER. On the Price Consciousness of Consumers. *Applied Statistics,* Vol. 10, No. 3, November 1961, pp. 170–188.

MAY, PAUL. Retail Pricing. *Gazette of the John Lewis Partnership,* Vol. 41, No. 35, October 1959, pp. 791–793.

PROGRESSIVE GROCER. How Much Do Customers Know About Retail Prices? *Progressive Grocer,* February 1964, pp. C104–106.

STOETZEL, J. Le Prix Comme Limite. In P. L. Reynaud. (Ed.), *La Psychologie Économique.* Paris: Marcel Rivière et Cie, 1954, pp. 184–188.

# G. Marketing Strategy

## 50. Systems Approach to Marketing

LEE ADLER

More and more businessmen today recognize that corporate success is, in most cases, synonymous with marketing success and with the coming of age of a new breed of professional managers. They find it increasingly important not only to pay lip service to the marketing concept but to do something about it in terms of (a) customer orientation, rather than navel-gazing in the factory, (b) organizational revisions to implement the marketing concept, and (c) a more orderly approach to problem solving.

In an increasing number of companies we see more conscious and formal efforts to apply rational, fact-based methods for solving marketing problems, and greater recognition of the benefits these methods offer. While these benefits may be newly realized, there is nothing new about the underlying philosophy; in the parlance of military men and engineers, it is the systems approach. For, whether we like it or not, marketing is, by definition, a system, if we accept Webster's definition of system as "an assemblage of objects united by some form of regular interaction or interdependence." Certainly, the interaction of such "objects" is product, pricing, promotion, sales calls, distribution, and so on fits the definition.

There is an expanding list of sophisticated applications of systems theory—and not in one but in many sectors of the marketing front. The construction of mathematical and/or logical models to describe, quantify, and evaluate alternate marketing strategies and mixes is an obvious case in point. So, too, is the formulation of management information systems[1] and of marketing plans with built-in performance measurements of predetermined goals. But no less vital is the role of the systems approach in the design and sale of products and services. When J. P. Stevens Company color-harmonizes linens and bedspreads, and towels and bath mats, it is creating a product system. And when Avco Corporation sells systems management to the space exploration field, involving the marriage of many scientific disciplines as well as adherence to budgetary constraints, on-time performance, and quality control, it is creating a *service* system.

In this article I shall discuss the utilization of the systems concept in marketing in both quantitative and qualitative ways with case histories drawn from various industries. In doing so, my focus will be more managerial and philosophical than technical, and I will seek to dissipate some of the hocus-pocus, glamor, mystery, and fear which pervade the field. The

---

◆ SOURCE: Reprinted by permission from *Harvard Business Review*, Vol. 45, No. 3, May-June 1967, pp. 105–118. © 1967 by the President and Fellows of Harvard College; all rights reserved.

[1] See, for example, Donald F. Cox and Robert E. Good, "How to Build a Marketing Information System," *Harvard Business Review*, Vol. 45, No. 3, May-June, 1967, p. 145.

systems concept is not esoteric or "science fiction" in nature (although it sometimes *sounds* that way in promotional descriptions). Its advantages are not subtle or indirect; as we shall see, they are as real and immediate as decision making itself. The limitations are also real, and these, too, will be discussed.

(Readers interested in a brief summary of the background and the conceptual development of the systems approach may wish to turn to the Appendix at the end of this article.)

## PROMISING APPLICATIONS

Now let us look at some examples of corporate application of the systems approach. Here we will deal with specific parts or "subsystems" of the total marketing system. Exhibit 1 is a schematic portrayal of these relationships.

### Products and Services

The objective of the systems approach in product management is to provide a complete "offering" to the market rather than merely a product. If the purpose of business is to create a customer at a profit, then the needs of the customer must be carefully attended to; we must, in short, study what the customer is buying or wants to buy, rather than what we are trying to sell.

In the consumer products field we have

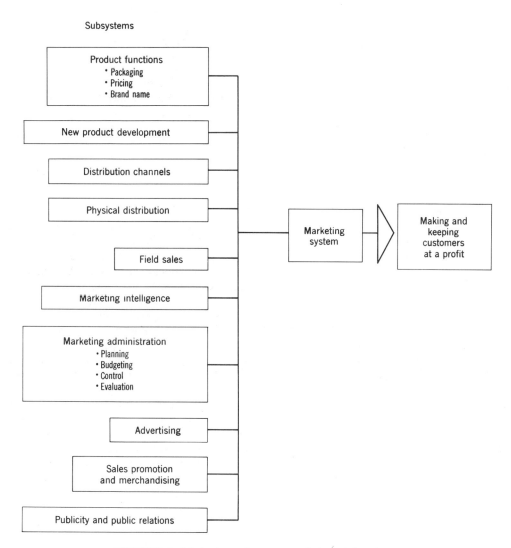

EXHIBIT 1. Marketing subsystems and the total system.

forged ahead in understanding that the customer buys nutrition (not bread), beauty (not cosmetics), warmth (not fuel oil). But in industrial products this concept has been slower in gaining a foothold. Where it has gained a foothold, it expresses itself in two ways: the creation of a complete product system sold (1) as a unit, or (2) as a component or components which are part of a larger consumption system.

Perhaps the most eloquent testimony to the workability and value of the systems approach comes from companies that have actually used it. For a good example let us turn to the case of The Carborundum Company. This experience is especially noteworthy because it comes from industrial marketing, where, as just indicated, progress with the systems concept has generally been slow.

**Birth of the Concept.** Founded in 1894, the company was content for many years to sell abrasives. It offered an extremely broad line of grinding wheels, coated abrasives, and abrasive grain, with a reputed capacity for 200,000 different products of varying type, grade, and formulation. But the focus was on the product.

In the mid-1950's, Carborundum perceived that the market for abrasives could be broadened considerably if—looking at abrasives through customers' eyes—it would see the product as fitting into *metal polishing, cleaning,* or *removal systems.* Now Carborundum is concerned with all aspects of abrading—the machine, the contact wheel, the workpiece, the labor cost, the overhead rate, the abrasive, and, above all, the customer's objective. In the words of Carborundum's president, W. H. Wendel:

That objective is never the abrasive per se, but rather the creation of a certain dimension, a type of finish, or a required shape, always related to a minimum cost. Since there are many variables to consider, just one can be misleading. To render maximum service, Carborundum (must offer) a complete system.[2]

**Organizational Overhaul.** To offer such a system, management had to overhaul important parts of the organization:

(1) The company needed to enhance its knowledge of the total system. As Wendel explains:

We felt we had excellent knowledge of coated abrasive products, but that we didn't have the application and machine know-how in

depth. To be really successful in the business, we had to know as much about the machine tools as we did the abrasives.[3]

To fill this need, Carborundum made three acquisitions—The Tysaman Machine Company, which builds heavy-duty snagging, billet grinding and abrasive cut-off machines; Curtis Machine Company, a maker of belt sanders; and Pangborn Corporation, which supplied systems capability in abrasive blast cleaning and finishing.

(2) The company's abrasive divisions were reorganized, and the management of them was realigned to accommodate the new philosophy and its application. The company found that *centering responsibility for the full system in one profit center* proved to be the most effective method of coordinating approaches in application engineering, choice of distribution channels, brand identification, field sales operations, and so forth. This method was particularly valuable for integrating the acquisitions into the new program.

(3) An Abrasives Systems Center was established to handle development work and to solve customer problems.

(4) Technical conferences and seminars were held to educate customers on the new developments.

(5) Salesmen were trained in machine and application knowledge.

**Planning.** A key tool in the systems approach is planning—in particular, the use of what I like to call "total business plans." (This term emphasizes the contrast with company plans that cover only limited functions.) At Carborundum, total business plans are developed with extreme care by the operating companies and divisions. Very specific objectives are established, and then detailed action programs are outlined to achieve these objectives. The action programs extend throughout the organization, including the manufacturing and development branches of the operating unit. Management sets specific dates for the completion of action steps and defines who is responsible for them. Also, it carefully measures results against established objectives. This is done both in the financial reporting system and in various marketing committees.

**Quantitative Methods.** Carborundum has utilized various operations research techniques,

---

[2] "Abrasive Maker's Systems Approach Opens New Markets," *Steel,* December 27, 1965, p. 38.

[3] Ibid.

like decision tree analysis and PERT, to aid in molding plans and strategies. For example, one analysis, which concerned itself with determining the necessity for plant expansion, was based on different possible levels of success for the marketing plan. In addition, the computer has been used for inventory management, evaluation of alternate pricing strategies for systems selling, and the measurement of marketing achievements against goals.

It should be noted, though, that these quantitative techniques are management tools only and that much of the application of systems thinking to the redeployment of Carborundum's business is qualitative in nature.

*Gains Achieved.* As a consequence of these developments, the company has opened up vast new markets. To quote Carborundum's president again:

Customers don't want a grinding wheel, they want metal removed. . . . The U.S. and Canadian market for abrasives amounts to $700 million a year. But what companies spend on stock removal—to bore, grind, cut, shape, and finish metal—amounts to $30 billion a year.[4]

Illustrating this market expansion in the steel industry is Carborundum's commercial success with three new developments—hot grinding, an arborless wheel to speed metal removal and cut grinding costs, and high-speed conditioning of carbon steel billets. All represent conversions from nonabrasive methods. Carborundum now also finds that the close relationship with customers gives it a competitive edge, opens top customer management doors, gains entrée for salesmen with prospects they had never been able to "crack" before. Perhaps the ultimate accolade is the company's report that customers even come to the organization itself, regarding it as a consultant as well as a supplier.

### Profitable Innovation

The intense pressure to originate successful new products cannot be met without methodologies calculated to enhance the probabilities of profitable innovation. The systems approach has a bearing here, too. Exhibit 2 shows a model for "tracking" products through the many stages of ideation, development, and testing to ultimate full-scale commercialization.

This diagram is in effect a larger version of the "New Product Development" box in Exhibit 1.

Observe that this is a logical (specifically, sequential), rather than numerical, model. While some elements of the total system (e.g., alternate distribution channels and various media mixes) can be analyzed by means of operations research techniques, the model has not been cast in mathematical terms. Rather, the flow diagram as a whole is used as a checklist to make sure "all bases are covered" and to help organize the chronological sequence of steps in new product development. It also serves as a conceptual foundation for formal PERT application, should management desire such a step, and for the gradual development of a series of equations linking together elements in the diagrams, should it seem useful to experiment with mathematical models.

### Marketing Intelligence

The traditional notion of marketing research is fast becoming antiquated. For it leads to dreary chronicles of the past rather than focusing on the present and shedding light on the future. It is particularistic, tending to concentrate on the study of tiny fractions of a marketing problem rather than on the problem as a whole. It lends itself to assuaging the curiosity of the moment, to fire-fighting, to resolving internecine disputes. It is a slave to technique. I shall not, therefore, relate the term *marketing research* to the systems approach—although I recognize, of course, that some leading businessmen and writers are breathing new life and scope into the ideas referred to by that term.

The role of the systems approach is to help evolve a *marketing intelligence* system tailored to the needs of each marketer. Such a system would serve as the ever-alert nerve center of the marketing operation. It would have these major characteristics:

1. Continuous surveillance of the market.
2. A team of research techniques used in tandem.
3. A network of data sources.
4. Integrated analysis of data from the various sources.
5. Effective utilization of automatic data-processing equipment to distill mountains of raw information speedily.
6. Strong concentration not just on reporting findings but also on practical, action-oriented recommendations.

[4] "Carborundum Grinds at Faster Clip," *Business Week,* July 23, 1966, pp. 58, 60.

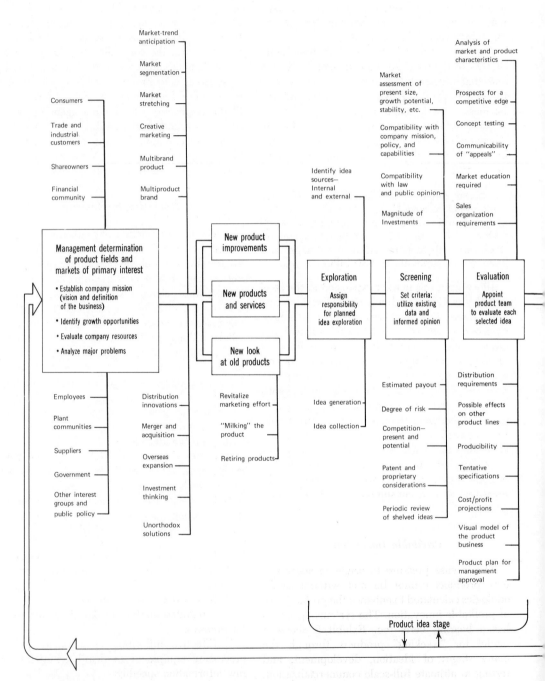

**EXHIBIT 2.** Work flow and systems chart for management of new products. (*Note:* This flow diagram was developed by Paul E. Funk, President, and the staff of McCann/ ITSM, Inc.)

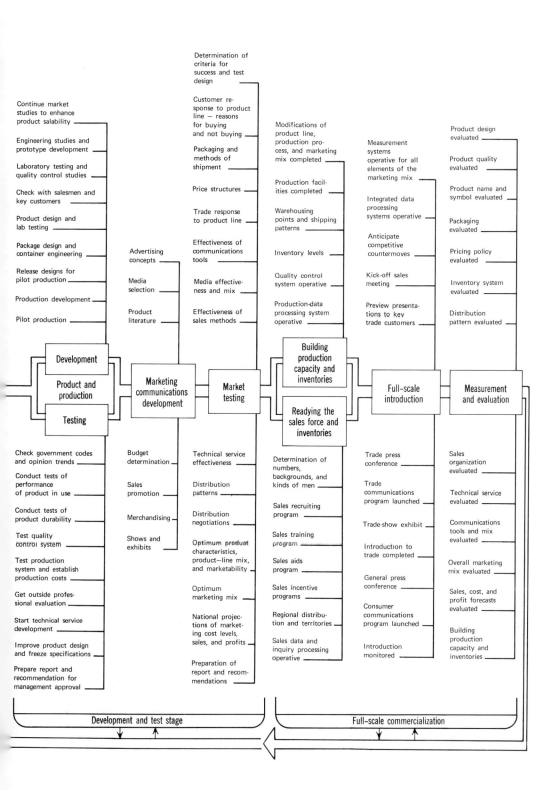

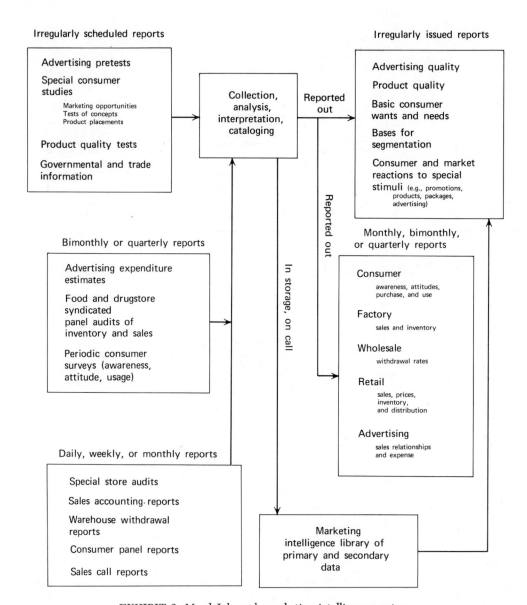

Irregularly scheduled reports

Advertising pretests

Special consumer studies

Marketing opportunities
Tests of concepts
Product placements

Product quality tests

Governmental and trade information

Collection,
analysis,
interpretation,
cataloging

Reported out

Irregularly issued reports

Advertising quality

Product quality

Basic consumer wants and needs

Bases for segmentation

Consumer and market reactions to special stimuli (e.g., promotions, products, packages, advertising)

Bimonthly or quarterly reports

Advertising expenditure estimates

Food and drugstore syndicated panel audits of inventory and sales

Periodic consumer surveys (awareness, attitude, usage)

In storage, on call

Reported out

Monthly, bimonthly, or quarterly reports

Consumer
awareness, attitudes, purchase, and use

Factory
sales and inventory

Wholesale
withdrawal rates

Retail
sales, prices, inventory, and distribution

Advertising
sales relationships and expense

Daily, weekly, or monthly reports

Special store audits

Sales accounting reports

Warehouse withdrawal reports

Consumer panel reports

Sales call reports

Marketing intelligence library of primary and secondary data

EXHIBIT 3. Mead Johnson's marketing intelligence system.

*Concept in Use.* A practical instance of the use of such an intelligence system is supplied by Mead Johnson Nutritionals (division of Mead Johnson & Company), manufacturers of Metrecal, Pablum, Bib, Nutrament, and other nutritional specialties. As Exhibit 3 shows, the company's Marketing Intelligence Department has provided information from these sources:

— A continuing large-scale consumer market study covering attitudinal and behavioral data

dealing with weight control.

— Nielsen store audit data, on a bimonthly basis.

— A monthly sales audit conducted among a panel of 100 high-volume food stores in 20 markets to provide advance indications of brand share shifts.

— Supermarket warehouse withdrawal figures from Time, Inc.'s new service, Selling Areas-Marketing, Inc.

— Salesmen's weekly reports (which, in addition to serving the purposes of sales management control, call for reconnaissance on competitive promotions, new product launches, price changes, and so forth).

— Advertising expenditure data, by media class, from the company's accounting department.

—Figures on sales and related topics from company factories.

— Competitive advertising expenditure and exposure data, supplied by the division's advertising agencies at periodic intervals.

— A panel of weight-conscious women.

To exemplify the type of outputs possible from this system, Mead Johnson will be able, with the help of analyses of factory sales data, warehouse withdrawal information, and consumer purchases from Nielsen to monitor transactions at each stage of the flow of goods through the distribution channel and to detect accumulations or developing shortages. Management will also be able to spot sources of potential problems in time to deal with them effectively. For example, if factory sales exceed consumer purchases, more promotional pressure is required. By contrast, if factory sales lag behind consumer purchases, sales effort must be further stimulated.

Similarly, the company has been able to devise a practical measurement of advertising's effectiveness in stimulating sales—a measurement that is particularly appropriate to fast-moving packaged goods. By relating advertising outlays and exposure data to the number of prospects trying out a product during a campaign (the number is obtained from the continuing consumer survey), it is possible to calculate the advertising cost of recruiting such a prospect. By persisting in such analyses during several campaigns, the relative value of alternative advertising approaches can be weighed. Since measurement of the sales, as opposed to the communications, effects of promotion is a horrendously difficult, costly, and chancy process, the full significance of this achievement is difficult to exaggerate.

**Benefits Realized.** Mead Johnson's marketing intelligence system has been helpful to management in a number of ways. In addition to giving executives early warning of new trends and problems, and valuable insights into future conditions, it is leading to a systematic *body* of knowledge about company markets rather than to isolated scraps of information.

This knowledge in turn should lead ultimately to a theory of marketing in each field that will explain the mysteries that baffle marketers today. What is more, the company expects that the system will help to free its marketing intelligence people from fire-fighting projects so that they can concentrate on long-term factors and eventually be more consistently creative.

Despite these gains, it is important to note that Mead Johnson feels it has a long road still to travel. More work is needed in linking individual data banks. Conceptual schemes must be proved out in practice; ways must still be found to reduce an awesome volume of data, swelled periodically by new information from improved sources, so as to make intelligence more immediately accessible to decision makers. And perhaps the biggest problem of the moment, one underlying some of the others, is the difficulty in finding qualified marketing-oriented programmers.

### Physical Distribution

A veritable revolution is now taking place in physical distribution. Total systems are being evolved out of the former hodgepodge of separate responsibilities, which were typically scattered among different departments of the same company. These systems include traffic and transportation, warehousing, materials handling, protective packaging, order processing, production planning, inventory control, customer service, market forecasting, and plant and warehouse site selection. Motivating this revolution are the computer, company drives to reduce distribution costs, and innovations in transportation, such as jet air freight, container ships, the interstate highway network, and larger and more versatile freight cars.

Distribution is one area of marketing where the "bread-and-butter" uses of the computer are relatively easily deployed for such functions as order processing, real-time inventory level reports, and tracking the movements of goods. Further into the future lie mathematical models which will include every factor bearing on distribution. Not only will packaging materials handling, transportation and warehouse, order processing, and related costs be considered in such models; also included will be sales forecasts by product, production rates by factory, warehouse locations and capacities, speeds of different carriers, etc. In short, a complete picture will be developed for management.

**Program in Action.** The experiences of the

Norge Division of Borg-Warner Corporation point up the values of the systems approach in physical distribution. The firm was confronted externally with complaints from its dealers and distributors, who were trying to cope with swollen inventories and the pressures of "loading deals." Internally, because coordination of effort between the six departments involved in distribution was at a minimum, distribution costs and accounts receivable were mounting persistently.

To grapple with this situation, Norge undertook a comprehensive analysis of its distribution system. Out of this grew a new philosophy. A company executive has described the philosophy to me as follows:

An effective system of physical distribution cannot begin at the end of the production line. It must also apply at the very beginning of the production process—at the planning, scheduling, and forecasting stages. Logistics, in short, is part of a larger marketing system, not just an evaluation of freight rates. We must worry not only about finished refrigerators, but also about the motors coming from another manufacturer, and even about where the copper that goes into those motors will come from. We must be concerned with *total flow.*

To implement this philosophy, the appliance manufacturer took the following steps:

(1) It reorganized the forecasting, production scheduling, warehousing, order processing, and shipping functions into *one* department headed by a director of physical distribution.

(2) The management information system was improved with the help of EDP equipment tied into the communications network. This step made it possible to process and report data more speedily on orders received, inventory levels, and the actual movement of goods.

(3) Management used a combination of computer and manual techniques to weigh trade-offs among increased costs of multiple warehousing, reduced long-haul freight and local drayage costs, reduced inventory pipeline, and the sales value of an improved "total" product offering. Also assessed were trade-offs between shorter production runs and higher inventory levels, thereby challenging the traditional "wisdom" of production-oriented managers that the longer the run, the better.

(4) The company is setting up new regional warehouses.

As a result of these moves, Norge has been able to lower inventories throughout its sales channels and to reduce accounts receivable. These gains have led, in turn, to a reduction of the company's overall investment and a concomitant increase in profitability.

It is essential to note that even though Norge has used operations research as part of its systems approach, many aspects of the program are qualitative. Thus far, the company has found that the development of an all-encompassing model is not warranted because of (a) the time and cost involved, (b) the probability that the situation will change before the model is completed, (c) a concern that such a model would be so complex as to be unworkable, and (d) the difficulty of testing many of the assumptions used. In addition, management has not tried to quantify the impact of its actions on distributor and retailer attitudes and behavior, possible competitive countermoves, and numerous other factors contributing to results.

### Toward Total Integration

The integration of systems developed for product management, product innovation, marketing intelligence, physical distribution, and the other functions or "subsystems" embraced by the term *marketing* creates a total marketing system. Thus, marketing plans composed according to a step-by-step outline, ranging from enunciation of objectives and implementational steps to audit and adjustment to environmental changes, constitute a complete application of systems theory. Further, as the various subsystems of the overall system are linked quantitatively, so that the effect of modifications in one element can be detected in other elements, and as the influences of competitive moves on each element are analyzed numerically, then the total scheme becomes truly sophisticated.

### PLUSES AND MINUSES

Two elements underlie the use and benefits of systems theory—order and knowledge. The first is a homely virtue, the second a lofty goal. Marketing is obviously not alone among all human pursuits in needing them; but, compared with its business neighbors, production and finance, marketing's need is acute indeed. The application of the systems concept can bring considerable advantages. It offers:

1. A methodical problem-solving orientation —with a broader frame of reference so that all aspects of a problem are examined.

2. Coordinated deployment of all appropriate tools of marketing.

3. Greater efficiency and economy of marketing operations.

4. Quicker recognition of impending problems, made possible by better understanding of the complex interplay of many trends and forces.

5. A stimulus to innovation.

6. A means of quantitatively verifying results.

These functional benefits in turn yield rich rewards in the marketplace. The most important gains are:

¶ A *deeper penetration of existing markets*—As an illustration, the Advanced Data Division of Litton Industries has become a leader in the automatic revenue control business by designing systems meshing together "hardware" and "software."

¶ A *broadening of markets*—For example, the tourist industry has attracted millions of additional travelers by creating packaged tours that are really product-service systems. These systems are far more convenient and economical than anything the consumer could assemble himself.

¶ An *extension of product lines*—Systems management makes it more feasible to seek out compatibilities among independently developed systems. Evidence of this idea is the work of automatic control system specialists since the early 1950's.[5] Now similar signs are apparent in marketing. For example, Acme Visible Records is currently dovetailing the design and sale of its record keeping systems with data-processing machines and forms.

¶ A *lessening of competition or a strengthened capacity to cope with competition*—The systems approach tends to make a company's product line more unique and attractive. Carborundum's innovation in metal-removal systems is a perfect illustration of this.

### Problems in Practice

Having just enumerated in glowing terms the benefits of the systems approach, realism demands that I give "equal time" to the awesome difficulties its utilization presents. There is no better evidence of this than the gulf between the elegant and sophisticated models with which recent marketing literature abounds and the actual number of situations in which those models really work. For the truth of the matter is that we are still in the foothills of this development, despite the advances of a few leaders. Let us consider some of the obstacles.

*Time and Manpower Costs.* First of all, the systems approach requires considerable time to implement; it took one company over a year to portray its physical distribution system in a mathematical model before it could even begin to solve its problems. RCA's Electronic Data Processing Division reports models taking three to five years to build, after which holes in the data network have to be filled and the model tested against history. Add to this the need for manpower of exceptional intellectual ability, conceptual skills, and specialized education—manpower that is in exceedingly short supply. Because the problems are complex and involve all elements of the business, one man alone cannot solve them. He lacks the knowledge, tools, and controls. And so many people must be involved. It follows that the activation of systems theory can be very costly.

*Absence of "Canned" Solutions.* Unlike other business functions where standardized approaches to problem solving are available, systems must be tailored to the individual situation of each firm. Even the same problem in different companies in the same industry will frequently lead to different solutions because of the impact of other inputs, unique perceptions of the environment, and varying corporate missions. These factors, too, compound time and expense demands.

*"Net Uncertainties."* Even after exhaustive analysis, full optimization of a total problem cannot be obtained. Some uncertainty will always remain and must be dealt with on the basis of judgment and experience.

*Lack of Hard Data.* In the world of engineering, the systems evolved to date have consisted all or mostly of machines. Systems engineers have been wise enough to avoid the irrationalities of man until they master control of machines. Marketing model-builders, however, have not been able to choose, for the distributor, salesman, customer, and competitor are central to marketing. We must, therefore, incorporate not only quantitative measures of the dimensions of things and processes (e.g., market potential, media outlays, and

[5] See *Automatic and Manual Control: Papers Contributed to the Conference at Cranford, 1951,* edited by A. Tustin (London, Butterworth's Scientific Publications, 1952).

shipping rates), but also psychological measures of comprehension, attitudes, motivations, intentions, needs—yes, even psychological measures of physical behavior. What is needed is a marriage of the physical and behavioral sciences—and we are about as advanced in this blending of disciplines as astronomy was in the Middle Ages.

Consider the advertising media fields as an instance of the problem:

¶ A number of advertising agencies have evolved linear programming or simulation techniques to assess alternate media schedules. One of the key sets of data used covers the probabilities of exposure to all or part of the audience of a TV program, magazine, or radio station. But what is exposure, and how do you measure it? What is optimum frequency of exposure, and how do you measure it? How does advertising prevail on the predispositions and perceptions of a potential customer? Is it better to judge advertising effects on the basis of exposure opportunity, "impact" (whatever that is), messages retained, message comprehension, or attitude shifts or uptrends in purchase intentions? We do not have these answers yet.

Even assuming precise knowledge of market dimensions, product performance, competitive standing, weights of marketing pressure exerted by direct selling, advertising and promotion, and so on, most marketers do not yet know, except in isolated cases, how one force will affect another. For instance, how does a company "image" affect the setting in which its salesmen work? How does a company's reputation for service affect customer buying behavior?

*Nature of Marketing Men.* Man is an actor on this stage in another role. A good many marketing executives, in the deepest recesses of their psyches, are artists, not analysts. For them, marketing is an art form, and, in my opinion, they really do not want it to be any other way. Their temperament is antipathetic to system, order, knowledge. They enjoy flying by the seat of their pants—though you will never get them to admit it. They revel in chaos, abhor facts, and fear research. They hate to be trammeled by written plans. And they love to spend, but are loathe to assess the results of their spending.

Obviously, such men cannot be sold readily on the value and practicality of the systems approach! It takes time, experience, and many facts to influence their thinking.

### Surmounting the Barriers

All is not gloom, however. The barriers described are being overcome in various ways. While operations research techniques have not yet made much headway in evolving total marketing systems and in areas where man is emotionally engaged, their accomplishments in solving inventory control problems, in sales analysis, in site selection, and in other areas have made many businessmen more sympathetic and open-minded to them.

Also, mathematical models—even the ones that do not work well yet—serve to bolster comprehension of the need for system as well as to clarify the intricacies among subsystems. Many models are in this sense learning models; they teach us how to ask more insightful questions. Moreover, they pinpoint data gaps and invite a more systematized method for reaching judgments where complete information does not exist. Because the computer abhors vague generalities, it forces managers to analyze their roles, objectives, and criteria more concretely. Paradoxically, it demands more, not less, of its human masters.

Of course, resistance to mathematical models by no means makes resistance to the systems approach necessary. There are many cases where no need may ever arise to use mathematics or computers. For the essence of the systems approach is not its techniques, but the enumeration of options and their implications. A simple checklist may be the only tool needed. I would even argue that some hard thinking in a quiet room may be enough. This being the case, the whole trend to more analysis and logic in management thinking, as reflected in business periodicals, business schools, and the practices of many companies, will work in favor of the development of the systems approach.

It is important to note at this juncture that not all marketers need the systems approach in its formal, elaborate sense. The success of some companies is rooted in other than marketing talents; their expertise may lie in finance, technology, administration, or even in personnel—as in the case of holding companies having an almost uncanny ability to hire brilliant operating managers and the self-control to leave them alone. In addition, a very simple marketing operation—for example, a company marketing one product through one distribution channel—may have no use for the systems concept.

## APPLYING THE APPROACH

Not illogically, there is a system for applying the systems approach. It may be outlined as a sequence of steps:

1. *Define the problem and clarify objectives.* Care must be exercised not to accept the view of the propounder of the problem lest the analyst be defeated at the outset.

2. *Test the definition of the problem.* Expand its parameters to the limit. For example, to solve physical distribution problems, it is necessary to study the marketplace (customer preferences, usage rates, market size, and so forth), as well as the production process (which plants produce which items most efficiently, what the interplant movements of raw materials are, and so forth). Delineate the extremes of these factors, their changeability, and the limitations on management's ability to work with them.

3. *Build a model.* Portray all factors graphically, indicating logical and chronological sequences—the dynamic flow of information, decisions, and events. "Closed circuits" should be used where there is information feedback or go, no-go and recycle signals (see Exhibit 2).

4. *Set concrete objectives.* For example, if a firm wants to make daily deliveries to every customer, prohibitive as the cost may be, manipulation of the model will yield one set of answers. But if the desire is to optimize service at lowest cost, then another set of answers will be needed. The more crisply and precisely targets are stated, the more specific the results will be.

5. *Develop alternative solutions.* It is crucial to be as open-minded as possible at this stage. The analyst must seek to expand the list of options rather than merely assess those given to him, then reduce the list to a smaller number of practical or relevant ones.

6. *Set up criteria or tests of relative value.*

7. *Quantify some or all of the factors or "variables."* The extent to which this is done depends, of course, on management's inclinations and the "state of the art."

8. *Manipulate the model.* That is, weigh the costs, effectiveness, profitability, and risks of each alternative.

9. *Interpret the results, and choose one or more courses of action.*

10. *Verify the results.* Do they make sense when viewed against the world as executives know it? Can their validity be tested by experiments and investigations?

### Forethought and Perspective

Successful systems do not blossom overnight. From primitive beginnings they evolve over a period of time as managers and systems specialists learn to understand each other better, and learn how to structure problems and how to push out the frontiers of the "universe" with which they are dealing. Companies must be prepared to invest time, money, and energy in making systems management feasible. This entails a solid foundation of historical data even before the conceptual framework for the system can be constructed. Accordingly, considerable time should be invested at the outset in *thinking* about the problem, its appropriate scope, operations, and criteria of choice before plunging into analysis.

Not only technicians, but most of us have a way of falling in love with techniques. We hail each one that comes along—*deus ex machina.* Historically, commercial research has wallowed in several such passions (e.g., probability sampling, motivation research, and semantic scaling), and now operations research appears to be doing the same thing. Significantly, each technique has come, in the fullness of time, to take its place as one, but only one, instrument in the research tool chest. We must therefore have a broad and dispassionate perspective on the systems approach at this juncture. We must recognize that the computer does not possess greater magical properties than the abacus. It, too, is a tool, albeit a brilliant one.

Put another way, executives must continue to exercise their judgment and experience. Systems analysis is no substitute for common sense. The computer must adapt itself to their styles, personalities, and modes of problem solving. It is an aid to management, not a surrogate. Businessmen may be slow, but the good ones are bright; the electronic monster, by contrast, is a speedy idiot. It demands great acuity of wit from its human managers lest they be deluged in an avalanche of useless paper. (The story is told of a sales manager who had just found out about the impressive capabilities of his company's computer and called for a detailed sales analysis of all products. The report was duly prepared and wheeled into his office on a dolly).

Systems users must be prepared to revise continually. There are two reasons for this.

First, the boundaries of systems keep changing; constraints are modified; competition makes fresh incursions; variables, being what they are, vary, and new ones crop up. Second, the analytical process is iterative. Usually, one "pass" at problem formulation and searches for solutions will not suffice, and it will be necessary to "recycle" as early hypotheses are challenged and new, more fruitful insights are stimulated by the inquiry. Moreover, it is impossible to select objectives without knowledge of their effects and costs. That knowledge can come only from analysis, and it frequently requires review and revision.

Despite all the efforts at quantification, systems analysis is still largely an art. It relies frequently on inputs based on human judgment; even when the inputs are numerical, they are determined, at least in part, by judgment. Similarly, the outputs must pass through the sieve of human interpretation. Hence, there is a positive correlation between the pay-off from a system and the managerial level involved in its design. The higher the level, the more rewarding the results.

Finally, let me observe that marketing people merit their own access to computers as well as programmers who understand marketing. Left in the hands of accountants, the timing, content, and format of output are often out of phase with marketing needs.

## CONCLUSION

Nearly 800 years ago a monk wrote the following about St. Godric, a merchant later turned hermit:

He laboured not only as a merchant but also as a shipman . . . to Denmark, Flanders, and Scotland; in which lands he found certain rare, and therefore more precious, wares, which he carried to other parts wherein he knew them to be least familiar, and coveted by the inhabitants beyond the price of gold itself, wherefore he exchanged these wares for others coveted by men of other lands. . . .[6]

How St. Godric "knew" about his markets we are not told, marketing having been in a primitive state in 1170. How some of us marketers today "know" is, in my opinion, sometimes no less mysterious than it was eight centuries ago. But we are trying to change that, and I will hazard the not very venturesome

forecast that the era of "by guess and by gosh" marketing is drawing to a close. One evidence of this trend is marketers' intensified search for knowledge that will improve their command over their destinies. This search is being spurred on by a number of powerful developments. To describe them briefly:

— The growing complexity of technology and the accelerating pace of technological innovation.
— The advent of the computer, inspiring and making possible analysis of the relationships between systems components.
— The intensification of competition, lent impetus by the extraordinary velocity of new product development and the tendency of diversification to thrust everybody into everybody else's business.
— The preference of buyers for purchasing from as few sources as possible, thereby avoiding the problems of assembling bits and pieces themselves and achieving greater reliability, economy, and administrative convenience. (Mrs. Jones would rather buy a complete vacuum cleaner from one source than the housing from one manufacturer, the hose from another, and the attachments from still another. And industrial buyers are not much different from Mrs. Jones. They would rather buy an automated machine tool from one manufacturer than design and assemble the components themselves. Not to be overlooked, in this connection, is the tremendous influence of the U.S. government in buying systems for its military and aerospace programs.)

The further development and application of the systems approach to marketing represents, in my judgment, the leading edge in both marketing theory and practice. At the moment, we are still much closer to St. Godric than to the millenium, and the road will be rocky and tortuous. But if we are ever to convert marketing into a more scientific pursuit, this is the road we must travel. The systems concept can teach us how our businesses really behave in the marketing arena, thereby extending managerial leverage and control. It can help us to confront more intelligently the awesome complexity of marketing, to deal with the hazards and opportunities of technological change, and to cope with the intensification of competition. And in the process, the concept will help us to feed the hungry maws of our expensive computers with more satisfying fare.

---

[6] *Life of St. Godric*, by Reginald, a monk of Durham, c. 1170.

## APPENDIX: WHAT IS THE SYSTEMS APPROACH?

There seems to be agreement that the systems approach sprang to life as a semantically identifiable term sometime during World War II. It was associated with the problem of how to bomb targets deep in Germany more effectively from British bases, with the Manhattan Project, and with studies of optimum search patterns for destroyers to use in locating U-boats during the Battle of the North Atlantic.[7] Subsequently, it was utilized in the defeat of the Berlin blockade. It has reached its present culmination in the success of great military systems such as Polaris and Minuteman.

Not surprisingly, the parallels between military and marketing strategies being what they are, the definition of the systems approach propounded by The RAND Corporation for the U.S. Air Force is perfectly apt for marketers:

An inquiry to aid a decision-maker choose a course of action by systematically investigating his proper objectives, comparing quantitatively where possible the costs, effectiveness, and risks associated with the alternative policies or strategies for achieving them, and *formulating additional alternatives if those examined are found wanting.*[8]

The systems approach is thus an orderly, "architectural" discipline for dealing with complex problems of choice under uncertainty.

Typically, in such problems, multiple and possibly conflicting objectives exist. The task of the systems analyst is to specify a closed operating network in which the components will work together so as to yield the optimum balance of economy, efficiency, and risk minimization. Put more broadly, the systems approach attempts to apply the "scientific method" to complex marketing problems studied *as a whole;* it seeks to discipline marketing.

But disciplining marketing is no easy matter. Marketing must be perceived as a *process* rather than as a series of isolated, discrete actions; competitors must be viewed as components of each marketer's own system. The process must also be comprehended as involving a flow and counterflow of information and behavior between marketers and customers. Some years ago, Marion Harper, Jr., now chairman of The Interpublic Group of Companies, Inc., referred to the flow of information in marketing communications as the cycle of "listen (i.e., marketing research), publish (messages, media), listen (more marketing research), revise, publish, listen. . . ." More recently, Raymond A. Bauer referred to the "transactional" nature of communications as a factor in the motivations, frames of reference, needs, and so forth of recipients of messages. The desires of the communicator alone are but part of the picture.[9]

Pushing this new awareness of the intricacies of marketing communications still further, Theodore Levitt identified the interactions between five different forces—source effect (i.e., the reputation or credibility of the sponsor of the message), sleeper effect (the declining influence of source credibility with the passage of time), message effect (the character and quality of the message), communicator effect (the impact of the transmitter—e.g., a salesman), and audience effect (the competence and responsibility of the audience.[10] Casting a still broader net are efforts to model the entire purchasing process, and perhaps the ultimate application of the systems concept is attempts to make mathematical models of the entire marketing process.

Mounting recognition of the almost countless elements involved in marketing and of the mind-boggling complexity of their interactions is a wholesome (though painful) experience. Nevertheless, I believe we must not ignore other ramifications of the systems approach which are qualitative in nature. For the world of marketing offers a vast panorama of non- or part-mathematical systems and opportunities to apply systems thinking. We must not become so bedazzled by the brouhaha of the operations research experts as to lose sight of the larger picture.

---

[7] See Glen McDaniel, "The Meaning of The Systems Movement to the Acceleration and Direction of the American Economy," in *Proceedings of the 1964 Systems Engineering Conference* (New York, Clapp & Poliak, Inc., 1964), p. 1; see also E. S. Quade, editor, *Analysis for Military Decisions* (Santa Monica, California, The RAND Corporation, 1964), p. 6.

[8] Quade, op. cit., p. 4.

[9] "Communications as a Transaction," *Public Opinion Quarterly*, Spring 1963, p. 83.

[10] See Theodore Levitt, *Industrial Purchasing Behavior* (Boston, Division of Research, Harvard Business School, 1965), p. 25ff.

# 51. New Criteria for Market Segmentation

## DANIEL YANKELOVICH

The director of marketing in a large company is confronted by some of the most difficult problems in the history of U.S. industry. To assist him, the information revolution of the past decade puts at his disposal a vast array of techniques, facts, and figures. But without a way to master this information, he can easily be overwhelmed by the reports that flow in to him incessantly from marketing research, economic forecasts, cost analyses, and sales breakdowns. He must have more than mere access to mountains of data. He must himself bring to bear a method of analysis that cuts through the detail to focus sharply on new opportunities.

In this article, I shall propose such a method. It is called *segmentation analysis*. It is based on the proposition that once you discover the most useful ways of segmenting a market, you have produced the beginnings of a sound marketing strategy.

### UNIQUE ADVANTAGES

Segmentation analysis has developed out of several key premises:

¶ In today's economy, each brand appears to sell effectively to only certain segments of any market and not to the whole market.

¶ Sound marketing objectives depend on knowledge of how segments which produce the most customers for a company's brands differ in requirements and susceptibilities from the segments which produce the largest number of customers for competitive brands.

◆ SOURCE: Reprinted by permission from *Harvard Business Review*, Vol. 42, No. 2, March-April 1964, pp. 83–90. © 1964 by the President and Fellows of Harvard College; all rights reserved.

¶ Traditional demographic methods of market segmentation do not usually provide this knowledge. Analyses of market segments by age, sex, geography, and income level are not likely to provide as much direction for marketing strategy as management requires.

Once the marketing director does discover the most pragmatically useful way of segmenting his market, it becomes a new standard for almost all his evaluations. He will use it to appraise competitive strengths and vulnerabilities, to plan his product line, to determine his advertising and selling strategy, and to set precise marketing objectives against which performance can later be measured. Specifically, segmentation analysis helps him to:

1. Direct the appropriate amounts of promotional attention and money to the most potentially profitable segments of his market;

2. Design a product line that truly parallels the demands of the market instead of one that bulks in some areas and ignores or scants other potentially quite profitable segments;

3. Catch the first sign of a major trend in a swiftly changing market and thus give him time to prepare to take advantage of it;

4. Determine the appeals that will be most effective in his company's advertising; and, where several different appeals are significantly effective, quantify the segments of the market responsive to each;

5. Choose advertising media more wisely and determine the proportion of budget that should be allocated to each medium in the light of anticipated impact;

6. Correct the timing of advertising and pro-

motional efforts so that they are massed in the weeks, months, and seasons when selling resistance is least and responsiveness is likely to be at its maximum;

7. Understand otherwise seemingly meaningless demographic market information and apply it in scores of new and effective ways.

These advantages hold in the case of both packaged goods and hard goods, and for commercial and industrial products as well as consumer products.

### Guides to Strategy

Segmentation analysis cuts through the data facing a marketing director when he tries to set targets based on markets as a whole, or when he relies primarily on demographic breakdowns. It is a systematic approach that permits the marketing planner to pick the strategically most important segmentations and then to design brands, products, packages, communications, and marketing strategies around them. It infinitely simplifies the setting of objectives.

In the following sections we shall consider nondemographic ways of segmenting markets. These ways dramatize the point that finding marketing opportunities by depending solely on demographic breakdowns is like trying to win a national election by relying only on the information in a census. A modern census contains useful data, but it identifies neither the crucial issues of an election, nor those groups whose voting habits are still fluid, nor the needs, values, and attitudes that influence how those groups will vote. This kind of information, rather than census-type data, is the kind that wins elections—and markets.

Consider, for example, companies like Procter & Gamble, General Motors, or American Tobacco, whose multiple brands sell against one another and must, every day, win new elections in the marketplace:

These companies sell to the whole market, not by offering one brand that appeals to all people, but by covering the different segments with multiple brands. How can they prevent these brands from cannibalizing each other? How can they avoid surrendering opportunities to competitors by failing to provide brands that appeal to all important segments? In neither automobiles, soaps, nor cigarettes do demographic analyses reveal to the manufacturer what products to make or what products to sell to what segments of the market. Obviously, some modes of segmentation other than demographic

are needed to explain why brands which differ so little nevertheless find their own niches in the market, each one appealing to a different segment.

The point at issue is not that demographic segmentation should be disregarded, but rather that it should be regarded as only one among many possible ways of analyzing markets. In fact, the key requirement of segmentation analysis is that the marketing director should never assume in advance that any one method of segmentation is the best. His first job should be to muster all probable segmentation and *then* choose the most meaningful ones to work with. This approach is analogous to that used in research in the physical sciences, where the hypothesis that best seems to explain the phenomena under investigation is the one chosen for working purposes.

### TEN MARKETS

In the following discussion we shall take ten markets for consumer and industrial products and see how they are affected by seven different modes of nondemographic segmentation. The products and modes are shown schematically in Exhibit 1. Of course, these segments are not the only ones important in business. The seven I have picked are only *examples* of how segmentation analysis can enlarge the scope and depth of a marketer's thinking.

### I. Watches

In this first case we deal with a relatively simple mode of segmentation analysis. The most productive way of analysis the market for watches turns out to be segmentation by *value*. This approach discloses three distinct segments, each representing a different value attributed to watches by each of three different groups of consumers:

1. *People who want to pay the lowest possible price for any watch that works reasonably well.* If the watch fails after six months or a year, they will throw it out and replace it.

2. *People who value watches for their long life, good workmanship, good material, and good styling.* They are willing to pay for these product qualities.

3. *People who look not only for useful product features but also for meaningful emotional qualities.* The most important consideration in this segment is that the watch should suitably

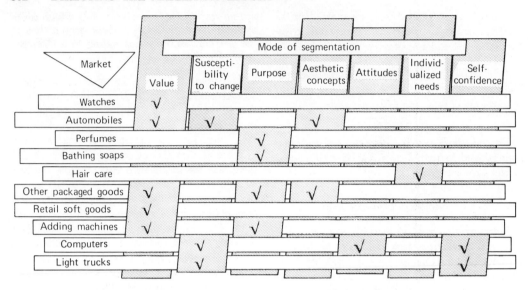

| Market | Mode of segmentation | | | | | | |
|---|---|---|---|---|---|---|---|
| | Value | Suscepti-bility to change | Purpose | Aesthetic concepts | Attitudes | Individ-ualized needs | Self-confidence |
| Watches | √ | | | | | | |
| Automobiles | √ | √ | | √ | | | |
| Perfumes | | | √ | | | | |
| Bathing soaps | | | √ | | | | |
| Hair care | | | | | | √ | |
| Other packaged goods | √ | | √ | √ | | | |
| Retail soft goods | √ | | | | | | |
| Adding machines | √ | | √ | | | | |
| Computers | | √ | | | √ | | √ |
| Light trucks | | √ | | | | | √ |

EXHIBIT 1. Example of segmentation in different industries.

symbolize an important occasion. Consequently, fine styling, a well-known brand name, the recommendation of the jeweler, and a gold or diamond case are highly valued.

In 1962, my research shows, the watch market divided quantitatively as follows:

Approximately 23% of the buyers bought for lowest price (value segment #1).

Another 46% bought for durability and general product quality (value segment #2).

And 31% bought watches as symbols of some important occasion (value segment #3).

Defining and quantifying such segments is helpful in marketing planning—especially if a watch company's product happens to appeal mostly to one segment or if the line straddles the three segments, failing to appeal effectively to any. Without such an understanding, the demographic characteristics of the market are most confusing. It turns out, for example, that the most expensive watches are being bought by people with both the highest and the lowest incomes. On the other hand, some upper income consumers are no longer buying costly watches, but buying cheap, well-styled watches to throw away when they require servicing. Other upper income consumers, however, continue to buy fine, expensive watches for suitable occasions.

*Timex's Timely Tactics.* The planning implications in value segmentation are very broad for the industry. For one thing, many of the better watch companies in the years between 1957 and 1962 were inadvertently focusing exclusively on the third segment described— the 31% of the market that bought a watch only as a gift on important occasions—thus leaving the bulk of the market open to attack and exploitation.

The U.S. Time Company took advantage of this opening and established a very strong position among the more than two-thirds of America's watch buyers in the first two segments. Its new low-price watch, the Timex, had obvious appeal for the first segment, and it catered to the second segment as well. At that time, higher-price watches were making the disastrous mistake in their advertising of equating product quality with water-proof and shock-resistant features. The Timex also offered these low-cost features, at lower prices, thus striking at a vulnerable area which the competition itself created. When Timex pressed its attack, it was able within a few years to claim that "Timex sells more watches than any other watch company in the world."

Even the *timing* of Timex's watch advertising was involved. Much of the third segment was buying watches only during the Christmas season, and so most of Timex's competitors concentrated their advertising in November and December. But since buying by the other two segments went on all the time, Timex advertised all year-round, getting exclusive attention ten months of the year.

Thus, nondemographic segmentation in the watch industry has directly affected almost every phase of marketing, including the composition of the product line. Major watch companies know that they must plan product line, pricing, advertising, and distribution within the framework of the three basic value segments of this market.

## II. Automobiles

The nondemographic segmentation of the automobile market is more complex than that of the watch market. The segments crisscross, forming intricate patterns. Their dynamics must be seen clearly before automobile sales can be understood.

Segmentation analysis leads to at least three different ways of classifying the automobile market along nondemographic lines, all of which are important to marketing planning.

*Value Segmentation.* The first mode of segmentation can be compared to that in the watch market—a threefold division along lines which represent how different people look at the meaning of *value* in an automobile:

1. *People who buy cars primarily for economy.* Many of these become owners of the Falcon, Ford, Rambler American, and Chevrolet. They are less loyal to any make than the other segments, but go where the biggest savings are to be found.

2. *People who want to buy the best product they can find for their money.* These prospects emphasize values such as body quality, reliability, durability, economy of operation, and ease of upkeep. Rambler and Volkswagen have been successful because so many people in this segment were dissatisfied.

3. *People interested in "personal enhancement (a more accurate description than "prestige").* A handsomely styled Pontiac or Thunderbird does a great deal for the owner's ego, even though the car may not serve as a status symbol. Although the value of an automobile as a status symbol has declined, the personal satisfaction in owning a fine car has not lessened for this segment of the market. It is interesting that while both watches and cars have declined in status value, they have retained *self-enhancement* value for large portions of the market.

Markets can change so swiftly, and the size of key segments can shift so rapidly, that great sensitivity is required to catch a trend in time to capitalize on it. In the automobile market, the biggest change in recent years has been the growth in segment two—the number of people oriented to strict product value. Only a few years ago, the bulk of the market was made up of the other segments, but now the product-value segment is probably the largest. Some automobile companies did not respond to this shift in the size of these market segments in time to maintain their share of the market.

*Aesthetic Concepts.* A second way of segmenting the automobile market is by differences in *style* preferences. For example, most automobile buyers tell you that they like "expensive looking" cars. To some people, however, "expensive looking" means a great deal of chrome and ornamentation, while to others it means the very opposite—clean, conservative lines, lacking much chrome or ornamentation.

Unfortunately, the same *words* are used by consumers to describe diametrically opposed style concepts. Data that quantify buyers according to their aesthetic *responses*—their differing conceptions of what constitutes a good-looking car—are among the most useful an automobile company can possess.

The importance of aesthetic segmentation can be pointed up by this example:

¶ When Ford changed from its 1959 styling to its 1960 styling, the change did not seem to be a radical one from the viewpoint of formal design. But, because it ran contrary to the special style expectations of a large group of loyal Ford buyers, it constituted a dramatic and unwelcome change to them. This essential segment was not prepared for the change, and the results were apparent in sales.

*Susceptibility to Change.* A third and indispensible method of segmenting the automobile market cuts across the lines drawn by the other two modes of segmentation analysis. This involves measuring the relative susceptibility of potential car buyers to changing their choice of make. Consider the buyers of Chevrolet during any one year from the point of view of a competitor:

At one extreme are people whose brand loyalty is so solidly entrenched that no competitor can get home to them. They always buy Chevrolets. They are closed off to change. At the other extreme are the open-minded and the unprejudiced buyers. They happened to buy a Chevrolet because they preferred its styling that year, or because they got a good buy, or because someone talked up the Fisher body to them. They could just as easily have purchased another make.

In the middle of this susceptibility continuum are people who are predisposed to Chevrolet to a greater or lesser degree. They can be persuaded to buy another make, but the persuasion has to be strong enough to break through the Chevrolet predisposition.

The implications of this kind of a susceptibility segmentation are far-reaching. Advertising effectiveness, for example, must be measured against each susceptibility segment, not against the market as a whole. Competitors' advertising should appear in media most likely to break through the Chevrolet predisposition of the middle group. In addition, the wants of those who are not susceptible must be factored out, or they will muddy the picture. Marketing programs persuasive enough to influence the uncommitted may make no difference at all to the single largest group—those who are predisposed to Chevrolet but still open enough to respond to the right stimulus.

If the marketing director of an automobile company does not break down his potential market into segments representing key differences in susceptibility, or does not clearly understand the requirements of each key segment, his company can persevere for years with little or no results because its promotion programs are inadvertently being aimed at the wrong people.

### III. Perfume

A segmentation analysis of the perfume market shows that a useful way to analyze it is by the different *purposes* women have in mind when they buy perfume.

One segment of the market thinks of a perfume as something to be added to what nature has supplied. Another segment believes that the purpose of fragrance products is to help a woman to feel cleaner, fresher, and better groomed—to correct or negate what nature has supplied. In the latter instance, the fragrance product is used to *cancel out* natural body odors; in the former, to *add* a new scent. To illustrate this difference in point of view:

¶ One woman told an interviewer, "I like a woodsy scent like Fabergé. It seems more intense and lingers longer, and doesn't fade away like the sweeter scents."

¶ But another woman said, "I literally loathe Fabergé. It makes me think of a streetcar full of women coming home from work who haven't bathed."

These differences in reaction do not indicate objective differences in the scent of Fabergé. They are subjective differences in women's attitudes; they grow out of each woman's purpose in using a perfume.

Purposive segmentation, as this third mode of analysis might be called, has been of great value to alert marketers. For instance:

A company making a famous line of fragrance products realized that it was selling almost exclusively to a single segment, although it had believed it was competing in the whole market. Management had been misled by its marketing research which had consistently shown no differences in the demographic characteristics of women buying the company's products and women buying competitors' products.

In the light of this insight, the company decided to allocate certain lines to the underdeveloped segments of the market. This required appropriate changes in the scent of the product and in its package design. A special advertising strategy was also developed, involving a different copy approach for each product line aimed at each segment.

In addition, it was learned that visualizations of the product in use helped to create viewer identification in the segment that used perfume for adding to nature's handiwork, but that more subtle methods of communication produced better results among the more reserved, more modest women in the second segment who want the "cancelling out" benefits of perfume. The media susceptibilities of women in the two segments were also found to be different.

Thus, from a single act of resegmentation, the advertising department extracted data critical to its copy platform, communication strategy, and media decisions.

### IV. Bathing Soap

A comparable purposive segmentation was found in the closely related bathing soap field. The key split was between women whose chief requirement of soap was that it should clean them adequately and those for whom bathing was a sensuous and enjoyable experience. The company (a new contender in this highly competitive field) focused its sights on the first segment, which had been much neglected in recent years. A new soap was shaped, designed, and packaged to appeal to this segment, a new advertising approach was evolved, and results were very successful.

## V. Hair-Care Market

The Breck-Halo competition in the shampoo market affords an excellent example of another kind of segmentation. For many years, Breck's recognition of the market's individualized segmentation gave the company a very strong position. Its line of individualized shampoos included one for dry hair, another for oily hair, and one for normal hair. This line accurately paralleled the marketing reality that women think of their hair as being dry, oily, or normal, and they do not believe that any one shampoo (such as an all-purpose Halo) can meet their individual requirements. Colgate has finally been obliged, in the past several years, to revise its long-held marketing approach to Halo, and to come out with products for dry hair and for oily hair, as well as for normal hair.

Other companies in the hair-care industry are beginning to recognize other segmentations in this field. For example, some women think of their hair as fine, others as coarse. Each newly discovered segmentation contains the seeds of a new product, a new marketing approach, and a new opportunity.

## VI. Other Packaged Goods

Examples of segmentation analysis in other packaged goods can be selected almost at random. Let us mention a few briefly, to show the breadth of applicability of this method of marketing analysis:

¶ In *convenience foods*, for example, we find that the most pragmatic classification is, once again, purposive segmentation. Analysis indicates that "convenience" in foods has many different meanings for women, supporting several different market segments. Women for whom convenience means "easy to use" are reached by products and appeals different from those used to reach women for whom convenience means shortcuts to creativity in cooking.

¶ In the market for *cleaning agents,* some women clean preventively, while others clean therapeutically, i.e., only after a mess has been made. The appeals, the product characteristics, and the marketing approach must take into account these different reasons for buying—another example of purposive segmentation.

¶ In still another market, some people use *air fresheners* to remove disagreeable odors and others to add an odor. A product like Glade, which is keyed to the second segment, differs from one like Airwick in product concept, packaging, and type of scent.

¶ The *beer market* requires segmentation along at least four different axes—reasons for drinking beer (purposive); taste preferences (aesthetic); price/quality (value); and consumption level.

## VII. Retail Soft Goods

Although soft-goods manufacturers and retailers are aware that their customers are value conscious, not all of them realize that their markets break down into at least four different segments corresponding to four different conceptions of value held by women.

For some women value means a willingness to pay a little more for quality. For others, value means merchandise on sale. Still other women look for value in terms of the lowest possible price, while others buy seconds or discounted merchandise as representing the best value.

Retailing operations like Sears, Roebuck are highly successful because they project *all* these value concepts, and do so in proportions which closely parallel their distribution in the total population.

## VIII. Adding Machines

In marketing planning for a major adding machine manufacturer, analysis showed that his product line had little relationship to the segmented needs of the market. Like most manufacturers of this kind of product, he had designed his line by adding features to one or several stripped-down basic models—each addition raising the model price. The lowest priced model could only add; it could not subtract, multiply, divide, or print, and it was operated by hand.

Since there are a great many features in adding machines, the manufacturer had an extremely long product line. When the needs of the market were analyzed, however, it became clear that, despite its length, the line barely met the needs of two out of the three major segments of the market. It had been conceived and planned from a logical point of view rather than from a market-need point of view.

The adding machine market is segmented along lines reflecting sharp differences in value and purpose.

¶ One buyer group values accuracy, reliability, and long life above all else. It tends to buy medium-price, full-keyboard, electric machines. There are many banks and other institutions in this group where full-keyboard operations are believed to ensure accuracy.

¶ Manufacturing establishments, on the other hand, prefer the ten-key machine. Value, to these people, means the maximum number of laborsaving and timesaving features. They are willing to pay the highest prices for such models.

¶ Both these segments contrast sharply with the third group, the small retailer whose major purpose is to find a model at a low purchase price. The small retailer does not think in terms of amortizing his investment over a period of years, and neither laborsaving features nor full-keyboard reliability count for as much as an immediate savings in dollars.

Despite the many models in the company's line, it lacked those demanded by both the manufacturer and small retailer segments of the market. But, because it had always been most sensitive to the needs of financial institutions, it had developed more models for this segment than happened to be needed. Product, sales, and distribution changes were required to enable the company to compete in the whole market.

### IX. Computers

One pragmatic way of segmenting the computer market is to divide potential customers between those who believe they know how to evaluate a computer and those who believe they do not. A few years ago only about 20% of the market was really open to IBM's competitors—the 20% who believed it knew how to evaluate a computer. By default, this left 80% of the market a virtual captive of IBM—the majority who did not have confidence in its own ability to evaluate computers and who leaned on IBM's reputation for personal appraisal.

Another segmentation in this market involves differences in prospects' attitudes toward the inevitability of progress. Although this factor has been widely ignored, it is a significant method for qualifying prospects. People who believe that progress is inevitable (i.e., that change is good and that new business methods are constantly evolving) make far better prospects for computers than those who have a less optimistic attitude toward progress in the world of business.

### X. Light Trucks

The market for light trucks affords us an-

other example of segmentation in products bought by industry. As in the computer example, there are both buyers who lack confidence in their ability to choose among competing makes and purchasers who feel they are sophisticated about trucks and can choose knowledgeably. This mode of segmentation unexpectedly turns out to be a key to explaining some important dynamics of the light truck market:

¶ Those who do not trust their own judgment in trucks tend to rely very heavily on both the dealer's and the manufacturer's reputation. Once they find a make that gives them reliability and trouble-free operation, they cease to shop other makes and are no longer susceptible to competitive promotion. Nor are they as price-sensitive as the buyer who thinks he is sophisticated about trucks. This buyer tends to look for the best price, to shop extensively, and to be susceptible to the right kind of competitive appeals, because he puts performance before reputation.

These ways of looking at the truck market have far-reaching implications for pricing policy, for product features, and for dealers' sales efforts.

### CONCLUSION

To sum up the implications of the preceding analysis, let me stress three points:

1. *We should discard the old, unquestioned assumption that demography is always the best way of looking at markets.*

The demographic premise implies that differences in reasons for buying, in brand choice influences, in frequency of use, or in susceptibility will be reflected in differences in age, sex, income, and geographical location. But this is usually not true. Markets should be scrutinized for important differences in buyer attitudes, motivations, values, usage patterns, aesthetic preferences, or degree of susceptibility. These may have no demographic correlatives. Above all, we must never assume in advance that we know the best way of looking at a market. This is the cardinal rule of segmentation analysis. All ways of segmenting markets must be considered, and *then* we must select out of the various methods available the ones that have the most important implications for action. This process of choosing the strategically most useful mode of segmentation is the essence of the marketing approach espoused in this article.

In considering cases like those described, we must understand that we are not dealing with different types of people, but with differences in peoples' *values*. A woman who buys a refrigerator because it is the cheapest available may want to buy the most expensive towels. A man who pays extra for his beer may own a cheap watch. A Ford-owning Kellogg's Corn Flakes-eater may be closed off to Chevrolet but susceptible to Post Toasties; he is the same man, but he has had different experiences and holds different values toward each product he purchases. By segmenting markets on the basis of the values, purposes, needs, and attitudes relevant to the product being studied, as in Exhibit I, we avoid misleading information derived from attempts to divide people into types.

2. *The strategic-choice concept of segmentation broadens the scope of marketing planning to include the positioning of new products as well as of established products.*

It also has implications for brand planning, not just for individual products but for the composition of a line of competing brands where any meaningful segment in the market can possibly support a brand. One explanation of the successful competing brand strategy of companies like Procter & Gamble is that they are based on sensitivity to the many different modes of market segmentation. The brands offered by P & G often appear very similar to the outsider, but small, marginal differences between them appeal to different market segments. It is this rather than intramural competition that supports P & G successes.

3. *Marketing must develop its own interpretive theory, and not borrow a ready-made one from the social sciences.*

Marketing research, as an applied science, is tempted to borrow its theoretical structures from the disciplines from which it derives. The social sciences offer an abundance of such structures, but they are not applicable to marketing in their pure academic form. While the temptation to apply them in that form is great, it should be resisted. From sociology, for example, marketing has frequently borrowed the concept of status. This is a far-reaching concept, but it is not necessarily the most important one in a marketing problem, nor even one of the important ones. Again, early psychoanalytic theory has contributed an understanding of the sexual factor. While this can sometimes be helpful in an analysis of buying behavior in a given situation, some motivation researchers have become oversensitive to the role of sex and, as a result, have made many mistakes. Much the same might be said of the concept of social character, that is, seeing the world as being "inner-directed," "other-directed," "tradition-directed," "autonomous," and so forth.

One of the values of segmentation analysis is that, while it has drawn on the insights of social scientists, it has developed an interpretive theory *within* marketing. It has been homegrown in business. This may explain its ability to impose patterns of meaning on the immense diversity of the market, and to provide the modern marketing director with a systematic method for evolving true marketing objectives.

# International Marketing and Economic Development

The role of marketing in expanding economies has not been adequately explored. Marketing in most countries has developed without any plan and too frequently without the realization that it has a positive role to play. Studies of international marketing have focused on the descriptive aspects of the national market. Certainly the individual differences among cultures and markets are important to an understanding of international marketing. For this reason, Part IV begins with the examination of these differences.

Important too is the role of marketing in a national market, which is examined in the second reading of Part IV. Finally, one of the most important marketing questions is discussed. What is the role of marketing in the economic development of a nation?

# 52. The World Customer

ERNEST DICHTER

Only one Frenchman out of three brushes his teeth.

Automobiles have become a must for the self-esteem of even the lowliest postal clerk in Naples or the Bantu street cleaner in Durban.

There is a supermarket in Apia, the capital of Western Samoa (which received its independence in January of this year). I found can openers and the cans to go with them in a remote village on the island of Upolu.

Four out of five Germans change their shirts but once a week.

Amazon Indians use outboard motors in deep green water alleyways.

What do these facts, and many others like them, portend for the future marketing manager? For top management in companies with foresight to capitalize on international opportunities? They mean that an understanding of cultural anthropology will be an important tool of competitive marketing. They mean that knowledge of the basic differences, as well as basic similarities, among consumers in different parts of the world will be essential. They mean that the successful marketer of the future will have to think not of a United States customer, nor even of a Western European or Atlantic community customer, but of a *world customer*.

For Western European countries, it is specific marketing facts and consumer purchasing behavior patterns which are of moment to today's businessman seeking new customers. At present, these countries comprise the biggest

‡‡ SOURCE: Reprinted by permission from *Harvard Business Review*, Vol. 40, No. 4, July-August 1962, pp. 113–122.

potential overseas market for most products. They are also the countries about whose consumers the most research information has been gathered. However, as some of the above examples illustrate, other parts of the world too are becoming potential markets, as human desires break the barricades of centuries in South America, Africa, and Asia.

Emergence of the European Common Market has forced businessmen and philosophers alike to take a look at the European as a distinct species. We now see the European as more than a Frenchman or an Austrian. The Atlantic community market and the world market may make us yet take a fresh look at what is alike and what is really different in humans, their desires, hopes, fears—in short, their motivations. Close observation of customers, and potential customers, all over the world reveals that there *are* some striking similarities, yet at the same time a considerable degree of permanent difference. From objective examination of these basic cultural similarities and differences, one may discern clues for serving the World Customer today.

In this article, I shall first point to a number of consumer behavior patterns relevant to international marketing, particularly within the Western European market but also in some of the less developed areas. Then I shall examine the differential role of national pride, which obviously affects and will affect the success of American-made products in Western European and other countries in the Atlantic market. Finally, in an effort to define and interpret the economic and psychological differences among world customers, I shall postulate six world market groups of nations, measured by the yardstick of middle class development.

## THE DISTINCTIVE EUROPEAN

The United States company going into Europe has to study the culture and the psychology of the people of the country, not just its manufacturing facilities and markets in the technological sense. The advertising and sales managers have to learn that reaching customers in a given country involves a real understanding of the basic motivations which operate within that country.

In dealing with various European markets, the American businessman must open his eyes to certain paradoxes, stereotypes, and hidden competitors.

### Apparent Paradoxes

There are paradoxes between the way in which American products are perceived and the way they are used. Thus, anti-Americanism is strongly coupled with a desire for many United States products, often out of pure snobbery, often because they are symbols of an affluent society. The Italian housewife considers her American sister a poor cook and a lady of leisure, but dreams day and night of owning a Hollywood kitchen.

A similar paradox is that of the West German businessman who scoffs at American know-how, pointing out the technical superiority of many of his national products, but proudly puts his elegantly uniformed chauffeur in a Ford, polished up to the last fold of its lacquered steel hull tuxedo.

### Ingrained Stereotypes

The American businessman must cast off deeply ingrained stereotypes in analyzing the purchasing behavior of European consumers, in reference to product meaning, "purchasing morality," and quality consciousness.

We all "know" that French women are very fashion conscious. Yet a study recently showed that this was exactly one of those glib stereotypes that have little if any basis in reality. The purchase of a dress or coat is much more of an investment for the Frenchwoman than for the American woman. This results from differences both in income and in prices of fashion products. It is not enough, therefore, to tell a French shopper that a garment is fashionable. She also

wants to know, in a way, the "trade-in value" of the dress or blouse. How long will the fabric last? How many years will she be able to wear it? These are promises and appeals which have to a very large extent lost their attraction to the American woman.

The European is very conscious of preservation. He collects and retains things. The only parallel that we have had in this country was during the period of World War II, when we developed a new kind of pride, a pride in doing without, a pride in not having bought a new car for several years, for example. This pride did not last very long. Just as soon as cars became available again, we reverted to our somewhat affluent American habit of replacing models quite rapidly. Yet this concept of "purchasing morality" still exerts influence in the United States for some products. For example, the average male still hesitates to buy two or three suits at one time because he feels that suits, together with many other articles of clothing, are highly overvalued, and therefore it is extravagant to buy more than one at the same time. On the other hand, most of us have learned that it no longer pays to resole shoes more than twice.

As for quality consciousness, as well as confidence in the trustworthiness of the manufacturer, this is quite different in different countries. In Australia or South Africa—and for that matter in England—you find on most toilet tissues the reassuring message that the manufacturer guarantees that the paper was not made out of secondhand rags, but only new rags and new raw materials.

Such a promise has become completely unnecessary in North America. Whatever advertising may be accused of, in many areas it provides the consumer, particularly in branded merchandise, with an assurance that he will not be cheated as long as he buys a well-known brand. It is true today that whether we buy a Westinghouse, a General Electric, or a Kelvinator refrigerator, we get more or less equal values as long as we pay about the same amount of money. What we have learned to buy is the freedom of individual choice. We buy images; we buy the sizzle because we have been reassured that the steak itself is of generally good quality. *In many European countries this confidence*, this almost blind reliance on the promise of the manufacturer, *has not yet been established*. Therefore, advertising approaches have to be based much more on definite proofs of quality.

### Hidden Competitors

Another problem facing Atlantic marketers is that in many areas they are still dealing with hidden competitors, lurking in places unfamiliar in domestic marketing. Taking toilet tissue again, in some recent motivational research done in West Germany I found it was much too premature to promise the German consumer luxury softness or colors compatible with the bathroom fixtures. Instead, the hidden but real competitor with which the toilet tissue manufacturer has to contend is the newspaper and the old standby of the German equivalent of the Sears, Roebuck catalog. The West German family feels that toilet tissue, particularly the American luxury type, is wasteful and unnecessary. The advertising approach, then, has to deal much more with providing absolution and selling the concept that good quality toilet tissue is a part of modern life.

## ETHOS OF NATIONALISM

Nationalism obviously plays a major role in determining consumer acceptance of nondomestically made products. Understanding its manifold aspects is a *sine qua non* for United States businessmen operating overseas.

National feeling manifests itself in many ways. Some of these have already been touched on briefly before. In this section, I shall show in greater detail how: (1) national pride can be a motivating sales factor employable by the astute overseas marketer as an asset; (2) longstanding cultural traditions in one nation can dictate the *discard* of advertising approaches proven successful in another nation; (3) stereotyped national *self*-illusions can alter the direction of marketing strategy.

### National Pride

*Admiration* of foreign products often goes together with *hidden inferiority feelings* which are overcompensated by tearing the foreigner down. These products are the tangible symbols of foreign superiority. For example:

¶ In Venezuela, despite various forms of anti-Yankee sentiment, it is considered chic to smoke United States cigarettes. Even when the American brand name is used and the Venezuelan smoker can discover the little phrase "Hecho en Venezuela" on his package, the almost completely identical cigarette suffers at least a 50% prestige loss. A successful approach used in overcoming this problem was to convince Venezuelans that the people they secretly admired in a form of love-hatred—the Americans—indeed liked Venezuelan tobacco, used it for their own cigarettes, and had no negative feeling toward Venezuelan cigarettes.

A similar solution was found in connection with Venezuelan rum by serving this rum in hotels in Caracas frequented by United States businessmen and tourists. The Venezuelan could be convinced that if it was good enough for the supposed foreign connoisseur, then it certainly ought to be good enough for him.

¶ The French gasoline, *Total*, had a domestic marketing problem arising from a national inferiority complex. Gasoline, to the Frenchman, was for a long time represented by American and British companies. Gasoline and oil (to a lesser extent) are symbols of power. The Frenchman was not convinced that his own gasoline would have the same power as the foreign brands. The approach calculated to overcome this sentiment was to present *Total* as an international brand that happened to originate in France and the Sahara, but was accepted and well-liked in many other countries.

¶ In Morocco, sales of French pasteurized milk had dropped considerably with the advent of Morocco's independence. This stemmed partly from the exodus of the French army with its families, and also from Moroccan unfamiliarity with drinking pasteurized milk.

But the drop in milk sales was also due to other factors, psychological in nature. One was the lack of confidence in the quality of pasteurized milk—Moroccan women were accustomed to buying from street vendors who milked the cows in front of their own eyes and then ladled the milk out of the pail. The soulless, odorless, clean pasteurized milk in bottles was simply too far removed from the original natural source of milk for the women to realize that they were still receiving the same quality of product.

But even more interesting was a factor dealing again with the phenomenon of national pride. The company had changed the lettering on its milk bottles and milk cartons from French to Arabic. The purpose was to please the newly independent consumers. Research showed, however, that instead of being pleased, consumers reacted negatively to this attempt at flattery. They stated it in the following way: "What is good enough for the French people is good enough for us. We don't want Arab milk. We want good French milk that the Frenchmen drink themselves."

For *marketing purposes* it thus was necessary to re-establish confidence in the naturalness of pasteurized bottled milk by showing cows and having street vendors also peddle pasteurized milk. A second measure was to change the lettering on the milk bottles back to French. Both steps resulted in increased sales.

The little phrase "Made in . . . " can have a tremendous influence on the acceptance and success of products over and above the specific advertising techniques used by themselves.

In a recent study in West Germany, this query was posed as part of a projective test: "An important discovery has been made in the technical field which has a great influence on our daily life. Which country has made this discovery?" As many as 78% answered: "Germany." (The study is being repeated in other countries. It will be interesting to examine the answers.) We also asked the Germans to think of a new product which through an error in production caused the death of several hundred people. The task of the respondents was to indicate which country would be most likely to manufacture such a product. We found that Germans considered this most likely to happen in the East zone, Russia, or the satellite countries, and then up to 30% in Italy or France.

The strong positive attitude evidenced by Germans toward their own technical product influenced an advertising approach developed for Ford in Germany. Research showed that the name Ford had a strong American association. The reaction of Germans was: "Americans drive our cars, Volkswagen and Mercedes; therefore they must be convinced that German cars are better than their own; so why should we buy their cars?" When the German Ford was presented as an example of cooperation between American ingenuity and know-how and German thoroughness and efficiency, considerable sales success was achieved.

### Inverted Morality

The influence of cultural traditions permeates a host of consumer behavior patterns.

The fact that 64% of Frenchmen don't brush their teeth is in part caused by the lack of running water in many communities. But a far more interesting aspect of this behavior could be explained on the basis of what I call "inverted morality." Here is an illustration of what can happen: In Puritanical cultures it is customary to think of cleanliness as being next to godliness. The body and its functions are covered up as much as possible.

But, in Catholic and Latin countries, to fool too much with one's body, to overindulge in bathing or toiletries, has the opposite meaning. It is *that* type of behavior which is considered immoral and improper. Accordingly, an advertising approach based on Puritanical principles, threatening Frenchmen that if they didn't brush their teeth regularly, they would develop cavities or would not find a lover, failed to impress.

To fit the accepted concept of morality, the French advertising agency changed this approach to a permissive one. The new approach presented the brushing of teeth as modern and chic but not as an absolute necessity which when neglected would result in dire consequences.

In line with the "inverted morality" notion is the fact that deodorant sales in France are lower than in most other countries. The majority, up to 80% of French housewives, use laundry soap instead of toilet soap. Only 20% of them have discovered perfumed, feminine soap which in the United States is frequently referred to as a "French type" of soap.

### Self-Illusions

Often nationals of a particular country are completely mistaken themselves about their own main characteristics. Successful marketers must be as cognizant of these national self-illusions as they must be aware of the mistaken stereotypes noted earlier. For example:

¶ Germans still refer to themselves as a nation of poets and thinkers; yet the largest selling newspaper, *The Bildzeitung*, has a circulation of 2½ million based largely on sensationalism and tabloid treatment of news. Even German *advertisers* had to be shown that this circulation, although proven by audits, was indeed psychologically possible. The only way this could be done was to force the German advertiser to look at his own people, including himself, without hypocrisy and in the harsh light of reality.

¶ All references to economy, comfort, and warmth had only a minimal effect in getting Englishmen to install central heating. They all ran up against a barrier of traditional self-illusion that Englishmen are of a hardy race that does not need the softening and effeminate effect of central heating. Inroads could be made only when the health of babies was used as a rationalization and after reassurance was given to the English "he-man" that to feel comfortably warm would not be detrimental to his self-image of virility.

¶ Most Europeans are convinced that they are individualists and nonconformists. Studies have shown that this is to a very large extent an illusion. There is a widely expressed fear of losing individuality, but right now it is the European who is becoming the representative of the mass market while it is the American market which in turn relies more and more on psychological segmentations. United States manufacturers may produce individuality on a mass scale, but individuality has become the decisive appeal in many products and services.

National self-illusions are hardly restricted to other nations. In the United States, as in quite a few other countries, many of our ethical principles are still based on the concept that we have to work by the sweat of our brow. In Germany, this is even more so. *The more you work, the more moral you feel.* Yet at the same time our modern psychological development and automation have resulted in a situation where fewer and fewer people work with their hands. Service fields are increasing, and we have more and more leisure time. The recent victory of the electricians' union in New York introducing a five-hour day aroused the nation for many reasons. Particularly pertinent here is that it clashed with most of our cherished beliefs of the importance of achieving happiness through work.

We are now confronted with increasing leisure time. Our discomfort results to a large extent from a lack of hedonistic morality such as prevailed among the Greeks for whom life was here to be enjoyed by a few people who did not have to work and did not have to feel guilty about it.

Leisure pursuits are spreading rapidly. Labor-saving devices are multiplying, and they are being adopted all over the world. The major difference lies in the degree of manifest or latent guilt feelings which are aroused:

Instant coffee is used by the Dutch housewife accompanied by the verbal protest that she only uses it in an emergency. What happens, however, is that the number of emergencies has increased amazingly.

French farmwives are inclined to say that they need large kitchen stoves in order to do the cooking for their large farm families. Young farmwives, however, have begun to admire and gradually buy the smaller units used by their city sisters. They have discovered that they do not have to stay as long behind the stove, and so are finding interests in other roles than that of a kitchen slave.

## BREAKING BOUNDARIES

Politically, in recent years we have watched a host of new nations emerge from erstwhile colonial status. It may be argued that many colonies would have been better off staying under the protection of enlightened colonial powers. Yet their desire for independence, no matter how premature we consider it to be, is so impulsive, explosive, and uncontrollable that no other solution remains than to satisfy this emotionally, humanly understandable hunger.

More important to the marketer is the fact that the same desire which spurred these political events has another dimension—viz., *in terms of consumption, whole centuries are being skipped in a world revolution of human expectations.*

Thus, from the viewpoint of the international psychologist's concern with the people still living in national units, we see the gradual development of the World Customer who breaks all boundaries:

¶ When a South African clothing manufacturer asks how to sell more long pants to previously half-naked Bantus, he is the first one to smash the barrier of apartheid, no matter how segregationistic his views may be. The moment one starts thinking of 10 million natives as consumers, one has to concern himself with their emotions and motivations.

Research revealed a greater psychological parallel between the emancipated Zulu and the emancipated white worker than between the nonemancipated Zulu and his emancipated tribal brother. The latter is ashamed when visited by his former ethnic peers. He has learned to speak English Afrikaans, has started to wear long pants, and often owns a car—a secondhand, dilapidated car, but nevertheless a car. He represents in many ways the same emotional conflict as that which existed between the first- and second-generation immigrants during the period of heavy immigration in the United States.

¶ In Australia until a few years ago 10% of the population was represented each year by newcomers, migrants, or—more euphemistically —"new Australians." These new Australians will change the basic Australian character in unrecognizable fashion within another ten years or so. As consumers, on the one hand, they want to eat, drink, and use the same products as the established Australians; on the other hand, they bring in their own customs and often superimpose Italian, German, or Spanish culture on the Australians.

## Six Market Groups

How can we locate the World Customer at various stages of development? How can we measure nations?

The "consumer revolution" which we are witnessing is basically not a proletarian one, but is *a revolution of the middle class*. It is the degree of development of a large middle class which makes the difference between a backward and a modern country both economically and psychologically. That is the clue for appraising and interpreting different cultures, for measuring their achievement.

The most important symbol of middle class development in the world today is the automobile. It is the automobile which represents achievement and personal freedom for the middle class. And this restless middle class is the most important factor in the constructive discontent which motivates people's desires and truly moves them forward. In some countries, like the United States, West Germany, Switzerland, Sweden, and Norway, most people have enough to eat and are reasonably well housed. Having achieved this thousand-year-old dream of humanity, they now reach out for further satisfactions. They want to travel, discover, be at least physically independent. The automobile is the symbol of mobility; the automobile has become the self-mobile!

Using middle class development as a measure of achievement, if we were to visualize the social composition of each country in terms of a scale showing the size of its middle class, upper class, and lower class, we could probably define some six groups.

*Group One: The Almost Classless Society, Contented Countries.* In this group we would include primarily the Scandinavian countries. The middle class takes up almost all of the scale, with very few people left who could be considered really poor and few who are really rich. We are dealing with a socialistic security and equalization which sounds like paradise, but often leads to loss of incentives.

In these countries, products are viewed in a rather sober fashion. The car, for instance, is strictly utilitarian, and showing off with one's auto is not considered correct.

Studies have shown that reliability and economy are very important. Attitudes toward products are rational: they do not represent a special status value. There is generally a conservative attitude toward new gadgets and styles. Second cars are practically nonexistent.

*Group Two: The Affluent Countries.* This group includes the United States, West Germany, Switzerland, Holland, and Canada. Few people starve, and there is still some room at the top. The top of the middle class itself, however, often is high and desirable enough so that there is no need to break through and trespass into the unpopular and threatened class of financial aristocracy.

Among these countries the most advanced is the United States. What happens in many areas in the United States represents the latest and leading trends and permits us to predict what will happen in the next few years in the other affluent countries. People in affluent countries want greater individuality in their products. They dream of high-quality, repair-proof, almost custom-tailored articles.

While the German still uses his car for prestige purposes, in the United States the status value of cars has substantially diminished and has been shifted to other products and services such as swimming pools, travel, and education. The average American considers his car more like an appliance than a status symbol. Conspicuous cars like the Cadillac or the Lincoln try to emphasize their quiet elegance to avoid being considered cars for show-offs. There is increased attention to functional values and integration in car designs. Cars are not pampered; they are expected to do their job.

*Group Three: Countries in Transition.* In this group we may place England, France, Italy, Autralia, South Africa, and Japan. These countries still have a working class in the nineteenth century sense. But this class is trying to break out of its bondage and join the comfortable middle class. The upper classes still have privileges and can afford maids, Rolls-Royces, and castles; but their privileges are being rapidly whittled away. These countries have not had complete social revolutions. (The Labor government in England represented such an attempt but failed). Servants are still cheap but rapidly getting more expensive and less easily available. Many wage-earning groups suffer from low wages. Living standards are behind those of the United States and West Germany. The white-collar worker often makes less money than the factory worker, but he has not integrated yet with the developing labor-based middle class. Prestige still plays an important role.

Cars are pampered in these countries. They are an extension of one's personality. They are given pet names. They represent major investments. Cars are outward symbols of success.

There are still many first-car people, who have only now bought their first proof of "having arrived." Price plays an important role as an invitation to enter the automobile world—upgrading the buyer from bicycles and motorcycles. For top classes, some very expensive cars are available. Style plays a role with certain groups; there is much experimentation, curiosity, and desire for product adventure. Markets are still fluid, have not stabilized yet. There is resistance in all these countries against planned obsolescence. A lot of people hold onto their cars for six to ten years or more. American cars are considered to be too flashy and also too expensive.

*Group Four: Revolutionary Countries.* Venezuela, Mexico, Argentina, Brazil, Spain, India, China, and the Philippines are in this group. In these areas large groups of people are just emerging from near-starvation and are discovering industrialization. Relatively speaking, there are more extremely rich people, a small but expanding middle class, and a very large body of depressed economic groups that are beginning to discover the possibilities of enjoying life through the revolution in industry.

In these countries large sections of the population have not even reached the level of being consumers. These are the Indians living in many South American countries, the people living in villages in India and Indonesia, and so on.

Automobiles are available only to a relatively small group. They are expensive and considered a luxury. They are taxed so highly that they are beyond the reach of most people. American cars are considered the ideal. People want to show off. Small cars are bought as a way to get started. As the middle class develops, there should be an even further increase in the sale of small and compact cars, with the really rich people preferring big American cars.

*Group Five: Primitive Countries.* The newly liberated countries of Africa and the remaining colonies comprise the fifth group. In these countries there exists only a very small group of wealthy indigenous and foreign businessmen, new political leaders, and foreign advisers. The rest of the population is most often illiterate and ignorant and exists in a preconsumer stage, characterized either by barter or by almost complete primitive "self-sufficiency." The few cars that are sold are primarily for the government bureaucracy. There is no real car market as yet.

*Group Six: The New Class Society.* In Russia and its satellite countries, there is emerging a class of bureaucrats who represent a new form of aristocracy, while everybody else represents a slowly improving, low middle class. True, in these countries the extremely low income and the starving proletarians have disappeared.

The automobile, the modern home with its mechanized kitchen and mass-produced food items, and supermarket distribution represent the symbols of a new industrial society. By understanding the basic position of a country on this scale of development one can understand the role of products at present and one can also predict their future possibilities.

There is an interest in prestige cars. All the bourgeois symbols of capitalist countries are being copied—particularly those of the United States.

### Our Greatest Opportunity

Many recent stories in the press—most of them picked up in foreign countries—make it appear that we ought to be ashamed of the good life we are leading. This recanting has its origin in a deep-seated guilt feeling which is unhealthy and dangerous. Some of the recanting is directed against a number of specific products, such as electrical gadgets, big cars, luxury and leisure time, and merchandise.

The real measuring rod of the success of one system over another should be based on the happiness of the citizens, their creativeness, and their constructive discontent. The desire to grow, to improve oneself, and to enjoy life to the fullest is at least equal, if not decidedly superior, to the goal of being ahead in a missile or a satellite program.

Our present life, therefore, should be presented as a challenge to the outside world— not in a boastful way, but as a life attainable by everyone through democratic and peaceful pursuits.

### CONCLUSION

In most countries I have visited, I find that human desires are pretty much alike. The big difference lies in the level of achievement, in its many different forms.

In Iquitos, on the Amazon River, I recently visited an Indian tribe. They live in blissful fashion, hunting and planting bananas and yuccas. Who is smarter—we, the hard-working "civilized people"—or the contented Indians? Part of the answer was provided by the fact that our guide complained that there were fewer and fewer Indians for tourists to see. They were becoming "too civilized." In other words, these primitive people who were supposed to be happy are caught in the inevitable maelstrom of development. They smoke cigarettes and are beginning to wear jeans and shirts.

Growth and progress are the only possible goals of life. I believe that the clue to man's destiny lies in his relentless training toward independence, not only politically, but also in the psychological sense. We are beset by fears, by inhibitions, by narrow-minded routine thinking.

Step by step, year by year, we free ourselves more and more. Jets reduce physical distances; international trade and mass communications break down barriers. The world is opening up. The Common Market will broaden into an Atlantic Market and finally into a World Market. In order to participate effectively in this progressive development of mankind, it is essential to have a creative awareness of human desire and its strategy throughout the world—to understand and prepare to serve the new World Customer.

# 53. The Challenge of the Underdeveloped National Market

### RICHARD D. ROBINSON

Marketing concepts most appropriate in the emerging states of Asia, Africa, and Latin America differ markedly from those to which we have grown accustomed in the United States. The difference begins with product design.

Rather than promoting products believed to generate the greatest financial return in the short run, Western firms selling in non-Western markets probably should place more emphasis on those products of greatest long-run benefit to the nations concerned and analyze most carefully the manner in which they are supplying those products to the market. Otherwise, Western managements may anticipate increasingly tight import restrictions for their products, blocked earnings, higher taxes, and eventual loss of foreign markets and assets.

The point is that one should expect heightened sensitivity to long-run national interests on the part of Asian, African, and Latin American governments as they become more sophisticated and skilled. Such sensitivity to national interest is what many unthinking Westerners have condemned with the epithet "nationalism."

A domestic marketing specialist in the United States may tend to look at the market from the point of view of the structure of present demand, so as to sell a new product or more of an existing product. The new might be new only in respect to style, brand, or packaging. Consumer wants are changed and expanded constantly in the process.

‡‡ SOURCE: Reprinted by permission from the *Journal of Marketing* (National Quarterly Publication of the American Marketing Association), Vol. 25, No. 6, October 1961, pp. 19–25.

But in India or Egypt, the marketing analyst —if sensitve to the national interest of the host country—must concern himself more with ascertaining what types of products would contribute most to increasing the national product, alleviating the nation's balance of payments situation, and sopping up inflationary pressures with a minimum commitment of scarce resources, including foreign exchange.

The stimulation of non-existing demands for new consumer goods or demands based on brand name, style obsolescence, or new packaging may well cause an unjustified waste of scarce materials and skills or an unnecessary commitment of them. Where resources are seriously limited in a per-capita sense, the Western businessman who remains insensitive to this national interest does so at his peril.

## THREE LEVELS OF MANAGEMENT SENSITIVITY

There are three levels of management sensitivity.

The first has to do with management's awareness of the need to modify or redesign *products* so as to make them really appropriate to the markets into which they are moving. The second has to do with management's awareness of the need to measure its products against the long-run interests of non-Western markets—in other words, *impact* of products. The third level of sensitivity is management's awareness of the extent to which its product is politically *vulnerable*.

Sensitivity on all levels may well lead to product modification—even to invention—or, on the other hand, to self-imposed limitation in certain cases. Perhaps within these underdeveloped national markets some products should not be promoted at all, however modified or redesigned.

## Product Design

Clearly, different United States products require different types of foreign markets. Some require large industrial markets; others, mass consumer markets. Still others need a professional or technical market, or a market in which public agencies buy, or a literate market, or a market in which the standard of living is high, and so on.

Since many of these characteristics are not found in markets outside of North America and Western Europe, the sales potential for certain products in many parts of the world is limited. Many American managements are well aware of the limitations placed on the degree to which they can expand foreign sales because of the special market characteristics demanded by the nature of their traditional products. Geographical and climatic conditions are also important variables; few American firms design products specifically for use in the jungle or the desert, or products for use by illiterates.

Generalizations that follow are based on the author's study of the attitudes and organization of 172 American companies in respect to overseas interests. This study was conducted over the 1956–58 period under the auspices of the Division of Research, Harvard Graduate School of Business Administration.

The necessity for substantially modifying or altering products to meet the specific demands of non-Western markets frequently discouraged American managements from taking serious interest in becoming active within these markets. It might be possible to service the European, Canadian, and Australian-New Zealand markets with surplus domestic production, but elsewhere such sales spillover was difficult to develop. The domestic product was simply not appropriate.

One executive pointed out that his company's principal product, asphalt roofing, was not appropriate in areas in which extreme heat was common, thereby ruling out much of the equatorial zone as a market.

Mining machinery produced by one firm could not be exported in large quantities because it was built specifically to fit conditions found in United States mines, conditions uncommon to other countries.

Management of a steel-castings company, the principal products of which were heavy castings for railway cars, cited many reasons why foreign customers did not wish to use cast steel, let alone the company's designs. Many foreign railways used buffers instead of couplers, rolled steel designs for the side frames instead of cast steel, and four-wheel freight cars instead of eight-wheel.

The president of one company stated that his firm's products were consumer goods and were to a very considerable extent culturally conditioned. "We block ourselves from many markets in South America, Africa, and other areas."

An American executive with a long experience in India commented that most United States companies were based on the North American customer. They had very little concern for customers elsewhere. Concrete evidence of such disregard was the little influence American firms had had in setting up world-wide standards. "United States industry has not even taken the trouble—or spent the money—to have its 1,700 national standards translated for use in foreign countries," the President of the American Standards Associations is reported to have said. "It is no coincidence that American industries doing the largest export business—the electrical and motion pictures industries, for example—are the ones that have developed international standards."[1]

In many cases where geographical and cultural influences on products were cited by management to explain their disinterest in foreign sales, the true reasons seemed to lie somewhat deeper. Too many managements had surmounted these difficulties. Asphalt roofing might not be good in extreme heats, but was it not impossible to develop a similar roofing which would be? Mining conditions might be quite different from those obtaining in United States mines, but surely appropriate machines could be built. Granted, the product of the steel castings company was not suited for sale in most foreign areas, but the development of an appropriate product was surely not as difficult as that encountered by such companies as the International Business Machines Company and the Westinghouse Electric Corporation.

One management was modifying the design

---

[1] *Time*, June 30, 1958, p. 74.

of its truck, which was to be produced and sold in Turkey. Changes were required by the rough roads, the high elevations, and extreme heat in some areas. Executives in a large automotive company observed that it was difficult for the larger, mass-production companies to alter products in this fashion to meet specific geographical and climatic conditions. But was great size necessarily related to inflexibility in this regard? The division manufacturing trucks in this case was probably little larger than the independent truck manufacturer who was modifying its product for the Turkish market.

Asked about the feasibility of manufacturing some sort of an intermediate type of machine in some foreign areas, a type no longer being used in the United States, a vice president of a farm machinery product replied that in a way his company was doing precisely that in Mexico; the tractor assembled in Mexico did not include all the latest hydraulic gadgets. Such a tractor would have required too much servicing and would have been too complicated for the ordinary Mexican farmer to operate.

Directly related to willingness to modify product design was the matter of quality. The experience of Corporation X in Africa is relevant.

The local African government had been buying from Corporation X, an American firm, hand-operated dusters for use in distributing pesticides in the cotton fields. The dusters were loaned to individual Negro farmers. The duster supplied by the corporation was a finely-machined device requiring regular oiling and good care.

But the fact that this duster turned more easily than any other duster on the market was relatively unimportant to the native farmers. Furthermore, the requirement for careful oiling and care simply meant that in a relatively short time the machines froze up and broke. The result? The local government went back to an older type French duster which was heavy, turned with difficulty, and gave a poorer distribution of dust, but which lasted longer in that it required less care and lubrication.

From the point of view of the small Negro cotton farmer, the quality of the French dusters was more appropriate than that of the American dusters. In this relative sense, the quality of the French machine was superior.

This view was reflected in a remark by the director of the international division of a large company to the effect that Europe could produce anything more cheaply and better than the United States. By "better" he meant better *relative to the demands of the foreign market.* He admitted that many American-made products were much better than their foreign counterparts in an absolute sense, but this superiority in quality was too expensive to be "within the circle of demand" of many foreign markets. For example, his company manufactured one item with an average life of thirty-five years. The trouble was that many people abroad could not afford to pay for a device lasting that long, and they were not impressed.

Another way of looking at quality was to consider that additional cost of a highly durable product represented an investment and, if the cost of capital were relatively high, as it was in many of the underdeveloped countries, it might not be economically feasible to purchase the more durable or higher-quality American product.

Some few firms had gone so far in product modification as to invent virtually new products. A pen company had designed a special, cheap, mass-produced pen for the Asiatic market. Landers-Frary and Clark was selling a newly-designed hand-operated corn mill in Latin America. Private Enterprise, Inc., had developed a wooden block with which to construct cheap housing in Central America. It was significant that those companies identified with substantial overseas interest demonstrated extraordinary ingenuity and flexibility in modifying their products so as to be appropriate to local geographical and cultural conditions. It was precisely those companies that had not been interested in foreign business which seemed to find their product most limited in respect to international sales.

Yet, in some cases, the problems faced by these latter firms did not seem nearly as great in this respect as those faced and overcome by the others. It seemed that *the fundamental interest and orientation of key members of management really determined the degree to which a product was limited geographically and culturally.*

An internationally minded management examined deliberately and systematically the products it intended to market within Country X from the point of view of the environment of Country X. It made no assumptions about the validity of an American-oriented product. Major environmental factors considered in relation to the design of a given product were:

Level of technical skills ⟶ Product simplification

Level of labor cost ⟶ Automation or manualization of product

Level of literacy ⟶ Remarking and simplification of product

Level of income ⟶ Quality and price change

Level of interest rates ⟶ Quality and price change
(Investment in high quality
might not be financially desirable.)

Level of maintenance ⟶ Change in tolerances

Climatic differences ⟶ Product adaptation

Isolation (heavy repair ⟶ Product simplification and reliability
difficult and expensive) improvement

Differences in standards ⟶ Recalibration of product and
resizing

Availability of other products ⟶ Greater or lesser product
integration

Availability of materials ⟶ Change in product structure and
fuel

Power availability ⟶ Resizing of product

Special conditions ⟶ Product redesign or invention

The added effort in developing an appropriate product, given the anticipated reward, might be thus measured. But it appeared that relatively few managements had analyzed the pros and cons of developing non-Western markets in these or similar terms.

### Product Impact

In designing, modifying, and promoting the sale of products in the underdeveloped markets, management should not assume that the economic and social benefits to be derived from these products are necessarily the same as when they are used within the American economy.

A representative of one firm explained that his company's export business was "absolutely nominal." Asphalt roofing, the firm's principal product, was expensive for a cheap labor market. It failed to compete with wood shake and slate. In most cases, there were few building code restrictions; and builders simply took the cheapest of the traditional products with little regard for comparative qualities or for the amount of labor required for installation. Although under some conditions asphalt roofing had absolute advantages over the traditional type of roofing, one of its principal advantages was that it required less labor than most other roofing for both manufacture and installation.

Outside of the United States and Western Europe, this labor-conserving feature of a product would not provide any significant economic advantage. The relationship of labor to the cost of materials is quite different from that in the Western European and American environment.

The point is that logically preceding any substantial commitment of company time and money to foreign sales projects should be a careful, impartial study of the impact of the products involved on the economies and societies in which they are to be sold. Sooner or later, the government of the recipient nation will awaken to its own interests. Products might well be analyzed in terms of their impact on production and upon the productivity of local labor. The introduction of some products might reasonably be expected to induce directly an expansion of employment. Others might have the effect of improving the quality of local labor. Luxury products and those of a fundamentally labor-saving nature might not be appealing under all circumstances to the development-conscious foreign government.

Each society develops its own peculiar wants in terms of non-essential, consumer goods. The satisfaction of at least part of this demand may be important to the national economy in order to maintain incentives and to sop up inflationary pressures. At least partial satisfaction may likewise be politically compelling.

By reason of the chronic pressure on investment and balance of payments in many underdeveloped countries, responsible governments are loathe to divert a greater share than is necessary of their already inadequate resources to the satisfaction of these demands. In order to relate the promotion of a non-essential consumer product in Country X to the national interest, two guides are useful: (1) Can the product be made available with a relative minor commitment of scarce local resources? (2) Does there already exist an unsatisfied popular demand for the product?

A product produced locally by presently unemployed labor and which upvalues locally available materials is quite different from an imported good, the price of which includes expensive foreign labor and scarce foreign exchange. Similarly, a non-essential product that is presently known and is in demand is quite different from a product for which demand will have to be stimulated.

Coca-Cola in Egypt is quite different from Coca-Cola in Turkey. In Egypt it has been known for many years' and is in great demand. The drink uses few resources and helps "soak up" inflationary pressure. In Turkey, the product would have to be promoted, thereby creating a *new* consumer demand. The economy is already straining to meet present consumer demands without cutting back investment in basic development. Clearly, the introduction of Coca-Cola is not necessary to induce incentive to produce. Of course, if it could be shown that Coca-Cola would constitute a consumption substitute for other goods, and involve fewer scarce resources than the others, then an argument might be made for the introduction of Coca-Cola.

Obviously the nature of a product may change substantially from one society to another. Both technical and social conditions may have a heavy impact. The type of mining involved may make it impossible to apply further units of labor, thereby giving an absolute advantage to mining machinery in terms of increasing production. Or the rural population in a particular area may not provide adequate labor to harvest and process the basic crops rapidly enough to prevent substantial damage in the case of adverse weather. This means that machines, which otherwise might have no impact on over-all production, would have substantial impact. These machines then change in nature from mere labor-saving devices into labor-creating ones in that they effect an absolute increase in production.

This discussion is occasioned by two observations: (1) Very few managements seem to be concerned about the nature of their product in relationship to total economic development, and specifically to the development of the country in which their product is marketed. (2) There seems to be little management awareness that a product might not have the same characteristics in relation to the American market as in a specific underdeveloped economy.

### Political Vulnerability of Product

Even though a product is appropriately designed for the market and its promotion is in the interest of the host society, a management may still run substantial risk if that product is politically vulnerable—that is, susceptible to public concern and governmental control.

The degree to which one is shielded from political interest is in part a function of the degree to which management has modified its product so as to be most appropriate to the market. It also depends on how well management has chosen it products from the point of view of their impact upon national economic interests.

But there are other criteria as well to be used in the determination of political vulnerability. Is the product of such a nature as to be politically important or to attract undue government attention? How irreplaceable is the foreign contribution contained in the product? Is local competition possible? Does the organization by which the product is made available recognize the interests of the host country?

Such public concern and control may on the one hand lead to protection within a market, or on the other hand to loss of market and assets. Some of the relevant criteria are suggested by the following questions:

1. Is the product ever the subject of important political debates in respect to adequacy of supply? (Sugar, salt, kerosene, gasoline, foodstuffs, transport facilities, public utilities, tires, medicines, etc.)

2. Is the production one on which other industries rest? (Cement, steel, power, machine tools, construction machinery, etc.)

3. Is the product one in which effective competition is difficult in small national markets?

4. Is the product one held to be essential either economically or socially? (Key drugs and medicines, laboratory equipment.)

5. Is the product important to agriculture? (Farm tools and machinery, pumps, fertilizers, seed, etc.)

6. Is the product of national defense significance? (Communications equipment, transport equipment, etc.)

7. Does the product include important components that would be available from local sources? (Labor, skills, materials.)

8. Is the product one for which competition from local manufacture may be reasonably expected in the foreseeable future?

9. Does the product relate to channels of mass communication media? (Newsprint, radio equipment, etc.)

10. Is the product primarily a service?

11. Does the use of the product, or its design, rest upon some legal requirement?

12. Is the product potentially dangerous to the user? (Explosives, drugs.)

13. Does the product induce a net drain on scarce foreign exchange?

If each of these questions were answered on a 1-to-10 scale, from a strong "yes" to a strong "no," the lowest scoring products would be among the most vulnerable to political pressures. It is often useful to ask how foreign ownership of a given industry or product source would be treated in the United States.

Political vulnerability may lead to labor agitation, public regulation (price fixing, allocation quotas, etc.); nationalization (in the sense of restricting ownership to local nationals); or socialization (public ownership) on the one hand—or on the other hand to favoritism and protection. Which way the pendulum swings depends largely upon the sensitivity and foresight of management in responding to political pressures before they become irresistible, also upon the effort management makes to relate its product to the specific needs of the market in respect to both design and impact.

Goods deemed to be essential (for example, high scores in questions 2, 4, 5, 6, and 9) often receive first claim to scarce foreign exchange in respect to importing. Likewise, these same products, if made within the country, often receive a high degree of encouragement and protection, up to and including government guarantee for the repatriation of profits and capital and an official prohibition against competing imports. Therefore, other than the possibility of national-

ization or socialization, the risk of investment abroad in the production of essential products is substantially less than that incurred in the case of less essential products.

## CONCLUSION

Relevant variables from management to management are really two: (1) degree of management sensitivity to the long-run interests and desires of the emerging countries of Asia, Africa, and Latin America, and (2) the degree of flexibility shown by management in product design and modification, as well as choice in the manner of supplying a market. Inasmuch as this article deals with product criteria only, there is no discussion of developing the most appropriate sources of supply (American, local, third country) or of organization (wholly-owned subsidiary, joint venture, mixed venture, contract manufacturing, license).[2]

The present study revealed that very few American managements are what one might call internationally minded. The foreign business of most is conducted simply as a spillover of the domestic.

This finding begs the question of why some few managements have shown such remarkable interest, flexibility, and sensitivity as to the needs of foreign markets while most remain callously indifferent. The answer is possibly to be found in a number of variables—the history of the firm, the way in which it is organized, the characteristics of its product, the nature of the productive processes, the sources of raw materials, and so on. But in the final analysis, the interest, flexibility, and sensitivity of management rests with individuals. It is they who make the relevant decisions.

The United States has been "caught short" in business personnel trained adequately in the proposition that the market place is the world. American business desperately needs more men who are thoroughly knowledgeable of Asia, Africa, and Latin America. Without them, it will be exceedingly difficult to build lasting markets in these areas for United States business.

---

[2] For further treatment of this subject, see the author's articles "Conflicting Interests in International Business Investment," *Boston University Business Review*, Vol. 7, Spring 1960, pp. 3–13, and "Organizing International Business from a New Point of View," *Oregon Business Review*, Vol. 19, August 1960, pp. 1–6.

# 54. Marketing and Economic Development

PETER F. DRUCKER

## MARKETING AS A BUSINESS DISCIPLINE

The distinguished pioneer of marketing, whose memory we honor today, was largely instrumental in developing marketing as a systematic business discipline—in teaching us how to go about, in an orderly, purposeful and planned way to find and create customers; to identify and define markets; to create new ones and promote them; to integrate customers' needs, wants, and preferences, and the intellectual and creative capacity and skills of an industrial society, toward the design of new and better products and of new distributive concepts and processes.

On this contribution and similar ones of other Founding Fathers of marketing during the last half century rests the rapid emergence of marketing as perhaps the most advanced, certainly the most "scientific" of all functional business disciplines.

But Charles Coolidge Parlin also contributed as a Founding Father toward the development of marketing as a *social discipline*. He helped give us the awareness, the concepts, and the tools that make us understand marketing as a dynamic process of society through which business enterprise is integrated productively with society's purposes and human values. It is in marketing, as we now understand it, that we satisfy individual and social values, needs, and wants—be it through producing goods, supplying services, fostering innovation, or creating

‡‡ SOURCE: Reprinted by permission from the *Journal of Marketing* (National Quarterly Publication of the American Marketing Association), Vol. 22, No. 3, January 1958, pp. 252–259.

satisfaction. Marketing, as we have come to understand it, has its focus on the customer, that is, on the individual making decisions within a social structure and within a personal and social value system. Marketing is thus the process through which economy is integrated into society to serve human needs.

I am not competent to speak about marketing in the first sense, marketing as a functional discipline of business. I am indeed greatly concerned with marketing in this meaning. One could not be concerned, as I am, with the basic institutions of industrial society in general and with the management of business enterprise in particular, without a deep and direct concern with marketing. But in this field I am a consumer of marketing alone—albeit a heavy one. I am not capable of making a contribution. I would indeed be able to talk about the wants and needs I have which I, as a consumer of marketing, hope that you, the men of marketing, will soon supply:—a theory of pricing, for instance, that can serve, as true theories should, as the foundation for actual pricing decisions and for an understanding of price behavior; or a consumer-focused concept and theory of competition. But I could not produce any of these "new products" of marketing which we want. I cannot contribute myself. To use marketing language, I am not even "effective demand," in these fields as yet.

## THE ROLE OF MARKETING

I shall today in my remarks confine myself to the second meaning in which marketing has become a discipline: The role of marketing in economy and society. And I shall single out as my focus the role of marketing in the economic development, especially of under-developed "growth" countries.

My thesis is very briefly as follows. Marketing occupies a critical role in respect to the development of such "growth" areas. Indeed marketing is the most important "multiplier" of such development. It is in itself in every one of these areas the least developed, the most backward part of the economic system. Its development, above all others, makes possible economic integration and the fullest utilization of whatever assets and productive capacity an economy already possesses. It mobilizes latent economic energy. It contributes to the greatest needs: that for the rapid development of entrepreneurs and managers, and at the same time it may be the easiest area of managerial work to get going. The reason is that, thanks to men like Charles Coolidge Parlin, it is the most systematized and, therefore, the most learnable and the most teachable of all areas of business management and entrepreneurship.

## INTERNATIONAL AND INTERRACIAL INEQUALITY

Looking at this world of ours, we see some essentially new facts.

For the first time in man's history the whole world is united and unified. This may seem a strange statement in view of the conflicts and threats of suicidal wars that scream at us from every headline. But conflict has always been with us. What is new is that today all of mankind shares the same vision, the same objective, the same goal, the same hope, and believes in the same tools. This vision might, in gross oversimplification, be called "industrialization."

It is the belief that it is possible for man to improve his economic lot through systematic, purposeful, and directed effort—individually as well as for an entire society. It is the belief that we have the tools at our disposal—the technological, the conceptual, and the social tools—to enable man to raise himself, through his own efforts, at least to a level that we in this country would consider poverty, but which for most of our world would be almost unbelievable luxury.

And this is an irreversible new fact. It has been made so by these true agents of revolution in our times: the new tools of communication—the dirt road, the truck, and the radio, which have penetrated even the furthest, most isolated and most primitive community.

This is new, and cannot be emphasized too much and too often. It is both a tremendous vision and a tremendous danger in that catastrophe must result if it cannot be satisfied, at least to a modest degree.

But at the same time we have a new, unprecedented danger, that of international and interracial inequality. We on the North American continent are a mere tenth of the world population, including our Canadian friends and neighbors. But we have at least 75 per cent of the world income. And the 75 per cent of the world population whose income is below $100 per capita a year receive together perhaps no more than 10 per cent of the world's income. This is inequality of income, as great as anything the world has ever seen. It is accompanied by very high equality of income in the developed countries, especially in ours where we are in the process of proving that an industrial society does not have to live in extreme tension between the few very rich and the many very poor as lived all earlier societies of man. But what used to be national inequality and economic tension is now rapidly becoming international (and unfortunately also interracial) inequality and tension.

This is also brand new. In the past there were tremendous differences between societies and cultures: in their beliefs, their concepts, their ways of life, and their knowledge. The Frankish knight who went on Crusade was an ignorant and illiterate boor, according to the standards of the polished courtiers of Constantinople or of his Moslem enemies. But economically his society and theirs were exactly alike. They had the same sources of income, the same productivity of labor, the same forms and channels of investment, the same economic institutions, and the same distribution of income and wealth. Economically the Frankish knight, however much a barbarian he appeared, was at home in the societies of the East; and so was his serf. Both fitted in immediately and without any difficulty.

And this has been the case of all societies that went above the level of purely primitive tribe.

The inequality in our world today, however, between nations and races, is therefore a new —and a tremendously dangerous—phenomenon.

What we are engaged in today is essentially a race between the promise of economic development and the threat of international world-wide class war. The economic development is the opportunity of this age. The class war is the danger. Both are new. Both are indeed so new that most of us do not even see them as yet. But they are the essential economic realities of this industrial age of ours. And whether we shall realize the opportunity or succumb to danger will largely decide not only the economic future of this world—it may largely decide its spiritual, its intellectual, its political, and its social future.

## SIGNIFICANCE OF MARKETING

Marketing is central in this new situation. For marketing is one of our most potent levers to convert the danger into the opportunity.

To understand this we must ask: What do we mean by "under-developed"?

The first answer is, of course, that we mean areas of very low income. But income is, after all, a result. It is a result first of extreme agricultural over-population in which the great bulk of the people have to find a living on the land which, as a result, cannot even produce enough food to feed them, let alone produce a surplus. It is certainly a result of low productivity. And both, in a vicious circle, mean that there is not enough capital for investment, and very low productivity of what is being invested—owing largely to misdirection of investment into unessential and unproductive channels.

All this we know today and understand. Indeed we have learned during the last few years a very great deal both about the structure of an under-developed economy and about the theory and dynamics of economic development.

What we tend to forget, however, is that the essential aspect of an "underdeveloped" economy and the factor the absence of which keeps it "under-developed," is the inability to organize economic efforts and energies, to bring together resources, wants, and capacities, and so to convert a self-limiting static system into creative, self-generating organic growth.

And this is where marketing comes in.

### Lack of Development in "Under-developed" Countries

First, in every "under-developed" country I know of, marketing is the most under-developed—or the least developed—part of the economy, if only because of the strong, pervasive prejudice against the "middleman."

As a result, these countries are stunted by inability to make effective use of the little they have. Marketing might by itself go far toward changing the entire economic tone of the existing system—without any change in methods of production, distribution of population, or of income.

It would make the producers capable of producing marketable products by providing them with standards, with quality demands, and with specifications for their product. It would make the product capable of being brought to markets instead of perishing on the way. And it would make the consumer capable of discrimination, that is, of obtaining the greatest value for his very limited purchasing power.

In every one of these countries, marketing profits are characteristically low. Indeed the people engaged in marketing barely eke out a subsistence living. And "mark-ups" are minute by our standards. But marketing costs are outrageously high. The waste in distribution and marketing, if only from spoilage or from the accumulation of unsalable inventories that clog the shelves for years, has to be seen to be believed. And marketing service is by and large all but non-existent.

What is needed in any "growth" country to make economic development realistic, and at the same time produce a vivid demonstration of what economic development can produce, is a marketing system:—a system of physical distribution, a financial system to make possible the distribution of goods, and finally actual marketing, that is, an actual system of integrating wants, needs, and purchasing power of the consumer with capacity and resources of production.

This need is largely masked today because marketing is so often confused with the traditional "trader and merchant" of which every one of these countries has more than enough. It would be one of our most important contributions to the development of "under-developed" countries to get across the fact that marketing is something quite different.

It would be basic to get across the triple function of marketing the function of crystallizing and directing demand for maximum productive effectiveness and efficiency; the function of guiding production purposefully toward maximum consumer satisfaction and consumer value; the function of creating discrimination that then gives rewards to those who really contribute excellence, and that then also penalize the monopolist, the slothful, or those who only want to take but do not want to contribute or to risk.

### Utilization by the Entrepreneur

Marketing is also the most easily accessible "multiplier" of managers and entrepreneurs in an "under-developed" growth area. And managers and entrepreneurs are the foremost need of these countries. In the first place, "economic development" is not a force of nature. It is the result of the action, the purposeful, responsible, risk-taking action, of men as entrepreneurs and managers.

Certainly it is the entrepreneur and manager who alone can convey to the people of these countries an understanding of what economic development means and how it can be achieved.

Marketing can convert latent demand into effective demand. It cannot, by itself, create purchasing power. But it can uncover and channel all purchasing power that exists. It can, therefore, create rapidly the conditions for a much higher level of economic activity than existed before, can create the opportunities for the entrepreneur.

It then can create the stimulus for the development of modern, responsible, professional management by creating opportunity for the producer who knows how to plan, how to organize, how to lead people, how to innovate.

In most of these countries markets are of necessity very small. They are too small to make it possible to organize distribution for a single-product line in any effective manner. As a result, without a marketing organization, many products for which there is an adequate demand at a reasonable price cannot be distributed; or worse, they can be produced and distributed only under monopoly conditions. A marketing system is needed which serves as the joint and common channel for many producers if any of them is to be able to come into existence and to stay in existence.

This means in effect that a marketing system in the "under-developed" countries is the *creator of small business*, is the only way in which a man of vision and daring can become a businessman and an entrepreneur himself. This is thereby also the only way in which a true middle class can develop in the countries in which the habit of investment in productive enterprise has still to be created.

### Developer of Standards

Marketing in an "under-developed" country is the developer of standards—of standards for product and service as well as of standards of conduct, of integrity, of reliability, of foresight, and of concern for the basic long-range impact of decisions on the customer, the supplier, the economy, and the society.

Rather than go on making theoretical statements let me point to one illustration: The impact Sears Roebuck has had on several countries of Latin America. To be sure, the countries of Latin America in which Sears operates—Mexico, Brazil, Cuba, Venezuela, Colombia, and Peru—are not "under-developed" in the same sense in which Indonesia or the Congo are "under-developed." Their average income, although very low by our standards, is at least two times, perhaps as much as four or five times, that of the truly "under-developed" countries in which the bulk of mankind still live. Still in every respect except income level these Latin American countries are at best "developing." And they have all the problems of economic development—perhaps even in more acute form than the countries of Asia and Africa, precisely because their development has been so fast during the last ten years.

It is also true that Sears in these countries is not a "low-price" merchandiser. It caters to the middle class in the richer of these countries, and to the upper middle class in the poorest of these countries. Incidentally, the income level of these groups is still lower than that of the worker in the industrial sector of our economy.

Still Sears is a mass-marketer even in Colombia or Peru. What is perhaps even more important, it is applying in these "under-developed" countries exactly the same policies and principles it applies in this country, carries substantially the same merchandise (although most of it produced in the countries themselves), and applies the same concepts of marketing it uses in Indianapolis or Philadelphia. Its impact and experience are, therefore, a fair test of what marketing principles, marketing knowledge, and marketing techniques can achieve.

The impact of this one American business which does not have more than a mere handful of stores in these countries and handles no more than a small fraction of the total retail business of these countries is truly amazing. In the first place, Sears' latent purchasing power has fast become actual purchasing power. Or, to put it less theoretically, people have begun to organize their buying and to go out for value in what they do buy.

Secondly, by the very fact that it builds one store in one city, Sears forces a revolution in retailing throughout the whole surrounding area. It forces store modernization. It forces consumer credit. It forces a different attitude toward the customer, toward the store clerk, toward the supplier, and toward the merchandise itself. It forces other retailers to adopt modern methods of pricing, of inventory control, of training, of window display, and what have you.

The greatest impact Sears has had, however, is in the multiplication of new industrial business for which Sears creates a marketing channel. Because it has had to sell goods manufactured in these countries rather than import them (if only because of foreign exchange restrictions), Sears has been instrumental in getting established literally hundreds of new manufacturers making goods which, a few years ago, could not be made in the country, let alone be sold in adequate quantity. Simply to satisfy its own marketing needs, Sears has had to insist on standards of workmanship, quality, and delivery—that is, on standards of production management, of technical management, and above all of the management of people—which, in a few short years, have advanced the art and science of management in these countries by at least a generation.

I hardly need to add that Sears is not in Latin America for reasons of philanthropy, but because it is good and profitable business with extraordinary growth potential. In other words, Sears is in Latin America because marketing is the major opportunity in a "growth economy" —precisely because its absence is a major economic gap and the greatest need.

### The Discipline of Marketing

Finally, marketing is critical in economic development because marketing has become so largely systematized, so largely both learnable and teachable. It is the discipline among all our business disciplines that has advanced the furthest.

I do not forget for a moment how much we still have to learn in marketing. But we should also not forget that most of what we have learned so far we have learned in a form in which we can express it in general concepts, in valid principles and, to a substantial degree, in quantifiable measurements. This, above all others, was the achievement of that generation to whom Charles Coolidge Parlin was leader and inspiration.

A critical factor in this world of ours is the learnability and teachability of what it means to be an entrepreneur and manager. For it is the entrepreneur and the manager who alone can cause economic development to happen. The world needs them, therefore, in very large numbers; and it needs them fast.

Obviously this need cannot be supplied by our supplying entrepreneurs and managers, quite apart from the fact that we hardly have the surplus. Money we can supply. Technical assistance we can supply, and should supply more. But the supply of men we can offer to the people in the "under-developed" countries is of necessity a very small one.

The demand is also much too urgent for it to be supplied by slow evolution through experience, or through dependence on the emergence of "naturals." The danger that lies in the inequality today between the few countries that have and the great many countries that have not is much too great to permit a wait of centuries. Yet it takes centuries if we depend on experience and slow evolution for the supply of entrepreneurs and managers adequate to the needs of a modern society.

There is only one way in which man has ever been able to short-cut experience, to telescope development, in other words, to *learn something*. That way is to have available the distillate of experience and skill in the form of knowledge, of concepts, of generalization, of measurement—in the form of *discipline*, in other words.

### THE DISCIPLINE OF
### ENTREPRENEURSHIP

Many of us today are working on the fashioning of such a discipline of entrepreneurship and management. Maybe we are further along than most of us realize.

Certainly in what has come to be called "Operation Research and Synthesis" we have the first beginnings of a systematic approach to the entrepreneurial task of purposeful risk-taking and innovation—so far only an approach, but a most promising one, unless indeed we become so enamored with the gadgets and techniques as to forget purpose and aim.

We are at the beginning perhaps also of an understanding of the basic problems of organizing people of diversified and highly advanced skill and judgment together in one effective organization, although again no one so far would, I am convinced, claim more for us than that we have begun at last to ask intelligent questions.

But marketing, although it only covers one functional area in the field, has something that can be called a discipline. It has developed general concepts, that is, theories that explain a multitude of phenomena in simple statements. It even has measurements that record "facts" rather than opinions. In marketing, therefore, we already possess a learnable and teachable approach to this basic and central problem not only of the "under-developed" countries but of all countries. All of us have today the same survival stake in economic development. The risk and danger of international and interracial inequality are simply too great.

Marketing is obviously not a cure-all, not a paradox. It is only one thing we need. But it answers a critical need. At the same time marketing is most highly developed.

Indeed without marketing as the hinge on which to turn, economic development will almost have to take the totalitarian form. A totalitarian system can be defined economically as one in which economic development is being attempted without marketing, indeed as one in which marketing is suppressed. Precisely because it first looks at the values and wants of the individual, and because it then develops people to act purposefully and responsibly—that is, because of its effectiveness in developing a free economy—marketing is suppressed in a totalitarian system. If we want economic development in freedom and responsibility, we have to build it on the development of marketing.

In the new and unprecedented world we live in, a world which knows both a new unity of vision and growth and a new and most dangerous cleavage, marketing has a special and central role to play. This role goes beyond "getting the stuff out the back door," beyond "getting the most sales with the least cost," beyond "the optimal integration of our values and wants as customers, citizens, and persons, with our productive resources and intellectual achievements"—the role marketing plays in a developed society.

In a developing economy, marketing is, of course, all of this. But in addition, in an economy that is striving to break the age-old bondage of man to misery, want, and destitution, marketing is also the catalyst for the transmutation of latent resources into actual resources, of desires into accomplishments, and the development of responsible economic leaders and informed economic citizens.

# 55. Marketing Processes in Developing Latin American Societies

CHARLES C. SLATER

In many underdeveloped areas of the world the lower two-thirds of the income groups in most urban areas spend two-thirds or more of their income on food. As much as half of this expenditure provides assembly, processing (including the waste and loss in transit), and distribution services to bring food from the rural areas to the cities. Cities in Latin America are growing at explosive rates in many underdeveloped areas as a result of migration from rural areas as well as population expansion within the cities. Yet, while these cities expand, the marketing systems often remain ancient and apparently inefficient. Thus, it appears that the expenditure of one of the largest "chunks" of disposable income in the urban areas of underdeveloped areas of Latin America is to be found in the food marketing system and manufactured nonfood consumption goods marketing system serving large urban areas.

Scholars studying the role of marketing in development have underscored the need for interdisciplinary approaches.[1] To date, however, relatively few large-scale systematic studies of *marketing's role in development* have been conducted.[2] This paper offers a way of describing internal marketing processes based on research done in Puerto Rico; La Paz, Bolivia; and Recife, Brazil.[3]

The proposition considered was that "bar-riers" exist along the channels by which farm products reach consumers and, similarly, "bar-riers" inhibit market participants from increasing the supply of farm inputs and nonfood consumption goods to rural areas. Study of the marketing systems can identify ways in which selective reforms can enhance market participation and lead to increased production and increased real income throughout the developing countries. The paper attempts to relate the development problem to internal market processes, then develops the relation of "bar-riers" to improved market performance, and finally presents a program to induce internal market integration.

## INTERNAL NATIONAL MARKET PROCESSES

The development process often consists of increasing the income of a region by utilizing the surplus agricultural product to create specialized capital-intensive tools, primarily for use in the urban sector. Wyn Owen, for example, has asked:

How can peasants be encouraged to produce a cumulative surplus of food and fibers over and above their own consumption, and how can this surplus largely be channeled to investment activity in the nonfarm sector without requir-

◆ SOURCE: Reprinted by permission from *Journal of Marketing* (National Quarterly Publication of the American Marketing Association, Vol. 32, July 1968, pp. 50–55.
[1] Berthold F. Hoselitz and Wilbert E. Moore, editors, *Industrialization and Society* (Paris: UNESCO, 1963), p. 364.
[2] John R. Wish, *Economic Development in Latin America: An Annotated Bibliography* (New York: Praeger, 1965), particularly Chapter 3, pp. 33–60.
[3] The results of these studies conducted at the Latin American Market Planning Center are expected to be published later this year. Also see *Proceedings* of the American Marketing Association (Fall, 1965), pp. 30–37, for a preliminary report of this research.

ing in exchange an equivalent transfer of productive value to the farm sector?[4]

Professor Owen also pointed out that, broadly speaking, there have been two models of development, the "Marx-Leninist" model and the "Mill-Marshallian" model. The former is characterized by direct intervention of the state in production planning, in the imposition of a first claim upon the output, and finally, in the rationing of the surplus in order to foster selected urban development goals. The "Mill-Marshallian" model is characterized by a family farm operating unit in which a large part of the output is exchanged for direct satisfaction of the producer's wants, as opposed to subsistence. These two ideal types of development models are rarely found in the pure state. Some degree of regulation hampers competition; also, market farming exists in most socialist agricultural areas. Some areas have experimented first with one and then with the other of these models. Yugoslavia has shifted from the "Marx-Leninist" model back to the "Mill-Marshallian" model. As reported by Fleming and Sertic, a "profit oriented" Yugoslavian farm production system has enabled the nation to achieve a domestic saving rate of about 29% of the total social product.[5]

Owen concludes:

. . . in the developing countries the emphasis clearly should be placed, not on immediate equity between farm and non-farm incomes, but on the maximization of the growth rate in agriculture and the maximum immediate diversion of the resulting increments to the protection and support of the emerging nonfarm sector and of the generally differentiated and interdependent features of a more highly developed economy. That is, the identified Mill-Marshallian model has been described not primarily to show how agriculture tends to be an unduly exploited sector in economically advanced countries, but rather to identify a tested and relatively painless method whereby the inevitably "painful" or sacrificial process of domestic capital accumulation can be set in self-sustaining motion and progressively accelerated in a traditional agrarian economy. But, first must come the will and the wit to effect those structural reforms which are necessary in most underdeveloped countries to condition the application of this method of accumulation.[6]

Walt W. Rostow probably has had the most influence in crystallizing understanding of the problems of reforming the marketing institutional structures of developing economies. In his book *The View from the Seventh Floor*, Rostow summarized his notions on the national market development process. He suggests:

. . . that there are four major jobs that must be done, and they should be done simultaneously as part of a conscious national strategy, shared by the public and private authorities. The four elements are these: a build-up of agricultural productivity; a revolution in the marketing of agricultural products in the cities; a shift of industry to the production of simple agricultural equipment and consumers' goods for the mass market; and a revolution in marketing methods for such cheap manufactured goods, especially in rural areas.[7]

Rostow's thesis stresses that unless the dynamic process is brought into operation, the transference of resources can affect income distribution but has little growth result. Without careful attention to the exchange process, for example, little has been gained by some land reform projects, resettlement programs, and colonization programs.[8]

## THE CRITICAL SEQUENCE TO THE INTERNAL DEVELOPMENT PROCESS

For the past two and one-half years a series of studies of the role of marketing in the development of San Juan, Puerto Rico; Recife, Brazil; and La Paz, Bolivia as well as a series of other more limited surveys of market institutions in other Latin American areas have been conducted. Based upon these studies, a process of inducing internal market development can be described as follows:

### 1. Map Market Channels

The first step of this process requires a careful mapping of the essential flow of products

[4] W. F. Owen, "The Double Developmental Squeeze on Agriculture," *American Economic Review*, Vol. LVI (March, 1966), pp. 43–44.

[5] J. M. Fleming and V. R. Sertic, "The Yugoslavic Economic System," *International Monetary Fund Staff Papers* (July, 1962), pp. 202–223.

[6] Owen, op. cit., p. 67.

[7] W. W. Rostow, *View from the Seventh Floor* (New York: Harper and Row, 1964), p. 136.

[8] "Factors Associated with Differences and Changes in Agricultural Production in Underdeveloped Countries." Development and Trade Analysis Division, U. S. Department of Agriculture (January, 1965).

through channels for important domestically produced food products. This mapping is useful to describe the quantities, the grading, the processing, and handling contributions as well as costs and prices at each step in the assembly and distribution cycle. Then as the products are observed moving through the market channel, the channel operators are induced to reveal the critical risks they see as the limiting factors or "barriers" which inhibit their accepting responsibility for more products being brought through the market channel. Some observers have suggested that the key barriers are the future price expectations; others seemingly are uncertain as to the level of demand relative to supply in distant markets. In short, there appears to be a lack of information about some marketing conditions and lack of insurance against market uncertainties. These market defects tend to minimize the market exposure or risk the market channel operators are willing to tolerate, given the sometimes stringent limits of their capital resources.

Studies in Puerto Rico have revealed that the most favorable effects upon the output rates of commodities occur when the risks are reduced or spread back up the channel, starting at the retail level and working backward up the supply channel. When market risks are reduced, producers and distributors seemingly are more willing to expand their output.[9]

It is relatively important to be assured that the risks along the channel are not removed "down" the market channel first (for example, producer first, then distributor), for the production responses which might occur would run into the still-existing market blocks further along the channel. Once frustrated, the producers and assembly market operators would then be very reluctant to expand output a second time after market failure the first time. Morton Paglin observed:

Since the farmer with a relatively large holding can eke out a moderate income without the trouble of hiring a high per cent of nonfamily labor, or the risk of borrowing additional working capital for other inputs associated with intensive cultivation, he frequently seems to prefer the low-effort, low-risk, low-output package to the higher-risk, higher-priced, higher-output combination.[10]

Mellor has described this preference for a minimum risk production option as a "low aspiration" pattern of behavior.[11]

## 2. Institute Selected Market Reforms

The second step in the process of inducing internal national market development is to inaugurate selected market reforms that will begin to provide assurances of market demand for products starting with retailer and going back up to the producer. When market reforms have spread or reduced risks, then added capital and options to utilize technology that will yield greater output may be more welcomed by innovators.

Again, it seems important at this stage to recognize innovators and to focus energies upon these more likely candidates for production and market channel expansion. In efforts to understand the differences in willingness to accept market risks, concepts of the diffusion of innovation developed by Everett Rogers and others can be useful.[12] The critical finding from these efforts to understand the diffusion of innovation is that there seem to be explainable and important differences in the rate of adoption of marketing innovations by retailers as well as others back up the commodity channel.[13]

## 3. Expand Market Capacity to Match Expanded Flow

The third event or step in the process is to adjust to the increased output that will likely enter the market channels if efforts to minimize perceived market risks have been successful. Thus, a second generation of market channel reforms may involve credit expansion and

[9] Kelly Max Harrison, "Agricultural Market Coordination in the Economic Development of Puerto Rico" (Unpublished Ph.D. dissertation, Department of Agricultural Economics, Michigan State University, 1966), p. 112ff.

[10] Morton Paglin, " 'Surplus' Agricultural Labor and Development: Facts and Figures," *American Economic Review,* Vol. LV (September, 1965), pp. 815–834.

[11] John W. Mellor, "The Use and Productivity of

Farm Family Labor in Early Stages of Agricultural Development," *Journal of Farm Economics,* Vol. 45 (August, 1963), pp. 517–534.

[12] Everett M. Rogers, *Diffusion of Innovations* (New York: Free Press of Glencoe, 1962).

[13] John R. Wish, "Food Retailing in Economic Development: Puerto Rico 1950–1965" (Unpublished Ph.D. dissertation, Department of Marketing and Transportation Administration, Michigan State University, 1967), pp. 144–188.

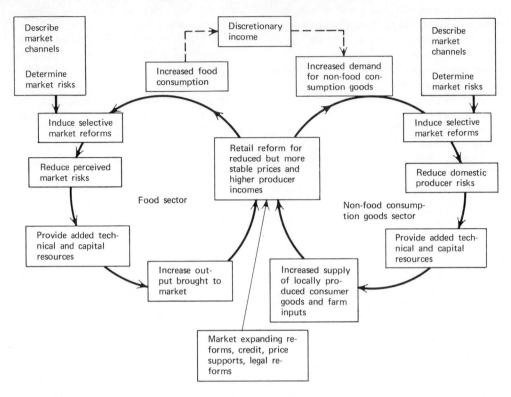

FIG. 1. Inducing internal national market development.

price supports to accommodate the almost certain stresses that will be put on the existing marketing system. Often storage and handling facilities have to be expanded to match the higher output—or at least indemnification provided until storage and handling facilities are expanded.

Often, legal reforms are needed as production expands. For example, a turnover tax on value added is applied in Brazil. In the state of Sao Paulo marketing cooperatives are usually taxed the full 15%, while small independent merchants sometimes sell cooperative members' output without paying full taxes. Thus, because of collection differences, a tax scheme is penalizing cooperative marketing programs which are supported by other government programs.

The impact upon producers of the higher output at lower prices is usually to increase their higher gross, and often higher net, incomes. The lower prices have to be understood

as necessary for the expansion of effective demand. The marketing of milk by producers in Puerto Rico is a case where output expanded at lower but more stable prices than producers had reasonably achieved prior to the installation of effective milk marketing programs.[14]

### 4. Retailing Reforms to Create Multi-Product Outlets with High Turnover-Low Margin Operations

A critical step in the process of reform of agriculture and food channels must take place at the retail level. Most developing societies are characterized by a multitude of small specialty merchants in public markets, who often sell small amounts daily at low margin, but do little to encourage suppliers by offering to buy large quantities of products of uniform quality at stable prices.

What appears to be needed are a few large multi-product merchants selling "lead" items at

[14] For a discussion of this problem of producer response to changes in price levels see Kelly M. Harrison, "Vertical Coordinations and Selected Product Markets 1950–1965," Robert Nason, editor,

*The Role of Food Marketing in Economic Development of Puerto Rico: A Seminar Summary* (East Lansing: Latin American Studies Center, 1966), pp. 55–66.

low margins to gain traffic and then gain profits from selling other, less frequently bought items at higher prices. Such large-scale retail operations need not cater only to the upper-income families. There are a few cases where such retail operations are affecting the marketing efficiency of communities.[15]

### 5. Expansion in Demand Due to Lowered Prices and Greater Discretionary Income

Finally, if the process has been organized appropriately, the increased consumption of food in the urban area yields higher levels of nutrition and productive energies. Of equal importance are the income elasticity effects. Robert D. Stevens found that in India the income elasticity for food was approximately 0.7.[16] Thus, while a larger stock of food at lower prices would induce increased consumption of food, it would also increase the discretionary income with the concomitant increases in demand for nonfood items. Therefore, a parallel analysis and planning task is needed to foster expansion of nonfood production and consumption based on a reduction in the perceived market risks faced by marketers of the locally-processed nonfood consumer goods and farm inputs.

The cycle of events can be illustrated schematically. (See Figure 1.) The task is one of identifying the appropriate sequence of risk reductions or "barrier" removals that will induce expansion of output. Price elasticity of demand will result in income gains for the producing sector, while income elasticity will result in increased discretionary income to foster growth in the nonfood sectors of the economy. This description is, of course, an oversimplification of the process. Quite likely, there are several discontinuities and, in some situations, disfunctional features apparent in the kind of change outlined above. This description of market processes seems useful in understanding communities as varied as San Juan, Recife, and La Paz. The barriers to growth in income are, however, different in each of these communities, though the techniques of identifying them are similar. Three broad problem areas may be encountered.

First, the lags in the diffusion of innovation can seriously reduce the effective response to the risk reductions fostered by the changes in the marketing system.[17] Consumers and distributors, as well as producers, have to adapt to changes in the marketing reforms.

Second, the transfer of resources as a result of changes in marketing institutions is neither automatic nor necessarily trouble-free. Of great importance is the fact that the food marketing systems of underdeveloped areas are usually very labor-intensive, and most reforms reduce the proportion of labor needed to carry forward the marketing tasks. Usually, the market people have few alternative occupational opportunities, and they are a vocal, urban group. Thus, marketing reforms may not automatically receive a welcome from those now responsible for the traditional marketing system. It is, therefore, important to know: (1) the extent of increased consumption due to income effects; (2) the amount of discretionary income diverted to nonfood consumption expenditures as a result of the lower-priced but more plentiful foods; and (3) the extent and timing of displacement and unemployment caused by the marketing institutional reforms. Some of these market reforms can be expected to displace labor, even though gross product changes may more than offset the unemployment. Therefore, coordinated labor-absorbing activities may be needed as reforms are implemented.

A third problem is that the cycle of effects outlined above requires the government to have some way to compare the costs and benefits that such a development approach would entail. Without such a basis for evaluation, competing priorities for development could break the cycle outlined above. For example, the short-term balance of payments problem could very well induce high short-term priorities to be placed upon export crops such as sugar in the Northeast of Brazil. Against this shift in resources must be weighed the import substitution effects of greater domestic production of farm and nonfarm products that the efforts to expand internal national markets

---

[15] Same reference as footnote 13.

[16] Robert D. Stevens, *The Elasticity of Food Consumption Associated With Changes in Income in Developing Countries,* Foreign Agricultural Economic Report No. 23, Economics Research Service (Washington: U. S. Department of Agriculture, 1965).

[17] R. Vincent Farace, "A Tentative Conceptual and Research Framework for the Analysis of the Economic Exchange in Developing Countries," paper presented to the International Communication Division, Association for Education in Journalism (Iowa: August 30, 1966).

Tasks

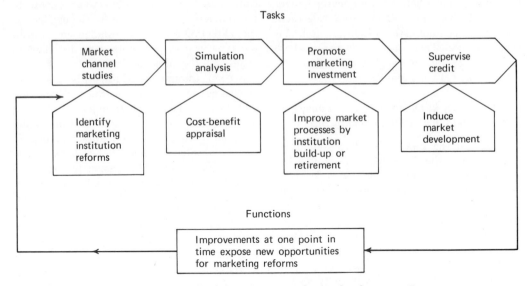

FIG. 2. Organization for continuing marketing development effort.

would induce. Similarly, import tax structures may be such that needed equipment for fostering more stable domestic production is denied entry on otherwise economically sound terms.

## CONCLUSIONS AND PROBLEMS OF APPLICATION

The development efforts of the past have overstressed the production problems of development at the expense of solving the various exchange problems. This appears to be correcting itself to some extent. There also appear to be the beginnings of a theory of national market development, which is generally consistent with the observations of economists—such as Owen, Paglin, and Rostow—who point out the need for new social and quantitative research skills to deal with exchange institution reforms. The interdisciplinary team approach is making some limited headway in making the theory operational. Finally, there is a growing recognition that a systems approach, utilizing computers to assist in simulating complex processes, may be needed to appraise costs and benefits of alternative developmental strategies.

The question of how to proceed becomes important, for there is as yet no sustaining tradition to implement national marketing development. Internal national market processes seemingly need to be institutionalized. The

critical problem is how to utilize government resources to foster the appropriate private sector growth. Here a page from the experience of Puerto Rico might be helpful. A series of development agencies "fomented" change. Observations "ex post" suggest a pattern which could be installed as a continuing task-oriented program. A four step program is shown in Figure 2.

The four steps can be described as follows:

1. Identify market development needs or opportunities by sustained research into marketing channels and the risks and bottlenecks seen by operators.

2. The costs and benefits attributable to the new (or continued) marketing institutional reforms can be evaluated—possibly using a simulation model as part of the decision processes of government and financial development officers.

3. For those projects that appear to have immediate merit, seek out and promote the participation of potentially interested investors and entrepreneurs. Here a different set of skills is needed because personnel evaluation and promotional efforts are not usually part of the marketing researchers' skills.

4. Finally, if the program is launched, supervised credit can be an important tool to foster the development goals and insure that operators (at least those who are in debt to the development agency) follow the desired rules

of business operation. It is useful to bear in mind that some marketing institutions will need to be "retired"—and the use of development funds to "retire" inefficient institutions may be cheaper and faster than political techniques.

Internal market processes, described as outlined in this paper, permit development planners to identify specific reforms to foster market integration. Further, this approach allows planners to foster private sector development.

# Marketing in Perspective and Challenging Issues

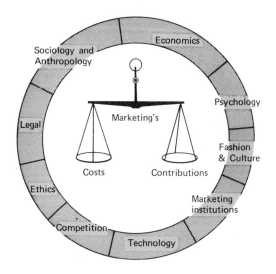

The sober task of evaluating the marketing function and issues of much concern are brought forth by the readings in this section. More in recent years than at any other time, academicians, students, and segments of the public at large have raised questions about our business system and specific matters on which there is diversity of viewpoint. Whether business can assume a dominant social role and still retain its essential economic function is a difficult matter. This basic issue has occupied the concern of marketing people as they consider the public interest versus the corporate (or industry) interest. The first four readings of this section represent a view of the issues that may continue to be with us for years to come.

The last three readings by eminent marketing scholars appraise the role of marketing today. Actually, to some degree consumers the world over appraise the marketing effort as they express satisfaction or dissatisfaction with the various aspects of the marketing effort. The marketing effort, as influenced by environmental forces, is immense and ever-changing; complete satisfaction with the effort is probably beyond the realm of possibility. Nevertheless, by constantly appraising contributions and costs of marketing, ways will doubtlessly be found to improve the total effort. Certainly, it is to this end that much of marketing education is devoted.

# 56. Is Advertising Wasteful?

## JULES BACKMAN

With some exceptions, economists generally have criticized advertising as economically wasteful. All the criticisms are not so extreme as one widely used economics text which states:

Overall, it is difficult for anyone to gain more than temporarily from large advertising outlays in an economy in which counteradvertising is general. The overall effect of advertising, on which we spent $14 billion [actually $15 billion—JB] in 1965, is to devote these productive resources (men, ink, billboards, and so forth) to producing advertising rather than to producing other goods and services.[1]

Most critics do not go this far in condemning advertising. However, they do emphasize that advertising may be wasteful in several ways: by adding unnecessarily to costs, by an inefficient use of resources, by promoting excessive competition, and by causing consumers to buy items they do not need. This article brings together the scattered criticisms of advertising and answers to them and thus presents an overview of the debate in this area. The nature of these criticisms and the significance of waste in a competitive economy are first reviewed. Attention is then given to the vital informational role played by advertising,

particularly in an expanding economy. Advertising is only one alternative in the marketing mix, and—hence its contribution must be considered among alternatives rather than in absolute terms.

## VARIATIONS ON A THEME

The criticism that advertising involves economic waste takes several forms.

### Competition in Advertising

The attack usually is centered on competition in advertising which some critics state flatly is wasteful.[2] Others have been concerned about the relative cost of advertising as a percentage of sales. Sometimes an arbitrary percentage, such as 5%, is selected as the dividing line between "high" and more "reasonable" levels of expenditure.[3]

Such cutoff points are meaningless, since the proper relative expenditures for advertising are a function of the product's characteristics. It is not an accident that relative advertising costs are highest for low-priced items which are available from many retail outlets and subject to frequent repeat purchases (for example, cosmetics, soaps, soft drinks, gum and candies, drugs, cigarettes, beer, etc.).

♦ SOURCE: Reprinted by permission from *Journal of Marketing* (National Quarterly Publication of the American Marketing Association), Vol. 32, January 1968, pp. 2–8.

[1] George Leland Bach, *Economics*, Fifth Edition (Englewood Cliffs, New Jersey: Prentice-Hall, Inc., 1966), p. 437. See also Kenneth Boulding, "Economic Analysis," Volume 1, *Microeconomics*, Fourth Edition, Vol. 1 (New York: Harper and Row, 1966), p. 513.

[2] Nicholas H. Kaldor, "The Economic Aspects of Advertising," *The Review of Economic Studies*, Vol. 18 (1950–51), p. 6.

[3] Joe S. Bain, *Industrial Organization* (New York: John Wiley & Sons, 1959), pp. 390–91. See also *Report of a Commission of Enquiry Into Advertising* (London, England: The Labour Party, 1966), p. 42. The Reith Report defined "substantially advertised products" at 5% or more.

Particularly criticized are emotional appeals, persuasion, and "tug of war" advertising where it is claimed the main effect is to shift sales among firms rather than to increase total volume of the industry. For example, Richard Caves states: "At the point where advertising departs from its function of informing and seeks to persuade or deceive us, it tends to become a waste of resources."[4]

In a competitive economy competitors must seek to persuade customers to buy their wares. We do not live in a world where a company stocks its warehouse and waits until customers beat a path to its doors to buy its products. If this is all that a business firm did, we would have economic waste in terms of products produced but not bought as well as in the failure to produce many items for which a market can be created. In the latter case, the waste would take the form of idle labor and unused resources.

### Inefficient Use of Resources

Economists have criticized advertising most vigorously as involving an inefficient use of resources. This criticism has been directed particularly against advertising where the main effect allegedly is a "shuffling of existing total demand" among the companies in an industry. Under these conditions, it is stated, advertising merely adds to total costs and in time results in higher prices. There undoubtedly is a shifting of demand among firms due to many factors including advertising. But this is what we should expect in a competitive economy. Moreover, there are many products for which total demand is increased (for example, television sets, radio sets, cars, toilet articles) for multiple use in the same home. In the sharply expanding economy of the past quarter of a century there are relatively few industries in which total demand has remained unchanged.

It must also be kept in mind that the resources devoted to competitive advertising usually are considered to be wasteful "in a full-employment economy" because they may be utilized more efficiently in other ways. Thus, the extent of "waste" involved also appears to depend upon whether the economy is operating below capacity. This point is considered in a later section.

### Adds to Costs

Sometimes, it is stated that if advertising succeeds in expanding total demand for a product, the result is a shift of demand from other products, the producers of which will be forced to advertise to attempt to recover their position. The net result of such "counter-advertising" is to add to costs and to prices.

But all increases in demand do not necessarily represent a diversion from other products. Thus, an expanded demand for new products is accompanied by an increase in income and in purchasing power flowing from their production. Moreover, during a period of expanding economic activity, as is noted later, the successful advertising may affect the rate of increase for different products rather than result in an absolute diversion of volume.

### Creates Undesirable Wants

Another variation is the claim that advertising is wasteful because it ". . . creates useless or undesirable wants at the expense of things for which there is greater social need. When advertising makes consumers want and buy automobiles with tail fins, tobacco, and movie-star swimming pools, there is less money (fewer resources) available to improve public hospitals, build better schools, or combat juvenile delinquency."[5] It is claimed that many of these types of products are useless and anti-social. Criticism of advertising is nothing new. In the late 1920's Stuart Chase claimed: "Advertising creates no new dollars. In fact, by removing workers from productive employment, it tends to depress output, and thus lessen the number of real dollars."[6]

These are value judgments reached by the critics on the basis of subjective "standards" which they set up. "What is one man's meat is another man's poison," as the old saying goes. The real question is who is to decide what is good for the consumer and what should he purchase?

In a free economy, there is a wide diversity

---

[4] Richard Caves, *American Industry: Structure, Conduct, Performance* (Englewood Cliffs, New Jersey: Prentice-Hall, Inc., 1964), p. 102.

[5] "Advertising and Charlie Brown," *Business Review,* Federal Reserve Bank of Philadelphia (June, 1962), p. 10.

[6] Stuart Chase, *The Tragedy of Waste* (New York: Macmillan Company, 1928), p. 112.

of opinion as to what combinations of goods and services should be made available and be consumed. Obviously, tastes vary widely and most persons do not want to be told what is best for them. In any cross section of the population of the country there will be a wide disagreement as to what constitutes the ideal components of a desirable level of living. Each one of us must decide what purchases will yield the greatest satisfactions. We may be misled on occasion by popular fads, advertising or even advice of our friends. But these decisions in the final analysis are made by the buyers and not by the advertisers, as the latter have found out so often to their regret.

## COMPETITION AND "WASTE"

The critics of advertising are really attacking the competitive process. Competition involves considerable duplication and "waste." The illustrations range from the several gasoline stations at an important intersection to the multiplication of research facilities, the excess industrial capacity which develops during periods of expansion, and the accumulations of excessive inventories.

There is widespread recognition that inefficiencies may develop in advertising as in other phases of business.[7] Mistakes are made in determining how much should be spent for advertising—but these mistakes can result in spending too little as well as too much.

We cannot judge the efficiency of our competitive society—including the various instrumentalities, such as advertising—by looking at the negative aspects alone. It is true that competition involves waste. But it also yields a flood of new products, improved quality, better service, and pressures on prices. In the United States, it has facilitated enormous economic growth with the accompanying high standards of living. The advantages of competition have been so overwhelmingly greater than the wastes inherent in it that we have established as one of our prime national goals, through the antitrust laws, the continuance of a viable competitive economy.

### Informational Role of Advertising

Advertising plays a major informational role in our economy because (1) products are available in such wide varieties, (2) new products are offered in such great numbers, and (3) existing products must be called to the attention of new consumers who are added to the market as a result of expansion in incomes, the population explosion, and changes in tastes.

The most heavily advertised products are widely used items that are consumed by major segments of the population. This does not mean that everyone buys every product or buys them to the extent that he can. Some of these products are substitutes for other products. For example, it will be readily recognized that cereals provide only one of many alternatives among breakfast foods. In some instances, heavily advertised products compete with each other like, for example, soft drinks and beer. In other instances, additional consumers can use the products so that the size of the total market can be increased (for example, toilet preparations).

Potential markets also expand as incomes rise and as consumers are able to purchase products they previously could not afford. As the population increases, large numbers of new potential customers are added each year. Continuous large-scale advertising provides reminders to old customers and provides information to obtain some part of the patronage of new customers. The potential market is so huge that large scale advertising is an economical way to obtain good results.

In addition, the identity of buyers changes under some circumstances and new potential buyers must be given information concerning the available alternatives. It has also been pointed out that some of these products are ". . . subject to fads and style changes" and that ". . . consumers become restive with existing brands and are prepared to try new varieties." Illustrations include cereals, soaps, clothing, and motion pictures.[8]

The consumer has a wide variety of brands from which to choose. Product improvements usually breed competitive product improve-

---

[7] Committee on Advertising, *Principles of Advertising* (New York: Pitman Publishing Corp., 1963), p. 34; and Neil H. Borden, "The Role of Advertising in the Various Stages of Corporate and Economic Growth," Peter D. Bennett, editor, *Marketing and Economic Development* (Chicago, Illinois: American Marketing Association, 1965), p. 493.

[8] Lester G. Telser, "How Much Does It Pay Whom To Advertise?", *American Economic Review, Papers and Proceedings* (December, 1960), pp. 203–4.

ments; the advertising of these improvements may result in an increase in total advertising for the class of products.

When any company in an industry embarks on an intensified advertising campaign, its competitors must step up their advertising or other sales efforts to avoid the possible loss of market position. This is a key characteristic of competition.

On the other hand, if any company decides to economize on its advertising budget, its exposure is reduced and its share of market may decline if its competitors fail to follow the same policy. Thus, for some grocery products it has been reported that ". . . competition within a sector may have established a certain pattern with regard to the extent of advertising, and any company dropping below this level faces possible substantial loss of market share.[9]

These results flow particularly if the industry is oligopolistic, that is, has relatively few producers who are sensitive to and responsive to actions of competitors. However, as the dramatic changes in market shares during the past decade so amply demonstrate, this does not mean that the companies in such oligopolistic industries will retain relatively constant shares of the market.[10]

The informational role of advertising has been succinctly summarized by Professor George J. Stigler:

. . . Under competition, the main tasks of a seller are to inform potential buyers of his existence, his line of goods, and his prices. Since both sellers and buyers change over time (due to birth, death, migration), since people forget information once acquired, and since new products appear, the existence of sellers must be continually advertised. . .

"This informational function of advertising must be emphasized because of a popular and erroneous belief that advertising consists chiefly of nonrational (emotional and repetitive) appeals.[11]

Elsewhere, Professor Stigler has pointed out that ". . . information is a valuable resource," that advertising is "the obvious method of identifying buyers and sellers" which "reduces drastically the cost of search," and that "It is clearly an immensely powerful instrument for the elimination of ignorance. . ." [12]

Often this information is required to create interest in and demand for a product. Thus, it has been reported:

. . . to a significant degree General Foods and the U.S. foodmarket created each other. Before a new product appears, customers are rarely conscious of wanting it. There was no spontaneous demand for ready-to-eat cereals; frozen foods required a sustained marketing effort stretching over many years; instant coffee had been around for decades, supplying a market that did not amount to a tenth of its present level. General Foods' corporate skill consists largely in knowing enough about American tastes to foresee what products will be accepted.[13]

Similarly, J. K. Galbraith, who has been very critical of advertising, has recognized that:

A new consumer product must be introduced with a suitable advertising campaign to arouse an interest in it. The path for an expansion of output must be paved by a suitable expansion in the advertising budget. Outlays for the manufacturing of a product are not more important in the strategy of modern business enterprise than outlays for the manufacturing of demand for the product.[14]

We live in an economy that has little resemblance to the ideal of perfect competition postulated by economists. However, one of the postulates of this ideal economy is perfect knowledge. Advertising contributes to such knowledge. Thus, in such an idealized economy, even though advertising may be wasteful it would still have a role to play. But in the world of reality, with all its imperfections, ad-

---

[9] National Commission on Food Marketing, *Grocery Manufacturing*, Technical Study No. 6 (Washington, D.C.: June, 1966), p. 14.

[10] Jules Backman, *Advertising and Competition* (New York: New York University Press, 1967), Chapters 3 and 4.

[11] George J. Stigler, *The Theory of Price*, Third Edition (New York: The Macmillan Company, 1966), p. 200.

[12] George J. Stigler, "The Economics of Information," *The Journal of Political Economy* (June,

1961), pp. 213, 216, 220. See also S. A. Ozga, "Imperfect Markets Through Lack of Knowledge," *Quarterly Journal of Economics* (February, 1960), pp. 29, 33–34, and Wroe Alderson, *Dynamic Market Behavior* (Homewood, Illinois: Richard D. Irwin, Inc., 1965), pp. 128–31.

[13] "General Foods Is Five Billion Particulars," *Fortune* (March, 1964), p. 117.

[14] J. K. Galbraith, *The Affluent Society* (Boston, Massachusetts: Houghton Mifflin Company, 1958), p. 156.

vertising is much more important. Advertising is an integral and vital part of our growing economy and contributes to the launching of the new products so essential to economic growth.

### How Much Is Informational?

In 1966, total expenditures for media advertising aggregated $13.3 billion.[15] It is impossible to determine exactly how much of this amount was strictly informational. However, the following facts are of interest.

Classified advertising was $1.3 billion

Other local newspaper advertising, largely retail, was $2.6 billion

Business paper advertising was $712 million

Local radio and TV advertising was $1.1 billion

Spot radio and spot TV advertising was $1.2 billion

National advertising on network TV, network radio, magazines and newspapers was $3.7 billion

Direct mail was $2.5 billion

Classified advertising and local advertising are overwhelmingly informational in nature. Certainly some part of national advertising also performs this function. These figures suggest that substantially less than half of total advertising is of the type that the critics are attacking as wasteful;[16] the exact amount cannot be pinpointed. Moreover, it must be kept in mind that a significant part of national advertising is for the promotion of new products for which the informational role is vital.

From another point of view, even if there is waste, the social cost is considerably less than suggested by these data. Thus, in 1966 about $10 billion was spent on advertising in newspapers, magazines, radio, and television; another $746 million was spent on farm and business publications. Without these expenditures, these sources of news and entertainment would have had to obtain substantial sums from other sources. It has been estimated that

". . . advertising paid for over 60% of the cost of periodicals, for over 70% of the cost of newspapers, and for 100% of the cost of commercial radio and TV broadcasting."[17] Thus, advertising results in a form of subsidization for all media of communication. Without it, these media would have to charge higher subscription rates or be subsidized by the government or some combination of both.

## ADVERTISING AND EXPANDING MARKETS

Economic growth has become a major objective of national economic policy in recent years. Rising productivity, increasing population, improving education, rates of saving, and decisions concerning new investments are the ingredients of economic growth. In addition, there must be a favorable political climate including tax policies and monetary policies designed to release the forces conducive to growth.

Advertising contributes to economic growth and in turn levels of living by complementing the efforts to create new and improved products through expenditures for research and development. One observer has described the process as follows:

. . . advertising, by acquainting the consumer with the values of new products, widens the market for these products, pushes forward their acceptance by the consumer, and encourages the investment and entrepreneurship necessary for innovation. Advertising, in short, holds out the promise of a greater and speedier return than would occur without such methods, thus stimulating investment, growth and diversity.[18]

Among the most intensive advertisers have been toilet preparations (14.7% of sales), cleaning and polishing preparations (12.6%), and drugs (9.4%). The markets for these products have been expanding at a faster rate than all consumer spending.

Between 1947 and 1966, personal consump-

[15] This total excludes a miscellaneous category of $3.3 billion.

[16] For the United Kingdom, the "disputed proportion" of advertising expenditures has been estimated at about 30% of the total. Walter Taplin, *Advertising, A New Approach* (Boston, Massachusetts: Little, Brown & Co., 1963), p. 126.

[17] Fritz Machlup, *The Production and Distribution*

*of Knowledge in the United States* (Princeton, New Jersey: Princeton University Press, 1962), p. 265.

[18] David M. Blank, "Some Comments on the Role of Advertising in the American Economy—A Plea for Revaluation," L. George Smith, editor, *Reflections on Progress in Marketing* (Chicago, Illinois: American Marketing Association, 1964), p. 151.

tion expenditures for these products increased as follows:[19]

|                                          | 1947  | 1955  | 1966  |
|------------------------------------------|-------|-------|-------|
|                                          | (millions of dollars) | | |
| Toilet articles and preparations         | 1,217 | 1,915 | 4,690 |
| Cleaning, polishing and household supplies | 1,523 | 2,480 | 4,487 |
| Drug preparations and sundries           | 1,313 | 2,362 | 5,062 |

As a share of total personal consumption expenditures, the increases from 1947 to 1966 were as follows:

Toilet articles and preparations
from 0.76% to 1.01%
Cleaning, polishing and household
supplies from 0.94% to 0.97%
Drug preparations and sundries
from 0.82% to 1.09%

These increases in relative importance are based upon dollar totals. However, the retail prices of these products rose less than the consumer price index during the postwar years.

Between 1947 and 1966, the price increases were as follows:

| Total consumer price index | 45.4% |
|----------------------------|-------|
| Toilet preparations        | 14.6  |
| Soaps and detergents       | 2.6   |
| Drugs and prescriptions    | 22.8  |

Thus, the increase in relative importance of these highly advertised products has been even greater in real terms than in dollars.

Between 1947 and 1966, the increase in *real* personal consumption expenditures has been:

Toilet articles and preparations
from 0.68% to 1.12%
Cleaning, polishing and household
supplies from 0.87% to 1.05%
Drug preparations and sundries
from 0.82% to 1.24%

Clearly, advertising appears to have contributed to an expansion in the demand for these products and to the growth of our economy with the accompanying expansion in job opportunities and in economic well-being.

There may have been some waste in this process—although all of such expenditures cannot be characterized as wasteful—but it appears to have been offset in full or in part by these other benefits.

The charge of large-scale waste in advertising appears to reflect in part a yearning for an economy with standardized, homogenous products which are primarily functional in nature. An illustration would be a refrigerator that is designed solely to be technically efficient for the storage of food. However, customers are also interested in the decor of their kitchens, in convenience and speed in the manufacture of ice cubes, in shelves that rotate, and in special storage for butter. These are additions to functional usefulness which "an affluent society" can afford but which a subsistence economy cannot.

### Advertising in a High Level Economy

The concept of waste must be related to the level achieved by an economy. Professor John W. Lowe has observed that "Perhaps a good deal of the 'wastefulness' assigned to advertising springs from the fact that a large part of the world's population cannot consider satisfying *psychological wants* when most of their efforts must be devoted to *needs*."[20] (Italics added.)

In a subsistence economy, scarcity is so significant that advertising might be wasteful, particularly where it diverts resources from meeting the basic necessities of life. Such an economy usually is a "full employment economy" in the sense that everyone is working. But the total yield of a full employment subsistence economy is very low, as is evident throughout Asia, Africa, and South America.

Professor Galbraith has noted that "The opportunity for product differentiation . . . is almost uniquely the result of opulence . . . the tendency for commercial rivalries . . . to be channeled into advertising and salesmanship would disappear in a poor community."[21]

In the high level American economy, there usually are surpluses rather than scarcity. The use of resources for advertising to differentiate products, therefore, is not necessarily a diver-

[19] *The National Income and Product Accounts of the United States, 1929–1965, Statistical Tables* (Washington, D.C.: United States Department of Commerce, August, 1966), pp. 44–49; and *Survey of Current Business* (July, 1967), pp. 23–24.

[20] John W. Lowe, "An Economist Defends Adver-

tising," *Journal of Marketing*, Vol. 27 (July, 1963), p. 18.

[21] John K. Galbraith, *American Capitalism: The Concept of Countervailing Power* (Boston, Massachusetts: Houghton Mifflin Company, 1952), pp. 106–07.

sion from other uses. Rather, it frequently represents the use of resources that might otherwise be idle both in the short run and the long run and thus may obviate the waste that such idleness represents.

### The Marketing Mix

The concept of waste cannot ignore the question—waste as compared with what alternative? Advertising cannot be considered in a vacuum. It must be considered as one of the marketing alternatives available. Generally it is not a question of advertising or nothing, but rather of advertising or some other type of sales effort.

It is a mistake to evaluate the relative cost of advertising apart from other marketing costs. It is only one tool in the marketing arsenal which also includes direct selling, packaging, servicing, product planning, pricing, etc. Expenditures for advertising often are substituted for other types of selling effort. This substitution has been readily apparent in the history of the discount house. These houses have featured well-advertised brands which were presold and, hence, virtually eliminated the need for floor stocks and reduced the need for space and many salesmen.

Advertising is undertaken where it is the most effective and most economical way to appeal to customers. It is a relatively low cost method of communicating with all potential customers and this explains its widespread adoption by many companies. To the extent that less efficient marketing methods must be substituted for advertising, we would really have economic waste.

## SUMMARY AND CONCLUSIONS

There is wide agreement that the informational role of advertising makes a significant contribution to the effective operation of our economy. There is also agreement that inefficiency in the use of advertising is wasteful, as are other types of inefficiencies that are part and parcel of a market-determined economy. The gray area is so-called competitive advertising, largely national, which is the main target of those who insist advertising is wasteful. Although precise data are not available, the estimates cited earlier indicate that the charge of competitive waste applies to substantially less than half of all advertising expenditures.

Competition unavoidably involves considera-ble duplication and waste. If the accent is placed on the negative, a distorted picture is obtained. On balance, the advantages of competition have been much greater than the wastes.

Advertising has contributed to an expanding market for new and better products. Many of these new products would not have been brought to market unless firms were free to develop mass markets through large-scale advertising. There may be some waste in this process, but it has been more than offset by other benefits.

Where burgeoning advertising expenditures are accompanied by expanding industry sales, there will tend to be a decline in total unit costs instead of increase, and prices may remain unchanged or decline. In such situations, it seems clear that advertising, while adding to total costs, will result in lower total *unit* costs, the more significant figure. This gain will be offset to some extent if the increase in volume represents a diversion from other companies or industries with an accompanying rise in unit costs. Of course, such change is inherent in a dynamic competitive economy.

Advertising expenditures have risen as the economy has expanded. At such times, the absolute increase in sales resulting from higher advertising expenditures need not be accompanied by a loss in sales in other industries. This is particularly true if a new product has been developed and its sales are expanding. In that event, new jobs probably will be created and help to support a higher level of economic activity generally.

The claim that resources devoted to advertising would be utilized more efficiently for other purposes ignores the fact that generally we have a surplus economy. All of the resources used for advertising are not diverted from other alternatives. Rather, it is probable that much of the resources involved would be idle or would be used less efficiently. Even more important would be the failure to provide the jobs which expanding markets create.

Finally, advertising does not take place in a vacuum. It is one of several marketing alternatives. The abandonment of advertising could not represent a net saving to a company or to the economy. Instead, such a development would require a shift to alternative marketing techniques, some of which would be less efficient than advertising since companies do not deliberately adopt the least effective marketing approach. On balance, advertising is an invaluable competitive tool.

# 57. Cigarette Smoking and the Public Interest: Opportunity for Business Leadership

HARPER W. BOYD, JR., and SIDNEY J. LEVY

What constitutes the responsibility of a business organization to the society of which it is a part? This question is not easily answered. Certainly, large corporations' conceptions of their duties and obligations have been modified to some degree in the transition from "robber baron" days to the present era of wider public stock ownership. Obvious reflections of this modification are increased dependence on buyers' goodwill and the growth of government regulation. In many cases, the increase of government control has been invited by business' refusal to show the kind of leadership that would make federal intervention unnecessary. A striking example is afforded by the current situation regarding cigarettes.

## THE DANGERS OF SMOKING

The habit of using tobacco in one form or another has been around for some 400 years. There have always been taboos against smoking, some of them based on assumptions regarding tobacco usage and health. In the opinion of many doctors these assumptions have recently become facts. Studies conducted over the past ten years or so leave little doubt in the minds of a substantial number of scientists and doctors that cigarette smokers have a higher death rate than nonsmokers. What makes this so frightening is that smoking is quite widespread. The U.S. Public Health Service estimates that 78 per cent of American

◆ SOURCE: Reprinted by permission from *Business Horizons*, Vol. 6, No. 3, Fall 1963, pp. 37–44.

men have a history of tobacco use and that, while the percentage of men smokers has in recent years been relatively stable, the percentage of women smokers has shown a steady increase.

The American public has been continuously exposed to these findings and to the warnings of leading medical researchers on the subject of smoking and health. In 1959, Dr. Leroy E. Burney, Surgeon General of the U.S. Public Health Service, stated in the *Journal of the American Medical Association* that "The weight of evidence at present implicates smoking as the principal . . . factor in the increased incidence of lung cancer."

E. H. Hammond, a well-known medical researcher, goes further in concluding that ". . . after reviewing the evidence, the mildest statement I can make is that, in my opinion, the inhalation of tobacco smoke produces a number of very harmful effects and shortens the life span of human beings." In a 1962 report entitled *Smoking and Health*, the Royal College of Physicians of London concluded that cigarette smoking is an important cause of lung cancer and that if the habit ceased, the number of deaths from the disease would decline significantly. The report goes on to say, "The chance of dying in the next 10 years for a man aged 35 who is a heavy cigarette smoker is 1 in 23 whereas the risk for a non-smoker is only 1 in 90. Only 15 per cent (one in six) of men of this age who are non-smokers but 33 per cent (one in three) of heavy smokers will die before the age of 65."

A study conducted by Hammond and Daniel

Horn of 187,783 men between the ages of 50 and 69 led to the conclusion that the total death rate from all causes was 1.57 times higher among men with a history of regular cigarette smoking and that death rates rose progressively as the numbers of cigarettes consumed daily increased. The relative death rate for lung cancer among regular cigarette smokers was 10.73 times greater than for non-smokers.

Deaths from lung cancer among males in the United States (36,000 in 1960) have increased 600 per cent since 1935. Lung cancer (a most unpleasant way to die) accounted for 2 per cent of all deaths in 1960 in the United States, but for about 6 per cent of deaths among men in their late 50's and early 60's. Cigarette smoking has also been linked to coronary heart disease, cancer of the male bladder, and cancer of the mouth, throat, and gullet.

If there were a way to treat tobacco or filter the smoke to overcome or even minimize the effects of smoking, the solution of the problem would be relatively simple. But to date, no method of treatment or filtering has been demonstrated to have any material effect. The best solution is to stop smoking; the evidence is that this action reduces the death rate substantially, even after long exposure. If one cannot stop smoking, the danger can be somewhat lessened by switching to pipes or cigars, which, because of infrequent inhalation, are reported to be less harmful.

Amazingly enough, despite the mass media's extensive coverage of the findings of the studies quoted earlier, not too many people (only 16 per cent, according to a recent American Cancer Society survey) believe that there is a correlation between cigarette smoking and lung cancer. This may be selective perception at work; that is, because the facts of the situation are totally unpleasant and affect a basic habit, the mind rejects the message or, in effect, never receives it. Domestic sales of cigarettes in 1963 hit a record 512 billion—up well over 100 billion in the past ten years. Cigarette consumption per capita according to the U.S. Department of Agriculture was about 4,025 in 1961, up 3 per cent over 1960 and 17 per cent over 1956. Decreases have occurred in only two years since 1935: 1953 and 1954, the years following the publicity given the earlier cancer studies. The increase since 1954 can no doubt be attributed in part to filters, which now account for over 50 per cent of all cig-

arette sales. While the filter has never been conclusively shown to be a health safeguard, it does permit smokers to rationalize the habit.

## SOLVING THE PROBLEM

We are actually concerned with two overriding questions: first, how can we prevent future generations from starting to smoke cigarettes, and second, how can we get people who are now cigarette smokers to terminate the habit or at least switch to cigars or pipes? The need for a solution to the first question is apparent in the fact that persons who begin to smoke do so at an ever younger age. It has been reported that 20 per cent of all boys have started smoking by the ninth grade and that almost 30 per cent of all girls smoke before they graduate from high school.

In attempting to solve these problems, we must recognize and understand that smoking is widespread and deeply entrenched and that it satisfies deep-seated human needs that have existed for a long period of time. Its existence is the direct result of strong forces operating in our culture. How else could the habit continue to exist when so many smokers classify it as being unhealthy, wasteful, dirty, and immoral? Certainly, powerful motivations must be operating to sustain cigarette smoking in the face of these negative attitudes.

Psychologists point out that cigarette smoking signifies energy and accomplishment and is deemed necessary to relieve tension. Thus, it is justified on the basis of its value as a reward or a means of self-gratification, and even as quasi-therapeutic.

Social Research, Inc., in a rather elaborate study entitled *Cigarettes, Their Role and Function*, divided the reasons why people smoke into two categories—personal and social. Under "personal," they note that cigarette smoking has many uses.

1. It is an intimate function and has the quality of a personal ritual. Like all rituals, it gives a sense of well-being, a feeling of security.

2. The process of smoking provides a variety of sensuous pleasures, including oral indulgence.

3. It provides a perverse pleasure that many people derive from punishing or endangering themselves in masochistic fashion.

4. It helps smokers tell what kind of people they are. Important here are the ideas of ma-

turity, virility, and aggressiveness among men, and poise, sophistication, and liberation, especially for women.

Under social meanings, the study reports that cigarettes can be equated with sociability, that they serve as gestures of affiliation or instruments of social interaction, and that they represent conformity. For the teen-ager, cigarette smoking serves as an initiation into the ranks of adults. Not to smoke is to be stigmatized as weak, prudish, or timid.

Whatever the reasons for smoking, it is clear that they are sufficiently powerful to make the habit difficult to break. So long as cigarettes have high personal and cultural values, individuals who now smoke them or who can be induced to smoke them will find the habit attractive. Thus, any remedial action must attempt to minimize the psychological and social values of cigarettes.

## RESPONSIBLE PARTIES

### *The Federal Government*

Given the above evidence, many persons would conclude that cigarettes should be classed as a harmful drug and so treated by the federal government, that is, their sale to the public should be prohibited. But such a solution ignores the facts that most adults smoke, that the habit is a strong one, and that cigarettes can be made from tobacco designed to be used for other forms of smoking. Extreme government action would probably end up worse than the diseases associated with cigarette smoking. Shades of the Volstead Act!

To be sure, the government has a distinct responsibility to protect the health and welfare of its citizens. To date, it has delayed action pending a "facts and recommendations" report from an advisory committee named by the U.S. Surgeon General. Perhaps some insight into possible action can be gleaned from the suggestions made to the British government by the Royal College of Physicians. These include: (1) preventing or at least restricting cigarette advertising; (2) more effectively regulating the sale of tobacco to children; (3) curtailing smoking in public places to alter its social acceptability; (4) placing a differential tax on cigarettes while reducing the tax on pipe tobacco and cigars; (5) organizing anti-smoking clinics; (6) informing purchasers of cigarettes of the tar and nicotine content of cigarette smoke; and (7) drawing the attention of the public to the dangers of smoking, with special care being taken to the education of school children.

It goes without saying that the government should continue and even expand its expenditures for research on cancer and other diseases to which smoking has been linked, which are currently only about $100 million annually. (In comparison, the government's tobacco price support program for the period from June 1, 1960 to April 30, 1961 totaled $42.8 million.) Any additional research costs could easily be financed by a special "medical research" tax per package; for example, at present consumption rates, a tax of $.05 per package would provide over $1 billion annually, even allowing for a tax reduction on cigars and smoking tobacco. Not all of this money would have to be spent on medical research. Some could be allocated to an intensive propaganda campaign designed to educate the public regarding the ill effects of cigarette smoking. The effectiveness of the tax could be increased by placing a tax stamp on each package with the statement, "Proceeds from this special tax are used to support cancer research." Hopefully, the additional tax (which would substantially raise the cost of a package of cigarettes) would cause some persons to quit or reduce their smoking because of the higher cost.

Certainly the government has the responsibility for issuing a definitive statement on smoking and health in a form that can easily be understood by the layman. In addition, the government could ban all cigarette advertising (as Italy has done) and could even use federal funds to "advertise" the ill effects of cigarette smoking. Such a campaign might include the use of scare posters similar to those issued by the British Ministry of Health. One poster shows the rise in lung cancer deaths from 5,303 in 1940 to 25,288 in 1961. The

figures are printed in gray on the lids of five coffins, which presumably will increase in size as the lung cancer death figures go up. This poster says: "The more cigarettes you smoke the greater risk. You have been warned."

In an effort to head off youngsters who might fall victims of the habit, the government could issue educational materials for use by the school. New York State has released a pamphlet warning youngsters of the "serious health hazard." The American Cancer Society has increased its showings of educational films to teen-agers on cancer and cigarettes and claims that they are having a considerable impact. But the likely response of many youths to such educational materials is, "Why worry about a disease that won't hit for 30 or 40 years?" Youngsters' smoking could be restricted by the enforcement of laws already on the books of most states that prohibit the sale of cigarettes to minors. Enforcement is difficult, however, because automatic vending machines are left unattended and cigarettes are readily available through casual adults.

The federal government has a unique role to play in helping to solve the cigarette problem, but its actions cannot get at the basic question of how to destroy the favorable image possessed by the cigarette in our culture. These actions can be important or even drastic, but much will depend on the consensus developed through cooperation from the industries involved.

### The Tobacco Industry

This embattled industry with some 65,000 employees and annual sales of nearly $8 billion has shown much anxiety over the cigarette problem but little tendency to accept any responsibility for solving it. In fact, many would argue that the industry has deliberately attempted to minimize or mask the various research findings regarding the harmful effects of cigarette smoking. It has played up the contention that other factors such as gas and industrial fumes are more likely causes of lung cancer than cigarettes and has argued that to date there is no proof that cigarettes are linked to cancer.

In 1954, in response to the initial research releases citing evidence of the dangers of cigarette smoking, the industry set up the Tobacco Industry Research Committee to finance scientific inquiry into the relationship, if any, between smoking and such maladies as lung

cancer and heart disease. Through 1962, total research expenditures made by TIRC have been only $5.5 million, considerably less than 1 per cent of the industry's approximately $170 million annual advertising expenditures. The tobacco industry could easily afford a larger research expenditure. Annual net profits of the "big five" (R. J. Reynolds Tobacco Co., Philip Morris, Inc., P. Lorillard Company, Liggett & Myers Tobacco Co., and The American Tobacco Co.) exceed $262 million and are thus in excess of twice the total yearly expenditures for cancer research in this country.

Although the storm warnings have been flying for some ten years, the major tobacco companies have done little to diversify. They are thus vulnerable to drastic outside action and reluctant to show initiative in facing up to the challenges of business statesmanship. Philip Morris has diversified into flexible packaging materials, chewing gum, chemicals and adhesives, and razor blades and shaving supplies to the extent that the sales of these products account for about 25 per cent of total sales. Reynolds, the only other major tobacco company to do much by way of diversification, has acquired Pacific Hawaiian Products Company with annual sales of under $30 million in fruit juice and cake mixes. Reynolds' Archer Aluminum Division is expanding and increased sales are expected, and U.S. Tobacco is now in the candy business.

For the most part, the tobacco companies have tried to meet the health issue on its own ground, that is, by launching new filter and king size brands. The filter tip market now represents 55 per cent of the total market, in contrast to about 1 per cent a decade ago. The nonfilter king size has about 20 per cent of the total—not because of its economy appeal, but because many smokers have apparently been attracted by the argument that the extra length serves as a natural filter.

The marketing of these new brands of cigarettes has been an expensive undertaking—over $10 million is often expended to introduce a new brand. The industry's attempt to solve its problems by more aggressive marketing is reflected, in part, by its substantial advertising expenditures. The cost per carton, as estimated by *Advertising Age*, varies widely among brands, ranging in 1961 from $.028 per carton for Camel and Lucky Strike to $.669 for Belair.

An ironical twist to the advertising situation is that from the late 1940's through 1954 the industry literally spent a small fortune creating doubts about the healthfulness of its products. Most of the advertising during this period featured doctors and filters that "really worked." Ads were filled with tars and resins presented so graphically as to convince some smokers that these were agents of destruction—as indeed they may well be. The Federal Trade Commission's rulings in 1955 and again in 1960, that, in effect, health cannot be dealt with in any cigarette advertising account for the present emphasis on pleasure. Perhaps the contrast suggests that the themes of health or pleasure per se affect smoking habits less than their widespread presentation, which lends public approval and acceptance to smoking. It seems clear that, although cigarette manufacturers should have a sense of public responsibility, they have given no evidence that they feel any real obligation to the public interest. This is not the case in other countries. Two Canadian cigarette manufacturers, following the example set in England, recently agreed to limit TV advertising to the hours after 9 p.m., when children are supposedly in bed.

### The Advertising Agency

The executives of many advertising agencies have long been defensive and insecure about the value to society of their role. They have often stated that the public doesn't understand their important contribution to "keeping the economy moving." And presumably they have reason to be on the defensive, given the public image of advertising executives as portrayed in the movies, in the popular literature, and on television.

It would surely contradict that image if the advertising industry could be persuaded to make a significant contribution to solving the cigarette problem. After all, it has been partially responsible for giving cigarette smoking a virile, socially acceptable, sensuous image. Certainly it would be difficult for an advertising agency executive to deny that the billions of dollars spent in advertising cigarettes over the past thirty years had made no impact on demand. An example of early cigarette advertising is the 1932 Lucky Strike ad in which the question was asked, "Do you inhale?" followed by the statement "What's there to be afraid of?" An earlier "Reach for a Lucky" campaign (circa 1930) described cigarettes as safe and even attributed medicinal values to them. In 1934, a Camel ad suggested that cigarettes

would alleviate jangled nerves, while a 1936 Camel ad identified smoking with doctors.

But to place the argument in this frame of reference is probably not fair. According to Neil Borden's classic study entitled *Economic Effects of Advertising*, advertising's part in expanding the market for cigarettes has been no more than an acceleration of a habit that has its roots in our culture. As our social environment has changed—especially in the breakdown of social restrictions upon personal behavior— the forces or prejudices against smoking have all but disappeared. Advertising men early perceived that smoking is a social habit and, as such, could be stimulated by making it socially acceptable, or by accelerating the forces already at work through emulation of well-known personages.

Now that smoking's link to cancer has been established, however, shouldn't this principle of emulation be dropped as the basis of advertising copy? At least one medical research authority on cancer believes that it should. Dr. Michael B. Shimkin, one of the senior directors of the National Cancer Institute of Bethesda, Md., has pleaded, "In fairness to our children the least the industry and the government should do is eliminate some of the shameful appeals from tobacco advertising such as those which equate smoking with bravery, sexual virility, and social status." Some of the present cigarette advertising unquestionably appeals to our youth—denials of the tobacco industry to the contrary. The TV advertising in the fall of 1962 that featured Paul Hornung is but one example.

To be sure, advertising men until recently didn't know, or suspect, the potential harm in cigarettes when they created their advertising claims. But they know it now—or at least should have strong doubts about the healthfulness of cigarette smoking. Yet they go on behaving as though cigarette smoking were harmless and even therapeutic. A few advertising agencies—all large—handle the bulk of cigarette advertising. Each could survive the resignation of their cigarette accounts. (Collectively, these accounts represent an income of about $30 million to the agencies involved.)

Imagine the furor that would follow the announcement of such a resignation—especially one accompanied by the statement, "We can no longer in good conscience continue to attempt to increase the demand for a product that possesses such potentially dangerous effects on users." It might even be argued that such leadership would be rewarded by its attraction of new accounts from business executives who admired such a stand.

Responsible agency leaders could go further and spark action by the Advertising Council, a nonprofit organization that marshals the forces of advertising for the social good. The council's unique and successful history of proven service is exemplified in the campaign to prevent forest fires (featuring Smokey the Bear) and the promotion of U.S. Savings Bonds. Leading advertising agencies could organize their talents behind an educational campaign designed to inform the public of the dangers of smoking and to play down the social role of cigarettes.

### Advertising Media

Resignation of the cigarette advertising accounts by agencies would not, of course, shut off the flow of advertising. The tobacco companies could hire other agencies, or, assuming an industry-wide boycott, set up "house agencies." Only if the mass media act collectively to refuse such advertising is there any chance of a really effective blackout action.

At least one industry representative has spoken out about the responsibility of the mass media with regard to cigarette smoking. LeRoy Collins, President of the National Association of Broadcasters stated in November, 1962 that radio and TV codes

should be much more than sets of legalistic standards and delineations of good taste and estimated public tolerance. I think the codes should serve as a broadcast conscience as well. Under them and to them, the individual broadcaster and all related enterprises should be able to look for, and find, ethical and unbiased leadership. For example, if we are honest with ourselves, we cannot ignore the mounting evidence that tobacco provides a serious hazard to health. Can we either in good conscience ignore the fact that progressively more and more of our high school age—and lower—children are now becoming habitual cigarette smokers? . . . We also know that this condition is being made continuously worse under the promotional impact of advertising designed primarily to influence young people.

As might be expected, the tobacco manufacturers accused Collins of having made a final judgment on a medical question that is still under study. They also denied advertising to American youth, although, according to Senator Maurine Neuberger (D., Ore.), some

40 per cent of all national advertising placed in college newspapers was sponsored by the tobacco companies. Only in recent months did the big five cigarette companies stop all campus advertising and promotion. This action was taken after a number of American universities banned cigarette advertising, largely at the urging of the American Cancer Society. Also within broadcasting's own ranks, many tried to minimize Collins' statements and publicly assured tobacco sponsors that the broadcast media were eager for their advertising dollars.

It would be a gigantic step forward to refuse cigarette advertising; it would be an even bigger step to provide free time to the Advertising Council for anti-smoking propaganda. But one is forced to conclude that, despite the fact that radio and TV networks and stations have by their own admission unique social responsibilities, it is unlikely that they, as a group, will ban cigarette advertising.

At least four major groups in our society have a responsibility for making a sincere effort to help solve the problem of cigarette smoking. Given the dimensions and roots of the problem, all four working together could accomplish more than any one working alone. It would be refreshing if the business groups were the first to act, for in so doing they would demonstrate that they were responsible agents of a free society. Too frequently, business is victimized by its inability to assume leadership. Thus, it falls into the position of criticizing action by the government without having an alternative offer. Businessmen could justify their actions by understanding that, in reality, they are acting only in their own interests and in the long-run interests of the free enterprise system that they claim is being continually eroded by the growth in power of the federal government. The opportunity afforded by the magnitude of the problem should excite, rather than inhibit, the relatively small group of men who can exercise effective leadership in this situation.

The last paragraph is likely to be misunderstood by many business leaders. The grounds on which the points advanced here will be repudiated are predictable:

"The link between cigarette smoking and lung cancer has not yet been proven."

"Advertising agencies act as agents for their clients; they work within regulations handed down by others."

"If we turn down the advertising, somebody else will accept it."

Unfortunately, the authors are forced to conclude that only the federal government will take action—and that business in general as well as many of those who consume or will consume cigarettes will be the losers. Intervention by the federal government into the problem of cigarette smoking will inevitably involve the various groups mentioned in this article, and any such intervention will be likely to serve as a precedent in cases of other products that can be shown to be potentially harmful. If the federal government acts in a way that is either not effective in solving the problem or that invades the domain of the agency or the media, then no one can be counted as the winner—least of all the cigarette smoker.

# 58. Applying Marketing Research Experience to the Race/Poverty Problem

DANIEL YANKELOVICH

We've been conducting research on urban problems of poverty and race for about three years, and even though this work represents a small fraction (about 10%) of our total research, we find ourselves deeply involved in it personally. The race/poverty issue is the dominant social problem of our times, and studying it opens a window on how the vital processes of government and society interact with each other. At the present time, for example, we are in the midst of a massive study, mandated by the U.S. Congress, to see what impact the Amendments to the Poverty Act of 1967 are having on more than 50 cities across the land. The purpose of the study is to assess what is happening now, and what is likely to happen in the future, both to the poverty populations of these cities, to city governments and to public and private agencies as more control of poverty programs is made available to local government.

We approached our first poverty study three years ago with considerable diffidence. Even though most of us in our organization have an academic background in social science, our professional lives have been largely devoted to business and marketing research. We are all too aware of the pitfalls in our own field which lay in wait for those who approach it without substantive business and marketing knowledge, however much technical skill in research they may have. We know how badly one can be misled in making marketing interpretations

◆ SOURCE: Reprinted by permission from the author, an unpublished paper presented before Boston Chapter, American Marketing Association, May, 1968.

if one doesn't understand the process of marketing itself. The fields of poverty, mental health and urbanology call for far more substantive knowledge over and above technical research competence. We were, therefore, surprised—and vastly relieved—to discover how many of the lessons we had learned from business research proved to be applicable to this new area. In science nowadays people trained in one branch of knowledge can often make discoveries in another branch, if they bring with them a new set of sensitivities to issues which might otherwise be bypassed. Fortunately, our business experience contributes something new, adding to rather than competing against existing expertise. I know that you would be interested in learning about how our mutual field of competence can be applied to social problems that are of the greatest urgency and importance to us all.

## RELEVANCE OF MARKET RESEARCH-TYPE DESCRIPTIONS

On the most elementary level, that of using research for purposes of description, we found that we were on quite familiar grounds. The poverty population may look homogeneous if seen from a distance, just as markets for products do. But once you come closer you begin to see its vast heterogeneity. As of now, 30 million people live below the poverty line in this country. And this official estimate greatly understates the problem. A family of four living in New York City on $65 per week, being forced to pay $150 per month for rent in a ghetto apartment, and being overcharged for food, clothing and credit is not considered be-

**415**

low the poverty line by current official standards.

What strikes one first from a research point of view, however, is that quite apart from having inadequate incomes, the poor are not in other vital respects a representative cross-section of the population.

They consist primarily of five groups:

1. Old people over 65.
2. Fatherless families.
3. Blacks and other non-whites.
4. Poorly-educated whites.
5. People living in rural areas.

These five groups, plus a small number added by the disabled and the mentally ill, make up the poverty population.

Furthermore, except for the old people and the mothers of small children, most of the poor are *not* unemployed. Government statistics show that 2/3 of the male heads of households in poverty families in the 22-54 age bracket work 39 weeks or more per year. Thus, the poverty population is made up of people who are *unemployable* (the old and the mothers of small children of fatherless families) plus people who *are employed but not making enough money* plus the small minority who are employable but *cannot find any work at all.*

Over and above the demographic factors, there are other important characteristics of the poverty population that should be mentioned:

### Being Poor and Being Blue Collar Are Not the Same

It need not be emphasized to this group that poverty and blue collar do not have the same meaning. Most blue collar workers do not fall below the poverty line; only about one-fifth of blue collar workers fall into the poverty category.

Most blue collar families are, of course, intact families. But the greatest difference between the blue collar population and the poverty population consists of intangibles: the values, the morale, the conceptions of themselves, the personality characteristics of the people involved. The non-poverty stable working class family has a far different outlook on life than that of the poverty group.

### SHARES VALUES

Some social scientists have questioned whether those in poverty share the assumptions and values of the majority of Americans

—a belief in the future, a faith in hard work, a belief in education, and a belief that most problems and difficulties can be overcome if one tries hard enough. I think it is important to emphasize that although the poor do not share all middle-class values, they *do* share most of the key values and beliefs of the vast majority.

In one national study the major felt needs of the poverty population at or above the 90% level were:

a. Helping their children to get more education;

b. Keeping their children out of trouble; and

c. Saving money on food and clothing.

Between 60% and 80% emphasized:

a. Making more money;
b. Having better medical care;
c. Having a more attractive home; and
d. Making the neighborhood a better place to live.

Even in the poorest segments of the population, we find the commonly shared American belief in the efficacy of self-help, in education, in progress, and in the future. Such shared beliefs, of course, serve to point up the discrepancy between a person's values and his situation—with the expected consequences on the person's self-esteem. Many of the poor share the middle-class point of view about themselves: that if they were capable, hard-working people, they wouldn't be poor—so there must be something wrong with them morally.

Some of the most striking differences between the values of the general population and the poverty population are these:

1. Twice as many of the general public as the poor are fully satisfied with their home life (49% to 27%); with their place in the community (28% to 15%); and with their achievement in life (20% to 11%).

2. There are also striking differences between the poor and the general public in the degree of satisfaction each group feels with their future opportunities, with their education and with being generally satisfied with their lot in life.

### The Poor Are Physically Sicker

Another characteristic of the very poor worth emphasizing is that they are physically sicker than the rest of the population.

1. Infant mortality in this country is in inverse ratio to the size of the family budget. (It is twice as high among the poor).

2. Persons and families with incomes under $2,000 are *five* times as likely to have a disabling heart condition as families with incomes of $7,000 or more.

3. They are *six* times as likely to be crippled by arthritis.

4. They are *six* times as likely to be crippled by nervous and mental conditions.

5. They are *nine* times as likely to have some form of visual impairment.

### There Are a Great Many Non-Economic Problems in Living in an Urban Slum

Having very little money is not the worst part of living in a city slum. Recent studies have shown that:

1. The poor are also exploited as consumers. The poor person pays more for credit than the middle-class person; mark-ups on products are as high as 100%, 200%, or even 300%. The food in supermarkets tends to be of poorer quality and higher prices; the furniture is of poor quality. Many well-known brand names of appliances are missing, and unknown brands are marked up beyond reason. The poor are subject to many unethical and illegal practices by storekeepers and landlords.

2. The poor believe they are being persecuted by the police and some of their other guardians; there is evidence to support this belief.

3. The poor in urban slums are prey to legal proceedings, such as having salaries garnisheed that deprive them of means for coping with their economic problems.

4. Most of the poor are not very good at communicating their needs, at making demands, and at availing themselves of existing services. In a time of professional shortage, they suffer the most. There are, of course, a small handful who have learned how to manipulate the system, but they seem to be a tiny minority.

## DIFFERENCES BETWEEN BLACK AND WHITE POVERTY

Since the race problem and the poverty problem are inextricably intertwined, it may be worth mentioning some of the differences between black and white poverty. Keep in mind this rule of thumb: except for the deep South, the problem of rural poverty is largely white; the problem of urban poverty is largely Negro.

We find some startling differences in Negro/white felt needs and attitudes.

1. Twice as many poor blacks as whites want a better education for themselves (60% vs. 30%).

2. Almost twice as many want special training to help them with a job (70% vs. 40%).

3. Almost twice as many want a better job (74% vs. 46%).

4. Making more money is the #1 felt need of poor blacks; it is #5 on the list for whites.

5. Significantly, more poor blacks than whites want to make their neighborhood a nicer place to live (74% vs. 50%), have better available medical care (73% vs. 59%) and nicer clothes (49% vs. 29%).

6. There are *no* differences on wanting to move out of the neighborhood. It is the lowest item on the felt need scale (28% for both poor whites and poor blacks).

It is interesting to note that poor blacks have a significantly greater degree of self-respect and sense of accomplishment as poor whites (as measured on a special scale we evolved after extensive depth interviewing).

Here is the conclusion we presented to the editors of *Fortune* in a recent study we conducted for them on the urban Negro:

Jobs, education for children and desegregation (in the sense of equal opportunity and respect, *not* in the sense of inter-marriage, socializing, and the taking over of white neighborhoods), represent the main objectives of the urban black today. Most blacks see some improvement for themselves mainly in the area of jobs, for which they give credit to themselves and their own efforts. Their present mood is activist, with a tinge of violence by a substantial minority. Black people feel that if they are going to make progress in education, housing, living conditions and the respect of the white community, they are going to have to fight for it themselves. The majority (60%) reject rioting and they also reject other forms of violence. But they do not reject other forms of fighting and black power.

Negroes are probably less divided today than they have been in the recent past. They are united on objectives; they are united in their mood of hopefulness; they are united in their anger. Even on the means of accomplishing their objectives, the division, though it is a real one, is fairly narrow. A majority would endorse aggressive but non-violent tactics; but a substantial minority (from a third to 40%) would go somewhat further in the direction of violence.

The study findings are pessimistic in the sense that they presage further violence and anger. But there is also some grounds for optimism; Negro attitudes of hope and progress currently coexist with attitudes of anger toward the white community. If, in the next few years, the more moderate activist but non-violent approach of the majority meets with cooperation and success, almost undoubtedly the anger and the violence will diminish. The study shows, we believe, that we are in a stage of transition and that the die is not cast. The white community has an even better chance of solving this problem than it did a few years ago. At that time, the mood of liberal *noblesse oblige* had to fail. Blacks can't get what they want most, which is what all other Americans want —a measure of self-respect and control over their own destiny—by having somebody else give it to them. They have to win it for themselves and they are currently in the mood to do so. How the white community responds in the immediate future will determine whether we shall experience a great social success for black and white alike, or whether this country will be rent by the violence and ugliness of racial revolution.

This sketch gives you a general picture of the poverty population as seen from a straightforward marketing research point of view. The problems one encounters in marketing, however, usually go far beyond the simple and straightforward task of describing a market or population. Some form of practical end result is almost always required. For example, we do considerable research in the new product area to learn what specifications new products and services should have to satisfy customer needs. We do this by analyzing the needs of the customer and we conduct marketing strategy studies to make sure that existing products or services fit these needs. One lesson all of us engaged in this type of research have learned many times is that the consumer does not buy products and services solely on the basis of his objective needs—i.e., automobiles are not merely transportation, food is more than nourishment. In the life insurance field, for example, there is less of a positive relationship between a family's *objective needs* for replacement income and the actual amount of life insurance purchased than there is between the

amount of life insurance purchased and certain intangible attitudes of the husband and father. This finding is, of course, typical; countless similar examples could be cited.

Consequently, we were not surprised to find this same phenomenon in the poverty and mental health areas. The people with the most severe emotional problems are not the ones who avail themselves of mental health services; and a wholly objective approach to poverty by offering housing, jobs, medical care, etc. fails to meet the full magnitude of the need. Don't get me wrong. Jobs, housing and medical care meet important objective needs, just as transportation meets an important objective need of the automobile buyer. But one can profoundly misunderstand how to cope with the poverty problem by focusing solely on objective needs, just as one can go bankrupt in the automobile market by providing nothing but stripped-down transportation.

Consider jobs. Follow-up studies of various jobs and job training programs show, time and again, that by themselves jobs like that of hospital orderly, dishwasher and parking lot attendant have astonishingly high dropout rates; and further, many better jobs which are not dead-end don't get filled because of fear, lack of self-confidence, a sense of shame about not being able to read or write, real or imagined racial tensions, etc.

Consider housing. In the 1930's, public housing was part of our national ideology. In those days people believed that if you took the person out of the slum and put him into a nice clean housing project, his world would change. As a consequence of this long-standing concern with housing, there are probably more social science studies on public housing than on any other comparable area. And they show, as our own recent studies on the Columbia Point housing project also show, that public housing by itself is not the answer. In fact, one runs the risk of *institutionalizing* poverty through certain types of housing rather than helping people to break out of the poverty cycle. Housing *does* solve certain problems. It keeps the rats out, and that's not a negligible benefit. On the other hand, many people living in housing projects have the impression of exchanging rats for filthy elevators, for hostile and indifferent neighbors, for bureaucratic caretakers who are just as unresponsive as slum landlords, and for delinquents collected *en masse*. In the old slum neighborhood the delinquents were spread out all over the neighborhood. In some of the new housing projects the delinquents are conveniently gathered together in the same location.

The demographic composition of the Columbia Point housing project is that of a typical poverty population: it is disproportionally black; mainly grade school education or less; the median income of those who *are* employed is about $46 per week and the median income of all households is about $35 per week; 25% of the population are elderly households, primarily widows; and 40% are families with female-only head of household. Columbia Point is a distillation of the northern urban poverty population—very high proportions of fatherless families with small children, blacks, old people, uneducated whites and men employed at below subsistence salary levels.

The major themes expressed by the residents of Columbia Point are those of powerlessness, feelings of vulnerability, and lack of control over their destiny.

Even the more optimistic and active speak of the inevitable disappointments that will come "in spite of whatever they do," and of futile hopes to own their own homes "which will never come true."

The women refer to the daily grind of their life with no prospect or hope for change, as if their lives were a jail sentence to which they are condemned. A few state overtly that they are depressed and nervous and may "break down" or "go crazy" if there is any more trouble. They speak of their inability to affect others in their world. To many of the women the least predictable element in their lives is a husband (if he is present) and children. Notably lacking is the middle-class effort to understand what role they themselves have had in creating the responses of their men and children, or what they might do to change them.

In some few of the interviews, there are expressions of being mistreated, abused and victimized. In these instances, it is the parents or husbands who victimize. The women express shame and inferiority and contrast their own lives with those of better-off relatives and speak of the stigma of being on A.D.C. Some refer to themselves as "nothing" or wonder why a "nobody" like themselves was even chosen to be interviewed. Some are "mad at the world." Others express anger at absent husbands or unknown neighbors who dirty the halls and get their children into trouble, while others state that they find themselves getting angry at their children for no good reason. Most of them report that anger comes in the form of occasional "blow-ups" and that the rest of the time they "ignore their husbands running around with other women"; they "avoid fights" with neighbors; they "don't like to argue or make a scene."

A number of the women express deep concern about bad influences in the environment on their children. Much of their lives seem to center around their children and the problem of protecting and controlling them. Very few express an active desire to overcome the obstacles and to achieve a better situation for themselves or their children. They are more concerned with achieving a modicum of stability and comfort than with moving up. Their hopes are confined to gaining a decent respectable life, a clean apartment, children who don't get into trouble, etc.

There is much comment, with varying degrees of vehemence, on other people living at Columbia Point: remarks on people in the project who are irresponsible, who dirty everything and who let their children run wild. Most residents keep to themselves. Some fear getting too close to their neighbors because they think this brings trouble or gossip. There is much talk of loneliness, of isolation, of going "stir crazy."

### The Poor Cope By Scaling Down

Most of the poor we have interviewed cope with their problems by a process of scaling down—scaling down their expectations, scaling down their future plans, scaling down their interests in their surroundings, in their neighborhoods, even in themselves. The scaling down takes several forms. One form is a kind of mental restriction—a lack of what might be considered ordinary levels of curiosity, of knowledge about the environment, of concern about body functions, of interests in their own health and welfare. With regard to planning for the future, there is a restriction of future time and a retreat into the most narrow and immediate concerns. Rather than concentrate on pie-in-the-sky and other unlikely projections in the future, many of the poor restrict their vision to the most immediate and concrete concerns and limit their interest to whatever is closely at hand.

Alongside of this kind of mental restriction there is an attempt to minimize feelings about personal problems—an unwillingness to dwell on the self and on one's own emotions.

This technique of coping by scaling down can often lead to an emotional impoverishment that matches the economic impoverishment.

### The Poor Shouldn't Be Romanticized

The poor should not be romanticized. You can't live the kind of life most of these people live in an urban slum without becoming frustrated, prejudiced, and aggressive. In a recent study of the poor (in the San Francisco area), the authors describe the differences between the very poor and the not-so-poor as:

1. A tendency to oversimplify the cause of events, including the causes of one's own situation;

2. A feeling of powerlessness, a "beggars-can't-be-choosers" kind of attitude; a feeling of impotence in dealing with the world;

3. A terrible kind of insecurity and pessimism; a conviction that emergencies are inevitable and can't be coped with;

4. A lack of confidence in dealing with people outside of one's immediate neighborhood or with people who are not in the same plight;

5. A marked anti-intellectualism; an anti-highbrow attitude;

6. A marked authoritarianism, intolerance, and prejudice against ethnic minorities;

7. Holding an image of the world as a jungle, and having a cynical and mistrustful attitude toward it;

8. Taking an aggressive, punitive attitude; a quickness to blame others; a certain kind of toughness and an ability to con others.

The urban poor are people who are off-balance; and being off-balance they are explosive. They are trying to maintain their sense of autonomy, independence, and manhood under tremendous pressures. Their situation isn't pretty and neither are they.

I emphasize these intangible factors because of our experience that the non-economic, psychological meaning of poverty has to be understood in relation to planning and evaluating programs aimed at breaking the poverty cycle.

In seeking to understand the quality of poverty as well as its objective characteristics, we have taken a page out of our market research experience. The ultimate objective of the research is to shape, test, and evaluate programs whose realistic aim is to help people to *help themselves* break out of the poverty cycle rather than to be passive recipients of services. The operative word here is self-help. More than 90% of the urban poverty populations we have interviewed want self-help methods of breaking out of the poverty cycle rather than handouts, and even though many of them are not in a good position to use self-help methods, a majority are. The marketing experience of shaping products and service to fit subjective as well as objective needs is directly relevant to planning programs in which people will actively participate.

## RESEARCH OF SOLUTIONS, NOT CAUSES

Let me now mention what is, we believe, the most important application of our business research experience. In the material I have covered up to now, there is considerable overlapping between our marketing research methods and the methods of social scientists working in these fields—and considerable overlap in findings. There is one application, however, where our methods are sharply differentiated from typical social science research: namely, that good marketing research is always concerned with *solutions* to problems rather than with discovering causes or adding to the store of knowledge. We have found with surprising frequency that an understanding of causes alone does *not* always lead to viable solutions to problems. Let me give you a simple example from business research. It has the virtue of making the point at issue clear because it is so simple.

¶ Several years ago, the Ford Motor Company found itself losing a share of the market for its light trucks to General Motors. It hypothesized that a price change was needed to stimulate sales: its trucks were priced several hundred dollars above the competing General Motors' trucks. Ford conducted a survey to test its hypothesis. The survey found that low price was indeed considered to be important to light truck buyers and was positively correlated with choice of make of truck (i.e., those who associated a lower purchase price with a particular make of truck were more likely to purchase that make than those who associated a higher price with it). In the light of these survey findings, and at a drastic sacrifice in profits, Ford lowered the price of its light trucks—and continued to lose exactly the same share of the market as before; no more, no less.

The survey had failed to show what later research (of a different kind) revealed: namely, that while price was a factor, it was secondary in importance to reliability of performance and the buyers' dependency on the dealer. Most light truck buyers are owners of small businesses, like dry cleaning establishments or TV repair services. For these small entrepreneurs, anxiety-reducing reliability of performance is much more important than a small price saving —because their business ceases to function if their truck breaks down.

This was a rather obvious research finding. It would have readily been discovered by a more flexible method that did not hypothesize in advance what the decisive variables might be. Yet, a startlingly large proportion of social science research is designed to measure correlations among variables assumed in advance of inquiry to be relevant and important. In recent years, for example, a spate of studies have measured the relationships between social class and mental health. These studies are enlightening and add to our store of knowledge. But they are largely irrelevant to the task of planning Mental Health Centers, even though many of them were designed for this purpose.

The point I wish to stress here is that those of us in the marketing research field who constantly have our findings put to the test have had a unique opportunity to find out what works and what doesn't. Every careful implementation of a study is, in effect, a crucial experiment. And, based on such experience we have been obliged to change somewhat radically conventional research methods—when research is used for solving problems rather than for gathering data. The fact is that conventional research methods are inadequate to solve either the problems of poverty or complex marketing problems. The classic method of the large-scale sample survey, with its major emphasis on sampling techniques, is, by itself, a clumsy, needlessly expensive, and inappropriate method for finding solutions to complex problems. I emphasize the phrase "by itself." For the sample survey, if used properly in conjunction with *other* research methods and for limited purposes, can be an invaluable tool. But what is required for the solution of any difficult problem that relates to planning programs for populations, whether the population be consumer or poverty, is not surveys alone but a rather complex research strategy that includes a mix of psychological research, field experiments, and analysis of the structure of

mediating institutions *plus* surveys—in a particular sequence with a particular division of effort.

As soon as we entered the poverty field, we discovered that the same basic methodological problem that we have been struggling with for twenty years in the marketing research field was also present here—in a more acute form. We also found, however, that social scientists typically do *not* distinguish between research aimed at winning knowledge and research aimed at producing change. And, even when the differences between these two objectives are acknowledged, their far-reaching methodological implications are rarely recognized.

As a dramatic illustration of this point, we recently had occasion to review three studies on cigarette smokers and smoking. One study was sponsored by the government; its purpose was to plan information programs aimed at *discouraging* cigarette smoking. A second project was sponsored by a cigarette company; its purpose was to find out how to *encourage* cigarette smoking. The third project was sponsored by a university; its purpose was to find out *how smokers differ from non-smokers*. All three projects used essentially the same research strategy. The major part of the research was a large-scale sample survey. All three studies had carefully drawn population samples, large enough in each instance to include adequate subsamples of smokers and non-smokers for purposes of comparison. The method of analysis called for contrasting smoker and non-smoker attitudes and behavior along a broad range of factors.

Now then, even though each study had a far different purpose—encouraging smoking versus discouraging smoking versus identifying differences between smokers and non-smokers —the research method and mode of analysis were the same in all three instances. Not surprisingly, since all three studies were technically well designed and executed, the findings largely replicated each other except for shadings of emphasis. Unfortunately, however, the data the manufacturer needed for his program were not the same as those the government needed, and neither of these duplicated the university's purposes.

Two of the three studies were aimed at creating change—how to get people to change their cigarette smoking habits. The university-based study was the only one that did not aim at creating change but creating knowledge. The key point, however, is that the design of all three studies followed the model of the university-based research, the one study that did not have the creation of change as its objective. All three studies investigated how smokers differ from non-smokers. The two studies aimed at creating change both failed in their objectives because they used the knowledge-for-its-own-sake model.

The conclusion I would like to emphasize here, without going into details, is that we in the marketing research field can contribute to social problems by bringing to bear our methods for researching solutions to problems, in sharp contrast to gaining information about causes or finding significant correlation among variables.

We call the research strategy we've worked out for finding solutions *Program Research*. It has eight steps, only one of which is a survey; and it has several features that may be worth noting in passing. The first is that it does not assume in advance of the research what the significant factors might be. We have learned, through long and hard experience, that it is extraordinarily dangerous to make such assumptions. The first three stages of our eight-stage system of Program Research are designed to isolate the crucial factors. And we don't begin a survey until we know what they are.

A second feature is that *evaluation* is built systematically into the research program. Ideas for programs which come from the research are tested against one another, and systematic evaluation gives the marketer an opportunity to get a constant flow of feedback for changing his programs and plans.

Although everyone doesn't use this particular method, other marketing research organizations have their own tested approaches. In my experience, even though the quality of research varies from company to company, the marketing research profession as a whole today, at least among its more experienced and reputable practitioners, has developed considerable sophistication in finding and researching solutions to problems. This sophistication is badly needed in the public domain.

## CONCLUSIONS

Let me briefly mention five conclusions we have tentatively reached on the nature of the poverty problem from our experience to date.

*First:* We must distinguish between *services* such as medical services, legal services, welfare services, etc., which have as their purpose alleviating the worst features of poverty, and *programs* aimed at helping people to break out of the poverty cycle and achieve some degree of economic self-sufficiency. With this distinction in mind, it becomes all too clear that while services can be given to the poor without far-reaching institutional changes in the society, breaking the poverty cycle for any large number of people has far different requirements. In other words, the institutions of the society as well as the poor themselves must change if the race/poverty problem is to be solved. Our educational system, our welfare system, our economic system (including marketing to ghettos), and our city/state/federal interrelationships must all undergo some degree of structural change.

*Second:* It is badly misleading to think of a single solution to the poverty problem, one panacea for all. There are at least *three* different types of solutions that must be put into practice. One segment of the poverty population is able to achieve economic self-sufficiency by direct and objective means—jobs, job training, etc.; but another segment, and possibly a majority of the total poverty population, requires a combination of direct and indirect programs. The same individual, in addition to a job opportunity, may also need some extra training, some remedial reading and writing, some successful experiences to bolster his self-respect and self-esteem, some hand-holding in the first few traumatic months of a new job, and maybe some medical care to get his teeth fixed. If you don't think it's worth this kind of effort, just do some fast arithmetic on the alternatives. The social cost of carrying an individual for a lifetime is many times that of helping him to become a productive taxpayer —like the rest of us. The third segment of the poor consists of those multiple-problem families and individuals who are old and sick, or single-parent families with large numbers of small children, or people who are too psychologically crippled to plan for economic self-sufficiency. These people desperately need services, not self-help programs. Incidentally, if the first two segments were to gain economic self-sufficiency, the burden of caring for the rest would not be great, and it could be done on a more generous scale than it is being done today.

*Third:* Some of the programs required to help people become economically self-sufficient have already been identified and pretested.

These include: (1) certain types of open-ended jobs with opportunities for advancement, with educational features and with on-the-job training built into them; (2) various forms of Day Care Centers and children's education programs such as Head Start; (3) programs of household management and financial planning to help make scarce means go further; (4) neighborhood centers where people who don't know where to go with their problems can find needed information, guidance, and help; (5) programs that use the poor to help other poor people through various forms of sub-professional training, etc.

Some needed programs, however, are still undefined or controversial. For example, programs of community involvement—to assure maximum feasible participation of the poor—may have some relevance to changing our institutions, but how much they actually contribute to the individual is highly problematic. Also, the whole issue of school integration and how much help to give to neighborhood schools presents a very mixed and confused picture indeed.

*Fourth:* No one—neither the federal government nor the cities nor industry—yet knows the most effective way to spend the vast amounts of money and human effort that will be required to solve the poverty problem. How many of the poor can hope to gain some form of economic self-sufficiency through self-help-type programs? How many can do it in one direct step and how many need indirect as well as direct programs? How do you achieve the coordination required between these programs and employers, educational institutions, government, etc.? How do you mobilize the cooperation of the community to carry out these programs? How do you design, in a practical fashion, the mix of programs appropriate for each individual? How do you make sure that the individual gets the form of help he needs to solve his particular problem? What is the best way of helping those who cannot hope to achieve some form of economic self-sufficiency? How much does it all cost, how long

will it take, and what resources are required to carry it out in the most effective and efficient fashion? To our knowledge, the answers to these questions are not yet known.

*Fifth:* We would like to emphasize that a combination of self-help on the part of the individual *plus* the right mix of practical programs *plus* various forms of institutional changes are all required to lick the problem. It is not easy to do three big jobs at once and we are not there yet. But there are some heartening signs. The most heartening sign to us personally is the increasingly active interest of the business community. Slowly but surely business is facing up to its own responsibilities and deep concerns, both from the point of view of enlightened self-interest but also, I think, from the broader point of view of a genuine concern with the community and the country apart from narrow business considerations. What the business community can do should not be underestimated. Its full-hearted contribution can make all the difference. In the past few months we have worked out an urban research program for sponsorship by business to investigate the poverty problems of their own community and to set guidelines so that business can choose among competing priorities. The interest in this approach is intense and very encouraging.

Finally, that part of the business community in which we find ourselves—the business and marketing research field—happens, by chance, to have the opportunity to play a crucially important role in solving this problem. In coming to understand the problem factually, in shaping up the solutions, in pretesting alternative programs, in providing systematic evaluation and feedback of results to effect planning—in all of these various and familiar facets of research—our profession can make a contribution that is far more important than may appear at first glance. Marketing research has, we believe, at least potentially, a decisive contribution to make to the public well-being.

# 59. Social Criticism and the Chemical Industry

## STEPHEN S. CASTLE

As a regular reader of printed mass media, I have been aware for some time that articles, columnists and commentators, news flashes, bulletins, and letters to the editors have contained a recurring theme. "Chemicals," they say, "do this and that." In frequency of appearance, the broadsides have become so commonplace that I have ceased collecting them. They are as much a part of the format on one significant metropolitan newspaper as the box score for the Kansas City Athletics.

The diligent scholar might find in substance a notable similarity between the performance of the chemical industry and that of the A's. This season, the Athletics have lost nearly two games for each league win. A content analysis of the chemical industry articles would likely show a similar record of accomplishment—for every celebrated achievement, "chemicals" suffer two sharp reverses.

Consistent performance of this sort wins last place in the league. And this is as true in the American Economic League as it is in the American Baseball League, except that in the former, the day may dawn when the industry can no longer "wait until next year."

The essays to which I have referred do not always say "chemical industry" if, indeed, this phrase is ever used. On occasion they do cite clusters of firms within the industry, but even this is subject to such irregularities as the intensity of a given Senate investigation and other worldly phenomena.

Taken singly, occasional criticisms are manageable. Often, they stimulate progress. They

◆ SOURCE: Reprinted by permission from Chemical and Engineering News, October 1965, pp. 144–148.

even may be argued away as normal discomforts of an industrialized society. Taken as a group, and inflicted upon society often enough and in sufficient volume, criticisms of air pollution, despoliation of the nation's water resources, and dangers of pesticides and insecticides are major threats to the American chemical industry. This is not to say that an extreme reaction of the public would lead to the disbanding of the industry—that's preposterous. But it is not preposterous to say that mounting criticisms can be real threats to the freedom to participate in the rewards of a competitive enterprise system.

If, in addition to correction of industrially promulgated evils, society were to demand vengeance as well, it would take a more inventive mind than mine to speculate profitably on the exact nature of the outcome. In any event, failure to broaden horizons beyond short-run profitability has serious implications for the long-run welfare of employees of the chemical industry, to say nothing of that of citizens at large.

### FIXING RESPONSIBILITY

Does the chemical industry pollute the air? Never! Does the chemical industry despoil the nation's waterways? Of course not!! Do the insecticides and pesticides developed in the chemical industry's laboratories also wipe out useful insect and animal life and threaten the adults and little children and infants of our republic? How absurd!!!

I know full well that when I am forced to cancel my classes because Newark's air is so foul that it is impossible to speak without gagging, the real fault lies with the automobile industry. You know and I know that the fault does not lie with the petro-chemical industry, for the industry has done a superb job of purifying its products and providing an almost endless list of superlative additives of every description. If there were no automobiles and no automobile assembly plants to spew smoke and noxious vapors, there would be no problem.

I also know that the layer of suds on what used to be a famous trout stream and now has ceased to be even an infamous carp stream is not the fault of the industrial chemicals industry. Rather it is the fault of America's soap triopoly and its satellites, and of municipal officials too worried about soaring taxes to build efficient sewage systems, and of citizens who use septic tanks instead of sewers.

I take a measure of joy in the suds I have now, for I know that soft detergents are on their way, thanks to industry's superhuman efforts, on-going and tireless since the late 1940's, when the almost eternal sudsing tendencies of hard detergents became apparent. I take my measure of joy now, because I know that when the suds are gone, I'll have to look at the filth underneath, if I can muster the courage to look at all. That bracing sight I will attribute to the papermaking industry, or some other industry, but not, to be sure, to the chemical industry.

## ROLE OF CHEMICAL MARKETING

By training and temperament, I look to marketing for the insights which I might properly bring to bear on social problems. By marketing, I mean that set of economic activities usually distinguished in economic theory from those of physical production and the precise act of consumption.

In the abstract, marketing is always a system of total corporate action operating in accordance with the appropriate social parameters, designed to transfer goods or services from the producer to the consumer, and in the process to advance, á la Adam Smith's "invisible hand," the best interests of the firm and of society.

In the particular, marketing is often a system of fragmented corporate frolic operating at or near the peril point of the antitrust laws. It is designed to outsmart and outmaneuver competitors and to transfer risk to someone else. And, in the process, it is designed to exalt the profit-making ability of incumbent manage-

ment, to pacify the labor union, to titillate the stockholder, and to avoid proximate contact with hoi polloi.

Thus, one hardly should be surprised to learn that the corporation falls halfway between good and evil, which is to say that it is imperfect as most of us and our works are imperfect in this real and imperfect world. After all, *the corporation has no soul and it has no conscience, if there's a difference.*

The corporation has no concept of—and no interest in—rightdoing. Equally important, it has no concept of—and no interest in—wrongdoing. Hence, the only way in which a corporation can influence a society which animates it is through the collective activity of the souls or consciences of the employees of the corporation.

Making an inert concept operate as a smoothly functioning viable economic unit requires a working program of a high order. A managerial approach to marketing is such a polished gestalt.

It is as intellectually stimulating as an equilibrium system in perfect competition. As an analytical tool in the real world, it is far more practical. The managerial approach to marketing has important implications as a prime contributor to the satisfaction of the profit motive, the mainspring of our competitive economic system.

## FAILURE OF COMMUNICATIONS

As a layman, I am quite willing to hold that the chemical industry is neither more nor less lax in the performance of most of the fundamental functions of managerial marketing than most other industrial goods manufacturers. In terms of many of the criticisms of the chemical industry, only one function, communications, really is at issue.

The communications function in a marketing system encompasses a variety of activities, including advertising, trade shows, personal selling activities, technical advice and assistance, research papers published in technical journals, and the like. These are the techniques which project the image of the corporation and its products to customers, and, in certain instances, to the world at large, external to the firm and its primary sphere of operations. This function also includes marketing research—the opposite side of the communications coin—the active search for market information.

In advertising, the firm attempts to convey information to its customers; in researching, the firm seeks to learn its customers' impressions of it, its products, and its services. These elements of projection and feedback form a complete communications system, the success of which depends upon the fidelity—or the degree of the absence of distortion—in the system.

Here, communications is segregated from the other marketing functions for two important reasons: First, communications, to be truly effective, cannot be inserted at just any point in the marketing process; it leads, accompanies, and follows the act of marketing goods and services. Second, communications is the single segment of the marketing process in which the chemical industry's firms have failed to perform adequately.

Taken as a group, the chemical companies' sales performance is impressive. The industry's profitability, growth, innovativeness, and world business leadership generally reflect this performance. Conversely, the industry's orientation to society, including its responsibility to exercise common sense in its economic activities, is considerably less apparent. From most of the chemical industry's communications efforts, for all that I can tell, the industry can be described best as crassly indifferent to the world outside its own selfish domain.

The industry's sales performance is excellent; its social posture is crude, at best.

Marketing in the chemical industry has failed to observe that the world has changed. In simplest and most obvious terms, there are more people in today's society. And more and more of this still growing population engages in intercommunication without regard to the industry and its feelings and desires. Distance no longer shields the chemical industry from the prying eyes of outsiders; silence by the industry no longer guarantees silence from society. Through default, industry runs a serious risk (if, indeed, it is not already at that point) of environmental obsolescence.

Since I have criticized the industry's—and particularly chemical marketing's—lack of communication with society, I feel obliged to offer my best suggestions for suitable topics to be exploited by the industry's present and prospective advertising agencies. (If there is a firm that does not have at least one advertising agency, that firm should hire an agency tomorrow. It's uncouth, if not un-American, to appear in public without a stylish advertising agency.)

## THE AIRPORT EFFECT

Build the first hard-hitting campaign around the Airport Effect! Airports are established in the suds-covered swamps and mosquito-free plains distant from our cities. In some instances, they are an hour away from the downtown core by fast transportation, and several hours away during peak traffic periods.

So what happens? Service industry springs up to soothe the weary traveler, and this is soon followed by astute land-jobbers who build (a) to house the service industry employees, and (b) because the land is cheap.

In short order, the area surrounding the formerly isolated airport is peopled by thousands of families with kids, cars, mortgages, and other success symbols. Their first civic act is to form a steering committee to secure petitions complaining about the noise of low-flying aircraft in the neighborhood. These citizen-activists rise to their finest civic hour when they picket Town Hall to have the airport closed forever when some sport splatters himself and his aircraft all over the enclave.

The chemical industry sometimes finds itself a victim of the airport effect. Manufacturing some things is simply a dirty, noisy, or stinking operation. If the manufacturer has a modest social conscience, he locates his plant in the vast reaches of no-man's land, there hopefully to stir up dirt, or to make noise, or to stink to his heart's content—all to his packet's gain and the economic betterment of society.

What's this? His employees regard the long commuting process with a lackluster eye. They edge in closer. The butcher, the baker, and the candlestick maker set up shop in the best traditions of marketing theory and practice. With these service facilities other industry arrives. Presto! Here's a petition from the League of Women Gardeners to the effect that factory dirt and smokestack stain are darkening their white azaleas. Here's another from the National Council for the Sanctity of Sleep decrying the tumult from the works when the graveyard shift roars in. And yet another arrives from the Clean Lungs Club decrying the fragrance of the week.

## THE OMELET EFFECT

Next, concentrate on the Omelet Effect! As an omelet can't be made without breaking the eggs, a person can't get clean without breaking out the detergent. And if the detergent of choice is synthetic detergent, rather than organic detergent, something's bound to give. Since, I'm told, cleanliness in America has reached such massive proportions that foreign psychologists suspect us of a national Lady MacBeth complex, we will have detergent. Furthermore, since we have a penchant for demanding the most effective from among a variety of products, we will continue to demand syndets.

It is time, therefore, to inspire the American people with visions of trout fishing trips to Manitoba, for who could abide a nation of dirty domestic trout fishermen at the expense of tattletale gray underwear? Nay, double the value of the omelet effect, by teaching us as a nation to pour our tap water down the middle of a glass. Once the 2-inch collar of suds in the dinner table stemware becomes appropriately fashionable, we will have progressed nicely toward adjusting society's taste to one of our more important products' little side effects.

## THE KIDS AND FOOLS EFFECT

But do not stop at that. Proceed to present the particulars surrounding the Kids and Fools Effect. There is a homely observation in the hill country to the effect that disaster in varying degrees may be anticipated from appropriate combinations of kids and fools and sharp-edged tools. The same might be said with respect to kids and fools and insecticides. I have the fleeting suspicion that warnings against the indiscriminate spraying of today's insecticides and pesticides have been grossly inadequate.

This observation, I realize, is colored by my having witnessed a Show and Tell Hour in my formative years. At Fort Leonard Wood, I watched a pair of photogenic adults of the genus *Capra* sent kicking into the Sweet Ultimately by a modest whiff of nerve gas. As an economic realist, I appreciate the value of these demonstrations to the goat-breeding industry. However, as a timid soul, I have recurring nightmares wherein I and mine are permanently upended because some simple-minded orchardist has loaded a peach tree with a massive overdose of a virulent bug bane.

Sleep would be sweeter and more restful if I could believe that every can of pesticide were to include a skull and crossbones brilliantly and contrastingly displayed on the container. I have a paranoid suspicion that there may be, somewhere, a farmer who can't read. Given the not-so-secret sign that the stuff in that can can kill, the odds in our favor might be marginally improved.

These, then, are some leads. The chemical industry—its communicators, its marketers—may use them as it will. There is no reason why the industry shouldn't use them, unless it perceives that there is something uncomfortable about them. If the suggestions have a common thread, they hint that improvements could be made (in some other company or industry, of course) for the betterment of conditions which these approaches excuse—but do not change.

Employees may also perceive that their corporation will not change things, because the firm is as unconcerned about the problems as though they did not exist. However, I am betting heavily that the corporation's employees will supply concern and will accomplish the necessary adjustments. I am betting that the employees will become the consciences where none now exist.

The power of positive advertising lies in truth. But if, at present, the industry goes in heavily for truth, its image can hardly sparkle. I hold that the first steps that the chemical industry must take are to adjust its products and processes to the needs of society. These needs are for pure, safe, effective products which leave the physical environment as clean as it was before they were used.

As some people in the chemical industry blame the container industry for beer cans that clutter the highways, I blame the chemical industry for the chemical trash that clutters the air we breathe. If the chemical industry does not befoul the atmosphere, the industry at least appears to me to be expert in the elements which do.

It is not too much to ask that the chemical industry justify its expertise by making something more than an uninspired economic contribution to the society which sustains and supports it. Moreover, until the industry has taken vigorous steps to correct shortcomings that in American society should be accomplished by institutions rather than by government, it does not seem to me that the industry should be particularly anxious to advertise.

Until the time comes when the chemical industry can truly "point with pride," I cannot see how it will have achieved its full marketing goal. On that score, let greed and avarice replace humanitarian impulses if they must. Remember that a firm which does a competent and complete job of marketing its products stands to win more often than it loses. With a part of the marketing process undone, the chemical industry has yet to achieve the best of which it is capable in a league where I would be most happy to see all the teams in first place at year's end.

## COURSE OF ACTION

As an outsider, I cannot command that the chemical industry do this or that. But as one convinced that the contributions of this industry should far outweigh any of its shortcomings, as one who has watched marketing folly in one segment of the industry lead that segment to the brink of economic calamity through present and potential legislation controlling it. I implore the chemical industry *to do* the following:

1. Lend to us, society, some portion of the industry's developmental genius to clean—and to keep clean—our air and water resources.

2. Re-emphasize the dangers of the intemperate use of some of the industry's best but potentially most harmful products.

3. Adjust the total corporate energy to encompass all of society, as well as that portion which the industry serves on a direct economic basis. Grow up, as it were, while developing a mature, competent marketing posture. Then grow beyond it still further, reaching the realm of mature corporate responsibility.

4. Recognize that all contributions—individually, as well as in the company and industry sense—are vitally important to all of American society, and hence to the Free World as well.

My motives in all of this article are intensely selfish ones. There is every reason to believe that the freedom which I, as an academician, desire for myself hinges directly upon the industrial freedom of the economy in which I live. It seems to me to be incumbent upon all of us to guard these freedoms well. In the process of the guarding, the chemical industry's responsibilities are no less well defined than are mine.

# 60. Efficiency Within the Marketing Structure

ROLAND S. VAILE

## THE NATURE OF MARKETING

Any consideration of efficiency of marketing must start with a clear recognition of the fact that there are two strikingly different aspects of marketing. In the first place the provision of time and place utilities requires certain physical functions in the movement and storage of commodities, while in the second place the use of these commodities by specific people requires change in ownership and market facilities for making such change. Efficiency may be considered with respect to either of these two general aspects of marketing.

Measurement of efficiency in the physical aspects of marketing involve such things as time and motion studies, the prevalence of cross-hauling, choice of channels of distribution so as to minimize effort and time, the extent to which advantage is taken of the economy of large-scale production in the handling processes, and the trends in the costs, both monetary and real, of performing the physical functions.

Measurement of efficiency of markets in respect of the necessary changes of ownership involves such things as:

1. The ease of making contact among prospective buyers and sellers.

2. The completeness of information concerning conditions of supply and demand and the promptness with which changes in these conditions are reported.

‡ SOURCE: Reprinted by permission from the *Journal of Marketing* (National Quarterly Publication of the American Marketing Association), Vol. 5, No. 4, April 1941, p. 350.

3. The adequacy of opportunity for "shopping" among different offerings in the formation of market judgments.

4. The existence and useableness of credit and similar facilitating instruments, one purpose of which is to provide a reasonable degree of equality in purchasing power as between buyers and sellers.

5. The accuracy with which prices reflect supply and demand conditions and thereby direct the use of resources not only in the physical aspects of marketing, but in other lines of production as well.

6. The extent to which the market organization permits manufacturing and similar production activities to be so carried out as to take advantage of the economies of large-scale production, but at the same time serves to prevent the effects of monopoly such as, for example, the restriction of output that results in a monopoly profit to the sellers.

7. The extent to which the market organization encourages the development of vertical integration and thereby avoids unnecessary changes in ownership.

8. The economic effects of attempts to shift the demand schedules for specific commodities —the effects, that is, upon individual sellers and individual buyers and business in general.

9. The extent or degree to which the market distributes income payments proportionally to the marginal product.

Neither of these two lists of consideration in the measurement of efficiency in marketing is complete. It is believed, however, that they illustrate the most important points of measurement in the test of efficiency.

# 61. Measuring the Cost and Value of Marketing

STANLEY C. HOLLANDER

When did marketing begin? When were the first criticisms of marketing voiced? We do not know the answer to either question, but we can be certain of two things. One is that the function of marketing, that is, trade and exchange, has been part of the human economic system for many thousands of years. The other is that criticisms and defenses of trading activities are almost as old as trade itself. In 1776, these criticisms provoked a thundering answer from Adam Smith:

The statute of Edward VI, therefore, by prohibiting as much as possible any middleman from coming in between the grower and the consumer, endeavoured to annihilate a trade, of which the free exercise is not only the best palliative of the inconveniences of a dearth, but the best preventative of that calamity: after the trade of the farmer, *no trade contributing so much to the growing of corn as that of the corn merchant.*[1]

Smith declared: "The popular fear of engrossing and forestalling [buying for resale] may be compared to the popular terrors and suspicions of witchcraft."[2] Today the fear of witchcraft seems to have abated; it has been many years since books attacking witches made the best-seller lists. But the persistent popularity of books attacking marketing suggests that

the fear of engrossers and forestallers has not vanished. The attacks have, of course, aroused a ready response, and the marketing journals have been filled with criticisms of the critics, interspersed with a modicum of self-criticism.

As is true of most such debates, the discussions have tended to generate considerably more heat than light. Only in fairly recent years have we had any really serious attempts to measure both the costs and the benefits of marketing in our society. The dearth of such studies is not the fault of the many serious and well-intentioned people who have debated the value of marketing. It is simply an indication of the complexity and magnitude of the problem.

## A PRODUCTIVITY ANALOGY

The difficulty of measuring marketing productivity may be illustrated by attacking a comparable problem: attempting to measure the productivity of a magazine article. An examination of the silent post-mortem in which you will indulge after finishing this or any other article will suggest some of the difficulties we face when we try to evaluate the marketing system.

In either case, we are trying to determine a ratio. On the one hand, we have the inputs into the system—the social and individual contributions to the product or process, and on the other hand, we have the outputs—the social and individual benefits. If the benefits are high in proportion to the inputs, we describe the article, the product, or the system in question as *highly productive*. But if the ratio is low, then the system is not very productive. The concept is simple to state; the real problems arise when we attempt to apply it.

---

[1] *The Wealth of Nations* (New York: Random House, 1937), p. 499. Emphasis supplied.

[2] *Ibid.*, p. 500.

◆ SOURCE: Reprinted by permission from the publisher, the Bureau of Business and Economic Research, Division of Research, Graduate School of Business Administration, Michigan State University. *Business Topics*, Vol. 9, No. 3, Summer 1961, pp. 17–27.

## Types of Input

The reading experiences that provide the final tests of a magazine article's value result from two major categories of inputs. One group consists of those supplied by the publisher and the people and firms associated with him. These include the work of paper and ink manufacturers, printers and production craftsmen, the postal service and the newsdealers, editorial employees, illustrators, and even authors. Supposedly the value of their services is measured by the prices and wages these contributors receive during the process of assembling and distributing the magazine. But this supposition involves a number of assumptions to which we will want to return shortly. Magazines, like every other product and service, present a number of unique problems in social cost measurement. For example, publications that derive much of their revenue from advertising may incur heavy production and promotional expenses so as to attract the readership that will attract advertising, which in turn, may, in various ways, affect the prices and sales of the commodities advertised. Under such circumstances it is often difficult to determine the exact inputs provided by each participant. A similar quandary arises out of the eternal debate between the publishers and the postmasters-general over the relationship of postal charges to the costs of furnishing postal services.

Another group of inputs is extremely important and many of these are often overlooked. These are provided by the readers, and include their time and effort as well as whatever they may pay, directly or indirectly, for the publication. These inputs are analogous to the time, effort and money expended by consumers in both the shopping and the consumption process. And, from the standpoint of the individual consumer, these are the personal costs that must be balanced against the personal benefits.

## Simple Evaluation

Let us start with the simplest version of this problem; the individual judgment each one of you will make after finishing this article or this issue of Business Topics. Undoubtedly, you will ask yourself whether it has been worth reading or not. Not *how* worthwhile, or *how* it compares with other things you might have read instead, but simply: am I pleased or not that I decided to take the time to read this article? This is the sort of judgment that we all make frequently.

Yet notice how often our reactions are ambivalent. We say of some experience or book or lecture, "I guess it was worthwhile," or "I don't know—it wasn't too bad," or "I'm rather glad I read it, and yet maybe I could have used the time more profitably."

Now it is no wonder that our judgments are sometimes vague. To decide that reading a particular article, or engaging in any other activity, is worthwhile involves a very complex accounting process. Very few of us have enough time to do all the things we would like to do, or to read all the things that we would like to read. The segments of time that we invest in reading a particular article may be especially precious segments, on a busy day or when there are many alternative activities clamoring for our attention. Then again, the time may consist of minutes spent in the dentist's anteroom, when there is little else that we can do and when we really only want a little intellectual anaesthesia before climbing into the chair. The article may demand considerable attention and intellectual effort, which we may consider as output, as a source of enjoyment (witness the pleasure many people derive from solving puzzles) or, under other circumstances and at other times, we may consider as input, as an unwarranted drain on our energies. The benefits of our reading are elusive and subtle. We may obtain intellectual exercise, new insight, stimulation and entertainment. Or our reading may prove stultifying, boring, or misleading. All of this we have to balance in some rough and ready fashion before we can say whether the magazine was, or was not, worthwhile.

## Complexities of Evaluation

However, this is still at the kindergarten level in productivity evaluation. Let us look at two more problems of greater complexity. One arises out of the fact that such rough balance sheets are really inadequate for comparative purposes or for social appraisals. Suppose, in the course of a year, that each of us reads two hundred magazine issues. Each issue consumes its own combination of time, money and energy; each yields its own patterns of information, insight and entertainment. How can we compare these two hundred: can we rank them in an ordinal line, and will our judgments be consistent each time that we express them? How can we add these two hundred patterns into a composite figure if we want to compare this year's reading with last year's, or with the magazines we read ten years ago? How can we make comparisons between, say, the magazines published in the U. S. and those published in other countries, or between publications issued under various auspices? What measures can we use to quantify either the inputs or the outputs, and how do we relate them to each other? It is perfectly apparent that these considerations are frivolous and frustrating, yet this is exactly the sort of problem we face when we try to make comparative judgments about the productivity of marketing.

But the problem is still more complex. Magazine articles are written in the hope of reaching large audiences. Each member of that audience is an individual. Each has his own standards, each has his own alternative ways of spending his time, each seeks his own particular satisfactions and ends. None is a replica of the others. In evaluating the effectiveness of an article, how can we add all of their tastes, inclinations and judgments into a single composite whole? Shall we regard one person's intense pleasure as the equivalent of several people's mild displeasure? Shall we allow extra, or reduced, weight in our calculus to the connoisseurs, to those who are the most sensitive to small differences, or to those whose swings on the manic-depressive axis are the widest?

## WEIGHING THE COSTS

Conceptualizing and evaluating are equally difficult in any attempt to aggregate all of the inputs and outputs of a complex economic systm. Given certain assumptions and conditions, it is relatively easy to measure the physical results of highly specific, small operations. For example, it is not too hard to determine which of two machines is more efficient at punching out sardine cans. This may involve some judgments about the relative cost of labor, capital and raw materials in the future. For example, one machine may be more efficient at low levels of output and the other at high levels, so some judgments have to be made about the nature of future demand for sardine cans. But practical, workable estimates can be made, and some of these judgments work out fairly well. Similarly, we can compare two different methods of putting those sardine cans on the supermarket shelves, subject to some assumptions as to the total number of cans to be stacked, the cost of labor, and the alternative uses for the stockmen's time in the store. But the only available mea-

sure, aside from miscellaneous hunches, guesses and opinions, of whether the whole operation is worthwhile is whether enough people buy those sardines to warrant allocating the social energies necessary to produce canned sardines instead of something else.

There seem to be only two measures by which we can evaluate the total inputs into the total marketing system. One is hours of labor, the other is monetary costs. Both have their limitations.

### Labor as a Measure

Labor hours are not all homogenous, and hence we have a problem if we try to use number of hours worked in marketing as the measure of marketing cost. How can we properly equate an hour of time worked by an unskilled laborer with an hour of time spent by a highly trained engineer or architect? They are both human beings. Moreover, the job that is assigned to the laborer may be far more burdensome than the work performed by the professional. But each hour of the skilled man's time represents an expenditure of the human capital invested in training, and so, in a sense, constitutes a higher cost than does an hour of common labor. The problem can be resolved through evaluating each hour of labor at its actual wage or salary rate, but this approach leads into the monetary problems we will face in a moment. Another difficulty, of somewhat less significance, bothers the statisticians who try to compute labor productivity figures. They argue whether it is more accurate to use actual hours worked as the labor investment, or whether paid vacations, holidays and sick leaves should be added. The issue is often described as the question of hours worked versus hours paid for. (Although it would drive the statisticians crazy, conceptually one might be justified in including some portion of the future hours to be spent in paid retirement as part of this year's "labor paid for.")

Another problem is more difficult. The number of hours invested in marketing measures, at any one moment, only a portion of the total cost of the system. Our economy also draws upon natural resources and upon the capital that the past has produced. We can only equate units of capital and units of labor by converting them to a common factor—their monetary value. This again leads us to the problems inherent in applying monetary measures to marketing input.

## Money as a Measure

Some of these problems are technical in nature. For example, should we evaluate the capital equipment used in any one year on the basis of its original cost, original cost minus depreciation (and if so, at what rate), cost to reproduce, or cost to replace with modern equipment? How shall we measure the labor of unpaid family workers? What shall we do about deferred compensation? More basic problems center around two major assumptions that underlie the use of monetary costs as a measure of input. When we use monetary costs expended in the private sector as our measure, we are, in effect, assuming that the government's contribution to marketing, which is considerable, is roughly equal to the net tax burden (also considerable), that is levied upon marketing. If the contribution and the taxes are unequal, then one party is, in a sense, contributing more to the bargain than it derives from the other. Our other assumption is that the costs represent free market values, that each dollar earned represents equal sacrifices, that each dollar spent obtains equal pleasure, and that there has been no exploitation of any of the participants in the system.

But there is an even more fundamental problem. The United States Census uses a monetary concept, "the value added by manufacturing," to measure the output of the manufacturing industry. The value-added figure is obtained by subtracting the total cost of the materials (and some services) that manufacturing industry purchases from the total amount of its sales. Many writers now advocate using a similar concept in marketing. A moment's reflection, however, shows that this concept of output is roughly equivalent to a monetary cost measure of input. Profits are usually a relatively small portion of the total figure and certainly are, at least in part, the price of certain managerial and entrepreneurial services. So, under this accounting, input and output will always be roughly equal.

## Consumer Satisfaction

The most difficult part of the whole business is to measure the real output of marketing. In spite of all talk about motivation research, hidden persuaders and the like, we really seem to know very little about what people want from the marketing system. An example from retail distribution may help to illustrate this point.

One school of thought holds that most people look upon stores very largely as places in which they can obtain merchandise. According to this point of view, people consider shopping as a nuisance, and are most satisfied when they can obtain their purchases with minimum expenditures of time, money, and effort. Some interesting experiments with shopping games and with records of consumer behavior tend to substantiate this view, although the results are by no means conclusive.[3] On the other hand, there is the view advanced by many motivational researchers and by some very successful merchants, that people like to shop. The advocates of this position maintain that shopping is an end in itself, apart from the goods that are purchased, and that the retail system should be designed to maximize the pleasures of shopping.[4] Now, of course, no hard and fast election can be made between these two approaches. Much depends upon the customer, the products being purchased, the place and the time. Some people seem to react to shopping differently than others.[5] Most people will display one attitude when buying antiques, and another when purchasing a tube of toothpaste. Some people, who normally try to rush in and out of the supermarket, will be willing, when traveling, to spend hours in the quaint native market place, probably much to the annoyance of the natives. If we have only ten minutes in which to catch a plane, we want the airport newstand to have our favorite magazine readily accessible; if we have two hours to kill between planes we like the airport bookstore that permits uninterrupted browsing. But even after allowing for all of these differences, we find that a fundamental question for both managerial strategy and social evaluation in retailing has been answered only indifferently and on an *ad hoc* basis. The devices for identifying and measuring consumer satisfaction in any general sense are limited to votes in the market place, which is probably the most significant single argument for a free market place.

---

[3] Wroe Alderson, *Marketing Behavior and Executive Action* (Homewood, Illinois: Richard D. Irwin, 1957), p. 183

[4] See, for example, Pierre Martineau, "A Store is More Than a Store," Motivation in Advertising, Ch. 20, (New York: McGraw-Hill, 1957), pp. 173–85.

[5] An interesting classification of shoppers appears in Gregory P. Stone, "City Shoppers and Urban Identification," *American Journal of Sociology*, July 1954, pp. 36–45.

## COST RESEARCH

A few unusually dedicated analysts have attempted to measure the costs of marketing in our society, in the face of all the difficulties we have noted and in spite of a number of technical obstacles we have not considered. In general, these people have been well aware of the problems and limitations inherent in their work. But they have felt that even a rough approximation of the actual figures would be ample reward for the herculean labors involved in such a task.

### Stewart and Dewhurst

By far the best known single study of this sort is *Does Distribution Cost Too Much?* (New York: Twentieth Century Fund, 1938), a study conducted by Professors Paul W. Stewart and J. Frederic Dewhurst under the sponsorship of the Fund. Stewart and Dewhurst worked with census figures on purchases and sales, and other data, to trace the 1929 flow of commodities in this country from original sources (agriculture, importation, and extractive industries) to final buyers (consumers, institutions, public utilities, and export) via such intermediate levels as manufacturing and trade. Increases in value resulting from transportation and from wholesale and retail trade were assigned as costs of marketing, increases at the manufacturing level were apportioned between marketing and processing. Stewart and Dewhurst estimated that, in 1929, final buyers absorbed $65.6 billion worth of finished tangible goods, of which three-fourths, or $49 billion, went to individual ultimate family consumers. These figures do not include the consumption of services, such as haircuts, medical attention or personal transportation. Total marketing costs for this $65 billion worth of goods were estimated at $38.5 billion.

In other words, according to this analysis, retailing, wholesaling, transportation, advertising, selling and other marketing activities took 59¢ out of every consumption dollar spent on goods or tangible commodities. This figure, which as we shall see has been subjected to some very serious criticism, included marketing and transportation expenses at all levels. Thus, it embraced practically all of the selling and distribution expenses involved in transferring cotton to the yarn spinner, in transferring cotton yarn to the fabric weaver, and in transferring fabric to the shirt manufacturer, as well as the marketing costs involved in moving finished shirts to the consumer. Stewart and Dewhurst were careful to point out that their figure, 59¢, was meaningless unless it was compared with what distribution did in return for its compensation. They also were careful to point out that a more efficient manufacturing system, turning out large quantities and obtaining economies of scale, would necessitate a more complex marketing system. Nevertheless, in reading their report one can sense a sort of physiocratic bias, a feeling that changes in form utility ought to be relatively more costly than changes in time, place and possession utility.

### Barger Study

In 1955, Harold Barger, relying on the vast data collections assembled by the National Bureau of Economic Research, published his *Distribution's Place in the American Economy since 1869* (Princeton: Princeton University Press, 1955). This is generally regarded as the most authoritative work yet published on the subject. Barger limited his analysis to wholesale and retail trade, and did not include manufacturers' marketing costs, as did Stewart and Dewhurst.

Barger was not overly impressed with distribution's performance in some respects. He concluded, for example, that labor productivity per man hour increased in commodity production at an annual rate of 2.6 percent per year from 1869 to 1949. Contrasted with this, he found that productivity in distribution went up only about 1 percent per year. The analysis is somewhat limited, since the measure used, total volume handled, does not allow for changes in functions performed. However, probably most of the difference is due to the greater relative application of machinery and other forms of capital in manufacturing than in trade.

However, he did find that wholesaling and retailing accounted for only about 35- 36¢ out of the consumer's dollar in 1929. Since he was working with only a portion of the total distributive activity for that year, rather than with the whole, we should expect his figure to be smaller than the Stewart and Dewhurst 59¢. However most analysts, including Barger, believe that part of the discrepancy is really a correction of the old figure, that would reduce it by an indeterminate amount, perhaps 8 or 9¢.

## Cox Study

For the last several years Reavis Cox and some of his associates at the University of Pennsylvania have been conducting an investigation of marketing costs to serve as a companion to, or as a revision of, the Stewart and Dewhurst study. Their work has not yet been published, although it should be released in the near future. Cox gave an advance presentation of some of their findings at the 1960 meeting of the American Statistical Association. There he disclosed that an analysis of the Bureau of Labor Statistics' massive input-output table for the U. S. economy in 1947 revealed that ultimate consumers that year took $96 billion worth of goods, of which $41 billion, or about 43 percent, went for distribution *activities*. This figure included the marketing expenses incurred by manufacturing firms, as well as the marketing activities of the distributive industries, i.e. wholesalers, retailers, transportation agencies and advertising agencies. The distributive industries themselves accounted for about 31.1 percent of the final value of all consumption goods, and a considerably smaller portion of the total final value of consumer services.[6]

## Department of Agriculture

In addition to these three studies and many smaller scale attempts there has been the massive work of the United States Department of Agriculture in measuring what it calls "marketing margins" for agricultural products. Unfortunately for our purposes, the Department uses the word "marketing" to embrace almost everything that can happen to agricultural products once they leave the farm. It determines its so-called marketing margin for consumer food products by subtracting the farm value of raw foodstuffs and by-products from the final retail value of agricultural foods. This margin thus includes, for example, both the cost of grinding wheat into flour and the cost of baking bread. The procedure is somewhat analogous to saying that the cost of manufacturing Ford cars is part of the cost of marketing iron ore.[7]

The economists who prepare the USDA marketing margin reports are always extremely careful in explicitly stating just what is included in their figures, although the same cannot always be said for the people who use those figures in political debate. But the agricultural definition yields results which simply are not comparable to the marketing cost studies we have examined, however useful the Department's work may be for other purposes. In 1939, for example, the Department said that 63 percent of the consumer's farm food dollar was absorbed by marketing costs, a slightly higher figure than has been reported for the last several years. Professors Beckman and Buzzell of Ohio State University reanalyzed the 1939 figures and found that just about one-third of the total 63 percent was the cost of processing prepared and semi-manufactured goods. The true marketing cost was about 41 percent, a figure much closer to those reported in the Barger and Cox studies for consumer goods in general.[8]

## THE ACTUAL OUTPUT

But even the most accurate marketing cost figure is relatively meaningless until it is compared with the work performed by marketing. Much of that work, as we have noted, consists of intangibles that resist quantification, and so we do not have an output figure to set against the cost percentage. But it is an inescapable fact that a dynamic, high level economy involves a very considerable amount of marketing work. Even the Soviets, who have not been outspoken admirers of our marketing system, are beginning

---

[6] 1960 Proceedings of the Business and Economics Section, ASA. Washington: American Statistical Association, 1961, pp. 319–22.

[7] The Department does usually make one reasonable but inconsistent adjustment in these figures. Consumer expenditures for restaurant meals are adjusted down to the retail store value of equivalent foodstuffs. The work of a restaurant chef is not treated as marketing, but the work of a cook in a frozen food plant is. In this connection though, it is only fair to say that increases in the sales of prepared food, the so-called "built-in maid services," fall short of explaining all of the recent changes in farm marketing and processing margins. Finally, we may note that in a recent unofficial study, two leading USDA economists added farmers' costs for machinery and purchased supplies into the total marketing margin reported for farm food products. Frederick V. Waugh and Kenneth E. Ogren, "An Interpretation of Changes in Agricultural Marketing Costs," *American Economic Review*, May 1961, pp. 213–27.

[8] T. N. Beckman and R. D. Buzzell "What Is the Marketing Margin for Agricultural Products?" *Journal of Marketing*, October 1955, pp. 166–68.

to pay us the compliment of imitation as their own economies emerge from the subsistence level. The western world is just beginning to notice such communist developments as a conference on advertising methods held in Prague in 1958, and attended by delegates from the Soviet Union, East Germany, Albania, Bulgaria, Poland, Czechoslovakia, Hungary, Rumania, Yugoslavia, China, Mongolia, North Korea and Vietnam.[9]

Dr. E. D. McGarry, of the University of Buffalo, has provided the best statement of what constitutes the actual output of marketing.[10] He lists six major functions of marketing which may be summarized as follows.

### Six Functions of Marketing

1. *The contactual function:* the searching out of buyers and sellers. This is a not inconsiderable task. A typical supermarket may carry five to six thousand items produced by hundreds of different processors.[11] One study of twelve representative drug stores found that each carried an average of 1,300 proprietary items (minerals, vitamins, patent medicines, etc.) alone, out of a selection of perhaps 20,000 or 30,000 such items produced for distribution through drug stores.[12] The American consumer draws upon a selection of literally tens, perhaps hundreds, of thousands of items. An elaborate and often unnoticed mechanism is needed to maintain contact between all of the people who use and produce both these items and their components, supplies and equipment.

2. *The pricing function:* in our society, the principal device for allocating our supply of scarce resources.

3. *The merchandising function:* the work of gathering information about consumer desires and translating it into practicable product designs.

4. *The propaganda function:* "the conditioning of the buyers or of the sellers to a favorable attitude toward the product or its sponsor." This is the most criticized of all the marketing functions. But probably few will dispute the need for some activity of this sort to support an economy in which consumption rises above subsistence and in which the advantages of scale are obtained through mass production in advance of sale.

5. *Physical distribution:* the brute job of transporting and storing goods to create time and place utility.

6. *The termination function:* something of a catch-all category, that includes both the process of reaching agreement in the case of fully negotiated transactions, and all of the contingent liabilities that remain with the seller after delivery takes place.

Since many of these functions are concerned with intangibles, facile evaluation of marketing performance seems unlikely, and perhaps impossible, even for the future. Probably room will always exist for debate concerning both the objectives of marketing and the means used to achieve these objectives. We may be certain that our present methods are not perfect. We may well anticipate the development of new and better techniques for the performance of many marketing tasks. Nevertheless, even though their work resists quantification, marketers need not apologize for their share of the consumer's dollar.

---

[9] Lazlo Sonkodi, "Advertising in a Socialist Economy," *Cartel*, July 1959, pp. 78–79. Sonkodi's source is, interestingly enough, a publication called *Magyar Reklam* (i.e. *Hungarian Advertising*). For a discussion of other Russian marketing developments, see Marshall Goldman, "Marketing—A Lesson for Marx," *Harvard Business Review*, January-February 1960, pp. 79–86.

[10] Reavis Cox and Wroe Alderson (eds.), "Some Functions of Marketing Reconsidered," *Theory in Marketing.* (Chicago: Richard D. Irwin, 1950), pp. 263–79.

[11] "The Dillon Study," *Progressive Grocer*, May 1960, p. D18.

[12] Burley, Fisher and Cox, *Drug Store Operating Costs and Profits* (New York: McGraw-Hill, 1956), p. 263.

# 62. Changing Social Objectives in Marketing

REAVIS COX

Much of our concern over the social objectives of marketing grows out of the fact that we are not satisfied as students and observers to confine ourselves to the problem of helping marketing serve as well as it can the narrowest interest of the most narrowly defined entity we can find to talk about—the individual worker or the particular firm. We must at some point subsume our ideas as to the functions of marketing into our ideas of what our whole society is supposed to achieve for us.

When Professor Bartels invited me to speak here today, the subject he suggested seemed interesting and not too difficult to handle effectively. Perhaps I was misled by the familiarty of the words into believing that I really knew what they meant. Certainly I fell into the common delusion that meetings of this sort are comfortably far off in the future, so that there will be plenty of time to work through uncertainties and ambiguities before the zero hour arrives.

On both counts I was overly optimistic. What I was asked to talk about has turned out to be extremely difficult to define and formulate. There has not been time to spell out in any detail precisely what we are to mean by "marketing" in this context or by the "social objectives" with which we are to be concerned.

Under some circumstances it might be feasible and useful simply to look systematically at the problems into which one runs when he tries to decide who it is that has social responsibilities in marketing, to whom these responsibilities run, what their precise nature is, and how

♦ SOURCE: Reprinted by permission from *Emerging Concepts in Marketing*, Proceedings of the Winter Conference, American Marketing Association, December 1962.

they have been changing. But the time allotted to me is too short for anything so ambitious, so I firmly put aside the temptation to go into these matters with any substantial degree of thoroughness. Instead I shall plunge directly and without further preamble into a consideration of several changes that have taken place since 1900 or so in our ideas as to what the social functions of marketing are and, therefore, how its social performance can be evaluated. These changes have not so much replaced old ideas with new ones as introduced new ideas to go along with the old or altered the relative emphasis placed upon established ideas.

## FROM PRODUCT ORIENTATION TO MARKET ORIENTATION

Consider, for example, the social implications of something we all talk about—the shift from product orientation to market orientation. The precise extent to which those who teach or practice marketing have made this shift is uncertain. We do know, however, that there have been significant changes in the points of view from which many people look at the flows that take place in marketing.

437

The traditional view is suggested clearly enough by the more or less official definition that says marketing is "the performance of business activities directed toward, and incident to, the flow of goods and services from producer to consumer or user."[1] The impetus for the study of marketing in its early days came from people who had goods to sell. There were the farmers, for example, who wanted to know more than they did about what happens to their products after they leave the country assembly points. Their primary objective was to increase their own share of the ultimate consumer's dollar. Then there were the sales managers and advertising managers, whose function was to move into consumption the goods produced by their employers, preferably in such a fashion as to increase both volume and profit margins. Distributors—wholesale and retail—emphasized their operations as sellers and merchandisers more than their operations as buyers, despite the claims they sometimes made to be purchasing agents for consumers and other users of goods. The basic question to be answered was, "How do we get rid of what we have to sell in satisfactory volume at a satisfactory profit?"

This way of looking at the marketing process has by no means disappeared; but there has been a significant increase in the extent to which marketing is treated as a flow *to* consumers rather than a flow *from* producers—a service of supply for users rather than a system of distribution for makers. The significance of this change for our problem of determining what marketing is supposed to accomplish and how well it does the job is self-evident. It takes us back to the old, familiar but often neglected idea that economic activity is engaged in not for its own sake but because something we call consumption happens at the end of the process. It argues that the true standard against which performance is to be measured is not the profitability of the enterprises that sell what the economy produces, but the quality, variety and quantity of satisfaction created for those who use it.

We can, of course, think of marketing as nothing more than an immensely complicated bridge whose work is done when traffic moves, without regard to what kind of traffic it is. "The function of bridges," says the *Encyclopaedia Britannica*, "may be described as the starting of a stream of human traffic hitherto impossible; the surmounting of a barrier, the linking up of two worlds divided by a gulf."[2] As to the nature and purpose of the traffic, the bridge is completely neutral. So by analogy marketing may be thought of as a system of communication whose objective is to transmit goods, people and messages without regard to their nature. Performance is to be measured by looking at such factors as the number of "bits" transmitted and the suppression of "noise" that interferes with communication.

In much of our thinking about marketing and its social objectives, however, we do not see it as neutral. We are likely to put a good deal of emphasis upon what is transmitted and with what results for the consumers at the end of the bridge, not merely upon how much is transmitted and how cheaply. In other words, marketing is judged to some extent by the end effects of the complex process of which it is a part. In this context, the social objectives of marketing must be defined to include the serving of socially desirable purposes well, not merely serving well whatever traffic offers itself. It must contribute to the flow of satisfactions reaching consumers, not detract from it.

Even with this definition, the shift of emphasis from product to market orientation does not solve all the problems raised by the evaluation of marketing. Defining the social objective to be attained in terms of satisfactions provided for consumers in general does not set up a schedule of priorities as between different consumers and as between different wants of particular consumers. We are left with a conflict between what have been called the economist's welfare approach and the politician's approach through arbitration or litigation.[3] When an economist guides our judgments as to the performance of marketing he falls back on some concept such as the principle that a society should seek to achieve the greatest good for the greatest number of its members. The politician is more likely to be governed by a desire to work out a viable compromise among conflicting interests and especially among or-

---

[1] "Report of the Definitions Committee," *Journal of Marketing*, 13: 209 (October, 1948).
[2] Article on bridges in *Encyclopaedia Britannica*, Vol. 4, p. 125 (1948).

[3] See the discussion of this problem in Donald J. Dewey, "Changing Standards of Economic Performance," *American Economic Review*, 50, No. 2: 1–12 (May, 1960).

ganized pressure groups. In more homely language, he is likely to think of quieting the squeaky wheel.

## FROM COST IMPOSED TO VALUE ADDED

We face similar problems of definition when we come to another of the shifts of emphasis we have made of late in our analyses of marketing. This is a preference for thinking of marketing as a process of adding value to goods and services rather than as a process of imposing costs upon those who buy these goods and services. Concentration of interest upon the seller's interest in marketing almost inevitably leads to the attitude that marketing is primarily something to be paid for. At some point, of course, attention must be given to why it is bought and how much it is worth to the buyer; but at least in the beginning emphasis is likely to be put upon how much must be paid and how to bargain so as to pay as little as possible.

A number of students, and notably Professor Beckman, have argued eloquently in recent years that marketing men do a gross injustice to themselves and to their field of study when they accept without serious question the convention of measuring the performance of marketing in terms of cost. Other sectors of the economy, it is said, are measured by the value they add to goods and services. Why treat marketing differently?

The proposition has much appeal to marketing men, who often find themselves on the defensive. Perhaps we are unduly sensitive to criticism. Perhaps we overestimate the extent of the hostility to marketing and all its works we hear expressed so often. Nevertheless, we shall lose nothing and gain something if we can persuade those who publish statistics about what marketing does, to do so in the same terms they use for statistics about what, say, manufacturing does.

For our purposes here today, the importance of the shift in concepts and in terminology that goes with talking about value added rather than cost lies in the effects it has upon our ideas of what the social objectives of marketing are and how its accomplishments can be measured. If we think of cost, the standard against which to evaluate performance must be some measure of efficiency. Given an output, the best per-

formance by marketing is the one that minimizes cost. Alternatively, given an expenditure for marketing, the best performance maximizes the amount of work done in return. Either way, what we seek is to minimize the ratio of expenditures for marketing to output delivered.

When we think of value added, the standard against which performance is best evaluated becomes productivity rather than efficiency. We think of what marketing does not as a set of undesirable though necessary activities but as the production of worthwhile values. Marketing in the end may still be judged as to whether it wastes resources by using more than it really needs to accomplish its results; but it starts with the assumption that what it does is desirable. So its students and practitioners find themselves under much less pressure to be defensive when they deal with its critics.

There remains, of course, the difficulty of defining and measuring the values marketing produces. The value system implicit in business and in much conventional economic analysis, leaves a great deal to be desired when applied to a social evaluation of marketing. This is true because it tends to encourage concentration upon marketable goods. Macroeconomics takes this point of view when it measures the national product by adding up all the purchases or, alternatively, all the sales made in the economy's markets during a given period.

This method of measuring GNP or its equivalent by-passes or ignores much that must be taken into account in evaluating the performance of the economy. Its limitations in measuring the true value of what is produced lead to pronouncements such as that of Ambassador Galbraith, who urges that strong efforts be made to enlarge the output of "public" as contrasted with "private" goods.[4] Such a shift inevitably would carry with it a reduction in the extent to which the economy depends upon markets and market procedures to direct its operations, as contrasted with governmental or other formal controls.

Whether we should regard this as also constituting a change in social objectives depends largely upon how we define "marketing." We can consider marketing to be merely one of the many ways in which a society of specialists organizes the necessary exchange of goods and services. In this view it stands on the same level as reciprocity, redistribution, householding and marketless trade. These are also ways

---

[4] J. K. Galbraith, *The Affluent Society* (Boston: Houghton Mifflin Company, 1958).

in which nations have organized this work.[5] In such a context its social responsibility is to maximize marketable values. If, on the other hand, we think of "marketing" as a generic term embracing all possible ways of handling exchange and directing the work of economic specialists, then we must correspondingly broaden our ideas as to what its social objectives are. It no longer is bound to the creation of marketable values alone.

## WHO IS IT THAT HAS SOCIAL OBJECTIVES?

Thus far we have spoken of marketing as though it is an organized entity of some sort to which social responsibilities have been assigned explicitly. In fact, we assign responsibilities to many different sorts of entities. The narrower the scope of the entity for which we try to set objectives, the more likely we are to accept definitions of its immediate objectives in terms of self-interest. The broader its scope, the more likely we are to insist upon defining its objectives in social rather than personal terms.

The social problem often becomes one of seeing how individual people with their self-centered interests tied into narrowly circumscribed units can be induced to seek social objectives broader than their own immediate wants. Inculcation of moral precepts or religious principles is one way of doing this. Another may be found in reliance upon Adam Smith's doctrine of the invisible hand, which holds that in a competitive society individuals pursuing their own narrow self-interest will drive each other to produce (as a sort of by-product) an overall result that is good. Yet another way is to use political instruments so as to constrain individuals and coerce them into serving some interest other than their own selfish ones.

Professor Krebs has pointed out how the objectives of economic activity change as we broaden the entity about which we speak.[6] Although he is not concerned specifically with marketing, much of what he has to say is germane to the subject we have under consideration here. He suggests that there are at least four different levels of generalization at which we can make meaningful statements concerning the objectives to be served, for whom the objectives are significant, and the sort of individual to whom we look for leadership.

At the lowest level, we consider individual enterprises. Here we think of the dominant interest to be served as being that of the owner or, in the corporate form of organization, the stockholder. The primary objective normally will be to maximize profit, the monetary income the owners derive from the operation of the business. This primary objective may be modified or supplanted, at least in the short run, by the desire simply to grow larger or to acquire more economic power for its own sake; but the assumption often is that these are merely indirect ways of enlarging profit in the long run. The active leader in all this is the business manager.

At the level of an industry or trade, performance is measured in somewhat different terms. Here the dominant interest is likely to be that of firms organized into more or less formal associations and particularly the larger, more powerful concerns that control such groups. The primary objective now may be to expand the markets of the industry as a whole. Perhaps it will be to make a more effective use of political instruments in the interests of the whole group, as by lobbying for tariffs to shut out foreign competition or for special concessions in some tax law. Its spokesman is the industrial leader or the trade association executive.

At a still higher level, we think of the whole economy. Here is where we take the dominant interest to be served as being that of the ultimate consumer. The objectives we spell out are sometimes mutually reinforcing, sometimes contradictory. We think of such objectives as maximizing the output of consumers goods, of optimizing their assortment or their allocation among consumers. We may emphasize either current output or growth. Perhaps we want to maximize or stabilize employment or to provide economic security at some minimal level for all. The spokesman for such interests as these is likely to be the economist or some comparable observer who stands on the sidelines as an observer rather than as a participant

---

[5] See Robert Bartels, *The Development of Marketing Thought* (Homewood, Ill. 1962), pp. 6–9, for a brief description of these various ways of organizing an economy. The discussion by Bartels is derived basically from the writings of Karl Polanyi

and his associates.

[6] Theodore J. Krebs, "Measurement of the Social Performance of Business," *Annals of the American Academy of Political and Social Science*, 343: 20–31 (September, 1962).

and evaluates what is happening on the field.

Finally, we can think of the entire nation in all its aspects as the entity whose objectives we want to define. Here the dominant interest to be served is everybody. The primary objectives must be stated in very broad terms indeed—elimination of duress and fraud, protection of the weak against the strong, the preservation and enlargement of human liberties. The spokesman for these interests is likely to be the statesman or, ideally, Plato's philosopher-king.

One of the reasons why we have difficulty in spelling out what we mean by the social objectives of marketing is the fact that we can think of so many different levels of generalization at which to cast our problem. We are caught in what we may call the horseshoe dilemma. The old nursery rhyme tells us that the loss of one horseshoe nail led to the loss of a kingdom. We can say correctly that the function of the nail was simply to hold the shoe to the horse's foot; but we also can say that its function was to preserve the horse or the rider or to contribute to the winning of the kingdom.

Much of our concern over the social objectives of marketing grows out of the fact that we are not satisfied as students and observers to confine ourselves to the problem of helping marketing serve as well as it can the narrowest interest of the most narrowly defined entity we can find to talk about—the individual worker or the particular firm. We must at some point subsume our ideas as to the functions of marketing into our ideas of what our whole society is supposed to achieve for us.

## MANAGEMENT BY MATHEMATICAL REASONING

In the light of what I have thus far said, we shall find it well worth while to consider one of the consequences flowing from the tremendous development of mathematical approaches to management that have become so conspicuous in recent years. This is a tendency to narrow rather than to broaden our view of marketing and its objectives. In this development we run counter to some of the trends we have already considered.

The nature of the danger to which the use of these techniques exposes us is stated graphically by Professor Rapoport in his comment upon the limitations of science as a guide to social action:

We live in an age of belief—in the omnipotence of science. This belief is bolstered by the fact that the problems scientists are called upon to solve are for the most part selected by the scientists themselves. For example, our Department of Defense did not one day decide that it wanted an atomic bomb and then order the scientists to make one. On the contrary, it was Albert Einstein, a scientist, who told Franklin D. Roosevelt, a decision maker, that such a bomb was possible. Today, in greater measure than ever before, scientists sit at the decision makers' elbows and guide the formulation of problems in such a way that scientific solutions are feasible. Problems that do not promise scientific solutions generally tend to go unformulated. Hence faith in the omnipotence of science.[7]

We have reason for concern over the danger that management in marketing also may concentrate its attention upon too small a part of its responsibility by formulating its pay-off matrices, decision rules, probabilities, constraints and all the rest in terms of objectives that make the problems analyzable. Important problems may be left unresolved for no better reason than that they cannot be reduced to analysis by these particular methods. Management's problems grow out of what management has to do, not out of what it can do by applying a specific, limited set of analytical tools.

The resultant danger is not a threat solely against the broad objectives we specify for marketing taken as a part of the social structure. It may threaten what the firm needs to do for itself in its own self-interest. In many particulars competition among firms resembles a game; but it is not really a game. Formulating the problems of the business manager in terms specified by game theory may help him work out answers to his problems but it simultaneously exposes him to serious danger. As has been said of war games used to train officers in the military services, one can sometimes win a war game on points by doing things that would lose the war itself, which does not have imposed upon it the formal definitions and rules characteristic of a game.

---

[7] Anatol Rapoport, "The Use and Misuse of Game Theory", *Scientific American*, 207, No. 6: R108

(December, 1962).

## CONCLUSION

It should now be apparent why I found the assignment so lightly undertaken one very difficult to fulfill. We are certainly very far from having a well-formulated set of social objectives for the guidance of students, practitioners and regulators of marketing. Whether we can ever have such a thing or whether we should have it, I shall not venture to state. I am willing to predict, however, that at least those of us whose lives are passed in the academic sectors of marketing will continue to try to find it.